T0340034

Global Agricultural Workers from the 17th to the 21st Century

Studies in Global Social History

VOLUME 50

The titles published in this series are listed at *brill.com/sgsh*

Global Agricultural Workers from the 17th to the 21st Century

Edited by

Rolf Bauer and Elise van Nederveen Meerkerk

BRILL

LEIDEN | BOSTON

European Research Council
Established by the European Commission

This book was realised with the support of ERC Consolidator Grant 2017 (Grant Number 771288).

This volume is published in collaboration with the International Conference of Labour and Social History (ITH) and arose out of the 55th ITH conference which took place in Linz, Austria on 5–7 September 2019.

Cover illustration: Unknown author, the photograph depicts a woman, a man and a kid ploughing a field. Fortepan Archive, 1929.

The Library of Congress Cataloging-in-Publication Data is available online at https://catalog.loc.gov
LC record available at https://lccn.loc.gov/2022055059

Typeface for the Latin, Greek, and Cyrillic scripts: "Brill." See and download: brill.com/brill-typeface.

ISSN 1874-6705
ISBN 978-90-04-52494-1 (hardback)
ISBN 978-90-04-52942-7 (e-book)

Contents

PART 1
The Agrarian Question and the Resilience of the Peasant Family Farms

Figures, Tables and Maps

Figures

Tables

Maps

Notes on Contributors

Karl Heinz Arenz

is Professor at the Federal University of Pará (UFPA), in Belém, working at the Faculty of History and the Postgraduate Program in Social History of Amazonia. The focus of his research is the Colonial Amazonian Society (seventeenth and eighteenth centuries), especially the complex relationship between Indigenous populations, Jesuit missionaries and Portuguese authorities. In 2019, he was co-editor of a colonial dictionary of the Tupi language, which was widely spoken in the Amazon Region.

Rolf Bauer

is an economic and social historian. He is interested in the history of modern South Asia, drugs, commodity frontiers, disasters and peasant studies. In 2019, he published his Ph.D. thesis *The Peasant Production of Opium in Nineteenth-Century India* with Brill. Currently, he is guest Professor for modern South Asia at the University of Vienna and visiting professor at the history department at Central European University.

Dina Bolokan

is Ph.D. candidate in Sociology and lecturer at the Centre for Gender Studies at the University of Basel, Switzerland. Bolokan's work deals with the political economy of labour migration within the agricultural sector in Europe. Her main research areas and interests are located within the fields of decolonial thought, postcolonial and post-Soviet studies, critical border studies, and feminist epistemologies.

Juan Carmona

is Associate Professor at the Universidad Carlos III de Madrid. He has published widely on rural institutions, organizations, and conflicts, including, with James Simpson, the book *Why Democracy Failed. The Agrarian Origins of the Spanish Civil War* (2020).

Debojyoti Das

is an anthropologist of South Asia with a focus on the borderlands of eastern India and the Indian Ocean world. His work is deeply interdisciplinary, bridging his training as an ethnographer with extensive use of visual media and action-based research. His current work focuses on land relations, climate change, migration, and sustainable development issues among marginalised littoral communities in the Bay of Bengal delta. He is the author of the book The Politics of Swidden Farming: Environment and Development in Eastern India (2018). He is currently exploring less glimpsed but important dynamics of climate migration in South Asia.

Josef Ehmer

is Professor Emeritus of Social and Economic History at the University of Vienna and Associate Fellow at the International Research Centre Work and Human Lifecycle in Global History at the Humboldt-University Berlin. His research encompasses European social history from the early modern period to the present day, which includes work and the worker, the family, ageing and old age, and migration. Currently, his main interest is in the implementation of the life course paradigm into labour history.

Sophie Elpers

works as researcher in ethnology at the Meertens Institute (Royal Academy of Arts and Sciences) in Amsterdam. In her doctoral thesis (University of Amsterdam, 2014) she has investigated the reconstruction of farmhouses in the Netherlands during and after the Second World War in the context of fierce discussions about national identity, tradition and modernization. Her current research focusses on (contemporary) rural vernacular architectures, everyday life in the countryside, images of rurality, processes of heritagization and musealization, and the history of ethnology. Sophie Elpers is section editor of the *Encyclopedia of Vernacular Architecture of the World*. She teaches critical heritage studies at the University of Bonn, Germany, and is executive vice president of the International Society for Ethnology and Folklore (SIEF). Sophie Elpers is also a staff member "research and development" at the Dutch Centre for Intangible Cultural Heritage where her research is on the relation between intangible and tangible heritage, with a specific focus on museum work.

Leida Fernandez-Prieto

is a Researcher at Institute of History at Higher Council for Scientific Research in Madrid. She holds a Ph.D. from the University of Havana, Cuba. She has been a Wilbur Marvin visiting scholar at DRCLAS, Harvard University, for the academic year 2015–16. She has also been visiting scholar at the Center for Latin American and Caribbean Studies at New York University. Fernandez is the author of two books, *Cuba Agrícola: mito y tradición, 1878–1920*, and *Espacio de poder, ciencia y agricultura: el Círculo de Hacendados*. Likewise, she is the author of "Islands of Knowledge: Science and Agriculture in the History of Latin America and the Caribbean" (*Isis*, 2013). Fernandez specializes in studies on the ethnobotanical legacies of Atlantic slavery, and in the multiplicity of knowledge, practices and agents that were part of the construction and circulation of global and local scientific tropical agriculture.

Katherine Jellison

is Professor of History and Director of the Central Region Humanities Center at Ohio University. She is past president of the Agricultural History Society and past co-chair of the Rural Women's Studies Association. Her publications include *Entitled to Power: Farm Women and Technology, 1913–1963* (1993), *It's Our Day: America's Love Affair with the White Wedding, 1945–2005* (2008), and a forthcoming book (with Steven D. Reschly) about Old Order Amish women. Her commentary on gender and politics appears frequently in such media outlets as the BBC, CNN, *The New York Times*, and *The Washington Post*.

Alexander Keese

is Professor of African History at the Université de Genève, Switzerland. He was the principal investigator of ERC Starting Grant ForcedLabourAfrica (n° 240898, 2010–2015) comparing forms of compulsory labour in West and Central Africa under colonial rule and beyond. He is the author of *Ethnicity and the Colonial State: Finding & Representing Group Identifications in Coastal West African and Global Perspective (1850–1960)* (2016).

Rachel Kurian

is International Labour Economics (emerita) at the International Institute of Social Studies of the Erasmus University Rotterdam. Recent relevant publications include (with Kumari Jayawardena) "Indebtedness, Sociocultural Hierarchies, and Unfree Labor on Nineteenth-Century Ceylonese Plantations" in Richard Allen (*eds*) *Slavery and Bonded Labour in Asia, 1250–1900* (2022), "Plantation Patriarchy and Structural Violence in Maurits Hassankhan et al, (eds) Social and Cultural Dimensions of Indian Indentured Labour and its Diaspora (2016), *Class, Patriarchy and Ethnicity on Sri Lankan Plantations: Two Centuries of Power and Protest* (2015) and "State, Citizenship and Democratic Deficits: Multiple Patriarchies and Women Workers on Sri Lankan Plantations" in Jayadeva Uyangoda (eds.), *Local Government and Local Democracy in Sri Lanka: Institutional and Social Dimensions* (2015).

A. Lozaanba Khumbah

was a Ph.D. candidate at the Centre for the Study of Regional Development, School of Social Sciences, Jawaharlal Nehru University, New Delhi. His primary research interests are studying state and market induced transformations of mountain economies, livelihood and ecological sustainability, institutional diversity and changing property rights relations especially in Northeast India. His MPhil and Ph.D. work focussed on agrarian change in shifting agriculture, also known as jhuming in Northeast India.

Rafael Marquese
is Professor of History at the University of São Paulo, Brazil. He is the author of *Administração & Escravidão. Ideias sobre a gestão da agricultura escravista brasileira* (1999); *Feitores do Corpo, Missionários da Mente. Senhores, letrados e o controle dos escravos nas Américas, 1660–1860* (2004); *Slavery and Politics. Brazil and Cuba, 1790–1850* (2016); *Os Tempos Plurais da Escravidão no Brasil. Ensaios de História e Historiografia* (2020); *Reconstructing the Landscapes of Slavery. A Visual History of the Plantation in the Nineteenth-Century Atlantic World* (2021). He is currently working on a book project on the global history of coffee and slavery.

Rogério Naques Faleiros
is Professor at the Department of Economics and at the Graduate Program in Social Policy at the Federal University of Espírito Santo (UFES), Brazil. He is currently the Dean of Planning and Institutional Development at UFES. He has researched economic history and Brazilian social thought.

Janina Puder
is a trained labour sociologist. Currently she is a research associate at the Institute of Sociology at the Friedrich Schiller University of Jena. She did her Ph.D. in the BMBF sponsored Junior Research Group "Bioeconomy and Social Inequalities." Thereby, she investigated in various field stays the exploitation of low-skilled migrant workers in the Malaysian palm oil sector. Here research interests include labour migration, political economy, theory of capitalism, socio-ecological transformation and social classes.

Alessandro Stanziani
is Professor, EHESS, in Global History and Research Director at CNRS. Since 2014, he is Leader and French leader of the international consortium Global History Collaborative (Princeton, Tokyo University, Humboldt and Freie University, EHESS, Paris). Since 2006 he is member of the steering committee of the European Network of Global History, he is member of the Indian labor History Association, the Economic History Association, International Labor Association and Network. His main Interests and fields are: Global history;

Labor history; Russian history, 18th-20th century; Indian ocean, labor, 18th-19th centuries; Economic, business and labor history, Europe (France, Britain), 18th early 20th century; Food history, 18th- 20th century. Among many other publications, he is the author of). *Labor in the fringes of Empire. Voice, exit and the law* (Palgrave: 2018); *Eurocentrism and the Politics of Global History* (Palgrave 2018). *Les entrelacements du monde* (2018) and *Les metamorphoses du travail constraint* (2020).

James Simpson

is Emeritus Professor at the Universidad Carlos III de Madrid. Among his many publications are *Spanish Agriculture: The Long Siesta, 1765–1965* (1995), *Creating Wine: The Emergence of a World Industry, 1840–1914* (2011) and, with Juan Carmona, *Why Democracy Failed. The Agrarian Origins of the Spanish Civil War* (2020).

Elise van Nederveen Meerkerk

is Professor of economic and social history at Utrecht University, The Netherlands. Among other publications, she authored the monograph *Women, Work and Colonialism in the Netherlands and Java. Comparisons, Contrasts, Connections, 1830–1940* (2019).

Bruno Gabriel Witzel de Souza

is Associate Researcher at the Institute for Economic & Social History at the University of Göttingen and member of the Centre for Global Migration Studies. The author received his Ph.D. in Development Economics from the same university. His research focuses on the relationship between economic history and long run development, particularly in nineteenth century Latin America. His fields of specialization are in migration economics, labor history, contract theory, and education history.

Introduction

Rolf Bauer and Elise van Nederveen Meerkerk

1   Why Global Agricultural Workers?*

Agriculture has historically been the largest economic sector, in terms of output volume and numbers of workers employed. Even today, about one billion people of working age (or, 26.7 per cent of the global labour force) are employed in agriculture, although they are extremely unevenly distributed over the globe.[1] Nevertheless, agricultural workers have long been underrepresented in the "old" as well as the "new" labour history.[2] This scholarly neglect of agriculture might be a result of what some have perceived as the slow death of agricultural work or a process of de-peasantisation – due to the effects of industrialisation and the rising productivity in agricultural production. However, for a long time, the decreasing importance of the agricultural sector has, in fact, been limited to a few highly industrialised nations. Everywhere else, agriculture is still a major economic sector and a source of income for a large part of the population. Although the share of people employed in the agricultural sector has been declining worldwide, and constitutes (far) below 5 per cent of the total working population in most high-income countries, their share is still considerable in most mid- and low-income countries, where the majority of the world population currently lives.[3] Besides their *quantitative* importance, there are several other *qualitative* considerations motivating the study of agricultural labourers. For this volume, we have identified three

* This research was conducted under the ERC-funded Consolidator Grant project "Race to the Bottom?" (Acronym TextileLab, Grant number #771288), of which the second author of this Introduction is the Principal Investigator. Open Access publication of this volume was made possible by the ERC funding. Furthermore, the editors would like to thank two anonymous referees of the volume for their valuable comments, in particular pertaining to this chapter. Meticulous language editing was done by Saskia Bultman, SWYM Editing.

1 "Employment in Agriculture (% of total employment) (modelled ILO estimate," International Labour Organization (via the World Bank), accessed 29 March 2022, https://data.worldbank.org/indicator/SL.AGR.EMPL.ZS. The figure refers to the year 2019.
2 For an excellent overview of "old" and "new" labour historiography, see Marcel van der Linden, "Labor History: The Old, the New and the Global," *African Studies* 66 (2007): 169–80.
3 To take some examples of countries represented in this volume: in 2010, the percentage of people working in agriculture was 16.7 in Brazil, 37.7 in Indonesia, 38.9 in Ghana, and 54.7 in India: "Share of Agriculture in Total Employment, 1961 to 2011," Our World in Data, accessed 23 November 2021, https://ourworldindata.org/grapher/share-of-agriculture-in-total-employment.

topical issues, which are very urgent in the present day and age but which call for more in-depth historical contextualisation.

First of all, in the context of worldwide population growth, rising food prices and environmental change, the issue of *food security* has appeared high on the political agenda over the past few decades. It was extensively discussed at the first World Food Summit (Rome, 1996) and has been one of the main concerns of the United Nations' "Millennium Development Goals" and "Sustainable Development Goals."[4] Food security is intrinsically – yet also ambivalently – related to the concept of *food sovereignty*, which can be defined as "the right of peoples to healthy and culturally appropriate food produced through ecologically sound and sustainable methods, and their right to define their own food and agriculture systems. It puts those who produce, distribute and consume food at the heart of food systems and policies rather than the demands of markets and corporations."[5]

Over the past decades, food sovereignty has become a major concern because small-scale farming has increasingly made way for large agro-industrial companies controlling the production of food in the name of guaranteeing "food security," particularly in the Global South. This monopolisation of food production by large companies creates pressing anxieties about the quality and quantity of food, the circumstances of its production and the ecological consequences of this system.[6] Food sovereignty has become a key concept of scholarly and political discourses and "now constitutes a powerful anti-capitalist vision for food system transformation."[7] Peasants not only play a central role in the political movement advocating food sovereignty. They are also seen as a possible solution to the many problems that the "corporate food regime" (see next section) has caused so far: political, economic and ecological. Small-scale, family-based agriculture is a specific form of agricultural engagement

---

4 Food and Agricultural Organization, *The State of Food Insecurity in the World: The Multiple Dimensions of Food Security* (Rome, 2013), 4, accessed 21 March 2022, https://www.fao.org/3/i3434e/i3434e.pdf.

5 Declaration of Nyéléni (2007), 1, accessed 21 March 2022, https://www.nyeleni.org/spip.php?article290.

6 At the 1996 World Food Summit in Rome, the transnational agrarian movement *La Via Campesina* (established 1993), coined the term "food sovereignty" for a broad audience. For a detailed account on the evolution of the term, see Philip McMichael, "Historicizing Food Sovereignty," *The Journal of Peasant Studies* 41, no. 6 (2014): 933–57. For more about the historical development of agro-business, see the next section.

7 Priscilla Claeys, Annette Aurélie Desmarais, and Jasber Singh, "Food Sovereignty, Food Security and the Right to Food," in *Handbook of Critical Agrarian Studies*, ed. A. Haroon Akram-Lodhi et al. (Northampton: Edward Elgar Publishing, 2021), 238.

and differs substantially from entrepreneurial farming. Strengthening small-scale peasant farming would not only guarantee sovereignty over food production but would make agricultural production ecologically more sustainable.[8] This perspective has been further developed by agroecology, sometimes also referred to as eco-agriculture.[9] Despite the upscaling of agriculture and the rise of "agribusiness," more than 95 percent of all those still employed in agriculture today are in fact smallholders in the Global South.[10] It is worthwhile investigating the resilience of smallholder and peasant producers in a long-term historical perspective in order to understand how and why, regardless of continuous upscaling and increasing capitalist relations of production, they have managed to survive.

A second highly urgent theme is coerced labour in the primary sector. Recent ILO estimates suggest that, in 2016, two million people worldwide were working under bonded or slave labour conditions in the private agricultural sector – thus excluding state-coerced programmes.[11] Apart from direct coercion, millions of other workers in the agricultural sector are working under shady contracts, through which they receive advances that grant labour contractors immense power over them to employ them whenever it suits them, under very poor living and working conditions.[12] For example, Oliver Pye quotes three different estimations that range from a few hundred thousand to ten million migrant plantation workers in the Malaysia-Indonesian region. Because many of them are undocumented labourers, their numbers are obscured, and they

---

8   As was already argued in the early 1980s: Harriet Friedmann, "Household Production and the National Economy: Concepts for the Analysis of Agrarian Formations," *The Journal of Peasant Studies* 7, no. 2 (1980): 159.

9   The Food and Agriculture Organization of the United Nations (FAO) lists nineteen different definitions of agroecology on its website. One definition that incorporates the main characteristics of agroecology was published by the United States Department of Agriculture (USDA): "Loosely defined, agroecology often incorporates ideas about a more environmentally and socially sensitive approach to agriculture, one that focuses not only on production, but also on the ecological sustainability of the productive system." Quoted on the FAO website, accessed 15 March 2022, https://www.fao.org/agroecology/knowledge/defi nitions/en/.

10   Eric Vanhaute, *Peasants in World History* (New York and London: Routledge, 2021), 3.

11   International Labour Organization (ILO), *Global Estimates of Modern Slavery: Forced Labour and Forced Marriage* (Geneva, 2017), 32, accessed 21 March 2022, https://www.ilo .org/wcmsp5/groups/public/---dgreports/---dcomm/documents/publication/wcms_575 479.pdf.

12   ILO, "Decent Work in Agriculture" (paper, International Workers' Symposium on Decent Work in Agriculture, Geneva, 2003), 23, accessed 22 March 2022, https://www.ilo.org/wcm sp5/groups/public/---ed_dialogue/---sector/documents/publication/wcms_161567.pdf.

are vulnerable to exploitation due to their often illegal status.[13] Likewise, the fruit and vegetable industries in Southern Europe rely heavily on migrant contract workers. According to CREA, a research organisation dedicated to the agri-food supply chains, the number of migrant workers in Italy's agricultural sector was recently estimated at over four hundred thousand: almost 50 per cent of the total labour force in Italy's primary sector.[14] The labourers come predominantly from Eastern Europe, the Maghreb, South Asia and sub-Saharan Africa, many of whom are undocumented migrants. Particularly in Southern Italy, where migrant workers are employed only temporarily – for the harvest of tomatoes, for instance – living conditions are abysmal, with workers frequently living in informal slums in isolated rural areas.[15] After abolition, contract labour was often framed as a voluntary alternative to slave labour.[16] Just like other recent historical studies, however, many of the contributions in this volume show that slavery and other forms of labour under (semi-)coerced conditions were omnipresent in the global countryside throughout the period under investigation. In this sense, there seem to be clear continuities with the past. This raises questions about why coerced labour in the agricultural sector has been so persistent, and how its appearance has changed over time under the influence of major economic, political and societal change.

Third, and closely related to the former point, the comparatively unprotected status of agricultural workers by governments and states stands out. Although many of the exploitative practices described above take place in the private sphere of agri-business, small-scale commercial agriculture or even in the household, many states turn a blind eye to these practices. In some cases, such as the Dominican Republic, the ILO found that the state has even explicitly facilitated forced labour in plantations since the 1980s.[17] Moreover, millions of waged agricultural workers – both men and women – do not receive crucial social benefits in their host countries, simply because current legislation often excludes (seasonal) migrants from social security schemes.[18] More

---

13   Oliver Pye, "Agrarian Marxism and the Proletariat: A Palm Oil Manifesto," *The Journal of Peasant Studies* 48, no. 4 (June 2021): 815.

14   Alessandra Corrado, "Migrant Crop Pickers in Italy and Spain" (E-paper, Heinrich Böll Foundation, 2017), 4–5, accessed 21 March 2022, https://www.boell.de/sites/default/files/e-paper_migrant-crop-pickers-in-italy-and-spain_1.pdf.

15   Corrado, "Migrant Crop Pickers," 4–5.

16   Alessandro Stanziani, "Introduction: Labour, Coercion, and Economic Growth in Eurasia, Seventeenth – Early Twentieth Centuries," in *Labour, Coercion, and Economic Growth in Eurasia, 17th–20th Centuries*, ed. Alessandro Stanziani (Leiden and Boston: Brill, 2013), 3.

17   ILO, "Decent Work in Agriculture," 23–24.

18   ILO, "Decent Work in Agriculture," 53.

in general, migration policies in many states keep a large part of the workforce in a highly vulnerable status, enabling employers to over-exploit the labourers and creating labour relations that some scholars refer to as "modern slavery."[19] Thus, apart from peasants, who are numerically over-represented in the global agricultural workforce, a huge landless agro-proletariat has come into existence in recent decades. This proletariat, partly consisting of illegal migrants, has not only been neglected and even exploited by states, but it has also been notoriously underrepresented in recent scholarship.[20] An important historical question arising in the context of this volume is to what extent we can discern continuities and changes in states' interferences with labour conditions in the agricultural sector, and how we might explain these.

This volume aims to highlight these three trends in agricultural labour: the resilience of the peasantry; coerced labour in agriculture; and the particular state (non-)intervention from a *historical* perspective. It tries to increase our understanding of the roots of these developments by bringing together studies on agricultural labour relations from all over the globe. The three sections in this book follow logically from the three questions posed in the previous paragraphs. However, before we contextualise the contributions in this volume further, we will first discuss some of the most recent insights about, as well as concepts surrounding, agricultural labour.

2   Labour Relations in Agriculture

The category of "agricultural worker" is fairly broad, and includes small peasant producers, those employed on family farms, and workers on plantations and other agro-industrial complexes. Furthermore, their labour relations are highly varied. They range from self-employment and wage labour to various forms of coerced labour relationships, such as slavery or indentured labour. Most of these different types of labour relations are represented in this volume: whether peasants under Eastern European serfdom, contract workers on colonial plantations in British India, or wage labourers in the nineteenth-century industrialising United States. In their introduction to the *Handbook Global History of Work* (2018), Karin Hofmeester and Marcel van der Linden provide a very useful definition of labour relations: "Labour relations define for

---

19   See, for example, Thomas Chesney et al., "Understanding Labour Exploitation in the Spanish Agricultural Sector Using an Agent Based Approach," *Journal of Cleaner Production* 214 (2019): 696.

20   Pye, "Agrarian Marxism," 816.

whom or with whom one works, and under what rules. Those rules, implicit or explicit, written or unwritten, determine the type of work, type and amount of remuneration, working hours, degrees of physical and psychological strain, and the degree of freedom and autonomy associated with the work."[21]

Over the past fifteen years, the International Institute of Social History (IISH) has brought together scholars in the context of the project "Global Collaboratory on the History of Labour Relations, 1500–2000," who have jointly developed a taxonomy of labour relations based on the above-mentioned definition.[22] Arriving at such a shared classification was an important step in the global history of labour relations. It allows scholars to use a common framework and language when analysing the labour relations of a specific population at a particular moment in time, or to determine how particular social, economic or political shifts impacted labour. Moreover, comparing various labour relations across space and time was thus made easier – enabling scholars to identify both regional differences and change over time.

When it comes to labour relations, it is complicated to categorise agricultural workers, as they typically pursue a livelihood by combining various income strategies: a worker might cultivate millet for household consumption, wheat for cash and sell her labour on a daily basis to a large landowner – all at the same time. The rules that determine the type of work, the amount of work, the remuneration or the degree of freedom differ in each case. Given the complexity of labour relations in agriculture, it may be useful to think in terms of labour *regimes*. A labour regime consists of various labour relations and can combine subsistence with commodity production and everything from so-called free wage labour to forced labour services.[23]

The following concepts and analytical tools have been fundamental in studying the spatial and temporal shifts in labour regimes. Immanuel Wallerstein's

---

21   Karin Hofmeester and Marcel Van der Linden, "Introduction," in *Handbook Global History of Work*, ed. Karin Hofmeester and Marcel van der Linden (Berlin and Boston: De Gruyter Oldenbourg, 2018), 4.

22   The project was an initiative of IISH staff member Jan Lucassen and includes key researchers such as Karin Hofmeester (coordinator), Christine Moll-Murata and, later, Rombert Stapel. For the project, its publications and its databases on labour relations, see the "Global Collaboratory" Dataverse, accessed 29 March 2022, https://datasets.iisg.amsterdam/dataverse/labourrelations.

23   In an essay on labour regimes in Northeast India, Willem van Schendel identified a colonial labour regime that included household self-employment, cash crop production, servile labour and communal labour: Willem Van Schendel, "Beyond Labor History's Comfort Zone?" in *The Life Work of a Labor Historian*, ed. Ulbe Bosma, and Karin Hofmeester (Leiden and Boston: Brill, 2018), 195.

World-Systems Analysis (WSA) is still a very powerful approach to understanding the links between emerging capitalism, an increasing demand for cash crops and shifting agricultural labour relations. WSA stresses the interlinkages between the emergence of global trade and merchant capitalism, inducing the extraction of minerals and agricultural products from the "periphery" in order to serve growing consumer and producer markets in the "core." Backed up by their merchant capitalist states in the seventeenth (Holland) and eighteenth (Britain) centuries, a new global division of labour came into being, in which African slave labour was employed to produce sugar and other cash crops on plantations in the Americas.[24] As the collaborative initiative SlaveVoyages has shown, the peak of the slave trade occurred in the eighteenth and early nineteenth centuries. Of the 10.64 million enslaved people recorded in the transatlantic slave trade database, 9.35 million embarked on the voyage to the plantations in the Caribbean, South and North America in the period 1700–1866.[25] After the slow abolition of the slave trade over the nineteenth century, a new source of cheap and exploitable labour was found, most notably in the agricultural workers of South and Southeast Asia. Two types of labour relations dominated the expanding cash crop markets: first of all, the self-exploiting peasant family cultivating produce on their own fields with their own means of production or in forms of sharecropping and, second, the indentured labourers who were shipped to plantations all over the globe.

WSA was an important step in understanding the global division of labour. It shifted our attention to periods when new zones were incorporated into the European-dominated world economy. These processes of incorporation were accompanied by the increasing coercion of the labour force in the peripheries.[26] That includes the obvious example of plantation slavery in the Caribbean but also peasant producers who were coerced to cultivate cash crops. A prime example which clearly depicts the mechanics of coercion many peasant producers in colonies faced is India's colonial opium industry. At the height of the industry, about 1.5 million peasant households cultivated poppy, the plant from which opium is extracted, for the British Indian government's Opium Department. While opium filled the government's treasuries, it impoverished

24   Charles Lemert, "Wallerstein and the Uncertain Worlds," in *Uncertain Worlds: World-Systems Analysis in Changing Times*, ed. Immanuel Wallerstein, Carlos Aguirre Rojas, and Charles C. Lemert (London and New York: Routledge, 2012), 158.

25   "Trans-Atlantic Slave Trade – Database," accessed 20 November 2021, https://www.slavevoyages.org/voyage/database.

26   Immanuel Wallerstein, *The Modern World-System III: The Second Era of Great Expansion of the Capitalist World-Economy* (San Diego: Academic Press, 1989), 137.

the peasantry, since the prices, dictated by the Opium Department were too low to even cover the costs of cultivation. North India's peasants clearly produced opium at a loss and they were forced to do so by the mechanics of a triangle of debt, power and dependency relations.[27] WSA enables us to view this form of coercion faced by peasants as well as indentured labour and enslaved labour as features of the same process: the incorporation of new zones into the global division of labour. Interestingly, this all occurred at a time when labour relations in the capitalist "core," northwestern Europe, became increasingly free and market-oriented.[28]

In the wake of WSA, a group of scholars has recently stressed the importance of studying "commodity frontiers." The global history of capitalism, Sven Beckert, Ulbe Bosma, Mindi Schneider and Eric Vanhaute argue, is a history of the expansion of commodity frontiers.[29] These frontier zones are characterised by the commodification of land and labour. What this approach adds to the WSA concept of incorporation is its emphasis on the ecological transformations that have accompanied the commodification of land and labour. While heavily influenced by the concept of the commodity chain, the commodity frontier approach starts the analysis in the countryside rather than in the industrial "cores" of the world economy. It has thus encouraged economic and social historians to study the history of capitalism by shifting their focus away from the urban industrial centres to the global countryside and, as a consequence, to labour relations in agriculture.[30]

Another important analytical device for studying shifts in agricultural labour relations, especially in the more recent period, is the concept of the "food regime," developed by Harriet Friedmann and Philipp McMichael. This concept allows us to analyse agricultural and food systems from a world-systems perspective and identify major hegemonic shifts. McMichael distinguishes "three phases of geo-political ordering of international food production and circulation": the British-centred imperial food regime, from the 1870s to the 1930s, the US-centred food regime from the 1940s to the 1970s and finally

---

27   For a detailed analysis of the peasant production of opium in nineteenth-century India, see Rolf Bauer, *The Peasant Production of Opium in Nineteenth-Century India* (Leiden and Boston: Brill, 2019).

28   Jan Lucassen, *The Story of Work: A New History of Humankind* (New Haven: Yale University Press, 2021), 194.

29   Sven Beckert et al., "Commodity Frontiers and the Transformation of the Global Countryside," *Journal of Global History* 16, no. 3 (2021): 435–50.

30   For an introduction to the concept of the "commodity chain," see Immanuel Wallerstein and Terence K. Hopkins, "Commodity Chains in the World-Economy Prior to 1800," in *The Essential Wallerstein*, ed. Immanuel Wallerstein (New York: The New Press, 2000), 221–33.

the corporate food regime, centred around the World Trade Organization (WTO), which has dominated global agriculture and food since the 1970s.[31] The major difference between the corporate food regime and the two former food regimes is the changing role of the state. While states dominated the agricultural and food markets during the British- and US-centred regimes, they became mere servants of global markets in the most recent regime. The WTO has represented the interests of transnational corporations in the liberalisation of global trading. In the name of "food security," countries in the Global South were pushed to open up their agricultural markets, leading to an expansion of agrarian exports and a penetration of large-scale enterprises at the cost of the displacement of small-scale farming. "Southern lands in particular," according to McMichael, "have been increasingly converted from local food provisioning to contract farming and agro-industrial estates."[32] In a similar vein, Jan Douwe van der Ploeg introduces the concept of "food empires" to analyse "the global and oligopolistic networks that control increasingly large parts of the production, processing, distribution and consumption of food."[33] Food empires, van der Ploeg argues, seek to control the linkages in agricultural and food systems and thus enable agribusiness to appropriate and centralise value.

3   Part 1: The Agrarian Question and the Resilience of Peasant Family Farms

In his recently published *Peasants in World History* (2021), Eric Vanhaute calls peasants the "single most important social group in world history since the advent of agriculture." He continues to argue that "[a]ll successful cultures and civilizations were based on extensive peasant economies comprising 90 percent or more of the population."[34] Besides the sheer magnitude of this group, there is another reason that the peasantry deserves scholarly attention: as mentioned above, the peasant mode of agricultural production could be a hopeful alternative to the current "corporate food regime."[35] Undoubtedly, peasants have been the most dominant group of agricultural workers in history. In

---

31   Philip McMichael, "Food Regimes," in Akram-Lodhi et al., *Handbook*, 218.

32   McMichael, "Food Regimes," 219.

33   Jan Douwe van der Ploeg, *The New Peasantries: Rural Development in Times of Globalization* (London and New York: Routledge, 2018), 245.

34   Vanhaute, *Peasants in World History*, 3.

35   Philip McMichael, "Global Development and the Corporate Food Regime," *New Directions in the Sociology of Global Development* 11 (2005): 265–99.

recent decades it has been increasingly acknowledged that "peasants" do not form a homogenous group, and that they work in a variety of rural (as well as non-rural) activities in both paid and unpaid, formal and informal sectors.[36] What most peasants do have in common, though, is the small scale of their business, their modest income and the importance of family and/or communal relations for their existence.[37]

The study of labour relations in agriculture arguably began with Karl Marx. While Marx paid demonstrably more attention to studying the urban working class, he nonetheless made some invaluable contributions to our understanding of rural social relations. His ideas about the proletarianisation of agricultural labour and the possible end of peasant family farms led to a long-lasting debate: the *agrarian question*. Both Marx and Lenin assumed that peasant families would eventually be swallowed by capitalism and spat out as capitalist farmers and wage workers, respectively. Unlike Marx and Lenin, Karl Kautsky believed in the survival of the self-sufficient family farm. Capitalism and the self-exploiting family farm would go well together, Kautsky argued: "a small holding cultivated on an intensive basis can constitute a larger enterprise than a bigger farm that is exploited extensively."[38] Indeed, more than a century later, peasant family farms are still the largest group in the agricultural sector, even though they have less land under cultivation than large commercial farms.[39]

The agrarian question – the issue of "whether and how agriculture provides surpluses over and above subsistence"[40] – is a longstanding debate in Marxist scholarship. It gained momentum when Karl Kautsky in his *Die Agrarfrage* (1899) questioned the idea that the transition to capitalist society would eventually rule out the model of peasant and family forms of (subsistence) agricultural production. A major contribution to this debate was Alexander Chayanov's *Theory of Peasant Economy* (1929). Based on extensive empirical data on Russian peasant families, Chayanov showed that peasants' economic behaviour differs from that of capitalist farmers. The goal of the former is self-reproduction while that of the latter is profit. Usually relying on the labour power of *the household unit*, the peasant will make decisions about – for

---

36   A. Haroon Akram-Lodhi et al., "An Introduction to the *Handbook of Critical Agrarian Studies*," in Akram-Lodhi et al., *Handbook*, 3.

37   Harriet Friedman, "Origins of Peasant Studies," in Akram-Lodhi et al., *Handbook*, 15.

38   Karl Kautsky, 1899, quoted in Jairus Banaji, "Summary of Selected Parts of Kautsky's *The Agrarian Question*," in *The Articulation of Modes of Production*, ed. Harold Wolpe (London: Routledge, 1980), 75.

39   Eric Vanhaute, "Agriculture," in *Handbook Global History of Work*, ed. Karin Hofmeester and Marcel van der Linden (Berlin and Boston: De Gruyter Oldenbourg, 2018), 230.

40   Michael Watts, "The Agrarian Question," in Akram-Lodhi et al., *Handbook*, 53.

example – the crops he/she cultivates or the intensity of the labour, not based on external market dynamics but, rather, on internal shifts in the household.[41] In Chayanov's own words, "the family's single indivisible labor product and, consequently, the prosperity of the farm family do not increase so markedly as does the return to a capitalist economic unit influenced by the same factors, for the laboring peasant, noticing the increase in labor productivity, will inevitably balance the internal economic factors of his farm earlier, i.e., with less self-exploitation of his labor power."[42] This flexibility allowed the peasant model to continue even in increasingly monetary societies, and monetisation arguably even strengthened, rather than weakened, communal and family ties in agricultural communities.[43]

Harriet Friedmann took up some of Chayanov's core ideas in the early 1980s. Her point of departure was that there is a wide variety of social and economic contexts in which agricultural household production has historically taken place. She sees agricultural labour relations as a continuum with "feudal relations of production at one extreme, and commercial relations of highly mechanised family farms within capitalist economies, at the other."[44] She argued that the internal composition and division of labour within productive households, and the characteristics of household members, are, to a large degree, determined by the external relations of households to each other and to other social groups. Like Chayanov, she distinguished the peasantry from other small-scale agricultural producers in the sense that peasant households have an ability to survive because they do not need to obtain an average rate of profit, unlike capitalist farmers. In some contexts, peasants even actively resist market penetration. According to Friedmann, peasant production can thus – and perhaps even needs to – continue to exist even under capitalist, highly commodified, agricultural production.[45]

The articles in the first part of this volume, all in their own way, try to empirically answer the question of how and why, regardless of continuous upscaling and increasing capitalist relations of production, peasant families have managed to survive. The section demonstrates that subsistence peasant

41   Alexander V. Chayanov, "On the Theory of Non-Capitalist Economic Systems," in *A. Chayanov: The Theory of Peasant Economy*, ed. Daniel Thorner, Basile H. Kerblay, and R. E. F. Smith (Homewood: AEA, 1966), 1–28.

42   Chayanov, "On the Theory," 6.

43   Harriet Friedmann, "Origins," 18–19.

44   Harriet Friedmann, "Household Production," 159.

45   Friedman, "Household Production," 163–67.

production did often indeed continue even under conditions of advancing commercialisation and industrialisation. Whereas, in Western Europe, commercialising agriculture resulted in peasant emancipation over the nineteenth century, peasant households in Eastern Europe, instead, faced increased coercion alongside growing production for an export market.[46] Joseph Ehmer's micro-historical study (Chapter 2) scrutinises the peasants of East-Elbia under serfdom, a highly oppressive form of bonded peasantry that persisted well into the nineteenth century. Contrary to some recent studies, in which oppressive forms of serfdom have been questioned, Ehmer reinforces the idea of the Baltic as a region marked by particularly coercive labour relations in agriculture. Under these harsh conditions, nevertheless, social mobility appears to have been more easily attainable for peasants than after the liberation of peasants, which actually solidified class relations and decreased the chances of climbing the social ladder.[47]

Outside Europe, too, peasants faced coercion in the context of the vast expansion of export markets. A notorious example is the Cultivation System, introduced by the Dutch colonisers on Java in 1830, which forced peasant households to produce exports crops such as coffee, tea, indigo or sugar. Peasants received some monetary compensation – although this was far under the market price – and the increasing cultivation of export crops put severe pressure on subsistence production. As Elise van Nederveen Meerkerk shows in Chapter 1, the additional labour demand imposed on households by the Cultivation System increasingly rested on women's shoulders. Women became more involved in household agricultural production – both subsistence and cash crops – and played a major role in the marketing of their produce as well as in cottage industries, such as textile production. In this way, women's work, both in subsistence agriculture and market production, actually prevented peasant families from starvation.[48]

In some cases, industrialisation and urbanisation could simultaneously lead to a return to forms of small-scale peasant production. An example is the American Northeast, where unemployment in cities led working-class families to frequently relocate between urban and rural areas, by way of a "safety valve." However, as Katherine Jellison shows in Chapter 3, this ideal of agrarian freedom existed only – and only partially – for white male landowners. Based on numerous letters written by members of a family living partly in New York City and partly in rural Massachusetts, Jellison presents the biographies of

---

46   Chayanov, "On the Theory," 1.
47   Ehmer, this volume.
48   Van Nederveen Meerkerk, this volume.

unsuccessful urban labourers, some of whom gave up life in the city in search of a better life in the countryside. Without any landed property, they all ended up at the bottom of the agrarian socio-economic order: as agricultural wage labourers. Women had even less room for manoeuvre, as their fate depended on their relationships with men – in rural areas even more so than in urban areas.[49]

Small-scale farming also persisted in the context of increasing commercialisation in agriculture in Western Europe. Although it is often held that either sharecropping or wage labour is preferred in viticulture, in Chapter 4 Juan Carmona and James Simpson show that – except in regions where top quality wines were produced – the majority of family farms in Southern Europe were, instead, tenant farms. This made sense both from the peasants' point of view and from that of most landowners. For the families, the diversification of agricultural activities, including subsistence as well as commercial activities other than viticulture were an important form of risk spreading, as grape yields were particularly volatile. Moreover, sharecropping contracts often reduced peasants' autonomy. For the landowners, due to the particularities of the vineyard crop, sharecropping could entail higher (instead of the usually assumed lower) transaction costs, making longer term tenant agreements more desirable in many regions.[50]

Like in the divergent cases of colonial Java under the Cultivation System and Southern European viticulture under conditions of commercialisation, the context of war could also prompt concern about issues of food security. As Sophie Elpers shows in Chapter 5, the destruction of and damage to impressive numbers of small-scale farms in the Netherlands as a consequence of the German occupation and warfare activities of the Second World War, the safeguarding of the food supply formed an important motor behind farm reconstruction. Simultaneously, the reconstruction of post-war farmhouses offered opportunities for the "modernisation" of the farm, which facilitated a clearer separation of the living and working quarters of the house, which were construed as, respectively, the "female" and "male" domains. To be sure, the breadwinner-homemaker ideal had already been propagated since the early twentieth century, for instance by farm household management schools and associations, but it increasingly became reality only after the war. The new farm architecture symbolised the abandonment of the centuries-old tradition of farm women working together with their husbands in agriculture,

---

49   Jellison, this volume.
50   Carmona and Simpson, this volume.

increasingly confining them, instead, to the sphere of domestic duties. Rising rural living standards as well as changing ideologies – also advocated by farmer women's organisations – enabled this shift.[51]

Chapter 6 provides a more contemporary history of Indian villages in the Eastern Himalayas that practise swidden ("slash-and-burn") agriculture, which has often been defined as traditional and "backward." In the context of colonial as well as post-colonial development schemes, peasants were either forced or trained to give up *"jhum"* in favour of irrigated paddy rice farming. This development led to the commodification of land and interference with age-old property relations, which involved communally held land. Permanent settlement and permanent cultivation turned land from a source of livelihood to a commodity. As a result, many cultivators were alienated from their land, which led to structurally new social relations in the village.[52] As opposed to the practice of swidden farming, which has often been framed as detrimental to the environment, the extension of agri-foresting and wet rice cultivation in these areas led to the depletion of land as well as a decreasing access to land for small-scale farmers. Thus, the demise of the peasant may well be detrimental to the environment as well as to social relations.

To the contrary, in Chapter 7 Lozaan Khumbah presents a case study of small-scale practitioners of swidden agriculture in Northeast India, who have adapted remarkably well to increasing market penetration in the region. Khumbah disrupts Esther Boserup's argument that demography is the decisive driver of change from swidden to permanent agriculture. Instead, distance to markets proved to be more decisive. While twenty-first-century Nagaland has certainly experienced population growth, it also experienced higher market integration and emigration to urban centres all over the subcontinent. The latter two developments created a market for foodstuffs produced by swidden cultivators who were able to gear their products to these new consumers, even creating niche markets for their traditionally produced foodstuffs. This allowed this seemingly outdated form of agricultural production to persist in the context of population growth and commercialisation.

To come back to the questions guiding this section, household peasant production continued all the way up to the present despite political, commercial and economic change. The main purpose of their small-scale production was subsistence food security but, whether in colonial Java, Europe or India, peasants also got involved in market production. In many instances, small-scale

51   Elpers, this volume.
52   Das, this volume.

production was also beneficial to employers or the state. Many peasant households accommodated to the altering conditions around them, which often meant combining different labour relations. Peasants supplemented subsistence household production with incidental wage labour, or marketed a share of their produce – sometimes voluntarily, in other contexts forced by authorities. A culmination of such force, by states, church institutions or individual entrepreneurs, can be found in the emergence of the large-scale cultivation of cash crops all over the Global South in the sixteenth century, particularly in the Americas. We will now turn to this specific form of labour relations, highlighting the role of slavery and other forms of coerced labour relations in agricultural production.

4   Part 2: Coerced Labour Relations in the Global Countryside

As mentioned, one of the important conundrums in the history of agricultural labour is why coercion – with slavery as its most extreme form – has been so persistent in this sector. In studying this question, the relatively novel concept of the "commodity frontier" has proven to be a useful analytical device. This concept is used to explore how capitalism in general, and the exploitation of land and labour at the frontier zones of the expanding world economy in particular, have affected labour and property relations as well as the natural environment. Commodity-centred histories have added to our understanding of the central role that coerced labour relations played in the development of capitalism.

In the early modern period, a specific group of commodities started to dominate world trade: psychoactive substances, the most important of which were coffee, tea, cacao, tobacco, opium and sugar.[53] Their value-to-weight ratio in addition to their addictive potential made them ideal commodities for the lucrative transoceanic commerce that was essential to empire building in the early modern period.[54] The production, trade and consumption of

---

53   Whether sugar can be regarded as a psychoactive substance in neurochemical terms is still debated. See, for example, Nicole M. Avena, Pedro Rada, and Bartley G. Hoebel, "Evidence for Sugar Addiction: Behavioral and Neurochemical Effects of Intermittent, Excessive Sugar Intake," *Neuroscience and Biobehavioral Reviews* 32, no. 1 (2008): 20–39. Understood as a "stimulant," sugar can be put in the same category as the other psychoactive substances mentioned above. See, for example, Mindi Schneider and Ulbe Bosma, "Stimulant Frontiers," *Commodity Frontiers* 2 (2021): i – iv.

54   For an excellent overview on the role of psychoactive substances in empire building, see David Courtwright, *Forces of Habit: Drugs and the Making of the Modern World* (Cambridge, MA: Harvard University Press, 2001).

psychoactive substances created enormous profits for traders and tax revenues for states. These profits and revenues relied first and foremost on "cheap
nature and cheap labour."[55] The political and economic realm of empires
offered ample opportunities for the expansion of this form of oceangoing commerce: consumers in the core on the one hand and cheap production in the
periphery through the violent appropriation of land and labour on the other.

There are a few explanations for why coercive labour relations were so persistent in agriculture. Land and labour were by far the two most important
factors in preindustrial agricultural production. In colonial contexts, land was
frequently available in abundance since it was acquired through violent means.
The Caribbean islands were made available for sugar production by killing or
expelling the indigenous population. Similarly, the rapid west- and southward
expansion of cotton production in nineteenth-century North America, was
only possible because indigenous people lost their land to violent frontier
men. In both cases, there was thus no shortage of land. Labour was the problem. Labour was the most expensive factor in these agricultural sectors and, as
a consequence, entrepreneurs had a huge incentive to keep labour costs as low
as possible: the result was maximum exploitation via coercion.[56]

While the expansion of the frontier zones made land available in abundance, this process often eliminated the local work force. On Caribbean sugar
plantations, for example, labour was simply not available locally after the
indigenous population had died. Labourers had to be recruited from distant
places and then kept confined to work on plantations in remote corners of the
world for long periods. This combination of mobility and immobility would
not have been possible without a high degree of coercion – be it in the form of
slavery or indentured labour.

However, not all kinds of agricultural production are suitable for extreme
forms of coercion. Vineyards, for example, demand a high level of care and
skills from the cultivators throughout the year. Employing coerced labourers
with little intrinsic motivation to carefully tend the vines would result in high
monitoring costs. This is why slavery was less likely to occur in wine production than, for example, in sugar, coffee or cotton. The cultivation of the latter

---

55   Jason W. Moore, *Capitalism in the Web of Life: Ecology and the Accumulation of Capital*
      (New York: Verso, 2015), 1–18.
56   The hypothesis that abundant free land will likely produce coerced labour relations is, of
      course, not new and was presented, for instance, by economist Evsday Domar in his paper
      "The Causes of Slavery or Serfdom," *The Journal of Economic History* 30, no. 1 (1970): 18–
      32. Some core ideas of Domar's paper can already be found in *Slavery as an Industrial
      System: Ethnological Researches*, published by Herman J. Nieboer in 1900.

crops is labour-intensive, but the actual labour of cutting cane, or picking coffee or cotton, is monotonous and easily monitored. This is particularly true for plantations where long rows of a single crop allowed overseeing large groups of workers at low costs. There is thus a certain crop-dependency in labour relations. That means that certain crops are more suitable for coerced labour than others. Most of the crops that dominated world trade in the early modern period fall into the category "very suitable for coerced labour."

The five chapters in this section deal with coerced labour in agricultural production in a colonial context from the seventeenth to the early twentieth century – a period that covers the rise and fall of the transatlantic slave trade and other forms of coerced labour. They show, first, that there was no simple and linear development from slavery to forms of less coerced labour in colonial agriculture and, second, that local ecological, economic and political circumstances heavily influenced labour relations and vice versa.

In the Amazon, for example, colonialists relied heavily on the know-how and traditional production methods of indigenous people when extracting and cultivating so-called *drogas do sertão* (forest products), such as cacao. In this case, slavery or indentured labour were no option, since the production of cacao was dependent on locally skilled labour. However, that does not mean that these indigenous labourers were actually free. In Chapter 8, Karl Heinz Arenz analyses the role of missions which, according to the author, should be understood as "efficiently functioning outposts of the Portuguese empire in the vast hinterland." The Jesuits built a network of farms or production centres that allowed them to exploit both the land and labour of this vast hinterland and to supply the metropole with *drogas do sertão*. An imperial law regulated the allocation of indigenous labourers, and the Jesuit missions were one of the major receiving parties. The labourers, while officially declared to be "free" people, were forced into highly exploitative and brutal labour relations. The missionaries made use of the labourers' know-how and skills, for instance in the seasonal collection of forest products. Native production methods became an integral part of the missionary network in the Amazon and were thus incorporated into the wider imperial economy.

The coexistence of vastly different forms of labour relations within one world economy becomes particularly apparent in Leida Fernandez-Prieto's case study of slavery on sugar plantations in Cuba (Chapter 9). Cuba, like Brazil, received enslaved people until well into the second half of the nineteenth century. Cuba's development of slave-based plantation agriculture coincided with industrial modernisation in Europe, that is, the period from the middle of the eighteenth century to the end of the nineteenth century. It is the interlinkages between Western science and industrial modernity, on the one hand, and ancestral local knowledge and practices in tropical plantation regions, on the other, that are of central interest to Fernandez-Prieto. From breeding and fertilising techniques to food provision for the enslaved labourers: knowledge and practices circulated between industrialising Europe and tropical Cuba, displaying the connections between "traditional" and "modern" modes of production and labour relations.

The abolition of the transatlantic slave trade in the early nineteenth century led to immediate labour shortages on many colonial plantations. One way in which planters – often backed by imperial states – solved this problem was by contracting migrant labourers to work on the plantations for a specific number of years, most notably in the West Indies/Caribbean but also in other parts of the globe. Migrant indentured workers often came from Asia: from other parts of the Empire (e.g., India in the case of the British West Indies and Java in the case of the Dutch East Indies), but also from China.[57] Adam McKeown has estimated that about 2.5 million migrants travelled as indentured labourers from South and East Asia to the Americas between 1840 and 1940, and that another 2.9 million Indians moved to other British colonies in Asia to perform contract labour.[58]

In Chapter 10, Rachel Kurian stresses the continuities from slavery to indentured labour. Certain methods of labour control employed on South Asia's plantations resembled those of slave plantations in the Caribbean. However, these were supplemented by "local forms of labour control," that is, those based on caste and religion. Kurian carves out another continuity: the role of the state. The case of Malaya, for example, shows how deeply involved the colonial state was in the recruitment of indentured labourers, both in terms of the legal framework and financial resources provided. Interestingly, this form of state recruitment of migrant labourers working on plantations in Malaysia has persisted until today, as shown in Chapter 16 by Janina Puder.

The Haitian Revolution, which began in 1791, was a crucial event, not only affecting slavery in the Caribbean but agricultural labour relations in other parts of the world too. It shifted the principal destination of the transatlantic slave trade from the Caribbean to Brazil. In 1790, the year before the Haitian Revolution broke out, the Caribbean slave trade had reached a height: 69,281 people disembarked and were sold as slaves on one of the Caribbean islands.[59]

---

57 Kay Saunders, "Introduction," in *Indentured Labour in the British Empire, 1834–1920*, ed. Kay Saunders (London and Canberra: Croom Helm, 1984), i–vii.

58 Adam McKeown, "Global Migration, 1846–1940," *Journal of World History* 15, no. 2 (2004): 157.

59 "Trans-Atlantic Slave Trade – Database," accessed 14 April 2022.

After that, the importance of the Caribbean as a destination for slave ships rapidly declined. Brazil, it seems, substituted the Caribbean as a buyer of enslaved people. Its rise as a slaving country was closely connected to one crop: coffee. Here, too, Brazil filled the vacuum left by the Caribbean in general and Haiti in particular. The revolution not only ended slavery in Haiti, but also its role as a leading producer of coffee (and sugar, cotton and indigo), since coffee production was based on slave labour. Newly independent Brazil emerged as the world's major coffee producer and exporter.[60] Brazil's rise in coffee correlated with rising slave imports. In 1790, Brazil was a comparatively small market in the transatlantic slave trade, with 10,633 enslaved people disembarking. After that, this number increased, reaching a height of 71,733 in 1828.[61]

However, Brazil was not the only emerging coffee producer. Ceylon was another. These two coffee economies differed in many respects but, most importantly, regarding their labour relations. While Ceylon's plantations owners hired seasonal labourers from South India through the Kangany System, Brazil's coffee was harvested by enslaved people. In Chapter 11, Rafael Marquese conducts a comparative analysis of Ceylon's and Brazil's nineteenth-century coffee economies. Marquese shows that these two different labour regimes not only had a varying impact on the design of the plantations – for instance, on how the coffee trees were planted – but also on the labour process and labour productivity. Seasonality and, accordingly, variations in labour demand – a problem that all agricultural producers have to deal with – led to different plantation types and harvesting systems. Since the enslaved labourers on Brazil's plantations could not simply be dismissed, the planters tried to postpone the harvest for as long as possible. In Ceylon, on the other hand, planters simply hired labourers for a period of a few months only. After the harvest, most labourers went back to their villages in South India, only to return for the coffee harvest in the following year.

While Chapter 11 deals with the coexistence of slavery and indentured labour, Chapter 12 sketches the transition from slavery to sharecropping arrangements – also in Brazil's coffee industry. Again, Brazil makes a particularly interesting case study, since the institution of slavery was only abolished in 1888, while the transatlantic slave trade had already been prohibited in the country since 1850. Against the backdrop of a booming coffee economy, the Brazilian planters were eager to find a new source of cheap labour: migratory labourers from Europe. Bruno Gabriel Witzel de Souza and Rogério Naques

---

60   Steven Topik, "Historicizing Commodity Chains," in *Frontiers of Commodity Chain Research*, ed. Jennifer Blair (Stanford: Stanford University Press, 2009), 44–49.

61   "Trans-Atlantic Slave Trade – Database," accessed 14 April 2022.

Faleiros begin their analysis in the 1840s, when a Brazilian firm started to offer migrant labourers sharecropping contracts. These contracts were interlinked with credits, which paid for the migrants' journey from Europe to Brazil. This system, the authors show, allowed the planters to bond the labourers to their farm until the debts were paid – a system not unlike the indentured labour system in South Asia at the time. Their analysis of these sharecropping contracts stretches until the 1930s, which allows them to delineate the continuities of this system but also the various refinements these contracts underwent during this period.

The case studies of this section are representative for agricultural production in the hinterlands of the global economy in the early modern period. They show how the frontiers of agriculture were constantly pushed, through which new land and labour were appropriated, often through the means of colonial conquest. Both cheap land and labour were crucial elements in the global desire for cash crops, and thus in the development of capitalism in this period of capital-extensive agrarian production. As land and labour were not necessarily voluntarily provided by indigenous populations, violence and force were typically used in their appropriation. In the production of sugar, coffee, cacao and many other colonial commodities, the (forced) mobility of the agricultural workers ensured that the constantly changing frontier zones were supplied with labour. The mobilisation of cheap labour under coercive relations, however, has remained a central feature of global agriculture up to the present, as becomes vividly clear when studying the role of the state in regulating agricultural workers' (im)mobility.

5   Part 3: State Intervention and Agricultural Labour Mobility

States have played a central role in the recruitment of agricultural labourers. They pass laws, provide resources and create networks to facilitate the supply of cheap labour in their agricultural sectors. Migration policies in particular have been a powerful tool that states have used to safeguard a mobile and cheap agricultural workforce. As discussed above, workers' mobility has been a key feature in agricultural production since the early modern period. This was not only because the expansion of frontier zones pushed production sites to remote corners of the world and, in the process of doing so, often decreased the availability of locally available labour. Also, seasonality – a feature that characterises agricultural work to a far greater degree than industrial production – creates a highly fluctuating labour demand. Seasonality determines when and where workers are needed. In some cases, technology has flattened out these fluctuations in labour demand. The greenhouses in Southern Spain, for example, allow the growth of fruit and vegetables throughout the whole year. However, in most cases, seasonality still largely determines the intensity of agricultural labour demand. Migration policies can help not only to satisfy agriculture's seasonal labour demands by, for example, issuing temporal visas, but also to keep the costs for the factor labour as low as possible. The production of "illegality" via migration policies keeps workers in a highly vulnerable status and thus forces them to accept low wages, long hours and substandard living conditions.

Accordingly, a major topic that runs through all four chapters of this section is the relation between labour, mobility and citizenship, and how state intervention has influenced these. Segregating labour rights along the lines of citizenship creates a status of high vulnerability for migrant workers and thus allows employers to create forced and exploitative labour relations. The need for particular forms of labour, be it in sugar cane production in the French Empire or on contemporary Malaysian oil palm plantations, seems to be fulfilled by drawing on migrants and other labourers with inferior citizenship status, whose exploitation is not prevented but, rather, enhanced by either the lack of protection of, or even active policies targeted at, migrant workers. Moreover, in rural communities in Ghana, old colonial practices of communal labour recently seem to be directed at migrant labourers, who, based on their citizenship status, have less capacity to resist such obligations than residents.

In Chapter 13, Alessandro Stanziani asks the question why, in the French Empire, despite the abolition of slavery, the use of coercion and restricting agricultural workers' mobility continued, both in the metropole and in its colonies. In France, the situation of rural labourers changed for the better after the 1789 Revolution, in the sense that *de facto* bondage was abandoned. Nevertheless, many forms of coercion continued, and agricultural workers' rights were much less protected by government measures than those of industrial workers. Thus, Stanziani concludes that "the Revolution of 1789 brought much more 'freedom' to urban than to rural workers." The metropole formed a blueprint for suppressed worker status throughout the French Empire. After 1848, thousands of freed slaves as well as new immigrants were put under contracts of *engagement*, which was, in fact, a form of bonded labour, under which labour conditions were hardly better than formerly under slavery. Legal restrictions for immigrants and non-French residents and a consistent negation of their rights in courts of law provided the institutional underpinnings for their inferior status in the colonies.

In Chapter 14, Alexander Keese investigates continuities and changes in what has been termed "communal labour" in Ghana, from the late colonial period to the very recent past. Under the label "communal labour," the state employed mandatory work programmes for the creation and maintenance of infrastructure. Developed in the colonial period, independent Ghana also implemented these mandatory work programmes, which helped to realise public infrastructural projects in rural areas at low costs. While Keese acknowledges major differences between the colonial and the postcolonial eras in terms of the physical exploitation of the workers, he also emphasises the continuities between these eras: both the colonial and the postcolonial state framed these mandatory work programmes as voluntary contributions for the rural community. In the recent past, the main target groups for these work programmes were immigrants and the descendants of immigrants, who, threatened by being expelled from Ghana, could be more easily forced to participate in "communal labour" than Ghanaian citizens. Although – with the exception of forced cultivation in some regions in colonial sub-Saharan Africa – not strictly agricultural in nature, these communal labour obligations impacted rural communities immensely. They drew labour away from agricultural work with little compensation in return, and restricted workers' mobility. These practices are another example of how states, instead of safeguarding agricultural labourers' rights, actively contributed to their exploitation.

Dina Bolokan (Chapter 15) takes labour relations in twenty-first-century European agriculture as the point of departure for her dissection of "neo-colonial labour regimes of im_mobilisation." What the vegetable and fruit industries in Italy or Spain and the meat industry in Saxony/Germany have in common is the coexistence of their workers' hypermobility and confinement. These workers are mobile because they migrate from Africa, Latin America, Asia or Eastern Europe to the production centres in the European Union; they are mobile because they follow the demand for their labour, from factory to slaughter house and from plastic tent to field. At the same time, the migrant workers are confined to these production sites, Bolokan argues, since they are closely monitored and allow little room for movement. The author traces the historical roots of this labour regime back to the nineteenth century, by looking at state interventions to recruit and regulate (migrant) agricultural labour in Switzerland and Prussia/Germany. Historically, too, Bolokan concludes, recruitment policies as well as migration restrictions both stimulated and confined migrants' labour mobility, in whatever way might have suited capitalists' and state interests.

Mobility and confinement also characterise the situation of the migrant labourers in the present-day Malaysian palm oil industry. In Chapter 16, Janina Puder describes a labour migration regime which is strongly supported by the Malaysian state. Palm oil production has become a major concern of Malaysia's economic development strategy – a trend that Puder traces back to the country's colonial past. As is common to production sites of the frontier zones of global capitalism, Malaysia's palm oil industry not only depends on inexpensive natural resources but also on cheap labour. The latter is primarily supplied by migrants from Indonesia. The powerful actors of this particular labour regime – the state in conjunction with plantation owners – developed various mechanisms to exploit these workers, from restrictive labour permits and low minimum wages to bureaucratic barriers to workers' formal organisation and their outright isolation.

The third and final question that is central in this volume concerns the changes and continuities in state interference with regard to (migrant) agricultural labour, and how we can explain these. In combination with the seasonality and absolute or relative scarcity of labour in particular branches of commercial agriculture, states have turned a blind eye to, or even facilitated, through particular labour or migration policies, the recruitment and exploitation of particular vulnerable groups of workers. Whether they were slaves from Africa, indentured labourers from South Asia or, like today, migrant workers from non-OECD countries working in relatively rich states, such as the European Union or Malaysia, the interests of merchants, planters and, more recently, agro-business have generally prevailed. In all chapters, the relationship with colonial pasts, and the changes and continuities with respect to these histories, become evident. Colonial or neo-colonial power relations were often in place to reinforce unequal measures and policies. This is not to say that the agency of agricultural workers has been completely absent. In the nineteenth century, indentured labourers in the French Empire sometimes dragged their employers to court if their payment was stalled or their contracts were breached; African migrant workers in Italy today protest against bad working conditions in fruit and vegetable companies. Likewise, Ghanaians have tried to resist having to take on communal labour duties. However, in many cases, even more vulnerable groups, often migrant labourers, are available to take on the work that others refuse to do.

6   Final Observations

This volume makes an important contribution to the study of agrarian labour relations in long-term, global perspective. Although being far from exhaustive, the chapters in this book highlight a number of continuities and discontinuities in the history of agricultural production. First of all, many of the contributions stress the importance of small-scale peasant production, in the past and present, for the safeguarding of food security – especially in the Global South – and highlight it as a possible solution to the further degradation of the natural environment. At the same time, this volume shows the longstanding historical trend of important currents *countering* the security and sovereignty of agricultural producers: the use of coercion as well as the lack of protection, and even the active facilitation, of agrarian labourers' precarity by state policies. Taking a long-term historical perspective is crucial because the problems of food security faced by the peasantry in the Global South today cannot be understood without analysing their colonial roots. As economist Utsa Patnaik has recently argued, the colonial past still determines "the present-day continuing thrust of Northern countries using new free trade regimes and income-deflating policies to access the products of the Global South."[62]

Can one indeed see the present-day "corporate food regime" as the continuation of earlier colonial power relations in the context of a globalising world economy? And does the role of the modern nation state, which, in many cases, enhances the interests of agro-business – for instance, through particular migration policies – parallel the coalition that existed between (capitalist) merchants and imperial states? Can "ensuring the viability of small-scale production ... and ensuring work and wages for rural labour"[63] indeed be a solution to effectively counter the pervasive exploitation of vulnerable groups in the countryside? More research is definitely desired to answer these questions. Perhaps "localisation" and small-scale production offer part of the key to solve these problems. However, additional structural solutions are likely needed and, here, globalisation, with its increasing means and speed of communication, might prove to be crucial. In fact, apart from the many similarities throughout time, there are also great contrasts with former historical periods. One important difference is that, nowadays, many NGOs, interest groups and researchers exist – ranging from the International Labour Organization and peasant interest groups to activist journalists – that are able to raise awareness, monitor and counter such abuses of agricultural workers. The United Nations Declaration on the Rights of Peasants and Other People Working in Rural Areas (UNDROP), adopted by the UN General Assembly in December 2018, could be seen as an important step towards protecting the rights of those working the land around the globe.

---

62   Utsa Patnaik, "An Alternative Perspective on the Agrarian Question in Europe and in the Developing Countries," in Akram-Lodhi et al., *Handbook*, 46.
63   Patnaik, "Alternative Perspective," 50.

Bibliography

Akram-Lodhi, Agha Haroon, Kristina Dietz, Bettina Engels, and Ben M. McKay, eds. *Handbook of Critical Agrarian Studies*. Northampton: Edward Elgar Publishing, 2021.

Avena, Nicole M., Pedro Rada, and Bartley G. Hoebel. "Evidence for Sugar Addiction: Behavioral and Neurochemical Effects of Intermittent, Excessive Sugar Intake." *Neuroscience and Biobehavioral Reviews* 32, no. 1 (2008): 20–39.

Bauer, Rolf. *The Peasant Production of Opium in Nineteenth-Century India*. Leiden and Boston: Brill, 2019.

Banaji, Jairus. "Summary of Selected Parts of Kautsky's *The Agrarian Question*." In *The Articulation of Modes of Production*, edited by Harold Wolpe, 45–93. London and New York: Routledge, 1980.

Beckert, Sven, Ulbe Bosma, Mindi Schneider, and Eric Vanhaute. "Commodity Frontiers and the Transformation of the Global Countryside: A Research Agenda." *Journal of Global History* 16, no. 3 (November 2021): 435–50.

Bosma, Ulbe, and Karin Hofmeester, eds. *The Life Work of a Labor Historian: Essays in Honor of Marcel van der Linden*. Leiden and Boston: Brill, 2018.

Chayanov, Alexander V. "On the Theory of Non-Capitalist Economic Systems." In *A. Chayanov: The Theory of Peasant Economy*, edited by Daniel Thorner, Basile H. Kerblay, and Robert E. F. Smith, 1–28. Homewood: AEA, 1966.

Chesney, Thomas, Keith Evans, Stefan Gold, and Alexander Trautrims. "Understanding Labour Exploitation in the Spanish Agricultural Sector Using an Agent Based Approach." *Journal of Cleaner Production* 214 (2019): 696–704.

Clayes, Priscilla, Annette Aurélie Desmarais, and Jasber Singh. "Food Sovereignty, Food Security and the Right to Food." In Akram-Lodhi et al., *Handbook of Critical Agrarian Studies*, 238–49.

Corrado, Alessandra. "Migrant Crop Pickers in Italy and Spain." E-Paper Heinrich Böll Foundation, 2017.

Courtwright, David T. *Forces of Habit: Drugs and the Making of the Modern World*. Cambridge, MA: Harvard University Press, 2001.

Domar, Evsey D. "The Causes of Slavery or Serfdom: A Hypothesis." *The Journal of Economic History* 30, no. 1 (1970): 18–32.

Friedmann, Harriet. "Household Production and the National Economy: Concepts for the Analysis of Agrarian Formations." *The Journal of Peasant Studies* 7, no. 2 (1980): 158–84.

Friedmann, Harriet. "Origins of Peasant Studies." In Akram-Lodhi et al., *Handbook of Critical Agrarian Studies*, 15–24.

Hofmeester, Karin, and Marcel van der Linden, eds. *Handbook Global History of Work*. Berlin: De Gruyter Oldenbourg, 2018.

Hofmeester, Karin, and Marcel Van der Linden, "Introduction." In Hofmeester and Van der Linden, *Handbook Global History of Work,* 1–14.

Hopkins, Terence K. and Immanuel Wallerstein. "Commodity Chains in the World-Economy Prior to 1800." In Wallerstein, *The Essential Wallerstein,* 221–33.

Lucassen, Jan. *The Story of Work: A New History of Humankind.* New Haven: Yale University Press, 2021.

McMichael, Philip. "Global Development and The Corporate Food Regime." *New Directions in the Sociology of Global Development* 11 (2005): 265–99.

McMichael, Philip. "Historicizing Food Sovereignty." *The Journal of Peasant Studies* 41, no. 6 (2014): 933–57.

McMichael, Philip. "Food Regimes." In Akram-Lodhi et al., *Handbook of Critical Agrarian Studies,* 218–31.

Moore, Jason W. *Capitalism in the Web of Life: Ecology and the Accumulation of Capital.* New York: Verso, 2015.

Nieboer, Herman Jeremias. *Slavery as an Industrial System: Ethnological Researches.* The Hague: M. Nijhoff, 1900.

Patnaik, Utsa. "An Alternative Perspective on the Agrarian Question in Europe and in the Developing Countries." In Akram-Lodhi et al., *Handbook of Critical Agrarian Studies,* 45–51.

Ploeg, Jan Douwe van der. *The New Peasantries.* London and New York: Routledge, 2012.

Pye, Oliver. "Agrarian Marxism and the Proletariat: A Palm Oil Manifesto." *The Journal of Peasant Studies* 48, no. 4 (June 2021): 807–26.

Saunders, Kay. "Introduction." In *Indentured Labour in the British Empire, 1834–1920,* edited by Kay Saunders, i–vii. London and Canberra: Croom Helm, 1984.

Schneider, Mindi, and Ulbe Bosma. "Stimulant Frontiers." *Commodity Frontiers* 2 (2021): i–iv.

Stanziani, Alessandro. "Introduction: Labour, Coercion, and Economic Growth in Eurasia, Seventeenth – Early Twentieth Centuries." In *Labour, Coercion, and Economic Growth in Eurasia, 17th–20th Centuries,* edited by Alessandro Stanziani, 1–26. Leiden and Boston: Brill, 2013.

Topik, Steven. "Historicizing Commodity Chains: Five Hundred Years of the Global Coffee Commodity Chain." In *Frontiers of Commodity Chain Research,* edited by Jennifer Bair, 37–62. Stanford: Stanford University Press, 2009.

Van Schendel, Willem. "Beyond Labor History's Comfort Zone?" In Bosma, Hofmeester, and Van der Linden, *The Life Work of a Labor Historian,* 174–208.

Vanhaute, Eric. "Agriculture." In Hofmeester and Van der Linden, *Handbook Global History of Work,* 229–47.

Vanhaute, Eric. *Peasants in World History.* New York and London: Routledge, 2021.

Wallerstein, Immanuel Maurice, ed. *The Essential Wallerstein.* New York: New Press, 2000.

Wallerstein, Immanuel Maurice. *The Second Era of Great Expansion of the Capitalist World-Economy, 1730–1840s*. San Diego: Academic Press, 1989.

Wallerstein, Immanuel Maurice, Carlos Antonio Aguirre Rojas, and Charles C. Lemert. *Uncertain Worlds: World-Systems Analysis in Changing Times*. Boulder, CO: Paradigm Publishers, 2012.

Watts, Michael. "The Agrarian Question." In Akram-Lodhi et al., *Handbook of Critical Agrarian Studies*, 53–66.

PART 1

The Agrarian Question and the Resilience of the Peasant Family Farms

∴

CHAPTER 1

Peasant Households under Pressure

Women's Work and the Cultivation System on Java, 1830–1870

Elise van Nederveen Meerkerk

1 Introduction: Colonial Extraction and Women's Work*

The costs and benefits of empire have been intensively debated by contemporaries as well as historians. Some historians have focused on the relatively high (especially military) costs of maintaining the British, French and Portuguese empires.[1] Others have argued, instead, that the costs were relatively minimal and that the net benefits for the metropole prevailed; if not in terms of economics, then at least in terms of political power and status.[2] Most scholars seem to agree, however, that, within metropolitan societies, the elites and capitalists had by far the most to gain from their nations' overseas possessions.[3] Apart from the costs and benefits for the *metropoles*, the costs and benefits for the inhabitants of the *colonies* are particularly relevant to this debate. In terms of natural resources and taxation in cash or in kind, ordinary colonised people generally paid a high price for colonialism, whereas the benefits they received were – at least until the early twentieth century – either negligible, or funded from their own contributions to the colonial state.[4] These issues are

---

* This research was conducted under the ERC-funded Consolidator Grant project "Race to the Bottom?" (Acronym TextileLab, Grant number #771288), of which the author is the Principal Investigator.

1 See, for instance, Patrick O'Brien, "The Costs and Benefits of British Imperialism 1846–1914," *Past & Present* 120 (1988): 163–200; Lance E. Davis and Robert A. Huttenback, *Mammon and the Pursuit of Empire: The Political Economy of British Imperialism, 1860–1912* (Cambridge: Cambridge University Press, 1986); Jacques Marseille, *Empire colonial et capitalisme français: Histoire d'un divorce* (Paris: Albin Michel, 1984).

2 Paul Kennedy, "Debate: The Costs and Benefits of British Imperialism 1846–1914," *Past & Present* 125 (1989): 186–92; Avner Offer, "The British Empire, 1870–1914: A Waste of Money?" *Economic History Review* 46, no. 2 (1993): 215–38; Philip J. Havik, "Colonial Administration, Public Accounts and Fiscal Extraction: Policies and Revenues in Portuguese Africa (1900–1960)," *African Economic History* 41 (2013): 171.

3 For instance, Davis and Huttenback, *Mammon*, 317.

4 For recent studies on the lack of investment in the well-being of indigenous populations, see, among others, Anne Booth, "Night Watchman, Extractive, or Developmental States? Some Evidence from Late Colonial South-East Asia," *Economic History Review*

---

at the heart of questions on the degree of colonial extraction, and how this affected the well-being of indigenous societies and economies.

One problem in answering these questions is that colonial extraction (and redistribution) is difficult to measure. Not only are the sources incomplete and often incomparable, there are also many different forms of extraction – ranging from sheer theft to indirect taxation – in cash or in kind. Also, it is often unclear which types of revenue historians include in their estimates of colonial extraction. In this chapter, I employ a broad definition of colonial extraction as "a net transfer of economically valuable resources from indigenous to metropolitan societies."[5] Such remittances generally consisted of tax revenues, returns from government monopolies on commerce, and unremitted government transfers.[6] In this broad definition of colonial extraction, indigenous labour services and *corvée* labour – be they for public works, as a form of non-monetary taxation, or systems of forced cultivation – ought to be included.[7] Often, colonisers legitimised practices of forced labour by claiming that these covered the costs of maintaining the empire, which included, for instance, investments in infrastructure or warfare in the colonies.

Towards the end of the nineteenth century, both with an eye to imperial competition and for humanitarian reasons, metropoles as well as the international community started to monitor excessive forms of extraction. However, the degree of control was amenable to definitions of what was considered extractive, and the ways in which "tradition" served to continue precolonial forms of taxation, such as *corvée* labour.[8] Especially with regard to building

---

60, no. 2 (2007): 257 (Dutch and British Southeast Asia); Elise Huillery, "The Black Man's Burden: The Cost of Colonization of French West Africa," *The Journal of Economic History* 74, no. 1 (2014): 1–38 (French West Africa); Havik, "Colonial Administration"; and Kleoniki Alexopoulou "An Anatomy of Colonial States and Fiscal Regimes in Portuguese Africa: Long-Term Transformations in Angola and Mozambique, 1850s–1970s" (PhD diss., Wageningen University, 2018) (Portuguese Africa).

5   Ewout Frankema and Frans Buelens, "Introduction," in *Colonial Exploitation and Economic Development: The Belgian Congo and the Netherlands Indies Compared*, ed. Ewout Frankema and Frans Buelens (London and New York: Routledge, 2013), 2.

6   Anne Booth, *The Indonesian Economy in the Nineteenth and Twentieth Centuries: A History of Missed Opportunities*; *A Modern Economic History of Southeast Asia* (London: Macmillan, 1998), 138–39.

7   See for a recent discussion of (forced) labour as a form of colonial taxation: Marlous van Waijenburg, "Financing the African Colonial State: The Revenue Imperative and Forced Labor," *The Journal of Economic History* 78, no. 1 (2018): 40–80, notably 41–42.

8   See, for instance, Alexander Keese, "Slow Abolition within the Colonial Mind: British and French Debates about 'Vagrancy,' 'African Laziness,' and Forced Labour in West Central and South Central Africa, 1945–1965," *International Review of Social History* 59, no. 3 (2014): 377–407; and Van Waijenburg, "Financing."

and infrastructure, imperial powers hid behind supposedly long-standing traditions of labour services, in which local elites demanded part of the (male) population to invest in public works.[9]

Despite the recent growing attention to forced labour in the colonial context, most studies tend to focus on the contributions of male workers, especially those working in the construction and maintenance of roads and infrastructure, or in mining.[10] More "hidden," indirect forms of labour extraction, such as the extra input of family members other than the male head of household due to shifts in his labour allocation, have often been overlooked, both by contemporaries and historians. By contrast, this chapter aims to connect the study of colonial extraction to indigenous women's work in agriculture, by investigating the case of Java under the Cultivation System. This system was introduced by the Dutch in 1830, and was highly profitable until the 1860s, which is why it has also been called a "classic piece of colonial exploitation."[11] At least until the 1870s, net remittances from Java to the Netherlands – after subtracting costs such as colonial administration and defence – were larger than in most other imperial contexts.[12] Between 1830 and 1870, the Cultivation System involved the labour of millions of Javanese households. A heavy mix of taxes and cultivation obligations burdened the majority of the Javanese peasant population.

In this chapter, I will present estimates of changing Javanese women's labour input under the influence of the Cultivation System. By estimating the amount of labour required for particular types of agricultural as well as non-agricultural production, and by an analysis of shifts in labour relations within households, a clearer picture will emerge of the labour burden on households, and particularly of the role Javanese women played in this crucial period of

9   For such indigenous labour services increasing under colonial rule, see, for instance, Peter Boomgaard, *Children of the Colonial State: Population Growth and Economic Development in Java, 1795–1880* (Amsterdam: Free University Press, 1989), 51 (Dutch East Indies); Keese, "Slow Abolition" (Central Africa) and Sarah Kunkel, "Forced Labour, Roads, and Chiefs: The Implementation of the ILO Forced Labour Convention in the Gold Coast," *International Review of Social History* 63, no. 3 (2018): 449–76 (Gold Coast).

10   For public works, see the works cited in the previous footnote. For a recent example of a study on forced labour in mines, see, for example, Kleoniki Alexopoulou and Dácil Juif, "Colonial State Formation without Integration: Tax Capacity and Labour Regimes in Portuguese Mozambique (1890s–1970s)," *International Review of Social History* 62, no. 2 (2017): 215–52.

11   Robert E. Elson, *Village Java under the Cultivation System, 1830–1870* (Sydney: Asian Studies Association of Australia [etc.], 1994), 303.

12   Angus Maddison, "Dutch Income in and from Indonesia 1700–1938," *Modern Asian Studies* 23, no. 4 (1989): 646; Booth, "Night Watchman," 257.

economic change. Most crucially, the increasing labour demands of the system led to a growing role for women in agriculture. First of all, their activities in subsistence agriculture increased, and, secondly, there were multiple ways in which they became involved in the production of cash crops, even if the colonial authorities eschewed recruiting women (or children) for this purpose. Apart from agriculture, the Cultivation System expanded women's activities in trade as well as domestic industries. As these were also important supplemental income-generating activities for peasant households, they will be briefly touched upon in this chapter.

2   Why Women, Work and Colonialism?[13]

Studying the agricultural work of women in a colonial context is important for several reasons. First of all, labour relations – and, in particular, the position of women in the household and the labour market – signify not only economic but also important social, cultural and political developments. Labour was often crucial in shaping colonial relations, as the scarcity of workers needed to obtain the natural resources the tropics had to offer was a constant concern of imperial rulers – whether they were Spanish, British, French, Portuguese, Dutch or Belgian. From the silver mines and the plantations in Latin America to the population-scarce and land-abundant areas of Africa, as well as in the labour-intensive rice planting economies in Southeast Asia, colonisers found it difficult to find and consolidate a labour force that was willing to work to their benefit.[14] For instance, the Dutch East India Company (VOC: *Vereenigde Oost-Indische Compagnie*) sailing to the coasts of what is nowadays called the Indonesian Archipelago, encountered communities that were overwhelmingly

---

13   The title of this section alludes to my recent monograph: Elise van Nederveen Meerkerk, *Women, Work and Colonialism in the Netherlands and Java: Comparisons, Contrasts, and Connections, 1830–1940* (London: Palgrave Macmillan, 2019). The current chapter draws heavily from the book, in particular chapter 3, but has been thoroughly revised for the purpose of this edited volume.

14   The literature on labour scarcity in European powers' overseas colonies is vast. Labour scarcity certainly predated the nineteenth century. See, for example, Rosanna Barragan, "Extractive Economy and Institutions? Technology, Labour, and Land in Potosí, the Sixteenth to the Eighteenth Century," in *Colonialism, Institutional Change, and Shifts in Global Labour Relations*, ed. Karin Hofmeester and Pim de Zwart (Amsterdam: Amsterdam University Press, 2018), 207–37; Ravi Ahuja, "Labour Relations in an Early Colonial Context: Madras, c. 1750–1800," *Modern Asian Studies* 36, no. 4 (2002): e.g., 797 (British India).

focused on agricultural production for subsistence and regional markets. It was difficult for the VOC traders to convince peasants to voluntarily cultivate cash crops, such as coffee, for export markets, and they resorted to alliances with local elites and forced labour in order to gain this high-profit tropical produce.[15] In the early nineteenth century, when the Dutch intensified their colonial administration on the island of Java, an even more stringent regime of forced cultivation, the notorious "Cultivation System" (*Kultuurstelsel*, c. 1830–1870) was implemented. Again, historians researching the Cultivation System have focused on the effects on male labour, or at best on indigenous *households*. As I will argue for the case of colonial Java, the reallocation of women's work facilitated part of the solution to this labour scarcity.

Second, "gender was an important axis along which colonial power was constructed."[16] Colonial encounters created "gender frontiers," in which "two or more culturally specific systems of knowledge about gender and nature met and confronted one another, forcing the invention of new identities and social practices."[17] These confrontations of different gender systems presented the problem of understanding the different expectations on either side regarding the roles of men and women. From the first colonial encounters onwards, European definitions of appropriate gender roles were used to "demasculinise" colonised men. This pertained to a whole range of gender-specific expectations,[18] but particularly when Europeans encountered gender-specific divisions of labour that were unusual to them. For instance, European colonists described African men who spun and washed as "womanly,"[19] or Indian men as "effeminate" and incapable of providing for their families.[20] In the case of colonial Java, many contemporary Dutch observers commented upon the

---

15   Jan Breman, *Koloniaal profijt van onvrije arbeid: Het Preanger stelsel van gedwongen koffieteelt op Java, 1720–1870* (Amsterdam: Amsterdam University Press, 2010).

16   Mrinalini Sinha, *Colonial Masculinity: The "Manly Englishman" and the "Effeminate Bengali" in the Late Nineteenth Century* (Manchester: Manchester University Press, 1995), 11.

17   Kathleen Wilson, "Empire, Gender, and Modernity in the Eighteenth Century," in *Gender and Empire*, ed. Philippa Levine (Oxford: Oxford University Press, 2004), 23.

18   For recent analyses of gender and empire, see Merry Wiesner-Hanks, "Crossing Borders in Transnational Gender History," *Journal of Global History* 6, no. 3 (2011); Elise van Nederveen Meerkerk, "Gender and Empire: Postcolonial Perspectives on Women and Gender in the "West" and the "East," 17th–20th Centuries," in *Vingt-cinq ans après: Les femmes au rendez-vous de l'histoire*, ed. Enrica Asquer et al. (Rome: École Française de Rome, 2019).

19   Susan D. Amussen and Allyson M. Poska, "Restoring Miranda: Gender and the Limits of European Patriarchy in the Early Modern Atlantic World," *Journal of Global History* 7, no. 3 (2012): 344.

20   Sinha, *Colonial Masculinity*, 55.

perceived "laziness" of indigenous men in contrast to the "industriousness" of their wives.[21] This was a way to represent dark-skinned Javanese men as less masculine than their white, European counterparts, confirming the latter's superiority and thus justifying their presence in the colony.

Third, studying the role of women in the household economy provides a more complete and accurate picture of the importance of the labour factor in practices of colonial extraction, as well as in the development of living standards. Many historians have contended that the living standards of the Javanese population deteriorated, or at best stagnated during the nineteenth and early twentieth centuries.[22] So far, Javanese women's economic activities and their contributions to the household income have generally not been accounted for in debates on the standard of living.[23] This is unfortunate, as the importance of women's work, either paid or unpaid, is increasingly being acknowledged in the more general literature on households' living standards.[24]

3   The Cultivation System in Java (1830 – c. 1870)

Dutch interference with the Indonesian Archipelago dates from the late sixteenth century. Although the VOC had established a few strongholds

21   See, for instance, H. W. Daendels, *Staat der Nederlandsche Oostindische bezittingen: Bijlagen, organique stukken, preparatoire mesures* (The Hague, 1814), 104; *Onderzoek naar de mindere welvaart der Inlandsche bevolking op Java en Madoera*, vol. Ixb3, *Verheffing van de Inlandsche vrouw* (Batavia: Kolff [etc.], 1914), 1; Philip Levert, *Inheemsche arbeid in de Java-suikerindustrie* (Wageningen: Landbouwhogeschool, 1934), 247.

22   Peter Boomgaard, *Children*; Booth, *Indonesian Economy*, 114; Pim de Zwart and Jan Luiten van Zanden, "Labor, Wages, and Living Standards in Java, 1680–1914," *European Review of Economic History* 19 (2015): 215–34.

23   This is also largely true for the standard literature on living standards in the Western world, which is often based on male wages. See, for instance, Robert C. Allen, "The Great Divergence in European Wages and Prices from the Middle Ages to the First World War," *Explorations in Economic History* 38, no. 4 (2001); Robert C. Allen, *The British Industrial Revolution in Global Perspective* (Cambridge: Cambridge University Press, 2009).

24   See, for example, for Britain, Sarah Horrell and Jane Humphries, "Women's Labour Force Participation and the Transition to the Male-Breadwinner Family, 1790–1865," *Economic History Review* 48, no. 1 (1995): 89–117; Jane Humphries, "The Lure of Aggregates and the Pitfalls of the Patriarchal Perspective: A Critique of the High Wage Economy Interpretation of the British Industrial Revolution," *Economic History Review* 66, no. 3 (2013): 693–714. For the Netherlands, see Van Nederveen Meerkerk, *Women, Work and Colonialism*, Chapter 5; Corinne Boter, "Living Standards and the Life Cycle: Reconstructing Household Income and Consumption in the Eearly Twentieth-Century Netherlands," *Economic History Review* 73, no. 4 (2020): 1050–73.

throughout the archipelago, and particularly on the most populous island of Java, it never gained full authority and relied on relationships with indigenous elites and indirect rule to be able to make its huge profits. In coalition with local rulers in the West-Javanese province of Priangan, for instance, forced coffee cultivation was implemented, which was lucrative for the elites and European traders but highly burdensome for the Priangan peasants, as it demanded more from their labour and land.[25] The voc went bankrupt by the end of the eighteenth century, and during the Napoleonic Wars the British took up rule in Java between 1811 and 1815. Following the Anglo-Dutch Treaty, the East Indies were returned to the Netherlands, and the newly installed Dutch King Willem I explicitly wished to make the colony gainful to the Dutch treasury. The metropole maintained the land tax the British had introduced in Java, and further aimed to stimulate bilateral trade with the colony. However, the Dutch failed to outcompete the British under the system of free trade, and Java became more of a burden than a cash cow in the 1820s, adding to the already large metropolitan state deficit.[26] To counter this problem, the Dutch designed more protective trade policies, in combination with forced cash crop cultivation; this became known as the "Cultivation System." This system, designed by one of the King's trustees, Johannes van den Bosch, involved Javanese households' forced cultivation of export crops, such as coffee, tea, indigo and sugar, in exchange for monetary compensation.

Van den Bosch was appointed Governor-General in Batavia (present-day Jakarta) in 1830. He was strongly convinced that Javanese peasants needed to be stimulated to cultivate cash crops for the world market instead of merely producing rice for their own subsistence. Enhancing their industriousness would benefit both the indigenous population and the Dutch state. To achieve this, Javanese peasants were expected to reserve a proportion of their land (ideally 20 per cent, although in practice this differed per region) as well as their labour to produce export crops for the Dutch colonial authorities. For their surpluses, peasants would receive monetary compensation, called "planter's wage" (*plantloon*).[27] However, in order for the colonial government to be able to make a profit, for most peasants this compensation was only two-thirds

---

25   Breman, *Koloniaal profijt*.

26   Janny de Jong, "Van batig slot naar ereschuld: De discussie over de financiële verhouding tussen Nederland en Indië en de hervorming van de Nederlandse koloniale politiek, 1860–1900" (Master's thesis, University of Groningen, 1989), 19–21.

27   Albert Schrauwers, "The 'Benevolent' Colonies of Johannes van den Bosch: Continuities in the Administration of Poverty in the Netherlands and Indonesia," *Comparative Studies in Society and History* 43, no. 2 (2001): 316.

of the market price for these export crops. Moreover, part of this money served to pay taxes to indigenous elites and Dutch civil servants. Thus, in practice, Javanese households only received about one-third of the market value for their produce.[28]

Although its impact varied greatly between the different regions of Java, overall, the Cultivation System widely impacted both the Javanese and the Dutch economies and, consequently, the work that was delivered by the men, women and children living in Javanese peasant households. Initially, the system was installed to replace the land tax, but, in fact, it functioned alongside it, and other forms of *corvée* labour for the community also continued to exist.[29] While the execution of the Cultivation System has been typified as "based upon an unsophisticated style of trial and error,"[30] including many failures and mishaps, its extractive effects are without a doubt. The fact that both Dutch administrators and village heads (*bupati*) received a percentage of the peasants' proceeds (*kultuurprocenten*) for their active interventions surely encouraged these overseers to continuously persuade peasants to deliver high yields.[31]

The success of the Cultivation System, in terms of the production volumes of cash crops, became evident within just a few years (Figure 1.1). Until the early 1840s, the forced cultivation of coffee was especially lucrative for the colonial authorities: the yield of coffee beans roughly quadrupled in the first decade of the system, from around twenty to eighty thousand tons per year. From then onwards, sugar gradually became the most prominent export product. In its final stage, the Cultivation System annually delivered about 160,000 tons of refined cane sugar to the Dutch state, to be sold on the world market, where the demand for sugar was rising rapidly.[32]

Over the decades, the net profits for the metropole were enormous (see Table 1.1 on page 40), as hundreds of millions of guilders landed in the Dutch state coffers.

---

28   Edwin Horlings, "Miracle Cure for an Economy in Crisis? Colonial Exploitation as a Source of Growth in the Netherlands, 1815–1870," in *Colonial Empires Compared: Britain and the Netherlands, 1750–1850*, ed. Bob Moore and Henk van Nierop (Aldershot: Ashgate, 2003), 154.

29   Cees Fasseur, *Kultuurstelsel en koloniale baten: De Nederlandse exploitatie van Java 1840–1860*. (Leiden: Universitaire Pers Leiden, 1992), 90. Ulbe Bosma, "Dutch Imperial Anxieties about Free Labour, Penal Sanctions and the Right to Strike," in *Labour, Coercion, and Economic Growth in Eurasia, 17th–20th centuries*, ed. Alessandro Stanziani (Leiden: Brill, 2013), 72.

30   Elson, *Village Java*, 82.

31   Elson, *Village Java*, 42, 44.

32   For a classic study of the importance of sugar in production, consumption and unequal economic relations, see Sidney Mintz, *Sweetness and Power: The Place of Sugar in Modern History* (New York: Viking, 1985).

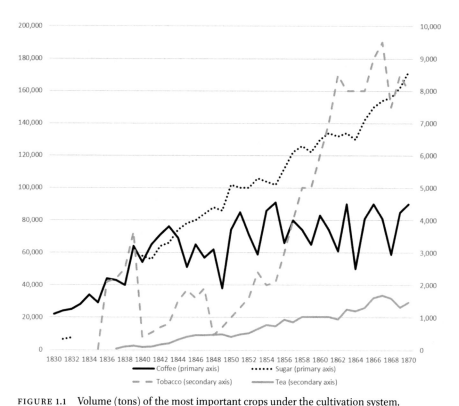

FIGURE 1.1   Volume (tons) of the most important crops under the cultivation system,
            1830–1870
            SOURCE: DATA FROM W. M. F. MANSVELT AND P. CREUTZBERG, *CHANGING
            ECONOMY OF INDONESIA: A SELECTION OF STATISTICAL SOURCE MATERIAL
            FROM THE EARLY 19TH CENTURY UP TO 1940*, VOL. 5, *INDONESIA'S EXPORT
            CROPS, 1816–1940* (THE HAGUE: MARTINUS NIJHOF, 1975), 52–53

Over the entire period, more than one billion Dutch guilders are estimated
to have been transferred to the Dutch treasury as *batig slot* (colonial surplus).
The colonial remittances formed a vital supplement to the state budget, which
allowed for restructuring the large public debt from 1843 onwards, and for
infrastructural improvements in the metropole.[33]

However, for Javanese peasants the system was much less profitable.
Although some historians have argued that the Cultivation System may have
enhanced the economic viability of Javanese villages, bringing, for instance,

---

33   Horlings, "Miracle Cure," 166.

TABLE 1.1   Net colonial remittances to the Dutch treasury, 1831–1877

Period	Net colonial surplus (million Dfl)	% of Dutch GNP	% of Dutch tax income
1831–1840	150.6	2.8	31.9
1841–1850	215.6	3.6	38.6
1851–1860	289.4	3.8	52.6
1861–1870	276.7	2.9	44.5
1871–1877	127.2	1.7	26.5

SOURCES: 1831–1870: ESTIMATES BY JAN LUITEN VAN ZANDEN AND ARTHUR VAN RIEL, *THE STRICTURES OF INHERITANCE: THE DUTCH ECONOMY IN THE NINETEENTH CENTURY* (PRINCETON: PRINCETON UNIVERSITY PRESS, 2004), 180, INCLUDING HIDDEN GOVERNMENT SUBSIDIES. 1870–1877: JANNY DE JONG, "VAN BATIG SLOT NAAR EERESCHULD: DE DISCUSSIE OVER DE FINANCIËLE VERHOUDING TUSSEN NEDERLAND EN INDIË EN DE HERVORMING VAN DE NEDERLANDSE KOLONIALE POLITIEK, 1860–1900" (MASTER'S THESIS, UNIVERSITY OF GRONINGEN, 1989) 133, 262; GNP: JAN-PIETER SMITS, EDWIN HORLINGS, AND JAN LUITEN VAN ZANDEN, *DUTCH GNP AND ITS COMPONENTS, 1800–1913* (GRONINGEN: GROWTH AND DEVELOPMENT CENTER, 2000), 173, 177

monetisation and infrastructural developments,[34] most scholars have, instead, pointed to the extractive and disruptive effects of the system for indigenous peasants.[35] Table 1.2 shows the number of households and amount of arable land involved in the Cultivation System after its installation in 1830, attesting to the quick spread and impact of the system. Of the more than 1.1 million households living in Java in the 1830s and 1840s, two-thirds up to almost three-quarters produced crops for the Dutch authorities, and, at its peak in the 1840s, over a quarter of all land suitable for agriculture was in use for forced cash crop cultivation.

Apart from the increasing demand for their labour for cash crop cultivation, both European and indigenous officials demanded extra labour services, for public works, such as road maintenance, but also – illegitimately – for private purposes, such as working their land.[36] On top of this, the land tax as well as

---

34   See, for instance, Elson, *Village Java*; Melissa Dell and Benjamin A. Olken, "The Development Effects of the Extractive Colonial Economy: The Dutch Cultivation System in Java" (NBER working paper no. 24009, 2017).

35   For instance, Boomgaard, *Children*; Booth, *Indonesian Economy*; De Zwart and Van Zanden, "Labor".

36   Robert Van Niel, *Java under the Cultivation System* (Leiden: KITLV Press, 1992), 81; Booth, *Indonesian Economy*, 21.

TABLE 1.2   Households and arable land engaged in forced cultivation, averages for Java 1836–1870

Year	% of households	% of total arable land
1836	67.1	18.3
1840	73.3	26.2
1845	69.5	24.8
1850	63.0	21.4
1855	61.0	21.2
1860	56.2	19.0
1865	54.1	16.4
1870	39.3	13.0

SOURCES: DATA FROM ROBERT E. ELSON, *VILLAGE JAVA UNDER THE CULTIVATION SYSTEM, 1830–1870* (SYDNEY: ASIAN STUDIES ASSOCIATION OF AUSTRALIA [ETC.], 1994), 185; F. VAN BAARDEWIJK, *CHANGING ECONOMY OF INDONESIA: A SELECTION OF STATISTICAL SOURCE MATERIAL FROM THE EARLY 19TH CENTURY UP TO 1940*, VOL. 14, *THE CULTIVATION SYSTEM, JAVA 1834–1880* (AMSTERDAM: KIT, 1993), 190–93

indirect levies on consumption and marketed products increased notably in the same period.[37] The outrageous demands on peasant households for labour services as well as cash payments led many of them into debt. Particularly men, who were pressed to provide labour services for the Cultivation System as well as being asked to perform other *corvée* duties, were unable to reserve sufficient time for subsistence production. This increasingly endangered peasants' food security. In the 1840s, the increased labour burden, in combination with bad weather conditions, epidemic diseases, crop failures and rising rice prices, led to successive famines in several residencies.[38] The inability to deal with these difficulties in ensuring food security, which led many people to migrate or even die, was closely linked to imbalances caused by the Cultivation System. Ironically, it was those peasants who fled their land to escape extortion, famine or epidemics, who ended up losing their rights to that land. As their land was usually claimed by the village elites, this led to increasing socio-economic polarisation.[39]

---

37   Van Niel, *Cultivation System*, 143.
38   Elson, *Village Java*, 119.
39   Elson, *Village Java*, 124–125.

As is evident, the effects of the Cultivation System on the labour time and economic well-being of Javanese households were tremendous, and, especially in its initial phase, the system led to serious problems for peasant households' livelihoods. Some studies have suggested that Javanese peasant households adjusted quite adequately to the increasing demands of the system;[40] however, the dynamics that were in place are still unclear. In the next section, I will argue that, to a large extent, the ability of households to adapt to new circumstances related to the flexibility with which women in particular employed their time.

4   Changes in Women's Work under the Cultivation System

Women in Southeast Asia have traditionally played a large role in subsistence agriculture, performing gender-specific tasks. Women, sometimes assisted by children, were responsible for the labour-intensive transplanting of young rice seedlings to the wet rice fields (*sawahs*), whereas men were in charge of maturing the crop in the following three months, in tasks such as weeding, tilling and irrigation. Harvesting was a community task, in which women and children, again, played an important role.[41] It is likely that an intensification of women's labour in subsistence rice cultivation occurred due to the labour demands the Cultivation System imposed on households and, in particular, on their adult male members, to grow cash crops. Although in some regions the system led farmers to plant their *sawahs* with sugar or indigo, this competition with subsistence crops was often avoided by creating new fields for rice.[42] Moreover, in principle, coffee was grown on drylands. All of this implies that the cultivation of cash crops, mostly done by men, came on top of rice cultivation. Of course, this seriously extended the total workload of households.[43] After 1830, obligations such as cash crop cultivation and other forced labour services greatly aggravated the additional labour burden on male peasants.[44] Especially sugar and indigo took much more than the anticipated sixty-six days' labour

---

40   Boomgaard, *Children*; Elson, *Village Java*.
41   Elson, *Village Java*, 6.
42   Elson, *Village Java*, 238–39.
43   Boomgaard, *Children*, 82–83.
44   Although *corvée* labour was intended only for the male breadwinner (*adjek*), there are indications that forced labour services increased to such an extent that household "dependants" (*afhangelingen*), too, were required to provide these services: Arsip Nasional Republik Indonesia (ANRI), Jakarta, Indonesia, K50 – Archief Directeur der Cultures (Cultures), file 1623, Residential report Tegal 1856.

to produce, and were more likely to consume between 120 and 130 days of an adult man's time.[45] In some regions, such as Pekalongan (North Central Java), male peasants had only fifty labour days left to spend on food production for their own use, where about ninety were required.[46]

As a consequence, women's involvement in agriculture increased. Around 1900, on average about 75 per cent of all hours spent on rice cultivation was performed by women,[47] compared with an estimated 50 per cent *before* the Cultivation System.[48] This also implied a change in gendered divisions of work. For example, harvesting – which, prior to the Cultivation System, had been done by men and women together – became a more exclusively female task.[49] By reallocating much of men's work in subsistence agriculture to women, Javanese women played an important role in restoring peasant households' food security after the first difficult years of the Cultivation System. It is likely that in the heyday of the system the corresponding figure was even slightly higher.

Although statistical information about the work of women in Java is notoriously lacking for the period of the Cultivation System, there are indirect ways to estimate their increased involvement in subsistence agriculture. By combining available information on the historical development of arable land and rice in Java[50] with more qualitative descriptions of women's involvement in rice cultivation,[51] we can arrive at aggregate estimates of the number of days women spent on subsistence production during the Cultivation System (see

45   Boomgaard, *Children*, 82.

46   Elson, *Village Java*, 88.

47   L. Koch, *Bijdrage tot de ontleding van het Inlandsch landbouwbedrijf* (Batavia: Landbouwvoorlichtingsdienst, 1919), 4–7.

48   Elsbeth Locher-Scholten, "Door een gekleurde bril ... Koloniale bronnen over vrouwenarbeid op Java in de negentiende en twintigste eeuw," *Jaarboek voor Vrouwengeschiedenis* 7 (1986): 39; Barbara Watson Andaya, "Women and Economic Change: The Pepper Trade in Pre-Modern Southeast Asia," *Journal of the Economic and Social History of the Orient* 38, no. 2 (1995): 167.

49   Peter Boomgaard and Jan Luiten van Zanden, *Food Crops and Arable Lands, Java 1815–1942: Changing Economy of Indonesia; A Selection of Statistical Source Material from the Early 19th Century up to 1940*, vol. 10 (Amsterdam: KIT, 1990), 17.

50   Most of this material was collected in the context of the research project *Changing Economy in Indonesia* and its subsequent publications. This series of publications of statistical source material relating to the Dutch East Indies for the period 1795–1940 was launched by W. M. F. Mansvelt in 1975, and the final volume appeared in 1996. See also Van Nederveen Meerkerk, *Women, Work and Colonialism*, Chapter 1, Section 1.6.

51   For example, Peter Boomgaard, "Female Labour and Population Growth on Nineteenth Century Java," *Review of Indonesian and Malayan Affairs* 15, no. 2 (1981): 19; Elson, *Village Java*.

Table 1.3). The table lists the available statistics on rice yields and arable lands (second and third columns) collected and published by Peter Boomgaard and Jan Luiten van Zanden, and lists the number of full-time (ten-hour) labour days needed for the cultivation of these amounts of rice (fourth column). From more descriptive literature, we know that, before the Cultivation System, women were involved in around 50 per cent of rice cultivation,[52] and that this rose over the nineteenth century (fifth column).[53] We can thus calculate the number of days women would have been involved in the different benchmark years (sixth column), and, relating this to the estimated number of adult women in the population, derived from the population statistics, we get an impression of what this meant in terms of number of days per adult woman per year (seventh column). In reality, of course, women did not work the land ten hours per day in the indicated number of days, as they were involved in many other, non-agricultural and household, tasks. They would have spread their agricultural activities over most of the year.

From these estimates, it can be concluded that the average adult Javanese peasant woman spent an increasing amount of time on rice cultivation, suggesting that the Cultivation System indeed impacted on the division of labour in peasant households. On average, due to the forced cultivations, men spent about twenty labour days less on rice cultivation, and this was presumably compensated by women, which would explain most of the rise in the number of labour days per adult woman between 1815 and 1836 shown in Table 1.3. The reallocation of women's time was caused by the additional tasks, such as weeding, that became necessary as many men were drawn into forced cultivation, and, as already mentioned, harvesting was also increasingly done by women.[54] In the residency of Pasuruan, for instance, colonial observers noted that, around 1840, women did all of the tasks, from transplanting the rice and weeding to harvesting.[55] Reforms to the Cultivation System, which were implemented after a severe subsistence crisis in the 1840s, seem to have temporarily interrupted this process, allowing men to spend some more time on rice production; however, after the 1860s, the relative involvement of women in subsistence production increased again, with rising per capita rice yields. It is, therefore, safe to say that the increasing time invested in rice production by

---

52   Locher-Scholten, "Door een gekleurde bril," 39.

53   Koch, *Bijdrage*, 4–7.

54   Boomgaard and Van Zanden, *Food Crops*, 17.

55   H. A. van der Poel, "Nota over de Rijstkultuur op Java," *Tijdschrift voor Nijverheid en Landbouw in Nederlandsch Indië* 11 (1865): 97–118.

TABLE 1.3   Estimated intensification of Javanese peasant women in rice cultivation, 1815–1880

Year	Rice yields (in 1,000 tons)	Ha of arable land	No. of labour days needed	% of women engaged in rice cultivation	Full-time labour days of women	No. of full-time days per adult woman	Index (1836 = 100)
1815	860.0	521,212	156,363,636	50	78,181,818	47	64
1836	1,202.6	884,265	252,015,441	70	176,410,809	72	100
1846	1,621.1	988,476	281,715,549	80	225,372,439	76	105
1860	2,051.2	1,235,663	352,163,855	80	281,731,084	74	102
1870	2,849.2	1,499,579	470,867,789	75	353,150,842	92	127
1880	3,816.2	1,684,857	529,044,945	70	370,331,461	90	124

SOURCES: RICE YIELDS AND ARABLE LAND: DATA FROM PETER BOOMGAARD AND JAN LUITEN VAN ZANDEN, *CHANGING ECONOMY OF INDONESIA: A SELECTION OF STATISTICAL SOURCE MATERIAL FROM THE EARLY 19TH CENTURY UP TO 1940*, VOL. 10, *FOOD CROPS AND ARABLE LANDS, JAVA 1815–1942* (AMSTERDAM: KIT, 1990), 41, 109, 112, 114, 116. REQUIRED LABOUR DAYS: PETER BOOMGAARD, *CHILDREN OF THE COLONIAL STATE: POPULATION GROWTH AND ECONOMIC DEVELOPMENT IN JAVA, 1795–1880* (AMSTERDAM: FREE UNIVERSITY PRESS, 1989), 221, 224, 227. POPULATION DATA: PETER BOOMGAARD AND A.J. GOOSZEN, *CHANGING ECONOMY OF INDONESIA: A SELECTION OF STATISTICAL SOURCE MATERIAL FROM THE EARLY 19TH CENTURY UP TO 1940*, VOL. 11, *POPULATION TRENDS 1795–1942* (AMSTERDAM: KIT, 1991)

women played a crucial role in safeguarding food security in the later decades of the Cultivation System.

The traditional gender-specific division of labour on Java meant that it was predominantly male peasants who cultivated crops destined for (local) markets, such as groundnuts, corn and cane sugar.[56] This division of labour remained in place when the Cultivation System was installed. Colonial officials even noted that women and children should not be involved in cash crop production under this system.[57] Nevertheless, in practice, women became increasingly involved in commercial agriculture for the Cultivation System. Many export crops simply turned out to be too labour-intensive to be exclusively cultivated by men. Women, and to a lesser extent children, were soon employed, both as unpaid members of the household economy and as wage workers. Wives regularly assisted their husbands in cultivation for export, for instance in the case of coffee. Furthermore, women were frequently engaged as wage workers on plantations. From the early days of the Cultivation System, tea cultivation required many extra labourers, especially for picking tea leaves, and, as it was hard to find male wage workers, women and children from the neighbourhood were often hired.[58] Finally, in sugar cultivation, which steadily increased during the Cultivation System, women were employed in all sorts of tasks, such as weeding and harvesting, with the exception of the very heavy labour of digging canals for irrigation.[59]

The existing information on women's work in cash crop production is scattered. Moreover, women's work varied strongly according to regional circumstances, such as crop type, soil suitability and the prevalent percentage of land/labour involved in forced cultivation. Nevertheless, we can make an educated guess about the minimum number of days Javanese peasant women spent, on average, working for the Cultivation System on an annual basis. A few assumptions have to be made, though, based on descriptions of women's tasks in particular forms of cash crop production and the proportion of households engaged in the Cultivation System (Table 1.2), as well as on the crop yields associated with the system.[60] Take, for instance, coffee cultivation. Coffee bean

---

56   Watson Andaya, "Women and Economic Change," 168.

57   Nationaal Archief (NA), The Hague, the Netherlands, Koloniën, 1850–1900, 2.10.02, file 5830, Geheime verbalen, no. 47, 12 February 1852.

58   ANRI, K3 – Batavia, file 2/1, General Report 1837/1838.

59   Peter Alexander, "Women, Labour and Fertility: Population Growth in Nineteenth Century Java," *Mankind: Official Journal of the Anthropological Societies of Australia* 14, no. 5 (1984): 367.

60   F. van Baardewijk, *Changing Economy of Indonesia: A Selection of Statistical Source Material from the Early 19th Century up to 1940*, vol. 14, *The Cultivation System, Java 1834–1880* (Amsterdam: KIT, 1993).

picking was highly labour-intensive and was often done by women. Depending on the region, coffee growing could require between 100 and 240 labour days per year.[61] Assuming that half of this labour was done by women, which is a minimum estimate, we multiplied the total number of labourers involved in forced coffee cultivation in a given year – as provided in the statistics by Van Baardewijk[62] – by 0.5 and thus arrived at a certain amount of women involved in this work per year. Furthermore, we know that women were involved in specific tasks in tea cultivation (leaf picking and sorting), tobacco cultivation (half of the irrigation and weeding, all of the sorting and bundling) and in cinnamon scraping (exclusively women). In sugar cultivation and processing, by contrast, they played a less important role – that is, compared to Javanese men.[63] Considering the changing mix of products under the Cultivation System in different years,[64] and assuming the minimum input of labour necessary to arrive at the yields registered,[65] a conservative estimate of the average number of full-time (ten-hour) days worked by women can be made for Java as a whole. The result of this exercise is shown in Table 1.4.

The involvement of the average Javanese peasant woman in commercial agriculture for the Cultivation System will have been around no more than one month per year. Initially, it was mostly the export of coffee and tea which involved an important share of female labour. Even though many more male than female labourers were involved in the cultivation and production of sugar, the sheer growth of the export volume of sugar from the 1840s (see Figure 1.1) made it important for women's work in cash crop cultivation too, as women were quite regularly hired for planting and weeding the sugar fields.[66] Over the 1850s, the number of days per capita seems to have dropped somewhat. This is consistent with the reduction in the total labour burden on households after the late 1840s, and also with the reported intensification of women's

---

61   Elson, *Village Java*, 89.
62   Van Baardewijk, *Cultivation System*, 190–93.
63   Elson, *Village Java*, 205.
64   For example, in 1836, 63 per cent of all forced labour used under the Cultivation System went towards coffee cultivation, and only 18 per cent was used for sugar cultivation. In 1870, these shares had risen to 73 per cent and 26 per cent. Still, the number of labour days for women declined overall because of their involvement in sugar cultivation, which became more important than tea or tobacco towards the end of the system, and because women were less prominent in the cultivation of sugar.
65   These are most probably underestimates, as Javanese rulers had an interest in reporting lower yields and labour input than the true figures. Van Baardewijk, *Cultivation System*, 24.
66   Roger Knight, "Gully Coolies, Weed-Women and *Snijvolk*: The Sugar Industry Workers of North Java in the Early Twentieth Century," *Modern Asian Studies* 28, no. 1 (1994): 58–59.

TABLE 1.4   Minimum estimates of labour days for adult women spent on cash crop
cultivation, Java 1815–1870

Year	Total no. of women involved in cash crops (minimum estimate)	No. of full-time days per adult woman under the cultivation system
1815	0	0
1836	236,326	35
1846	293,770	36
1860	284,948	27
1870	323,162	31

Note: author' s own calculations, based on: minimum estimate labour input van baardewijk, *the cultivation system*, 190–93; population figures boomgaard and gooszen, *population trends*; information on women's involvement in cash crop production: robert e. elson, *village java*

involvement in rice cultivation. In the later days of the Cultivation System, the involvement of women in cash crops increased again, mainly owing to the rise in coffee cultivation on private coffee plantations owned by Europeans, which were permitted in Java after the second half of the 1860s. Strictly speaking, this form of women's work was not directly prompted by the Cultivation System, but it was a type of commercial agriculture that would not have been in place without colonialism.

Last but not least, the Cultivation System also impacted Javanese women's work in other economic sectors. Traditionally, women were very active in selling whatever small surpluses the household generated from the land, such as rice, vegetables and fruit, at local markets.[67] Two important side effects of the Cultivation System facilitated trade: first of all, the investments in infrastructure that were done to facilitate the transportation of export crops from the fields to the harbours and, second, the increasing monetisation due to the cash payments of *plantloon* to the peasants. As a consequence, more markets (*pasars*) arose, and these were more frequently visited.[68] The growing circulation of money led to an increase in the number of shops (*warung*), which were run by both men and women; in some regions the number of shops even

---

67   Watson Andaya, "Women and Economic Change," 172.
68   Boomgaard, *Children*, 113–14.

doubled within ten years.[69] Moreover, women took the opportunity presented by the increasing number of seasonal migrant workers travelling several miles from their villages to work on coffee or sugar plantations. They started selling food, such as rice dishes or fried peanuts or bean cakes, along the roads towards the plantations.[70] For many women, the preparation of food – which was traditionally a task carried out by women in the domestic sphere – thus became a way to earn some extra cash.

Apart from economic activities in (retail) trade, women also became increasingly active in cottage industry. As my previous research has shown, after a few decades of downturn, industrial activity recovered after the 1850s, for instance in aspects of textile production such as weaving and batiking (wax printing and dyeing) of cotton cloth, in which women played a crucial role.[71] Besides textiles, there were many other cottage industries, such as straw-mat-making and bamboo-working, that showed increased activity in the later years of the Cultivation System, be it out of opportunity – increasing welfare and commercialisation[72] – or out of the necessity to supplement household income.[73] The increased monetisation and the growing local demand for indigenous products, as well as the rising number of landless peasants, who sought alternative work opportunities in wage labour and cottage industries, stimulated local industrial activity.

5 Conclusion

Javanese women's work was vital in the context of economic change induced by colonial extraction under the Cultivation System in a number of ways. The system put immense pressure on peasant households, by increasingly calling upon labour for cultivating export crops. Although the system was mainly intended towards having men respond to the labour demands of the system, women's economic role increased in numerous ways. First of all, the reallocation of men's labour to cash crop production meant that women's already

---

69   Elson, *Village Java*, 263.

70   NA, Koloniën 1850–1900, 2.10.02, file 559, Verbaal van 27-11-1856, no. 24.

71   Elise van Nederveen Meerkerk, "Challenging the De-Industrialization Thesis: Gender and Indigenous Textile Production in Java under Dutch Colonial Rule, c. 1830–1920," *Economic History Review* 70, no. 4 (2017): 1219–43.

72   As is posed by Elson, *Village Java*, 270–271.

73   As is argued by Boomgaard, *Children*, 134.

substantial activities in subsistence agriculture intensified further. Second, women became involved in the production of cash crops, most notably tea and coffee, even though the colonial government did not actively recruit women (or children) for this purpose. However, the labour intensity of these cultivations was such, that the demand for unpaid family labour as well as wage labour increased due to the Cultivation System. Third, women's activities in market and retail trade expanded due to the increasing monetisation of the economy. Finally, most notably, from the late 1840s, women were found to be increasingly performing non-agricultural activities in the countryside, such as textile production and straw plaiting, for their own use, but certainly also to be sold on local markets.

Figure 1.2 shows my estimates of what this implies for the increase of women's labour time in terms of average days per year. This figure suggests that the total time women spent on economic activities for subsistence and for the market over the entire course of the Cultivation System rose considerably. At first, this related mainly to an intensification in the forms of agriculture, with women replacing and assisting men deployed in forced cultivation. Subsequently, after the reforms of the late 1840s, there was more leeway to increase commercial activities. Whereas Javanese households were greatly affected by the Cultivation System because much extra labour was demanded from them, women formed an important factor in providing both labour and extra income – by intensifying as well as by reallocating their economic activities.

Of course, these are rough estimates, and highly aggregate figures: not *all* Javanese households were affected to the same degree. But as (depending on the time period) half to three-quarters of all households on Java were involved in the Cultivation System, we can safely conclude that the majority of women were highly impacted regarding their input and work pace. During the system's most stringent decades – the 1830s and 1840s – women had to increasingly step in to make sure the production of rice and other foodstuffs for the household's own consumption was safeguarded, thus trying to prevent the strained indigenous living standards from further deteriorating. They also put in hours of work in cash crop production, either to help their husbands or to earn some extra cash on neighbouring farms. At the same time, following the monetisation brought about by the Cultivation System, opportunities to earn some extra cash in retail trade or proto-industry emerged. All in all, to come back to the issue of colonial extraction that was raised in the introduction, it is clear that not only indigenous men but, perhaps even more so, indigenous women, carried the burden of Java's highly extractive Cultivation System.

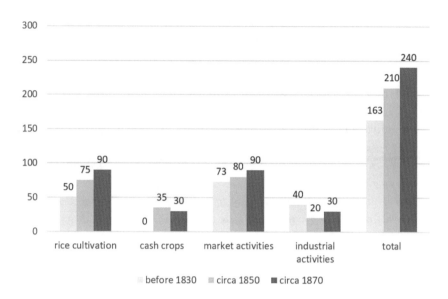

FIGURE 1.2   Estimates of number of full-time (ten-hour) days worked by Javanese women, 1830–1870

Bibliography

Archival Material

Arsip Nasional Republik Indonesia (ANRI), Jakarta, Indonesia:

ANRI, K3 – Batavia, file 2/1, General Report 1837/1838.

ANRI, K50 – Archief Directeur der Cultures (Cultures), file 1623, Residential report Tegal 1856.

Nationaal Archief (NA), The Hague, The Netherlands:

NA, Koloniën 1850–1900, 2.10.02, file 559, Verbaal van 27-11-1856, no. 24.

NA, Koloniën, 1850–1900, 2.10.02, file 5830, Geheime verbalen, no. 47, 12 February 1852.

Printed Material

Ahuja, Ravi. "Labour Relations in an Early Colonial Context: Madras, c. 1750–1800." *Modern Asian Studies* 36, no. 4 (2002): 793–826.

Alexander, Peter. "Women, Labour and Fertility: Population Growth in Nineteenth Century Java." *Mankind: Official Journal of the Anthropological Societies of Australia* 14, no. 5 (1984): 361–71.

Alexopoulou, Kleoniki. "An Anatomy of Colonial States and Fiscal Regimes in Portuguese Africa: Long-Term Transformations in Angola and Mozambique, 1850s–1970s." PhD diss., Wageningen University, 2018.

Alexopoulou, Kleoniki, and Dácil Juif. "Colonial State Formation without Integration: Tax Capacity and Labour Regimes in Portuguese Mozambique (1890s–1970s)." *International Review of Social History* 62, no. 2 (2017): 215–52.

Allen, Robert C. "The Great Divergence in European Wages and Prices from the Middle Ages to the First World War." *Explorations in Economic History* 38, no. 4 (2001): 411–47.

Allen, Robert C. *The British Industrial Revolution in Global Perspective.* Cambridge: Cambridge University Press, 2009.

Amussen, Susan D., and Allyson M. Poska. "Restoring Miranda: Gender and the Limits of European Patriarchy in the Early Modern Atlantic World." *Journal of Global History* 7, no. 3 (2012): 342–63.

Baardewijk, F. van. *Changing Economy of Indonesia: A Selection of Statistical Source Material from the Early 19th Century up to 1940.* Vol. 14, *The Cultivation System, Java 1834–1880.* Amsterdam: KIT, 1993.

Barragan, Rossana. "Extractive Economy and Institutions? Technology, Labour, and Land in Potosí, the Sixteenth to the Eighteenth Century." In *Colonialism, Institutional Change, and Shifts in Global Labour Relations*, edited by Karin Hofmeester and Pim de Zwart, 207–37. Amsterdam: Amsterdam University Press, 2018.

Boomgaard, Peter. "Female Labour and Population Growth on Nineteenth Century Java." *Review of Indonesian and Malayan Affairs* 15, no. 2 (1981): 1–31.

Boomgaard, Peter. *Children of the Colonial State: Population Growth and Economic Development in Java, 1795–1880.* Amsterdam: Free University Press, 1989.

Boomgaard, Peter, and Jan Luiten van Zanden. *Changing Economy of Indonesia: A Selection of Statistical Source Material from the Early 19th Century up to 1940.* Vol. 10, *Food Crops and Arable Lands, Java 1815–1942.* Amsterdam: KIT, 1990.

Boomgaard, Peter, and A. J. Gooszen. *Changing Economy of Indonesia: A Selection of Statistical Source Material from the Early 19th Century up to 1940.* Vol. 11, *Population Trends 1795–1942.* Amsterdam: KIT, 1991.

Booth, Anne. *The Indonesian Economy in the Nineteenth and Twentieth Centuries: A History of Missed Opportunities; A Modern Economic History of Southeast Asia.* London: Macmillan, 1998.

Booth, Anne. "Night Watchman, Extractive, or Developmental States? Some Evidence from Late Colonial South-East Asia." *Economic History Review* 60, no. 2 (2007): 241–66.

Bosma, Ulbe. "Dutch Imperial Anxieties about Free Labour, Penal Sanctions and the Right to Strike." In *Labour, Coercion, and Economic Growth in Eurasia, 17th–20th Centuries*, edited by Alessandro Stanziani, 63–86. Leiden: Brill, 2013.

Boter, Corinne. "Living Standards and the Life Cycle: Reconstructing Household Income and Consumption in the Early Twentieth-Century Netherlands." *Economic History Review* 73, no. 4 (2020): 1050–73.

Breman, Jan. *Koloniaal profijt van onvrije arbeid: Het Preanger stelsel van gedwongen koffieteelt op Java, 1720–1870.* Amsterdam: Amsterdam University Press, 2010.

Daendels, H. W. *Staat der Nederlandsche Oostindische bezittingen: Bijlagen, organique stukken, preparatoire mesures*. The Hague, 1814.

Davis, Lance E., and Robert A. Huttenback. *Mammon and the Pursuit of Empire: The Political Economy of British Imperialism, 1860–1912*. Cambridge: Cambridge University Press, 1986.

Dell, Melissa, and Benjamin A. Olken. "The Development Effects of the Extractive Colonial Economy: The Dutch Cultivation System in Java." NBER working paper no. 24009, 2017.

Elson, Robert E. *Village Java under the Cultivation System, 1830–1870*. Sydney: Asian Studies Association of Australia [etc.], 1994.

Fasseur, Cees. *Kultuurstelsel en koloniale baten: De Nederlandse exploitatie van Java 1840–1860* . Leiden: Universitaire Pers Leiden, 1992.

Frankema, Ewout, and Frans Buelens. "Introduction." In *Colonial Exploitation and Economic Development: The Belgian Congo and the Netherlands Indies Compared*, edited by Ewout Frankema and Frans Buelens, 1–17. London and New York: Routledge, 2013.

Havik, Philip J. "Colonial Administration, Public Accounts and Fiscal Extraction: Policies and Revenues in Portuguese Africa (1900–1960)." *African Economic History* 41 (2013): 159–221.

Horlings, Edwin. "Miracle Cure for an Economy in Crisis? Colonial Exploitation as a Source of Growth in the Netherlands, 1815–1870." In *Colonial Empires Compared: Britain and the Netherlands, 1750–1850*, edited by Bob Moore and Henk van Nierop, 145–67. Aldershot: Ashgate, 2003.

Horrell, Sarah, and Jane Humphries. "Women's Labour Force Participation and the Transition to the Male-Breadwinner Family, 1790–1865." *Economic History Review* 48, no. 1 (1995): 89–117.

Huillery, Elise. "The Black Man's Burden: The Cost of Colonization of French West Africa." *The Journal of Economic History* 74, no. 1 (2014): 1–38.

Humphries, Jane. "The Lure of Aggregates and the Pitfalls of the Patriarchal Perspective: A Critique of the High Wage Economy Interpretation of the British Industrial Revolution." *Economic History Review* 66, no. 3 (2013): 693–714.

Jong, Janny de. "Van batig slot naar ereschuld: De discussie over de financiële verhouding tussen Nederland en Indië en de hervorming van de Nederlandse koloniale politiek, 1860–1900." Master's thesis, University of Groningen, 1989.

Keese, Alexander. "Slow Abolition within the Colonial Mind: British and French Debates about 'Vagrancy,' 'African Laziness,' and Forced Labour in West Central and South Central Africa, 1945–1965." *International Review of Social History* 59, no. 3 (2014): 377–407.

Kennedy, Paul. "Debate: The Costs and Benefits of British Imperialism 1846–1914." *Past & Present* 125 (1989): 186–92.

Knight, Roger. "Gully Coolies, Weed-Women and *Snijvolk*: The Sugar Industry Workers of North Java in the Early Twentieth Century." *Modern Asian Studies* 28, no. 1 (1994): 51–76.

Kunkel, Sarah. "Forced Labour, Roads, and Chiefs: The Implementation of the ILO Forced Labour Convention in the Gold Coast." *International Review of Social History* 63, no. 3 (2018): 449–76.

Levert, Philip. *Inheemsche arbeid in de Java-suikerindustrie*. Wageningen: Landbouwhogeschool, 1934.

Locher-Scholten, Elsbeth. "Door een gekleurde bril ... Koloniale bronnen over vrouwenarbeid op Java in de negentiende en twintigste eeuw." *Jaarboek voor Vrouwengeschiedenis* 7 (1986): 34–51.

Maddison, Angus. "Dutch Income in and from Indonesia 1700–1938." *Modern Asian Studies* 23, no. 4 (1989): 645–70.

Mansvelt, W. M. F. and P. Creutzberg. *Changing Economy of Indonesia: A Selection of Statistical Source Material from the Early 19th Century up to 1940*. Vol. 5, *Indonesia's Export Crops, 1816–1940*. The Hague: Martinus Nijhof, 1975.

Marseille, Jacques. *Empire colonial et capitalisme français: Histoire d'un divorce*. Paris: Albin Michel, 1984.

Mintz, Sidney. *Sweetness and Power: The Place of Sugar in Modern History*. New York: Viking 1985.

Nederveen Meerkerk, Elise van. "Challenging the De-Industrialization Thesis: Gender and Indigenous Textile Production in Java under Dutch Colonial Rule, c. 1830–1920." *Economic History Review* 70, no. 4 (2017): 1219–43.

Nederveen Meerkerk, Elise van. *Women, Work and Colonialism in the Netherlands and Java: Comparisons, Contrasts, and Connections, 1830–1940*. London: Palgrave Macmillan, 2019.

Nederveen Meerkerk, Elise van. "Gender and Empire: Postcolonial Perspectives on Women and Gender in the 'West' and the 'East,' 17th–20th centuries." In *Vingt-cinq ans après: Les femmes au rendez-vous de l'histoire*, edited by Enrica Asquer, Anna Bellavitis, Isabelle Chabot, and Cristina La Rocca, 397–416. Rome: École Française de Rome, 2019.

O'Brien, Patrick. "The Costs and Benefits of British Imperialism 1846–1914." *Past & Present* 120 (1988): 163–200.

Offer, Avner. "The British Empire, 1870–1914: A Waste of Money?" *Economic History Review* 46, no. 2 (1993): 215–38.

Onderzoek naar de mindere welvaart der Inlandsche bevolking op Java en Madoera. Vol. 1xb3, *Verheffing van de Inlandsche vrouw*. Batavia: Kolff [etc.], 1914.

Poel, H. A. van der. "Nota over de Rijstkultuur op Java." *Tijdschrift voor Nijverheid en Landbouw in Nederlandsch Indië* 11 (1865): 97–118.

Schrauwers, Albert. "The 'Benevolent' Colonies of Johannes van den Bosch: Continuities in the Administration of Poverty in the Netherlands and Indonesia." *Comparative Studies in Society and History* 43, no. 2 (2001): 298–328.

Sinha, Mrinalini. *Colonial Masculinity: The "Manly Englishman" and the "Effeminate Bengali" in the Late Nineteenth Century.* Manchester: Manchester University Press, 1995.

Smits, Jan-Pieter, Edwin Horlings, and Jan Luiten van Zanden. *Dutch GNP and Its Components, 1800–1913.* Groningen: Growth and Development Center, 2000.

Van Niel, Robert. Java under the Cultivation System. Leiden: KITLV Press, 1992.

Waijenburg, Marlous van. "Financing the African Colonial State: The Revenue Imperative and Forced Labor." *The Journal of Economic History* 78, no. 1 (2018): 40–80.

Watson Andaya, Barbara. "Women and Economic Change: The Pepper Trade in Pre-Modern Southeast Asia." *Journal of the Economic and Social History of the Orient* 38, no. 2 (1995): 165–90.

Wiesner-Hanks, Merry. "Crossing Borders in Transnational Gender History." *Journal of Global History* 6, no. 3 (2011): 357–81.

Wilson, Kathleen. "Empire, Gender, and Modernity in the Eighteenth Century." In *Gender and Empire*, edited by Philippa Levine, 14–45. Oxford: Oxford University Press, 2004.

Zanden, Jan Luiten van, and Arthur van Riel. *The Strictures of Inheritance: The Dutch Economy in the Nineteenth Century.* Princeton: Princeton University Press, 2004.

Zwart, Pim de, and Jan Luiten van Zanden. "Labor, Wages, and Living Standards in Java, 1680–1914." *European Review of Economic History* 19 (2015): 215–34.

CHAPTER 2

Peasant Life Courses and Social Mobility in Serfdom

The Baltic Provinces of the Russian Empire in the Eighteenth and Nineteenth Centuries

Josef Ehmer

1 Introduction

Over the last three decades an intensive scholarly discussion has taken place in European historiography about the so-called second serfdom in the territories east of the river Elbe; that is, the early modern re-establishment of peasant bondage in the context of market production and economic globalisation.[1] The results of these debates and of a wave of empirical research questioned the previous hegemonic concept of "agrarian dualism," that is, the distinction between a long-term trend towards peasant emancipation in Western Europe and the opposite trend in the east, as well as the assumption of absolute power of estate owners over their peasants.[2] By contrast, more recent research has stressed the high regional diversity within "the East" and painted early modern East-Elbian agrarian relations in a more positive light, ascribing more room for manoeuvre to peasant serfs and portraying them as having a more balanced relationship to their lords.[3] In this context, the form of bondage known

---

1   I am grateful for the support of the International Research Centre "Work and Human Lifecycle in Global History" at Humboldt University Berlin (re:work).
2   Markus Cerman, *Villagers and Lords in Eastern Europe, 1200–1800* (Basingstoke: Palgrave Macmillan, 2012), 1–3, 14.
3   Many examples of diversity are presented in Jan Peters, ed., *Gutsherrschaftsgesellschaften im europäischen Vergleich* (Berlin: Akademie Verlag, 1997), especially in the chapters by William W. Hagen, "Die brandenburgischen und großpolnischen Bauern im Zeitalter der Gutsherrschaft 1400–1800: Ansätze zu einer vergleichenden Analyse," in Peters, *Gutsherrschaftsgesellschaften,* 17–28; and Edgar Melton, "Gutsherrschaften im ostelbischen Deutschland und in Rußland: Eine vergleichende Analyse," in Peters, *Gutsherrschaftsgesellschaften,* 29–44. Of course, high regional diversity also characterised many, if not most other parts of Europe. Furthermore, in some regions, free peasants might have coexisted with tenants, and various forms of bondage may have occurred alongside each other. See, for instance, for Sweden, Christina Prytz, "Life-Cycle Servant and Servant for Life: Work and Prospects in Rural Sweden c. 1670–1730," in *Servants in Rural Europe, 1400–1900,* ed. Jane Whittle (Woodbridge: The Boydell Press, 2017), 99–100.

© JOSEF EHMER, 2023 | DOI:10.1163/9789004529427_004

as "Baltic serfdom" – which, for centuries, appeared to Western observers as the most oppressive form of East-Elbian serfdom – has been questioned and even dispelled as a myth by some historians.[4] However, a close look at social-historical studies on and from the Baltic, and at primary sources, reinforces the assumption of a particularly harsh bondage in this region. The aim of this chapter is to approach these debates from a life course perspective and to reveal the impact both of serfdom and of peasants' emancipation on life course regimes.

2   The stabilisation of Peasants' Life Courses in Western and
       Central Europe

I start with a brief and simplistic glance at Western European developments. The long-term transformation of feudal domination in Western and Central Europe throughout the early modern period had a profound impact on the life courses of peasants and on social mobility in rural societies. The relative freedom and independence of peasants in the management of daily work routines and the trend towards hereditary possession stabilised both the individual life courses of peasants and the class barriers between the peasantry and the – rapidly growing – sub-peasant social groups of smallholders, cottagers and agricultural labourers.

In early life phases, this is reflected in the decrease of life-cycle service of sons and daughters of peasants. When the institution of life-cycle service emerged in the Middle Ages, presumably already in the ninth century, it represented an exchange of children between peasant households of a more or less homogeneous peasantry.[5] Farmhands and maids were the sons and daughters of peasants, who were not needed in their own families or who were required or forced to serve in the manor or in another farm. The growing social differentiation of early modern rural societies changed the social origins and the status of servants. Leaving one's own family at an early age and working and living in the household of an employer for many years became the typical life course trajectory of landless people's children.[6] Sons and daughters of land-rich

---

4   Marten Seppel, "Die Entwicklung der 'Livländischen Leibeigenschaft' im 16. und 17. Jahrhundert," *Zeitschrift für Ostmitteleuropa-Forschung* 54, no. 2 (2005): 174–75.
5   Michael Mitterauer, *Why Europe? The Medieval Origins of its Special Path* (Chicago: Chicago University Press, 2010), 59.
6   For an illustrative example, see Jürgen Schlumbohm, "Micro-History and the Macro-Models of the European Demographic System: Life Course Patterns in the Parish of Belm, Germany – Seventeenth to the Nineteenth Centuries," *The History of the Family* 1, no. 1 (1996): 85.

peasants, by contrast, generally remained in their parents' home until they inherited the holding and became peasants themselves, or until they married off into another farmstead of similar size and status. If both of these strategies failed, they might remain single and living in the family home. The stability of social status continued in later life phases.[7] When a child of a "full" peasant had taken over a farmstead, he or she would normally keep this position for life or at least until retirement, in places in which the institution of retirement had come into existence.[8] The typical life course pattern of a peasant in the highly stratified rural societies of early modern Western and Central Europe involved belonging to the peasant class from the cradle to the grave.

The typical life course pattern of children of sub-peasant classes, by contrast, would consist of leaving their families of origin and entering into service at an early age, and working as single live-in farmhands or maids into their twenties or early thirties. When they left service, they usually married and settled down as cottagers and casual day labourers. Servants in eighteenth- and nineteenth-century England, for instance, "were sons and daughters of labourers, destined to become labourers themselves."[9]

3   Life Course Regimes in East-Central and Eastern Europe

In most early modern Eastern European regions, agriculture was embedded in feudal manorial systems. In these regions, like in the West, peasant families and households were the basic units of production. However, they had to dedicate considerable parts of their labour power to demesne land, and various degrees of dependency vis-à-vis their manorial lords existed: from relative autonomy in practical labour issues to full serfdom and personal bondage. With respect to life courses, roughly three different types may be distinguished.

---

7   This assertion, of course, does not apply for tenants with short-term leases.
8   In the early modern rural world, retirement meant the withdrawal of a peasant (whether a widow, a widower or a married couple) from the headship and ownership of farmstead by leaving or selling it to a successor in exchange for accommodation, board and care on the farm for the rest of his/her life. On early modern rural retirement practices in East-Central Europe, see Hermann Zeitlhofer, *Besitzwechsel und sozialer Wandel: Lebensläufe und sozi-oökonomische Entwicklungen im südlichen Böhmerwald, 1640–1840* (Vienna: Böhlau, 2014); and, more generally, Josef Ehmer, "Life interest," in *Encyclopedia of Early Modern History Online*, ed. Friedrich Jaeger (Leiden: Brill, 2019) – even if the translation of the German term *"Ausgedinge"* into the English term "Life interest" is somewhat misleading.
9   Ann Kussmaul, *Servants in Husbandry in Early Modern England* (Cambridge: Cambridge University Press, 1981), 10.

Firstly, parts of East-Central Europe show a development similar to that of the West: a growing social differentiation of rural societies, from large and affluent farmers to small peasants and cottagers, most of them casual wage labourers, all the way down to labourers without any land and the poor.[10] In these highly stratified areas big farmers had both a favourable position vis-à-vis their lords and stable life courses. Children of lower-class families almost exclusively went into life-cycle service, similar to the practices in Western European regions.[11] For example, in the Bohemian lands and the western and central parts of today's Poland, the "life-cycle servant" prevailed well into the nineteenth and early twentieth centuries.[12] In the region which is today's central and southern Poland, for instance, in the late eighteenth century more than 20 per cent of the boys aged ten to fourteen and about 40 per cent of young men aged fifteen to twenty-four were live-in farm servants, and a still remarkable but continuously declining number remained in this position into their late twenties and early thirties. In this region, "a significant fraction of young movers left the household of origin to spend an intermediate stage as unmarried farm servant prior to completing other transitions."[13] Young women also left home in this region and became farm maids, but to a lesser extent than men: less than 20 per cent in the age group of ten to fourteen, about 25 to 30 per cent aged between fifteen and twenty-four, and only very few in their late

---

10   For the East Elbian regions, see Edgar Melton, "*Gutsherrschaft* in East Elbian Germany and Livonia, 1500–1800: A Critique of a Model," *Central European History* 21, no. 4 (1988): 315–49; Melton, "Gutsherrschaften,"; Hagen, "Bauern"; and, generally, Peter Kriedte, *Peasants, Landlords and Merchant Capitalists: Europe and the World Economy 1500–1800* (Cambridge: Cambridge University Press, 1984).

11   The most important recent contribution to the prevalence of life-cycle service in early modern East-Central Europe stems from Mikolaj Szoltysek, *Rethinking East-Central Europe: Family Systems and Co-Residence in the Polish-Lithuanian Commonwealth*, vol. 1 (Bern: Peter Lang), 2015. His comprehensive study on family systems in the Polish-Lithuanian Commonwealth covers a large part of this state, which included most parts of today's Poland, Lithuania and Belarus, and the western parts of today's Ukraine. Szoltysek's analysis is based on a large number of population listings mainly from the last decade of the eighteenth century, which include almost twenty-seven thousand peasant households from various parts of the Polish-Lithuanian Commonwealth; see, particularly, 113–117 and 125.

12   Szoltysek, *Rethinking East-Central Europe;* and Eduard Maur, "Das Gesinde in Böhmen nach dem Soupis poddaných podle viry aus dem Jahre 1651," in *Soziale Strukturen in Böhmen: Ein regionaler Vergleich von Wirtschaft und Gesellschaft in Gutsherrschaften, 16.–19. Jahrhundert*, ed. Markus Cerman and Hermann Zeitlhofer (Vienna and Munich: Verlag für Geschichte und Politik/R. Oldenbourg Verlag, 2002), 111–25.

13   Szoltysek, *Rethinking East-Central Europe*, 312.

twenties and thirties.[14] However, in addition to farmhands and maids in peasant households, who were used both for work on the farmstead and for *corvée* labour at the demesne, we also find agricultural servants who worked (and lived) directly at the seigniorial estate or on manor farms (*Meierhöfe*). This was particularly true for dairy production, in which maids lived at the manor and slept in special servants' sheds or in the stables.[15] Often, the adolescent children of peasants, and particularly those of the sub-peasant classes, were forced to work at the manor for two to five years, due to the institution of compulsory service (*Gesindezwangsdienst*). When servants were not needed permanently at the manor, they might also eat and sleep at their parental farmstead.[16]

Secondly, in the eastern fringe of today's Poland and in Belarus and Ukraine a household's labour force consisted almost entirely of a peasant's family and relatives, while life-cycle service was an exception.[17] The same is true for rural southern Russia, which was characterised by large and complex multigenerational peasant households, which "were entitled to a share of communal land which was periodically (partially) redistributed."[18] In this system, the size of the land allotted to a family was the flexible variable which was enlarged or downsized by the village community in accordance with the size and composition of each individual family.[19] Therefore, there was no need for an adjustment of the household's labour force by taking in servants or by employing agricultural labourers.[20]

---

14   Szoltysek, *Rethinking East-Central Europe,* 312.

15   Jürgen Kocka, *Arbeitsverhältnisse und Arbeiterexistenzen: Grundlagen der Klassenbildung im 19. Jahrhundert* (Berlin: J. H. W. Dietz, 1990), 158 (for East-Holstein around 1800).

16   On *Gesindezwangsdienst* see Cerman, *Villagers,* 72; Maur, "Gesinde," 120–121; Jan Peters, "Ostelbische Landarmut – Statistisches über landlose und landarme Agrarproduzenten im Spätfeudalismus," *Jahrbuch für Wirtschaftsgeschichte* 10, no. 1 (1970): 217, 227–230; Klaus Tenfelde, "Ländliches Gesinde in Preußen: Gesinderecht und Gesindestatistik 1810–1861," *Archiv für Sozialgeschichte* 19 (1979): 197–99, 222–24.

17   Szoltysek, *Rethinking East-Central Europe,* 306–10.

18   Kersti Lust, "How Permanent were Farms in the Manorial System? Changes of Farm Occupancy in the Nineteenth-Century Russian Baltic Provinces of Estland and Livland," *Continuity and Change* 35 (2020): 217.

19   Peter Czap, "'A large family: the peasants' greatest wealth': Serf Households in Mishino, Russia, 1815–1858," in *Family Forms in Historic Europe,* ed. Richard Wall, Jean Robin, and Peter Laslett (Cambridge: Cambridge University Press, 1983), 105–51.

20   Michael Mitterauer and Alexander Kagan, "Russian and Central European Family Structures: A Comparative View," *Journal of Family History* 7, no. 1 (1982): 125–27.

4 The Baltic Provinces of the Russian Empire

A third and very distinct pattern prevailed in the Baltic region. The three Baltic governments of the Russian Empire, namely Estland (today's northern Estonia), Livland (today's southern Estonia and northern Latvia, both of which were under Russian rule from 1721) and Kurland (Courland, today's southern Latvia, included in the Russian Empire in 1795), represent a very special case. The agrarian labour relations in this region were characterised by a commercial manorial economy (*Gutswirtschaft*) based on personal bondage until well into the nineteenth century. The provinces were ruled by a German Baltic nobility whose estates were split up into demesne land and land leased to peasant serfs of Estonian or Latvian ethnicity who were "hereditarily servile" (*erbuntertänig*) and regarded as the property of the landowners.[21] Peasants had no property rights at all on "their" land nor any right to move, and were obliged to perform demesne labour.[22] The focus of the manorial economy was the export-oriented production of grain, particularly rye. In the sixteenth and seventeenth centuries, grain was exported to Western Europe by water, via several ports, the most important ones being Riga, Tallinn and Pärnu. In the eighteenth century, under Russian rule, the production of rye brandy (vodka) and its export to the Russian lands became dominant.

There has been a long tradition of research on household structures and labour relations in the Baltic region. Research on the eighteenth and nineteenth centuries has been stimulated by the existence of excellent historical sources. These include head-tax censuses, so-called "soul revisions," which had been implemented by Tsar Peter I, as part of his state reforms. From 1722 until 1858, ten soul revisions were held more or less uniformly throughout the Russian Empire. In Estonia and in Livonia, the soul revisions of 1782 and 1795 were carried out particularly precisely and thoroughly by the Baltic German nobility, listing the entire population (both genders and all ages) in the German language, and the same is true for Kurland's first census in 1797.[23] Manorial lords registered all their serfs, village after village and farmstead after

---

21 Andrejs Plakans, "Peasant Farmsteads and Households in the Baltic Littoral, 1797," *Comparative Studies in Society and History* 17, no. 1 (1975): 9.

22 The clear ethnic distinction between peasant and lord resembles patterns of colonial rule outside Europe.

23 Plakans, "Peasant Farmsteads," 5–7; Juhan Kahk and Halliki Uibi, "Familiengeschichtliche Aspekte der Entwicklung des Bauernhofes und der Dorfgemeinde in Estland in der ersten Hälfte des 19. Jahrhunderts," in *Familienstruktur und Arbeitsorganisation in ländlichen Gesellschaften*, ed. Josef Ehmer and Michael Mitterauer (Vienna: Böhlau, 1986), 37.

farmstead, by name, age, social position, marital status and occupation – when it differed from the category peasant. Moreover, the particularly accurate ones linked two subsequent soul revisions, making a note of why somebody was no longer at his previous place of residence or, vice versa, where somebody had lived previously. As mobility beyond an estate was a rare exception, estate owners maintained an overview of their serfs' social and spatial moves within the estate, which were usually induced or enforced by the lords themselves.[24]

Such sources are well suited for the partial reconstruction of individual and family life courses. Most research, however, has done a cross-sectional analysis of one (or more) soul revisions, simulating aggregated life courses on the basis of age. There have only been a few attempts, so far, to follow single individuals over successive revisions, thus partially reconstructing actual life courses.[25] In addition to nominal population listing, there is also a rich ethnographic literature dating from the eighteenth century onwards, starting in the 1770s with August Wilhelm Hupel's *"Topographische Nachrichten von Lief- und Ehstland"* (Topographic notices from Livonia and Estonia).[26]

5   Peasant Life Courses in the Baltic Provinces: A Local Case Study

This chapter examines how serfdom impacted the life courses of the various groups of the peasant population. For a detailed analysis of how life courses and social mobility were intertwined, I selected a number of Estonian parishes. One of these is the parish and estate of Sangaste (*Sagnitz*) in the *Livländische Gouvernement* (in northern Livonia, today's southern Estonia), half-way between Riga and lake Peipus. Sangaste was located in an area of extensive export-oriented agricultural production. It became famous in the eighteenth century (and is still known) for its brandy made from winter rye.[27] Its flourishing demesne economy was based on relatively large peasant farmsteads. The

---

24   This analysis, and parts of the following paragraphs below, are based on my own work with these sources, which I conducted at the Estonian Academy of Sciences in Tallinn during the winter of 1977/1978. The soul revisions are kept at the Estonian National Archives in Tartu: Eesti NSV – Riiklik Ajaloo Keskarhiv (ENSV RAKA).

25   The most important work in this area is by two Estonian scholars, Juhan Kahk and Halliki Uibu, who already in the 1980s, linked the soul revisions of 1816, 1834, and 1850; see Kahk and Uibu, "Familiengeschichtliche Aspekte." My own unfinished research (see below) links the soul revisions of 1782 and 1795.

26   August Wilhelm Hupel, *Topographische Nachrichten von Lief- und Ehstland*. Vols. 1–3 (Riga: Johann Friedrich Hartknoch, 1774/1777/1782).

27   All details are from Kahk and Uibu, "Familiengeschichtliche Aspekte".

soul revision of 1816 registered a serf population of 5,731 persons in 521 households, which means an average household size of eleven.

The social hierarchy which estate owners (or their staff or the parish priest) had in mind when they carried out soul revisions – in Sangaste as well as in the whole region – consisted of three major groups. The highest rank in the serf population was held by the head of each farmstead, the *Wirt* (or *Wirth*), and – although to a minor extent – the members of his family.[28] The *Wirt* was responsible towards the lord of the manor for the functioning of the farmstead and particularly for the provision of demesne labour.[29] He had no personal rights vis-à-vis his lord and no property rights to "his" farmstead, but he exercised authority over the members of his family and over the servants, including the right to corporal punishment.[30] Among Sangaste's serf population in 1816 about 50 per cent were registered as belonging to the family of the *Wirt*, who represented the core of the estate's labour force.

The second group were male and female servants, *Knechte* and *Mägde*, and, when they were married, their children. About 90 per cent of all households included male and female farm servants, with roughly four servants per household. Together with their children they made up about 35 per cent of the estate's labour force, which is a very high proportion compared to the rest of Europe. Servants were the sons and daughters of peasants, of married servants or of *Lostreiber* (see below), who were shifted between farmsteads according the will of their lord.[31] Servants were usually hired for one or more years and, in addition to food and lodging, they received a small amount of money, and sometimes even a tiny piece of land for their own use.[32] However, they were not allowed to move to another *Wirt* of their own accord. A Livonian manor law of the 1790s, for instance, stipulated that servants were only allowed to ask

---

28   In the following paragraphs, I give preference to the terms "*Wirt*" and "*Lostreiber*," which appear in the sources, over translations such as "peasant" or "inmate/cottager," as these might hide the very specific meaning of these status groups under the conditions of Baltic serfdom.

29   Jürgen Freiherr von Hahn, *Die bäuerlichen Verhältnisse auf den herzoglichen Domänen Kurlands im XVII. und XVIII. Jahrhundert* (Karlsruhe: G. Braunsche Hofbuchdruckerei und Verlag, 1911); Elina Waris, "The Family and Marriage in Southern Estonia," in *Family Life on the Northwestern Margins of Imperial Russia*, ed. Tapio Hämynen, Jukka Partanen, and Yuri Shikalov (Joensuu: Joensuu University Press, 2004).

30   Hupel, *Topografische Nachrichten*, vol. 3, 625; Kahk and Uibi, "Familiengeschichtliche Aspekte," 58, 70.

31   Kahk and Uibu, "Familiengeschichtliche Aspekte," 85–63.

32   Kahk and Uibu, "Familiengeschichtliche Aspekte," 65–67; Hahn, *Die bäuerlichen Verhältnisse*, 58.

for permission to move to another farmstead.[33] In contrast to agricultural servants in Central and Western Europe they did not have the freedom to choose
another employer after a contracted term had come to an end. Indeed, while
servant work under Baltic serfdom was a form of wage labour, it lacked any
element of free wage labour.

The size of the household and the large portion of servants in Sangaste
reflects the requirements of the demesne economy.[34] To master the burdens
of demesne labour and to produce enough food for a large peasant household, a labour force of about four adult men was required on average, usually
consisting of two members of the peasant's family – the head (*Wirt*) himself
and an adult son or brother – and two male servants (*Knechte*).[35] The number
of servants was flexible and directly proportional to the number of workable
members of the head's family. Some servants were very young, from four years
upwards, and the age group from ten to twenty was relatively large. However,
the bulk of male servants was between twenty and fifty years old, with hardly
any variation in that wide age range. Service in Sangaste was certainly not life-
cycle service.

In all, 44 per cent of the male servants were married, which amounts to
almost all of the male servants in the higher age groups.[36] Most of them lived
in their peasant's farmstead together with their wives – who worked as maids –
and their children, before they became servants themselves elsewhere.[37] Being
married, however, did not mean that servants had a household of their own.
Eighteenth-century Estonian farmhouses usually consisted of only one large
room with one common hearth where meals were cooked for all household

---

33   Kahk and Uibu, "Familiengeschichtliche Aspekte," 59.

34   For another Livonian estate, Pinkenhof, in 1816, see Andrejs Plakans and Charles
      Wetherell. "Family and Economy in an Early Nineteenth-Century Baltic Serf Estate," In
      The European Peasant Family and Society, ed. Richard L. Rudolph (Liverpool: Liverpool
      University Press, 1995), 172–73.

35   Kahk, and Uibu, "Familiengeschichtliche Aspekte," 55; Waris, "Family and Marriage," 342.

36   Married servants also existed in other parts of Europe, for instance in the Austrian Alpine
      regions, but they were a clear exception. Moreover, married servant couples were usu-
      ally not allowed to live together. They served at different farmsteads, visiting each other
      on Sundays or holy days; see Michael Mitterauer, "Gesindeehen in ländlichen Gebieten
      Kärntens: Ein Sonderfall historischer Familienbildung," in *Historisch-anthropologische
      Familienforschung. Fragestellungen und Zugangsweisen*, ed. Michael Mitterauer
      (Vienna: Böhlau, 1990), 233–56.

37   See Heldur Palli, "Estonian Households in the Seventeenth and Eighteenth Centuries,"
      in *Family Forms in Historic Europe,* ed. Richard Wall, Jean Robin, and Peter Laslett
      (Cambridge: Cambridge University Press, 1983).

members. During the nineteenth century, separate chambers for *Wirte* and their wives were established very slowly.[38]

The third and lowest social group within the serf population were the so-called *Lostreiber*, *Badstüber* and *Einwohner*.[39] This was a heterogeneous group of landless serfs, most of whom were in the higher age groups, with the men being aged between forty and seventy or beyond, whereas the women were in their thirties and upwards. Many of them were widows or widowers or single persons, but there were also married couples with children. They lived as lodgers in farmhouses or in sheds of their own, or in the village's steam bath hut or in the hut for drying flax – when these were not in use for their proper purpose. Both socially and economically, and sometimes also geographically, *Lostreiber* lived at the fringe of the demesne economy. They had no access to land or only to tiny plots and were obliged to work on demesne fields or on farmsteads when needed, and when physically able to do so, particularly in times of peak labour demand during summer. Five per cent of Sangaste's population were counted as *Lostreiber*, along with a few persons labelled as beggars.[40]

At first glance, this social hierarchy and classification looks similar to social structures in early modern Western and Central European rural populations. The combination of a peasant family as the stable core of the labour force with servants as an element of medium-term flexibility and a floating group of potential labourers on demand seems to be functional for market-oriented agricultural family production in various contexts. However, there are two major differences. Firstly, the bulk of the labour force consisted of peasant families and servant families. The group of *Lostreiber* was too small, too old and often not physically suited to fulfil the work of agricultural labourers. Secondly, in the Baltic commercial demesne economy neither the position of *Wirt* nor that of servant was stable. The social hierarchy of the village population was counterbalanced by the fact that all three groups were serfs without any personal or property rights and that they were equal in that respect vis-à-vis their lords.[41] The ambivalence between social distinction on the one hand, and collective

38   Plakans, "Peasant Farmsteads," 10; Andrejs Plakans, "Identifying Kinfolk beyond the Household," *Journal of Family History* 2, no. 1 (1977): 7; Kahk and Uibu, "Familiengeschichtliche Aspekte," 48–50.

39   For descriptions of this group, see Hupel, *Topographische Nachrichten*, vol. 1, 54–55, 61; vol. 2, 127; vol. 3, 632; Hahn, *Die bäuerlichen Verhältnisse*: 61ff.; Kahk and Uibu, "Familiengeschichtliche Aspekte," 68–69.

40   The remaining 10 per cent of Sangaste's serf population do not clearly fit into a particular category. They are registered as domestic service staff in the manor house, craftsmen, orphans, foster children, widows, and others.

41   Kahk and Uibu, "Familiengeschichtliche Aspekte," 58ff.

subordination under the lord on the other, is reflected in a limited stability of life courses and in a high enforced social mobility.[42]

6   Life Courses and Enforced Social Mobility in a Micro-historical Perspective

The following partial reconstruction of life course patterns is based on the linkage of the soul revisions from 1782 and 1795 of the parish of Ambla (*Ampel*) in northern Estonia, about sixty kilometres southeast of Tallinn. In 1782, this parish consisted of thirty estates (*Erbgüter und Beigüter*).[43] For the following investigation I selected six estates with a total of 2,049 inhabitants, whose owners registered their serfs particularly accurately; and for closer inspection I concentrated on two of them: for close reading, I focused on a rather small one, Reesna, with only 124 souls; and for a minor statistical analysis, I examined the three united estates of Tois, Regaffer and Porrick.[44]

That personal bondage was prevalent in all these estates becomes visible in entries in the soul revisions about serfs who were no longer there in 1795 or, vice versa, who had come to the estate after 1782, and is particularly evident in the way in which the writers of the soul revisions explain why somebody left and somebody else showed up. The main reason was, besides death, the will of the lord. Over and over again, one reads entries such as the following: "A domestic servant, given to me by my father"; "A cook, pledged to the colonel"; "Daughter of the *Wirt*, given as a gift to Miss Müller"; "Daughter of the *Wirt*, sold to Major Wrangel in Reval" (Tallinn); "The whole family given to me as a gift by Kurro estate"; "Son of the coachman, now owned by the assessor in the city of Waremsberg, sold to the assessor"; "*Wirt*, bought from Jämper estate"; or, simply "*Wirt*, was sold, his wife now *Lostreiber*"; or "*Wirt*, was bought from xy."[45] However, quite a large number of mainly young serfs, be it daughters or

---

42   Waris, "Family and Marriage," 347–49.

43   Kirchspiel Ambla/Ampel, http://www.mois.ee/deutsch/kirchsp/ambla.shtml.

44   ENSV RAKA F. 1864, nim 2, su. V-52.

45   In the original German: "*Aufwärter, ist mir von meinem Vater geschenkt*"; "*ein Koch, dem Obristen verpfändet*"; "*Tochter des Wirts, an Fräulein Müller geschenkt*"; "*Tochter des Wirts, ist nach Reval an Major Wrangel verkauft*"; "*Sohn des Kutschers, gehört jetzt dem Assessor in der Stadt Waremsberg, ist an den Assessor verkauft*"; "*Wirt, vom Gut Jämper gekauft*"; and "*Wirt, ist verkauft, sein Weib jetzt Lostreiberin*"; "*Wirt, von xy gekauft.*" Late eighteenth-century Baltic authors, such as Hupel, who were committed to the spirit of the Enlightenment, no longer took the right to purchase and sell individuals or whole families for granted or viewed it as legitimate. Nevertheless, they justified this practice by means of demographic and economic arguments. They argued that an estate might

sons of *Wirte* or male farmhands or maids, took their fate into their own hands and ran away (*"weggelaufen," "verlaufen," "nach Schweden entlaufen"*), although some of them were caught and brought back, or returned voluntarily (*"war verlaufen"; "vorher verlaufen"*).[46]

Female life courses reveal a further aspect of bondage, namely an exchange of women for marriage between estates, be it daughters or widows of *Wirte* or of servants. Frequently, one finds entries such as: "married into Noemküll estate" or vice versa "his wife, from Reesna estate" (*"nach Noemküll verheiratet"; "Weib, vom Gut Reesna"*). One has the impression that a kind of mutual exchange of young women took place between two estates.[47] In farmstead number five of Koik & Arro estate, in 1782, lived a servant aged forty and his wife, aged thirty, and a younger single servant aged twenty-three. Sometime after 1782, the older servant had died and his widow "was married into Korkus estate" (*"ist auf dem Gut Korkus verheiratet"*). The *Wirt* of this farmstead also lost his position sometime after 1782 and was transferred to a *Lostreiber* hut (*"jetzt Lostreiber"*), presumably after the death of his wife. The younger servant (aged thirty-six in 1795) became his successor as *Wirt* and received a wife from Korkus estate (aged twenty-nine) (*"29, Weib, vom Gut Korkus"*). Our sources do not tell us whether such marriages were forced or voluntary. However, as the mobility of serfs was strictly limited to an estate, and as many of these bride exchanges involved estates further away and not even from the same parish, one might assume that involuntary unions were more likely and that particularly women were shifted between estates, whether they liked it or not.

As already mentioned, I chose Reesna estate to illustrate the life courses of the various groups of serfs. This estate was owned as a hereditary estate (*Erbgut*) by the "Lieutnant Gustav von Müllern" in 1782 and was pledged to

---

otherwise suffer from a lack of peasants, while another estate, by contrast, might suffer from an abundance of people. See, for instance, Hupel, *Topographische Nachrichten,* vol. 3, 625, 632–33: *"Dem Verkauf einzelner Personen oder ganzer Familien, so sehr sie auch die Menschheit herabwürdiget, muß dennoch für einige Zeit noch nachgesehen werden [...] da in einigen Gebieten schon ein lästiger Ueberfluß an Menschen sich äußert, in anderen hingegen wohl die Hälfte der Bauerstellen noch wüste liege. Bey solchen Umständen ist die Freiheit, Menschen zu verkaufen, noch das einzige Mittel, diesem dem Staat nachtheiligen Fehler einigermaßen abzuhelfen"*.

46 For the practice of running off (*"Läuflingswesen"*), see Hahn, *Die bäuerlichen Verhältnisse,* 29–32.

47 This practice seems to have had a legal basis. Hupel, *Topographische Nachrichten,* vol. 1, 590, quotes an eighteenth-century Livonian law, which confers on a peasant serf the right to marry a farm servant from another estate: *"Kein Hof darf einem fremden Gebietsbauern eine zur Ehe begehrte Magd verweigern, um so viel mehr, als eben das Recht den Abgang bald wieder ersetzen kann. "* See also Plakans, "Identifying," 8.

"Baron Matthias Stachelberg" in 1795. The estate was characterised by comparably small households and a low number of servants. It had a serf population of 120 persons in 1782, of whom nine lived and worked at the manor house, while 111 persons belonged to the sixteen farmsteads of the manor. In 1795, the population had risen to 130 persons (six of whom lived at the manor house) and, in addition to the farmsteads, three *Lostreiber*-positions had been established.

If we look, first, at the sixteen heads of the peasant households (*Wirte*) in 1782, we see that six of them were no longer alive in 1795 – an expression of high mortality. Another six had kept their position as *Wirt*. Most interesting are those four *Wirte* who changed their position: the first one was transferred to the manor to serve as a herdsman and a coachman (*Viehhüter und Kutscher*) together with his wife, who was now registered as a herdswoman (*Viehhüterin*). This couple replaced the previous coachman and his wife, who had been designated for the position of *Wirt* in a newly established farmstead (*neugepflanztes Gesinde*). The second *Wirt* and his wife were demoted and went to work as servants (*Knecht* and *Magd*) in another farmstead. The third one was moved, after the death of his wife, to one of the new *Lostreiber* sheds. The fourth *Wirt* and his wife remained in their farmstead but handed over the headship to their son, who became the new *Wirt*. One might see this as a kind of retirement. The retired couple was aged forty-eight (husband) and fifty-three (wife) in 1795, their son and successor was twenty-eight, and his wife was thirty years old. If we include the six deceased *Wirte*, a total of ten changes in headship took place at Reesna estate between 1782 and 1795. Six of these new *Wirte* were sons of *Wirte*, but only two of them became *Wirte* on the farmstead of their fathers; the other four became *Wirte* at different farmsteads. Two of the remaining four new *Wirte* were former servants, one was the coachman mentioned above, and one (and his wife) had been bought from another estate. This shows that servants did have chances to become *Wirte*, even if the sons of *Wirte* seemed to have better ones. However, the majority of *Wirte*'s sons ended up as servants on the estate, were sold to other estates or remained in their father's or brother's farmsteads until they reached a higher age. They were usually married and had children of their own.

In 1782, we find only ten male servants in Reesna, two of them "boys" (*Jung*) aged nine and thirteen, and eight *Knechte* aged twenty to forty-nine. In 1795, three of these male farmhands were deceased, two had become *Wirte*, two were now servants on farmsteads other than where they had been working in 1782, two had become *Lostreiber*, and one had been sold to another estate. Looking at the social background of the same number of servants in 1795, we find one former *Wirt*, five former sons of *Wirte* and four former servants, including one boy. Three of these ten *Knechte* were married with children of their own. There were only eight farm maids in Reesna in 1782. Their life courses differed remarkably from those of male servants: the maids were clearly younger, all of them aged ten to twenty-nine; by 1795, two of them had run away, four had been married into other estates, one had disappeared from the sources, and only one had married the son of a *Wirt* (who later became a *Wirt* himself) and thus remained at the estate.

Reesna is certainly too small a sample to allow generalisations. However, the group of the three estates of Tois, Regaffer and Porrick (including Arrohof), which were pledged to and jointly managed by Friedrich Adolph Baron of Dellinghausen in 1795, is large enough for modest quantification. In 1795, the population of this group of estates consisted of seven "free persons" (*freie Leute*), among which were a "governess from Hamburg" and a "chambermaid from Arensberg" (*Gouvernante, Kammerjungfer*). Among the 742 serfs there were seventeen "*Hofdomestiken*," who lived and worked in the manor house, mainly domestic servants and maids, but also a cook, a coachman and some herdsmen. All others belonged to the different categories of "peasants" (*Bauern*), even if some of them practised a trade. The soul revisions registered three weavers, three cabinet makers, a gardener, a shoemaker, a miller, a "windmiller," a smith and a tanner – which points to a remarkable amount of non-agricultural activities.

To analyse these individuals' social mobility and life course trajectories from 1782 to 1795, I restrict myself to those (male) categories, which are most clearly defined: *Wirte* (as heads of peasant farmsteads), sons of *Wirte*, and male servants on farmsteads. The results essentially confirm the observations already made in connection with the Reesna estate. These concern, firstly, the very high mortality in this period and region. Of the seventy-one *Wirte* in 1782, only forty-seven were still alive in 1795; almost a third (32.4 per cent) had died within these thirteen years. Sons of *Wirte* show lower death rates, even though this category included very young children (twenty individuals out of 117 died, which is 17.1 per cent). One has to keep in mind, however, that children who were born and died between the two soul revisions were not recorded. Servants (*Knechte*) showed the highest survival rates (three out of thirty-seven died, 8.1 per cent), which is certainly due to the fact that this category included neither very young children nor elderly persons.

Table 2.1 summarises the position changes of the surviving *Wirte*, sons of *Wirte*, and *Knechte* (male servants). In these estates, too, social positions were not stable. Hardly two-thirds of *Wirte* kept their status, and there was a real risk

TABLE 2.1   Social mobility in the parish of Ampel (Ambla, Estonia) 1782–1795 (only surviving
             males): Tois (Pruuna), Regaffer (Rägavere), Porrick and Arrohof (Pöriki and Aru)
             estates

	Wirte	Sons of *Wirte*	Servants (*Knechte*)
remain or become *Wirte*	65.9	27.8	26.5
remain sons of *Wirte*	---	39.2	---
remain or become servants	12.8	28.9	67.6
become *Lostreiber*	4.3	4.1	---
become others	17.0[a]	---	5.9[b]
N 1782 (= 100)	47	97	34

a *Wirte*: three living as father in a farm of a son; one taken along ("*mitgenommen*") from the
   former owner; one transferred to the inn as a new innkeeper; one fled ("*verloffen*");
b servants (*Knechte*): two fled ("*verloffen*").
SOURCE: THE AUTHOR'S OWN CALCULATIONS BASED ON THE SOUL REVISIONS: EESTI
NSV – RIIKLIK AJALOO KESKARHIV (ENSV RAKA), 1864/2/VIII-146

of being downgraded to the position of servant.[48] Servants, in turn, had
serious chances to become or replace *Wirte*, even if two-thirds of them
kept their status. Sons of *Wirte* had equal chances to become *Wirt* or servant, but they had a third option as well, namely to remain "son" even at an
advanced age and even when they were married and had children of their
own. Whether or not one retained one's social status was hardly foreseeable,
as it depended on the will of the lord. The life courses of the serf population
were shaped by unforeseen social rise and descent, as the "lords played ...
providence."[49]

   In addition to these status changes, soul revisions reveal the clear impact of
age on work status in the case of very young and very old serfs. Below age fourteen, almost all farmhands were not denoted as "servants" (*Knecht* or *Magd*)

---

48   Degradations (*Absetzungen*) were justified both in contemporary discourse and in later
      historiography with the argument that lazy or inefficient peasants must be replaced and/
      or demoted to servant status for the sake of maintaining or raising the productivity of a
      farmstead; see, for instance, Melton, "*Gutsherrschaft*," 340; or the doctoral dissertation by
      Hahn, *Die bäuerlichen Verhältnisse*, 45–46, 59, who himself descended from a noble Baltic
      estate owners' family; on the Hahn family see Plakans, "Identifying," 9.
49   Hahn, *Die bäuerlichen Verhältnisse*, 46, Fn. 1.

in the soul revisions, but as "boy" (*Jung*) or "foster child" (*Aufzögling*), or as "nanny" (*Kinderwärterin*), in the case of a nine-year-old girl who took care of the two children of a *Wirt*, aged two and four. Elderly persons often figure as "old man," "old hag" or "old broad" (*alter Kerl, altes Weib*). Such terms seem to denote persons who were no longer fully usable in the labour process. From about age fifteen onwards, one might occupy the position of a farm servant, and from about twenty years of age onwards the status of *Wirt* or *Wirt*'s wife, as long as one could maintain one's working power – or, rather, as long as one could meet the expectations of the lord.

7   The Impact of Peasant Liberation on Social Mobility and Life Course Transitions

The period 1782–1795 has been characterised as "the height of Baltic serfdom"[50] (*Erbuntertänigkeit; Leibeigenschaft*). What changed with peasant emancipation? The abolition of serfdom in the Baltic provinces of the Russian Empire was a complicated and lengthy process, which started in 1816 (Estonia), 1817 (Courland) and 1819 (Livonia), and was not completed before 1863.[51] There were two main obstacles to full freedom, which were only gradually let go of: firstly, "all the farmland remains in the ownership of the landlords."[52] Peasants' access to land became regulated by lease contracts, which still forced them to spend a considerable part of their labour power on manor land. Secondly, their freedom of movement remained strictly limited and was only extended step by step over several decades: first, they were granted free movement within the parish; then within the court district; then within the entire province (in Estonia with the exception of towns and cities); and, finally, in 1863 they were granted the right to move freely in the whole Russian Empire. Nevertheless, the family-land bond became strengthened during this long period of transition and, from 1849 onwards, peasants were entitled to buy land from their landlord and to acquire full ownership.[53] What did this mean for the social mobility and life courses of peasants and servants?

---

50   Plakans, "Peasant Farmsteads," 3.
51   Valdis Bluzma, "Legal Regulation of the Abolition of Serfdom in Baltic Governorates of the Russian Empire in Early 19th Century: Historic Background, Realisation, Specific Features and Effect," in *Social Changes in the Global World: 6th International Scientific Conference; Proceedings* (Shtip: Goce Delcev University, 2019), 585.
52   Bluzma, "Legal Regulation," 575.
53   Bluzma, "Legal Regulation," 585.

To answer that question, we can draw on research by two Estonian scholars, Juhan Kahk and Halliki Uibu, cited above, who linked the 1816, 1834 and 1850 soul revisions of various Livonian and Estonian parishes, including the parish and estate of Sangaste, which I dealt with above. Table 2.2 compares the social mobility from 1816 to 1834 and from 1834 to 1850, thus covering a large part of the transition period towards peasant emancipation. It shows a clear trend towards stabilisation of status and a reduction of social mobility. The proportion of *Wirte* and their sons who kept their position increased significantly, while the share of those who experienced downward mobility towards servant or *Lostreiber* positions declined. Vice versa, the chances for servants to become *Wirte* deteriorated considerably. In other words, "[t]he social boundaries between the categories of the peasantry strengthened."[54] One might describe these changes as a process of class formation in the transition from feudal to bourgeois labour relations. The lines between *Wirte* and servants became less porous than they were in serfdom. Life courses now unfolded within classes, while life course transitions between status groups became an exception.

To sum up: the sources used in this chapter, and the application of a life course perspective, indicate that the form of bondage known as "Baltic serfdom" was no myth. Oppressive serfdom shaped social relations in the rural societies of the Baltic provinces of the Russian Empire well into the nineteenth century. This implied an insecure social position for peasant *Wirte,* who lived under the threat of becoming downgraded to the position of servant or *Lostreiber,* if they did not meet the expectations and demands of their lords. However, this also implied chances for upward mobility for farmhands (*Knechte*), who might gain the position of peasant head of a farmstead (*Wirt*). Both shifts in position, however – reflecting both downward and upward mobility – depended primarily on decisions by the lord of the manor and only secondarily – if at all – on the individual aspirations of serfs. The peasant liberation of the nineteenth century, in sharp contrast to the previous period, stabilised individual life courses as well as social class inequalities.

---

54   Kahk and Uibu, "Familiengeschichtliche Aspekte," 94.

TABLE 2.2   Social mobility in the parish Sangaste (Sagnitz, Livonia), 1816–1834 and 1834–1850

	1816–1834	1834–1850
Wirte-couple (head and wife)		
N 1834 = 321		
remain *Wirte*	51.7	73.2
become servants	6.8	2.6
become *Lostreiber*	11.8	0.9
become others[a]	29.7	23.3
	100.0	100.0
Sons of household heads (*Wirte*)		
N 1834 = 387		
remain sons or become *Wirte*	55.9	86.6
become servants	44.1	13.4
	100.0	100.0
Male servants (*Knechte*) and their sons		
N 1834 = 513		
become *Wirte*	23.0	8.2
remain or become servants	77.0	90.8
	100.0	100.0

a   Estate personal ("*Hofdomestiken*"), relatives of new head, widows, beggars.
SOURCE: THE AUTHOR'S OWN CALCULATION BASED ON JUHAN KAHK AND HALLIKI UIBI, "FAMILIENGESCHICHTLICHE ASPEKTE DER ENTWICKLUNG DES BAUERNHOFES UND DER DORFGEMEINDE IN ESTLAND IN DER ERSTEN HÄLFTE DES 19. JAHRHUNDERTS," IN *FAMI-LIENSTRUKTUR UND ARBEITSORGANISATION IN LÄNDLICHEN GESELLSCHAFTEN*, ED. JOSEF EHMER AND MICHAEL MITTERAUER (VIENNA: BÖHLAU, 1986), 80–81 (TABLES 15 AND 16).

Bibliography

Bluzma, Valdis. "Legal Regulation of the Abolition of Serfdom in Baltic Governorates of the Russian Empire in Early 19th Century: Historic Background, Realisation, Specific Features and Effect." In *Social Changes in the Global World: 6th International Scientific Conference; Proceedings*, 575–88. Shtip: Goce Delcev University, 2019.

Cerman, Markus. *Villagers and Lords in Eastern Europe, 1200–1800*. Basingstoke: Palgrave Macmillan, 2012.

Czap, Peter. "'A large family: the peasants' greatest wealth': Serf Households in Mishino, Russia, 1815–1858." In *Family Forms in Historic Europe*, edited by Richard Wall, Jean Robin, and Peter Laslett, 105–51. Cambridge: Cambridge University Press, 1983.

Ehmer, Josef, and Michael Mitterauer, eds. *Familienstruktur und Arbeitsorganisation in ländlichen Gesellschaften.* Vienna: Böhlau, 1986.

Ehmer, Josef. "Life Interest." In *Encyclopedia of Early Modern History Online*, edited by Friedrich Jaeger. Leiden: Brill, 2019.

Hagen, William W. "Die brandenburgischen und großpolnischen Bauern im Zeitalter der Gutsherrschaft 1400–1800: Ansätze zu einer vergleichenden Analyse." In Peters, *Gutsherrschaftsgesellschaften*, 17–28. Berlin: Akademie Verlag, 1997.

Hahn, Jürgen Freiherr von. *Die bäuerlichen Verhältnisse auf den herzoglichen Domänen Kurlands im XVII. und XVIII. Jahrhundert.* Karlsruhe: G. Braunsche Hofbuchdruckerei und Verlag, 1911.

Hupel, August Wilhelm. *Topographische Nachrichten von Lief- und Ehstland.* Vols. 1–3. Riga: Johann Friedrich Hartknoch, 1774/1777/1782.

Kahk, Juhan, and Halliki Uibi. "Familiengeschichtliche Aspekte der Entwicklung des Bauernhofes und der Dorfgemeinde in Estland in der ersten Hälfte des 19. Jahrhunderts." In *Familienstruktur und Arbeitsorganisation in ländlichen Gesellschaften*, edited by Josef Ehmer and Michael Mitterauer, 31–101. Vienna: Böhlau, 1986.

Kocka, Jürgen. *Arbeitsverhältnisse und Arbeiterexistenzen: Grundlagen der Klassenbildung im 19. Jahrhundert.* Berlin: J. H. W. Dietz, 1990.

Kriedte, Peter. *Peasants, Landlords and Merchant Capitalists: Europe and the World Economy 1500–1800.* Cambridge: Cambridge University Press, 1984.

Kussmaul, Ann. *Servants in Husbandry in Early Modern England.* Cambridge: Cambridge University Press, 1981.

Lust, Kersti. "How Permanent Were Farms in the Manorial System? Changes of Farm Occupancy in the Nineteenth-Century Russian Baltic Provinces of Estland and Livland." *Continuity and Change* 35 (2020): 215–43.

Maur, Eduard. "Das Gesinde in Böhmen nach dem Soupis poddaných podle viry aus dem Jahre 1651." In *Soziale Strukturen in Böhmen: Ein regionaler Vergleich von Wirtschaft und Gesellschaft in Gutsherrschaften, 16.–19. Jahrhundert*, edited by Markus Cerman and Hermann Zeitlhofer, 111–25. Vienna and Munich: Verlag für Geschichte und Politik/R. Oldenbourg Verlag, 2002.

Melton, Edgar. "*Gutsherrschaft* in East Elbian Germany and Livonia, 1500–1800: A Critique of a Model." *Central European History* 21, no. 4 (1988): 315–49.

Melton, Edgar. "Gutsherrschaften im ostelbischen Deutschland und in Rußland: Eine vergleichende Analyse." In Peters, *Gutsherrschaftsgesellschaften*, 29–44. Berlin: Akademie Verlag, 1997.

Mitterauer, Michael, and Alexander Kagan. "Russian and Central European Family Structures: A Comparative View." *Journal of Family History* 7, no. 1 (1982): 103–31.

Mitterauer, Michael. "Gesindeehen in ländlichen Gebieten Kärntens: Ein Sonderfall historischer Familienbildung." In *Historisch-anthropologische Familienforschung: Fragestellungen und Zugangsweisen*, edited by Michael Mitterauer, 233–56. Vienna: Böhlau, 1990.

Mitterauer, Michael. *Why Europe? The Medieval Origins of Its Special Path*, Chicago: Chicago University Press, 2010.

Palli, Heldur. "Estonian Households in the Seventeenth and Eighteenth Centuries." In *Family Forms in Historic Europe*, edited by Richard Wall, Jean Robin, and Peter Laslett, 207–16. Cambridge: Cambridge University Press, 1983.

Peters, Jan. "Ostelbische Landarmut – Statistisches über landlose und landarme Agrarproduzenten im Spätfeudalismus." *Jahrbuch für Wirtschaftsgeschichte* 10, no. 1 (1970): 97–126.

Peters, Jan, ed. *Gutsherrschaftsgesellschaften im europäischen Vergleich*. Berlin: Akademie Verlag, 1997.

Plakans, Andrejs. "Peasant Farmsteads and Households in the Baltic Littoral, 1797." *Comparative Studies in Society and History* 17, no. 1 (1975): 2–35.

Plakans, Andrejs. "Identifying Kinfolk beyond the Household." *Journal of Family History* 2, no. 1 (1977): 4–30.

Plakans, Andrejs. "The Familial Contexts of Early Childhood in Baltic Serf Society." In *Family Forms in Historic Europe*, edited by Richard Wall, Jean Robin, and Peter Laslett, 167–206. Cambridge: Cambridge University Press, 1983.

Plakans, Andrejs, and Charles Wetherell. "Family and Economy in an Early Nineteenth-Century Baltic Serf Estate." In *The European Peasant Family and Society*, edited by Richard L. Rudolph, 165–87. Liverpool: Liverpool University Press, 1995.

Prytz, Christina. "Life-Cycle Servant and Servant for Life: Work and Prospects in Rural Sweden c. 1670–1730." In *Servants in Rural Europe, 1400–1900*, edited by Jane Whittle, 95–112. Woodbridge: The Boydell Press, 2017.

Schlumbohm, Jürgen. "Micro-History and the Macro-Models of the European Demographic System: Life Course Patterns in the Parish of Belm, Germany – Seventeenth to the Nineteenth Centuries." *The History of the Family* 1, no. 1 (1996): 81–95.

Seppel, Marten. "Die Entwicklung der 'livländischen Leibeigenschaft' im 16. und 17. Jahrhundert." *Zeitschrift für Ostmitteleuropa-Forschung* 54, no. 2 (2005): 177–93.

Szoltysek, Mikolaj. *Rethinking East-Central Europe: Family Systems and Co-Residence in the Polish-Lithuanian Commonwealth*. Vol. 1. Bern: Peter Lang, 2015.

Tenfelde, Klaus. "Ländliches Gesinde in Preußen: Gesinderecht und Gesindestatistik 1810–1861." *Archiv für Sozialgeschichte* 19 (1979): 189–229.

Waris, Elina. "The Family and Marriage in Southern Estonia." In *Family Life on the Northwestern Margins of Imperial Russia*, edited by Tapio Hämynen, Jukka Partanen, and Yuri Shikalov, 333–85. Joensuu: Joensuu University Press, 2004.

Zeitlhofer, Hermann. *Besitzwechsel und sozialer Wandel: Lebensläufe und sozioökonomische Entwicklungen im südlichen Böhmerwald, 1640–1840*. Vienna: Böhlau, 2014.

CHAPTER 3

Escape from New York

Gender and the Rural Safety Valve, 1856–1884

Katherine Jellison

In a box in a cupboard in a seaside cottage in Maine lie dozens of letters written in the second half of the nineteenth century by members of the Chauncey (Cheney) Janes Sherman family of New York City and rural western and south-central Massachusetts. The letters primarily represent correspondence to former clothing shop proprietor Cheney Sherman from his children George William Sherman, Emma Sherman and Caroline (Caddie) Sherman. Cheney's children, born in New York City in the 1830s and 1840s and raised there as members of the petite bourgeoisie, demonstrated in their lively letters the extent to which frequent relocation from the countryside to the city and back again remained a feature of life in the industrial Northeast during the American Civil War and Reconstruction eras. Their letters also demonstrate the extent to which one's gender determined the character of those relocation experiences.[1]

The frequent movement between city and country of Sherman family members resulted, in part, from a belief that the rural landscape provided a safety valve for unemployed urban workers. Although the term *safety valve* is most closely associated with historian Frederick Jackson Turner and his 1893 frontier thesis, the general concept had been familiar to Americans since at least the 1840s.[2] The belief that superfluous urban wage earners could find success as agrarians, however, depended on the availability of inexpensive land – a

---

1 The Sherman letters belonged to Marion (Polly) Echols, Cheney Sherman's great-granddaughter, and the person who built the Maine cottage, christened it "Timberock" and retired there in 1960. It is now a vacation rental cottage. The author thanks Linda Hanna Holmes – current owner of the cottage – for permission to use the Sherman letters, Sharon Wood for photographing the letters and Sherry Gillogly for her assistance with genealogical research on the Sherman family. For discussion of the characteristics of middle-class shopkeeper family life during the Sherman children's upbringing, see the following classic studies: Paul E. Johnson, *A Shopkeeper's Millennium: Society and Revivals in Rochester, New York, 1815–1837* (New York: Hill and Wang, 1978) and Mary P. Ryan, *Cradle of the Middle Class: The Family in Oneida County, New York, 1790–1865* (Cambridge: Cambridge University Press, 1981).
2 Fred A. Shannon, "A Post Mortem on the Labor-Safety-Valve Theory," *Agricultural History* 19, no. 1 (January 1945): 31.

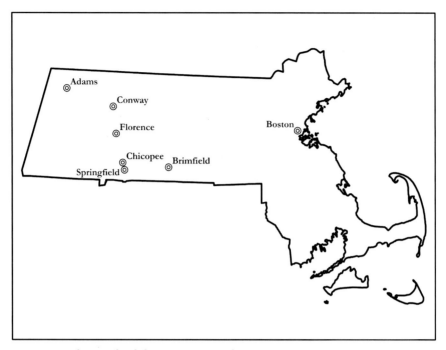

MAP 3.1   Sherman family locations in Massachusetts
            SOURCE: MAP BY SEAN HOLLOWELL.

scarce commodity in nineteenth-century Massachusetts. Nevertheless, some
members of the extended Sherman family continued to believe in the illusory
safety valve and to adhere to the Jeffersonian image of farmers as the epitome
of rugged American individualism. Some family members also subscribed to
pastoral notions, portraying the countryside as a wholesome alternative to
the unhealthy city. To the extent that this vision of agrarian freedom, opportunity and vitality existed, however, it existed only for White male landowners. Women, persons of colour and landless White men could not achieve
this agrarian ideal. And in an increasingly urban, industrial America, even
those who had access to the ideal might reject it in favour of city dreams. The
Sherman family letters demonstrate all these nineteenth-century American
themes and developments in dramatic fashion as they moved from New York
City to various locations in Massachusetts.[3]

---

3   I capitalise the terms *White* and *Black* throughout this chapter to emphasise that these racial
    categories are not natural phenomena but instead socially constructed.

The Shermans' correspondence begins in the closing years of the antebellum period. While visiting his in-laws' Conway, Massachusetts, farm home during the Fourth of July holiday in 1856, twenty-four-year-old factory machinist George William Sherman wrote home to his pregnant wife Sarah, who was apparently staying with George's family in New York City. He reported seeing a campaign flag for Republican presidential candidate John C. Fremont on the village green, but farm work rather than national politics merited George's most vivid commentary. He had travelled to the farm to assist his father-in-law – who had no living sons – with the summer haying. The scorching July sun was taking a toll, however, on the complexion of a man accustomed to indoor, industrial labour. Before signing off as Sarah's "Affectionate Husband," George closed his letter with thoughts of his mother and younger siblings, telling Sarah, "Give my love to mother & the children & tell her I'll be so black when I get back she won't know me."[4]

For George, life as a farm labourer – even a temporary one – perhaps did not conform to his image of himself as a modern man in an industrial age. During a time when political debate raged over extending enslaved Black labour beyond the South to the Union's newly admitted territories and states – a question that had indeed spurred the creation of the Republican Party and Fremont's candidacy – George possibly viewed farm labour as inappropriate work for an ambitious White man. His statement that field labour would dramatically darken his skin perhaps acknowledged that he was performing work strongly associated with African American labourers in the political rhetoric of the day. By contrast, factory labour, which was strictly reserved for White workers at this time, beckoned George back to the city.

Following the October 1856 birth of their daughter, whom they named for George's sister Emma, George and Sarah Sherman pursued their version of the era's urban domestic ideal in the small manufacturing city of Springfield, Massachusetts. George's employer, the Springfield Armory, was a national centre for innovation and development in America's Industrial Revolution and was the country's premier arms manufacturer. For a young man with George's ambitions, it was undoubtedly the right place to be. Nevertheless, the young couple maintained regular contact with Sarah's parents, Dexter and Sarah

---

4   George W. Sherman to Sarah Bartlett Sherman, 6 July 1856, Sherman Family Letters, Timberock Cottage, New Harbor, Maine. Hereafter cited as Sherman Family Letters. For information on Dexter Bartlett, see Charles Stanley Pease, ed., *History of Conway (Massachusetts), 1767–1917* (Springfield, MA: Springfield Printing and Binding Company, 1917), 255, and the Dexter Bartlett entry on findagrave.com, https://www.findagrave.com/memorial/81462314/dexter-bartlett.

Bartlett, and periodically made the thirty-five-mile journey north by train to visit their farm at Conway. For the next two decades, in fact, the Bartletts' farm would be a rural refuge for members of the Sherman family, and Sarah Sherman and her daughter Emma spent large portions of their summers there. During those times, Sarah wrote back to Springfield to inform George about life on her father's farm, including the fresh cucumbers her father had picked for her or the colt he had recently sold. In contrast to George's quest for success in industry, Dexter Bartlett was seemingly living out an older American dream as a member of Thomas Jefferson's nation of farmers. Occasional lapses occurred in the idyllic life portrayed in letters from the farm, such as the sleighing accident that temporarily left Dexter milking cows with only one hand. Otherwise, he appeared to be living the life of the exemplary yeoman farmer.[5]

Meanwhile, back in New York, the Sherman family, like the nation itself, was coming apart at the seams. In a letter that George's younger sister Emma Sherman White wrote from New York City on 25 June 1860, she did not express concerns about sectional strife or that year's upcoming presidential election but focused instead on the breakdown of her parents' marriage. Writing to George's wife Sarah at her parents' farm, Emma opened her letter cheerfully, telling her sister-in-law that she would like to visit Sarah at the farm and "get some flesh on" her after a recent weight loss but did not want to spend time away from her husband Johnnie, whom she adored "more than all the world." In contrast to her own happy marriage, however, Emma reported that her parents' union was beyond repair and that Cheney and Marion Caldwell Sherman "had agreed to separate ... entirely." As a result, Emma noted, her unemployed, fifty-three-year-old father was now "dying by inches" in New York. Family correspondence never explains the cause of Cheney's failure as a businessman and husband, but the consequences of his downfall are clear: the former New York clothier left the city to return to the countryside of his native Brimfield, Massachusetts. Indeed, until his death nearly a quarter century later in 1884, Cheney Sherman remained in south-central Massachusetts, boarding with neighbours or relatives in exchange for farm labour and receiving gifts of clothing and sympathetic letters from his adult children.[6]

---

5 Entry for Emma Sherman Echols, in Gertrude B. Darwin, *Lineage Book: National Society of the Daughters of the American Revolution*, vol. 31 (Harrisburg, PA: Telegraph Printing Company, 1910), 213. Sarah Bartlett Sherman to George W. Sherman, 26 July, no year; Sarah Bartlett Sherman to George W. Sherman, 19 June 1859; Dexter and Sarah Bartlett to George W. and Sarah Bartlett Sherman, 5 February 1860, Sherman Family Letters.

6 Emma Sherman White to Sarah Bartlett Sherman, 25 June 1860, Sherman Family Letters; *The New York City and Co-Partnership Directory for 1843 & 1844*, vol. 2 (New York: John Doggett, Jr., Publisher, 1843), 306.

As an itinerant farm labourer, Cheney Sherman now resided at the bottom of Massachusetts' rural socio-economic system and at the bottom of the masculinity scale. With no farm or home of his own, and separated from his wife and children, Cheney represented the antithesis of the rural masculine ideal. He was not a sturdy yeoman farmer and family provider but a boarder in other people's homes and a labourer on other people's land. No longer "dying by inches" as a failed businessman in New York City, he was now an aging labourer in rural exile. Unlike his daughter Emma, who had mused about gaining weight and improving her health in the wholesome countryside, Cheney found little comfort there.[7]

At the same time, George and Sarah Sherman continued their pursuit of the urban domestic ideal in Springfield, where, a month after the Civil War began, Sarah gave birth to George William Sherman, Jr., in May 1861. Unfortunately, it was a difficult birth that left both mother and baby in precarious health, and George, Jr., died in early October. Writing from New York City late that month, George's mother Marion shared her sympathies with her son and daughter-in-law and asked after her estranged husband, encouraging George to write a long letter telling her how and what Cheney was doing in the countryside. Marion ended her letter noting that it was "hard times for some in New York," including an uncle who had lost his business in May and friends who had volunteered to fight in the war rather than face continuing unemployment. From Marion's perspective, Cheney had likely been wise to seek rural refuge, and she added a poignant postscript: "Remember me kindly to your father."[8]

Urban life proved no less difficult for George, even in a small city. In the aftermath of their son's birth and death in Springfield and Sarah's own continuing health problems, George and Sarah now also looked to the countryside for relief. In what must have been an agonising decision for the young couple, Sarah left Springfield in November 1861 to try to recover her health at her parents' farm. She took their daughter Emma with her, leaving George alone in Springfield as the family breadwinner. George's letters to Sarah through the remainder of that year reveal the growing strain as he tried to balance his duties to his wife and to the Springfield Armory, which was operating around the clock to supply the Union military. Writing on 19 November, he reported, "I will be up there Thanksgiving hit or miss. Our foreman wouldn't give me permission

7   Colin R. Johnson, "Masculinity in a Rural Context," in *The Routledge History of Rural America*, ed. Pamela Riney-Kehrberg (New York: Routledge, 2016), 155.

8   George William Sherman, Jr., entry, findagrave.com, https://www.findagrave.com/memor ial/81462363/george-william-sherman; Marion Caldwell Sherman to George W. Sherman, 27 October 1861, Sherman Family Letters.

even under the circumstances, but I went and saw the Master Armorer & got leave ...." In an undated letter written sometime between Thanksgiving and Christmas, George voiced concern over Sarah's persistent cough, described the Christmas presents he was sending to the farm and told his wife, "I believe Sarah that I'm thinking of you every minute in the day ... I will not neglect you my dear girl for all the armory." On 29 December, George asked whether Sarah had received the cod liver oil he had sent, and he promised to send some type of "inhaling apparatus" that would ease her troubled breathing. George also reported that he had finally stood up to his foreman, telling his superior that he "had sacrificed enough to him and the armory and should do it no longer." Under these stressful circumstances, George perhaps now envied his yeoman father-in-law, who did not report to a supervisor and could be at Sarah's bedside every day. In the end, however, Sarah did not regain her health at her father's farm and died there at age twenty-six in January 1862.[9]

Several months later, as the war raged on, Emma finally informed her father of George's recent tragedies. As writer Lillian Smith once commented, while much of men's Civil War-era writing focused on the "group sameness" of political speeches and military battles, women's personal writing recorded the "individual differences" in how particular families, neighbourhoods and communities experienced the war. Smith's observations certainly hold true for the letters Emma sent to Cheney Sherman during the war. Writing from New York City to her father in the farming village of East Brimfield, Massachusetts, Emma only briefly mentioned the war news – including casualties at the recent Second Battle of Bull Run – before launching into lengthy discussion of family matters. She reported that her husband Johnnie – unemployed in the city for two months – would soon be joining the Union Navy and that her grief-stricken brother George had "broke[n] up housekeeping" in Springfield following his wife's death. Emma noted, however, that while George had left for employment as a machinist at the Colt Armory in Hartford, Connecticut, he had placed his five-year-old daughter "little Emma" in a more stable and wholesome environment – her maternal grandparents' Conway, Massachusetts, farm home.[10]

9   George W. Sherman to Sarah Bartlett Sherman, 19 November 1861; George W. Sherman to Sarah Bartlett Sherman, [November/December?] 1861; George W. Sherman to Sarah Bartlett Sherman, 29 December 1861, Sherman Family Letters; Sarah S. Bartlett Sherman entry, findagrave.com, https://www.findagrave.com/memorial/81462365/sarah-s-sherman.

10   Lillian Smith, "Autobiography as a Dialogue between King and Corpse," in *The Winner Names the Age: A Collection of Writings by Lillian Smith*, ed. Michelle Cliff (New York: W.W. Norton, 1978), 190–91; Emma Sherman White to Cheney J. Sherman, [September?] 1862, Sherman Family Letters.

Cheney, in the meantime, continued his life of intense physical labour, and Emma's plans for ending her father's toil on the land came to naught. Writing from her lodgings in Harlem to her father on 5 September 1864, Emma reported that her husband Johnnie had made it through the Battle of Mobile Bay without "a scratch" and would be using a portion of the $15,000 promised him for capture of a Confederate vessel to purchase a home of their own where Cheney could come and live with his daughter and son-in-law and "not have to work much longer." Approximately a week later, however, Emma's husband came home to New York seriously wounded. Following the Union victory, Acting Ensign Johnnie White had been among those clearing Mobile Bay of Confederate torpedoes when one exploded. Writing to her father in East Brimfield on 10 October, Emma told him that she, Johnnie and their two-year-old daughter Carrie were in nearby Chicopee, Massachusetts, where they hoped a "change of air" might ease her husband's suffering before a possible return to the Brooklyn Naval Hospital. The story did not have a happy ending. Writing on black-bordered stationery from the home of her brother's in-laws at Conway, Emma mused on 16 August 1865: "Father I am very sorry that you have to work as hard in your old day's [sic] .... How much Johnnie and I anticipated having a pleasant home so that we might have you with us. You were always connected with all our future plans but it was not to be so. [H]is death has made a sad change."[11]

Unlike his brother-in-law Johnnie, George Sherman enjoyed a measure of financial security during the war. He remained a civilian but nevertheless believed he was fulfilling his masculine duty to the Union cause through his work as a skilled operative in an arms factory, first in Springfield, then Hartford and later at the Starr Armory in Yonkers, New York. He continued to harbour large ambitions, writing to his father from Yonkers early in 1864 that he was working on a secret invention that would have a major impact on manufacturing – if only he could raise the money to finish the project and patent it.[12] By the end of the year, he was working at yet another weapons factory, this time in Chicopee, Massachusetts. Writing on 4 December, George

11   Emma Sherman White to Cheney J. Sherman, 5 September 1864; Emma Sherman White to Cheney J. Sherman, 10 October 1864; Emma Sherman White to Cheney J. Sherman, 16 August 1865, Sherman Family Letters; Report of Lieutenant Commander J.E. Jouett to Rear Admiral D.G. Farragut, 8 August 1864, in Frank Moore, ed., *The Rebellion Record: A Diary of American Events*, vol. 8 (New York: D. Van Nostrand, Publisher, 1865), 124; Rear Admiral D.G. Farragut to Secretary of the Navy Gideon Welles, 29 August 1864, in *Annual Report of the Secretary of the Navy* (Washington, DC: Government Printing Office, 1864), 476.

12   George W. Sherman to Cheney J. Sherman, 8 January 1864, Sherman Family Letters.

lamented that his recent move had prevented him from voting in the presidential election. He assured Cheney, however, that although he had "always had been a [D]emocrat," he would have voted for "*Old Abe*" [George's emphasis] and the Union cause. George also reported that he was one of three men who inspected the monthly shipment of two thousand breech-loading carbine rifles to the U.S. Army post on New York's Governor's Island. He then closed his letter with an arms-related pun about General William Tecumseh Sherman's on-going March to the Sea and the importance of weapons manufacturing to a Union victory: "The General who bears the same name with ourselves is at present the *big gun* [George's emphasis] among them. He is giving the Rebels all they desire, and I hope he as well as all the rest of our soldiers will continue to do so until they are glad to come under. [I]f no lack of good arms is all that is necessary to end the war, it will not last a great while longer."[13]

With the end of the war came an end to George's steady munitions factory employment. From the U.S. Combination Lock Company in Providence, Rhode Island, in 1866 to the Remington Armory in Ilion, New York, in 1867 and then on the road looking for new employment in 1868, George continued to pursue a life in urban manufacturing while his young daughter remained on the farm in Conway. In a letter he wrote from New York City's National Hotel on 17 May 1868, George congratulated his daughter Emma on having her own pet "little *Bossie* [George's emphasis] calf," noting she would never be able to enjoy such a luxury if she were with him in the big city. As he told the child, "I see [calves] often here but the poor little things are in the street, and almost scared to death, at so many [horse] teams, which they have to keep dodging about or they will get run over."[14]

While George Sherman remained a city dweller following the war, his sister Emma, like her father, was living a life of hard labour in the Massachusetts countryside. While staying in western Massachusetts following her husband Johnnie's death, Emma married a man named Clark Rice, who, like Cheney Sherman, earned his living primarily as a farm labourer. Unlike her marriage to Johnnie White, which she described in highly affectionate terms, this match was one of convenience rather than love, and subsequent letters to Cheney Sherman from both Emma and her younger sister Caddie indicate that Emma's second husband was an undependable provider and an indifferent stepfather to Emma's daughter Carrie. Writing from Williamsburg, Massachusetts, near the Conway home of her brother George's in-laws, Emma reported to her father

13   George W. Sherman to Cheney J. Sherman, 4 December 1864, Sherman Family Letters.
14   George W. Sherman to Emma Sherman, 17 May 1868, Sherman Family Letters.

on 19 August 1869, that her husband Clark was "hard at work this summer ... farming most of the time and getting out timber." She also made reference to her own labour as the hired man's wife, remarking that she had recently cut her fingers when the axe slipped while she was splitting kindling.[15]

As a farm labourer's wife, Emma's fate was tied to that of a man who was at the bottom of the agrarian socio-economic order. Historian Nancy Grey Osterud has noted that in the nineteenth-century Northeast, "rural women were defined through their relationships with men .... They gained access to land, the most important resource in an agricultural society, only through husbands and sons, fathers and brothers." For Emma, who lacked access to land through her father Cheney, her brother George and her husband Clark, economic options were limited. She would never be a member of a landowning family, and, as Osterud has observed, "it was almost impossible for rural women to support themselves outside male-headed farm households."[16]

Emma's life in western Massachusetts proved difficult in multiple respects. In February 1870, when Caddie wrote to Cheney Sherman that Emma now had "a very pleasant home" on the farm that employed Clark, she apparently did not understand that the owner also expected Emma to do the women's work of the farm: gardening, caring for poultry, doing a portion of the milking and cooking for field workers. If Clark and Emma's house was typical of hired labour housing, its kitchen lacked a water pump and a sink with a drain. That meant that Emma spent a great deal of time fetching clean water from an outdoor source and dumping dirty water into the yard. According to a prominent physician of the era, the daily hauling in and out of water buckets could turn a rural woman into a "laboring drudge." Although she did not describe herself as a drudge in the letter she wrote to her father on 3 July 1870, Emma admitted that work on the farm was taking a toll. Reporting that she had been "very, very busy" cooking for field hands during haying season and had been unable to engage a "hired girl" to help her, Emma confided to Cheney that she was "not very strong and never was used to such life as one has to do on a farm."[17]

Dissatisfied with their life on the farm, Emma's husband at one point moved his small family to Little Rock, Arkansas, where he laboured on the police force until the city's hot weather and high cost of living caused him "to dissipate."

---

15   Emma Sherman Rice to Cheney J. Sherman, 19 August 1869, Sherman Family Letters.
16   Nancy Grey Osterud, *Bonds of Community: The Lives of Farm Women in Nineteenth-Century New York* (Ithaca, NY: Cornell University Press, 1991), 1–2.
17   Osterud, *Bonds of Community*, 142–43; Caddie Sherman Spooner to Cheney J. Sherman, 27 February 1870; Emma Sherman Rice to Cheney J. Sherman, 3 July 1870, Sherman Family Letters.

As Caddie described the "dreadful" situation in a long letter to their father, her sister's Arkansas sojourn brought both Clark and Emma "to their senses" and made them realise "that all this western life and success was a myth." Back in Massachusetts, Emma continued her life as a farm labourer's wife, while Caddie worried in a letter to their father that "country life" was not good for Emma: "[It] is hard work and it begins to tell on her. [M]akes her grow old. Clark is a good enough fellow but not the one for Em I am sorry to say." Several years later, Caddie was still expressing concern for Emma, telling Cheney that her sister found it "tough ... to live and work so hard in the country" and reporting that she was the one who provided Emma's family with all their clothing. When Emma herself wrote her father from the tiny western Massachusetts village of Florence on 27 October 1878, she was working as a seamstress, sixteen-year-old Carrie was earning $5.50 a week at the local silk mill, and Clark was once again searching for work, now hoping to rent or labour on a farm near his father-in-law Cheney.[18]

By the time Emma wrote to her father in October 1878, the Rices were living out the worst-case circumstances for a farm labourer's family. Clark was between farmhand jobs, and Emma and Carrie were the ones contributing to the family coffers. Emma was working as a seamstress, which, along with domestic work, was one of the few types of wage labour available to a married woman in a rural neighbourhood. Carrie, at sixteen, was now old enough to work in one of the many textile mills that dotted the Massachusetts countryside and had been hiring single rural women since the 1820s. As Emma's sister Caddie had correctly noted, "country life" was indeed "hard work" for the women of the Rice family.[19]

Urban life proved no easier. Unlike her older sister, Caddie remained a city dweller, apparently working in a series of low-paying jobs until she married Frederick B. Spooner, a man she described to her father as loving her "dearly." Writing her father from New York City in the late 1860s, Caddie hoped her upcoming marriage would ease her financial concerns, noting, "I hate to give up my liberty but I must have a home. I cannot work always. I must get someone to take care of me." Unfortunately, however, Caddie ended up following

---

18   Caddie Sherman Spooner to Cheney J. Sherman, 6 July 1871; Caddie Sherman Spooner to Cheney J. Sherman, 11 February 1872; Caddie Sherman Spooner to Cheney J. Sherman, 5 February 1877; Emma Sherman Rice to Cheney J. Sherman, 27 October 1878, Sherman Family Letters.

19   For an overview of employment options for both rural and urban women in nineteenth-century New England, see Thomas Dublin, *Transforming Women's Work: New England Lives in the Industrial Revolution* (Ithaca, NY: Cornell University Press, 1994).

her loving but unlucky husband from Boston to New York City as he pursued one underpaid job after another. Her misfortunes in the city – and those of her father and sister in the countryside – left Caddie with an ambivalent attitude toward rural life. In a letter written a few years into her marriage, Caddie told her father he was too old to do farm work, "particularly now that warm weather is coming on," but she extolled the virtues of the farm in upstate New York where she was boarding to recover her own health "in lovely country near Poughkeepsie – on very high ground – [where] they keep a great many cows and I have all the milk I want to drink." Several months later, in the same letter in which she worried that country life was destroying her sister Emma's health, Caddie observed that in the aftermath of the Wall Street financial panic of 1869 business was "very dull" and "money very tight" in New York City. She now told Cheney to "[c]onsider yourself fortunate Father that you are a farmer and no such care as business on your mind." Closing another letter to her father, Caddie summarised a year in which her husband had been unemployed for six months and she had been obliged to return to her mother's New York City home with an unspecified gynaecological ailment: "Oh, I have seen terrible trouble lots of it in one short year. [B]ut it is peculiar to our family – so I must take my share. I am only twenty two but I feel thirty – and I guess I look it."[20]

Like her sister Emma before her, Caddie had once hoped that she and her husband would be able to provide her father with a stable and prosperous home, but that was not to be. A decade after the letter in which Caddie despaired about her health and premature aging, Cheney was still on his own in the countryside near East Brimfield, and Caddie was still living with relatives in New York City alongside her "kind and devoted" travelling salesman husband and their two-and-a-half-year-old son Hoyt. She was also still fretting about her sister, telling Cheney, "Em's marriage has proved very unfortunate and I am sorry for all parties."[21]

In the meantime, Caddie's brother George continued to avoid country life, moving from one industrial job to another in cities and towns throughout New England and the state of New York. Unable to secure a civilian position as a machinist around the time of the 1869 panic, he even did a brief stint in

---

20   Caddie Sherman to Cheney J. Sherman, 17 November 1867; Caddie Sherman Spooner to Cheney J. Sherman, 6 July 1871; Caddie Sherman Spooner to Cheney J. Sherman, 11 February 1872; Caddie Sherman Spooner to Cheney J. Sherman, 14 November 1869, Sherman Family Letters.

21   Caddie Sherman Spooner to Cheney J. Sherman, 31 January 1880, Sherman Family Letters; 1880 U.S. Census, New York City, New York, Schedule 1, Enumeration District 573, Dwelling 140, Family 198.

the U.S. Navy, where he sailed to Santo Domingo as part of President Ulysses S. Grant's ill-fated empire-building scheme. Caddie reported to her father that the Navy had treated George "very badly indeed" before she somehow finagled his discharge, and he was "now at Hazardville Conn[ecticut] in a machine shop doing as well as usual." She despaired, however, that her brother would ever fulfil the role of securely employed urban householder, writing her father that she wished that George "would marry some nice energetic woman – settle down – and look after his daughter – it is certainly time. [A]nd I very often lose all patience with George." A few years later, in April 1877, George was indeed married again, but to a sickly woman whose strained relationship with his daughter Emma obliged the girl to remain in Conway as George and his second wife settled into their South Adams, Massachusetts, home, and George once again looked for industrial employment. Writing to his daughter back in Conway, George noted that outdoor "chopping and shoveling" work had recently left him with a swollen arm and wrist and had once more convinced him that farm work would never be for him. As he told his daughter, "My Wife's relations once advised me to go to farming. What a farmer I'd make!! And how true the old saying 'You cannot learn and [sic] old dog new tricks.'"[22]

Regardless of the peacetime instability of his work as a machinist, George Sherman did not view the countryside as a safety valve for the economic challenges of urban industrial life. A farm might provide a safe haven for his motherless daughter or a healthy temporary residence for his ailing sister Caddie, but – as the experiences of Cheney Sherman and Clark Rice indicated – it might only mean hard work, low pay and lack of prestige for a landless man. If the "Wife's relations" who urged George to take up farming were his second wife's family, they obviously hoped he would fare better than his father and brother-in-law. If, instead, he was referring to his first wife's relatives in his April 1877 letter, they likely hoped that George would replace his sonless father-in-law, who had died three months earlier, and take over the Bartlett family farm at Conway. For a man in the prime of life with access to his own farmland, maybe the countryside could provide a refuge from urban storms, but it was one that George adamantly rejected.[23]

---

22   Caddie Sherman Spooner to Cheney J. Sherman, 6 July 1871; George W. Sherman to Emma Sherman, 9 April 1877, Sherman Family Letters.

23   Caddie Sherman Spooner to Cheney J. Sherman, 5 February 1877, Sherman Family Letters. George's father-in-law Dexter Bartlett, who outlived his wife and all his children, died at age 76 on 3 January 1877. See Pease, *History of Conway*, 255, and Dexter Bartlett entry, findagrave.com.

George Sherman spent the fifteen years between his first and second marriages residing in hotels and boarding houses as he futilely pursued urban success. While the yeoman ideal of an earlier era may have been appropriate for his father-in-law Dexter Bartlett, George firmly rejected this model of masculinity in favour of a newer one that centred on industrial know-how. Even in the face of failure, George never gave up on his adherence to this new masculinity, rejecting advice that the countryside might be an appropriate refuge for himself as well as his daughter.

Perhaps the experiences of his father Cheney and brother-in-law Clark further influenced George's rejection of country life. Unlike Dexter Bartlett, Cheney Sherman and Clark Rice were not farm owners but farm labourers. As such, George likely saw them as examples of failed masculinity. His younger sister Caddie certainly viewed them in this way. The pitying tone of her letters to Cheney and her scornful comments about Clark indicate that she saw both men as failures. Her assessment of George, however, proved no better. As she told their father, she had given up "all patience" with her brother over his futile pursuit of success in industry and – briefly – in the U.S. Navy. By contrast, she viewed her own husband, Fred Spooner, as a good and competent man whose failure to conform to the urban masculine ideal was not the result of weak character but of unfortunate circumstances.

Unlike George, his sisters did not have the option of choosing the countryside as a place of permanent or semi-permanent refuge. Like most nineteenth-century women, their economic fates were tied to those of their husbands. As their correspondence indicates, Caddie and her sister Emma had adopted the urban middle-class notion of marriage as a companionate relationship, but they also viewed it as an economic imperative. As Caddie correctly noted in a letter to her father, a good marriage was the most acceptable means for a woman to improve her economic situation in nineteenth-century America. Caddie aspired to the domestic ideal of the urban middle class and believed she was marrying a young businessman who would sufficiently support his own household. Even when her dream was not realised and they continued to reside with relatives, Caddie's faith in Fred Spooner never wavered. She continued to believe in the urban domestic ideal, and she and Fred apparently never considered a permanent escape to the countryside. When her health weakened, however, a short-term stay in the country – with its abundant supply of fresh air and milk – provided Caddie with the tools for recovery.

Perhaps her sister Emma's experience dissuaded Caddie and Fred from considering permanent relocation to the countryside as an answer to their woes. Like her sister's fate, Emma's economic destiny was tied to that of her husband. In their loving marriages to Johnnie White and Fred Spooner, the sisters were yoked to men who managed the vagaries of urban employment as well as they could. In her marriage of last resort to farm labourer Clark Rice, Emma followed her unsteady provider from the New England countryside to the city of Little Rock, Arkansas, and back again. There, she milked cows, tended chickens, hauled countless buckets of water and performed other typical women's work on the farms that employed her husband. To help make ends meet, she also earned money as a seamstress. As Caddie described her, Emma now resembled the farmwife drudge that reformers of the era feared selfish husbands were overloading with too many chores. Emma's role as a hard-working farmwoman bore little resemblance to the middle-class housewife she had envisioned becoming back when she believed Johnnie White would survive the Civil War and claim his bounty on a Confederate ship.

Throughout their peripatetic existence, members of the Sherman family maintained their kinship ties by naming their children after one another and sending informative and opinionated letters to each other across the urban/ rural divide. Following Cheney Sherman's business failure, they frequently resided on the edge of poverty, which sometimes necessitated industrial employment (in a silk mill or a gun factory) and other times required labour on the land. As the Sherman family's correspondence suggests, for White men and women in the American Northeast, one's identity as a farm or industrial labourer – or as a rural or urban dweller – remained necessarily flexible during this period of geographic mobility, national crisis and economic change. As their correspondence also illustrates, however, the extent to which a person had agency in moving across urban/rural boundaries, and the experiences they encountered in these relocations, varied significantly according to one's age, marital status and – especially – her or his gender.[24]

Bibliography

1880 U.S. Census. New York City, New York. Schedule 1. Enumeration District 573.
Annual Report of the Secretary of the Navy. Washington, DC: Government Printing Office, 1864.

---

24   For an in-depth exploration of kinship as a category of analysis for understanding nineteenth-century U.S. history, see Carolyn Earle Billingsley, *Communities of Kinship: Antebellum Families and the Settlement of the Cotton Frontier* (Athens, GA: University of Georgia Press, 2004). Although Billingsley focuses on the American South, many of her insights also apply to families in the North.

Billingsley, Carolyn Earle. *Communities of Kinship: Antebellum Families and the Settlement of The Cotton Frontier*. Athens, GA: University of Georgia Press, 2004.

Darwin, Gertrude B. *Lineage Book: National Society of the Daughters of the American Revolution*. Vol. 31. Harrisburg, PA: Telegraph Printing Company, 1910.

Dublin, Thomas. *Transforming Women's Work: New England Lives in the Industrial Revolution*. Ithaca, NY: Cornell University Press, 1994.

Johnson, Colin R. "Masculinity in a Rural Context." In *The Routledge History of Rural America*, edited by Pamela Riney-Kehrberg, 165–78. New York: Routledge, 2016.

Johnson, Paul E. *A Shopkeeper's Millennium: Society and Revivals in Rochester, New York, 1815–1837*. New York: Hill and Wang, 1978.

Moore, Frank, ed. *The Rebellion Record: A Diary of American Events*. Vol. 8. New York: D. Van Nostrand, Publisher, 1865.

The New York City and Co-Partnership Directory for 1843 & 1844. Vol. 2. New York: John Doggett, Jr., Publisher, 1843.

Osterud, Nancy Grey. *Bonds of Community: The Lives of Farm Women in Nineteenth-Century New York*. Ithaca, NY: Cornell University Press, 1991.

Pease, Charles Stanley, ed. *History of Conway (Massachusetts), 1767–1917*. Springfield, MA: Springfield Printing and Binding Company, 1917.

Ryan, Mary P. *Cradle of the Middle Class: The Family in Oneida County, New York, 1790–1865*. Cambridge: Cambridge University Press, 1981.

Shannon, Fred A. "A Post Mortem on the Labor-Safety-Valve Theory." *Agricultural History* 19, no. 1 (January 1945): 31–37.

Sherman Family. Letters. Private collection.

Smith, Lillian. "Autobiography as a Dialogue between King and Corpse." In *The Winner Names the Age: A Collection of Writings by Lillian Smith*, edited by Michelle Cliff, 187–98. New York: W.W. Norton, 1978.

CHAPTER 4

Landlords and Sharecroppers in Wine Producing Regions

Beaujolais, Catalonia and Tuscany, 1800–1940

Juan Carmona and James Simpson

1 Introduction

The economic significance of sharecropping, a type of farming in which families rent small plots of land from a landowner in return for a portion of their crop, has been reinterpreted over the past couple of decades.[1] A long tradition of considering the sharecropping contract as an explanation of agrarian backwardness and an obstacle to economic development has been replaced by a more favourable view, in which it is seen as a useful contract for resolving problems associated with moral hazard or risk.[2] The literature has insisted on the advantages of its use for a crop such as the vine, whose output is highly sensitive to the quality and timing of labour inputs and the fact that the plant can be easily and permanently damaged if the operations are badly carried out. Moreover, viticulture is very labour-intensive and has been difficult to mechanise until recently. Studies on sharecropping in the Tuscan wine region since the Middle Ages, or in the Catalonia vineyards in the last two centuries, have shown the advantages of this contract, especially when compared to fixed rent tenancy.[3] However, a limitation of these studies is that sharecropping is less common in European vineyards than the literature suggests.[4] Certain

---

1 An earlier version of this chapter was presented at the EURHO Conference 2019, Paris, 10–13 September 2019. We wish to thank Rolf Bauer for his comments. The authors have benefitted from financial assistance from the Ministerio de Ciencia e Innovación PID2019-104869GB-100.
2 Douglas W. Allen and Dean Lueck, *The Nature of the Farm* (Cambridge: The MIT Press, 2002).
3 Daniel A. Ackerberg and Maristella Botticini, "The Choice of Agrarian Contracts in Early Renaissance Tuscany: Risk Sharing, Moral Hazard or Capital Market Imperfections?" *Explorations in Economic History* 37 (2000): 241–57, for Tuscany. Juan Carmona and James Simpson, "The Rabassa Morta in Catalan Viticulture: The Rise and Decline of a Long-Term Sharecropping Contract, 1670s–1920s," *The Journal of Economic History* 59, no. 2 (1999): 290–315; for Beaujolais, Philip Hoffman, "The Economic Theory of Sharecropping in Early Modern France," *The Journal of Economic History* 42, no. 1 (1984): 155–62.
4 Juan Carmona and James Simpson, "Explaining Contract Choice: Vertical Coordination, Sharecropping, and Wine in Europe, 1850–1950," *The Economic History Review* 65, no. 3

difficulties exist with the contract, such as the problem of dividing the harvest, the risks associated with specialising in a commercial crop or moving up the quality ladder. In the first case, while the costs of supervising the quality of the sharecropper labour inputs are lower than for other types of contracts, those related to the division of the harvest can be very high, especially when wine quality is important. On the other hand, the fluctuation of grape production is much higher compared to other products, and family farmers who tend to be risk averse will not specialise, forcing the landowners to supply a multicropping farm to potential tenants. Finally, the preference for sharecropping over fixed rent tenancy usually does not take into account the possibility that the landowner is not indifferent to whether the rent is in kind or in cash, especially when grape quality is high. These factors could explain why share-cropping is less common in commercial viticulture, and that, in certain cases, landowners prefer to devise alternative labour contracts which can solve the problems associated with the transaction costs of labour-intensive cultivation. Sharecropping is thus more often found in polyculture farms where the vineyard plays a complementary role.

The factors offered in the previous part explain why the sharecropping contract was common in a number of important wine regions, such as Beaujolais in France, the Italian region of Tuscany (Chianti) or Catalonia in Spain, but mainly absent in others. Although the contract originated in the Middle Ages in Tuscany, and from the seventeenth century in the other two cases, these regions not only survived without major changes until the 1940s but successfully helped displace other types of local wine producers, adapted to the profound changes in viticulture in this period, and were capable of producing premium wines. For the reasons we have already indicated, usual explanations are not enough to explain the survival of the form of organisation occurring in these regions, and we offer a different one. One crucial characteristic of wine production in these three regions was its concentration in large properties that centralised the production process of all or part of the harvest in order to enjoy the advantages offered by the integration of the production of grapes thanks to the nature of the contract, which gave the landowners great freedom to control the production of sharecroppers. On the other hand, the three regions shared a particularly hilly landscape which made labour-intensive viticulture and mechanisation expensive. Moreover, the nature of the terrain led to high levels of human specificity and explains the fact that most sharecroppers

---

(2012): 887–909; Samuel Garrido, "Sharecropping Was Sometimes Efficient: Sharecropping with Compensation for Improvements in European Viticulture," *The Economic History Review* 70, no. 3 (August 2017): 997.

remained on the same farm for very long periods. These exogenously given long-term contracts stand as most important difference with similar contracts in tropical plantations or even in the southern United States, where land flatness reduces monitoring costs, thus allowing shorter contracts.

In this chapter, we will first show the factors that explain the presence and absence of sharecropping in viticulture. Next, we will show which types of contracts vineyard landowners could use to maintain the advantages offered by sharecropping without its disadvantages. Finally, we will show how the landowners of Beaujolais, Tuscany and Catalonia solved the problems of division of harvest, specialisation and wine production in a context of technical change. We will pay special attention to the role of the supervision of sharecroppers, which was done in order to favour technical change and the reduction of transaction costs.

2   Sharecropping and Viticulture

The family farm is the most widespread form of organisation in agriculture because of the low costs of supervising labour. In farming, output is highly sensitive to the timing and quality of effort, and often deficiencies in these areas only become apparent after the harvest. Even then, it can be difficult to determine whether a poor crop was caused by the worker's negligence or by exogenous factors, such as adverse weather conditions.[5] The family farm provides strong incentives for labour to carry out tasks diligently and over time, and members can acquire important human asset specific skills linked to their land, which allow them to be more productive than if they have to keep changing farms each year.[6] Furthermore, until recently there were few economies of scale in most types of agriculture, allowing the family farm to compete successfully with large estates or plantations.[7] In addition, the fact that workers prefer to work their own land in order to increase their income and gain security for old age implies that in traditional economies the majority of farms are worked by their owners. Therefore, in order to be viable, land or labour contracts have to replicate the advantages that family farms enjoy.

5   Allen and Lueck, *Nature*, 6–7; Yujiro Hayami and Keijiro Otsuka, *The Economics of Contract Choice: An Agrarian Perspective* (Oxford: Clarendon, 1993), 12–16.

6   For asset specificity, see Oliver Williamson, *The Economic Institutions of Capitalism: Firms, Markets, and Relational Contracting* (New York, Free Press: 1985), 242.

7   Debraj Ray, *Development Economics* (Princeton: Princeton University Press: 1998), 453–55; Hayami and Otsuka, *Economics*, 6–7.

The major advantage of rental contracts is that they provide the best incentives for farmers to maximise output, but not to maintain soil fertility or care for fixed assets (buildings, trees, vines, etc.) compared, for instance, to small landowner cultivators.[8] Wage labour, at the other end of the spectrum of contract choice, provides fewer incentives to apply a sufficient effort and care for fixed assets without the need for careful supervision. Sharecropping, by contrast falls between these extremes, and the literature provides two broad additional explanations for the sharecropping contract: risk sharing, and the presence of market imperfections for inputs other than land.

Agriculture is a risky economic activity, not just because of output sensitivity to weather or disease, but also because price variability can have a big impact on farm income. National and international market integration can increase income variability as a poor harvest is no longer offset by high local prices. In this sense, the advantage of sharecropping compared to fixed rental tenancies, is that it shifts part of the risk of harvest or price failure to a less risk-averse landowner.[9] However, there are a number of objections to the tenant's risk aversion as being the determining factor in contract choice. First, fixed rent tenants can expect to be helped in case of poor harvests.[10] Second, recent studies have questioned that sharecroppers are more risk averse than fixed rent tenants or even the landowners. Small owner-occupiers typically reduce risk by using the family endowments of land, labour and capital to produce a variety of different income streams, a characteristic found especially in the case of wine, whose output fluctuated considerably more than other crops. In France, like in Spain or Italy, most vineyards were minuscule and worked by part-time producers.[11] Therefore, if large landowners wanted to attract potential tenants, they had to allow multicropping (polyculture) in sufficiently large holdings or to permit sharecroppers to work outside the exploitation, despite

---

8   Allen and Lueck, *Nature*, 58–61.

9   French literature has noted the expansion of the contract in times of difficulty; see Fabien Connord, *La terre des autres: Le métayage en France depuis 1889* (Montrouge, Editions du Bourg: 2018), 98–99.

10   Elizabeth Griffiths and Marc Overton, *Farming to Halves: The Hidden History of Sharefarming in England from Medieval to Modern Times* (Basingstoke, Palgrave: 2009), 127–30.

11   In France there were 1.6 million hectares of vines and 1.6 million growers in the 1900s. Marcel Lachiver, *Vins, vignes et vignerons: Histoire du vignoble français* (Paris, Fayard: 1988), 583. Vine scattering was an additional risk-minimising device in Italy. Giovanni Federico and Pablo Martinelli, "Italy to 1938," in *Wine Globalization: A New Comparative History*, ed. Kym Anderson and Vicente Pinilla (Cambridge: Cambridge University Press, 2018), 190–91.

the increasing monitoring costs. For this reason, it was common in France and Tuscany to offer farms large enough to employ the sharecropper's family full time, and prohibit them from working elsewhere.

A second kind of explanation is related to transaction costs. According to Alfred Marshall, transaction costs with sharecropping were particularly high because neither the landowner nor tenant received the full marginal return from increased labour and capital inputs, encouraging both to be undersupplied.[12] However, the transaction costs associated with effort are actually lower on a family farm worked by sharecroppers, than using wage labour. More recently, transaction costs explanations have been used for preferring sharecropping contracts instead of tenancy when it is possible to damage fixed assets which affect future harvests (buildings, trees, soil, etc.). For example, with a crop such as the vine, output is highly sensitive to the quality and timing of labour inputs and the plant itself can be easily and permanently damaged if the pruning, ploughing and hoeing operations are carried out badly.[13] This explains why rental contracts were not common in viticulture, while the use of wage labour was rare because the close monitoring required to reduce the risks of opportunistic behaviour on the part of the workers was too costly for most landowners.[14] However, the relatively high figures for vineyards under fixed rent tenancy contracts found in French statistics in 1892 (8 per cent) suggest that the effect was limited in certain contexts.[15] Sharecropping also created transaction costs associated with the division of the harvest, which was an important factor in limiting its use with viticulture.[16] If the division took place in the vineyard, the landowner needed to be present to avoid theft and ensure that the different varieties, together with under- and over-ripe fruit, were divided equally between the two parties. For exogenous reasons, vineyards were usually highly fragmented, and the landowner would have considerable difficulties in monitoring a number of geographically dispersed plots throughout the village since most were located only on certain parts of the hillsides (generally south-facing), and on marginal land. The grapes then needed to be transported quickly to the landowner's cellar to prevent fermentation. A less time-critical moment for dividing the harvest was after fermentation, but the

12   Alfred Marshall, *Principles of Economics: An Introductory Volume* (Basingstoke, [1890] 1990), 534–37.
13   Carmona and Simpson, "Rabassa Morta," 292–93.
14   See, especially, Jules Guyot, *Étude des vignobles de france pour servir a l'enseignement mutuel de la viticulture et de la vinification françaises*, vol. 3 (Paris, 1868), 292–93.
15   Garrido, "Sharecropping Was Sometimes Efficient," 980.
16   Allen and Lueck, *Nature*, 53–55.

possibilities for sharecroppers to cheat were even greater. Wine could be stolen, and the small scale of production implied that there were usually plenty of winemaking facilities in a village for sharecroppers to hide part of their harvest from the landowner. As wine quality varied considerably, and good wine could be removed before the division by a dishonest tenant and replaced with poorer wines brought from elsewhere or even by inferior wines obtained from the second pressing, such as *vinello* in Italy. Landowners were obliged to accept these wines as rental payment from their tenants, unlike the merchants, who could reject inferior wines.

Market imperfections for factor inputs such as technical know-how, managerial skills or capital provide a third type of explanation. Farm management might involve not only organising the timing of activities, such as the start of the harvest, but also planning responses to exogenous shifts in factor and commodity prices or the appearance of new biological or labour-saving technologies, skills that were not easily accessible to sharecroppers.[17] Capital market imperfections are another explanation in cases in which tenants were too poor to accept fixed rental contracts and sharecropping allowed landowners to advance farm equipment and working capital, with the future harvest used as security.[18] However, on occasions, sharecroppers also had access to credit markets, sometimes because they owned some land, while, over time, market imperfections might be eliminated, leading to sharecropping disappearing locally.[19]

By contrast, too little attention has been given to two other factors that influence the nature of contracts in viticulture. First, contract choice needs to be linked to the nature of vertical co-operation and integration associated with the production and marketing arrangements of individual crops and livestock. The literature assumes that the landowner was indifferent to receiving payment in cash or kind but, while this might have been the case with crops such as cereals where spot markets existed, it was not with crops which required immediate processing and demanding a high degree of vertical coordination. Therefore, decisions on contract choice sometimes carried important implications concerning the extent that they were to be involved in downstream operations associated with processing and marketing farm produce. A second factor is the role of human asset specificity in long-term contracts. These contracts allowed sharecroppers to become more productive as they accumulated human asset specificity linked to the land, which encouraged them

---

17   James Roumasset, "The Nature of the Agricultural Firm," *Journal of Economic Behavior and Organization* 26 (1995): 161–77.

18   Ray, *Development Economics*, 564–68; Hayami and Otsuka, *Economics*, Chapter 5.

19   Connord, *La terre des autres*, 48–51.

to undertake non-observable investments, which was especially important, as new biological technologies were often required just to maintain yields.[20] These restrictions are especially important in the case of vines, which were often grown on hillsides under specific conditions and were difficult to mechanise until the 1950s. Long-term contracts reduced the incentives for tenants to overexploit assets, such as existed with short-term ones. Long-term contracts and high human asset specificity do, however, have an important drawback, which is the absence of a farm ladder or lifetime earning patterns. It is implied, therefore, that stable lifetime incomes for tenants, and a guaranteed skilled labour force for the landowner, could end suddenly if the contract was brought to a premature conclusion.[21]

3   Contract Choice in Commercial Viticulture From 1850

Problems such as the division of the harvest, the tenant's desire to multicrop to reduce risk, or the monitoring of effort on highly fragmented plots all help to explain why sharecropping was comparatively rare. In France in 1892, according to the official statistics, only 8.3 per cent of the total area of vines were cultivated using sharecropping contracts, and these were concentrated in a few regions.[22] Spanish statistics on contract choice are very poor, but sharecropping appears to have been rare, and geographically highly concentrated.[23] In Italy, sharecropping was more widespread, but rarely used in commercial viticulture, despite the crop representing 20 per cent of the total agricultural output in 1911.[24] Therefore, how were vines cultivated if sharecropping was so rare? By far the most common were owner-occupiers who made their own wines, generally of low quality, using only family labour. However, fine wines were often made on large estates, and specific labour contracts were more common than sharecropping or fixed rent tenancy. Finally, from 1860, technological change allowed

---

20   Oriana Bandiera, "Contract Duration and Investment Incentives: Evidence from Land Tenancy Agreements," *Journal of the European Economic Association* 5, no. 5 (2007): 956–57 stresses the importance of non-observable investments.

21   In the US South, the contract is usually explained as a rung on a farm ladder that saw the tenant move from labourer, to sharecropper, tenant and, finally, landowner, as they accumulated capital, skills and reputation over their working life. Lee Alston and Joseph Ferrie, "Time on the Ladder: Career Mobility in Agriculture, 1890–1938," *The Journal of Economic History* 65, no. 4 (2005): 1058–81.

22   Connord, *La terre des autres*, 44–48.

23   Zoilo Espejo, *Costumbres de derecho y economía rural* (Madrid, 1900).

24   Federico and Martinelli, "Italy to 1938," Table 5.1.

significant scale economies in viticulture and the possibility to enjoy low-cost production even using wage labour and sharecropping occasionally.

The typical organisation structure in the late nineteenth century was a family-operated vineyard making its own wine, much of it consumed by the family. Increasing amounts, however, were sold to wholesale merchants, who blended these different types of wine for the hundreds of thousands of small retailers in urban areas, to be sold as common wine.[25] Fine wine production was organised differently, since there was a strictly limited area of favourable land to produce these wines, and considerable care was required in carrying out the different activities. This led landowners to create sophisticated labour contracts to resolve problems of moral hazard and monitoring, and creating incentives for vineyard workers to acquire, and utilise, human asset specificity. Fine wine production also required large amounts of capital as producers deliberately reduced output to improve quality, and high-quality winery equipment was needed.[26] Sharecropping could have provided the high levels of human asset specificity that were required, but its use was absent in Bordeaux and Champagne, and vineyard workers lacked the skills and capital required to transform quality grapes into fine wine. Fine wine producers also wanted to protect their brand names, and therefore did not want sharecroppers to be able to sell their share on the market. As a result, the landowner kept the whole harvest and hired skilled winemakers, while vineyard workers received high wages. In Bordeaux, the *prix-faiteurs* were given the responsibility on the large estates for all the skilled operations on a fixed area of vines. In Burgundy, the *vigneron a prix d'argent* was given this responsibility, while the Champagne *maisons* outsourced the production of their grapes to small growers, although they remained under their supervision.[27]

But even in the case of common wine, new technologies changed the nature of vineyard supervision and reduced transaction costs between 1860 and 1914, encouraging the creation of large estates and use of wage labour and sometimes sharecropping contracts, especially in the French Midi.[28] In the Midi, economies of scale began to be important on vineyards of over thirty hectares that were established on the fertile plains rather than the hills, and growers used large quantities of pesticides, fungicides and artificial fertilisers, as well

25   Henri Sempé, *Régime économique du vin: Production, consommation, échange* (Bordeaux and Paris, 1898), 104–6.

26   Carmona and Simpson, "Explaining Contract Choice," 896.

27   Carmona and Simpson, "Explaining Contract Choice," 896–98.

28   James Simpson, *Creating Wine: The Emergence of a World Industry, 1840–1914* (Princeton: Princeton University Press, 2011).

as irrigation and light pruning, to improve yields.[29] As wine prices fell relative to wages from the late nineteenth century, some landowners turned to share-cropping contracts to reduce costs. However, in the years of poor harvests and low prices in the early 1900s, landowners were obliged to provide a guaranteed salary to their sharecroppers, limiting interest in the contract.[30]

These factors suggest why sharecropping contracts were not widely used in commercial vine cultivation. Yet in a few important wine regions, notably Beaujolais in France, Tuscany (Chianti) in Italy and Catalonia in Spain, share-cropping was the most common contract. Furthermore, it managed to survive the profound technical and commercial changes in wine production over sev-eral centuries, and remained important until after the Second World War. At first glance, this seems to be the only element these very different contracts had in common, especially with respect to the degree of specialisation and the share of the production delivered to the owner. Nevertheless, sharecroppers in all three regions worked for large landowners who centralised the production process for all or part of the harvest, and produced a medium-quality wine for the market. The rest of the chapter shows how this type of organisation solved the problems of transaction costs associated with the supervision of work, management and the division of the harvest, together with the incentive structure for sharecroppers.

4   The *Vigneronnage*

The vineyards of Beaujolais were close to navigable water, and from the sev-enteenth century viticulture grew rapidly in response to the Parisian market. The region, in particular Haut (northern) Beaujolais where the hillside was especially steep, benefitted from a growing reputation and high prices from the mid-nineteenth century.[31] Sharecropping represented between 30 and 40 per cent of all vines of the *département* of Rhône in 1882, but reached 80 per cent in the district of Villefranche-sur-Saône, in the north.[32] Beaujolais

---

29   Carmona and Simpson, "Explaining Contract Choice."

30   Carmona and Simpson, "Explaining Contract Choice," 903.

31   Gilbert Garrier, *Paysans du Beaujolais et du Lyonnais: 1800–1970*, vol. 1 (Grenoble: Presses Universitaires de Grenoble, 1973), 270, notes that planning vines (the *minage*) cost between eight and ten times more than further south.

32   Pierre Galet, *Les vignobles de France*, vol. 1, *Méditerranée, Rhône-Alpes, Bourgogne, Franche-Comté, Alsace-Lorraine* (Paris: Éditions Tec & Doc, 2004), 1100. The area of vine-yards in Villefranche increased fourfold, from 6,643 hectares in 1827 to 26,396 in 1905.

wines, although inferior to French fine wines, were called *le grand ordinaire de France*, and large landowners using sharecropping obtained prices that were at least double what owner-occupiers achieved in the same region, with the difference increasing between 1850 and 1940.[33] Just like in Catalonia, landowners had started to market their own wines from the eighteenth century.[34] Between the late nineteenth century and 1940, land concentration and sharecroppers increased dramatically, especially for the better wines.[35] By contrast, sharecropping stopped being used for cereal production in the same area from around 1800.[36]

A typical property in Beaujolais had between twelve and forty hectares of vines, which were sub-divided and cultivated by between five and fifteen sharecroppers in standard units called *vigneronnage*.[37] Tenants were given about two hectares of vines, and one-and-a-half hectares of pasture for livestock, which was sufficient to keep a family and a domestic servant fully employed. The sharecropper was required to reside on the farm, and the family was prohibited from working elsewhere. Although the milk, butter and cheese production was of poor quality, they provided an important dietary supplement and helped them survive phylloxera or periods of abnormally low wine prices.[38] If the sharecroppers owned land themselves, they were expected to rent it to others.[39] Landowners were responsible for all the major production decisions, including the choice of grape varieties and pruning methods used, as well as the timing and methods to be used in replanting after phylloxera (1875–1890), the degree of mechanisation, and when to begin the grape harvest.[40] Landowners often advanced capital because of the high cost of harvesting for the sharecropper, and sometimes because of crop destruction by hail storms. However the role of the sharecropper was decisive. The hills and the high density of vines made viticulture in Beaujolais especially labour-intensive and made mechanisation expensive. The sharecropper was responsible not just for working the vines but also for supervising the harvest and winemaking,

---

33   Jacques Burel, *Le vignoble Beaujolais* (Lyon: Riou, 1941), 71–72.

34   Garrier, *Paysans*, vol. 1, 138.

35   Especially during the mid-nineteenth century. Garrier, *Paysans.*, vol. 1, 605 and vol. 2, Table 6.

36   Garrier, *Paysans*, vol. 1, 269.

37   François Myard, *Le vigneronnage en Beaujolais* (Lyon, 1907).

38   Humbert Chatillon, *Le Beaujolais viticole* (Paris, 1906), 67.

39   Cheysson, *L'habitation du métayer vigneron du Beaujolais autrefois et aujourd'hui* (Paris, 1899), 221.

40   Myard, *Vigneronnage*, 208–9. For the increasing landowner participation in sharecroppers' expenses, see Connord, *La terre des autres*, 52.

which could involve as many as twenty people, and was required to be married, so that his wife could provide food for the workers.[41] Contracts were annual, but the hilly nature of the terrain led to high levels of human specificity, and explains why most sharecroppers remained on the same farm for long periods, sometimes even for several generations.[42]

The landowner played a crucial part in the winemaking process. The harvest was collected rapidly, and sharecroppers made the wine using their own equipment although, to avoid cheating, this was always located within the landowner's winery. Sharecroppers were not allowed to have winemaking equipment in their own cellars, and for this reason the wineries of large estates sometimes had to accommodate more than a dozen wine presses.[43] Winemaking was managed personally by the landowner or their agent, and after fermentation the wine from each vat was divided by somebody considered independent, with the landowner and sharecropper both present.[44] Only then could the sharecropper take possession of their wine, to either sell on the market or to the landowner.[45] Although these measures helped reduce the monitoring costs associated with dividing the harvest, they increased production costs compared to large growers without sharecroppers.[46]

An important feature of the contract for landowners was that labour costs were borne by the sharecroppers, including those of the harvest and winemaking. Therefore, when the poor harvests and exceptionally low prices of the 1900s ruined many sharecroppers, landowners had to offer a different contract called *grands gages*, which guaranteed a salary.[47] These contracts were similar to the *prix-fait* found in Bordeaux or the *vigneron a prix d'argent* found in Burgundy, although they contained only limited incentives for good work for the sharecropper. While both landowners and tenants might have preferred

---

41   Myard, *Vigneronnage*, 193. The harvest represented about 25 to 30 per cent of the sharecropper's annual farm costs. Garrier, *Paysans*, vol. 1, 391.

42   Garrier, *Paysans*, vol. 1, 152–53. An enquiry carried out in 1898 showed that some families had been working the same farm for more than 150 years: Myard, *Vigneronnage*, 305.

43   Paul Ferrouillat and M. Charvet, *Les celliers: Construction et matériel vinicole avec la description des principaux celliers du Midi, du Bordelais, de la Bourgogne et de l'Algérie* (Montpellier: Paris, 1896), 380 and Cheysson, *L'habitation*, 230.

44   Myard, *Vigneronnage*, 193.

45   Garrier, *Paysans*, vol. 1, 390.

46   Winemaking at Château Malescot in Bordeaux in the late nineteenth century, for example, cost 437 francs per hectare, against 657 francs on the Deleche estate: Ferrouillat and Charvet, *Les celliers*, 360, 388.

47   M. V. Vermorel and M. R. Danguy, *Les vins du Beaujolais, du Mâconnais et du Chalonnais* (Dijon, 1894), 17; Myard, *Vigneronnage*, 262–63.

sharecropping contracts, fixed wage contracts were an acceptable substitute when market conditions were especially volatile and tenants required a guaranteed income.

Finally, the vignerons might have preferred to be landowner-occupiers themselves. In fact, sharecroppers owned very little land, just 1.5 per cent of the Beaujolais land market during the nineteenth century, less than day labourers.[48] Sharecroppers were able to save money after the First World War, but land concentration continued to increase during the interwar period.[49] Not only did small growers lack the skills to produce quality wine and the capital to establish a cellar, but there were economies of scale associated with marketing it.[50] One possibility was to move down the quality ladder, which had the added advantage of requiring less labour. Indeed, on the plains of the Bas-Beaujolais, which were well suited to mechanisation and producing large quantities of cheap wines, sharecropping was less common and disappeared after 1900. However, the area of vines in this region also declined because production costs were high compared to those of the Midi with which it competed.[51] Sharecropping in Beaujolais was, therefore, linked to the production of better quality wines requiring the presence of a specialist winemaker to supervise operations and the need for a labour-intensive viticulture to provide a supply of suitable grapes. Yet the northern Beaujolais was an exception: its wines were superior to most other French wines (although inferior to those of Bordeaux or Burgundy, where direct cultivation was practised). Landowners were highly active in monitoring both the grape and winemaking process, as well as selling the wines.[52] Sharecroppers preferred increasing human asset specificity than moving to other wine producing regions and becoming owner-occupiers. Despite the advantages, in times of low prices landowners had to be prepared to guarantee a salary to attract and retain workers.

---

48   Garrier, *Paysans*, vol. 1, 360.

49   Garrier, *Paysans*, vol. 1, 605.

50   Hubert Clique, *Les caves coopératives de vinification en Bourgogne* (Paris, 1931), 97, 141.

51   After the phylloxera, vineyards in the *Bas Beaujolais* declined by 25 per cent compared to an increase of 18 per cent in Villefranche. Garrier, *Paysans*, vol. 1, 429.

52   According to Goujon, most of them were *négociants*, or needed a professional manager to supervise the cellar. Paul Goujon, *La cave et le grenier: Vignobles du Chalonnais et du Mâconnais au XIXe siecle* (Lyon: Presses Universitaires de Lyon, 1989), 216.

5   The *Rabassa Morta*

The *rabassa morta* began to be used throughout Catalonia from the end of the seventeenth century to meet the rapid increase in the demand for wines and spirits. Most contracts were found in the districts where vines were planted on the hillsides, especially in the province of Barcelona and parts of Tarragona. In 1920, in many regions, including Penedès, between 60 to 80 per cent of all vines were cultivated by sharecroppers.[53] Landowners were able to obtain a common wine of better quality and price compared to those produced by the new, large-scale cooperatives which started appearing during the first third of the twentieth century and, despite the intense conflicts that brought *rabassers* and landowners head to head, the contract seems to have reached its greatest geographical spread in the 1930s.[54]

The *rabassa morta* contracts originally required the grower or *rabasser* to clear the land, which was generally marginal land, and wooded, to plant vines within a fixed period (usually between two and ten years), to cultivate them in accordance with the customs of the region, and to hand over between one-fifth and one-third of the annual harvest to the owner.[55] The farms covered between two and four hectares, often in different plots cultivated by a single sharecropper. The contracts were originally valid until two-thirds of the vines had died and, in theory, this implied that the contacts were indefinite, lasting for generations.[56] Several factors explain how the contract was successful in reducing the different types of transaction costs associated with sharecropping. First, the absence of economies of scale in traditional viticulture and the scale of winemaking was low enough to allow sharecroppers to produce their own wine.[57] Second, by guaranteeing a separated possession of the vines from the land, including the right to sell them, the contract provided strong motivation for labourers to care for the vines. Monitoring was therefore enforced through the market, and gave "high powered" incentives to apply more labour in the vineyard rather than in other activities, in contrast to the situation

---

53   According to Raimon Soler-Becerro, *Viticultura, desigualtat i conflicte agrari: La lluita per la terra a la Catalunya vitícola, 1900–1936* (Tarragona: Publicacions URV, 2019), Appendix 5, in 26 villages of Penedès.

54   Juan Carmona and James Simpson, "Cuando el rentista no es derrotado: El caso de la rabassa catalán, 1890–1936" (IFCS – Working Papers in Economic History, WH 31891/ UC3M, Universidad Carlos III de Madrid, Instituto Figuerola, 2020), Table 1.

55   Emili Giralt, "El conflicto 'rabassaire' y la cuestión agraria en Cataluña hasta 1936," *Revista de trabajo* 7 (1964): 51–72.

56   Hence the Catalan name, *rabassa morta*, meaning "dead vine."

57   Carmona and Simpson, "Rabassa Morta," 297.

in Beaujolais.[58] The use of a sharecropping contract instead of a fixed rent tenancy contract had a major advantage in that it avoided the problem of establishing a rent which satisfied both tenants and landlord. It also allotted landowners the grapes necessary to produce and sell their own wine.[59] Finally, the success of the contract, which was generally an oral agreement, rested on the existence of face to face trust that avoided short-term opportunism and ensured the survival of the contract for generations.[60] It should be emphasised that the clearing of the marginal land to plant the vines, and the fact that a vineyard took at least four years to produce a substantial harvest, explains both the low rent and the relatively high value of the vineyard compared to the land.

In the wine districts, land concentration was on the rise, which gave the landowners the opportunity to process a significant amount of wine, even if they only received a relatively small share of the total harvest. Initially, quality was not relevant because exports from the region consisted of *aguardiente* (spirits), rather than wines. However, the building of new roads connecting the vineyards with Barcelona and other ports by the early nineteenth century allowed growers to switch to the production of table wines, for which they obtained better prices. Better quality wines were initially achieved without technological change, but wine production was increasingly centralised in the wineries of the *mas*, under the supervision of a *masover*, with the landowner, who usually lived locally, also taking an active role.[61] The appearance of new vine diseases and pests – and, particularly, the destruction of all the vineyards by phylloxera between 1880 and 1900 – led to greater involvement of growers in grape production. Landowners and sharecroppers maintained their contracts, despite the opportunity offered to the landlords to recover the land when two-thirds of the vines had died. However, the planting and cultivation of the new American strains was more capital-intensive and required chemical fertilisers, which further increased the intervention of the landowner.[62] Like in Tuscany and Beaujolais, the particularities of the mountainous landscape, which made

---

58   Carmona and Simpson, "Rabassa Morta," 293.
59   Carmona and Simpson, "Explaining Contract Choice." Among recent works, Garrido, "Sharecropping Was Sometimes Efficient," or Josep Colomé et al., "The *Rabassaire* Struggle: Long Term Analysis of a Social and Political Movement," *International Review of Social History* 63, no. 1 (2018): 1–27 ignored the role of landlords as winegrowers.
60   Carmona and Simpson, "Rabassa Morta," 294.
61   Most landlords were growers who advertised in the trade directories and sold on Barcelona's expanding market: Carmona y Simpson, "Cuando el rentista." The information on the place of residence of the landowners is based on Soler-Becerro, *Viticultura*, Appendix 2.
62   Carmona y Simpson, "Rabassa Morta," 303–4.

mechanisation difficult, explain the importance of human capital specificity and, consequently, the landlord's interest in maintaining the long duration of the contracts.[63]

Despite the difficulties created by the low wine prices during the interwar period, the landowners' wineries using the *rabassa morta* contract were more successful than the cooperative wineries that spread throughout the Catalan wine-growing areas from the early twentieth century.[64] Like in Tuscany, cooperatives had more difficulty establishing themselves in sharecropping areas. Despite having modern facilities and enjoying enormous economies of scale, cooperatives had trouble competing with low-cost regions, such as La Mancha. In particular, while Catalan cooperatives failed to supply economic incentives to independent growers to improve grape quality, large growers using sharecropping contracts were able to guarantee the quality of the grapes through vertical integration across the different farms in their property. The *rabassa morta* contract clauses allowed the landowner to enter the farm in order to supervise the various tasks, to fix the harvest date, and to control the winemaking process in the vats of each sharecropper.[65] This supervision indirectly benefitted the *rabassers* themselves, as it allowed them to produce better quality wines – and explains their reluctance to join the cooperatives, considering that their product was of better quality.[66] Landowners were also able to make marketing decisions autonomously, having the ability to control their product, while cooperative managers usually struggled to justify their decisions to their members, given the large price fluctuations.[67]

However, like in Tuscany, the increasing costs of chemical products and depressed wine prices from the early twentieth century decreased the return on unit labour input in viticulture compared to what unskilled wage labour in industry could earn, especially in the rapidly growing city of Barcelona, whose population quadrupled between 1887 and 1930. Although yields per hectare

---

63   Giralt, "El Conflicto," 56–57.

64   For Catalan cooperatives, see Jordi Planas, "Els inicis del cooperativisme vitivinícola," in *Vinyes, vins i cooperativisme vitivinícola a Catalunya*, ed. Josep Colomé Ferrer, Jordi Planas Maresma, and Francesc Valls Junyent (Barcelona: Publicacions de l'Abadia de Montserrat, 2015), 369–401.

65   Mancomunitat de Catalunya, *Projecte de regulació dels censos, rabassa morta i terratge a Catalunya* (Barcelona, 1923), 38–47, Instituto de reformas sociales, *La "Rabassa morta" y su reforma* (Madrid, 1923).

66   Jordi Planas, *Viticultura i cooperativisme: La comarca d'Igualada, 1890–1939* (Barcelona: Publicacions de l'Abadia de Montserrat, 2013), 384–85, notes that few sharecroppers joined cooperatives.

67   Simpson, *Creating Wine,* 74.

were somewhat higher than in other areas of Catalonia, unlike in Beaujolais there is no evidence that the price differential obtained by the landowners increased during the interwar period, making it possible to compensate for the fall in the relative prices of wine with respect to labour.[68] Both sharecroppers' autonomy and the fact that sharecroppers processed a greater share of the harvest explain that, unlike the Tuscan case, the demands of sharecropper organisations such as the *Union de Rabassers* (created in 1923) were not limited to an improvement of the expenses and product distribution, preserving the centralised processing system. Instead, these organisations adopted a more radical stance, demanding full landownership at the expense of the farms' unity.[69] As a result, the passing of a land reform act (*Llei de contractes de conreu*) in 1934 made it possible for sharecroppers to substitute the payment of rent in grapes for the payment of rent in cash and enabled them to redeem their farms, which would have meant the potential disappearance of the large private wineries, if this law had not been annulled.[70]

6   The *Mezzadria Poderale* in Tuscany

The *mezzadria poderale* was a medieval sharecropping contract, widely found in the provinces of central Italy, particularly in the mountainous regions of Tuscany, Umbria and Marche. In a similar way to the large French *métairies*, farmers practised multicropping (polyculture) and self-sufficient agriculture. In the case of Tuscany, and, more specifically, in the Chianti regions of Florence, Arezzo, Pisa and Siena, there was a growing trend towards wine specialisation and the expansion of the contract between 1830 and 1940, while preserving the multicropping characteristics of the contract. Like Beaujolais, Chianti sold at a higher price than common wine, with a premium of up to one hundred per cent in the 1930s, and in Italy in 1938 it represented 34 per cent of premium wine produced in wineries of more than 500 hl.[71]

---

68   Tenants would complain about the landlord's failure to get good prices.

69   A different interpretation is based on the increasing autonomy of the sharecroppers. For example, see Ramon Garrabou, Jordi Planas, and Enric Saguer, "Sharecropping and Management of Large Rural Estates in Contemporary Catalonia," *Journal of Peasant Studies* 28, no. 3 (2001): 101. However, in this study the role of the landowner as grower is, again, completely ignored.

70   Carmona and Simpson, "Cuando el rentista," 22–28.

71   Istituto Centrale di Statisticca del Regno d'Italia, *Annuario Statisco dell'Agricoltura italiana 1936–1938* (Roma, 1939), 103. For the percentage of quality wine in Federico and Martinelli, Italy until 1938, see Table 5.4.

Tuscany was a region of large estates, most of which had self-sufficient farms (*podere*), which were cultivated by sharecroppers (*mezzadre*) and organised around administrative centres (*fattorie*) with processing facilities. Despite their medieval origins, the maximum expansion of the *fattorie* occurred in recent times: between 1830 and 1930, their number quadrupled in Florence, and they occupied more than 60 per cent of the province's cultivated area.[72] In Tuscany, 60 per cent of the *fattorie* had more than five hundred hectares, but in the more specialised wine-growing areas (such as Florence) the average was just one hundred hectares with ten *poderes* each.[73] Sharecroppers were offered annual contracts, varying in size from six to twenty-six hectares, sufficient to support a family and perhaps a few farm servants, although larger farms were rarer in wine-growing areas.[74] The sharecropper was required to reside on the farm and, like in Beaujolais, the family was prohibited from working elsewhere.[75] The *fattorie* usually produced a variety of products, especially wheat, wine and olive oil, but the weight of each of them varied locally, and, in the case of Chianti in 1900, wine often represented a larger share of the production value.

Although sharecroppers had ample autonomy to choose the crops, landowners could ask them to increase the production of more commercial ones. Landowners could modify the size of the *podere* in order to make them suited to more labour-intensive crops or a smaller family, and, in certain cases, they supplied basic food in exchange for an increase in the production of commercial crops.[76] With the increased commercialisation of Tuscan wines in the national and international market from the last third of the nineteenth century, landowners started to play a greater role in key production decisions, such as the choice of grape varieties needed to produce Chianti, the pruning system used or the control of the harvest.[77] In addition, the *fattorie* were equipped

---

72   Sandro Rogari, *Le campagne toscane nel ventennio postunitario: Rivista di storia dell'agricoltura*, vol. 2 (2009), 103; Istituto Centrale di Statisticca, *Annuario Statisco*, 103, and Ministro per la Costituente, *Rapporto della Commissione económica* (Roma, 1947), 213.

73   The Riccoli, one of the best known, had two thousand hectares in three *fattorie* in 1838: Giulana Biagioli, "Storie di aziende agrarie," in *Marche* 7 (2016): 177.

74   Francesco Galassi, "Stasi e sviluppo nell'agricoltura toscana, 1870–1914: Primi resultati di uno studio aziendale," *Rivista di storia economica* 3 (1986): 304–37; Giuliana Biagioli, "La mezzadria poderale nell'Italia centro-settentrionale in età moderna e contemporanea (secoli xv – xx)," *Rivista di storia dell'agricoltura* 42, no. 2 (2002): 83.

75   Biagioli, "La mezzadria poderale," 54–55.

76   Luporini and Parigi, "Multi-Task Sharecroppping Contracts: The Italian Mezzadria." *Economica* 63 (1996): 445–57; Biagioli, "Storie di aziende," 185; Frank Snowden, *The Fascist Revolution in Tuscany 1919–1922* (Cambridge: Cambridge University Press, 1989), 28.

77   Ricasoli's role in the definition of the varieties of grapes that make up the "Chianti Classico" was crucial: Biagioli, "La mezzadria poderale,"2000. For Chianti and sharecropping, see

with technicians or administrators.[78] Unlike in Beaujolais or Penedès, the vine was a promiscuous crop, especially in the Chianti production areas (99 per cent of the vineyards of Florence in 1929), and the destruction by phylloxera was delayed until the 1930s.[79] In general, the cultivation of wine in this region was very labour-intensive, given the steep hillsides and dispersed vineyards. This made mechanisation difficult and human specificity high, which explains why, despite the contracts being annual, farms were worked by the same families for generations.[80]

Winemaking was originally carried out by both sharecroppers and landowners, but as wine quality and demand increased, it was carried out by the sharecroppers in the central winery, where the division took place under the supervision of the farm manager (*fattore*).[81] As Chianti wine is a mixture of different varieties, its production required great control. Sharecroppers often took out loans with the *fattore* against commercial crops such as wine, which were settled annually after the harvest.[82]

The landowners of the *fattorie*, which were closely linked to the production and export of Chianti, benefitted from their greater economies of scale in winemaking, their capacity to produce a sufficient variety of grapes, and the advantages in marketing they provided.[83] Despite the growing criticism in the nineteenth century of the *mezzadrie poderale* because of their supposed inefficiency and conservatism, the number of sharecroppers increased as a share of the labour force, from 42 per cent in 1882 to 55 per cent in 1911. Just like in the Penedès region, cooperatives did not compete with the private wineries in sharecropping regions.[84]

Luca Mocarelli and Manuel Vaquero Piñeiro, "Viticulture in the Italy of the Mezzadria," in *A History of Wine in Europe*, ed. Conca Messnia (London: Palgrave, 2018); on pruning, see Galassi, "Stasi e sviluppo," 322.

78   In 1902, the demands for reform called for greater sharecropper participation in the major production decisions. Snowden, *Fascist Revolution*, 52. Ministro, *Rapporto*, 214–15.

79   Promiscuous cultivation was greatest in the Chianti production areas: Yearbook, 1939, 272. For promiscuous cultivation as a way to reduce erosion, see Dario Gaggio, *The Shaping of Tuscany: Landscape and Society between Tradition and Modernity* (Cambridge: Cambridge University Press, 2017), 116.

80   Evictions were very rare, although there was some mobility within the *fattorie* themselves: Snowden, *Fascist Revolution*, 30.

81   Biagioli, "La mezzadria poderale," 77–78.

82   Biagioli, "La mezzadria poderale," 85.

83   Giulia Meloni and John Swinnen, "Trade and Terroir: The Political Economy of the World's First Geographical Indications," *Food Policy* 81 (2018): 1–20. It was marketed at higher prices; the price was double that of ordinary wine in the 1930s: Istituto Centrale di Statisticca, *Annuario Statisco*, 406–7.

84   The competitive advantages in Biagioli, "La mezzadria poderale," 63–64.

Like in Catalonia, the major conflicts in the 1920s are generally attributed to the need for greater labour inputs, higher expenses for chemicals to fight phylloxera (which reduced sharecroppers' income), as well as sharecroppers' loss of independence on the better managed estates.[85] Moreover, the prohibition on working outside the *poderale* became costlier as industrial wages increased.[86] The most important conflicts occurred in Florence, in 1906, and after the First World War, with the triumph of the Socialist Party in more than half of the Tuscan municipalities. Their demands included shifting the cost of chemicals to the landowners and ending payments for using their processing facilities.[87] The expenditure on copper sulphate and sulphide to combat phylloxera could represent up to 15 per cent of the value of the harvest in the first decades of the twentieth century, increasing the debt of the sharecroppers to their landowners.[88] However, in contrast with Catalonia, Tuscan sharecroppers wanted to be more involved in the management of the *fattorie*, keeping the organisational advantages of large-scale processing.[89]

7   Conclusions

Although sharecropping was generally rare in viticulture, it was widely found in the important European regions of Beaujolais, Chianti and Penedès, where it showed significant capacity to adapt to the profound changes in viticulture between 1830 and 1930. Geographical restrictions made viticulture especially labour-intensive and limited mechanisation in these regions, thus explaining the importance of human asset specificity and long-term contracts. Furthermore, in these three regions landowners centralised winemaking, which allowed them to enjoy the advantages of greater economies of scale and enabled them to control the grape quality of their tenants. However, their success was linked to being located in the vicinity of Lyon, Florence and Barcelona. These were their main markets and were close enough to the vineyards that landowners did not need to create sophisticated marketing networks to sell their premium wines. By contrast, while the local cooperative wineries had the economies of scale to create such networks, they failed to create economic

---

85   Biagioli, "La mezzadria poderale," 65.

86   Luporini and Parigi, "Multi-Task Sharecropping Contracts," 455.

87   Ministro, *Rapporto*, 221; Biagioli, "La mezzadria poderale," 92 and 66.

88   For an average of the expenditure of four large *fattorie* at the beginning of the twentieth century, see Galassi, "Stasi e Sviluppo," 324.

89   For the sharecroppers' demands, see Snowden, *Fascist Revolution*, 44–47.

incentives to improve grape quality, while their managers had trouble making autonomous marketing decisions.

A further consideration is the increasing long-term instability in the day-to-day relations between landlords and vine growers. The combination of low wine prices, growing capital requirements, higher opportunity costs of labour (because of industrialisation) and the barriers to exit led to collective action to improve contractual conditions. In particular, sharecroppers wished to take action because their autonomy, a characteristic of these long-term contacts, was threatened by the greater involvement of landlords in the management of their estates. While this allowed sharecroppers to produce better quality wines, it also limited their possibilities for negotiating changes and devising alternative contracts.

Bilbiography

Ackerberg, Daniel A., and Maristella Botticini. "The Choice of Agrarian Contracts in Early Renaissance Tuscany: Risk Sharing, Moral Hazard or Capital Market Imperfections?" *Explorations in Economic History* 37 (2000): 241–57.

Allen, Douglas W., and Dean Lueck. *The Nature of the Farm*. Cambridge: The MIT Press, 2002.

Alston, Lee, and Joseph Ferrie. "Time on the Ladder: Career Mobility in Agriculture, 1890–1938." *The Journal of Economic History* 65, no. 4 (2005): 1058–81.

Bandiera, Oriana. "Contract Duration and Investment Incentives: Evidence from Land Tenancy Agreements." *Journal of the European Economic Association* 5, no. 5 (2007): 953–86.

Biagioli, Giuliana. "La mezzadria poderale nell'Italia centro-settentrionale in età moderna e contemporanea (secoli xv-xx)." *Rivista di storia dell'agricoltura* 42, no. 2 (2002): 53–101.

Biagioli, Giuliana. "Storie di aziende agrarie." *Marche* 7 (2016): 169–91.

Burel, Jacques. *Le vignoble Beaujolais*. Lyon: Riou, 1941.

Carmona, Juan, and James Simpson. "The Rabassa Morta in Catalan Viticulture: The Rise and Decline of a Long-Term Sharecropping Contract, 1670s–1920s." *The Journal of Economic History* 59, no. 2 (1999): 290–315.

Carmona, Juan, and James Simpson. "Explaining Contract Choice: Vertical Coordination, Sharecropping, and Wine in Europe, 1850–1950." *The Economic History Review* 65, no. 3 (2012): 887–909.

Carmona, Juan, and James Simpson. "Cuando el rentista no es derrotado: El caso de la rabassa catalán, 1890–1936." IFCS – Working Papers in Economic History, WH 31891/UC3M, Universidad Carlos III de Madrid, Instituto Figuerola, 2020.

Chatillon, Humbert, *Le Beaujolais viticole*. Paris : Imp. De A.Davy, 1906.

Cheysson, Émile. *L'habitation du métayer vigneron du Beaujolais autrefois et aujourd'hui*. Paris, 1899.

Clique, Hubert. *Les caves coopératives de vinification en Bourgogne*. Toulouse: impr. F. Boisseau, 1931.

Colomé, Josep, Jordi Planas, Raimon Soler-Becerro, and Francesc Valls-Junyent. "The *Rabassaire* Struggle: Long-Term Analysis of a Social and Political Movement." *International Review of Social History* 63, no. 1 (2018): 1–27.

Connord, Fabien. *La terre des autres: Le métayage en France depuis 1889*. Montrouge: Éditions du Bourg, 2018.

Espejo, Zoilo. *Costumbres de derecho y economía rural*. Madrid, 1900.

Federico, Giovanni, and Pablo Martinelli. "Italy to 1938." In *Wine Globalization: A New Comparative History*, edited by Kym Anderson and Vicente Pinilla, 190–220. Cambridge: Cambridge University Press, 2018.

Ferrouillat, Paul, and M. Charvet. *Les celliers: Construction et matériel vinicole avec la description des principaux celliers du Midi, du Bordelais, de la Bourgogne et de l'Algérie*. Montpellier, 1896.

Gaggio, Dario. *The Shaping of Tuscany: Landscape and Society between Tradition and Modernity*. Cambridge: Cambridge University Press, 2017.

Galassi, Francesco. "Stasi e svilupp' nell'agricoltura toscana, 1870–1914: Primi resultati di uno studio aziendale." *Rivista di storia economica* 3 (1986): 304–37.

Galet, Pierre. *Les vignobles de France* Paris: Éditions Tec & Doc, 2004, 2 vols.

Garrabou, Ramon, Jordi Planas, and Enric Saguer. "Sharecropping and Management of Large Rural Estates in Contemporary Catalonia." *Journal of Peasant Studies* 28, no. 3 (2001): 89–108.

Garrido, Samuel. "Sharecropping Was Sometimes Efficient: Sharecropping with Compensation for Improvements in European Viticulture." *Economic History Review* 70, no. 3 (2017): 977–1003.

Garrier, Gilbert. *Paysans du Beaujolais et du Lyonnais: 1800–1970*. Grenoble: Presses Universitaires de Grenoble, 1973.

Giralt, Emili. "El conflicto 'rabassaire' y la cuestión agraria en Cataluña hasta 1936." *Revista de trabajo* 7 (1964): 51–72.

Goujon, Paul. *La cave et le grenier: Vignobles du Chalonnais et du Maconnais au XIXe siecle*. Lyon: Presses Universitaires de Lyon, 1989.

Griffiths, Elizabeth, and Mark Overton. *Farming to Halves: The Hidden History of Sharefarming in England from Medieval to Modern Times*. Basingstoke: Palgrave, 2009.

Guyot, Jules. *Étude de vignobles de France: Pour servir a l'enseignement mutuel de la viticulture et de la vinification françaises*. Paris, 1868.

Hayami, Yujiro, and Keijiro Otsuka. *The Economics of Contract Choice: An Agrarian Perspective*. Oxford: Clarendon, 1993.

Hoffman, Philip. "The Economic Theory of Sharecropping in Early Modern France." *The Journal of Economic History* 42, no. 1 (1984): 155–62.

Istituto Centrale di Statisticca del Regno d'Italia. *Annuario Statisco Statistico dell'Agricoltura italiana, 1936–1938.* Roma: Failli, 1939.

Lachiver, Marcel. *Vins, vignes et vignerons: Histoire du vignoble français.* Paris: Fayard, 1988.

Luporini, Annalisa, and Bruno Parigi. "Multi-Task Sharecroppping Contracts: The Italian Mezzadria." *Economica* 63 (1996): 445–57.

Mancomunitat de Catalunya. *Projecte de regulació dels censos, rabassa morta i terratge a Catalunya.* Barcelona: Imp. Casa Caritat, 1923.

Marshall, Alfred. *Principles of Economics: An Introductory Volume.* Basingstoke: Macmillan, [1890] 1990.

Meloni, Giulia, and John Swinnen. "Trade and Terroir: The Political Economy of the World's First Geographical Indications." *Food Policy* 81 (2018): 1–20.

Ministro per la Costituente. *Rapporto della Commissione económica.* Roma: Istituto poligrafico dello stato, 1947.

Mocarelli, Luca, and Manuel Vaquero Piñeiro. "Viticulture in the Italy of the Mezzadria." In *A History of Wine in Europe,* edited by Conca Messina, 227–52. London: Palgrave, 2018.

Myard, François. *Le vigneronnage en Beaujolais.* Lyon: Impr. réunies, 1907.

Planas, Jordi. "Els inicis del cooperativisme vitivinícola." In *Vinyes, vins i cooperativisme vitivinícola a Catalunya,* edited by Josep Colomé Ferrer, Jordi Planas Maresma, and Francesc Valls Junyent, 369–401. Barcelona: Publicacions de l'Abadia de Montserrat, 2015.

Planas, Jordi. *Viticultura i cooperativisme: La comarca d'Igualada, 1890–1939.* Barcelona: Publicacions de l'Abadia de Montserrat, 2013.

Ray, Debraj. *Development Economics.* Princeton, Princeton University Press, 1998.

Rogari, Sandro. "Le campagne toscane nel ventennio postunitario." *Revista di storia dell'agricoltura* 2 (2009): 99–107.

Roumasset, James. "The Nature of the Agricultural Firm." *Journal of Economic Behavior and Organization* 26 (1995): 161–77.

Sempé, Henri. *Régime économique du vin: Production, consommation, échanges.* Bordeaux and Paris, 1898.

Simpson, James. *Creating Wine: The Emergence of a World Industry, 1840–1914.* Princeton: Princeton University Press, 2011.

Soler-Becerro, Raimon. *Viticultura, desigualtat i conflicte agrari: La lluita per la terra a la Catalunya vitícola, 1900–1936.* Tarragona: Publicacions URV, 2019.

Snowden, Frank. *The Fascist Revolution in Tuscany 1919–1922.* Cambridge: Cambridge University Press, 1989.

Stiglitz, Joseph. "Incentives and Risk Sharing in Sharecropping." *Review of Economic Studies* 41, no. 2 (1974): 219–56.

Vermorel, M. V. and M. R. Danguy. *Les vins du Beaujolais, du Mâconnais et du Chalonnais*. Dijon : H. Armand, DL, 1894.

Williamson, Oliver. *The Economic Institutions of Capitalism: Firms, Markets, and Relational Contracting*. New York: Free Press, 1985.

CHAPTER 5

Co-producers of Architects

The Role of Farm Women in the Reconstruction of Farmhouses in the Netherlands after the Second World War

Sophie Elpers

In the autumn of 1945 a number of farm women arrived – unannounced – at the Department of Agriculture in The Hague. They had come to make clear the extent to which they – as housewives on Dutch farms – were interested in, and had a stake in, the plans relating to the reconstruction of the farmhouses that had been destroyed.

∴

This is how, in 1946, an employee of the Ministry of Agriculture, Fisheries and Food Supply described a protest action by farm women who were keen to play a role in the reconstruction of farmhouses which were destroyed during the Second World War.[1] A handful of individual women were behind this protest action, which was labelled spontaneous and amateurish. Whether the Ministry advised the women to work on a larger scale and adopt a more considered approach or whether their visit to the Ministry was part of a bigger plan that was already in place, is unclear. Whichever is true, women's activities in relation to the reconstruction of farmhouses were characterised by large-scale organisation and well-considered arguments. Ultimately, their actions contributed to the modernisation and rationalisation of farmhouses.

In this chapter I describe the demands that farm women made with regard to the reconstruction of farmhouses, analyse and contextualise the origins of these demands, and explain what influence the women actually had on the

---

1 Letter from Annet Schaik to the Federation of Christian Farm Women, Farmers' Daughters and Other Rural Women and Girls, 7 September 1946, in: Archive of Atria, Institute on gender equality and women's history (Atria), Archive of the Christian Rural Women's Federation (CPB), file 73.

construction process. [2] The analysis exposes underlying power relations that were intertwined with knowledge. I show who exactly produced what knowledge and who classified this knowledge as meaningful. First, I give some general information on the destruction and reconstruction of the farmhouses.

1   Destruction and Reconstruction

During the Second World War approximately 9,000 farmhouses in the Netherlands were totally destroyed. Only a few hours before the German invasion in May 1940, a Dutch army unit burned down some one hundred farmhouses so that their own defence would not be hindered and the enemy could not hide behind or in the buildings. Another few hundred farmhouses were ruined during the actual invasion. However, most of the farmhouses, about 8,500, were lost in the context of the liberation in 1944 and 1945, when fierce battles took place on Dutch territory, and parts of the land were flooded as a defence tactic. In all parts of the country, destruction took place, but especially the southern and the eastern parts of the Netherlands suffered badly; 9,000 farmhouses were completely destroyed, 40,000 were damaged. In relation to the total number of about 192,000 farms in that period, these numbers accounted for 4 per cent and 17 per cent of the total, respectively. However, these numbers give a somewhat skewed impression due to the geographically unequal distribution of the destruction.

In order to guarantee the food supply for the country, the ruined farms had to be rebuilt as soon as possible. To this end, the Dutch government set up the Agency for the Reconstruction of Farmhouses (*Bureau Wederopbouw Boerderijen*) as early as July 1940. This agency was given the task of organising and coordinating the reconstruction, designing strict guidelines for this process and making sure the guidelines were followed. After 1945 the agency was also responsible for all those farms that had been destroyed during the last year of the war. All destroyed farms were reconstructed individually – rather than through serial construction – in a process which involved more than six hundred architects from all regions in the Netherlands.

Besides this government institution, other actors were also involved in the reconstruction. These included individual local architects; the Institute of Dutch Architects; local planning authorities responsible for the aesthetic

---

2 Parts of this chapter were published in Dutch in Sophie Elpers, *Wederopbouwboer-derijen: Agrarisch erfgoed in de strijd over traditie en modernisering, 1940–1955* (Rotterdam: Naio10 Publishers, 2019), 204–18.

criteria of new architecture; the Dutch Association for the Protection of Cultural Heritage; the consultant for farmhouses at the National Information Service for Agriculture; between 1940 and 1945 (before the liberation of the Netherlands): the occupying authority, Nazi agricultural organisations, and Nazi ethnologists and folklorists; and, finally, the individual farmers and farm women who had lost their farmhouses, as well as the Farmers' Union and other organisations for farmers and farm women. These actors and institutions each developed their own ideas, wishes and demands regarding the reconstruction, based on their own analysis of the present situation and based on their visions about the future of the Netherlands. Also, they tried to get their ideas and demands realised in different ways. One of the possibilities was to present their ideas directly to the Agency for the Reconstruction of Farmhouses and its advisory boards (consisting of agricultural experts, veterinary surgeons and financial experts). Another possibility was to use the media directed at the civil servants working at the Agency for the Reconstruction or directed at local architects, farmers and farm women.

As the destroyed farmhouses were reconstructed individually, farming families could influence the reconstruction of the individual farmhouses. For every new farmhouse, an individual building plan was made by – in most cases – a local architect, who was free to develop the plan together with the farming families concerned but who also had to follow the guidelines of the Agency for the Reconstruction of Farmhouses. These guidelines stated that the new buildings had to be cheap, that they had to be fireproof and hygienic, and that they had to allow for efficient working processes. The individual farmers had to give their permission and sign the plans before the reconstruction could start.

In order to provide a profound analysis of the reconstruction of the farmhouses and an understanding of its complexity and dynamics, a research approach is needed that includes all the different actors, their ideas and demands, their motivations, the power relations in which they were embedded, and their negotiations among each other.[3] The focus on the role of farm women in this chapter contributes to a deeper understanding of these dynamics and the complexity of the reconstruction, both of which were determined

3   Elpers, *Wederopbouwboerderijen*. For post-war reconstruction in the Netherlands in general, see Antia Blom, Simone Vermaat, and Ben de Vries, eds, *Post-War Reconstruction in the Netherlands 1945–1965: The Future of a Bright and Brutal Heritage* (Rotterdam: Nai010 Publishers, 2016); Koos Bosma and Cor Wagenaar, eds, *Een geruisloze doorbraak: De geschiedenis van architectuur en stedebouw tijdens de bezetting en de wederopbouw van Nederland* (Rotterdam: NAi Uitgevers, 1995).

by a fierce debate about tradition and modernisation amongst the different actors. In the late 1940s, this debate even turned into a battle.

2   The Two Functions of Farmhouses

The conflict about modernisation and tradition was strongly connected with the functions of farmhouses during the period under consideration. At the time, farmhouses had two functions. On the one hand, they were agricultural buildings: objects for daily use which had to foster and guarantee the (economic) well-being of the farming families and which had to contribute to the modernisation of Dutch agriculture on a micro and macro level. On the other hand, the buildings were objects with an explicit symbolic function. As such, they represented certain traditions, values and identities, and had to contribute to the formation of a national community and the strengthening of a national identity.

2.1   *Traditional Reconstruction*
Despite initial optimism about the "New Netherlands" after the Second World War, representatives of the political and intellectual elite, proponents of the cultural heritage protection movement and some prominent architects began to voice cultural pessimism. They had concerns about possible negative effects of the modernisation processes, people's moral decadence, and a lack of national cohesion. In their eyes, the promotion of rural traditions could create a new sense of national cohesion and national belonging and a new moral order in the post-war society. The idea was that a national "mental reconstruction" was to be realised alongside the material reconstruction. A traditional, regionally typical reconstruction of farmhouses (using traditional, regionally typical exterior forms and floor plans and traditional materials for the exterior) could both symbolise *and* generate national unity (in this, the notion of "unity through variety" was key), cohesion and morality. Furthermore, it was hoped that a traditional reconstruction would counteract the "creeping" loss of "traditional" rural culture in the wake of modernisation. This "creeping" loss was considered a much more serious challenge than the loss of the farms caused by the war.[4]

---

4   Elpers, *Wederopbouwboerderijen*, 116–19.

2.2   *Modernisation*

At first, the advocates of traditional reconstruction and those whose primary concern was modernisation tried to come to compromises. The traditional *exteriors* were indeed compatible with the modern *in*teriors the "modernisers," who mainly came from the organised agricultural sector, requested. However, in the late 1940s, these "modernisers" introduced entirely new forms of farmhouses (modular systems), with the aim of making farm buildings cheaper, more hygienic, more fire-safe and more efficient. They hoped that this would lead to an increase in professionalism and productivity, and that it would thus facilitate economic progress on both the micro and macro level. In their view, particularly the living and working conditions of small farmers had to be improved. The destruction of the farms was considered an opportunity in that sense – even though the financing of the reconstruction was so complex that it became a challenge in itself.[5]

In the end, most of the reconstructed farmhouses got a modern interior enclosed by a traditional design; however, traditional elements were increasingly abandoned – and farming families generally supported this development. The destructions during the Second World War and the daily experiences in temporary shelters after the destruction made farming families aware of the central role the farmhouses played in their lives and work and motivated them to request innovation. However, this was certainly not a *new* topic. The agricultural sector, including associations for farmers and farm women, had already engaged in promoting and realising the urgently needed modernisation of farmhouses before the war.

3   Women's Study Committees

Immediately after the Second World War, around fifty thousand farm women were members of various rural women's federations. These federations had been founded in the 1920s and 1930s[6] and had worked to improve living

---

5 The reconstruction was partly funded by the state and partly paid by the farmers concerned – the percentage was dependent on the size of the farms: Elpers, *Wederopbouwboerderijen*, 56–61.

6 From 1930, there was a joint body representing farm women: the non-denominational Dutch Federation of Farm Women and Other Rural Women (Nederlandse Bond voor Boerinnen en andere Plattelandsvrouwen). Farm women's federations were also established as part of the provincial Catholic federations of farm women. In 1939, a national federation was founded for Protestant Christian farm women: the Federation of Christian Farm Women, Farmers' Daughters and Rural Women and Girls (Christen Boerinnen, Boerendochters, Plattelandsvrouwen en -meisjes Bond – CBPB). Together with the umbrella consultation

conditions in rural areas from their inception. They organised various activities to this end, such as lectures and courses on educational, domestic and social themes. Members also carried out a great deal of work to promote the development of rural women, including setting up nursery schools, reading rooms and child health clinics, and maintaining close contact with institutions offering farm household management education.[7] The foundation of the Centre for Farm Women and Other Rural Women's Organisations (*Centrale van Boerinnen en andere Plattelandsvrouwenorganisaties*, hereafter referred to as "the Centre") in 1946 brought into being an umbrella organisation for these federations, as well as giving them a shared mouthpiece.

One of the Centre's first activities involved coordinating a large-scale, nationwide project relating to the reconstruction of farmhouses. This project had been initiated in the autumn of 1945 by the executive committee of the Dutch Federation of Farm Women and Other Rural Women (*Nederlandse Bond van Boerinnen en andere Plattelandsvrouwen*) (from 1946: Dutch Federation of Rural Women (*Nederlandse Bond van Plattelandsvrouwen*)) and was taken over one year later by the Centre. Specifically, the project involved gathering information on farm women's demands with regard to the reconstruction of farmhouses, via specially established provincial study committees. This information was ultimately passed on to the Agency for the Reconstruction of Farmhouses (*Bureau Wederopbouw Boerderijen*) and was published in two brochures.[8] Even though some provinces, like the northern province of Friesland, had been much less seriously affected by the destruction than others, such as Gelderland in the central eastern Netherlands and the southern provinces of North Brabant and Limburg (over six thousand farmhouses had been destroyed in total in these three provinces alone), study committees were set up in every province. Each one consisted of three to seven women: farm women from the

---

body, the Centre for Farm Women and Other Rural Women's Organisations (founded in 1946, after the first steps towards its foundation had been taken in 1940), this meant that an extensive network was in place that linked farm women across the whole country.

7 Margreet van der Burg, *"Geen tweede boer": Gender, landbouwmodernisering en onderwijs aan plattelandsvrouwen in Nederland, 1863–1968* (Wageningen: Afdeling Agrarische Geschiedenis, Wageningen Universiteit, 2002), 262–68.

8 A. C. Wiersma-Risselada, *Het aandeel der vrouw bij de wederopbouwboerderijen* (Den Haag: Nederlandse Bond van Plattelandsvrouwen, 1946); Centrale van Boerinnen en andere Plattelandsvrouwenorganisaties/Ministerie van Landbouw, Visserij en Voedselvoorziening, in *De boerin en haar huis* (= *Landbouw* 10) ('s-Gravenhage: Staatsdrukkerij- en Uitgeverijbedrijf, 1949).

rural women's associations (with preference given to those whose farmhouses had been destroyed), at least one teacher of farm household management education and, in some cases, a social worker. Involving teachers was important, as, amongst other things, they could easily catalogue, via their students, the demands being made with regard to reconstruction. The Centre also ensured that the various religions were well represented within the committees – an important consideration in a pillarised country such as the Netherlands.[9] To aid opinion formation, the Centre had formulated specific points on which the study committees should focus their attention:

> 1. Determination of the existing type of dwelling. 2. Identification of any deficiencies or shortcomings. 3. Determination of the most practical design for the living quarters. 4. The number of rooms and their position in relation to each other. 5. Open-plan kitchen or separate kitchen and living room. 6. Position of kitchen, cellar, washing area and other storage areas (for fuel, vegetables, potatoes) in relation to each other and the facilities present. 7. Link between living quarters and working area. 8. Joinery used for windows, doors, skirting boards, corners, etc. 9. What improvements and simplifications are desirable in the light of an anticipated shortage of domestic help, also in the future?[10]

Two points stand out that are characteristic of the contribution made by women to the reconstruction of farmhouses. The first relates to the gender-specific appropriation of space that resulted from the Centre's focus on the living quarters of the farmhouse and, consequently, its neglect of the working area. The living quarters were regarded as the woman's domain and the working area as that of the man. Research has shown, however, that this strict gender-related segregation between the household and the farm tended to be much more of an ideal and did not reflect the day-to-day social reality of rural women.[11] Secondly, what was expected was an analysis of the situation

---

9   Centrale van Boerinnen en andere Plattelandsvrouwenorganisaties/Ministerie van Landbouw, Visserij en Voedselvoorziening, *De boerin en haar huis*, 1949, 3; see also Bé Lamberts, *Boerderijen: Categoriaal onderzoek wederopbouw 1940–1965* (Zeist: Rijksdienst voor het Cultureel Erfgoed, 2007), 76.

10   These guidelines were drawn up by A.C. Wiersma-Risselada: Atria, CPB, file 722; adapted version in *De Plattelandsvrouw* 4 (1946): 64.

11   The living quarters were, however, where the tasks were carried out for which farm women had primary responsibility: housekeeping and looking after the children. See, for example, Van der Burg, *"Geen tweede boer,"* 325; Margreet van der Burg and Krista Lievaart, *Drie generaties in schort en overall: Terugblik op een eeuw vrouwenarbeid in de landbouw*

prior to the destruction of farmhouses and a problem-oriented approach to their reconstruction. This required the women to draw on knowledge that they had accumulated through many years of experience on farms and in gender-specific household management education.

4   The Gender-Specific Appropriation of Space

The stereotypical, gender-specific appropriation of space forms part of the views propagated by farm household management schools and associations. The first household management course for farm women and farmers' daughters was offered in 1909. From 1913 onwards, farm household management teachers were trained to educate rural women, and farm household management schools were founded. These institutions trained young women – usually over a two-year period – to prepare them for their future role as a mother, housewife and farm woman. Adult women were able to follow abridged courses covering similar subject matter.[12] The education offered also dealt with farming, although it was not the intention for the students to become a "second farmer" in the household, alongside their (future) husbands. A clear – and largely ideal – separation was maintained between the woman's and the man's sphere of work, as historian Margreet van der Burg has demonstrated in her study on the education of rural women.[13] The content of the education was based on the bourgeois ideal that women should deal first and foremost with the family, the household and the agricultural community – an ideal that was very favourably received in farming circles, particularly amongst landowners and farmers with large farms. In their view, the farm woman's role as housewife and mother had a positive impact on the well-being of the farming family and, consequently, on the well-being of the rural community as a whole. Women were considered to have natural virtues and morals and were expected to pass these on to their children. They could only do so, however, if they led a "civilised" life and had duties in keeping with this. These certainly did not include

---

(Wageningen: Afdeling Agrarische Geschiedenis, Wageningen Universiteit, 1998), 21; Lorraine Garkovich and Janet Bokemeier, "Agricultural Mechanization and American Farm Women's Economic Roles," in *Women and Farming: Changing Roles, Changing Structures*, ed. Wava Haney and Jane Knowles (Boulder, CO and London: Westview Press, 1988), 212.

12   From 1935 to 1945, approximately two hundred thousand women took part in fourteen thousand household management courses. See "Huishoudelijke voorlichting ten plattelande," *De nieuwe veldbode*, 26 August 1948, 571.

13   Van der Burg, *"Geen tweede boer."*

tough, physical work on the land.[14] Nevertheless, this ideal did not match with social reality within the agricultural sector. After all, many farms relied on the assistance of farm women and farmers' daughters, particularly during the "Crisis Years" before the Second World War and during the war. The assumption that, after the war, women barely helped out on their farms, due to the impact of ongoing mechanisation and modernisation, also does not hold, as was demonstrated by Van der Burg and Lievaart.[15]

Whereas farm household management education trained women to enter the "female" work domain, agricultural education for men focused on the farm, which was considered to be the "male" domain. This resulted in a gender-related segregation that prevented people – and particularly, men – from seeing the farm as a single entity whose two constituent elements, the living quarters and working area, were inextricably linked by mutually dependent and overlapping fields of work.[16] These two types of vocational training relating to the farm remained strictly separated into the 1960s. In accordance with the curriculum drawn up for farm household management education, the activities of rural women's associations also emphasised the role of the woman as a mother and housewife and, therefore, predominantly focused on the tasks carried out in the living quarters.

5   Demands Relating to Reconstruction

The data collected by the provincial study committees through surveys and interviews contained extremely detailed information on the living quarters of the farmhouses to be reconstructed.[17] A rather diverse wish list had emerged, as views differed from one region to another, but there was agreement on numerous basic issues.[18] These included standards relating to the number and size of the rooms in the living quarters, which were discussed with the afore-mentioned reconstruction advisory committees.[19] The standards regarding

---

14   Van der Burg and Lievaart, *Drie generaties*, 20–21. Incidentally, the discussion about the ideal role for women was not initially conducted amongst farm women themselves, but amongst well-to-do women who were participating in the growing women's movement.

15   Van der Burg and Lievaart, *Drie generaties*, 28.

16   Van der Burg and Lievaart, *Drie generaties*, 20–28, 112; Van der Burg, "*Geen tweede boer*," 313.

17   See, for example, the reports of the Gelderland, Limburg and Groningen study committees in: Atria, CPB, file 722.

18   Lamberts, *Boerderijen*, 77.

19   "Verslag van de vergadering van de boerderijencommissie en afgevaardigden van Verenigingen van Plattelandsvrouwen en door oorlogsgeweld gedupeerden," 13 November

the volume of the dwelling were eventually laid down in the government's reconstruction guidelines. Depending on the size of the farm, the volume of the dwelling could be between 315 and 600 cubic metres. In the case of smaller farms with more than seven people in the family, for every two children it was permitted to build dwellings 25 cubic metres bigger than prescribed in the guidelines, up to a maximum of 400 cubic metres.[20]

However, other issues that the women had identified, including the urgent need to avoid windows with glazing bars (as found in traditional farmhouses) because they made farmhouses too dark and the windows difficult to keep clean, were not included in the guidelines.[21] For that reason, in 1946, A.C. Wiersma-Risselada, who held administrative functions both within the Centre and within the Dutch Federation of Rural Women and who was an enthusiastic supporter of involving women in the reconstruction, noted that she was unhappy about the cooperation with the advisory committees of the Agency for the Reconstruction of Farmhouses. In her view, the committees were primarily focused on the working area, the farmer's domain, and did not pay enough attention to the living quarters (Figure 5.1).[22]

1946, in: Nationaal Archief (NA), The Hague, the Netherlands, Directie van de Landbouw: Veeteelt, 2.11.05, file 204; Bureau Wederopbouw Boerderijen, "Uittreksel uit de rapporten van de boerinnenbonden etc. betreffende de grootte van boerenwoningen," in: NA, Directie van de Landbouw: Veeteelt, 2.11.05, file 204.

20 "Algemene regelen en voorwaarden voor de financiering van de herbouw van door oorlogsgeweld geheel of gedeeltelijk verwoeste of onherstelbaar beschadigde boerderijen (1948)," 4, in: NA, VROM, 2.17.03, file 5052. See also "Financierings- en premiumregeling oorlogsschade boerderijen," *Nederlandse Staatscourant*, 21 May 1952, 5; Wiersma-Risselada, *Aandeel der vrouw*, 9–11; Centrale van Boerinnen en andere Plattelandsvrouwenorganisaties/ Ministerie van Landbouw, Visserij en Voedselvoorziening, *De boerin en haar huis*, 1949, 21–25; A. D. van Eck, "Nota," 11, in: RCE (Cultural Heritage Agency of the Netherlands), collection SHBO/BWB, no file number.

21 In the conservative Catholic agricultural journal *Boer en tuinder* (Farmer and Horticulturist), farm women were asked to accept farmhouse designs with small windows in the living quarters so that the intimate, enclosed character of historic farmhouses could be retained. See the articles in *Boer en Tuinder*: "Heemkunde," "Heemkunde," 3 April 1948, 7; "Wederopbouw Boerderijen en het aandeel van de vrouw," 28 August 1948; "Boereninterieur: Inrichting van de boerenwoning," 31 December 1948; "Nieuwe ideeën en moderne huizen," 28 January 1950. The cultural heritage organisation Bond Heemschut and conservative architects were also proponents of small glazing bar arrangements. Farm women opposed them, stating: "... you come to enjoy this seclusion once a year on your holidays, while we have to live with it all year round." Cited from N. B. Goudswaard, *Naar een goede en goedkope boerderij* (Meppel: N.V. Noord-Nederlandse Drukkerij, 1950), 12.

22 Wiersma-Risselada, *Het aandeel der vrouw*, 12–16.

FIGURE 5.1   Caricature to encourage women to make
their voices heard on the subject of the
reconstruction, 1946
SOURCE: A. C. WIERSMA-RISSELADA,
HET AANDEEL DER VROUW BIJ DE
WEDEROPBOUWBOERDERIJEN (DEN
HAAG: NEDERLANDSE BOND VAN
PLATTELANDSVROUWEN, 1946), 13

Within the context of the individual approach taken to the reconstruction of the farmhouses, however, the demands of women that had been catalogued would be drawn on extensively. The government also appears to have seen opportunities here. The Ministry of Agriculture, Fisheries and Food Supply had ensured that farm household management teachers could participate in the reconstruction study committees.[23] Alongside their role as inventory takers,

---

23   Report on the period from March to July 1946 by Annet Schaik, in: Atria, CPB, file 73.

they could contribute new ideas to the study committees on how farmhouses should be laid out and equipped. Furthermore, via their students they would be able to disseminate the demands that the study committees ultimately laid down with regard to the reconstruction, and, in this way, reach the individual farm women on the ground. This was in keeping with the general expectations placed on them in their role as teachers; the teachers were expected to visit farming families to get to know the different regional living conditions and then derive their students' needs from these visits. The teachers were also supposed to offer individual on-the-spot advice.

In 1946 and 1949, two booklets were published containing detailed summaries of women's demands relating to the reconstruction, as collected by the study committees: *Het aandeel der vrouw bij de wederopbouwboerderijen* (Women's part in the reconstruction of farmhouses) and *De boerin en haar huis* (The farm woman and her home).[24] The first of these was published by the Dutch Federation of Rural Women and reported on the study committees' initial findings. These were presented in further detail in the second booklet, published by the Centre in cooperation with the Ministry of Agriculture, Fisheries and Food Supply. The publications were mainly intended for farm women whose farmhouses had been destroyed, as well as architects and contractors, and served as a guide during the individual approach to the reconstruction. Above all, the reconstruction of a farm had to result in living quarters that were efficiently laid out; moreover, the reconstructed building needed to promote hygiene and morality. Both publications opted for a form of argumentation and presentation that compared the old and new farmhouses. Here, the emphasis was placed on the shortcomings of the old farmhouses: "With regard to the layout of the living quarters, existing good forms should be perfected, deficiencies remedied and shortcomings that have arisen over time in existing dwellings due to changing living habits addressed."[25]

In principle, the Housing Act ("*Woningwet*," adopted in 1901 and amended in 1921 and 1931) was already applicable to dwellings before the war.[26] This Act

24   Wiersma-Risselada, *Het aandeel der vrouw*; Centrale van Boerinnen en andere Plattelands-vrouwenorganisaties/Ministerie van Landbouw, Visserij en Voedselvoorziening, *De boerin en haar huis,* 1949.

25   Wiersma-Risselada, *Het aandeel der vrouw,* 5.

26   The aforementioned focus on the working area can also be attributed to the fact that the Agency for the Reconstruction of Farmhouses and the advisory committees relied on the Housing Act as far as the living quarters were concerned. See A. D. van Eck, "Nota," 16, in: RCE, collection SHBO/BWB, no file number. For information on the Housing Act see Noud de Vreeze, ed. *6,5 miljoen woningen: 100 jaar woningwet en wooncultuur in Nederland.* Rotterdam: Uitgeverij 010, 2001; Karin Gaillard, "De ideale woning op papier," in *Honderd*

imposed conditions relating to hygiene and safety and required dwellings to be a certain size. The construction of box beds was also prohibited. In *De boerin en haar huis*, however, it was noted that, since the introduction of the Housing Act, progress "in the countryside [had lagged] well behind that seen in cities."[27] The reconstruction of the farmhouses now presented an opportunity to make significant improvements to the living quarters of farming families. For example, farm women no longer wanted: "a. box beds. b. unpartitioned sleeping areas for boys and girls. c. the toilet to be in the barn or outside. d. open access to the loft via a stairway from the living room or raised-level room. e. sleeping areas above the cellar with insufficient floor insulation. f. direct entry into the living room without a hall or porch."[28]

The following were regarded as inadequate: "a. the number of sleeping areas, the washing and bathing facilities. b. the light and ventilation levels. c. the water supply throughout the house. d. waste disposal. e. the number of fitted cabinets for clothes, kitchen utensils and work equipment. f. the partitioning of the loft between the living quarters and working area."[29]

In the second edition of *De boerin en haar huis*, published in 1956, these arguments were also supported by photographs in which the old situation and the new, improved situation were placed side by side (Figures 5.2a and b).[30]

The reference to "deficiencies and shortcomings" from the past was based on knowledge that women had acquired from their experience of carrying out everyday housework in the living quarters of their farmhouses.[31] Such knowledge appeared to be an insufficient argument on its own, however. Indeed, the influence and expertise of farm household management teachers were cited to substantiate the demands being made by farm women. Women's demands relating to the reconstruction were being cultivated "thanks to the information communicated through farm household management education and associations," which, to a large extent, supplemented or broke the cycle of knowledge

jaar wonen in Nederland 1900–2000, ed. Jaap Huisman, Irene Cieraad, and Karin Gaillard (Rotterdam: Uitgeverij 010, 2000), 111–71; J. G. M. Keesom, *Wonen. Woning. Wet. Wij wonen: 100 jaar Woningwet* (Amsterdam: Stedelijke Woningdienst Amsterdam, 2000).

27   Centrale van Boerinnen en andere Plattelandsvrouwenorganisaties/Ministerie van Landbouw, Visserij en Voedselvoorziening, *De boerin en haar huis*, 1949, 6.

28   Wiersma-Risselada, *Het aandeel der vrouw*, 5.

29   Wiersma-Risselada, *Het aandeel der vrouw*, 6.

30   Centrale van Boerinnen en andere Plattelandsvrouwenorganisaties/Ministerie voor Landbouw, Visserij en Voedselvoorziening, *De boerin en haar huis*, 1956.

31   Wiersma-Risselada, *Het aandeel der vrouw*, 5.

FIGURES 5.2A AND B   Illustrations of the old situation and the new, desirable situation in
farmhouses
SOURCE: CENTRALE VAN BOERINNEN EN ANDERE
PLATTELANDSVROUWENORGANISATIES/MINISTERIE
VAN LANDBOUW, VISSERIJ EN VOEDSELVOORZIENING,
DE BOERIN EN HAAR HUIS (= *LANDBOUW* 10) ('S-
GRAVENHAGE: STAATSDRUKKERIJ- EN UITGEVERIJBEDRIJF,
1956), 51, 56

passed on from mothers to daughters – and, thereby, stopped the reproduction
of unchanging knowledge.[32]

Institutionalised education, as a place where knowledge was generated,
legitimised women's demands, particularly those regarding the efficient
layout and equipping of the living quarters. The Nieuw Rollecate institute,

---

32   Wiersma-Risselada, *Het aandeel der vrouw*, 12; see also Greta Smit, "Veranderingen in de
huishoud," in *Nederlandse Bond van Plattelandsvrouwen 1930–1955*, ed. Nederlandse Bond
van Plattelandsvrouwen (Groningen, 1955), 74–75.

the national training college for farm household management teachers in Deventer, had calculated how much time and energy could be saved in the new farmhouses compared with the old ones. Some of the results, for which the housework had been broken down into different steps, were published in the booklet *Het aandeel der vrouw bij de wederopbouwboerderijen*:

> For example, a supply of water for mopping and washing on the first floor would save 43 hours per year, based on 10 buckets per week, each containing 10 kg of water, being carried over a distance of 5 metres [which was the distance that would have to be covered if the buckets had to be carried upstairs, as was the case in the old farmhouses]. The same applies to drainage on the first floor. If the cellar door does not open into the kitchen and you have to walk 2½ m back and forth to the cellar with an estimated frequency of ten times per day, this equates to 50 m per day. Two doors also have to be opened each time. The distance covered can be limited by ensuring that the cellar door opens into the kitchen.[33]

To cite another example, it was specified that installing central heating would save an estimated 3,750 working minutes (62.5 working hours) per year, as the farm women would no longer need to keep stoves burning.[34]

Calculations such as these added an analytical dimension to the knowledge that women had acquired through experience.

6 The Rationalisation of the Household

As was the case in other countries, since the beginning of the 1920s there was a lot of interest in the topic of the rational household in the Netherlands. This interest began with the publications of the American home economist Christine Frederick, who advocated applying insights from business economics to the household; in Frederick's view, the housewife should function as a manager and work in accordance with an efficient work schedule.[35] In 1928, a Dutch translation of Frederick's 1915 book *Household Engineering: Scientific Management in the Home* was published under the title *De denkende huisvrouw*.

---

33 Wiersma-Risselada, *Het aandeel der vrouw*, 11–12.
34 For the other results of the study conducted by Nieuw Rollecate, see the documents in: Atria, CPB, file 722.
35 This was based on the scientific management theory of the engineer Frederick Winslow Taylor.

Nieuwe inzichten (The thinking housewife. New insights).[36] German economist Erna Meyer's work on the *"neue Haushalt"* (new household), in which she demonstrated – in a more concrete way than Frederick – what rationalisation meant in household practice and in which she divided up housework into sub-tasks was also published in Dutch, in 1929, as *De nieuwe huishouding* (The new household).[37] Theda Mansholt (1879–1956), director of the Rollecate training institute and aunt of Sicco Mansholt, the future Minister of Agriculture, Fisheries and Food Supplies, had written the foreword to this Dutch version. From this, we can already see the important role that the rationalisation of the household would play at the institute. In 1930, Rollecate adapted its curriculum in line with the "well-considered household," as it was named by Theda Mansholt, one of the principal advocates of rationalisation.[38]

Rationalisation also meant paying attention to how the kitchen was equipped. Based on the concept of "efficiency," Frederick had designed a kitchen that was small, orderly and practical, to allow the housewife to carry out her chores in a logical order and without too much toing and froing, bending and stretching.[39] In Germany, this concept was emulated in 1926 in the famous kitchen design of architect Margarete Schütte-Lihotsky, the *Frankfurter Küche*. In the Netherlands, following experiments in various locations and using various methods, a rational kitchen was designed that the company *Bruynzeel* put into series production in 1938.[40] The design took the housewife's needs into account, emphasising efficiency, hygiene and comfort. Its basic elements were a worktop with two cupboards underneath and a sink in the middle. There was often a pull-out chopping board at the top of the right-hand cupboard. The sink and worktop were made of artificial stone and under the sink there was

---

36   Christine Frederick, *De denkende huisvrouw: Nieuwe inzichten* (Haarlem: Tjeenk Willink, 1928).

37   Erna Meyer, *De nieuwe huishouding* (Amsterdam: Van Holkema & Warendorf, 1929). A third guide that largely corresponded to the other two was translated from French in 1932: Paulette Bernège, *Orde en methode in de gezinshuishouding* (Haarlem: Tjeenk Willink, 1932). See also Margrieth Wilke, "Kennis en kunde. Handboeken voor huisvrouwen," in *Schoon genoeg: Huisvrouwen en huishoudtechnologie in Nederland 1898–1998*, ed. Ruth Oldenziel and Carolien Bouw (Nijmegen: SUN, 1998), 72–80.

38   Van der Burg, *"Geen tweede boer,"* 248–58.

39   Frederick, *De denkende huisvrouw*, 42.

40   Mayke Groffen and Sjouk Hoitsma, *Het geluk van de huisvrouw* (Amsterdam: SUN, 2004), 109–14; Marja Berendsen and Anneke van Otterloo, "Het 'gezinslaboratorium': De betwiste keuken en de wording van de moderne huisvrouw," *Tijdschrift voor sociale geschiedenis* 28, no. 3 (2002): 301–22; Irene Cieraad, "Het huishouden tussen droom en daad: Over de toekomst van de keuken," in *Schoon genoeg: Huisvrouwen en huishoudtechnologie in Nederland 1898–1998*, ed. Ruth Oldenziel and Carolien Bouw (Nijmegen: SUN, 1998), 40–44.

a small shelf for storing buckets and the like. This basic configuration could be expanded by adding more cupboards under the worktop, as well as wall cupboards, large freestanding cupboards and pot racks. Standardised dimensions and the interchangeability of the elements made the kitchen easy to use in construction. The "Bruynzeel kitchen" was installed in a large proportion of post-war social housing, although often it was not the original version that was fitted but, instead, smaller, simpler and cheaper variants. "Bruynzeel kitchens" were also incorporated into farmhouses. The possibility of combining the individual kitchen elements in various ways, depending on the space available, was a major advantage.[41] After all, kitchens of various types were found in farmhouses: working kitchens as well as open-plan kitchens with a dual function (kitchen and living room) in a single space, which meant there was sometimes more space and sometimes less space available for the kitchen facilities.

The same was also true of the farmhouses to be reconstructed. Arguments in favour of the working kitchen and the open-plan kitchen had been collected by the study committees. The choice ultimately made "will depend ... on what is customary in a particular region, the size of the dwelling and the financial means of the future residents," Wiersma-Risselada announced in the booklet *Het aandeel der vrouw bij de wederopbouwboerderijen*. She also proposed a third version: a living room with an adjacent kitchen area that could be sealed off by means of a sliding door or curtain.[42] All three of these options were actually created during the reconstruction, with the first two being the most common.[43] With regard to the equipping of kitchens, we can assume that the original "Bruynzeel kitchen" was by no means applied in all cases, but that the kitchens in the reconstructed farmhouses were, nevertheless, equipped in accordance with the same principles of efficiency, hygiene and comfort. This was recommended in *De boerin en haar huis*, which included precise details relating to the worktop and sink, amongst other things. These had to be seventy-five to eighty-five centimetres in height, and the worktop needed to be at least two hundred centimetres long and the sink sixty centimetres long, with a distance of fifty centimetres from the chrome-plated tap to the sink. The sink had to be made of granite, asbestos cement, artificial stone, stainless steel or glazed earthenware and have concave corners. Next to the sink, a tile-shaped soap

---

41   "Het keukenprobleem," *Goed wonen* 1 (1948): 185–88.

42   Wiersma-Risselada, *Het aandeel der vrouw*, 7. See also A. C. Wiersma-Risselada, "Woonhuis of kamer met kooknis," *De Plattelandsvrouw* 5, no. 7 (1947): 102–3.

43   F. Sander, "Wederopbouw Boerderijen 1940–1956," in: RCE, collection SHBO/BWB, no file number. The working kitchen was mainly constructed in the northern provinces, in Zeeland and on small farms.

dish could be integrated into the wall. The distance to the cooker and kitchen cupboards had to be as short as possible.[44] By providing this degree of precision, the farm women presented themselves as experts (above the architects) who did not allow any alternatives.

7   The Impact on Reconstruction

That the two booklets mentioned above were actually used in the reconstruction and that the demands of rural women were largely taken into account is apparent not just from the interviews I have conducted with architects involved in the reconstruction,[45] but also from the handful of reconstructed farmhouses that did not undergo conversion.

FIGURE 5.3   Interior of a reconstructed farmhouse in Maarheeze
SOURCE: SERGE TECHNAU, *INTERIOR OF A RECONSTRUCTED FARMHOUSE IN MAARHEEZE*, NORTH BRABANT, 2017 (IMAGE ARCHIVE OF THE CULTURAL HERITAGE AGENCY OF THE NETHERLANDS (RCE), OBJECT NUMBER 14299−61961)

---

44 Centrale van Boerinnen en andere Plattelandsvrouwenorganisaties/Ministerie van Landbouw, Visserij en Voedselvoorziening, *De boerin en haar huis,* 1949, 35.
45 See the interview with Oldhoff, Rikken and Van Rijsbergen, in: Meertens Institute, collection "Erfenis van het verlies," file 1012.

Although the farmhouses differed from one region to another, as traditional forms were used during the reconstruction in most cases, there were certain characteristics that could be seen throughout the country. Behind the front door of the living quarters there was usually a hall with textured plaster panelling, which was easy to keep clean. This hall, which kept the home relatively free of draughts, led to the rooms. On the ground floor, these consisted of a working or open-plan kitchen with a worktop, a sink and a number of (fitted) cupboards, one or two living/sitting rooms or studies, often with fitted cupboards and, in some cases, a bedroom or a shower room, as well as a toilet and a utility room linking the living quarters and the working area. On the upper floor, there were several bedrooms equipped with fitted cabinets and, sometimes, a washbasin. In some cases there was also a bathroom. All the bedrooms opened directly onto a landing or hallway leading to the top of the stairs. Ceiling heights of at least two-and-a-half metres and large windows ensured sufficient light and ventilation. The use of cavity walls meant the farmhouses were well insulated (Figure 5.4).

AFB. 9. KLEIN BEDRIJF MET TOEPASSING VAN EEN WOONKEUKEN	FIG. 9. SMALL FARM INCORPORATING AN OPEN-PLAN KITCHEN
koestal	cowshed
spoelplaats	utility room
gang	hall
kamer	room
woonkeuken	open-plan kitchen
slaapk / slaapkamer	bedroom
badkam	bathroom
Woonkeuken $18–26\,m^2$	Open-plan kitchen $18–26\,m^2$
Kamer (event. slaapkamer ouders) $14–18\,m^2$	Room (possibly parents' bedroom) $14–18\,m^2$
3–4 slaapkamers $12–14\,m^2$ voor slaapkamer ouders	3–4 bedrooms $12–14\,m^2$ for parents' bedroom
$9–12\,m^2$ voor 2 pers. slaapkamers	$9–12\,m^2$ for 2-person bedrooms
$12–16\,m^2$ voor 4 pers. slaapkamers	$12–16\,m^2$ for 4-person bedrooms
$6\,m^2$ voor 1 pers.slaapkamer	$6\,m^2$ for 1-person bedroom

Badkamertje	2,80 m² (min. afmeting 1,50–1,85 m)
W.C.	1 m² min.
Kelder	9 m²
Bijkeuken	10–12 m²
Gang of portaal	2 m² min. breedte minstens 1 m

Een woning volgens bovenstaande indeling vraagt een vloeroppervlak van circa 58 m² en de inhoud ervan bedraagt ongeveer 390 m³ (excl. spoelplaats).

Bathroom	2.80 m² (min. dimensions 1.50–1.85 m)
W.C.	1 m² min.
Cellar	9 m²
Pantry	10–12 m²
Hall or porch	2 m² min., at least 1 m wide

A dwelling with the above layout requires a floor area of approximately 58 m² and has a volume of around 390 m³ (excl. utility room).

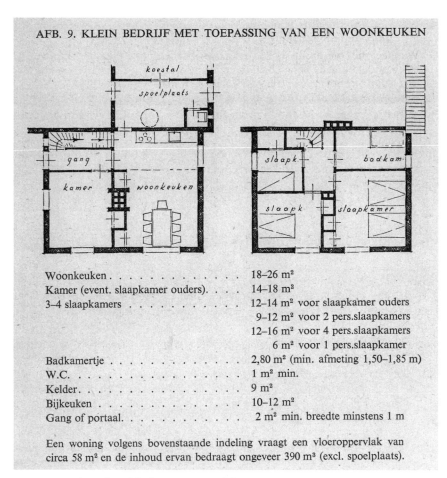

AFB. 9. KLEIN BEDRIJF MET TOEPASSING VAN EEN WOONKEUKEN

Woonkeuken	18–26 m²
Kamer (event. slaapkamer ouders)	14–18 m²
3–4 slaapkamers	12–14 m² voor slaapkamer ouders
	9–12 m² voor 2 pers.slaapkamers
	12–16 m² voor 4 pers.slaapkamers
	6 m² voor 1 pers.slaapkamer
Badkamertje	2,80 m² (min. afmeting 1,50–1,85 m)
W.C.	1 m² min.
Kelder.	9 m²
Bijkeuken	10–12 m²
Gang of portaal.	2 m² min. breedte minstens 1 m

Een woning volgens bovenstaande indeling vraagt een vloeroppervlak van circa 58 m² en de inhoud ervan bedraagt ongeveer 390 m³ (excl. spoelplaats).

FIGURE 5.4 Floor plan of the living quarters of the reconstructed farmhouse of a small farm
SOURCE: *DE BOERIN EN HAAR HUIS* (1949), 21

As the farmhouses that had been destroyed were around sixty-five years old on average, their reconstruction often involved far-reaching modernisation. This applied, in particular, to small farms that, before the war, still had living quarters with tiled floors laid directly onto the sand, low ceilings, box beds, sleeping areas in open lofts and insufficient lighting and ventilation: "Just some of the major shortcomings associated with the dwellings," as the Agency for the Reconstruction of Farmhouses pointed out.[46] In many cases, the barns were in poor condition too. Against this background it is, therefore, unsurprising that some farming families regretted the fact that their farmhouses had not been destroyed and that, consequently, they did not qualify for reconstruction.

When it came to satisfying the farm women's demands, however, certain restrictions applied: while the farm women ideally wanted to have electricity in their homes, in 1947 some 28 per cent of Dutch farmhouses had not yet been connected to the grid. In most regions this situation did not change immediately as a result of the reconstruction. Although 78 per cent were also not connected to mains water,[47] this did not mean that water pipes and sanitary facilities could not be installed and used. After all, individual (electric) pump systems could be used to pump water around the home.

Within the context of the reconstruction, the following were also discouraged by the government due to financial reasons: central heating; more than one toilet in the home; baths and double (from 1950 also single) washbasins; more than one lighting point and one socket in living rooms, with the exception of the open-plan kitchen, where there could be two lighting points, and the "main living rooms," where two sockets could be installed.[48]

8 "Prompters" of the Architects

Farm women's organisations saw the reconstruction of farmhouses as an opportunity to fundamentally improve farmhouses and actively involve farm

---

46   A. D. van Eck, "Nota," 16, in: RCE, collection SHBO/BWB, no file number; see also Centrale van Boerinnen en andere Plattelandsvrouwenorganisaties/Ministerie van Landbouw, Visserij en Voedselvoorziening, *De boerin en haar huis*, 1949, 6–7.

47   Evert W. Hofstee, *Rural Life and Rural Welfare in the Netherlands* (Den Haag: Government Printing and Publishing Office, 1957), 130.

48   A. D. van Eck, "Nota," appendix 2, in: RCE, collection SHBO/BWB, no file number. See also the letter from the Minister for Reconstruction and Public Housing to the Minister of Finance, 14 September 1949, appendix 1: Bureau Wederopbouw Boerderijen: "Korte omschrijving van de sobere uitvoering van een boerderij, tevens richtlijn voor het samenstellen van het bestek," in: NA, VROM, 2.17.03, file 5052.

women and give them a say in this process. The demands relating to the reconstruction that the study committees collected were based on knowledge that
farm women had acquired through years of practical experience. In addition,
they were underpinned by knowledge stemming from gender-specific farm
household management courses. These courses promoted a gender-related
segregation between the household and the farm, which was evident from,
and even reinforced by, the explicit focus of women on the living quarters during the reconstruction. In all likelihood, farm women who were not members
of the rural women's associations, or had contact with the associations or the
farm household management schools in another way, were not questioned
about the reconstruction. These associations and schools led the way; it was
members of rural women's associations and teachers who took on the central
role when it came to cataloguing, selecting and adding to demands relating
to the reconstruction, as well as making these demands publicly known. They
can, therefore, be regarded as elites who ultimately determined what demands
were made. These demands were centred around the modernisation and
rationalisation of farmhouses. As a result, traditional farmhouse forms were
dispensed with. Although the 1949 publication *De boerin en haar huis* contained a chapter describing historical types of farmhouses in the Netherlands,
this was provided to convince readers that new solutions were needed. The
desired modernisation could "build ... on an age-old farming tradition" by
striving to replicate the same "strong, authentic spirit," but certainly not by
copying old forms, which would amount to little more than "imitation," which
was described as a "futile endeavour, vapid and superficial."[49] However, it could
not be assumed that a homogeneous approach would be employed: certain
provincial study committees recommended retaining the farmhouses typical
of the region, for example. Several years later, an article appeared in the magazine *De Plattelandsvrouw* (The Rural Woman) extolling the virtues of "modern
farmhouses in accordance with the old tradition" – according to this article,
current practice was demonstrating that traditional, regional types of farmhouse could easily be adapted to modern-day demands.[50] Here, we can see the
battle between tradition and modernisation that played out throughout the
whole of the reconstruction period and defined the construction of the new

---

49   Centrale van Boerinnen en andere Plattelandsvrouwenorganisaties/Ministerie van
      Landbouw, Visserij en Voedselvoorziening, *De boerin en haar huis*, 1949, 8.
50   See the reports of the study committees of the Gelderland, Limburg and Groningen
      farm women's federations in: NA, Directie van de Landbouw: Akkerbouw en Weidebouw,
      2.11.01, file 372; "Moderne boerderijen Nederland."

farmhouses, which generally combined tradition and modernisation but, over time, abandoned traditional elements more and more obviously.

Guided, or at least advised, by the aforementioned elites, farm women were able to assume the role of co-producers of the farmhouses within the context of the reconstruction. This is what a journalist from the *Nieuwe Rotterdamse Courant* newspaper was referring to in 1946 when he talked about the farm woman as the "prompter" of the architect.[51] This "prompting" was done in various ways: by influencing the guidelines for the reconstruction of the farmhouse and by engaging in individual negotiations with architects and contractors, for which the two publications described here served as a guide. Earlier, in 1934, the booklet *De plattelandswoning* (The rural home) had been published, which was also intended to serve as a guide for the construction and equipping of the living quarters of farmhouses. This was a publication by H. A. de Vries, a teacher at the national farm household management teacher training college Nieuw Rollecate, and the architect Jan Jans. Theda Mansholt had contributed to the foreword. It can be inferred from the use of language in this booklet that the task of women was mainly seen as ensuring that the living quarters were *used* correctly. The *construction* was a matter for (male) architects, and Jans and De Vries were clearly asking them to build principal forms that were typical of the region concerned.[52] In the publications mentioned previously, this was not an issue anymore.

Whereas the 1946 booklet *Het aandeel der vrouw bij de wederopbouwboerderijen* focused exclusively on the reconstruction of farmhouses, the other booklet, *De boerin en haar huis,* was also intended to reach those who would be "involved in designing, building and equipping farmhouses in the future."[53] After the publication of this second booklet, the interest that organised rural women showed in house building increased further. From the late 1940s, rural women's organisations held regular exhibitions and special information evenings on practical homes and facilities and how to use them efficiently. This was also the case in Zeeland, for example, after the 1953 North Sea flood, when hundreds of farmhouses were destroyed by a huge storm surge and had to be reconstructed.[54] Model homes were also set up in various parts of the country,

51   "De wederopbouw van boerderijen. Plattelandsvrouwen wensen een adviserende stem," *Nieuwe Rotterdamse Courant*, 29 April 1946.

52   H. A. de Vries and Jan Jans, *De plattelandswoning* (= *Bibliotheek voor de huisvrouw op het platteland* 3) (Zwolle: Tjeenk Willink, 1934).

53   Centrale van Boerinnen en andere Plattelandsvrouwenorganisaties/Ministerie van Landbouw, Visserij en Voedselvoorziening, *De boerin en haar huis*, 1949, 51.

54   "Om de Watersnood," *De nieuwe veldbode*, 30 April 1953, 631.

with support from the Ministry of Agriculture, Fisheries and Food Supply. Accompanying instructions were provided by teachers and special household management advisors.[55]

In 1956, when the last of the destroyed farmhouses had been reconstructed, a second, revised edition of *De boerin en haar huis* was published. C.W. Willinge Prins-Visser, a professor teaching in the farm household management programme established in 1952 at Wageningen Agricultural College, had provided additional chapters for this second edition.[56] This programme played an important role in providing information on household management within the context of the "regional improvement" measures undertaken from the mid-1950s, which aimed to improve problem areas where agricultural production was lagging behind by means of land consolidation and intensive education programmes. The demands of rural women that had been collected prior to the reconstruction also remained important within this context.[57]

9   A "Civilisation Offensive"

For the agricultural organisations, modernisation and rationalisation were the main priorities during the reconstruction of the farmhouses. Reconstructed farmhouses had to allow modern approaches to farming, meaning that

---

55   Lamberts, *Boerderijen*, 79. A comparison with women's activities in the area of urban house building reveals that, shortly after the Second World War, the strategies adopted by the Dutch Housewives' Association and women's house building advisory committees geared towards the urban context showed similarities with the strategies of rural women. However, there is no evidence of any closer collaboration between rural and urban women within the context of the reconstruction. See, for example, Liesbeth Bervoets and Ruth Oldenziel, "Vrouwenorganisaties als producenten van consumptie en burgerschap 1880–1980," *Tijdschrift voor Sociale Geschiedenis* 28, no. 3 (2002): 273–300; Elisabeth M. L. Bervoets, Marije Th. Wilmink, and Frank C. A. Veraart, "Coproductie: Emancipatie van de gebruiker? 1920–1970," in *Techniek in Nederland in de twintigste eeuw*, vol. VI, *Bouw*, ed. E. M. L. Bervoets (Zutphen: Walburg Pers, 2003), 161–95; Wies van Moorsel, *Contact en controle: Het vrouwbeeld van de Stichting Goed Wonen* (Amsterdam: SUA, 1992), 131. For construction activities of women in Northwest Germany in preindustrial times, see Thomas Spohn, "Bauherrinnen: Materialien zum Anteil von Frauen am Bauen in Westfalen," *Rheinisch-westfälische Zeitschrift für Volkskunde* 57 (2012): 35–74.

56   Centrale van Boerinnen en andere Plattelandsvrouwenorganisaties/Ministerie van Landbouw, Visserij en Voedselvoorziening, *De boerin en haar huis*, 1956, 7.

57   Erwin H. Karel, "De maakbare boer: Streekverbetering als instrument van het Nederlandse landbouwbeleid 1953–1970," *Historia agriculturae* 37 (Groningen/Wageningen: Nederlands Agronomisch Historisch Instituut, 2005), 244.

traditional, regional types of farmhouse were allowed to be or even had to be abandoned – a view that came into ever sharper relief over the course of the reconstruction (with some exceptions). However, it was not just a question of the new farmhouses *allowing* modern farming: they also needed to *encourage* it or even make it compulsory.[58]

The habits and lifestyles of farming families could also be influenced by the new farmhouses. This can be demonstrated by a number of examples relating to family life, health, personal care, hygiene and morality: the rationalisation of the home was meant to reduce the amount of time that farm women spent on housework and was, therefore, intended to allow them to dedicate more time to the family, which needed to be nurtured,[59] and more time to personal development. Bedrooms (instead of box beds and sleeping in open lofts) and adequate washing facilities in the living quarters were supposed to lead to good health and good personal hygiene. Separate bathrooms were intended to allow intimacy to be respected, with separate bedrooms for boys and girls serving the same purpose.[60] These elements of the reconstructed farmhouses had the potential to change the behavioural patterns of farming families. That did not by any means always happen immediately, however; sometimes there was resistance to change. Some of the reconstructed farmhouses had a shower room, for example. (In the absence of water pipes, a shower bucket was raised and a handle was then pulled to let the water flow out.) However, it was not uncommon for such rooms to be used for other purposes: "In practice, these proved to be ideal for storing toys, begonias or clover seed," reported G. J. A. Bouma, a National Agricultural Advisor for Farmhouse Construction, before providing information on the correct use of these rooms, in an article on bath and shower facilities in farmhouses.[61] A second typical example is the traditional "best room," which was still found in old farmhouses and which the

---

58   This highlights the interaction and reciprocity between people and artefacts: on the one hand, people shape objects and give them meanings; on the other, objects influence people, both through their physical manifestation and the meanings they have acquired.

59   Gerrie Andela, *Kneedbaar landschap, kneedbaar volk: De heroïsche jaren van de ruilverkavelingen in Nederland* (Bussum: THOTH, 2000), 133.

60   For information on this topic, for Belgium, see Sofie de Caigny and Wouter Vanderstede, "Spiegel van het hemelhuis: De wisselwerking tussen woonideaal en sociale rollen bij de Belgische Boerinnenbond (1907–1940)," *Tijdschrift voor sociale en economische geschiedenis* 2, no. 1 (2005): 11.

61   Bouma, G. J. A., "Een badprobleem," *De nieuwe veldbode*, 14 Feburary 1952; see also G. J. A. Bouma, "Het Rijkslandbouwconsulentschap voor Boerderijbouw" (= chapter from *7000 jaar bouw van boerderijen in Nederland*, manuscript), 4, in: RCE, collection SHBO/Bouma, no file number, box 2.

Agency for the Reconstruction of Farmhouses regarded as superfluous. They believed that every room in the home should be used every day, as communicated in 1944.[62] Since the "best" room had more of an aesthetic function, however, it was only used to receive notable visitors or on special holidays. Consequently, no space was allocated to this function in many of the reconstructed farmhouses. Nevertheless, it seems that some farming families did declare a room within the farmhouse to be the "best room" and, to allow this, did without the living room, thereby holding on to a significant ritual of home life.[63] The architectural changes were made before sociocultural adaptations had taken place, and, consequently, to prompt people to change their behaviour, the government felt the need to provide people with more information.

This was an outright "civilisation offensive." Supported by information that familiarised the farmers and farm women with the way these farmhouses worked (as a form of "follow-up care"), the reconstructed farmhouses were intended to contribute to the modernisation of agriculture and, at the same time, at the initiative of rural women's organisations, to an increase in general well-being in rural areas. Within the context of regional improvement, from the second half of the 1950s onwards steps were taken, structurally and on a broad basis, to bring about this increase in general well-being.[64]

Besides this, the reconstruction of the farmhouses was linked to another agenda, which became apparent in the information that agricultural organisations provided about the reconstruction and that was linked to the aims described above: strengthening the independence and self-sufficiency of farmers and farm women. This represents the emergence of the aim of promoting a far-reaching change in the mentality of farmers and farm women, something that would later become a key area of focus of the regional improvement measures: farmers and farm women had to be given a "taste for modernisation"; they should not merely be open to modernisation, but should, above all, actively pursue it themselves.[65]

---

62   André Geurts, *Boerderijen in de Noordoostpolder: Bouwhistorie en vormgeving 1942–1962* (Lelystad: Uitgeverij De Twaalfde Provincie, 2003), 31; Letter from A. D. van Eck to the "Director-General for Agriculture," 5 April 1944, 3, in: HFA (Flevoland Archive), Directie van het Openbaar Lichaam De Wieringermeer (Ijsselmeerpolders), 0714, file 1716.

63   See, for example, the interview with Van Maurik (1 h 14 min), in: Meertens Institute, collection "Erfenis van het verlies," file 1012.

64   Andela, *Kneedbaar landschap, kneedbaar volk*, 128–151. See also Kees Schuyt and Ed Taverne, *1950: Welvaart in zwart-wit* (Den Haag: Sdu Uitgevers, 2000), 214.

65   Andela, *Kneedbaar landschap, kneedbaar volk*, 148. See also Ton Duffhues, *Voor een betere toekomst: Het werk van de Noordbrabantse Christelijke Boerenbond voor bedrijf en gezin, 1896–1996* (Nijmegen: Valkhof Pers, 1996), 222; Karel, *De maakbare boer*, 1–20, 27.

With respect to labour aspects, the reconstruction process of farmhouses in the Netherlands consolidated ideas about gender-specific work on farms – women should be responsible for family and household tasks, men for farming. This work division was propagated by the farmers' and farm women's associations and schools that had a powerful role in the field of agriculture in the middle of the twentieth century. However, those ideas did not reflect the everyday working situation of rural women, neither during the "Crisis Years" before the Second World War and during the war, nor after the war when agriculture underwent mechanisation and modernisation. The support of women on the farm, for instance in the care for animals, was often still self-evident.

The reconstruction of the farmhouses, the living quarters and the stables enabled farm women and farmers to work more efficiently and thus to spend less time on work.

From the interviews I have conducted, we know that maidservants who had helped the farm women with their work before the war, often did not or could not come back when the farmhouses were reconstructed. In the reconstructed farmhouses, farm women's work became less time consuming, partly because the new living rooms could be cleaned much more easily due to the new hygiene standards which were followed in the reconstructed farmhouses. Also, the rationalisation of the composition of the new kitchens led to more time-effective work. Women were required to carry out their work in the family and household in a professional manner – the new rationalised kitchens could help in that sense.[66]

Bibliography

Andela, Gerrie. *Kneedbaar landschap, kneedbaar volk: De heroïsche jaren van de ruilver-kavelingen in Nederland*. Bussum: THOTH, 2000.

Berendsen, Marja, and Anneke van Otterloo. "Het 'gezinslaboratorium': De betwiste keuken en de wording van de moderne huisvrouw." *Tijdschrift voor sociale geschiedenis* 28, no. 3 (2002): 301–22.

Bernège, Paulette. *Orde en methode in de gezinshuishouding*. Haarlem: Tjeenk Willink, 1932.

Bervoets, Liesbeth, and Ruth Oldenziel. "Vrouwenorganisaties als producenten van consumptie en burgerschap 1880–1980." *Tijdschrift voor Sociale Geschiedenis* 28, no. 3 (2002): 273–300.

---

66   Van der Burg, "*Geen tweede boer*," 332–33.

Bervoets, Elisabeth M. L., Marije Th. Wilmink, and Frank C. A. Veraart. "Coproductie: Emancipatie van de gebruiker? 1920–1970." In *Techniek in Nederland in de twintigste eeuw*. Vol. VI, *Bouw*, edited by E. M. L. Bervoets, 161–95. Zutphen: Walburg Pers, 2003.

Blom, Anita, Simone Vermaat, and Ben de Vries, eds. *Post-War Reconstruction in the Netherlands 1945–1965: The Future of a Bright and Brutal Heritage*. Rotterdam: Nai010 Publishers, 2016.

"Boereninterieur: Inrichting van de boerenwoning." *Boer en Tuinder*, 31 December 1948.

Bosma, Koos, and Cor Wagenaar, eds. *Een geruisloze doorbraak: De geschiedenis van architectuur en stedebouw tijdens de bezetting en de wederopbouw van Nederland*. Rotterdam: NAi Uitgevers, 1995.

Bouma, G. J. A. "Een badprobleem." *De nieuwe veldbode*, 14 Feburary 1952.

Burg, Margreet van der. *"Geen tweede boer": Gender, landbouwmodernisering en onderwijs aan plattelandsvrouwen in Nederland, 1863–1968*. Wageningen: Afdeling Agrarische Geschiedenis, Wageningen Universiteit, 2002.

Burg, Margreet van der, and Krista Lievaart. *Drie generaties in schort en overall: Terugblik op een eeuw vrouwenarbeid in de landbouw*. Wageningen: Afdeling Agrarische Geschiedenis, Wageningen Universiteit, 1998.

Caigny, Sofie de, and Wouter Vanderstede. "Spiegel van het hemelhuis: De wisselwerking tussen woonideaal en sociale rollen bij de Belgische Boerinnenbond (1907–1940)." *Tijdschrift voor sociale en economische geschiedenis* 2, no. 1 (2005): 3–29.

Centrale van Boerinnen en andere Plattelandsvrouwenorganisaties/Ministerie van Landbouw, Visserij en Voedselvoorziening. *De boerin en haar huis* (= *Landbouw 10*). 's-Gravenhage: Staatsdrukkerij- en Uitgeverijbedrijf, 1949.

Cieraad, Irene. "Het huishouden tussen droom en daad: Over de toekomst van de keuken." In *Schoon genoeg: Huisvrouwen en huishoudtechnologie in Nederland 1898–1998*, edited by Ruth Oldenziel and Carolien Bouw, 31–58. Nijmegen: SUN, 1998.

"De wederopbouw van boerderijen. Plattelandsvrouwen wensen een adviserende stem." *Nieuwe Rotterdamse Courant*, 29 April 1946.

Duffhues, Ton. *Voor een betere toekomst: Het werk van de Noordbrabantse Christelijke Boerenbond voor bedrijf en gezin, 1896–1996*. Nijmegen: Valkhof Pers, 1996.

Elpers, Sophie. *Wederopbouwboerderijen: Agrarisch erfgoed in de strijd over traditie en modernisering, 1940–1955*. Rotterdam: Nai010 Publishers, 2019.

"Financierings- en premiumregeling oorlogsschade boerderijen." *Nederlandse Staatscourant*, 21 May 1952, 5.

Frederick, Christine. *De denkende huisvrouw: Nieuwe inzichten*. Haarlem: Tjeenk Willink, 1928.

Gaillard, Karin. "De ideale woning op papier." In *Honderd jaar wonen in Nederland 1900–2000*, edited by Jaap Huisman, Irene Cieraad, and Karin Gaillard, 111–71. Rotterdam: Uitgeverij 010, 2000.

Garkovich, Lorraine, and Janet Bokemeier. "Agricultural Mechanization and American Farm Women's Economic Roles." In *Women and Farming: Changing roles, Changing Structures*, edited by Wava Haney and Jane Knowles, 211–28. Boulder, CO and London: Westview Press, 1988.

Geurts, André. *Boerderijen in de Noordoostpolder: Bouwhistorie en vormgeving 1942– 1962*. Lelystad: Uitgeverij De Twaalfde Provincie, 2003.

Goudswaard, N. B. *Naar een goede en goedkope boerderij*. Meppel: N.V. Noord-Nederlandse Drukkerij, 1950.

Groffen, Mayke, and Sjouk Hoitsma. *Het geluk van de huisvrouw*. Amsterdam: SUN, 2004.

"Heemkunde." *Boer en Tuinder*, 3 April 1948, 7.

"Het keukenprobleem." *Goed wonen* 1 (1948): 185–88.

Hofstee, Evert W. *Rural Life and Rural Welfare in the Netherlands*. Den Haag: Government Printing and Publishing Office, 1957.

"Huishoudelijke voorlichting ten plattelande." *De nieuwe veldbode*, 26 August 1948, 571.

Karel, Erwin H. "De maakbare boer: Streekverbetering als instrument van het Nederlandse landbouwbeleid 1953–1970." *Historia agriculturae* 37. Groningen/ Wageningen: Nederlands Agronomisch Historisch Instituut, 2005.

Keesom, J. G. M. *Wonen. Woning. Wet. Wij wonen: 100 jaar Woningwet*. Amsterdam: Stedelijke Woningdienst Amsterdam, 2000.

Lamberts, Bé. *Boerderijen: Categoriaal onderzoek wederopbouw 1940–1965*. Zeist: Rijksdienst voor het Cultureel Erfgoed, 2007.

Meyer, Erna. *De nieuwe huishouding*. Amsterdam: Van Holkema & Warendorf, 1929.

"Moderne boerderijen Nederland." *De Plattelandsvrouw*, December 1953.

Moorsel, Wies van. *Contact en controle: Het vrouwbeeld van de Stichting Goed Wonen*. Amsterdam: SUA, 1992.

"Nieuwe ideeën en moderne huizen." *Boer en Tuinder*, 28 January 1950.

"Om de Watersnood." *De nieuwe veldbode*, 30 April 1953.

Schuyt, Kees, and Ed Taverne. *1950: Welvaart in zwart-wit*. Den Haag: Sdu Uitgevers, 2000.

Smit, Greta. "Veranderingen in de huishoud." In *Nederlandse Bond van Plattelandsvrouwen 1930–1955*, edited by Nederlandse Bond van Plattelandsvrouwen, 73–77. Groningen, 1955.

Spohn, Thomas. "Bauherrinnen: Materialien zum Anteil von Frauen am Bauen in Westfalen." *Rheinisch-westfälische Zeitschrift für Volkskunde* 57 (2012): 35–74.

Vreeze, Noud de, ed. *6,5 miljoen woningen: 100 jaar woningwet en wooncultuur in Nederland*. Rotterdam: Uitgeverij 010, 2001.

Vries, H. A. de, and Jan Jans. *De plattelandswoning* (= *Bibliotheek voor de huisvrouw op het platteland* 3). Zwolle: Tjeenk Willink, 1934.

"Wederopbouw Boerderijen en het aandeel van de vrouw." *Boer en Tuinder*, 28 August 1948.

Wiersma-Risselada, A. C. *Het aandeel der vrouw bij de wederopbouwboerderijen*. Den Haag: Nederlandse Bond van Plattelandsvrouwen, 1946.

Wiersma-Risselada, A. C. "Woonhuis of kamer met kooknis." *De Plattelandsvrouw* 5, no. 7 (1947): 102–3.

Wilke, Margrieth. "Kennis en kunde. Handboeken voor huisvrouwen." In *Schoon genoeg: Huisvrouwen en huishoudtechnologie in Nederland 1898–1998*, edited by Ruth Oldenziel and Carolien Bouw, 59–90. Nijmegen: SUN, 1998.

CHAPTER 6

Planting the Land and Shifting the Cultivator

Labour, Land and Environment in Eastern Nagaland

Debojyoti Das

1   Introduction

Since the early 1990s, the globalisation of farming has ensured that the interests of agribusiness are premised on a highly contested neoliberal approach to development, one that naturalises food scarcity imaginaries as the justification for the expansion of global agricultural value chains.[1] This agenda is also premised on a framing of "smallholder farmers like shifting cultivators, as 'backwards,, inefficient and non-productive which, in turn, renders these farmers and their practices as obstacles to development."[2] In the context of British India, development programmes targeted at rural agrarian improvement were initiated during the late 1940s by the Food and Agricultural Organisation (FAO) and the Ford Foundation. These organisations attempted to discredit shifting cultivation, describing it as unproductive, backward, harmful and bad for the mountain environment, as they rolled out the Grow More Food Programme.[3]

In the Naga Hills, slash-and-burn farming, a way of life and a technique integral to the reciprocal redistributive village economy, was disrupted by the promotion of plantation cash crops and wet terrace rice cultivation, beginning in the late 1950s. Today, land use in the slash-and-burn landscape is complicated by the interplanting of cash crops with plantations in the hills and wet paddy cultivation in the foothills. These changes reflect a relentless effort made by external actors to transform people's food habits, land use, land relation and priorities of crop cultivation. This is not only unique to Nagaland per se, but has happened in swidden cultivation landscapes across South and Southeast Asia.[4]

---

1 This chapter draws heavily on my book *The Politics of Swidden Farming*, published in 2018 with Anthem Press, but has been thoroughly revised for the purpose of this edited volume.

2 Gabay Clive and Susan Llcan, "Leaving No-One Behind? The Politics of Destination in the 2030 Sustainable Development Goals," *Globalization* 14, no. 3 (2017): 337.

3 Hodge James Morgan, *Triumph of the Expert: Agrarian Doctrines of Development and the Legacies of British Colonialism* (Ohio: Ohio University Press, 2007).

4 Dove Michael Roger, "A Revisionist View of Tropical Deforestation and Development," *Environmental Conservation,* 20, no. 1 (1993): 17.

In this chapter, I will engage with the question of power and the characteristic ways it operates in upland settings to bring into being the notion of a
simple, powerless people who are engaged with the state and the market. The
territorialisation process and informal, personalised lines of patronage are two
forms of power that hinge on the real and supposed ignorance and isolation of
uplanders. The definition of uplanders as a "backward" people has legitimated
both harsh measures such as land expropriation and forced settlement as well
as benevolent forms of paternalism and control through subsidies, grants and
micro-credit.[5] The questions I try to answer in this chapter are, first, do farmers
who belong to a particular mode of production adapt to changes immediately
when they are introduced under state-sponsored schemes and programmes?
And, second, how does agrarian change take shape?

Theories of agricultural change and social stratification among highland
communities in the Global South have been offered since the early 1930s, with
considerable emphasis on an evolutionary model that places paddy peasantry
or settled irrigated farming at the top of the pyramid in primary production.
Edmund Leach proposed a model in the early 1940s that posited the Shans
and the Kachins as two social systems determined by geographical barriers.
The relations between Shan paddy farming and Kachin swiddeners were,
in the first place, ecological, and reflected two distinct political orders, one
democratic and the other, authoritarian.[6] This functionalist framework finds
reflection in Audrey Richards' work on Bemba swidden cultivation in Africa.[7]
Richards makes a connection between labour supply, nutrition and diet to
show that the shortage of male labour in the north province of Zambia caused
Bemba swidden agriculture to break down under population pressure and
migration. Henrietta Moore and Megan Vaughan, while revisiting Richards'
work on swidden farming in Zambia, argue that her claims were more cultur-
ised and linked ethnic identity with their mode of livelihood. Thus, both were
co-constituent in producing Bemba identity as savage, vulnerable and wild.
While the natural scientists pointed to the physical limits of the viability of
citemene (swidden), Richards pointed to the social limits by looking at labour
migration and, chiefly, power. Richards reinscribed a standard understanding

5   Li Tania Murray, *Land's End: Capitalist Relation on an Indigenous Frontier* (London: Routledge,
    2014), 15.
6   Edmund Ronald Leach, *Political Systems of Highland Burma: A Study of Kachin Social
    Structure* (London: G. Bell, 1954), 29.
7   Richards Audrey, *Land, Labour and Diet in Northern Rhodesia: An Economic Study of the
    Bemba Tribe* (Oxford: Oxford University Press, 1939), 21.

of swidden as a single process of "cutting and burning trees" that was on the verge of "breakdown."[8]

Similarly, unlike the standard use of "involution" that dominated for a decade to distinguish between "swidden and *swahi*"[9] – that is, hill farming and valley agriculture – "plain emulation" was largely presented as a factor of sociocultural change in a number of case studies on Southeast Asian agriculture.[10] All these studies present a synchronic social history of highland agriculture based on the teleology of "evolution." These explanations of agricultural intensification ignored the colonial practice of constructing "social and ethnic hierarchy" and diachronic interventions[11] that produce difference and identities, characterising the people who inhabited the forest landscape as *jangly* (wild) food gatherers and semi-nomadic settlers, as opposed to the settled agriculturists on the plains.

Agrarian intensification in the Naga Hills is today defined by growing market demand for long beans and people changing their taste towards rice, as the "crop of civilisation." Its easy accessibility and increasing popularity in farmers' cuisines has replaced the traditional food crop from farmers' culinary habits. Although farmers still grow millet as a supplement to the dominant rice cultivation in the area, it is no longer the staple food crop. Simultaneously, cultural values and state policies concerning the popularisation of horticulture and settled wet terrace rice cultivation have been mediated by village elites and the Baptist Church to produce land use changes and land relations that make agricultural intensification and social differentiation in a Naga village more complex than when explained from a standard evolutionary model. Here, I find Sturgeon's use of the term "landscape plasticity" useful to understanding how land use changes in the Southeast Asia highlands are influenced by local factors in different socio-political contexts that reflect the negotiating role of human agency and the global and national state agendas that aim to territorialise the landscape and the people. Sturgeon goes on to show how Akha land

---

8   Henrietta Moore and Megan Vaughan, *Cutting Down Trees: Gender, Nutrition, and Agricultural Change in the Northern Province of Zambia, 1890–1990* (Cambridge: Cambridge University Press, 1993), 49.

9   Clifford Geertz, *Agricultural Involution: The Process of Ecological Change in Indonesia* (Berkeley: University of California Press, 1963), 17.

10   Ian Iijana, "Socio Cultural Change among the Shifting Cultivators through the Introduction of Wet Rice Cultivation – A Case Study of Kerens in Northern Thailand," *Memoirs of the College of Agriculture* 79, no. 3 (1970): 1.

11   Sumit Guha, *Environment and Ethnicity in India 1200–1900* (Cambridge: Cambridge University Press, 1999), 5.

use in China and Thailand is influenced both by state policies and the negotiating role played by the Akha community leaders themselves.[12]

Similarly, other works in recent years have given alternative explanations to the practices of social differentiation in highland swidden farming, claiming that there can be no uniform evolutionary model that explains how farming systems have developed and intensified. The changes in farming and land use practices are determined by the local history of migration, settlement, state policies and institutional interference, which are mediated by the changing attitudes and perceptions of farmers.[13] They are also determined by the networks of patronage that link the global and the local by integrating the village economy with the discourses of regional, local and global markets. I will focus on the practices of articulation that rural elites and intermediaries adopt in the study village, in order to examine emerging inequalities based on class relations and property rights that define access to and control over land and forest resources.[14] Hence, resource access and control is not determined by neat class relations but, rather, by the power of individuals to control labour relations. This power is not codified under common laws but defined by customary practices.

I will use life histories and the case studies of individual farmers and then bring into context the overall argument of my paper. Life histories help in explaining the underlying complexity of farming that occupies much of the *jhum*[15] farming landscape, where quantified data analysis does not produce satisfactory results because of the complexity involved in people's use of and dependence on the land.

2 A backdrop to *Jhum* in Leangkangru and the Shamator Region

The diffusion of rice agriculture was formally undertaken by the Agriculture Department in the newly formed Indian state of Nagaland during the 1970s through the Wet Terrace Rice Intensification Programme in the Tuensang and Mon districts. In the post-independence period, tour reports confirm that

12   Janet Sturgeon, *Border Landscapes: The Politics of Aka land use in Burma and China* (University of Washington Press: Seattle, 2005), 160.

13   Philip Hirch, "Forests, Forest Reserve, and Forest Land in Thailand," *The Geographical Journal* 56, no. 2 (1989): 166.

14   Jesse Ribot and Nancy Lee Peluso, "A Theory of Access," *Rural Sociology* 68, no. 2 (2003): 153.

15   *Jhum* is the local name for swidden or slash-and-burn farming, used across north-eastern part of India.

in the unadministered Naga Hill areas that were placed under NEFA (North Eastern Frontier Area) administration, the encouragement for *jhummias* to adopt terrace cultivation had already begun. Man Bahadur Rai, the Assistant Political Officer of the NEFA, gives insightful references in his tour diary to state interventions taking shape in that area as early as 1956: "At 0700 hrs we left for Pangsha village. On the way villagers were seen working in their cultivations. They are now burning *jhooms*. I met one Noklak Agricultural Demonstrator who was going to Pangsha to start his WTC [Wet Terrace Cultivation] project. Along the bank of river Lang Pangsha, people have started WTC in quite a number of plots." (emphasis added).[16]

In other tour reports produced by the NEFA administration, touring officials were often accompanied by Agricultural Department Village Level Workers (VLW), who would train local *jhum* farmers in the art of paddy cultivation and willing headmen and village chiefs in the art of terrace farming. Irrigation incentives were also proposed to intensify paddy cultivation in the flatlands, provided that villagers promised to work these fields year after year. In his 1951 tour diary, the Additional Deputy Commissioner (ADC) of Tuensang Frontier Division writes that one of the Pangsha men requested that he open a terrace rice cultivation plot in their area. In return, he promised that he would ask the government to grant subsidies, provided that the villagers give him their word that the fields, once opened, would be continuously cultivated.[17] Since the mid-1950s, the postcolonial Indian frontier administration had started the diffusion of modern ideas of farming on a small scale, under the five-year plans for the development of tribal and backward areas. These policies were broadly framed under a policy of paternalism advanced by Verrier Elwin, who was appointed as Special Adviser for Tribal Affairs in the North Eastern Frontier Agency (NEFA). In 1956, Elwin submitted his policy dossier, which contained a "new deal" for the economic upliftment and development of the tribal areas of the North Eastern Frontier of India.[18] His assignment in the NEFA sanctioned Nehru's principle of "unity in diversity" and the idea of *panchsheel* – the five strategies for tribal development.[19] The Yimchunger *jhummias* were, once

---

16   Mon Bahadur Rai, Assistant Political Officer, Noklak, 1956, Department of Art and Culture, Record Room, Nagaland, 10.

17   Tour Diary of A.D.C. Tribal Area, Tuensang, 1951. Government of Arunachal Pradesh, Directorate of Research, Itanagar. Records of Research Reports, Papers and Articles.

18   Verrier Elwin, *A New Deal for Tribal India* (India: Ministry of Foreign Affairs), 1–10.

19   These ideas were developed and crystallised by Verrier Elwin: 1) People should develop along the lines of their own genius, and the imposition of alien values should be avoided. Try to encourage in every way their own traditional arts and culture. 2) The tribal rights in land and forest should be respected. 3) Train and build up a team of their own people

again, classified as a "backward and isolated hill people." The "new deal" also endorsed the popularisation of highland wet terrace rice farming among *jhummias*. As a result of this policy initiative, two kinds of paddy farms developed among the upland Yimchunger *jhummia* settlements: paddy farms in lowland marshy swamps and terraces on steep mountain slopes. The former were more productive, yet vulnerable to flooding. The latter were protected from floods but were often damaged by landslides before they stabilised. The success of farming in these landscapes was often an individual achievement, depending on the resource mobilisation done by a farmer with government officials through networks of patronage, unlike in *jhum* fields, where we see collective action and participation from entire villages and clans. The rice intensification programme among Yimchunger *jhummias* developed in three phases. The first phase was under the NEFA administration (1950–1960) and the second phase began in the 1970s, after the Yimchunger area was separated from the NEFA administration. The third phase started in the 1990s, when all farmers started to take an active interest in paddy farming, as a result of their increasing interest in the consumption of rice, as a superior and tastier food crop, and because of incentives coming from the Baptist Church. Here, I will reflect on individual life histories of farmers and on how *pani kheti* (wet terrace rice cultivation) has evolved through agricultural demonstrators locally known as *kelu babu*. The growth of *pani kheti* has remarkably changed the agrarian land use, as it sustains the plantations and orchards that squats *jhum* fallows (uncultivated land). Farmers are increasingly dependent on government subsidies and schemes that target the popularisation of agroforestry and horticultural crops. Since the late 1980s, the Agriculture Department has reduced terrace wetland subsidies and has focused on promoting horticulture and plantation farming. The policy is also endorsed in recent changes in forest rights and regulation passed by the state legislature. The Nagaland Tree Felling Regulation 2002, which is an amendment of earlier *jhumland* regulation, states that: "All horticulture species will not require permission for felling, from non-forested areas including plantation of such species, excluding the following species: (a) *aam* (Magnifera indica) and (b) wild apple."[20]

---

to do the work of administration and development. Try to avoid introducing too many outsiders into tribal territory. 4) We should not over-administer tribal areas or overwhelm them with a multiplicity of schemes. Administrate in accordance with their own social and cultural institutions. 5) We should judge the result, not by statistics or the amount of money spent, but by the human character that is evolved. *A New Deal for Tribal India* (India: Ministry of Foreign Affairs), 1–10.

20   Zepto Angami, *Nagaland Village Empowerment Rules* (Kohima: Novelty Printing Press, 2008), 163.

In Yimchunger paddy farms, *aam* (mango) co-evolved after seeds were supplied by the Agricultural Department and privately procured by farmers from nurseries in Dimapur town. Nurseries have boomed in Dimapur over the last decade, as they find a ready market in *jhum* farmers in the uplands. The State Agricultural Department procures *pullies* (saplings) from plains nursery planters and supplies them at a subsidised price to promote horticultural crops among *jhum* cultivators. The intensification of agroforestry has led to the scarcity of free land (commons) in the uplands, which is pushing farmers to choose more commercial crops. However, intensification does not reflect a substantial increase in farm productivity, as many farmers responded that their output is far less than the inputs in agriculture. Rice cultivation is not gaining popularity because of productivity. Rather, it is the vicious cycle of patronage created by state officials, development programmes and political party workers in the village that sustains this practice. Similarly, the popularity of rice over other crops in recent years is attached to prestige and linked to social capital, as recognised by Baptist Church deacons and pastors, who promote rice over other crops in their Sunday prayer sermons as the crop of the civilised people. In addition to this, the symbolic capital that rice consumption provides to famers has added to its consumption value as the "food grain of civilisation." Despite this, villagers still depend on millet, buckwheat, maize and long beans as substitutes for rice during times of scarcity at the end of the agricultural cycle. For many families, cash income from government jobs has promoted the reliance on imported market rice, commonly known in the village as "ration rice" also ocasionally supplied by government's Public Distribution System (PDS) under Priority Household (PHH) and Antyodaya Anna Yojana (AAY) programme. While, in traditional Yimchunger society, millet and buckwheat were combined, the demise of buckwheat and millet cultivation has come with the popularisation of rice. This keeps poor and landless farmers in Yimchunger villages dependent on coarser grains such as maize and long beans, which are generally meant for fattening animals.

3   Diversifying Slash-and-Burn Land Use in Leangkangru: Ethnographic Evidence

Far away from the state capital Kohima (approximately 290 kilometres) lies the village of the Yimchunger Nagas, Leangkangru. I explored the village with a Yimchunger resident of Shamator town who was working as a facilitator of community conservation in the Nagaland Environment Protection and Economic Development (NEPED) project. He described Leangkangru as the most successful village in the whole Shamator area, as they had delivered results by successfully participating in government- and community-driven development programmes. Leangkangru, I soon realised, represents the promised land for immigrants, who migrated to this village from neighbouring villages. This resulted in its composite identity as a "collection village": a village that has grown with migrants coming in search of their clan members and relatives and as refugees from their natal villages and clans.

The settlement became a refuge for people who had been orphaned by colonial raids and the practice of headhunting in their native village. Some came to take shelter in the homes of their kin, while others migrated because they had lost all family members in their own villages. In addition, a good number of people migrated from faraway places, changed villages and, finally, settled in Leangkangru. The first settlers of this new village came from the surrounding villages. Shiponger was the biggest donor of land. For this act of generosity, the village elders explained that their parents and first settlers offered *mithuns*, chicken and pigs in exchange for land to Shiponger village headmen. In the initial years, the settlement was located at a much lower altitude: around 1100 metres. That later changed as raids and headhunting diminished. The first settlers were frequently challenged by other tribes. Villagers narrate tales of many heads being taken in the headhunting raids and heads taken by truce and by men camouflaged in the bridal paths (footpaths create by Nagas over hill slopes), as villagers crossed over from one village territory to another. Head-taking declined in the late 1940s as the evangelists came through Shiponger to Shamator and Sikur village, which had a significant Sema population. The Assam Rifles established its camp in Shamator town in 1952. At that time, Leangkangru was a small, new settlement near Sangpurr and Shamator, more prominent and numerically larger Yimchunger villages.

The village where I undertook research to understand land relations was originally a small village that came into existence as a collection of villages in 1938. The year of settlement is engraved in the village "Citizen pillar" that was set up by the village headman in the centre of the village to commemorative the fifty years of its existence. My host, Nikon, was also an immigrant who had come from Shiponger village after the raid of 1942 by troops led by a British officer, whose name, he recalled from popular tales in the village, was "Adam Saho." We do get a reference to a Colonel Adams in official colonial correspondences, who toured the region and carried out punitive raids on head-hunting villages. A significant proportion of the villagers who now inhabited the upper

Khel[21] were from that village. Nineteen families from Sangpurr had migrated to join Leangkangru. The affiliation that brought them together was their clan patronage and reciprocity. Most of the migrants belonged to the Jangra clan. The Jangra clan is not the numerically most dominant in Sangpurr village, but it was in Leangkangru. When Nikon first came to the village, his father had taken shelter in the lower *khel* with another Jangra clan household. They provided them with shelter and a *jhum* plot. During the 1980s, my host had moved to the upper *khel* to make his own *khel*. His brother had also become a *gau burah* (village headman) and another of his brothers had joined the Nagaland police. His elder brother became a village guard in the late 1970s and today he works as the VG commander. His own upbringing was meagre. However, he had the fortune to study in an Ao Baptist missionary school. His sister was married to the head *dobashi* (people who can speak two languages: the official language of administration and their native tongue and acted as go-between in village disputes) in the town, and he himself enjoys a commanding position among his clansmen. In 2000, he separated his *khel* from that of his brother, who acts as one of the village headmen in the area. His social mobility in the village is reflective of the shifting power relations in the village and represents the changing dynamics of land relations in the village.

A narration of his life story shows how farming that was once based on the power of the chief's command and control over labour power was dissolved with the emergence of the Baptist Church and the entry of development programmes through political party workers and government intermediaries in the village. New land relations have emerged, and these are reflected in the nature of "access control" over resources, particularly land and labour,[22] exercised by patrons in the village through different community-driven development schemes. In contemporary Naga villages, the village development board and village council are the most important legislative bodies: they implement and oversee externally funded development programmes through the selection of beneficiaries, mediating claims and village disputes and by setting up rules and regulation in the village. The village council is composed of both *gau buras* and nominated village council members (VCM).

If we read classic ethnographies on the Naga Hills, land relations are always spoken of in terms of mutualistic communal ownership (clan land), rather than private revenue land.[23] There were three classes of land use: (1) village land (2) clan land and (3) individual land. Indigenous Naga scholars such as

---

21   Naga villages are divided into *khel,* meaning village ward and colonies dominated by a
      particular clan or kinship network.
22   Jesse Ribot and Nancy Lee Peluso, "A Theory of Access," *Rural Sociology* 68, no. 2 (2003): 153.
23   John Philip Mills, *The Lotha Nagas* (London: Macmillan, 1922).

Shimrey[24] observed that education and Christianity brought about change by introducing a monetised economy, all of which led to the change in land use system. He notes:

> These changes have resulted in the emergence of a so-called "elite" in the village. This has contributed much to the change in land use system. The "power" and "statuses" attached to the land was affected by money coming into the village. From such as transition emerged elite households with a monetary economy. Land that was considered the most important symbol of influence and status in the society is being challenged by wealth based on money. This brings inevitable changes to land ownership system .... Land that was once considered livelihood is now available as a commodity that can be bought and sold. Today, the best portion of the terrace field is owned by rich households .... The result is internal land alienation within the tribe.[25]

In addition to this, land alienation has occurred because of customary rules that allow ancestorial property to be inherited only by male members in Naga society; females have no right.[26] While interacting with villagers, I realised that these three kinds of land arrangement were prevalent in the hilly swidden fields but not in wet terrace rice fields. Fixed private landownership had emerged since the government had started popularising wet terrace rice cultivation during the 1950s. Before that period, these lands were not cultivated, as they were not suitable for *jhum* cultivation, due to the annual inundation. In the initial years, as tour diaries suggest, the promotion of wet terrace rice cultivation was contested by some village headmen. The government was keen to settle *jhum* cultivators as this was seen as the first step towards containing *jhum* fellow and bringing about improvement.[27] It was very difficult to get labourers to do *pani kheti*, as their chiefly loyalty was attached to the *jhum* fields.

---

24 Ursula Shimrey, "Land Use System in Manipur Hills: A Case Study of Thangkul Naga," in *Land, People and Politics: Contest over Tribal Land in Northeast India*, ed. Walter Fernandes and Sanjoy Barbora (Guwahati: Northeast Social Research Centre; Copenhagen: International Working Group for Indigenous Affairs, 1999), 88–122.

25 Shimrey, "Land Use System."

26 Ltu Vizokhole, "Women, Property and Angami Naga Customary Law," in *Unequal Land Relations in North East India: Custom, Gender and the Market*, ed. Erik de Maaker and Meenal Tula (Guwahati: Northeast Social Research Centre, 2020), 62.

27 A number of tour reports prepared by the 1950s by the Additional Deputy Commissioner, A.D.C. Tribal Area, Tuensang, refer to the difficulties of attracting commoners to do *pani kheti*.

During the 1950s, when the ideas of wet terrace rice cultivation were first promoted in Yimchunger villages, the villagers were brought into conflict with the habitat of the *mithun*, a wild buffalo widely found in *jhumland*. This resulted in the slow but gradual decline of the *mithun* population. During the fieldwork, my interlocuters expressed grief that *mithuns* could only rarely be spotted in villages. Except for in Sangpurr village, where paddy cultivation occupies a very limited amount of land use, *mithuns* can only still be spotted in the wild. The problem has a longer history linked to the promotion of settled agriculture that has brought about human-wildlife conflict with the intensification of paddy and plantation agriculture. The change in land use is best narrated by an anonymous Assistant Deputy Commissioner (ADC) for Tuensang Tribal Area in his tour diary dated 20 February 1950. On arrival at the Yimchunger village Huchirr he observes:

> The keeping of *mithuns* is also becoming a serious problem. There are only 114 houses but because of *mithuns*, it is very difficult to open *pani kheti*, since fences has [sic] to be constructed round the fields. All GBs [*gau burah*] are against the keeping of *mithuns*. The cultivators [*pani khets*] has [sic] to set up the fences for themselves round their fields which make [sic] their fields look like gardens. I have told the villagers that in the future, *mithun* keepers will have to fix up the fence around the fields if they were to keep *mithuns* and that regarding *mithuns* belonging to other villages the owners should be told to remove their *mithuns*. Huchirr has not got much land and I am afraid *mithuns* and *pani kheti* cannot remain together here. One has to go. The village is a poverty-stricken village. There are no village reserves around the village. I have ordered the villagers to keep an area with a radius of 150 yard [sic] free around the village to raise a village reserve. *Dobashis* are to see that they keep this order.[28]

The instructions from the Assistant Deputy Commissioner were directed towards the opening up of *pani kheti* and suited the interests of village headmen and village patrons, who were now going to gain from settled terrace cultivation. With the rise of plantation farming and terrace rice cultivation and the proliferation of *cartos* (ammunition) in the hands of the village guards, the degraded forest had depleted the abundance of wild animals. The proliferation

---

28   Tour Diary of A.D.C Tribal Area, Tuensang, Government of Arunachal Pradesh, Directorate of Research, Itanagar, Records of Research Reports, Papers and Articles.

of guns also meant a decline in bushmeat. In addition, the decline in *mithun* has facilitated the proliferation of *pani kneti*. Correspondingly, since the 1990s, changes in farmers' crop choices and land use have affected household cattle supply. This land use and these cropping changes are linked to a host of other factors that link people's belief system and the changes brought on by institutional intervention. These changes, though subtle, are mediated by human agency.

Leangkangru presents a characteristic case study of agricultural intensification that shows a complex history of how land relations and land use changes have been affected by migration, changing landownership patterns and clan dynamics in the village, which are based on lineage history and mother village affiliation. Comparably, villagers' association with government intermediaries, political party patrons and the church has played an important role in establishing patron-client relations within the village among clan households.

4   The Case of Nikon: The Second Settler

Here, I present the case study of one farmer to illustrate how, despite their late arrival in the village, farmers have achieved high social mobility and have become important decision makers and landed elite in the village through brokerage in development programmes.

Nikon was my host and I had spent considerable time with him in the village. He was a latecomer – the second person to come to the village from Sangpurr village. His father first came to Leangkangru after the 1942 Sangpurr raid. When I asked Nikon why he had migrated to the upper *khel*, he smiled and said he intended to live close to the church and moved with the plan to establish his own *khel*, where he could establish his own patron-client relations with his clan members and kin. His children defended his relocation by observing that, although they were the second settlers, not a single villager can benefit without their father's role as broker in development programmes. Nikon's brother had also become a village headman by the time they relocated. Many other villagers who lived surrounding his settlement claimed through hearsay that, until the late 1980s, Nikon's family was very modest. His father had given him two plots of land for cultivation and his other brother did not get any. One of his brothers joined the Nagaland police. His other brothers worked as village guard commandants. Nikon was the political intermediary in the village and benefitted from his political patrons' successive election victories from 1989 to 2009. During this phase, he, along with his brothers, consolidated assets and bought multiple plots of land in all parts of the village, with the consent of the village headmen. Today, he owns more than fourteen plots of land in the village.

During our stay in the village, he light-heartedly remarked that, whenever a villager needed money, he gave them cash in return for mortgaging their land. He was also well-connected with the public servants and Agriculture Department staff, who would bring schemes and programmes of improvement to the village in return for electoral support during general elections. During my stay in the village, the Flood and Irrigation Department officials visited the village to conduct a prospective survey for irrigation. Nikon welcomed the guests and introduced the village headman to the officials. In the previous years, he had established irrigation, fisheries and other household assets by diverting resources through the formation of a self-help group with his daughter as chairman. In 1978, he got married in the village church. In those days, "holy marriages" were unheard of in Yimchunger villages. During that year, he also became the Sunday school master in the village church. Since then, he has held many positions in the village, including secretary of the village development board, which he occupied from 1990–1999. He was also the planning committee chairman of the church's Golden Jubilee celebrations. Over the years, he has amassed enormous support among his kinsmen. He was the owner of the largest *khel* and had nineteen families under his direct influence. In 1978, the same year he got married, he bought one plot of land. At the time, he was the president of the village student union. The crops that he grew were millet, buckwheat corn and long beans. In 1980, he bought a *pani kheti* (paddy plot) by paying a little cash to a distressed seller. That year, he cultivated paddy for the first time. In 1989, one of the clansmen from his village of origin won the legislative assembly elections and appointed him as his chief political liaison in the village. From then on, he started buying many plots of land. He then became the vice president of the All India Congress Committee of the Shamator area. His political links with the legislative assembly member and later minister brought him many incentives to expand his land holdings in the village. In 1986, he experimented with planting pine trees in one of his *jhum* fields for the first time. In subsequent years, he planted *gamoria* and teak. In 1999, he experimented with running orange plantations and became the de facto officer in charge of sapling redistribution for beneficiary households. Since 2003, he has diversified his upland farming through hollock, jatropha, banana, pineapple and increased long bean cultivation.

Over the past forty-four years, he has consolidated his land holding in the village from one plot of land to fourteen and has diversified his cropping with state support and the patronage he received from his political patron. Land is unequally distributed in the village, with 60 per cent of households owning over ten plots of land, as opposed to the 18 per cent of the households that are landless. During this period, many other farmers lost their land. This has been the consequence of privatised land holding, which has helped influential clan members to consolidate land, while others have been left behind. State support has helped those farmers who network effectively and have the social capital to negotiate with the political actors that form the patron-client relations in contemporary Naga villages. Due to Nikon's political influence and his close ties with the village church, one of his sons joined the Assam Rifles, while his daughter started the theology programme in Kohima town. In the 1990s, when long bean cultivation became a major source of income for Leangkangru farmers, he worked as a go-between for town merchants in the supply chain. During his two terms as village development board secretary, his wife recalls he was always running between the village and the administrative headquarters, negotiating seed supplies and procuring subsidies for the village.

In the late 1990s, upland agricultural intensification on a large scale had started with schemes provided by various government departments. These schemes were implemented in highland villages through their village councils, village development board and, on a more informal level, through the *khel* heads that have control over their clan members. The labour supply is controlled by the church, student bodies, Citizen (village headman), the family and, within the *khel*, through reciprocity between families. Nikon's success comes from his rise in the village as a political actor and a patron. From a simple party foot soldier, he rose to the post of vice president. His fluency in the Ao Naga dialect also made him popular among Ao officers and district administrators (75 per cent of all top government jobs in Nagaland are held by Ao Nagas, who are also responsible for distributing development money). He has used these skills to act as a contact point and intermediary for various projects and programmes implemented in the village. He once explained to me in passing that, although the first founders still own the village, they could not bring development, as they were uneducated and were unacquainted with modern-day patronage politics. Joseph's agricultural success closely corresponded to land consolidation in every post-election season during the last three decades. During an election, a huge amount of cash passes through the village economy, and he is assigned the role to consolidate votes for his party. Because the majority of the public in the village belong to the Jangra clan, Nikon's political leadership in the village mattered.

Nikon's agricultural success also comes from the patronage he has built within his clan members. In the last decade, when his party's legislative assembly member and former minister were in power, his lineage members became beneficiaries. Besides plantation seeds, agricultural subsidies went to members of his clan. While his farm benefitted from the subsidised seed supplies, landless farmers benefitted from cash subsidies. This made him a prominent plantation landlord in the village. During the 2009 cropping season, he cultivated five plots of land: three upland *jhum* fields and two lowland paddy fields. Only in one farm had he done mixed cropping of chillies, tubers, white oats and other vegetables along with millet. In other agricultural fields, he planted jatropha curcas (a diesel crop), maize, long beans, Naga chillies and rice in his wet paddy field. His paddy field, located in the Nyaporo side of the village, was one of the largest, with two fishery ponds. One was functional while the other lay barren, as the self-help group (SHG) did not work as well as intended. He explained that when a SHG is formed, people are very enthusiastic. However, after some time, public participation fades away, as people take less interest in the fields. He was sharing one portion of his land with a clan member, the Public Works Department driver and one landless relative. In return, these people were helping him with free labour. His other *pani kheti* was offered to the former church pastor on similar terms. These lands were all provided free of rent. In lieu of rent, help was expected during the sowing and harvesting season in addition to building huts and farm rest houses. In 2009, Joseph had built a new two-storeyed rest shed in his *pani kheti*. He charged rent on none of them. Rather, all tenants contributed family labour to his field.

Nikon strongly believed that land relations among the Nagas were not the same as in the caste-based society of the plains. He explained that there is no sharecropping among Yimchunger Nagas and, hence, there is no exploitation of labour among *jhummias*. Land relations cannot be understood in pure class-caste binaries in the upland Naga Hills. Many authors have tried to see land relation in idiosyncratic class-caste terms, and they have failed to demonstrate how labour relations are mediated by kinship ties and clan patronage politics. The web of power in *jhummed* landscapes is exerted through the "bundle of rights" that community members hold over resources achieved by controlling labour relations. The changes in land relation reflect the shifts in labour relations within *khel*s and clans, now determined by the new patronage links established by the village headman with government intermediaries and their schemes and programmes of *jhumland* development.

Reciprocal inter-household exchange of land in return for labour brought success to individual families who were working just like the chiefs, but reciprocity was now based on patronage that linked state schemes and programmes with the villagers, who participated in programmes in the hope of getting loans and subsidies. Resource access was thus facilitated by people in the village who could attract subsidies, seed supplies, loans and cash payments. In the past, before the establishment of the village church and the rise of newcomers such as Nikon, the village headman was the most powerful person in the village. Nikon's father had originally taken shelter in the house of one the chief's brothers. Slowly, through his association with the church, formal education and his association with the political party, he had emerged as the public leader in the village. He had been responsible for bringing development projects and schemes to the village. The political parties developed a link with the people by supporting them by means of agricultural subsidies, tree crops, tree saplings and promises of development, roads and horticultural plants before elections.

For Nikon, plantations were important, as these were assets for the future, while his landless kin depended on subsidies for their immediate household needs. These subsidies helped in building patronage between the landless and the landed, and helped produce tangible assets. Farmers such as Nikon had built their access and control over village resources through the expansion of their farms. In 2008, when the Village Council ordered a *neelam* (auction) of all cattle in the village, the decision had not come as a surprise. Cattle that had been introduced in the village under the Animal Husbandry programme were destroying and eating away the saplings of new plantations, damaging crops that were now growing close to the village boundary and grazing in areas that were now settled as reserve and private forest. At a much earlier date, *mithun* had vanished from Leangkangru forest because of the opening of new paddy fields.

For Nikon, these patronage affiliations were important, as they sustained modern agroforestry promoted by state schemes intended to shift cultivation. Class formation between households in swidden cultivation landscapes is thus produced by the practice through which development subsidies are appropriated by key village patrons. During my interviews, I could only gather data from individual households on the amount of subsidies each farmer got; I was unable to obtain information on the seed supplied to promote tree plantation and horticulture crops. I later solved this conundrum after interviewing a slightly aged man who explained that landless farmers could also become the beneficiaries of plantation programmes by demonstrating their de facto ownership over land that was not formally their own. In such cases, the landless farmers became the beneficiaries of financial assistance while their landed kinsman appropriated the seed supplies. In this way, both parties benefitted from the programme through the mutual exchange of subsidies. Thus, access to resources was not determined by property rights but by knowledge of how to capitalise on claims to development assistance and free seed supplies. Forest reserves were also claimed by people who were not part of the village.

In such cases, large tracts of forest were reserved by outsiders and local politicians. Here, again, subsidies were used to bring about afforestation in the village. There was an extreme shortage of firewood in Leangkangru, as plantation reserves that were coming up in the village did not allow households to collect minor forest products, as these reserve forests were no longer part of the village commons. Trees were fenced and fines were imposed on trespassers and illegal woodcutters. In the past, access had been free, as the trees had little economic value. Now, however, women and children had to walk a long distance to collect firewood from the forest, as the commons were shrinking with the growing agroforestry programme. Even Nikon's family had problems in collecting firewood, as they had reserved their private forest for timber. Wild trees that produced excellent fuel wood were never replanted, as they were seen as wild and non-economical. Subsequently, some people started selling fuel wood to outsiders, as the townspeople needed cash for their children's education.

As my study shows, the consolidation and privatisation of land holding leads to rural class formation. Consolidation is linked to cash inflow, patronage and state support, which are utilised by farmers according to their affiliation to their lineage and clan. *Jhum* farming landscapes in Nagaland are evolving as sites of agricultural transformation. Conventional studies of lowland agriculture were based on technological changes; however, neither the notion that the green revolution induced social differentiation in predominantly rice-growing lowlands nor the classic model of agricultural involution, as proposed by Geertz,[29] explain the historical specificity and cultural dimensions of highland societies which are based on lineage and clan affiliation, as opposed to the caste- and class-based societies in the plains. In recent years, many studies have investigated these questions by refocusing on local-level case studies and on the power structures within which agrarian change occurs.[30] Thus, the focus has shifted from studies of agrarian changes based on the social and political structure of society to processes that bring about inequalities in society. Studies also examine how lineages, institutional interventions and clan structures allow patronage politics to shape affiliation and difference.

Class relations are not well defined in lineage-based societies, nor does an evolutionary model fit the nature of agricultural change. Agrarian change is

---

29 Clifford Geertz, *Agricultural Involution: The Process of Ecological Change in Indonesia* (Berkeley: University of California Press, 1963), 39.

30 Joel S. Kahn, "Cultarising the Indonesian Landscape," in *Transforming the Indonesian Upland: Marginality, Power and Production*, ed. Tania Murray Li (London: Routledge, 1999), 81–106.

influenced by interactions that are built through patronage and kinship ties, in which the relations of power are defined by personal networks and contacts. Many farmers in Yimchunger villages have articulated that "there is no inequality in Naga society, as it is class-less and caste-less." This statement, at face value, stands true. Despite this belief, however, disparate inequalities are rapidly emerging. Social dynamics and agrarian change in the highlands must be understood in relation to both these changing dynamics and the bundle of rights and access to resources articulated under customary laws and age-old traditions.

In Leangkangru village today, eighteen households (nearly 16 per cent) are reported to be landless, while the Nagaland Environment Protection through Economic Development (NEPED) survey has placed this at 30 per cent. Landlessness is quite unusual in communities that have village forests, clan forests and community forests. However, in Leangkangru village, every land holding is private. Reserve forests belong to individuals, headmen, first settlers and project beneficiaries. Out of the 106 households surveyed during my fieldwork, excepting the eighteen households who are landless, every farmer has a plantation in his *jhum* fields. A few farmers have large reserves that contain teak, *gamoria*, orange, pineapple, banana, cardamom, ginger and many other crops introduced through government schemes. Paddy farming has already individualised landholding in the valleys. A similar phase is building up in the hills through afforestation and agroforestry, where access and control over resources are highly individualised. Although farmers in Leangkangru always claimed to have established private landholdings, "access control" over private *jhum* land was communal and flexible. Every farmer in the village had the right to take minor forest products from the fields of another farmer. With the establishment of plantation timber trees and orchards, access to forest resources in fallow *jhum* plots began to be restricted. These changes must be understood as part of the state's panoptic control over unruly spaces. The local colonial officials accomplished their dual objectives of "conservation" and "fixity" by promoting wet terrace cultivation, as, inherently, this process produced a fixed assessment of tenure, which was easier to control than *jhum* fields, which were constantly mobile.

In traditional Yimchunger society, *khels* were an area of land defined by a *khel* boundary and a *murung* house with a village chief or first settler, who claimed to be the owner of the village and who was the de jure custodian of land and forest resources. Today, the *khels* have been fragmented by new settlers, existing families and by people acting as political intermediaries and government servants, including people who have been appointed as Village Council members and the politically appointed village headman. As one of the headmen remarked, "it is leadership that is counted in the village; the traditional first settlers are illiterate, they don't know the government procedures to write applications, meet government officials and explain them about their needs. An educated, literate person is more important and wiser to bring about development."[31]

The relationship between the paddy fields and the *jhum* plots are thus a reflection of the social networks that have been built between the patrons and their clients in the village. Landlessness fosters patronage and dependence; government subsidies and the distribution of seedlings and loans under the capacity-building and communitisation programmes have a similar effect. For example, some farmers expressed that landlessness was no issue in getting agricultural subsidies for tree plantation under various agriculture department schemes. The landless farmers enjoyed the subsidies by becoming beneficiaries, as they showed their landed kin's property as their own while applying for subsidies. Landowners parted with their share of subsidies but became the long-term beneficiaries of orchards. This way, they could make multiple claims to subsidies and seed supplies under different government programmes for agricultural development over time.

Farmers such as Nikon, the village headman, and other influential men, such as the former regional council members, some deacons and the schoolteacher, who had the opportunity to capitalise on state schemes, were well off, even during the worst dry season. The irrigated channels were watering their fields from the Yayi river. In the early twentieth century, when wet rice was experimentally promoted among the Semas, Ao and Lotha Nagas of the Mokokchung sub-division, the colonial hill administrators reported similar successes. Only the *jhum* crops failed. In a report prepared by H.J. Mitchell et al. (1943) submitted to Robert Reid, it was observed that:

> In the Sema Naga area where the land has become exhausted and the people were faced with starvation, one or two Angami villagers, experienced in the art of terracing, were engaged to teach the Semas how to make terraces. They selected sites with constant water supply, they showed the Semas how to make terraces and channels and how to plant and they explained what ceremonies and sacrifices the Angamis performed to further the growth of the crop. All these took a long time, owing to the strong conservatism of the Semas. But once the [influential man] accepted the

---

31   As narrated by Tohinba in his testimony on village programme and functioning.

new idea they were soon followed by the rest. Now large areas are under terraces and villages have their granaries full.[32]

These narratives were based on the specific success stories of "influential men" who were part of the colonial patronage politics. In the decolonisation phase, we see that wet terrace rice boomed and was diffused through these networks of intermediaries, who were the educated men of the village, party workers and government servants attached to the district and circle/block administration. The village church record clearly confirms the popularity of rice over other traditional *jhum* crops, which have slowly come to decline in production with changing land use and Yimchunger Naga society's preference of rice over other *jhum* crops. Likewise, there has been an expansion of plantation and non-traditional food crops in the region.

5 Conclusion

With the coming of state-backed subsidies and new legislation that formally recognised the village council, relations of power and reciprocity as well as land relations were rearranged, meaning that new landholding arrangements were produced. New categories of people (second settlers) rose to positions of influence within the existing social institutions in the village, as they gained access to new forms of wealth and capital, as reflected in Nikon's life history. This also had an impact on land relations and is reflected in the landholding pattern in the study village. Before the advent of colonial administration, usufruct rights over land were stronger and more established, as they defined the land relations between families. During my field study, these were shrinking, as more and more upland farms were brought under permanent cultivation through agroforestry programmes. The establishment of permanent rights over *jhum* land gradually destroyed the land entitlements formally established as a bundle of rights, based on reciprocity between the chiefs and his subjects, the second settlers. The introduction of new crops, such as wet rice, led to permanent rights being established over lowland fields, which once had been barren forestland.

---

32   Messrs H. J. Mitchell, O.B.E, B. Fr. S and R. E. Mc Guire, O.B.E., I.C.S. in Assam to study the administration of the Excluded and Partially Excluded Areas, February – March 1943, Government of Burma, Reconstruction Department Report, IOR, M/3/1457 – Frontier Excluded areas of Assam and Burma.

In analysing the shifting land relations in Leangkangru, with the access of power transferring from the first settlers to the second settlers, I was inspired by studies that focused on control over the access to and use of land and resources. For African or Southeast Asian highland societies, where land relations cannot be understood using the Western nomenclature of rights over land or tenure, several studies have defined the unique land relations and the customary tradition of access to land.[33]

By contrast, for Northeast India, there are limited sets of studies that engages with the critical debate on land, tenure and rights in the upland areas inhabited by the "Scheduled Tribes."[34] The understanding of land relations in Nagaland are based on Western notions of property and colonial classifications that were documented in colonial tour diaries and monographs. Even – and especially – where legislation sought to recognise and protect "customary" land rights, these Western, colonial notions were already modifying their nature and paved the way for further changes. These standard classifications in the present land-tenure context misrepresent the complex power structure and labour relations exercised through land-based property relations. The egalitarian nomenclature used to understand land relations is clearly not applicable to the contemporary social context, where the village headmanship has been institutionalised in Nagaland. Customary land relations and principles of justice based on tradition are mediated by the district administration. The local *dobashi* courts do not operate within the mainstream judicial framework that compartmentalises the judiciary and the executive. In fact, under the guise of "customs," decisions are made by executives who interpret customs based on the knowledge of *dobashis*. Faith-based institutions such as the church also exercise enormous control over land-based social relations, as they control labour distribution through age sets which are organised in the village to provide free labour for these religious organisations. Similarly, land relations are increasingly being defined by the growing commercial value of the land and the growing trend of establishing rights to control access to it.

In this chapter, I have discussed the ways in which land and property relations have altered over time in the Yimchunger Naga shifting cultivation village, with a shift towards private property. The colonial interpretation of land relations and the recognition of village headmen as village patrons gave the headmen (chiefs) both the legal and customary writ to make decisions on

---

33   Anna Lowenhaupt Tsing, *In the Realm of the Diamond Queen: Marginality in an Out-of-the-Way Place* (Princeton: Princeton University Press, 1993), 20–35.

34   Erik de Maaker and Meenal Tula, eds., *Unequal Land Relations in Northeast India: Custom, Gender and the Market* (Guwahati: North Eastern Social Research Institute, 2020), 1–30.

community land. With the upsurge of the money economy and state assistance for permanent settlement through the promotion of terrace cultivation, the value attached to land has changed, as it has become alienable: land has become a "commodity" that can easily be exchanged, mortgaged and permanently developed. The institutionalisation of private property has led to increasing landlessness and to control over community land by those villagers who can establish that they have the resources to develop the land permanently by cultivating wet rice in irrigated terraces or by establishing tree plantations and horticultural programmes. In other words, it was via the promotion and adoption of wet terrace rice cultivation and tree plantations that permanent individual rights were established and that the new regime of alienable proprietorship, in which the value of land is determined through exchange and sale, was put in place.

Bibliography

Angami, Zepto. *Nagaland Village Empowerment Rules.* Kohima: Novelty Printing Press, 2008.

Dove, Michael Roger. "A Revisionist View of Tropical Deforestation and Development." *Environmental Conservation* 20, no. 1 (1993): 17–56.

Elwin, Verrier. *A New Deal for Tribal India.* India: Ministry of Foreign Affairs, 1–10.1.

Gabay, Clive, and Susan Llcan. "Leaving No-One Behind? The Politics of Destination in the 2030 Sustainable Development Goals." *Globalization* 14, no. 3 (2017): 337–42.

Geertz, Clifford. *Agricultural Involution: The Process of Ecological Change in Indonesia.* Berkeley: University of California Press, 1963.

Guha, Sumit. *Environment and Ethnicity in India 1200–1900.* Cambridge: Cambridge University Press, 1999.

Hirch, Philip. "Forests, Forest Reserve, and Forest Land in Thailand." *The Geographical Journal* 56, no. 2 (1989): 166–74.

Hodge, James Morgan. *Triumph of the Expert: Agrarian Doctrines of Development and the Legacies of British Colonialism.* Athens, OH: Ohio University Press, 2007.

Iijana, Ian. "Socio Cultural Change among the Shifting Cultivators through the Introduction of Wet Rice Cultivation – A Case Study of Kerens in Northern Thailand." *Memoirs of the College of Agriculture* 79, no. 3 (1970): 1–35.

Kahn, Joel. "Culturalising the Indonesian Landscape." In *Transforming the Indonesian Upland: Marginality, Power and Production,* edited by Tania Murray Li, 79–104. London: Routledge, 1999.

Leach, Edmund Ronald. *Political Systems of Highland Burma: A Study of Kachin Social Structure.* London: G. Bell. 1954.

Li, Tania Murray. *Land's End: Capitalist Relations on an Indigenous Frontier.* London: Routledge, 2014.

Ltu, Vizokhole. "Women, Property and Angami Naga Customary Law." In *Unequal Land Relations in North East India: Custom, Gender and the Market,* edited by Erik De Maaker and Meenal Tula, 62–86. Guwahati: Northeast Social Research Centre, 2020.

Maaker, Erik De, and Meenal Tula, eds. *Unequal Land Relations in Northeast India: Custom, Gender and the Market.* Guwahati: North Eastern Social Research Institute, 2020.

Mills, John Philip *The Lotha Nagas.* London: Macmillan, 1922.

Moore, Henrietta, and Megan Vaughan. *Cutting Down Trees: Gender, Nutrition, and Agricultural Change in the Northern Province of Zambia, 1890–1990.* Cambridge: Cambridge University Press, 1993.

Ribot, Jesse, and Nancy Lee Peluso. "A Theory of Access." *Rural Sociology* 68, no. 2 (2003): 153–81.

Richards, Audrey. *Land, Labour and Diet in Northern Rhodesia: An Economic Study of the Bemba Tribe.* Oxford: Oxford University Press, 1939.

Shimray, Ursala, A. "Land Use System in Manipur Hills: A Case Study of Thangkul Naga." In *Land, People and Politics: Contest over Tribal Land in Northeast India,* edited by Walter Fernandes and Sanjoy Barbora, 88–112. Guwahati: Northeast Social Research Centre; Copenhagen: International Working Group for Indigenous Affairs, 1999.

Sturgeon, Janet. *Border Landscapes: The Politics of Aka Land Use in Burma and China.* Seattle: University of Washington Press, 2005.

Tsing, Anna Lowenhaupt. *In the Realm of the Diamond Queen: Marginality in an Out-of-the-Way Place.* Princeton University Press: Princeton, 1993.

CHAPTER 7

Agrarian Change in the Hills of Northeast India

The Unlikely Story of Shifting Agriculture

A. Lozaanba Khumbah

Shifting agriculture is widely known as *jhuming* in Northeast India. It is a contested practice. It is integral to the livelihoods and landscapes of the hilly regions of India's Northeast. At the same time, it has also been the site of active state interventions, from colonial times to the present.[1] The ecological question, specifically the sustainability of the agrarian system in the face of population growth, has been a major reason for debate. However, the rapidly transforming *jhumscapes*[2] of the region, especially in the face of intrusive state-driven markets, suggest a significant divergence from the prevailing narratives.

Since the turn of the century, an increasing number of studies have come to recognise the central role of the market in transforming local practices of shifting agriculture.[3] This is hugely significant since much of the debate on shifting agriculture hinges on demography as the most important driver of change. Following Boserup's thesis,[4] increasing population pressure was expected to lead to shorter and shorter fallows, effectively undermining the sustainability

---

1 Examples of state intervention during colonial times can be found in Verrier Elwin, *The Baiga* (Delhi: Gian Publishing House, [1931] 1986), 100–31. Government interventions post-independence are examined by Debojyoti Das, "Demystifying the Myth of Shifting Cultivation Agronomy in the North-East," *Economic and Political Weekly* 41, no. 47 (November – December 2006): 4912–17, amongst others.

2 Or "*jhuming* landscape." The idea of "*jhumscape*" is further developed in the paper.

3 The Task Force on Rehabilitation of Shifting Cultivation Areas (2006) reported that farmers were cultivating lesser areas for food crops, giving way to vegetables or other crops with a higher market value. In the West Garo Hills District of Meghalaya, farmers are slowly "reviving" cash crop cultivation, which had met with limited success a few decades earlier. Amba Jamir, "Shifting Options: A Case Study of Shifting Cultivation in Mokokchung District in Nagaland, India," in *Shifting Cultivation, Livelihood and Food Security: New and Old Challenges for Indigenous People in Asia*, ed. Christian Erni (Bangkok: Food and Agricultural Organization, International Work Group for Indigenous Affairs and Asia Indigenous Peoples Pact, 2015), 175, also found that farmers were capitalising on local tastes and food habits by adding value to crops that ensured good returns from the market.

4 Ester Boserup, *The Conditions of Agricultural Growth: The Economics of Agrarian Change under Population Pressure* (London: George Allen & Unwin, 1965).

of the system over a period of time. It formed the basis for most state interventions in the post-colonial era, as well as predictions of an "ecological disaster" in the region by some experts.[5]

The predicted disasters, however, have not occurred.[6] On the contrary, it has become evident that shifting agriculture is transforming in ways that experts had not anticipated. For instance, in a study on Nagaland, Amba found that fallow lengths were increasing instead of decreasing.[7] The present study also confirms a similar trend of increasing fallow lengths, much against the grain of the prevailing narrative. While this may not be the case everywhere, it does hint that there is no single trajectory of change.

Evidence from other countries, most notably Southeast Asia, indicate that changes in shifting agriculture are multilayered and uneven across space, especially with respect to market access.[8] Cramb et al. write that simplistic linear narratives that equate increasing demographic pressure with shortening fallows and environmental destruction require more qualification.[9] Such narratives fail to account for the movement of population within a country and the various factors that drive rural migration to urban areas.

In other words, shifting agriculture in Northeast India is affected by larger socio-economic and political changes in the country even though its practice may be confined largely to a geographical region. Indeed, farmers innovate precisely in response to these larger changes. Shifting agriculture, therefore, does not operate in isolation.[10] This is mainly due to the ease with which markets can now be accessed, made possible by the robust network of roads developed by the state after Independence. While upland farmers have always interacted with markets,[11] the nature and scale of present-day exchanges

---

5   Malcolm Cairns and Harold Brookfield, "Composite Farming Systems in an Era of Change: Nagaland, North-East India," *Asia Pacific Viewpoint* 52, no. 1 (2011): 57.

6   Cairns and Brookfield, "Composite Farming Systems," 57.

7   Jamir, "Shifting Options."

8   Nathalie van Vliet et al., "Trends, Drivers and Impacts of Changes in Swidden Cultivation in Tropical Forest Agriculture Frontiers: A Global Assessment," *Global Environmental Change* 22 (January 2012): 418–29.

9   R. A. Cramb et al., "Swidden Transformations and Rural Livelihoods in Southeast Asia," *Human Ecology* 37 (May 2009): 323–46.

10   Perhaps one of the most enduring assumptions or myths about shifting agriculture is that it operates in isolation. This is, of course, closely linked to similar views on indigenous communities who tend to be located on the frontiers of nation states, and away from mainstream imaginations of the country. For instance, the most prominent criticism of shifting agriculture – that it becomes unsustainable with increasing population – assumes a closed and static system, isolated from the rest of the world.

11   See Michael R. Dove, "Theories of Swidden Agriculture, and the Political Economy of Ignorance," *Agroforestry Systems* 1 (1983): 85–89; S. N. Mithra, "Arunachal's Tribal

mediated by radically improved roads and communication services is unprec-edented. For instance, the growth of domestic flight services in the past few years has led to high demand for *jhum* products from the Northeast in cer-tain pockets of metro cities, such as Delhi, Mumbai and Bangalore, populated by people from the region, creating a market for *jhum* products that did not exist before. Commenting on the nature of agrarian change, Harris-White et al. argue that the transformation of shifting agriculture is essentially a transition to a capitalist economy.[12]

This chapter situates shifting agriculture within these larger socio-economic contexts, specifically that of increased market penetration. It seeks to identify drivers of change that are transforming shifting agriculture, characterise the changing agrarian practices, and understand the implications of these changes both on society and the environment. To make up for the lack of temporal data, and to factor in the role of geography and terrain, the study maps trans-formations in shifting agriculture over space. It is based on extensive fieldwork, which was carried out as part of the author's doctoral work.

1   The Area of Study

Six villages from the hilly districts of Tamenglong and Noney, Manipur form the study area.[13] These two districts are populated mainly by four ethnic Naga communities of Inpui, Liangmei, Rongmei and Zeme, who are traditional prac-titioners of shifting agriculture. *Jhuming* continues to be integral to the rural economy along with wet rice cultivation,[14] horticulture and market-oriented

---

Economic Formations and their Dissolution," *Economic and Political Weekly* (October 1983): 1837–46; Jelle J. P. Wouters, "Keeping the Hill Tribes at Bay: A Critique from India's Northeast of James C. Scott's Paradigm of State Evasion," *European Bulletin of Himalayan Research* 39 (2012): 41–65.

12   Barbara Harris-White, Deepak K. Mishra, and Vandana Upadhyay, "Institutional Diversity and Capitalist Transition: The Political Economy of Agrarian Change in Arunachal Pradesh, India," *Journal of Agrarian Change* 9, no. 4 (2009): 512–47.

13   Noney district was carved out of Tamenglong district in 2016. In instances where informa-tion is not available for the newly formed district, data for Tamenglong is used for both districts. K. Sarojkumar Sharma, "Okram Ibobi Singh Inaugurates Two More Districts," *Times of India*, 17 December 2016, https://timesofindia.indiatimes.com/city/imphal/okram-ibobi-singh-inaugurates-two-more-districts/articleshow/56030775.cms.

14   Wet rice cultivation or terrace cultivation is not a traditional practice in the study area. It was introduced by the government with the help of other communities from the Northeast, like the Angamis from Nagaland, who are traditional practitioners of wet rice cultivation.

farming which have emerged in the past few decades due to a combination of government policy and better access to markets. The districts represent, at a micro level, the larger socio-economic changes taking place in the region.

As mentioned earlier, the study seeks to map transformations in shifting agriculture over space. Hence, an important criterion for selecting the study villages was the "distance" from the market centres – Tamenglong district headquarter and Noney bazaar. Tamenglong is a Census Town, with a steadily expanding population that was just under twenty thousand, according to the 2011 Census. It is 164 km away from Imphal, the state capital. Noney bazaar, on the other hand, is an emerging market along National Highway 53. It is much closer to Imphal (sixty kilometres) and is, therefore, a convenient stopping point for food for travellers en route to and from Imphal. With its numerous hotels providing "home food," a thriving hospitality industry has mushroomed in Noney with the highway as its lifeline.

The six villages chosen for the study are Chiuluan, Akhui, Karuangmuan, Ijeirong, Bakuwa and Shingra. These villages, located at varying "distances" from the market centres reflect unequal access to space – an element which is usually ignored in most studies.[15] "Distance" is conceptualised not only "as the crow flies" but also in relative terms. Bad roads (unmetalled or seasonal) have further bearing on transport costs, influencing access and time taken to reach markets.

Table 7.1 details the important variables of road length and quality, transport availability and costs to arrive at an indicator of accessibility. The indicator gives an approximate measure of the ease or difficulty of accessing nearby markets, ranked on a scale of D1 to D5, where D1 is most accessible and D5 is least accessible. This may be elaborated on with an example. Farmers from Chiuluan and Karuangmuan village (D1) hardly spend ten rupees to go to the market at any time of the year. By contrast, farmers from Shingra village have to either walk for a whole day or spend around four thousand rupees to hire a four-wheel drive vehicle to access the market. But this is possible only in the dry autumn and winter seasons. At the peak of the monsoon season, roads become practically unusable and any significant interaction with the market is effectively brought to a stop.

The case of Shingra village (D5) needs to be highlighted. Shingra farmers prefer to sell their produce at Leimakhong market in Imphal, not at Noney bazaar, which is the nearest market, because they get better prices there. However, this requires a dawn-to-dusk march on foot, one way, not to mention that the goods are carried by the person him- or herself. Thus, for Shingra farmers, "going to the market" requires two complete days and involves

---

15   Or, assumed to be uniform, which is not the case.

FIGURE 7.1   "Distance" mediates access to markets
              Left: A temporary bamboo bridge connecting Karuangmuan village and
              Noney bazaar. It is most likely to be swept away during the monsoon. Right: A
              particularly bad section of the road between Shingra/Bakuwa village and
              Noney bazaar

considerable physical effort.[16] This is in stark contrast with other villages, especially Chiuluan and Karuangmuan, where markets can be accessed in a few minutes' time. Accessing markets in such contrasting ways has significant implications for the kind of products that farmers can sell and, therefore, on agricultural practices and agrarian change.

The bulk of the fieldwork was carried out from February to May 2018. The study used a mixed-methods approach, combining both quantitative, questionnaire-based household-level surveys and qualitative interviews. The household survey was carried out over two stages. The first stage was a complete census of the village.[17] This included basic information concerning

---

16   Shingra village provides a glimpse of how upland farmers usually interacted with markets
      before modern-day roads.
17   A census of the villages was necessary because official numbers in the census did not
      match with the reality in the villages for two important reasons. First, negligence on the
      part of government officials who, in most cases, do not go to the villages but instead sum-
      mon the village Chairman and Secretary to the towns, where details of everyone in the
      village are entered. Apart from the census, many families whose doors were marked as
      having been surveyed by the National Health and Family Survey (NHFS) reported that
      they were not interviewed. Second, conducting a census from afar works to the advantage
      of village authorities who intentionally swell household numbers so that the village can
      receive a greater share from various government schemes. In all the villages, the number
      of households reported in the census is much higher than the real number of households
      in the village. The village authority members were open about their practice of swelling
      household numbers to get more grants.

TABLE 7.1 Characteristics of the study villages

Market centre	Villages	No. of HH	Main economic activity	Road condition	Transport service	Distance (km)	Cost of transport (Rs.)	Accessibility index	Ethnic community
Tamenglong	Chiuluan	95	Govt. jobs, *jhuming*, Barak river-valley vegetable cultivation, orange orchards; Supplies vegetable to Tamenglong town	Metalled, district highway	Daily/ hourly/ on demand	3.5	10	D1	Rongmei
Tamenglong	Akhui	72	Govt. jobs, potato farms, *jhuming*, orange orchards; Military check-post acts as local market	Metalled, district highway	Daily	18	60	D2	Rongmei
Noney	Karuang muan	88	Wet rice, banana farms, vegetable *jhum*; Situated on railway project	Unmetalled, all-weather road	Daily/ hourly/ on demand	2	10	D1	Inpui

TABLE 7.1 Characteristics of the study villages (*cont.*)

Market centre	Villages	No. of HH	Main economic activity	Road condition	Transport service	Distance (km)	Cost of transport (Rs.)	Accessibility index	Ethnic community
Noney	Ijeirong	43	Wet rice, *jhuming*, cane and orange orchards; Situated on ADB road project	Unmetalled, all-weather road	Daily	14	80	D3	Inpui
Noney	Bakuwa	36	Wet rice, *jhuming*, turmeric fields, bamboo shoot; Situated on ADB road project	Unmetalled, fair weather road; gentle gradient;	Daily in autumn; Hire 4x4 vehicles in rainy season	14	100 or 2500	D4	Inpui
Noney	Shingra	68	*Jhuming*, chilli fields, NTFP (mushroom); Mithun rearing; 1-day trek to market	Unmetalled, fair weather road; steep gradient	Hire – only 4x4 vehicles	25	4000	D5	Liangmei

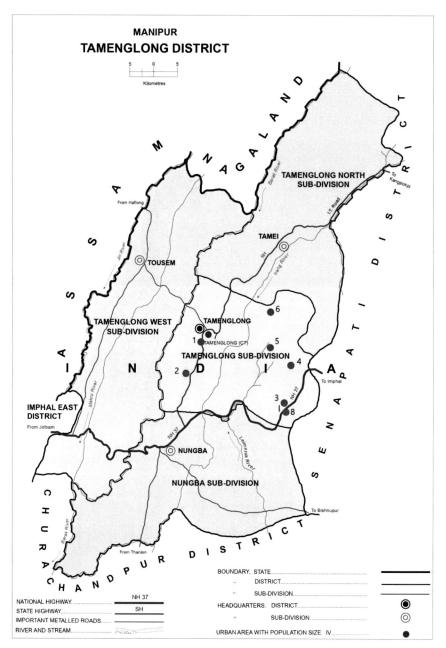

MAP 7.1   Locating the field

SOURCE: CENSUS OF INDIA 2011. ADMINISTRATIVE ATLAS – MANIPUR,
(DIRECTOR OF CENSUS OPERATIONS, MANIPUR), 30

household size, sources of income, agricultural output (*jhum*, wet rice field, horticulture) and food security. Forty per cent of the households were interviewed in detail in the second stage, selected through stratified random sampling. The qualitative aspect of the fieldwork involved participant observation, key informant and in-depth interviews with different categories of people, informal conversations both with individuals and groups, visits to the fields, and photographs. Interviews were also conducted across different age groups, including between fathers, sons and grandsons to gain an intergenerational view of agrarian change. The stories, songs and life experiences of older people, farmers both men and women, and traders provided a wealth of information that complemented data from questionnaires.

2   Drivers of Change: Significant Divergences

Most studies on shifting agriculture assume a direct correlation between population and the sustainability of the agrarian system. As pointed out earlier, this is possible only in a closed system without any movement of people or other qualitative changes. That is hardly the case: I found considerable movement of youth from the villages to towns and cities. This is push migration, due to the lack of good schools in the villages; those leaving are mainly in search of quality education, and employment (Table 7.2).

The table shows that in the area of study, on average 40 per cent of all family members live outside the village for most of the year, ranging from 38.7 per cent in Karuangmuan village to 53.9 per cent in Akhui village. Of all migrants, students account for no less than 57 per cent (Chiuluan) and up to 90 per cent (Shingra village).[18] Access to good education is, therefore, one of the most important reasons for migration. This has resulted in the mass exodus of young people, who make up the core of the working age group, giving

---

18   By virtue of being close to the town, students from Chiuluan village have access to good quality primary and secondary education. This explains the lower percentage of students in the migrated group. Student migration consists mainly of those seeking a Bachelor's or Master's degree in metro cities. By contrast, most student migration from Shingra village is for primary and secondary education within the state. There are very few instances of migration to metro cities for higher studies. The comparatively low proportion of students among the total migration in Ijeirong village (61.4 per cent) may be attributed to the presence of a private school in the village that started a few years ago.

TABLE 7.2   Migration in the study villages

Village	Average family size	Average no. of people migrated per family (% of total)	% of students in the migrated group
Chiuluan (D1)	5.7	40.4	57.3
Akhui (D2)	6.3	53.9	76.4
Karuangmuan (D1)	6.2	38.7	66.3
Ijeirong (D3)	5.8	46.6	61.4
Bakuwa (D4)	6.3	52.4	68.8
Shingra (D5)	5.8	43.1	90.7

rise to the feeling of an "empty village."[19] During the course of the fieldwork, it was very common to find mostly middle-aged parents living in the village and working in the fields, while all or most of the children lived outside the village in the nearby towns to study.

This trend is certainly not an anomaly. Cramb et al. also found localised population decline due to out-migration in Southeast Asia.[20] The immediate impact of this widespread out-migration is the loss of valuable labour. As shifting agriculture is highly labour-intensive, it has resulted in farmers cultivating smaller fields.[21] The decrease in *jhum* field sizes has also been accelerated by farmers diversifying to wet rice cultivation, horticulture and the cultivation of high-value crops, further reducing the labour required for *jhuming*. Thus, the overall population increase in the village has not resulted in a corresponding intensification of shifting agriculture and decreasing fallow lengths, as

---

19   Older people very often referred to this feeling of an "empty village," contrasting this to, and longing for, the winter season, in which young people return to the village during the holidays, especially for Christmas.

20   Cramb et al., "Swidden Transformations," 323–46.

21   Mr Hungamang Thiumei, aged eighty, from Shingra village points out that four to five families presently cultivate the same patch of land that he and his family cultivated while he was in his prime, some forty years ago. He attributes this change to education, which has broken up the family labour. Other, older farmers have similar opinions.

TABLE 7.3   Fallow length in the study villages

Village	Fallow length (years)	Trend
Chiuluan (D1)	10–12	Increasing
Akhui (D2)	9–10	Increasing
Karuangmuan (D1)	12 +	Increasing
Ijeirong (D3)	10 +	Increasing
Bakuwa (D4)	10 +	Increasing
Shingra (D5)	8–9	Stable

Boserup postulated.[22] On the contrary, much against popular perceptions, fallow lengths are either increasing or stable (Table 7.3).[23]

This counter-intuitive finding is also reported by Amba for Mokukchung, Nagaland, where *jhum* cycles were lengthening from eight to fourteen years due to a combination of decreasing field sizes and families leaving shifting agriculture.[24] The table further suggests that accessibility to markets plays a role in the fallow cycle. Villages closer to the market (Chiuluan, Karuangmuan) have lengthier fallow period than villages further away (Shingra). This may be explained by the fact that farmers with lesser access to markets are more dependent on traditional *jhuming* and, therefore, cultivate it more intensively.

On the other hand, farmers living closer to towns have greater incentive to diversify towards more market-friendly practices. Even within *jhuming*, farmers are moving away from traditional cereal crops that ensured food security (e.g., paddy) to crops that provide good monetary returns (e.g., vegetables).

---

22   Boserup, *Conditions.*

23   Quite significantly, Shingra farmers narrated that they "borrowed" forest land from a neighbouring village for *jhuming* for a particular year because their own forests were not "mature enough" yet. This prevented the *jhum* cycle from becoming non-sustainable. A similar instance was also reported in Puichi village (not a part of this study). These instances are highly significant for three reasons. First, they show that farmers are keenly aware of the ecological limitations of *jhuming* and work to safeguard it. Second, robust traditional institutions are central for sustainably managing resources, especially during such crucial moments. And third, most studies that simply predict decreasing fallows do not appreciate local realities, such as property rights regimes, in which it is possible for a village to "lend" a significant area of forest to another village for a particular year.

24   Jamir, "Shifting Options," 175.

They cater to the demands of an emerging educated, middle class population who have moved out of the villages to live in the nearby towns. This population, many of them with white-collar jobs, continue to maintain strong connections with their parental villages. They also retain their culinary taste for "home food." In other words, the much-maligned practice of shifting agriculture has, quite remarkably, found a ready market at the turn of the twenty-first century.

But *jhum* markets are not confined to towns and market centres close to the villages. The metro cities of Delhi, Mumbai and others with a significant proportion of the population in the Northeast have also become major consumers of *jhum* goods.[25] Apart from the cultural and regional connection, *jhum* produce has an extra appeal in a health-conscious era because it is "fertiliser free."[26] One can also sense a certain degree of legitimacy being imparted to traditional agriculture by pitching it in this manner. This urban-based population with traditional tastes has become one of the most important markets for *jhum* products.

The sudden marketability of *jhum* produce has led to what Delang calls a "cash orientation" where farmers "sell most of the crops that they grow, using the income earned to purchase food and other necessities."[27] This, of course, depends on whether markets can be accessed and is, therefore, more pronounced in villages closer to the towns. As was mentioned earlier and will be discussed in detail later, this is leading to changes in the way in which farmers make choices about crops on *jhum* fields. In other words, while population development does play a significant role in determining agrarian change,[28] it is markets and access to markets that is driving qualitative changes in the *jhum* field.

The significance of roads and access to markets in transforming traditional agriculture can hardly be overstated, even though it is scarcely mentioned in literature in the Indian context. Up until the middle of the twentieth century, markets were not easily accessible for upland farmers. Due to barriers posed

---

25   This is a recent development that is perhaps only a decade old. It began as more frequent (daily) flights enabled faster communication with the region.

26   Or "chemical free." Local farmers use this as an effective sales pitch in the towns. They do not use the term "organic," which consumers in the metro cities use. It is also highly ironic, because shifting agriculture is considered to be ecologically destructive.

27   Claudio O. Delang, "Social and Economic Adaptations to a Changing Landscape: Realities, Opportunities and Constraints," in *Living at the Edge of Thai Society: The Karen in the Highlands of Northern Thailand,* ed. Claudio O. Delang (London: Routledge Curzon, 2003), 155–82.

28   Though, in the case of the study area, it has led to change in a direction, contrary to what is generally assumed.

FIGURE 7.2   A "Northeast" shop in New Delhi
Note: A new "Northeast" shop is all set to start
operations in Kishangarh, New Delhi, a locality with a
high density of people from the region. The name of
the shop "*Roots – Flavors of the Northeast*" captures the
sentiment that accompanies these shops

mainly by terrain, distance and concerns over safety,[29] "going to the market" was usually an annual event.[30] It would be undertaken mostly during the dry autumn season at the end of the agricultural calendar,[31] in groups for the sake of security and involved at least three to four days of walking.[32] Due to the considerable hardships involved, no more than four to five trips could be made in a year.

To a large extent, the season of marketing, the distance involved and the mode of transportation dictated the nature of goods that were traded. Farmers mostly sold non-perishable items, such as dry king chilli, oilseeds, forest produce, such as cane, cinnamon barks and seasonal fruits, such as oranges and *parkia* (stink bean or bitter bean). In return, farmers mainly purchased essential items such as salt, clothes, oil, dry fish and agricultural implements. In most cases, farmers themselves carried these goods on foot.

Interacting with markets at this scale had little or no bearing on the agricultural practice in the hills. It is also helpful to remember that *jhuming* was not only pre-capitalist, it also operated in a pre-monetised economy. With reference to the Mizo hills, Jackson writes that salt was locally valued more than cash as late as the beginning of the twentieth century: "Coins were more likely to be fashioned into necklaces or hammered into bullets than to play any meaningful role in financial transactions .... Money – the thing and the concept – arrived gradually and took time for the local populace to understand and trust it as a 'purchasing medium.'"[33]

However, all these circumstances have radically changed over the last few decades, especially after Independence. Money has become the sole way of

---

29   Safety was a significant concern then, which can be easily overlooked today. The danger posed by wild animals was very real. But more than wild animals, farmers risked head-hunting or being caught up in inter-tribe warfare. Adequately armed menfolk were, therefore, an essential part of the marketing group.

30   It appears to have been an important part of their annual calendar, but not only due to practical reasons or compulsions. Older respondents recall their trips to the market with more than nostalgia, imparting a festive hue to the whole "occasion," both in gearing up for the trip and in the warm welcome extended by the children to the returning elders. The experience and expectations, especially for children, of "*keithian kanu*," an Inpui term for "going to the market," was an essential part of the lived agrarian stories.

31   Marketing in the middle of an agricultural season was rare. A popular saying of the time, recalled by Mr Keihiamang Thiumai, aged ninety-one (born 1926), from Shingra village reflects this: "If you take two-three trips to the market, weeds will overtake your field."

32   Considering all the preparations required, a single trip to the market could easily take up a week.

33   Kyle Jackson, "Globalizing an Indian Borderland Environment: Aijal, Mizoram, 1890–1919," *Studies in History* 32, no. 1 (2016): 48.

payment. At the same time, the concerted efforts of the government to build roads have brought markets "nearer." Most villages have daily access to local markets, while some villages are situated right at the edge of newly emerging towns. Markets are now accessible in a matter of hours, or even minutes. Farmers close to towns are able to sell their produce – including perishable items, such as vegetables – on a daily basis, generating good income. They are also able to hire autos, sumo pick-up trucks or even trucks collectively or individually to market their produce.

The scale of market-induced changes in traditional agricultural practices is perhaps captured by a line oft-quoted by the women of Chiuluan village: "We have raised our children by selling vegetables ..." It is an unmistakable indicator that the traditional role assigned to shifting agriculture as subsistence agriculture is changing – *jhum* fields have become an important source of monetary income. Therefore, the dominant narrative of agrarian change simply based on demographic pressure needs to be revisited.

3   Characterising Agrarian Change

This section highlights three major ways in which shifting agriculture and the larger hill economy is changing: diversification away from *jhuming*, mainstreaming of horticulture and the transition from subsistence towards producing for the market within *jhuming*. There are variations across space due to physiological (topographical) constraints and cultural reasons (tribe, agricultural history), apart from "distance" to markets. Despite these specificities, current *jhumscapes* are generally characterised by these three features.

3.1   *Diversification Away from* Jhuming
The multiplicity of agrarian practices is one of the most conspicuous characteristics of present-day hill economies. There is a multitude of agrarian practices in the study area, where shifting agriculture was once the most dominant and the only agricultural practice, particularly before the 1960s.[34] Apart from traditional *jhuming*, one can also find non-paddy or vegetable-only *jhum* fields, wet rice cultivation, different types of horticulture, and fields for specific

---

34   Older respondents from different villages concur that wet rice cultivation was introduced to the region through government initiatives in the 1960s. Before this, shifting agriculture was the sole agrarian practice. Mr Keihiamang Thiumai from Shingra village (born 1926) actively persuaded his contemporaries to take to wet rice farming in his capacity as chairman of the village during that period.

high-value crops such as chilli, turmeric, potato and ginger, as well as vegetable fields and kitchen gardens (Table 7.4).

This is perhaps best understood as diversification away from *jhuming* towards more market-friendly practices. Many of these practices, however, are minor modifications of traditional *jhuming* and closely resemble it in many respects, especially in field preparation. Horticulture has emerged out of the local practice of growing fruit trees, though government policies accelerated its growth. Wet rice cultivation is the only practice that was introduced top-down by the government, and has now become an intrinsic part of the hill economy.

In most villages, the importance of traditional *jhuming* has been overshadowed and even replaced by some of these new practices. In fact, as later discussions show, horticulture has become the most dominant practice in the study area in terms of the number of families involved. In areas with favourable terrain, wet rice cultivation is highly sought after as a reliable source of food security. It has become an integral part of three villages in the study area (Karuangmuan, Ijeirong and Bakuwa), with terraces dominating in Ijeirong.

Farmers have also built on existing practices, adapting them to suit the local ecology, adjusting to labour constraints and in response to market opportunities. *Jhuming* without paddy or only for vegetables is one of these new practices and is likely to become more popular. Potato cultivation by Akhui farmers and chilli cultivation by Shingra farmers are traditional practices which have intensified recently. However, turmeric cultivation in Bakuwa village and vegetable cultivation on the banks of the Barak river by Chiuluan farmers are new practices that have emerged in response to demand from the market.

Diversification can also be seen in the way in which farmers have started to cultivate multiple varieties of fields at the same time. Each household manages three fields and farms on average. Ijeirong farmers have a remarkable 3.4 plantations to add to two fields per household. This trend suggests that farmers no longer depend exclusively on shifting agriculture. This is perhaps what Ramakrishnan meant when he argued for diversification "to take the pressure off shifting agriculture."[35]

Across space, farmers with better access to markets (Chiuluan, Karuangmuan, Akhui) have diversified away from *jhuming* more than others (Shingra). Shingra is the only village in the study area where *jhuming* is more important

---

35   P. S. Ramakrishnan, "Shifting Agriculture in Transition: The Way Forward," in *Shifting Agriculture in Asia: Implications for Environmental Conservation and Sustainable Livelihood*, ed. K. G. Saxena, Luohui Liang, and Kanok Rerkasem (Dehra Dun: Bishen Singh Mahendra Pal Singh, 2007), 1–16.

TABLE 7.4   Diversity of agrarian practices in the study area

Field type	Chiuluan (D1) No. of HHs	% of total	Akhui (D2) No. of HHs	% of total	Karuangmuan (D1) No. of HHs	% of total	Ijeirong (D3) No. of HHs	% of total	Bakuwa (D4) No. of HHs	% of total	Shingra (D5) No. of HHs	% of total
Total farming HHs	78		69		83		43		36		68	
Horticulture	67	85.9	65	94.2	81	97.6	42	97.7	36	100	57	83.8
Jhum paddy	43	55.1	52	75.4	2	2.4	25	58.1	14	38.9	64	94.1
Jhum veg. field	6	7.7	2	2.9	43	51.8	12	27.9	9	25.0	4	5.9
Wet rice/terrace	-	-	-	-	45	54.2	36	83.7	32	88.9	9	13.2
Jhum + Wet rice	-	-	-	-	-	-	26	60.5	10	27.8	7	10.3
Potato field	-	-	57	82.6	-	-	-	-	-	-	1	1.5
Chilli field	-	-	4	5.8	-	-	-	-	3	8.3	23	33.8
Turmeric field	-	-	-	-	-	-	-	-	27	75.0	1	1.5
Vegetable field	16	20.5	-	-	-	-	-	-	-	-	-	-
Others	8	10.3	6	8.7	2	2.4	-	-	-	-	1	1.5
Avg. no. of fields per farming HH	1.3		2.2		1.6		2.0		2.4		1.6	
Avg. no. of plantations per farming HH	1.5		1.7		3.1		3.4		1.9		1.5	

TABLE 7.4   Diversity of agrarian practices in the study area (*cont.*)

Field type	Chiuluan (D1)		Akhui (D2)		Karuangmuan (D1)		Ijeirong (D3)		Bakuwa (D4)		Shingra (D5)	
	No. of HHs	% of total	No. of HHs	% of total	No. of HHs	% of total	No. of HHs	% of total	No. of HHs	% of total	No. of HHs	% of total
Total HHs surveyed	95		72		88		43		36		68	
No agriculture	17		3		5		1		0		0	

Notes:

"HHs" denotes "Households." Also in other tables.

Farming households include any household involved in any form of agricultural work. One household may have *jhum* fields, wet rice fields and plantations.

Other households may be managing with only one plantation or a potato field.

Others include ginger fields, kitchen garden and sugar cane fields

than horticulture with 94 per cent of households still involved in it. As later discussions show, they are also more dependent on it. Even though a handful of households are experimenting with new practices, the bulk of their labour is still directed towards ensuring food security. By contrast, all other villages have more families involved in horticulture. Qualitatively though, the villages of Chiuluan, Karuangmuan and Akhui have benefitted most from diversification, aided by easy access to markets.

3.2   Mainstreaming of Horticulture

Perhaps the most distinctive marker of the shift away from *jhuming* is the way in which horticulture has become mainstream. It has overtaken *jhuming* to become the most prominent agrarian practice with more than 80 per cent of farming households managing at least one plantation across all the villages (Table 7.4). Many families have, in fact, moved out of *jhuming* to focus on horticulture. The economy of Karuangmuan village, for instance, is almost entirely based on banana plantations. Many salaried households have also invested in plantations with the aim of making a profit.

The almost ubiquitous presence of horticulture in the region is unique to the present. Fruit trees have always been an essential part of the home garden. In the past, growing fruit trees was a secondary activity that mainly completed the food basket and supplemented monetary income. However, the rise of urban centres of demand coupled with improved access to these areas, along with government incentives, have quickly propelled horticulture as the most important agrarian practice today.

This is highly significant because it marks a radical shift from producing to fulfil subsistence needs, as in traditional *jhuming*, to producing for the market for monetary income. Table 7.6 shows the distribution of plantations and horticultural farms by type. It provides a broad glimpse of the scale of horticulture in the study area. The cultivation of native species, such as orange, banana, and timber trees, is most common.[36] Cane is, however, native to and cultivated on a large scale only in Ijeirong village. Farmers are also experimenting with other varieties, mainly in response to demands from the market. For instance, *galgal*, also known as hill lemon (*Citrus Pseudolimon*), fetches a better price than oranges and has prompted many farmers to start cultivating it on a large scale. Other emerging

---

36   *Parkia* (stink bean) was an important cash crop till the 1990s before they died en masse in the region due to various diseases. There are few surviving trees from that period. It discouraged farmers from investing in *parkia* though it does fetch a good price.

TABLE 7.5   Distribution of plantations by type (number of farms)

Plantation type	Chiuluan (D1)	Akhui (D2)	Karuangmuan (D1)	Ijeirong (D3)	Bakuwa (D4)	Shingra (D5)
Orange	82	88	10	40	2	54
Banana	10	19	233	22	6	14
Timber	3	1	4	25	42	27
Parkia	2	4	3	1		7
Pineapple	1		1	5	1	1
Bamboo	3				8	
Cane				44		
Others	17	9	1	6	12	1
Total plantations	118	121	252	143	71	104
Total farming HHs	78	69	83	42	36	68
Avg. plantations per farming HH	1.5	1.7	3.1	3.4	1.9	1.5

Note: "Others" include *galgal*, or hill lemon, jackfruit, litchi, mango, *heiribob* and *gan-lwak*.

varieties include pineapple, mango, litchi, jackfruit, *heiribob* (*Citrus Latipes*)[37] and *gan-lwak*.[38]

The villages closest to the market (Chiuluan and Karuangmuan) also have the biggest orange orchards and banana plantations. While local climatic factors have played a role (oranges are favoured in the cooler climate of Chiuluan and bananas are favoured in the warmer climate of Karuangmuan), the growth of horticulture, especially that of banana plantations in Karuangmuan is best explained through the lens of market penetration. In fact, the growth of these two horticultural crops needs to be explored in some detail.

---

37   *Heiribob* is a citrus fruit whose thick skin is dried and used to flavour non-vegetarian dishes.
38   *Gan-lwak* (in Rongmei) is a semi-wild plant with distinctive pungent leaves that are consumed mostly as chutney in early spring and rainy season. These trees grow up on their own in the first year of fallow following *jhuming*. However, some farmers have domesticated it and grow it in in plantations in order to maximise on the good price that it commands on the market.

Oranges (*Citrus Reticulata*)[39] are native to Tamenglong[40] and have been grown for more than a hundred years.[41] The seasonal nature of oranges (November to February) allows for easier marketing in the dry winter months when more labour is available. They were perhaps the most important horticultural crop in the past.[42] Today, the state promotes horticulture as an alternative to *jhuming* by sponsoring the annual "Orange Festival" of Tamenglong. The incentives provided by the state, however, benefit those who have access to capital and market mainly due to the peculiarities of growing oranges.

It takes ten years or more for orange trees to mature before farmers can begin to get profitable returns. But orange trees are highly sensitive to weedicides and, therefore, require manual weeding three to four times a year. In a context where labour has become scarce due to the out-migration of youth, poor farmers are unable to manage large farms without extra labour. As a result, the salaried rich who have access to capital and can afford to hire wage labourers manage the biggest orchards. This is seen in Chiuluan village, which has the largest orange orchards in the study area (Table 7.6). Out of the sixteen families managing a minimum of five hundred orange trees, only four families actually depended on the orchard as a major source of income. The rest of the families were salaried, with the orange orchard as an investment for additional income and for profit. This translates to a gradual cementing of economic inequality in a society which has otherwise been known to be relatively egalitarian.

The banana plantations of Karuangmuan village give rise to a different challenge. Bananas have grown in popularity recently, as an alternative to oranges. Unlike oranges, banana cultivation provides returns within a year of planting. Bananas are also harvested throughout the year and are a consistent source of income. They have become highly sought after and are especially popular

---

39   "Tamenglong Orange / Mandarin (Citrus reticulata)," Manipur Organic Mission Society, accessed 1 June 2021, https://momamanipur.com/tamenglong-orange/.

40   Sobhapati Samom, "Manipur Expects GI Tag for Its Unique Orange in Tamenglong," *Hindustan Times*, 3 September 2020, https://www.hindustantimes.com/india-news/mani pur-expects-gi-tag-for-its-unique-orange-in-tamenglong/story-4YtoxfVOJ5xmtshfUYa jsN.html.

41   Akhui village has many orange trees that are more than a hundred years old.

42   It was an important item of trade for farmers in the study region in the past. Older respondents from Shingra and Chiuluan village narrated how they would undertake a full day's journey to Phalok or Sonparam village to buy oranges at the rate of Rs. 1 for one hundred pieces. They would return to their villages, rest a day and then travel to Imphal or Sekmai to sell them at around Rs. 4–5 per one hundred pieces. The whole thing easily took up five man days, but, despite the physical rigours involved, it was considered highly profitable.

TABLE 7.6   Who owns the largest orange orchards in Chiuluan village?

Income source 1	Income source 2	No. of trees (P1 + P2 + P3)
Government job	Government job	3000 + 1000
Government job	Government job	2500 + 300 + 50
Government job	Pension	1000 + 1000 + 1000
Wage labour	Plantation (Orange)	1200 + 100
Government job	Pension	1000 + 900
Government job	Jhum vegetable and NTFP	1000 + 400
Government job	Government job	1000 + 100 (Others)
Government job	Government job	900 + 500 + 200
Government job	Government job	800 + 500
Government job	Government job	800 + 100 (Other fruits)
Pension	Vehicle owner	700 + 200 (Banana)
Plantation (Banana)	Plantation (Orange)	500 + 200 (Banana)
Private-sector job	Plantation (Orange)	500 + 100 (Banana)
Government job	Jhum vegetable and NTFP	500
Vegetable farm	Plantation (Orange)	500

Note:
"p" denotes "Plantation." also in Table 7.7.
All plantations are orange plantations unless otherwise indicated. Only plantations with five hundred trees or more on a single farm were chosen. The plantations in the table do not account for the age of the trees, which would reflect returns.

when market access is good.[43] This is exemplified by Karuangmuan village, where banana plantations exploded in the last ten years to replace shifting agriculture almost completely.

Many families manage plantations at a commercial scale with more than a thousand banana groves. These are managed with the widespread use of weedicides, such as "Roundup" by Bayer (earlier, Monsanto), and pesticides. The extensive use of these inputs levels the playing field by drastically reducing the need for labour to clear weeds. As a result, there is not too much difference in

---

43   One respondent, in fact, calculated that owning three to four hundred banana groves is equal to being a Class C primary school teacher with the government.

TABLE 7.7   Who owns the largest banana plantations in Karuangmuan village?

Income source 1	Income source 2	No. of groves (P1 + P2 + P3)
Private-sector job	Plantation (Banana)	1000 + 200
Plantation (Banana)	Private-sector job	750 + 200 + 50
Plantation (Banana)	Private-sector job	700 + 500 +400
Private-sector job	Plantation (Banana)	700 + 500 + 200
Plantation (Banana)		600 + 500 + 400
Construction worker	Plantation (Banana)	500 + 500 + 400
Plantation (Banana)		500 + 450 + 200
Plantation (Banana)		500 + 400 + 300
Private-sector job	Plantation (Banana)	500 + 400 + 350
Compensation money	Plantation (Banana)	500 + 400 + 300
Government Job	Plantation (Banana)	500 + 400 +200
Private-sector job	Plantation (Banana)	500 + 300 + 300
Plantation (Banana)		500 + 150 + 80
Mason	Plantation (Banana)	500
Animal husbandry	Plantation (Banana)	500

the economic profiles of families involved in banana plantations (Table 7.7). Those owning large banana plantations in the village included a construction worker, a mason and others engaged in private-sector jobs (private school, shops, etc.).

However, the traditional system of land rights and the process by which land is allocated for cultivation has been disregarded in favour of profit making from the plantations.[44] In addition, the large-scale use of the weedicide Roundup is bound to have implications for the health of the farmers[45] and the

---

44   In an interview, the chairman of the village Mr Jonesh Khumba replied that there has been no "*ramrai nu*" in the village for the last two years. "*Ramrai nu*" is the tradition in Inpui villages in which the elders of the village sit together and decide on which part of the village to allocate for *jhuming* that particular year. This was central to maintaining the *jhum* cycle with an appropriate fallow length.

45   Roundup is reported to have cancer-causing components and the company is being sued in various courts. Patricia Cohen, "Roundup Maker to Pay $10 Billion to Settle Cancer Suits," *New York Times*, 24 June 2020, https://www.nytimes.com/2020/06/24/business/roundup-settlement-lawsuits.html.

soil. While the long-term effects on the soil and local ecology are yet unknown, it appears that these are significant. Chiuluan and Akhui farmers report that the sustained use of Roundup hardens the soil and makes it unfit for cultivation – due to which they had given up its use. Regarding the short term, farmers from Karuangmuan report that Roundup softens the soil a few days after it has been sprayed. This has resulted in a few incidents of banana plants collapsing under their own weight on steeper slopes.

The orange orchards of Chiuluan village and the banana plantations of Karuangmuan village illustrate that horticulture has become mainstream. Most farmers are likely to shift away from traditional *jhuming* and into horticulture as roads improve and markets become more accessible. Agriculture in the region is likely to change in this direction. However, these developments also give rise to new challenges of socio-economic differentiation and ecological sustainability. In all likelihood, the current scenarios in Chiuluan and Karuangmuan are a precursor to change that will engulf the region in a short period of time.

3.3   *From Subsistence Farming to Production for Market*

The shift away from traditional *jhuming* can not only be seen in the changes outside the *jhum* field. It is also evident in the changing cropping patterns, specifically the diminishing role of paddy in the *jhum* field. In the past, food security was the primary motive for production, with almost all of the produce being consumed by the family. As farmers adapt to take advantage of market opportunities, this is no longer the case. Farmers' priorities are being reordered in such a way that crops generating good monetary returns (vegetables) are increasingly preferred over those that ensure food security (cereals).

Paddy is no longer the most important crop in a *jhum* field, except in Shingra village. This can be seen both in terms of the quantity produced and the number of months it sustains a family.[46] A family in Shingra village produces an average of 145 *tins* of paddy, more than twice the amount of paddy produced

---

46   Every family was asked about the number of months they can subsist from the paddy they produced. They were also asked about the quantity of rice they need to buy from the market in a year. This was matched with the estimated food requirements of the family, arrived at through thorough calculation. After cross-checking with various responses, it was calculated that, on average, 0.25 kilograms of rice was needed for a person for the morning meal. The amount gets reduced to 0.20 kilograms for the evening meal. A larger quantity of rice is usually prepared in the morning, keeping in mind both lunch and the midday meal. Thus, a family of five would need 1.25 kilograms (5 * 0.25) for the morning and 1 kilogram (5 * 0.20) in the evening, or a total of 2.25 kilograms a day. Of course, there are variations in the amount consumed by men, women and children. The same amount

FIGURE 7.3 *Jhum* fields in Shingra village, 2016
Note: The wet rice fields of a neighbouring village along the banks of the iring
river can be seen in the background. Shingra village has the largest *jhum* fields in
the study area and produces the maximum quantity of paddy

by Chiuluan (sixty-nine *tins*) and Akhui (seventy *tins*) (Table 7.8). The paddy
produced sustains a family for an average of almost eleven months for Shingra
village and six months for Chiuluan village (Table 7.10).

Shingra farmers cultivate paddy extensively due to the prohibitively high
costs involved in buying and transporting rice from the market.[47] On the other
hand, Chiuluan and Akhui farmers do not put as much emphasis on paddy
production, as rice can be easily procured from the market. They focus more on
growing market-friendly crops with high returns. Many farmers, especially in
Chiuluan and Akhui village, explain that paddy is grown mainly out of concern

is not consumed on a non-working day either. At the same time, most families also factor
in the needs of pets (dogs and cats, especially). Keeping in mind all these considerations,
calculations derived from this amount (250 grams for the morning and 200 grams for the
evening) generally matches the food estimates of most families.

47   A fifty-kilogram bag of rice, which costs Rs. 1,000 at Noney bazaar, incurs a transportation
cost of at least Rs. 200 when it reaches Shingra village, making the effective price Rs. 1,200.
Shingra farmers, therefore, have to spend more money than others to buy the same quantity of rice from the market. But they have to spend more time and effort compared to
others to earn the same amount of money (walking for two days to Leimakhong, Imphal).

for "health,"[48] taste, and to give "company" or "aid" in the growth of other high-value crops, such as chilli. In other words, in places with good access to markets, paddy has already taken a secondary role in the *jhum* field.

In villages such as Karuangmuan, Ijeirong and Bakuwa, where suitable terrain is available, the burden for paddy production is being shifted to wet rice fields (Table 7.9). Farmers prefer cultivating paddy in wet rice or terrace fields over *jhum* fields for a number of reasons: it is less labour-intensive both in field preparation and weeding, paddy production is more consistent over time, and paddy from wet rice fields is softer and tastier. Though suitable land for wet rice fields is scarce, the fields are central to the food security needs of the farmers who own them. For instance, the bulk of paddy that sustains Bakuwa farmers for 10.8 months is derived from wet rice paddy (tables 7.9, 7.10). In addition, 55 per cent of Karuangmuan households who cultivate wet rice paddy depend on it to provide food for 8.4 months (Table 7.10).

Table 7.10 suggests that the degree of market accessibility determines whether farmers produce for the market or for subsistence. In villages with good market access (Chiuluan, Akhui and Karuangmuan), at least 70 per cent of families depend on the market for food. By contrast, when markets are relatively difficult to access (Ijeirong, Bakuwa and Shingra) farmers prioritise being self-sufficient in food production (67 per cent of families and above), through *jhum*, wet rice cultivation or a combination of both.

With reference to the Southeast Asian context, Cramb et al. note that there are two stages of transition from subsistence to production for the market.[49] The first stage involves farmers using spare land and labour to produce for the market – a characteristic of Shingra, Bakuwa and Ijeirong farmers. The second stage involves using spare land and labour for subsistence – found in Chiuluan and Karuangmuan village, and to an extent in Akhui village. In the study area, however, both stages seem to be at work simultaneously, mediated by unequal access to markets.

The obvious advantage of generating income from *jhuming* in villages close to the market is reflected in Figure 7.4.[50] The huge gap in earnings amongst the villages can be properly appreciated in the context of Table 7.4 (which details the number of families engaged in *jhuming*) and Table 7.8 (which shows

---

48   Food is prepared by mixing rice produced from the *jhum* field and rice bought from the market.
49   Cramb et al., "Swidden Transformations," 327.
50   Karuangmuan village is an outlier, because it has mostly given up on traditional *jhuming*. Their *jhum* vegetable fields are small scale and done mainly for subsistence, as maximum labour is devoted to banana plantations.

TABLE 7.8 Paddy production from *jhum* fields

Harvest (in *tins*)	Chiuluan		Akhui		Ijeirong		Bakuwa		Shingra	
	No. of HHs	% of total farming HHs	No. of HHs	% of total farming HHs	No. of HHs	% of total farming HHs	No. of HHs	% of total farming HHs	No. of HHs	% of total farming HHs
0–50	24	55.8	22	42.3	19	76	10	83.3	8	12.5
51–100	12	27.9	22	42.3	6	24	2	16.6	15	23.4
100–150	3	6.98	6	11.5					15	23.4
151–200	1	2.33	2	3.8					16	25.0
> 200	3	6.98							12	18.7
Total harvest	2977		3642		944		316		9287	
Jhuming HHs	43		52		25		12		64	
Total HHs	95		72		43		36		68	
Average production per farming HH	69.23		70.0		37.8		26.3		145.1	

TABLE 7.9   Paddy production from wet rice or terrace fields

Harvest (in *tins*)	Karuangmuan		Ijeirong		Bakuwa		Shingra	
	No. of HHS	% of total farming HHS	No. of HHS	% of total farming HHS	No. of HHS	% of total farming HHS	No. of HHS	% of total farming HHS
0–50	11	23.4	7	20	2	6.3	1	14.3
51–100	12	25.5	10	28.6	11	34.4	2	28.6
101–150	9	19.1	12	34.3	5	15.6	1	14.3
151–200	5	10.6	6	17.1	9	28.1	3	42.9
> 200	10	21.4			5	15.6		
Total Harvest	6293		4201		4815		880	
HHS doing WR	47		35		32		7	
Total HHS	88		43		36		68	
Average production per farming HH	133.9		105.0		150.5		125.7	

Note:
1 *tin* holds approximately 7 kg of paddy (or, approx. 14 kg of rice)
1 tin = 7 kg; 100 kg = 1 quintal; 50 *tins* = 3.5 quintals
200 *tins* = 14 quintals = 1.4 metric tons
9287 *tins* = 650 quintals = 65 metric tons
6293 *tins* = 440 quintals = 44 metric tons

the production of paddy). A typical *jhum* farmer from Chiuluan village earns almost five times more cash than his counterpart in Shingra village with a larger field (even though Shingra farmers produce twice as much paddy; see Table 7.8). A closer analysis reveals that farmers from Chiuluan and Akhui village sell mostly vegetables and other perishable goods. By contrast, Shingra farmers mostly sell non-perishable goods such as ash gourd, dried beans and dried chilli in the dry winter months.[51]

---

51   The relatively higher average income of Shingra farmers as compared to Ijeirong and Bakuwa farmers must be understood in the context of much larger *jhum* fields in Shingra village. Farmers in these two villages distribute their labour across wet rice fields.

TABLE 7.10   Main sources of food security

| Villages | Paddy from field (*Jhum* + wet rice) | | | Rice from the market |
	Paddy cultivating HHS (% of total)	Avg. no. of months sustained by local paddy	HHS dependent on local paddy (% of total)	HHS (farming + non-farming) dependent on rice from the market (% of total)
Chiuluan (D1)	45.3	5.9	13.7	86.3
Akhui (D2)	72.2	7.1	29.2	70.8
Karuangmuan (D1)	55.6	8.4	28.4	71.6
Ijeirong (D3)	95.3	10.1	67.4	32.6
Bakuwa (D4)	100	10.8	88.9	11.1
Shingra (D5)	97.1	10.7	77.9	22.1

Note: A family is considered to be primarily dependent on locally produced paddy (*jhum* + wet rice) if it sustains them for at least eight months or two-thirds of the year

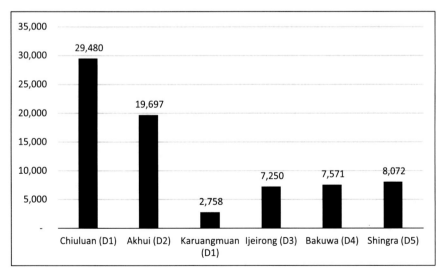

FIGURE 7.4   Graph showing the income of *jhum* farmers from different villages

The changing role of the *jhum* field as a source of income is captured by the story of Mrs Kambuiliu Gangmei (forty-three years old), a *jhum* farmer from Chiuluan village. Her work cycle incorporates both farming and marketing, as she takes on the dual role of a farmer as well as a vegetable vendor in Tamenglong bazaar. Prior to the weekly "market day,"[52] she harvests crops that can be sold at the market. These include green leaves, vegetables, maize and chilli, depending on the season. After returning home, she organises and arranges the vegetables, preparing them for sale the next day. On the "market day" she makes her way to the market at dawn. In the past, she would walk along with other women, but commercial vehicles that started plying the route recently bring her to the market in minutes. By eight o'clock in the morning, she has either finished selling her vegetables or sold the unsold ones to a retailer at a wholesale rate. After arriving back home and refreshing herself, she heads to her field where she spends half the day tending to it. The other half is spent in gathering crops and vegetables that can be sold the next day. This routine is repeated throughout the year with variations depending on the peaks and troughs of labour requirements.

Over the course of the whole season (2017–2018), Mrs Gangmei earned approximately seventy thousand rupees from the *jhum* field alone. This was more than twice the value of the 160 *tins* of paddy that she harvested the same year.[53] This weekly, if not daily, income from the sale of *jhum* vegetables pays the school fees for her children and helps run the family. It also goes without saying that the field provided for the kitchen needs of the family throughout the year. As *jhum* produce becomes "marketable," a subsistence form of agriculture has completely transformed into a viable source of income. It is for this reason that Chiuluan women folk often say that "we have raised our children by selling vegetables ..."

By contrast, the farmers of Shingra village are forced to sell mostly non-perishable items at the end of the year to traders who come to the village and buy from the farmers at wholesale rates. Hence, it is very common to hear Shingra farmers lamenting the terrible condition of the roads time and time again. Easy access to markets means that shifting agriculture is becoming increasingly cash oriented. In fact, farmers are innovating in order to take advantage of the new opportunities by introducing non-traditional crops, including hybrid varieties, in their *jhum* fields. At the same time, the lack of

---

52   Tamenglong bazaar has three "market days," on Tuesday, Thursday and Saturday. Though the vegetable market is open every day, the market day attracts more shoppers as well as sellers.

53   160 *tins* = Rs. 32,000 at Rs. 200 per *tin*.

access means that Shingra farmers continue to *jhum* in the traditional way. Agrarian change in the Northeastern hills of India is likely to fall somewhere between these two extremes.

4   The Implications of Agrarian Change

The unique characteristics of present-day agrarian change open up a new set of challenges that are yet to be completely understood. The traditional question of sustainability, centred on decreasing fallow length, is now open for debate, though we are faced with new questions. The immediate consequences of current agrarian change are twofold. The first is the unravelling of traditional institutions due to the rise of commercial agriculture. The second major consequence, accentuated by the breakdown of traditional institutions, pertains to the environment. The present section attempts to provide pointers in uncovering these challenges.

4.1   *Unravelling Institutions and Ramifications*
Traditional institutions that regulated shifting agriculture have come under great strain. Changing agricultural practices inform changing ideas of land and resources and, therefore, necessarily have a bearing on the efficacy of traditional institutions.[54] The fault lines are visible in the study area, where a special provision of the Constitution of India (Article 371C) allows villages to manage resources according to their traditional norms and customs.

First, as agriculture becomes market driven, it also becomes more privatised. This is more evident in horticulture, which is transitioning into a capital-intensive practice. Increased privatisation, in turn, usually involves the side-stepping of traditional practices in favour of greater returns from the land. As communal safeguards are set aside to ensure profit making, communities are in danger of descending into a cycle of unsustainable resource use and exploitation. This can have long-term repercussions both on the local ecology and society. Such a scenario is highly likely in Karuangmuan village.

Second, property rights regimes, which are generally a mix of communal-private ownership and management, are being reworked comprehensively. This is largely driven by the emergence of the permanent and semi-permanent land use systems of wet rice cultivation and horticulture. In most such cases,

---

54   Mariteuw Chimère Diaw, "Si, Nda Bot and Ayong: Shifting Cultivation, Land Use and Property Rights in Southern Cameroon" (network paper 21e, Rural Development Forestry Network, Summer 1997).

communal control is becoming redundant as the rights of individuals become more pronounced. This, in turn, is excluding farmers who do not own land from certain agrarian practices. It must be pointed out here that farmers regularly "borrow" plots of land for shifting agriculture.[55] However, this is not extended to plantations or wet rice fields, as they involve more permanent use of land.

Thus, commercial and increasingly capital-intensive agriculture is effectively restructuring society. For example, the largest owners of orange farms in Chiuluan village or Akhui village are government employees who are able to hire labour and invest in inputs. This trend is found across the board in all the villages to varying degrees. One can observe the gradual concretisation of socio-economic inequality in these once egalitarian societies. This is bound to have long-term social and ecological side effects because effective management of communal resources is not possible in a community where every member does not have an equal stake.

Third, the current study has also found cases in which traditional institutions have not evolved to meet the challenges brought on by changing agrarian practices. For instance, the system of annually demarcating areas for the purpose of shifting agriculture is not done for cultivating chilli fields (Shingra village) and turmeric fields (Bakuwa village), unlike in Akhui village, which regularly sets aside the colder, mountainous regions for potato fields. This leaves a lot of ambiguity, which farmers can exploit to their own benefit and to the detriment of the environment. Both chilli and turmeric require fresh fields every year and will most likely result in the increased fragmentation of forests in the absence of any regulation.

Fourth, institutional efficacy is also often undermined by internal contradictions, which get further accentuated by market forces, including global capital. In the region where the present study was conducted, disputes that

---

55   The six villages under study generally follow a combination of private and communal landownership and management. There are tracts of land that belong to the village, whose usage and management is directly under the village. In addition, families also own one or several plots of land in different areas of the village. However, these plots of land cannot be utilised by the family at their discretion. The community "grants" a family access to their land when their plot of land falls under the area marked by the village council for *jhuming* for that particular year. Farmers, therefore, freely "borrow" plots of fields for *jhuming* without any written agreement, with the land returning to the owner the following year. There are no costs involved in borrowing, and no share of crops given to the owner. Sometimes a token of one kilogram of sugar or chicken is given to the owner of the plot. However, fields are usually not "borrowed" for farming, as this involves a more permanent use of land. This is leading to privatisation of land with little or no communal control.

sometimes turn bloody and lengthy legal battles over ownership rights to land and resources are not uncommon. This is exacerbated by the fact that traditional rights are oral and unwritten and, therefore, open to interpretation and manipulation. Karuangmuan village had a protracted and acrimonious dispute between two clans over landownership. While the inner contestations were always present, it was triggered in 2006 when monetary compensation was announced for constructing railway tracks and a platform on the village land. The dispute resulted in a severe erosion of social capital represented by a split in the church, amongst other things.

The direct fallout of this dispute is that Karuangmuan village has not been able to continue with the traditional system of *ramrai nu*, in which the village council identifies land to be cultivated in a particular year. The situation is further exacerbated by the desire to cultivate as many banana plantations as possible. As a result, farmers are given a free hand to "open up" forests for all kinds of agrarian activity without any sort of community-imposed checks. While this may lead to short-term individual profit, it will most certainly lead to significant ecological problems later.

While the inner contestations played out in the open in the case of Karuangmuan village, there is simmering tension in almost every village. These situations threaten to get out of control and disrupt the social fabric from time to time, especially with respect to the allocation, extraction and exploitation of resources. Another potential trigger, which adds to institutional strain, is the construction of the World Bank-funded Asian Highway passing through Ijeirong and Bakuwa village.

Proactive communities and villages have sought to minimise conflict and confusion by drafting traditional rules and regulations in the form of a village constitution. Chiuluan village has written a constitution that clearly defines the norms that govern resource use. During the fieldwork, Bakuwa village was actively deliberating writing one such document. Such initiatives hint at the huge gap between constitutional provisions granting traditional institutions the right to manage their own resources and the challenges faced by local institutions in adapting to the changing socio-economic contexts driven by the market and, in some cases, by global capital.

4.2   The Ecological Consequences of Commercial Agriculture

The current agrarian changes have affected the environment in two important ways. First, the changes have led to a loss of species diversity. Second, in the context of ineffective institutions, they have led to increased forest fragmentation and the overexploitation of available land and resources. The new, "cash-oriented" nature of shifting agriculture is leading to crop specialisation;

FIGURE 7.5   The constitution of Chiuluan village

and farmers have become particularly focused on producing crops with a high
market value. The increasing number of fields dedicated to specific high-value
crops points to this trend. Farmers are cultivating less of a variety of crops as
they focus on marketability.

As a result, the genetic pool, represented by the diversity of seeds, is becoming depleted, as crops that are no longer sown are lost forever. This reduced crop diversity is clearly visible in farming communities that live closer to the market. For instance, *jhum* paddy is almost extinct in Karuangmuan village. Even in Chiuluan village, where paddy continues to be grown, only three varieties of paddy were reported by the majority of respondents. By contrast, Shingra farmers have a rich pool of over twenty varieties of paddy, not to mention other crops.

The shrinking gene pool is perhaps one of the most significant fallouts of agrarian change in the hills. However, not enough attention has been given to it. It is an invaluable loss, which compromises the resilience of the shifting agricultural system and negatively impacts farmers' food and livelihood security. It makes fields more vulnerable to pests and weeds, while exposing farmers to market uncertainties and climatic variations at the local level. At the macro level, the loss of species severely impacts efforts to mitigate the effects of climate change.

Second, the emergence of intensive commercial cultivation is likely to lead to the overexploitation and fragmentation of forests. Banana plantations in Karuangmuan village are causing pressure due to a combination of unrestricted access to forest land and the widespread use of weedicides in the plantations. As farmers prefer plantations close to the village for easy transportation, these are situated in a five-kilometre radius from the village. Land close to the village is thus in danger of overexploitation in a few years' time, as farmers have to shift to a new plot every three to five years. The likelihood of ecological challenges in the near future is exacerbated by the fact that farmers extensively employ weedicides, such as Roundup by Bayer (Monsanto), in managing banana plantations. As mentioned earlier, the commercialisation of banana plantations has been made possible by the widespread use of labour-saving techniques such as weedicides and pesticides. However, these have implications on the health and well-being of farmers as well as the environment.

The pace of forest fragmentation is also being hastened by the cultivation of turmeric, chilli and potatoes. Though the fields on which these crops are grown are usually smaller in size, they are not cultivated over compact areas, like the traditional *jhum* fields. In addition, they require fresh plots every year. In fact, farmers report that a plot of land used to grow turmeric cannot be used to grow any other crop in the next two to three years, as soil fertility is completely exhausted. In case of king chilli, farmers seek plots of land which have not been cleared for ten years or more.

The full impact of commercial farming and plantations on the environment and, in certain cases, the health of farmers is yet to be fully known. Many practices have emerged only in the last few years. However, in their wake, fragile and sensitive ecologies have come under extreme pressure. Across the board, there is a loss of crop diversity. Additionally, in cases where local traditional institutions are rendered ineffective, the environment is left to the mercy of private interests. In a context where property rights regimes are not well defined, the overexploitation of available land and resources, leading to long-term environmental degradation, is highly likely.[56]

5   Conclusion

Present-day agrarian changes in the hills of Northeast India are multilayered and uneven across space. They are driven by a host of factors, such as education, which has caused large-scale out-migration from villages to towns and cities, leading to localised population decline and contributing to lengthening fallow lengths. The improvements in connectivity, particularly roads, have also radically transformed agrarian practices as *jhum* produce found a niche market among the rapidly expanding middle class.

The present study mapped changing agrarian practices across villages with varying degrees of access to markets. It found that there is a general shift away from traditional *jhuming* towards more market-friendly practices, such as horticulture. In fact, more families are involved in orange orchards, banana plantations and other horticultural farms as compared to shifting agriculture. This is highly significant because it marks the turn from subsistence farming to producing for the market, which Harris-White et al. call a "transition to the capitalist economy."[57] This is visible within the *jhum* field itself, where farmers prefer crops with a high market value to those which ensure food security.

Agrarian transition, however, is far from uniform across space, especially with respect to distance from the market. As a result, the two distinct stages of agrarian transition identified by Cramb et al. are at work within the study area.[58] Shingra, Bakuwa and Ijeirong farmers use spare land and labour to produce for the market, while Chiuluan, Karuangmuan and Akhui farmers use their spare land and labour for subsistence. In other words, farmers who live close to towns and marketplaces prioritise income security, while those who do not have easy access to markets prioritise food security. These choices play out in the *jhum* fields and shape the *jhumscapes* – orchards and plantations on

---

56   Diaw, "Si, Nda Bot and Ayong."

57   Harris-White, Mishra and Upadhyay, "Institutional diversity," 512–47.

58   Cramb et al., "Swidden Transformations," 327.

the edge of towns, and paddy fields as one moves further away from market centres.

The current pattern of agrarian change, driven by an increasingly "cash-oriented" agriculture, is undermining the efficacy of local traditional institutions. This has ramifications for society as a whole, in which inequality is becoming concretised. Ineffective and weakened institutions are also unable to regulate private interests for sustainable resource use. In the absence of a well-defined legal framework, individual villages are responding to powerful market and global forces on their own. In the present context, efficacious and robust institutions are central to both societal and environmental sustainability.

To conclude, the transformation of shifting agriculture has taken an unlikely turn from what was expected by many experts. It has neither become obsolete nor has it disintegrated into a cycle of unsustainable resource use. On the contrary, two decades into the twenty-first century, it continues to be an important source of livelihood for farmers in the hills of Northeast India. While the geographical peculiarities of the region have certainly played a role in this transformation, the agency of farmers needs to be recognised. In fact, the large-scale disruption of markets caused by the pandemic-imposed lockdowns is expected to push farmers to *jhum* more intensely in the next few years.

In the context of climate change on the one hand and increasing market penetration on the other, the pace of agrarian change is likely to pick up. The next few decades will be crucial for sustainability, not only with respect to the environment, but also concerning the communities engaged in shifting agriculture. As traditional property rights regimes get reworked in the face of a market-driven capitalist system of production, issues of social differentiation and economic inequality are likely to become more prominent. Shifting agriculture in Northeast India is, therefore, faced with new questions of sustainability that go far beyond that of decreasing fallow lengths.

Bibliography

Boserup, Ester. *The Conditions of Agricultural Growth: The Economics of Agrarian Change under Population Pressure*. London: George Allen & Unwin, 1965.

Cairns, Malcolm, and Harold Brookfield. "Composite Farming Systems in an Era of Change: Nagaland, North-East India." *Asia Pacific Viewpoint* 52, no. 1 (2011): 56–84.

Census of India 2011. *Administrative Atlas – Manipur*. Director of Census Operations, Manipur. https://India-Census of India 2011-Administrative Atlas-Manipur (censusindia.gov.in).

Cohen, Patricia. "Roundup Maker to Pay $10 Billion to Settle Cancer Suits." *New York Times*, 24 June 2020. https://www.nytimes.com/2020/06/24/business/roundup-set tlement-lawsuits.html.

Cramb, R. A., Carol J. Pierce Colfer, Wolfram Dressler, Pinkaew Laungaramsri, Quang Trang Le, Elok Mulyoutami, Nancy L. Peluso, and Reed L. Wadley. "Swidden Transformations and Rural Livelihoods in Southeast Asia." *Human Ecology* 37 (May 2009): 323–46.

Das, Debojyoti. "Demystifying the Myth of Shifting Cultivation Agronomy in the North-East." *Economic and Political Weekly* 41, no. 47 (November – December 2006): 4912–17.

Delang, Claudio O. "Social and Economic Adaptations to a Changing Landscape: Realities, Opportunities and Constraints." In *Living at the Edge of Thai Society: The Karen in the Highlands of Northern Thailand*, edited by Claudio O. Delang, 155–82. London: Routledge Curzon, 2003.

Diaw, Mariteuw Chimère. "Si, Nda Bot and Ayong: Shifting Cultivation, Land Use and Property Rights in Southern Cameroon." Network Paper 21e, Rural Development Forestry Network, Summer 1997.

Dove, Michael R. "Theories of Cassava and the Political Economy of Ignorance." *Agroforestry Systems* 1 (1983): 85–89.

Elwin, Verrier. *The Baiga*. Delhi: Gian Publishing House, [1931] 1986.

Government of India. *Report of the Inter-Ministerial National Task Force on Rehabilitation of Shifting Cultivation Areas*. Director General of Forests and Special Secretary, Ministry of Environment and Forests, 2006.

Harris-White, Barbara, Deepak K. Mishra, and Vandana Upadhyay. "Institutional Diversity and Capitalist Transition: The Political Economy of Agrarian Change in Arunachal Pradesh, India." *Journal of Agrarian Change* 9, no. 4 (2009): 512–47.

Jackson, Kyle. "Globalizing an Indian Borderland Environment: Aijal, Mizoram, 1890–1919." *Studies in History* 32, no. 1 (2016): 39–71.

Jamir, Amba. "Shifting Options: A Case Study of Shifting Cultivation in Mokokchung District in Nagaland, India." In *Shifting Cultivation, Livelihood and Food Security: New and Old Challenges for Indigenous People in Asia*, edited by Christian Erni, 159–202. Bangkok: Food and Agricultural Organization, International Work Group for Indigenous Affairs and Asia Indigenous Peoples Pact, 2015.

Mithra, S. N. "Arunachal's Tribal Economic Formations and their Dissolution." *Economic and Political Weekly* 18, no. 43 (October 1983): 1837–46.

Ramakrishnan, Palayanoor S. "Shifting Agriculture in Transition: The Way Forward." In *Shifting Agriculture in Asia: Implications for Environmental Conservation and Sustainable Livelihood*, edited by Krishna Gopal Saxena, Luohui Liang, and Kanok Rerkasem, 1–16. Dehra Dun: Bishen Singh Mahendra Pal Singh, 2007.

Samom, Sobhapati. "Manipur Expects GI Tag for Its Unique Orange in Tamenglong." *Hindustan Times*, 3 September 2020, https://www.hindustantimes.com/india-news/manipur-expects-gi-tag-for-its-unique-orange-in-tamenglong/story-4YtoxfVOJ5xmtshfUYajsN.html.

Sharma, K. Sarojkumar. "Okram Ibobi Singh Inaugurates Two More Districts." *Times of India*, 17 December 2016, https://timesofindia.indiatimes.com/city/imphal/okram-ibobi-singh-inaugurates-two-more-districts/articleshow/56030775.cms.

Vliet, Nathalie van, Ole Mertz, Andreas Heinimann, Tobias Laganke, Unai Pascual, Birgit Schmook, Cristina Adams et al. "Trends, Drivers and Impacts of Changes in Swidden Cultivation in Tropical Forest Agriculture Frontiers: A Global Assessment." *Global Environmental Change* 22 (January 2012): 418–29.

Watson, James W. "Geography – A discipline in distance." *Scottish Geographical Magazine* 71 (1955): 1–13.

Wouters, Jelle J. P. "Keeping the Hill Tribes at Bay: A Critique from India's Northeast of James C. Scott's Paradigm of State Evasion." *European Bulletin of Himalayan Research* 39 (2012): 41–65.

PART 2

Coerced Labour Relations in the Global Countryside

∵

CHAPTER 8

Cassava, Cacao and Catechesis

Agriculture and Extractivism in the Jesuit Missions on the Amazon in the Seventeenth and Eighteenth Centuries

Karl Heinz Arenz

1 Introduction

Many of the Jesuit missions that were scattered throughout the Amazon valley during the seventeenth and eighteenth centuries are considered by historians to be the "cradles" of present-day cities in the northern part of Brazil.[1] In fact, the widespread network of these religious settlements, known as *aldeamentos*, interlinked the most important strategic points within the vast Amazonian floodplain. This unique environment guaranteed good conditions for agricultural and extractivist activities due to the annual flooding of the Amazon River and the humid tropical conditions. Some of the first descriptions of the region clearly indicate its natural richness and economic potential,[2] rather than predominantly referring to the legendary city of *El Dorado*.[3] Thus, regardless of their inherent capacity for later urban development, the missions, as they were conceived by the religious, had, above all, a rural character which they maintained up to their official transformation into *vilas*, that is, semiurban

---

1 Rhuan Carlos dos Santos Lopes, "'Novos ditames de racionalidade': O Diretório dos Índios e a urbanização na Amazônia colonial (1751–1759)," *Perspectiva Amazônica* 2, no. 3 (January 2012): 31–45; Décio de Alencar Guzmán, "A primeira urbanização: Mamelucos, índios e europeus nas cidades pombalinas da Amazônia, 1751–1757," *Revista de Cultura do Pará* 18, no. 1 (January 2008): 75–94; Renata Malcher de Araújo, "A razão na selva: Pombal e a reforma urbana na Amazônia," *Camões – Revista de Letras e Culturas Lusófonas* 15–16 (January/June 2003): 151–65; Manuel Nunes Dias, "Estratégia Pombalina de urbanização do espaço amazônico," *Brotéria – Cultura e Informação* 115, no. 2–4 (August – October 1982): 239–305.

2 Symão Estacio da Sylveira, *Relação sumaria das cousas do Maranhão* (Lisbon: Imprensa Nacional, [1624] 1911); Luís Figueira, "Memorial sobre as terras, e gentes do Maranhão, Grão-Pará, e Rio das Amazonas [1637]," *Revista do Instituto de História e Geografia Brasileiro* 94, no. 148 (1923): 429–32; Maurício de Heriarte, *Descripção do estado do Maranhão, Pará, Coropá e rio das Amazonas* (Vienna: Impr. De Karl Gerold, [1664] 1874).

3 Neide Godim, *A invenção da Amazônia* (São Paulo: Marco Zero, 1994), 11–138.

communities under direct civil administration, from 1756 onwards.[4] It is worth mentioning that, in this process, certain traditional production methods of the indigenous peoples, such as the gathering – or extraction – of plants, roots and oils in the tropical rainforest, were integrated into the colonial economy, which was based on strategic commercialisation. This junction of traditional activities and mercantilist logic is comprised in the term "extractivism."[5]

This chapter analyses the multiple agricultural and extractive activities in the missions, with special regard to the gathering and planting of cacao along the swampy riverbanks and the nearby rainforest, as well as the cultivation of cassava on the rather poor sandy soil of the Amazon basin, in the context of colonisation during the second half of the seventeenth and the first half of the eighteenth century. This period can be considered as a time of profound crisis on account of the uninterrupted series of wars, epidemics and conquests that affected large areas of nearly all continents. With its global network of trade routes and trading posts, the Portuguese Empire was not exempt from the impact of these crises.

Thus, a long-lasting economic depression (1670–1700) accompanied the successive decline of Lusitanian influence during the second half of the seventeenth century, especially in Southern Asia, and its subsequent concentration on the Atlantic space. There were several reasons for this development: first, the growing competition between the French, English and Dutch, installed in the Caribbean islands, and their Luso-Brazilian counterparts, when it came to sugar and tobacco production; second, the indebtedness of the Portuguese Crown as a consequence of the constant quarrels with the Castilians (from the ascent of the Bragança dynasty in 1640); finally, the suppression of the long tolerated and profitable smuggling of slaves to the Spanish colonies in South America. In response, Portugal began to centralise and rationalise its administrative structures and to launch new economic initiatives, like other Western European countries at that time.[6]

The policy of the king, Dom Pedro II, and his finance minister, Luís de Meneses, Count of Ericeira, has to be highlighted in this context. From the

---

4   Rafael Chambouleyron, Karl Heinz Arenz, and Vanice Siqueira de Melo, "Ruralidades indígenas na Amazônia colonial," *Boletim do Museu Paraense Emílio Goeldi – Ciências Humanas* 15, no. 1 (January 2020): 7–12.

5   Martine Droulers, *Brésil: Une géohistoire* (Paris: Presses Universitaires de France, 2001), 71.

6   Luiz Felipe de Alencastro, "L'économie politique des découvertes maritimes," in *L'autre rive de l'Occident*, ed. Adauto Novaes (Paris: Métailié, 2006), 71–74; Jean-François Labourdette, *Histoire du Portugal* (Paris: Fayard, 2000), 343–423; Frédéric Mauro, *Des produits et des hommes: Essais historiques latino-américains XVIe – XXe siècles* (Paris and The Hague: Mouton/ École pratique des Hautes Études, 1972), 70.

1670s, the Crown sought to promote domestic production in continental Portugal (mostly textile and wine) to equalise the trade balance, marked by an excess of imports and a decline in net exports. The measures had clear mercantilist characteristics and were also aimed at stimulating the consumption of domestic products, both in the motherland and the colonies. In this context, the Crown gave priority to overseas production, and was particularly focused on agricultural and silvicultural output from its two American possessions, Brazil and Maranhão.[7] However, another commercial depression, following an overproduction of sugar and tobacco, two key commodities during the 1680s, and the suicide of the Count of Ericeira in 1690, compromised the economic recovery of Portugal.[8]

Throughout this period, the Society of Jesus proved to be a loyal supporter of the Bragança dynasty that came to power in 1640. Father António Vieira (1608–1697) had been one of the closest counsellors of Dom João VI, its first king, before crossing the ocean, in 1652, in order to re-establish the Jesuit Maranhão Mission, which officially comprised the entire Amazon region under Portuguese rule.[9] In 1655, Vieira even obtained the official tutorship of the Society of Jesus over the colony's indigenous populations. This momentous decision played an important role in the application of the economic plans conceived under Dom Pedro II between 1676 and 1682. Thus, in 1680, Vieira helped to conceive a law that intended to create a flexible labour market by declaring the indigenous people free, but maintained the fathers' control over them. However, the growing discontent of the local Portuguese settlers, who felt marginalised by the Crown, led to an uprising, during which the Jesuits were expelled from São Luís, in 1684. Subsequent negotiations in Lisbon resulted in the *Regimento das Missões*, a statute that granted considerable autonomy to the missions and regulated the annual allocation of indigenous labourers to settlers and authorities. Apart from some substantial modifications, this law was valid until 1755, when the Jesuits lost the temporal, that is, civilian, administration over the *aldeamentos*. Up until then, the *Regimento*

---

7   From 1621 to 1772, the Portuguese possessions in South America consisted of two separated administrative entities: the State of Brazil and the State of Maranhão and Grão-Para (since 1751, Grão-Pará and Maranhão). Most of the Amazon basin was located in the latter state.

8   Joel Serrão and António Henrique de Oliveira Marques, eds., *Nova história de Portugal*, vol. 7 (Lisbon: Presença, 2001), 197–213, 271–74; Albert-Alain Bourdon, *Histoire du Portugal* (Paris: Chandeigne, 1994), 70–74; Rafael Chambouleyron, *Povoamento, ocupação e agricultura na Amazônia colonial (1640–1706)* (Belém: Açaí, 2010), 77–169.

9   Alencastro, "L'économie politique," 80–81.

also constituted the legal framework for the economic ventures of the Society of Jesus in the region.[10]

In order to analyse these activities, the chapter mainly draws on Jesuit sources, especially the chronicle and the reports of Father João Felipe Bettendorff (1625–1698), the treatises of Father João Daniel (1722–1776) and, to a lesser degree, the notes of Fathers Lourenço Kaulen (1716–1799) and Anselmo Eckart (1721–1809). Father Bettendorff, who was born in Luxembourg, spent nearly four decades (1661–1698) in the Amazon region. Father Daniel, who was from Portugal, lived in the colony for fifteen years (1744–1759), before being expelled in 1757. Fathers Kaulen and Eckart, who were both of German origin, spent a rather brief time in the colony (1751/1753–1757), and were also among the expellees of 1757.[11] First, the chapter examines the missions as relevant production sites and as the living places of the indigenous labour force. After that, it investigates first the extractive and then the agricultural activities. As we will see, these overlap and are actually difficult to separate, although the extraction of vegetal products from the rainforest has generally been identified as the most common form of economic production in colonial Amazonia.[12] In the analysis, the chapter does not only consider commercial and technical aspects, but also the impact of indigenous traditions and knowledge.

2   The Mission Network and the Indigenous Labour Force

The main purpose of the missions was the evangelisation of the indigenous populations and their submission to a Catholic sovereign by confining them

---

10   Karl Heinz Arenz and Diogo Costa Silva, *"Levar a luz de nossa santa fé aos sertões de muita gentilidade": Fundação e consolidação da missão jesuíta na Amazônia portuguesa (século XVIII)* (Belém: Açaí, 2012), 52–68; Beatriz Perrone-Moisés, "Índios livres e índios escravos: os princípios da legislação indigenista do período colonial (séculos XVI a XVIII)," in *História dos índios no Brasil*, ed. Manuela Carneiro da Cunha (São Paulo: Companhia das Letras, 1992), 117–23.

11   Karl Heinz Arenz, "Do Alzette ao Amazonas: Vida e obra do padre João Felipe Bettendorff (1625–1698)," *Revista Estudos Amazônicos* 5, no. 1 (2010): 25–78; Karl Heinz Arenz, "A vasta Amazônia em poucas páginas: Os tratados do padre João Daniel da Vice-Província do Maranhão (século XVIII)," in *Escritas e leituras: temas, fontes e objetos na Iberoamérica, séculos XVI – XIX*, ed. Eliane Cristina Deckmann Fleck and Mauro Dillmann (São Leopoldo: Oikos/Unisinos, 2017), 91–118; Karl Heinz Arenz, "O 'tapuitinga' Anselm Eckart e os índios da Amazônia portuguesa (1753–1757)," in *Anais do 30° Simpósio Nacional de História: História e o futuro da educação no Brasil*, ed. Márcio Ananias Ferreira Vilela (Recife: Associação Nacional de História – ANPUH, 2019), 1–16.

12   Droulers, *Brésil*, 71.

within an extensive network of interconnected rural settlements. There, they lived as neophytes and catechumens according to a routine of repetitive catechesis and compulsory labour. For example, in all missions, before going to the fields or workshops (for example pottery and carpentry), the Indians were obliged, even before dawn, to attend mass and listen to a catechetical lesson, which was repeated in the evening followed by baroque devotional practices (mainly processions, litanies and chants).[13] In order to maintain this convent-like way of life, preferably without external interference, the fathers used to set up the missions at some distance from the European settlements (small towns, farms and forts), but always alongside the strategic natural axis constituted by the Amazon River and its numerous tributaries.

According to their specific tasks, there were, roughly speaking, four types of missions: a) the farms, or *fazendas*, attached to one of the two urban Jesuit colleges in Belém and São Luís (generally situated in the surroundings of these towns); b) the villages exclusively dedicated to royal service (such as the saltworks on the Atlantic coast); c) the so-called *aldeamentos de repartição*, missions whose male labour force was annually inventoried and assigned to either external (to settlers or authorities) or internal work; d) the *aldeamentos de doutrina*, small establishments dedicated to religious instruction, especially for groups who had recently come into contact with the missionaries and who were exempt from external labour for at least two years.[14]

In the eighteenth century, the farms played an essential role in the subsistence of the urban colleges and in the production of supplies for the missions in the distant backcountry, known as *sertão*. The larger ones possessed sugar mills, sugar cane, cacao and cassava plantations, as well as facilities and pasture for livestock breeding and small workshops for the production of canoes, furniture, ceramics or cotton cloth.[15] Internal statistics from 1747 mention fourteen important farms: five in the Maranhão captaincy, on the outskirts of São Luis (Anindiba, São Brás, Amandijuí, São Marcos and Maracu), and nine in the Pará captaincy, near Belém (Marajoaçu, Arari, Mortigura, Samaúma, Jaguarari,

13   "Direção do que se deve observar nas Missões do Maranhão," in Serafim Leite, *História da Companhia de Jesus no Brasil*, vol. 4 (Rio de Janeiro and Lisbon: Instituto Nacional do Livro/Livraria Portugalia, 1943), 112–113 (pars. 14 and 16).

14   Leite, *História*, vol. 4, 99–103; Johannes Meier and Fernando Amado Aymoré, *Jesuiten aus Zentraleuropa in Portugiesisch- und Spanisch-Amerika: ein bio-bibliographisches Handbuch*, vol. 1 (Münster: Aschendorff Verlag, 2005), 106.

15   Leite, *História*, vol. 3, 249, 279–280; Dauril Alden, *The Making of an Enterprise: The Society of Jesus in Portugal, its Empire and beyond, 1540–1750* (Stanford: Stanford University Press, 1996), 421.

Ibirajuba, Mamaiacu, Gibirié and Curuçá).[16] These farms, run by the missionaries, are frequently cited in official documents from the eighteenth century as
objects of constant contention, as they concentrated most of the labour force
that was urgently needed by the settlers (as farm workers) or by the authorities
(as rowers, auxiliary soldiers or workers for the construction of public buildings). Within this context, the Jesuits were charged for accumulating wealth
and retaining native workers for their own ventures.[17]

By contrast, in the seventeenth century, the *fazendas* of the religious orders,
as well as all agricultural and extractivist activities, were still mainly projects
involving the cooperation of missionaries and colonial authorities. At the same
time, even if it seems contradictory, the Jesuits never forbade compulsory work
and even allowed the enslavement of indigenous people under certain conditions. In this regard, they largely agreed with the settlers and the authorities on
the exploitation and integration of the native populations into colonial society.
The principal disagreement was over the interpretation and implementation of
indigenous labour laws. Father Vieira, superior of the Jesuit missions from 1653
to 1661, clarified his order's position in Lisbon in January 1662, after having been
expelled from the Amazon region for categorically rejecting any kind of illegal
Indian slavery, in the following terms: "It is not my intention that there may not
be any slaves; after all, I tried at this royal court [in 1655], as it is well known and
one can see from my proposal, that a council of the greatest scholars should be
established for this item and that the cases of legal captivity should be defined
by law. But because we [the Jesuits] want the legal ones and are against the
illegal ones, they [the settlers] don't like us in that colony and, therefore, they
throw us out of it."[18]

Shortly after his arrival in the region in 1653, Vieira drew up a regulation
(although his authorship has not clearly been proved) obliging the authorities to make sure that the Indians who had been "rescued" – that is, purchased from other Indians who had kept them as prisoners – should always
be given sufficient time and land to plant and harvest what they needed for

---

16   "Catalogus brevis Personarum V. Provinciæ Maragnonensis, 1747," *Biblioteca Pública de
      Évora*, cod. CXV/2-11, n. 8, fols. 165v–166r; Leite, *História*, vol. 3, 135–142, 235–252, 299–311.
17   José Alves de Souza Júnior, *Tramas do cotidiano: Religião, política, guerra e negócios no
      Grão-Pará dos setecentos* (Belém: Editora da UFPA, 2012), 143–329; Raimundo Moreira das
      Neves Neto, *Um patrimônio em contendas: Os bens jesuíticos e a magna questão dos dízi-
      mos no Estado do Maranhão e Gráo-Pará (1650–1750)* (Jundiaí: Paco Editorial, 2013), 17–109.
18   Antônio Vieira, *Sermões escolhidos: Texto integral* (São Paulo: Martin Claret, 2004), 175.
      Translated from Portuguese by the author.

their livelihood.[19] It is worth mentioning that this proposal was conceived in the early stages of colonisation, when there was a dynamic of extreme mobility of Indians, missionaries and soldiers. Some years later, between 1658 and 1660, when the network of the *aldeamentos* was already being consolidated and most of the Indians were, accordingly, confined within them, Father Vieira wrote a statute which simply presupposed agricultural activities in and around the missions. By the way, the very few direct economic instructions, that are mentioned in the document, relate exclusively to outside services.[20]

Unfortunately, we know very little about the specific working conditions of indigenous workers within the *aldeamentos*, as the missionaries' reports do not point out every detail of daily life. In this regard, the letter that Father Ascenso Gago wrote on the strategic mission in the Ibiapaba Hills in 1694, is very instructive. This report is about the introduction of agricultural methods, the distribution of tools and, above all, the implementation of a strict work routine within this village.[21] The letter methodically shows the various steps involved in setting up a mission. Thus, after the act of vassalage and the execution of the first catechetical instructions and sacramental rites (such as baptisms and marriages), the missionary in charge introduced a severe timetable in order to accustom the Indians, who were considered to be undisciplined, to daily discipline. After that, the priest provided the Indian chiefs with tools, which he received from the authorities and nearby living settlers, so that the cultivation of fields could begin, along with the teaching of craft skills. The document also mentions that the *Tapuias*, as indigenous speakers of non-Tupi languages were called, were purposely overlooked during the distribution of plots of land and tools, as they were considered less reliable due to their nomadic way of life (which actually revolved around regular seasonal migrations), which was interpreted as evidence of inconstancy.[22]

---

19 "Modo como se há de governar o gentio que há nas aldeias de Maranhão e Pará," *Biblioteca da Ajuda*, Lisbon, cod. 49-IV-23, nr. 30, fols. 137r/v [pars. 1, 4, 7 and 12].

20 "Direção do que se deve observar nas Missões do Maranhão," in Leite, *História*, vol. 4, 121 [pars. 42 and 43].

21 "Carta ânua do que se tem obrado na missão da Serra de Ibiapaba," in Leite, *História*, vol. 3, 38–56.

22 In general, the Jesuits and other religious orders preferred and promoted the Tupi-speaking populations. Communication with these peoples was easier, as there already existed a lingua franca known as "*Língua Geral*," whose use was systematically propagated by the missionaries. See: José Ribamar Bessa Freire, *Rio Babel: A história das línguas na Amazônia* (Rio de Janeiro: EduERJ, 2011), 15–42. As an example, we can cite Father João Felipe Bettendorff, who refers to the marginalisation of Tapuia peoples (Cambocas and Nheengaíbas) in the mission farm of Mortigura. See: João Felipe Bettendorff, *Crônica dos*

In a certain way, more than fierce competitors, settlers and missionaries were close and interdependent partners, at least as far as the regional economy was concerned. Thus, every year they did not only divide the indigenous workers among themselves according to the applicable provisions – even if they very often disagreed on the terms of allocation, treatment and remuneration –, but they also produced and commercialised nearly the same commodities. Nevertheless, it was mainly traditional indigenous know-how that enabled a relatively stable food production (primarily, manioc flour, the main staple food) as well as the seasonal gathering of tropical rainforest products (especially cacao, clove bark, sarsaparilla roots and copaiba oil). For this reason, in the early days of colonisation, formal alliances with the most important indigenous groups were vital for the European colonisers, as they enabled the settlers to establish themselves in the still unfamiliar tropical environment. To use a metaphor of Nádia Farage, certain native peoples were their "bulwark in the hinterland."[23] From the mid-seventeenth century onward, the insertion of more and more indigenous groups into colonial society, primarily by confining and supervising them in the missions, was the fundament for its further economic development, as has already been emphasised.

Until recently, the scholarship tended nearly exclusively to stress, according to the established logic of mercantilism, the importance of extractivism and the exportation of the *drogas do sertão* (forest products), and overlooked the contribution of Amazonian Indians to the colonial economy. Contemporary Jesuit documents and Portuguese trade registers, however, show how European and native production methods intermingled and diversified, thus ensuring not only the subsistence of the mission villages, but also the provisioning of local markets and even global commercial networks. Occupying strategic points in the *várzea* (the fertile floodplain along the riverbanks), in close linkage to the surrounding *sertão* (the vast backcountry covered with dense tropical forest), these rural settlements turned out to be the territorial – or, more adequately, the fluvial – basis for the complex system of socio-economic dynamics that was emerging in the Amazon region. Mainly for that reason, at the end of the seventeenth century, the tropical colony was gaining importance within the Atlantic-centred Portuguese Empire.

Among the different commodities, it was, without any doubt, cassava and cacao that made the colony work. In fact, cassava, with its many varieties,

---

     Padres da Companhia de Jesus no Estado do Maranhão (Belém: Fundação Cultural do Pará Tancredo Neves/Secretaria de Estado da Cultura, [1698] 1990), 157.

23   Nádia Farage, *As muralhas dos sertões: Os povos indígenas no rio Branco e a colonização* (Rio de Janeiro: Paz e Terra/ANPOCS, 1991).

was the most important staple food all over the northern and central parts of South America, and also spread to Africa and Asia relatively fast, thanks to the intense Portuguese trading dynamics. At the same time, cacao was appreciated as one of the most profitable tropical commodities in Europe's aristocratic and bourgeois circles. As the two plants both have their origin in the Amazon basin, the indigenous peoples of the region had, over the course of hundreds, if not thousands of years accumulated a vast knowledge related to these two tropical products. Especially the cassava with its many by-products, such as starch, tapioca, *beiju* (flat cakes), *cauim* (a fermented beverage) and, above all, flour (made by toasting and granulating the pulpy mass squeezed out of the smashed roots), was an essential component of the regional diet, both for the natives and for the colonisers. Fathers Anselm Eckart and João Daniel describe the production procedures of manioc flour, reputed as being the "bread of the region," and other correlated products in great detail, as well as the various indigenous methods of cultivating and gathering cacao.[24] Thus, in the truest sense of the word, all the knowledge about what to do with the cassava roots and where to find the cacao trees in the rainforest was concentrated in the *aldeamentos* run by the missionaries.

3   The Extractivist Activities and the Importance of the *Sertões*

Even more than the network of military forts, the missions proved to be efficiently functioning outposts of the Portuguese empire in the vast hinterland. The *padroado*, i.e., the patronage of the Crown over ecclesiastical and missionary activities, is at the origin of this strategic task of the *aldeamentos*, at least until the mid-eighteenth century.[25] Thus, the numerous catechetical settlements along the Amazon River and its main tributaries constituted a kind of corridor that can be characterised, according to the words of Daniel Nordman,

---

24   "Papeis do P. Ancelmo Eschard," *Instituto das Arquivos Nacionais/Torre do Tombo*, Lisbon, sec. Ministério dos Negócios Eclesiásticos e da Justiça (MNEJ)/Papéis Pombalinos (PP), cod. 59, no. 4; João Daniel, *Tesouro descoberto no máximo rio Amazonas*, vol. 1 (Rio de Janeiro: Contraponto, 2004), 413–19.

25   The British historian Charles Ralph Boxer defined the Portuguese patronage "as a combination of rights, privileges and duties granted by the papacy to the Crown of Portugal as patron of Roman Catholic missions and ecclesiastical institutions in vast regions of Asia and Brazil": Charles Ralph Boxer, *O Império colonial Português: 1415–1825* (Lisboa: Edições 70, 1981), 227.

as a "granular frontier."[26] In fact, the effective presence of the colonisers in this space was reduced to a number of strategic spots interlinked with one another by very risky waterways that passed through nearly impenetrable forests and vast floodplains. This tropical "frontier" gained importance within the Portuguese colonial empire when the loss of trading posts to the Dutch on the island of Ceylon and in the Malay Archipelago, in the 1640s, and to the English in India, in the 1660s, resulted in a considerable decrease in the supply of spices, especially clove (from the Moluccas) and cinnamon (from Ceylon). At the royal court in Lisbon, therefore, the plan was drawn up to focus on the Amazon basin, from where the Dutch had just been expelled and where the captain Pedro Teixeira had unilaterally set the first boundary marker between the zones respectively claimed by the Castilian and the Portuguese Crown during his expedition to Quito in 1639, rather than on the South Asian coasts. The discovery of some highly valued spices in the Amazon rainforest, such as cacao, clove bark, sarsaparilla, vanilla, Copaiba oil, and a native cotton variety brought the region into focus; all the more because the introduction of Asian spices in the Amazon region, such as Indian clove, cinnamon, nutmeg and pepper, was not very successful.[27] Thus, Father João Felipe Bettendorff reports that he planted the seedling of a cinnamon tree from India, which the king himself had given to him, in the patio of the college in São Luís in 1689, but there are no records of a significant production of this spice.[28] In fact, the early interest in native plants from the rainforest prevailed, as is shown by official documents that stimulate their collection and eventual cultivation with the clear intention of exporting them to European markets.[29] The sources also

---

26   Daniel Nordman, *Frontières de France: De l'espace au territoire (XVIe – XIXe siècle)* (Paris: Gallimard, 1998), 40–43.

27   Jaime Cortesão, *História da expansão portuguesa* (Lisbon: Imprensa Nacional/Casa da Moeda, 1993), 462–63; Leite, *História*, vol. 4, 158–61. Concerning the spices in the Amazon basin, see: *Arquivo Histórico Ultramarino*, Lisbon, sec. ACL-CU-009: 05/09/1648, cx. 3, doc. 00265 (native products near Gurupá on the Amazon); 18 September 1648, cx. 3, doc. 00267 (products in the coastal plain of Maranhão); 25 November 1650, cx. 3, doc. 00291 (products in the region of Gurupá); 8 August 1652, cx. 3, doc. 00265 (cultivation of Moluccan clove, pepper and nutmeg in the region); 4 August 1661, cx. 4, doc. 00437 (demand to fix the price of native cotton).

28   Bettendorff, *Crônica*, 454.

29   Arquivo Histórico Ultramarino, Lisbon, sec. ACL-CU-009: 20/09/1677, cx. 5, doc. 00614 (insistence on collection of cacao and vanilla); 28 July 1681, cx. 6, doc. 00654 (projects to cultivate cacao, vanilla and indigo); 10/02/1984, cx. 6, doc. 00693 (tax exemption for cacao and clove bark from Franciscan farms); 18 September 1690, cx. 7, doc. 00820 (insistence to export more spices despite Dutch competition); 10 January 1693, cx. 8, doc. 00859 (production of dye from *urucum* and other native plants).

stress the necessity of discovering new areas, reputed to be rich in all sorts of *drogas do sertão*, throughout the vast tropical plain.[30]

In actual fact, from the end of the seventeenth century the rainforest products were very popular in Europe both as ingredients of remedies and as food refiners or preservatives.[31] Except for some, such as the so-called *cacau manso*, that is, cultivated cacao (differing from the "wild" or *bravo* variety), most of the native spices were gathered in the *sertões* and transported in canoes, rowed by Indians from the missions, to the seaport in Belém in order to be shipped to the metropole. Indeed, colonial sources, especially those written by missionaries, denounce, mostly without any result, the brutal methods of exploitation of the labour force – that is, those who were responsible for gathering the forest products, rowing the canoes or cultivating the crops on plantations – in order to increase export volumes.[32] In addition to hard work and harsh punishments, the withholding of salaries and non-compliance with the legally regulated working periods (depending on the type of work, between four and six months) were common. We find an example of the extreme working conditions in the report of Father Lourenço Kaulen, who administered the Piraguiri Mission on the Xingu River between 1754 and 1756:

> Dragged, cruelly, to work like mules, they [indigenous labourers] can hardly produce anything other than manioc flour (which, moreover, is often missing). Even so, they are forced to work. There is no intention of giving them a fair remuneration, unless, by chance, the 8 fathoms of extremely coarse cloth, which they receive from the royal servants, could be called a fair salary for a continuous nine-month job. One can buy it for just three *cruzados* of our currency. Or what is worse: they send a tiny piece of paper to a poor widow, whose husband had fallen ill because of the hard work or who had died, just to warn her, this way, that she should

---

30 Arquivo Histórico Ultramarino, Lisbon, sec. ACL-CU-009: 16/10/1674, cx. 5, doc. 00590 (density of native products in the Tocantins valley); 13 January 1696, cx. 9, doc. 00907 (wood and tobacco designated as new and profitable *drogas*); Biblioteca da Ajuda, Lisbon, cod. 51-V-44, fol. 124v, 9 February 1684 ("discovery" of pepper on the seashore of Maranhão and sarsaparilla in the Amazon valley); Bettendorff, *Crônica*, 464 (abundance of "wild" cacao in the Madeira valley in the 1680s).

31 For the medical-therapeutic effects attributed to Amazonian spices, see: Karl Heinz Arenz, "Casca de cravo, óleo de copaíba e raiz de salsaparrilha: Especiarias amazônicas em tratados médico-botânicos da Europa (séc. XVII e XVIII)," in *Anais do X Simpósio de História – ANPUH-Seção Pará*, ed. Davison Hugo Rocha Alves and Thiago Broni de Mesquita (Belém: Paka-Tatu, [2016] 2017), 530–41.

32 Farage, *As muralhas dos sertões*, 24–26.

not go to care for the sick or the dead, because, if she does, she will have to pay for the transport to the village, etc. These are the things that they grant as reward to the Indians, who try to flee in order to not be subjected to services, which they call royal ones; and – oh, what a shame! – they constantly insist that the missionary has to tell these unfortunate Indians to endure such things. With broken bones, dislocated nerves, sick or completely naked, they return to their families. Anyway, they will only come back, if they did not manage to escape.[33]

One of the most common services executed by indigenous labourers for colonial authorities, private merchants and religious orders was the gathering of cacao. In fact, among the forest products, cacao played a key role, as it was rather abundant in the vast *sertões*. The Indians knew where to find the widely scattered cacao groves and how and when to collect their fruits. Fathers João Felipe Bettendorff (in the seventeenth century) and João Daniel (in the mid-eighteenth century) mention the considerable amount of cacao orchards along the riverbanks of the Amazon and its huge tributaries, especially in the western part of the basin around the Madeira River.[34] Official records from 1743–1745 show that the Jesuits played an important role in the commercial exchanges between Belém and Lisbon. They were responsible for four-fifths of the exports dispatched by the religious orders in these years. Cacao made up 78.7 per cent of the products, followed by clove bark (16.1 per cent), sugar (2.7 per cent), sarsaparilla (2.1 per cent) and coffee (0.4 per cent).[35] The two non-forest products, sugar and coffee, were produced, along with tobacco and cotton, on the Jesuit farms, where cacao was also increasingly being cultivated. By contrast, the systematic collection of the *drogas do sertão* predominated in the inland missions. Planting and gathering thus became complementary activities in the economy of the missions at the end of the seventeenth century.[36]

---

33   Lourenço Kaulen, "Carta-ânua da missão de Piraguiri," in "A expulsão de um missionário 'tapuitinga' da Amazônia pombalina: A carta-ânua do padre Lourenço Kaulen (1755–1756)," translated and commented on by Karl Heinz Arenz and Gabriel de Cassio Pinheiro Prudente, *Revista História* (USP) 178 (2020): 25.

34   Bettendorff, *Crônica*, 464; Daniel, *Tesouro*, vol. 2, 83, 467.

35   Droulers, *Brésil*, 102–3; Alden, *Making*, 547.

36   Ciro Flamarion Cardoso, "La forêt, les Indiens et l'Amazonie portugaise," in *Pour l'histoire du Brésil: hommage à Katia de Queirós Mattoso*, ed. François Crouzet, Philippe Bonnichon, and Denis Rolland (Paris: Harmattan, 2000), 172–73; Leite, *História*, vol. 4, 153–64; João Lúcio de Azevedo, *Os jesuítas no Grão-Pará: Suas missões e a colonização* (Coimbra: Imprensa da Universidade, 1930), 153–57.

In fact, from the 1670s onwards, cacao was, definitively, the most important product of the region that was exported to Lisbon. The Jesuits had been among the first to become aware of the success of this commodity on the European markets and started to cultivate it systematically, involving even the settlers in this venture. In a letter from 1677, Father Bettendorff informed the General Superior Giovanni Paolo Oliva that he had introduced the cacao tree, very common in Pará (eastern part of the Amazon basin), on the coastal plain of neighbouring Maranhão:

> Three years ago [1674], I twice planted one thousand cacao seedlings, of which one thousand turned into trees. Besides the blossoms, they are already producing fruits which are called cacao and of which is made the chocolate beverage. All inhabitants of the Maranhão captaincy are very content with this new subsidy for their livelihood and their businesses which was brought, thanks to my care and zeal, from Pará to Maranhão. I have given to certain persons cacao fruits, of which each specimen contains at least forty-six grains. These fruits produce an equal number of trees. And as I am willing to go on sharing with these people, they will have something to become rich in the future or, at least, to live from more decently in the present. Six or, at most, ten trees produce per year one *arroba* [c. fifteen kilograms], as the weight measure is called here. One thousand trees will give one hundred *arrobas* [of cacao beans], which are sold for more than one thousand *cruzados*. This year I intend to plant at least six thousand trees as a source of income for the Mission. God may provide for their growth, for they will be planted for His greater glory.[37]

In another report, written one year later, Bettendorff clarifies that his initiative to plant the cacao trees and, especially, to involve the settlers was due to a request of "the Governor to satisfy the wish of the Most Serene Prince [future king Dom Pedro II]."[38] Many other letters in his official correspondence as superior refer to cacao as one of the most valuable products for the sustenance

---

37   Archivum Romanum Societatis Iesu, Rome, cod. Bras 26, fol. 43v, 10 September 1677. Translated from Latin by the author. One *arroba* corresponds to approximately fifteen kilograms.

38   Archivum Romanum Societatis Iesu, Rome, cod. Bras 26, fol. 47r, 7 May 1678. The prince the letter refers to is Dom Pedro, who was regent from 1667 to 1683, before declaring himself king.

of the mission and the colony.[39] His successor, Italian-born Father Pedro Luís Consalvi, also stressed the role of Bettendorff in the cacao enterprise in a letter to the general superior in which he wrote that "in a very innovating way, Father Rector planted cacao, from which is made the beverage known as chocolate."[40]

The steadily growing demand of cacao in Europe even motivated the colonial authorities to transfer the capital of the colony from São Luís to Belém, because the harbour in the Amazon delta gave better access to the cacao producing forests and plantations.[41] Nevertheless, the production and exportation of cacao was not as successful as described in the first letters from the 1670s. The oscillations of the colonial market also affected this rather new economic activity. In 1691, Father Aloísio Conrado Pfeil mentions a local commercial crisis on account of the lack of cacao and clove bark for exportation after bad harvests.[42] But just thirteen years later, at the beginning of the eighteenth century, the settlers complained about the over-commitment of the Jesuits to the commercial production of cacao, reminding them of their spiritual obligations. With regard to this growing discontent, Dauril Alden explains that the "Jesuits, along with the other Orders active in the Amazon, produced some cacao on their own plantations, but they depended primarily upon their Amerindian charges in the interior missions to collect it. Such reliance brought the fathers into direct conflict with vested settler interests."[43]

These tensions point to the increasing profit prospects of cacao and explain the interest of orders, settlers and authorities to increase its quantity by adapting the once wild tree to plantation modes. Referring explicitly to the experience of the Spaniards in the neighbouring colonies, even the prince regent, Dom Pedro, insisted in 1675 that cacao should be cultivated in the Amazon region "as it is done in the Indies of Castile."[44] Nonetheless, as already mentioned, the continuity of seasonal gathering in the *sertão* missions linked indigenous

---

39   Archivum Romanum Societatis Iesu, Rome, cod. Bras 27, fol. 2v, 1671; cod. Bras 26, fol. 27r, 21 July 1671; cod. Bras 9, fol. 298r, 15 January 1672; cod. Bras 26, fol. 43v, 20 September 1677; cod. Bras 26, fol. 47r, 7 May 1678; cod. Bras 26, fol. 48v–49r, 1678.

40   Archivum Romanum Societatis Iesu, Rome, cod. Bras 26, fol. 53v, 2 August 1678. Translated from Latin by the author.

41   Joaquim Romero Magalhães, "Le Portugal et les dynamiques de l'économie atlantique du XVe au XVIIIe siècle," in *Le Portugal et l'Atlantique: XVe – XXe siècles*, ed. Fundação Calouste Gulbenkian (Lisbon and Paris: Centre culturel Calouste Gulbenkian, 2001), 8; Bettendorff, *Crônica*, 648.

42   *Archivum Romanum Societatis Iesu*, Rome, cod. Bras 26, fol. 366v, 27 February 1691.

43   Alden, *Making*, 546.

44   Arquivo Histórico Ultramarino, Lisbon, cod. 268, fol. 9v–10r, 3 April 1675. With regard to the importance of cacao in the Spanish colonies, see: Eduardo Arcila Farías, *Comercio entre Venezuela y México en los siglos XVII y XVIII* (México: El Colegio de México, 1950);

practices and knowledge with the far-reaching intercontinental trading system that developed around cacao. The rural character of the missions was thus retained and even strengthened due to the non-circulation of metal coins and restricted access to iron tools.[45] For example, already in the 1650s cotton cloth served as substitute for money to remunerate the services of the indigenous labourers, who worked outside the missions, and was used in small commercial exchanges.[46] Decades later, in the eighteenth century, cacao beans substituted the cloth rolls as "natural currency."[47] This parallel system of traditional trade without the use of coined money and with hardly any investment in new tools or methods, contributed to producing a rural colonial environment with pronounced indigenous features.

From the end of the seventeenth century, the Jesuits had followed the growing extractivist activities of the settlers and colonial authorities, who were dispatching more and more canoe flotillas to the hinterland, with suspicion. The fathers did not shy away from reporting them to high-ranking church officials. Thus, in 1701, an anonymous document from the Maranhão Mission denounced the alleged greed of the settlers for "spices" and the abuse of indigenous people as compulsory workers to the papal authorities in Rome: "The main business in these Portuguese towns [Belém and São Luís] was to make, by all means, profit with the aromatic clove bark and with cacao, i.e., the famous and aromatic beans from which chocolate is made. A huge quantity of these substances is extracted from the forests by Indian labourers and then sent to Portugal."[48]

Between the lines, the complaint alludes to the harsh competition that existed between settlers and missionaries in producing and commercialising these two important Amazonian products. However, although the Jesuits' contribution to the exportation of commodities was less than many researchers, such as Alden Dauril,[49] have presumed, they were perceived as serious

---

Marcy Norton, *Sacred Gifts, Profane Pleasures: A History of Tobacco and Chocolate in the Atlantic World* (Ithaca, NY: Cornell University Press, 2010).

45 Frédéric Mauro, *Le Portugal et l'Atlantique au XVIIᵉ siècle (1570–1670): Étude économique* (Paris: SEVPEN/École pratique des Hautes Études, 1960), 424–28.

46 Heriarte, *Descripção*, 9.

47 Charles-Marie de La Condamine, *Voyage sur l'Amazone* (Paris: La Découverte, [1752] 2004), 117; Raimundo Moreira das Neves Neto, *"Em aumento de minha fazenda e do bem desses vassalos": A coroa, a fazenda real e os contratadores na Amazônia Colonial (séculos XVII – XVIII)* (Jundiaí: Paco Editorial, 2019), 16.

48 "Informatio de Marañonensis Missionis Statu," *Archivio Storico de Propaganda Fide*, Rome, cod. Scritture riferite nei Congressi – America Meridionale, vol. 1, fol. 518r, 1701.

49 Dauril Alden, "Aspectos econômicos da expulsão dos jesuítas do Brasil," in *Conflito e continuidade na sociedade brasileira*, ed. Henry H. Keith and S. F. Edwards (Rio de Janeiro: Civilização Brasileira, 1970): 31–78.

competitors, especially during the first half of the eighteenth century, when cacao commerce became of growing importance. In fact, "[c]rude exports data exist only from 1730 onwards and reveal how cacao became the most important product of Amazonian economy. The fluctuation of its position within the totality of the region's exports for the period 1730–1755, however, is significant, ranging from 97 per cent in 1736 to 44 per cent in 1753. Only in two years, cacao represented a little less than half of the entire exports of the Amazon region. In fifteen years, it represented more than 80 per cent of all the products shipped from the Amazon region to Portugal."[50]

Around 1732, Governor Alexandre de Sousa Freire (1728–1732), a tenacious foe of the Jesuits, set up a list of the estates (farms and other properties) that belonged to the Society of Jesus with details of their production activities. Sousa Freire certainly exaggerated the fathers' economic output when trying, unlike his Jesuit-friendly predecessor, João da Maia da Gama, to prove to the Crown that the Jesuits tried to bypass the Royal Treasury by systematically avoiding or refusing the payment of tithes. According to Sousa Freire, the fathers produced only around 500 *arrobas* of cacao on their estates (*fazendas*) each year. Additional to that, up to 5,400 *arrobas* of wild cacao came from the missionary villages upstream on the banks of the Amazon River and its southern tributaries Tocantins, Xingu, Tapajós and, mainly, Madeira.[51]

According to Father João Daniel, the annual expeditions to gather cacao in the central and western parts of the Amazon basin, that is, in rather remote areas abundant with cacao orchards, meant a deep cut in the daily routine of the missions, the "main nerve of the State," and brought much suffering to the Indians, who were classified as being "the feet and hands of the white settlers." The missionary complained that the only people to get rich through this activity were the commanders of the *canoas* (transport boats). For this reason, he implicitly suggested the planting of cacao in a system of crop rotation on the fields around the inland missions. As an example, he related the successful experience of a certain missionary (probably he himself) in Cumaru on the Tapajós River, in the mid-1750s, where the planting of *macaxeira* (a kind of cassava), cacao seedlings (which produced "10,000 trees") and banana alternated annually on the partially flooded and sandy terrains that surrounded the

---

50   Rafael Chambouleyron and Karl Heinz Arenz, "Frontier of Expansion, Frontier of Settlement: Cacao Exploitation and the Portuguese Colonisation of the Amazon Region (17th and 18th centuries)," 6, accessed 21 November 2020, https://commoditiesofempire .org.uk/publications/working-papers/working-paper-29/.

51   Arquivo Histórico Ultramarino, Lisbon, sec. Pará-Avulsos, cod. 13, doc. 1223, c. 1732.

mission. However, this form of cultivation did not prevail, nor did it expand, since the Jesuits were expelled a few years later in 1759.[52]

4 The Agricultural Activities and the Persistence of Indigenous Traditions

Contemporary sources, such as the report of the judge Maurício de Heriarte from 1664, describe the central valley of the Amazon basin with its mighty tributaries Tapajós, Trombetas and Rio Negro as an extreme fertile plain, ideal for growing wild rice, sarsaparilla, cacao, manioc and maize, or for breeding livestock.[53] He also points to the systematic cultivation of native vegetal dye substances, such as annatto, as well as profitable plants from other tropical or semi-tropical regions, such as indigo, sugar cane and tobacco. For this purpose, the royal official proposed the implementation of huge plantations or farms on the riverbanks and islands throughout the vast floodplain: "There are many and good sites to build big settlements."[54] When Heriarte wrote these words, the Jesuits had already established a series of small rural settlements in the *várzea* regions of the Amazon valley. In fact, during the 1650s alone, according to Dauril Alden, more than fifty missions had been founded by order of Father Antônio Vieira.[55] Over the years, many of these settlements specialised in a specific activity, be it agricultural (cultivating cotton or cacao, preparing manioc flour or drying fish) or artisanal (building canoes or producing ceramics).[56] However, in all of them, cassava, rice, beans and maize were planted for their own consumption.[57]

The mission network thus became important for agricultural production, especially in the decades after the first uprising of the settlers and the expulsion of Vieira and, at least temporarily, that of most of the Jesuit fathers, in 1661. Father Bettendorff, who had managed to escape the persecution and became the local superior in Belém (1662–1663) and São Luís (1663–1668), described his efforts to reconstruct the economic and infrastructural base of the two urban communities during the 1660s in detail.[58] For that reason, he

---

52   Daniel, *Tesouro*, vol. 2, 244, 248, 259, 449, 465.
53   Heriarte, *Descripção*, 37–39 and 45.
54   Heriarte, *Descripção*, 69.
55   Alden, *Making*, 113.
56   Leite, *História*, vol. 3, 99–366.
57   Daniel, *Tesouro*, vol. 1, 429.
58   Bettendorff, *Crônica*, 513–14.

invested in the farms that were situated near the two towns, planting diverse fruit trees (among them, orange trees from China), (re)building small sugar mills, promoting livestock breeding and even acquiring enslaved Africans as a permanent labour force. These activities, which had the character of a diversified economy of subsistence, show that local necessities had priority. As has already been emphasised, the farms provided the Jesuit communities in Belém and São Luís with food, furniture, ceramics and other items for daily use. Furthermore, they delivered all sort of products needed to guarantee the functioning of the remote inland missions, to satisfy the indigenous groups at the moment of first contact or to meet the needs of the crew members of the many transport convoys that went up and down the Amazon River.

Bettendorff himself experienced how useful the chain of well-functioning farms was for the missionaries. For instance, in 1661, when he was appointed to the Tapajós mission, in the present-day city of Santarém, he stopped on his way upstream at the mission farms of Mortigura and Cametá. First of all, he received manioc flour as provisions for his journey, and, subsequently, he got some living turtles, that had either been captured in the river or bred at the farm, as meat supply.[59] In another report, written in 1665, just four years after his arrival, the missionary from Luxembourg, by then already the rector of the central residence in São Luís, provides a general view of the economic conditions of the mission, detailing the high productivity of some farms.[60] Bettendorff's report starts with one of the most relevant and prosperous rural establishments in the Maranhão captaincy:

> Seven miles from the town, we possess a farm called Anindiba. It has a chapel dedicated to Saint Ignatius where the [indigenous] servants attend divine services and instruction of the doctrine. The whole property occupies one square mile and is very fertile, ideal for manioc and sugar cane. It has many trees that can be cut easily. Four villages of Indians inhabit our property. At that farm, we have more than sixty servants, children and adults all together, to cultivate the fields. A *curiboca* or *cafuzo*, that is, a son of an African man and an Indian woman, who is our servant, administers the farm. The poor ones, although born more to sleep, eat and drink

---

59   Bettendorff, *Crônica*, 159.
60   Two years before, he engaged in the reconstruction of the central Jesuit residence and the farms in Maranhão after the uprising of the settlers. See: Bettendorff, *Crônica*, 303–8. Bettendorff's interest in economic issues was clearly emphasised by the Jesuit historian Serafim Leite. See: Leite, *História*, vol. 4, 317–18.

than to work, provide us with manioc flour, enough for one year, maize, oil, and brandy, as well as cloth made of cotton and other things.[61]

The report also mentions smaller properties on the outskirts of São Luís. One of them occupied an entire island of one-and-a-half square miles on which "lives a fisherman with his wife and children, an African, with an African wife, a daughter and other descendants, and also three servants, and he takes care of a herd of cattle, which includes 67 animals, some goats, about 30 pigs and chicken. The women are our laundresses and weavers."[62] The document continues by succinctly presenting various rural scenes on farms and missions throughout the delta and the Amazon valley, revealing a clear concern with the precarious and constantly oscillating supplies of manioc flour and fish for the mission, and also for the colony in general.[63]

In the official annual statistics, or *Catalogus*, that Bettendorff sent to the general superior in Rome in 1671, he reports the existence of several small properties which had been donated by benefactors from Belém and São Luís. Like on their big farms, the Jesuits produced a large variety of food on these strips of land to sustain the residents of the urban colleges (mainly young students and novices, but also a growing number of elderly and sick missionaries), and, to a lesser degree, they produced products to be exported. Bettendorff particularly emphasises the production of salt (actually a royal monopoly) and livestock breeding in Maranhão and that of sugar, cotton and cacao, as well as manioc flour, in Pará. He also registers that the Jesuits' Indian workers in Maranhão were mainly legal slaves, while those in Pará were officially free, but obliged to live on the farms, just like the Indians in the inland missions.[64]

Bettendorff's descriptions do not only have an economic dimension, but also a sociocultural one, for they provide details, as we can see, about the complex system of cross-cultural interactions between Jesuit missionaries, indigenous groups and even persons of African origin. Furthermore, the reports refer to the rather difficult period between 1663 and 1680, when the Jesuits had temporarily lost the control, granted to them by law in 1655, over the indigenous labour force and their annual repartition and distribution. Only in 1686,

---

61 Archivum Romanum Societatis Iesu, Rome, cod. Bras 26, fol. 12v, 11 August 1665. Translated from Latin by the author.

62 Archivum Romanum Societatis Iesu, Rome, cod. Bras 26, fol. 12v–13r, 11 August 1665.

63 Archivum Romanum Societatis Iesu, Rome, cod. Bras 26, fol. 13v,16v,14r and 17v, 11 August 1665.

64 Archivum Romanum Societatis Iesu, Rome, cod. Bras 27, fol. 2v, 1671.

they recovered the so-called "double administration" (concerning spiritual and temporal/secular matters) over the missions.[65]

Another report from 1671 on the general visitation carried out by Bettendorff as superior of the missions also reveals, between the lines, the behaviour of the Indians in relation to the mission system. Instead of accepting the role of subordinate labourers, some native groups tactically negotiated their entry into the *aldeamentos* motivated by their own interests. Three examples can be pointed out. First, remote missions, whose fathers were frequently absent due to pastoral obligations or sickness, admitted the presence of not yet converted or baptised Indians, not respecting the official principle of segregation between Christians and "pagans." This occurred in the faraway Tupinambaranas mission near the mouth of the Madeira River. Bettendorff disapprovingly remarks that "those who call themselves Christians live mixed up with the heathens, more than in other villages."[66] Second, certain groups set clear conditions before settling down in a mission. Bettendorff mentions the Nhunhuns from the Xingu River who, although they had only recently come into contact with the missionaries, insisted on forwarding a delegation in order to inspect the *aldeamento* and demanded the allocation of fertile plots of land close to the river prior to moving to the mission. The father also reports his encounter in Cametá with a group of Aruaquis from the Tocantins valley who declared their interest to settle down in the *aldeamento* because they had to recover from the attacks of slave hunters and a hostile neighbouring group.[67] Third, shamanist rites persisted in the missions in spite of the daily catechetical instructions and ludic devotions. Bettendorff refers to a secret (and syncretic) ceremony held by shamans that he interrupted in Tapuitapera, one of the oldest missions, near São Luís. While the shamans were arrested, he himself was, according to his report, nearly lynched by his own Indian rowers who, very attached to their shamans, were eager to take revenge.[68] Although these observations are not directly related to agriculture they reveal, nevertheless, the social and cultural background in which the economic activities took place. To a certain extent, they show a typical feature of rural communities, in which the persistence of traditions was still strong, even if these were passing through constant

---

65   Arenz, "Do Alzette ao Amazonas," 34–36, 57.
66   Archivum Romanum Societatis Iesu, Rome, cod. Bras 9, fol. 263v, 21 July 1671. Translated from Latin by the author.
67   Archivum Romanum Societatis Iesu, Rome, cod. Bras 9, fol. 260r and 262r, 21 July 1671.
68   Archivum Romanum Societatis Iesu, Rome, cod. Bras 9, fol. 264r/v, 21 July 1671.

resignification due to frequent interferences – mainly (moral) interdictions and (technical) innovations – from outside.[69]

Two decades later, in the beginning of the 1690s, describing the "rich and beautiful gardens" surrounding the older *aldeamentos*, Bettendorff emphasised that more and more native groups were becoming reluctant to move to the missions. As an example, he mentions the reaction of the Guanases, who argued that they were already living on extremely fertile lands and did not see any reason for them to settle down in a missionary village. Other groups, also full of distrust, preferred to send a vanguard ahead to the nearest mission to "plant their [own] maizes and maniocs," as a precautionary measure.[70] The growing suspicion of the Indians was not only due to the fact that they were more and more aware of the functioning of the mission system with its various constraints, but also due to the effects of the new law, the *Regimento das Missões*, which, in 1686, established new labour conditions, especially those concerning the outside services. In fact, the law redefined the rules for the annual distribution of male workers and the respective periods of permitted absence from the mission. These could vary, according to the commodity to collect or cultivate, from four to six months, instead of two to four.[71]

Another factor which made life in the missions extremely precarious were the epidemics. Three outbreaks of contagious diseases, in 1661/1662, 1695/1696 and 1748/1749, depopulated entire *aldeamentos*. Beside the high mortality, the number of Indians who fled from the missions in these periods was considerable.[72] But despite these nearly regular catastrophic interruptions, the economy tended to develop advantageously. Thus, in 1697, at the very end of the seventeenth century, Bettendorff wrote that a ship bound for Portugal could only be loaded with one-third of all the "sugars, tobaccos and, particularly, clove bark and cacao" which had been piled up in the ports of São Luís and Belém.[73] This brief mention reveals, on the one hand, how much agriculture (sugar, tobacco and cultivated cacao) and extractivism (clove bark and wild cacao)

---

69   Paula Montero, "Índios e missionários no Brasil: Para uma teoria da mediação cultural," in *Deus na aldeia: Missionários, índios e mediação cultural*, ed. Paula Montero (São Paulo: Globo, 2006), 44–66.

70   Bettendorff, *Crônica*, 510–511, 618.

71   Yllan de Mattos, "Regimento das Missões do Estado do Maranhão e Grão-Pará, de 21 de dezembro de 1686," *Revista 7 Mares* 1, no. 1 (October 2012): 119 [pars. 14–15].

72   Tamyris Monteiro Neves, "A ira de Deus e o fogo que salta: A epidemia de bexigas no Estado do Maranhão (1695)," *Amazônica – Revista de Antropologia* 5, no. 2 (2013): 344–61; Bettendorff, *Crônica dos Padres da Companhia de Jesus*, 214–216, 587–588; Daniel, *Tesouro*, vol. 1, 385–86.

73   Bettendorff, *Crônica*, 648–49.

intermingled around the turn of the seventeenth to the eighteenth century and, on the other hand, how much the Amazon region was far from being a miserable and precarious periphery.[74]

In the 1720s, when the self-proclaimed procurator of the settlers, Paulo da Silva Nunes, accused the Jesuits of being responsible for the "ruin" of the regional economy, the pro-Jesuit governor João da Maia da Gama (1722–1728) defended the order, stressing that the fathers had "made come down"[75] from the hinterland more than four thousand Indians and, through this labour force, had contributed to increase the profit for the Crown. Implicitly, the governor affirmed that this had enabled him to annually dispatch ships with "twenty, twenty-five and even thirty thousand *arrobas* of cacao, and eight thousand *arrobas* of sugar" to Lisbon, ironically remarking that "this is, according to Paulo da Silva Nunes, the ruin of the colony."[76]

Despite the great importance attributed to export commodities, it should not be forgotten that cassava was one of the main agricultural products. In fact, the term *roças* (fields), is omnipresent in colonial documents. In most cases, it is employed as synonym for small or medium-sized plots of land prepared according to the common slash-and-burn method for manioc planting. From a traditional nourishment of the Indians, cassava flour turned into the main staple food of the whole colony, mainly due to its good storage conditions. This turned it into an ideal food supply for the many expeditions and voyages.[77] A missionary source from the 1750s, written a few years before the fathers' expulsion, conveys a rather clear picture of the importance of cassava in the daily life of the Indians. In 1753–1754, Father Anselmo Eckart described

---

74   For the diversity of aspects of the economy in the Amazon region and its central position within the Portuguese trade system, see: Chambouleyron, *Povoamento*, 121–69.

75   There were three manners to obtain indigenous workers: "making them come down" (*descimento*) through persuasion by a missionary, "rescuing them" (*resgate*) by acquiring indigenous prisoners of intertribal conflicts and, finally, "captivating them" in the context of a so-called just war (*guerra justa*). While the first ones were considered free persons (although they were under tutorship of the priests), the other two groups were regarded as legal slaves belonging to those who had "rescued" or captured them. In addition, illegal expeditions, in which Indian villages were raided or chiefs were manipulated to obtain slaves, were common. A network of human trafficking developed, which was largely tolerated by the colonial authorities. See: Perrone-Moisés, "Índios livres," 123–28.

76   "Parecer de João da Maia da Gama, governador que foi do Maranhão, sobre os requerimentos que a El-Rei apresentou Paulo da Silva Nunes contra os missionários," in *Chorografia histórica, chronográphica, genealógica, nobiliária e política do Império do Brasil*, vol. 4, ed. Alexandre José de Mello Moraes (Rio de Janeiro: Tipografia Americana, 1858), 260–61.

77   Roberto Borges da Cruz, "Farinha de 'pau' e de 'guerra': Os usos da farinha de mandioca no extremo Norte (1722–1759)" (Master's thesis, Universidade Federal do Pará, 2011), 21–130.

how the many derivative products of manioc were prepared. Besides the elaborate process of flour production (washing, grinding, squeezing and toasting), he highlights the making of "wine" or *cauim*, an alcoholic beverage made by chewing and cooking the manioc mush, to guarantee its fast fermentation. According to Eckart, this work was mainly done by "older women, who already stood with one foot in the boat of Charon [mythological helper of Hades]," as the evaporation of the brew released the cyanide contained in the toxic cassava species.[78]

The report reveals the still widespread consumption of this traditional and, in many cases, also ceremonial beverage, even in the interior of the missions at the end of the Jesuit period. Up to the last years of their presence, the fathers used to complain about the constant "dancing and boozing sessions" that were clandestinely held in the villages, especially since they were aware that these assemblies had a clear ritual character.[79] According to Father Jacinto de Carvalho, other "heathen" rites prevailed more or less openly in the missions, such as the veneration of mummified bodies as "god of the maize, god of the cassava, god of the rain and god of the sun" among the Tapajós.[80] This example shows that, in addition to economic aspects, the symbolic dimension has to be taken into account in order to more profoundly understand the agricultural and extractivist activities in colonial societies in the Americas, especially in places where the Indians constituted the majority of the labouring and resident population, like in the Amazon region.

5   Conclusions

In summary, we can draw four important conclusions. First, the widespread rural mission settlements under Jesuit (and, to a lesser extent, under Franciscan, Carmelite and Mercedarian) administration played a far greater role in the colonial occupation and exploitation of the Amazon region than

---

78   "Papeis do P. Ancelmo Eschard," *Instituto das Arquivos Nacionais/Torre do Tombo*, Lisbon, sec. Ministério dos Negócios Eclesiásticos e da Justiça (MNEJ)/Papéis Pombalinos (PP), cod. 59, no. 4.

79   Father João Daniel notes that "while the Indians are laughing [during their feasts], the missionaries are crying." Daniel, *Tesouro*, vol. 1, 289, 362.

80   Father Jacinto de Carvalho alluded to the mummified corpses, which are also mentioned in the writings of Bettendorff and Daniel, in his report to the superior general Michelangelo Tamburini (21 March 1719). Archivum Romanum Societatis Iesu, Rome, cód. 10 I, 204r. Bettendorff and Daniel also mention the veneration of the mummified corpses of the ancestors among the Tapajós.

the system of fortifications along the Amazon River or around the two main urban agglomerations, Belém and São Luís, on the Atlantic seashore. Indeed, the very first reports on the Amazon valley already pointed out in detail the economic potential of the region's backcountry. Second, the large network of interconnected Jesuit missions, which was founded in the 1620s and expanded in the 1650s, consisted of rural production centres and contributed, despite all precarities, to establishing the long-lasting success of this vast "granular" frontier, whose natural axis was the Amazon River. Third, the agricultural and extractivist activities were, at least throughout the second half of the seventeenth century, a kind of joint venture involving missionaries, settlers and colonial authorities. Despite the constant tensions between these agents, each depended entirely on the indigenous labour force – which, for a long time, was the only labour force that was available. As for the Indians, even those submitted to obligatory confinement and compulsory labour held to their main traditions and were able to articulate and negotiate their interests. Fourth, indigenous knowledge and practices adapted to the necessities of mercantilist trading, forming a new production system which had a specific regional character in accordance with the processing methods of the commodities, mainly cacao and cassava.

The agency of the indigenous populations within the mission is implicitly noticeable in most reports of Jesuit authors, although the fathers normally tended to emphasise "inconstancy" and "rusticity" when writing about the Indians. In this context, the contribution of Father João Felipe Bettendorff must be stressed, for, in the second half of the seventeenth century, this missionary from Luxembourg was a central figure in the consolidation process of the Jesuit mission network. His voluminous chronicle and many of his over fifty official letters reveal his evident interest in economic issues and thus testify to his historical role in the development of the Amazon region.

Bibliography

Alden, Dauril. "Aspectos econômicos da expulsão dos jesuítas do Brasil." In *Conflito e continuidade na sociedade brasileira*, edited by Henry H. Keith and S. F. Edwards, 31–78. Rio de Janeiro: Civilização Brasileira, 1970.

Alden, Dauril. *The Making of an Enterprise: The Society of Jesus in Portugal, its Empire and beyond, 1540–1750*. Stanford: Stanford University Press, 1996.

Alencastro, Luiz Felipe de. "L'économie politique des découvertes maritimes." In *L'autre rive de l'Occident*, edited by Adauto Novaes, 67–81. Paris: Métailié, 2006.

Araújo, Renata Malcher de. "A razão na selva: Pombal e a reforma urbana na Amazônia." *Camões – Revista de Letras e Culturas Lusófonas* 15–16 (January/June 2003): 151–165.

Arcila Farías, Eduardo. *Comercio entre Venezuela y México en los siglos XVII y XVIII.* Mexico: El Colegio de México, 1950.

Arenz, Karl Heinz, and Diogo Costa Silva. *"Levar a luz de nossa santa fé aos sertões de muita gentilidade": Fundação e consolidação da missão jesuíta na Amazônia portuguesa (século XVIII).* Belém: Açaí, 2012.

Arenz, Karl Heinz. "A vasta Amazônia em poucas páginas: Os tratados do padre João Daniel da Vice-Província do Maranhão (século XVIII)." In *Escritas e leituras: Temas, fontes e objetos na Iberoamérica, séculos XVI – XIX*, edited by Eliane Cristina Deckmann Fleck and Mauro Dillmann, 91–118. São Leopolto: Oikos/Unisinos, 2017.

Arenz, Karl Heinz. "Casca de cravo, óleo de copaíba e raiz de salsaparrilha: Especiarias amazônicas em tratados médico-botânicos da Europa (séc. XVII e XVIII)." In *Anais do X Simpósio de História – ANPUH-Seção Pará*, edited by Davison Hugo Rocha Alves and Thiago Broni de Mesquita, 529–42. Belém: Paka-Tatu, [2016] 2017.

Arenz, Karl Heinz. "Do Alzette ao Amazonas: Vida e obra do padre João Felipe Bettendorff (1625–1698)." *Revista Estudos Amazônicos* 5, no. 1 (2010): 25–78.

Arenz, Karl Heinz. "O 'tapuitinga' Anselm Eckart e os índios da Amazônia portuguesa (1753–1757)." In *Anais do 30° Simpósio Nacional de História: História e o futuro da educação no Brasil*, edited by Márcio Ananias Ferreira Vilela, 1–16. Recife: Associação Nacional de História – ANPUH, 2019.

Azevedo, João Lúcio de. *Os jesuítas no Grão-Pará: Suas missões e a colonização.* Coimbra: Imprensa da Universidade, 1930.

Bettendorff, João Felipe. *Crônica dos Padres da Companhia de Jesus no Estado do Maranhão.* Belém: Fundação Cultural do Pará Tancredo Neves/Secretaria de Estado da Cultura, [1698] 1990.

Bourdon, Albert-Alain. *Histoire du France.* Paris: Chandeigne, 1994.

Boxer, Charles Ralph. *O Império colonial Português: 1415–1825.* Lisboa: Edições 70, 1981.

Cardoso, Ciro Flamarion. "La forêt, les Indiens et l'Amazonie portugaise." In *Pour l'histoire du Brésil: Hommage à Katia de Queirós Mattoso*, edited by François Crouzet, Philippe Bonnichon, and Denis Rolland, 171–80. Paris: Harmattan, 2000.

Chambouleyron, Rafael, and Karl Heinz Arenz. "Frontier of Expansion, Frontier of Settlement: Cacao Exploitation and the Portuguese Colonisation of the Amazon Region (17th and 18th centuries)." Accessed 21 November 2020. https://commodit iesofempire.org.uk/publications/working-papers/working-paper-29/.

Chambouleyron, Rafael, Karl Heinz Arenz, and Vanice Siqueira de Melo. "Ruralidades indígenas na Amazônia colonial." *Boletim do Museu Paraense Emílio Goeldi – Ciências Humanas* 15, no. 1 (January 2020): 1–22.

Chambouleyron, Rafael. *Povoamento, ocupação e agricultura na Amazônia colonial (1640–1706).* Belém: Açaí, 2010.

Cortesão, Jaime. *História da expansão portuguesa.* Lisbon: Imprensa Nacional/Casa da Moeda, 1993.

Cruz, Roberto Borges da. "Farinha de 'pau' e de 'guerra': Os usos da farinha de mandioca no extremo Norte (1722–1759)." Master's thesis, Universidade Federal do Pará, 2011.

Daniel, João. *Tesouro descoberto no máximo rio Amazonas*, vols. 1–2. Rio de Janeiro: Contraponto, 2004.

Dias, Manuel Nunes. "Estratégia Pombalina de urbanização do espaço amazônico." *Brotéria – Cultura e Informação* 115, no. 2–4 (August-October 1982): 239–305.

Droulers, Martine. *Brésil: Une géohistoire*. Paris: Presses Universitaires France, 2001.

Farage, Nádia. *As muralhas dos sertões: Os povos indígenas no rio Branco e a colonização*. Rio de Janeiro: Paz e Terra/ANPOCS, 1991.

Figueira, Luís. "Memorial sobre as terras, e gentes do Maranhão, Grão-Pará, e Rio das Amazonas [1637]." *Revista do Instituto de História e Geografia Brasileiro* 94, no. 148 (1923): 429–32.

Freire, José Ribamar Bessa. *Rio Babel: A história das línguas na Amazônia*. Rio de Janeiro: EdUERJ, 2011.

Godim, Neide. *A invenção da Amazônia*. São Paulo: Marco Zero, 1994.

Guzmán, Décio de Alencar. "A primeira urbanização: Mamelucos, índios e europeus nas cidades pombalinas da Amazônia, 1751–1757." *Revista de Cultura do Pará* 18, no. 1 (January 2008): 75–94.

Heriarte, Maurício de. *Descripção do estado do Maranhão, Pará, Coropá e rio das Amazonas*. Vienna: Impr. de Karl Gerold, [1664] 1874.

Kaulen, Lourenço. "Carta-ânua da missão de Piraguiri." In "A expulsão de um missionário 'tapuitinga' da Amazônia pombalina: A carta-ânua do padre Lourenço Kaulen (1755–1756)." Translated and commented on by Karl Heinz Arenz and Gabriel de Cassio Pinheiro Prudente. *Revista História* (USP) 178 (2019): 19–29.

Labourdette, Jean-François. *Histoire du Portugal*. Paris: Fayard, 2000.

La Condamine, Charles-Marie de. *Voyage sur l 'Amazone*. Paris: La Découverte, [1752] 2004.

Leite, Serafim. *História da Companhia de Jesus no Brasil*. Vol. 3. Rio de Janeiro/Lisbon: Instituto Nacional do Livro/Livraria Portugalia, 1943.

Leite, Serafim. *História da Companhia de Jesus no Brasil*. Vol. 4. Rio de Janeiro/Lisbon: Instituto Nacional do Livro/Livraria Portugalia, 1943.

Lopes, Rhuan Carlos dos Santos. "'Novos ditames de racionalidade': O Diretório dos Índios e a urbanização na Amazônia colonial (1751–1759)." *Perspectiva Amazônica* 2, no. 3 (January 2012): 31–45.

Magalhães, Joaquim Romero. "Le Portugal et les dynamiques de l'économie atlantique du XVe au XVIIIe siècle." In *Le Portugal et l'Atlantique: XVe – XXe siècles*, edited by Fundação Calouste Gulbenkian, 3–10. Lisbon/Paris: Centre culturel Calouste Gulbenkian, 2001.

Mattos, Yllan de. "Regimento das Missões do Estado do Maranhão e Grão-Pará, de 21 de dezembro de 1686." *Revista 7 Mares* 1, no. 1 (October 2012): 112–22.

Mauro, Frédéric. *Des produits et des hommes: Essais historiques latino-américains XVIe–XXe siècles*. Paris and The Hague: Mouton/École pratique des Hautes Études, 1972.

Mauro, Frédéric. *Le Portugal et l'Atlantique au XVI Ie siècle (1570–1670): Étude économique*. Paris: SEVPEN/École pratique des Hautes Études, 1960.

Meier, Johannes, and Fernando Amado Aymoré. *Jesuiten aus Zentraleuropa in Portugiesisch- und Spanisch-Amerika: Ein bio-bibliographisches Handbuch*. Vol. 1. Münster: Aschendorff Verlag, 2005.

Montero, Paula. "Índios e missionários no Brasil: Para uma teoria da mediação cultural." In *Deus na aldeia: Missionários, índios e mediação cultural*, edited by Paula Montero, 31–66. São Paulo: Globo, 2006.

Neves Neto, Raimundo Moreira das. *"Em aumento de minha fazenda e do bem desses vassalos": A coroa, a fazenda real e os contratadores na Amazônia Colonial (séculos XVII – XVIII)*. Jundiaí: Paco Editorial, 2019.

Neves Neto, Raimundo Moreira das. *Um patrimônio em contendas: Os bens jesuíticos e a magna questão dos dízimos no Estado do Maranhão e Grão-Pará (1650–1750)*. Jundiaí: Paco Editorial, 2013.

Neves, Tamyris Monteiro. "A ira de Deus e o fogo que salta: A epidemia de bexigas no Estado do Maranhão (1695)." *Amazônica – Revista de Antropologia* 5, no. 2 (2013): 344–61.

Nordman, Daniel. *Frontières de France: De l'espace au territoire (XVIe – XIXe siècle)*. Paris: Gallimard, 1998.

Norton, Marcy. *Sacred Gifts, Profane Pleasures: A History of Tobacco and Chocolate in the Atlantic World*. Ithaca, NY: Cornell University Press, 2010.

"Parecer de João da Maia da Gama, governador que foi do Maranhão, sobre os requerimentos que a El-Rei apresentou Paulo da Silva Nunes contra os missionários." In *Chorografia histórica, chronográphica, genealógica, nobiliária e política do Império do Brasil*. Vol. 4, edited by Alexandre José de Mello Moraes, 258–74. Rio de Janeiro: Tipografia Americana, 1858.

Perrone-Moisés, Beatriz. "Índios livres e índios escravos: Os princípios da legislação indigenista do período colonial (séculos XVI a XVIII)." In *História dos índios no Brasil*, edited by Manuela Carneiro da Cunha, 115–32. São Paulo: Companhia das Letras, 1992.

Serrão, Joel, and António Henrique de Oliveira Marques, eds. *Nova história de Portugal*. Vol. 7. Lisbon: Presença, 2001.

Souza Júnior, José Alves de. *Tramas do cotidiano: Religião, política, guerra e negócios no Grão-Pará dos setecentos*. Belém: Editora da UFPA, 2012.

Sylveira, Symão Estacio da. *Relação sumaria das cousas do Maranhão*. Lisbon: Imprensa Nacional, [1624] 1911.

Vieira, Antônio. *Sermões escolhidos: Texto integral*. São Paulo: Martin Claret, 2004.

CHAPTER 9

A Laboratory of Colonial Agricultural Modernity

Environment, Sugar and Slavery in Cuba

Leida Fernandez-Prieto

1 Introduction

Cuba emerged as the world's leading cane sugar producer in the early nineteenth century.* This was achieved as a result of the void left in the international market by the collapse of the French colony of Saint-Domingue (now Haiti), the transfer and circulation of know-how, expert personnel and technologies in the adoption of the Caribbean sugar plantation model, and Cuba's insertion within transatlantic slave trade and trafficking circuits. Brazil and Cuba were the last two countries to receive enslaved Africans who were forced to work on agricultural plantations. Over more than three centuries, some eight hundred thousand enslaved Africans were brought to the Caribbean island.[1] Sixty per cent of them were the result of illicit trade after the signing of the Anglo-Spanish treaty prohibiting slave trade in 1817. From then on, the *ingenio* (sugar mill), a central part of the slave-based sugar agro-industrial complex, was the flagship of modernity on both sides of the Atlantic until the abolition of slavery in 1886.

---

* This work is part of the Special Intramural Project, "Tropical Nature, Colonial Science and Agro-Botanical Expertise in the Making: Spain and the Hispanic Caribbean in the 19th Century," financed by the Spanish National Research Council (CSIC). A draft was presented at the workshop "Colonial Agricultural Modernities 1750s–1870s: Capital, Concepts, Circulations," which was held at Wissenschaftskolleg zu Berlin/Institute for Advanced Study in 2018. I would like to thank Kris K. Manjapra, Sascha Averbach, Ulbe Bosma and other colleagues for the invitation and helpful comments during the meeting. Also, I want to thank Rolf Bauer for the invitation to participate in this book, and Erin Goodman for the translation.

1 Philip D. Curtin, *The Atlantic Slave Trade: A Census* (Madison: University of Wisconsin Press, 1969); Juan Pérez de la Riva, *El monto de la inmigración forzada en el siglo XIX* (Havana: Editorial de Ciencias Sociales, 1979); José Luciano Franco, *Comercio clandestino de esclavos* (Havana: Editorial de Ciencias Sociales, 1980). For a recent overview of the numbers of enslaved Africans introduced to America, see David Eltis and David Richardson, *Atlas of the Transatlantic Slave Trade* (New Haven: Yale University Press, 2015).

This chapter seeks to situate the place of tropical agriculture and slavery within the period of modernity and the industrial sugar revolution, departing from the dialogue between the global history of labour relations, studies of slavery and science, commodity histories and environmental histories. The commodification of the tropical environment and the enslaved population were constitutive elements of the production chain and the consumption of sugar as a commodity destined for the international market. According to the taxonomy established by Karin Hofmeester and Marcel van der Linden, slave labour not only produced commodities for the world market but was also conceived as a commodity in itself within slave plantation design.[2] At the same time, this chapter underscores the elaboration of a grand narrative centred on the environment to conceptualise, justify, classify, and control slave labour relations in tropical sugar agriculture, and researches slave agency through African practices and knowledge about crops and food. The chapter also illuminates new global-local connections among different labour relations and commodity production chains along the axis of Cuba, Uruguay and Europe, and examines how they are woven into the visual representation of slavery in the context of modern industrial agriculture and debates on the science of nutrition.

Conceptual history establishes the transition towards the language of political modernity in Latin America between 1770 and 1870.[3] These years coincide with the rise and fall of slave-based sugar plantations in Cuba. Some authors identify the sugar boom with colonial reinforcement in the era of the Atlantic revolutions.[4] Other scholars highlight the contribution of the *indianos* – Spanish emigrants in the Americas who returned with large fortunes – to the modernisation of cities such as Barcelona and Asturias.[5] At the same time, Havana's transformation into a modern port city is owed to the capital accumulated through slave agriculture. Agrarian, economic and commodity histories highlight the analysis of slave plantation crops that are key to European expansion and the development of capitalism as a world system.

2 Karin Hofmeester and Marcel van der Linden, "Introduction," in *Handbook Global History of Work*, ed. Karin Hofmeester and Marcel van der Linden (Berlin and Boston: De Gruyter Oldenbourg, 2018), 1–14.

3 Javier Fernández Sebastián, ed., *Diccionario político y social del mundo iberoamericano: Conceptos políticos fundamentales, 1770–1870* (Madrid: Centro de Estudios Políticos y Constitucionales – Universidad del País Vasco, 2014).

4 Ada Ferrer, *Freedom's Mirror: Cuba and Haiti in the Age of Revolution* (New York: Cambridge University Press, 2014).

5 Martín Rodrigo Alharilla and Lizbeth Chaviano, eds., *Negreros y esclavos: Barcelona y la esclavitud atlántica, siglos XI – XIX* (Barcelona: Icaria, 2017).

Studies on Cuba pay little attention to identifying the contributions of various agents (landowners, experts, slaves, etc.) and technologies in tropical agriculture in the context of the "second slavery" and the environmental conquest during the industrialisation of the nineteenth century from the perspective of labour relations in conversation with other methodological approaches. This is most likely due to the influence of the thesis on the immobility of tropical agriculture associated with dependency theory.[6] Sugar's industrial modernity was surely co-constitutive of racial agricultural capitalism based on African slavery and other forms of coerced labour, as was the case with Asian labour. Some texts observe the colonies as authentic laboratories of modernity to emphasise the presence of multiple and heterogeneous modernities in the face of the Western Eurocentric gaze. Mintz, for example, argues that the Caribbean sugar slave plantation represented the beginning of modernity.[7] Other studies argue for the possible colonial origin of the modern factory system based on the existence of different forms of coerced labour in the colonies that were constitutive of the wage worker training process.

Labour history has focused on the working class and its struggles after the 1959 Cuban Revolution, whose narrative responded to Marxist endeavours but also to Eurocentric ones that excluded other labour relations, including slavery.[8] Slavery studies, on the other hand, highlight resistance tactics used by slaves, which ranged from rebellions and maroonage – slaves who fled and took refuge in the countryside – to demonstrate their access to various mechanisms to achieve freedom.[9] More recently, geographers, botanists and

---

6   For a historiographical analysis of labor relations and slavery in Latin America and the Caribbean, see James P. Brennam, "Latin America Labor History," in *The Oxford Handbook of Latin America History*, ed. José C. Moya (New York: Oxford University Press, 2011), 342–63; Rossana Barragán and David Mayer, "Latin America and the Caribbean," and Patrick Manning, "Slave Labour," in *Handbook Global History of Work*, ed. Karin Hofmeester and Marcel van der Linden (Berlin and Boston: De Gruyter Oldenbourg, 2018), 83–110 and 377–94.

7   Sidney Mintz, *Sweetness and Power: The Place of Sugar in Modern History* (New York: Viking, 1985).

8   Joan Casanovas Codina, *Bread, or Bullets! Urban Labor and Spanish Colonialism in Cuba, 1850–1898* (Pittsburgh, PA: University of Pittsburgh, 1998); Robert J, Alexander, *A History of Organized Labor in Cuba* (Westport, Conn: Praeger, 2002).

9   Rebecca Scott, *Slave Emancipation: The Transition to Free Labor, 1860–1899* (Pittsburgh, PA: University of Pittsburgh Press, 2000); Manuel Barcia, *Seeds of Insurrection: Domination and Resistance on Western Cuban Plantations, 1808–1848* (Baton Rouge: Louisiana State University Press, 2009); and Alejandro de la Fuente and Ariela J. Gross, *Becoming Free, Becoming Black: Race, Freedom, and Law in Cuba, Virginia, and Louisiana* (New York: Cambridge University Press, 2020). A recent study offers new insights into the efforts and mechanisms carried out by the slaves to achieve freedom. See Claudia

historians of science have examined the transmission of medicinal, nutritional and religious knowledge of enslaved Africans in the Americas.[10]

This chapter examines the creation of a narrative centred on the idealisation of the environment to organise the tropical agrarian space in the context of industrial modernity in Cuba. This was in contrast to the introduction of technologies and expert personnel in response to the deterioration of natural production conditions. The second section highlights the control mechanisms of slave labour relations exercised by the landowners, but, above all, it illuminates the gaps in the plantation system itself that allow slaves to be valued as human beings rather than as machines, which is one of the prevailing theses in sugar historiography. A final section analyses Cuba's connection with various global-local production chains and labour relations through the promotion and sale of Liebig's Extract of Meat Company products on the European market, the success of the livestock industry in Uruguay, and the illegal transatlantic slave trade.

2　The Commodification of the Environment: The Invention of Prodigal Tropical Agriculture

The benign climate and extremely fertile land of Cuba – benefitted from what I term "prodigal tropical agriculture" – were heralded by various institutional and private agents as the ideal natural conditions to support the thesis of Cuban exceptionalism, which was centred on the consolidation of the sugar plantation. In 1768, Agustín Crame published a report to promote the development of agriculture with the information collected during a reconnaissance and exploration trip throughout the entire colonial territory.[11] Crame, a Spanish-Flemish

Varela and Manuel Barcia, *Wage-Earning Slaves: Coartacion in Nineteenth-Century Cuba* (Gainesville: University Press of Florida, 2020).

10　Judith A. Carney and Richard Nicholas Rosomoff, *In the Shadow of Slavery: Africa's Botanical Legacy in the Atlantic World* (Berkeley, Los Angeles, and London: University of California Press, 2009); Robert Voeks and John Rashford, *African Ethnobotany in the Americas* (New York: Springer, 2013); Leida Fernández Prieto, "Plantas, plantas y saberes en la red del tráfico negrero: Cuba-España-África," in *Cádiz y el tráfico de esclavos: De la legalidad a la clandestinidad,* ed. Martin Rodrigo y Alharilla and Maria del Carmen Cózar Navarro (Madrid: Silex, 2018), 295–321.

11　Agustín Crame, *Discurso político sobre la necesidad de fomentar la isla de Cuba acompañado de una breve descripción de sus principales pueblos y planos de toda la Isla,* Archivo General de Indias (AGI), SD, Materias Gubernativas, leg. 1157, fols. 120–177; Leida Fernández Prieto, "Crónica anunciada de una Cuba Azucarera," in *Francisco Arango y la*

military engineer, was part of the group of colonial officials in charge of imple-
menting the Bourbon reforms after the British returned Havana to Spain. He
was also a representative of the English trading houses that introduced slaves
from the island of Jamaica, one of the routes that blurred imperial frontiers
in the sugar business early on. Crame highlighted the supposed superiority of
the fertility of Cuban lands compared to those of the British colony to ensure
the success of the slave plantation system. He associated that fertility with the
abundance of virgin woodlands, although he was aware of the productive limits when he mentioned the use of fertiliser in Jamaica.

Cuba illustrates the place of ecology as a central analytical category in the
creation of the environmental concept of "prodigal tropical agriculture" and
racialised labour relations as part of industrial modernity that rested on an
unprecedented drive for slavery through the illicit trade of human beings. On
the one hand, I have chosen this term because tropical agriculture encompasses
colonial agriculture. On the other hand, I want to underscore the value of tropical ecosystems in the production of agricultural commodities destined for the
world market through the design of the slave plantation system. This concept
is built on the foundation of multiple and contradictory qualifications that
continue to this day. For instance, talking about the tropics evokes notions of
abundance, lavishness, exuberance and fertility and, at the same time, of decadence, backwardness, and the supposed absence of scientific innovations in
the collective imagination, in a way that crosses historical analyses. The term
reflects various tensions between temperate and tropical agriculture, between
modernity and backwardness, domination and tutelage, and the racial division
of labour common to colonial agriculture. All of these notions made up the language of slave-based industrial agricultural modernity between 1750 and 1870.

The Creole statesman and landowner Francisco de Arango y Parreño argued
for the exceptionality of Cuba's natural conditions from a free trade position
applied to export agriculture. Arango defined this system as "branches of
extraction," thinking of it as a form of "plantation agriculture" that he associated with "prosperity" and the "happiness" of obtaining free trade from Spain,
greater facilities for the introduction of slaves, and greater possibilities to
convince landowners to adopt all of the advances of the Industrial Revolution
for the development of slave-based sugar production.[12] He was considered

---

         invención de la Cuba azucarera, ed. María Dolores González-Ripoll and Izaskun Álvarez
         Cuartero (Salamanca: Universidad de Salamanca, 2009), 55–65.

12   Francisco Arango y Parreño, *Obras* (Havana: Ministerio de Educación, 1952); María Dolores
         González-Ripoll and Izaskun Álvarez Cuartero, eds., *Francisco Arango y la invención de la
         Cuba azucarera* (Salamanca: Universidad de Salamanca, 2009).

the ideologue responsible for the invention of a "sugar producing" Cuba. For Arango, the island had "vastness, a happy location, fertile soil, a variety of productions and abundant and beautiful ports," which distinguished it from the rest of the Antilles when it came to developing plantation agriculture based on slavery. In his view, blacks were the "necessary evil" because they were best able to withstand the rigours of the climate. Thus, Arango followed in the wake of those who justified the myth of European whites' inability to perform agricultural work in tropical zones. He also defended the supposed kindness of the Spaniards towards the slaves as opposed to the French people's inhumane treatment, a "black legend" repeated in numerous later works.

Arango proposed to transplant the slave plantation model to the European industrial centres and the British and French sugar colonies, and put forward a plan for the creation of a local board for the protection of agriculture. The objective of the expedition was to become familiar with industrial advances because "even in the fertile lands, this fertility ends and here industry enters to replace it." Like Cramer, Arango was aware of the limits of the commodification of tropical nature. Historians have analysed the industrial espionage trip as part of the landowners' local strategies to catapult the island as the primary producer of cane sugar in the world, after the Haitian Revolution.[13] This expedition illustrated the circulation of knowledge through the recruitment of expert personnel among the Caribbean sugar colonies. For example, Julien Lardière, a French sugar technician, was contacted in Jamaica for the subsequent modernisation of the so-called new mills in Cuba at the end of the eighteenth century and the beginning of the nineteenth century.[14] The landowners created the *Real Junta de Fomento de la Habana* (Royal Board of Development of Havana) with the approval of the Spanish Crown. This institution and the *Real Sociedad Económica de Amigos del País* (Royal Economic Society of Friends of the Country) were spaces for the dissemination and creation of agro-industrial knowledge, although it is better to study these institutions in terms of industrial modernity rather than agricultural improvements. The landowners prioritised the introduction of industrial technologies, since they understood that obtaining sugar relied on factory processing. They relied on the benign climate

---

13   María Dolores González-Ripoll, "Dos viajes, una intención: Francisco Arango y Alejandro Oliván en Europa y las Antillas azucareras (1794 y 1829)," *Revista de Indias* 62, no. 224 (2002): 85–102.

14   Leida Fernández Prieto, "Mapping the Global and Local Scientific Archipelago: Agriculture, Knowledge and Practices, 1790–1870," in *Global Scientific Practice in an Age of Revolutions, 1750–1850*, ed. Patrick Manning and Daniel Rood (Pittsburgh, PA: University of Pittsburgh Press, 2016), 181–98.

and the fertility of the soil for their achievements in agriculture. This idea has been confirmed above all by economic historians, who have insisted that the landowners did not introduce agricultural reforms. References to their role in the introduction and/or acclimatisation of plants, successful or not, and the participation of various agents in local trials and experiments are found in memoirs and reports from the two institutions, which merit further study.

Arango was one of the local informants who hosted the well-known Baron Alexander von Humboldt, who more precisely defined the role of tropical regions for the production of "agricultural types," or "colonial productions," destined for European industrial manufacturing.[15] Humboldt witnessed the major capital investments that went into modernising the mill factories. At the same time, he recognised the fertility of Cuban lands that produced for more than twenty years without the need for replanting. In his essay, however, he warned about deforestation and fuel shortages as problems for the island's sugar industry. Von Humboldt was critical of the slave trade and how landowners considered slaves "beasts of burden," criticisms that earned him initial censorship in Cuba. Writing from a Eurocentric point of view, the German traveller suggested the formation and training of *criollos* (creoles, or locally-born people) in European laboratories to achieve improvements in the manufacturing of beet sugar to cane sugar, rather than depending on more or less successful local experiments. This proposal had previously been defended by important landowners from the *Sociedad Económica de Amigos del País* and the *Real Junta de Fomento de la Habana*.

In 1840, Spanish chemist José Luis Casaseca described the so-called Cuban Industrial Revolution, based on the installation of steam engines in the mills to increase industrial yields. Previously, in 1837, the introduction of the railroad extended the boundaries of sugar plantations. That is how landowners in Cuba consolidated the strategy of industrial technological development and the "art of making sugar," understood as the empirical skills of the sugar master responsible for manufacturing and/or applied chemistry to the industry by specialised workers, almost always from industrial centres. In other words, the term worked interchangeably both to designate amateur knowledge and specialised knowledge.

---

15   Miguel Ángel Puig-Samper, Consuelo Naranjo Orovio, and Armando García González, eds., *Ensayo Político de la isla de Cuba, Alexander von Humboldt* (Aranjuez: Doce Calles, Junta de Castilla y León, 1998).

In recent decades, new studies maintain that the colony was not a simple recipient of the advances of the industrial sugar revolution.[16] The texts highlight the role of the local elite as agents of enlightenment and modernisation based on the introduction of European and American ideas and machinery, the translation of reference works, research trips, and data collection endorsed by the Spanish empire. These approaches continue to privilege the industrial process. Other debates revolve around profitability and the impossibility of adopting new technological advances with the use of slave labour.[17] On the other hand, some authors observe the correlation between the greater technological impulse and the so-called second slavery, which strengthened American industrial capitalism.[18] The studies exclude technological changes in agriculture and the participation therein of farmers, skilled personnel and slaves.

In 1845, Ramón de la Sagra was the first to define tropical agriculture based on biological, social and racial ideas in the context of the Industrial Revolution and the European division of labour. Sagra was the director of the Botanical Garden in Havana, a colonial institution that developed the plan for scientific reforms based on slavery. He employed the work of so-called emancipated Africans, those Africans whom the British located on slave ships and declared free under abolitionist treaties.[19] In reality, they were again enslaved, forced to work in the construction of urban sites and on plantation agriculture. For the Spanish botanist and agronomist, the overpopulation and food shortage in Europe could be solved by a division between agricultural colonies and manufacturing empires, between the Old World and the New World. Sagra justified the colonial function of producers of raw materials for the European market

---

16   María M. Portuondo, "Plantation Factories: Science and Technology in Late-Eighteenth-Century Cuba," *Technology and Culture* 44 (April 2003): 231–57; Jonathan Curry-Machado, *Cuban Sugar Industry: Transnational Networks and Engineering Migrantsin Mid-Nineteenth Century Cuba* (New York: Palgrave Macmillan, 2011); Adrian Leonard and David Pretel, eds., *The Caribbean and the Atlantic World Economy: Circuits of Trade, Money and Knowledge, 1650–1914* (Basingstoke: Palgrave Macmillan, 2015).

17   Laird W. Bergad, Fe Iglesias García, and María del Carmen Barcia, *The Cuban Slave Market, 1790–1880* (New York: Cambridge University Press, 1995).

18   Dale W. Tomich, *Through the Prism of Slavery: Labor, Capital, and World Economy* (Lanham, Md.D: Rowman & Littlefield, 2004); Dale W. Tomich, ed., *New Frontiers of Slavery* (New York: SUNY Press, 2016); Dale W. Tomich, ed., *Slavery and Historical Capitalism during the Nineteenth Century* (Lanhan, MD: Lexington Books, 2017).

19   Inés Roldán de Montaud, "The Misfortune of Liberated Africans in Colonial Cuba, 1824–76," in *Liberated Africans and the Abolition of the Slave Trade, 1807–1896*, ed. Richard Anderson and Henry B. Lovejoy (Rochester, NY: University of Rochester Press, 2020), 153–73.

because: "the intertropical regions seem to be nature's laboratory, and the temperate and cold [regions are] the manufacturers of art," or "nations that change the products of their labour industry for the exclusives of a prodigal nature little supported even by human ingenuity," in a clear allusion to slavery.[20] It was probably the first time that the term *ingenio* was tied to intelligence and the first time that scientific practice was applied to agriculture in Cuba.

For the botanist, colonial agriculture was in its "infancy" because it did not include cattle ranching, which was common in intensive farming in Europe in order to maintain the soil's fertility rather than abandoning it in search of virgin lands to clear and cultivate. Thus, Sagra clearly warned readers about the negative effects of deforestation that characterised plantation agriculture:

> Devastating logging and the system of unpredictability that directs it are transformed into barren and scorched plains that were formerly thick and leafy. And successively temperatures will rise and the precipitation will be reduced ... where the trees are annihilated a scene of loneliness and death will replace the laughing spectacle of a young and wild nature that offered to reward with usury the efforts of well-managed industry.[21]

Sagra believed that prodigal nature had triumphed over a "vicious organisation" with regard to slavery. He argued that slaves belonged to a "savage race" that made the "progress of cultivation impossible," and wrote about "the basis of their backwardness and the great and insurmountable obstacle that has always been experienced in the Antilles to constitute agriculture as a science, as it is practised in Europe," the "paralysing" element of "the soil's natural forces and the intellectual means of man," and "the building of tropical agriculture on the absurd foundation of force, ignorance, and the unforeseen." In other words, he put forward the thesis of the impossibility of introducing scientific advances with slave labour, which has cut through historical debates to this day. By contrast, European white settlers were portrayed as "active, honest, industrious and able to withstand the milder climate of those regions," debunking the myth of the rigours of the tropical climate for white settlement.

The farmers' search for solutions to lower production costs in the face of competition from beet sugar and Spain's supposed prohibition of the slave trade, facilitated the entry of European white settlers, Yucatecans and Chinese

---

20   Ramón de la Sagra, *Estudios coloniales con aplicación a la isla de Cuba* (Madrid: Imprenta de D. Dionisio Hidalgo, 1845).

21   Ramón de la Sagra, *Historia económico-política y estadística de la Isla de Cuba* (Havana: Imprenta de la Viuda de Arazoza y Soler, 1831), 84–85. My translation.

coolies in the context of the second slavery. In 1847, for example, the *criollo* landowner Pedro Diago brought in more than five hundred Chinese coolies from Amoy to work in his mill, with the support of the *Real Junta de Fomento*. From then on, the country saw the arrival of thousands of Chinese coolies on English and North American ships. Therefore, we should not be surprised by Sagra's defence of the immigration of Chinese coolies – the "Asian race," which he defined as "a crucial element for the recent improvements in agriculture" – as opposed to slavery.

The French publishers Eduardo Laplante and Luis Marquier and the Creole landowner Justo G. Cantero presented the industrial modernity of the mills as a symbol of prosperity to an international audience.[22] Cantero described the relationship between sugar cane, tropical climate and fertility that fed the discursive myth of earthly paradise and prodigal nature common to tropical agricultural colonies. His descriptions of the sugar mills, however, alluded to frequent episodes of droughts, soil exhaustion and hurricanes that affected the plantations. This translated into greater attention from farmers to agricultural experimentation, the hiring and participation of expert personnel, the introduction and dissemination of equipment, the use of fertilisers, and the coexistence of slavery with other types of labour, such as Asian workers in a degree of semi-slavery, involved in the production of goods for the world market.

Tropical agriculture more clearly reflected the periphery/periphery, Atlantic/Pacific and centre/periphery connections through biological transfers and the introduction and diffusion of mechanical farming and modern practices with the participation of landowners, who were experts in plantations and slaves. Tracing these exchanges documents the global and local debates associated with the application of scientific knowledge to solve the ecological, economic and social problems of industrial slave-based agriculture. Here, I refer to the global diffusion of sugar cane varieties, the introduction and application of fertilisers and technologies – hallmarks of modern agriculture – but also to the fragility of the tropical environment.

The Caribbean islands proved the ideal homeland for the acclimatisation of sugar cane, to the point that many naturalists and travellers were unsure

---

22 Luis Miguel García Mora and Antonio Santamaria García, eds., *Los ingenios: Colección de vistas de los principales ingenios de azúcar de la isla de Cuba*, ed. Justo G. Cantero and Eduardo Laplante (Madrid: CSIC-Doce Calles, 2005). New studies highlight the place of lithography for analysis of the control of the industrial landscape of plantation and slave labour. See Dale W. Tomich et al., *Reconstructing the Landscapes of Slavery: A Visual History of the Plantation in the Nineteenth-Century Atlantic World* (Chapel Hill: University of North Carolina Press, 2021).

whether the plant was indigenous or exotic. This issue became very important when the Otaheiti variety, key to the development of the Caribbean
sugar industry, degenerated on the oldest sugar cane plantations. The Otaheiti
variety had first entered Cuba via the transatlantic sugar and slave trade circuits in 1789. During his sugar expedition, Arango had learned of the Otaheiti
cane variety's advantage in adapting to the machinery established in Cuba.
Thereafter, he ordered a large quantity of seeds from the slave trader Philip
("Felipe" to the Cubans) Allwood. Alexander von Humboldt also confirmed
that the sugar cane variety had debunked his fear that it would degenerate
in the New World. Even so, landowners chose to sow different varieties in the
plantations in Cuba, which turned the plantations into true fields of experimentation in the context of industrialisation, including Cristalina (from Java),
and that ultimately prevailed on the exhausted soil. Landowners also organised expeditions to search for new Otaheiti canes in the original domestica-
tion sites, an aspect that is hardly considered in historiography. This was the
case with the successful expedition of Tomás de Juara y Soler, who ordered
cane from Otaheiti (now Tahiti) to be delivered to the Pacific islands. The
seed arrived in fifteen boxes through the Tahiti route – California – Panama –
Colon – New Orleans – Havana. The whole trip took four months. Others tried
to bring seeds from the United States and even devised a (failed) expedition to
the island of Tahiti via France.

In 1846, the first sugar plague broke out, affecting the Otaheiti cane on the
British island of Mauritius and the French island of Bourbon (now Réunion).
The overall strategy was the introduction of new varieties from Java, other
regions of Southeast Asia and Oceania, Brazil and Egypt. At the same time,
institutional and private agents began to pay more attention to scientific study
and global-local experimentation. Cuba was not affected by the plague but it
raised the issue of the plant's degeneration on exhausted soils and, with it,
the beginning of debates on the cane's supposed infertility when seeds were
obtained from the crossing of several varieties. For example, Cantero recalled
that Leonard Wray did not understand why agronomists wanted to obtain
seed when it was impossible and he recommended the Otaheiti and Salangore
varieties in the main sugar treatise of the period.[23] The sugar cane hybrid was
likely obtained in Barbados and Java in the late nineteenth century.

---

23   Leonard Hume Wray, *The Practical Sugar Planter: A Complete Account of the Cultivation
        and Manufacture of the Sugar cane, According to the Latest and most Improved Processes*
        (London: Smith, Elder, 1848); Stuart G. McCook, *States of Nature: Science, Agriculture and
        Environment in the Spanish Caribbean 1760–1940* (Austin: University of Texas Press, 2002);

Cuba became a laboratory and a meeting place between the practices of European and domestic landowners, between the global and the local, with the introduction and application of organic and chemical fertilisers. The landowners tried different types of fertilisers, including guano, due to its high level of organic matter, when they found that the "prodigal" nature of the country was not exempt from the increasing decline in agricultural yields. The application of organic and chemical fertilisers favoured the entry of scientific sugar agriculture into the Spanish colony. This made the overlapping of circuits visible to consolidate both industrial and agricultural modernity. For example, in 1840, Pedro Diago used the same transatlantic sugar and slave networks for the acquisition and commercialisation of Peruvian guano fertiliser through the New York firm A.B. Allen.[24] At the same time, the landowners once again relied on the recruitment of workers and experts from the industrial centres for their farms. At his Las Cañas sugar mill, Juan Poey tested manure compost prepared according to the European model, that is, in pits made on his own farms, under the direction of Edgar Carbonne, a French engineer based in Cárdenas, Cuba. This mill, like others, was financed with capital from the slave trade.

Likewise, the progressive generalisation of certain mechanical equipment (ploughs and rollers, among others), illustrates the connections with industrial centres in the United States and England, but it also highlights how the tropical agrarian space responded to local demands. The English firm Fowler and Company commissioned the in situ construction of special ploughs for the terrain conditions in Cuba, including the steam plough tested at the plantation owned by Miguel Aldama in 1863. By contrast, the diffusion of the mechanical plough reflected the multidirectional connections that existed: periphery/periphery, Atlantic/Pacific and centre/periphery. This was the case with the Messrs Ransome Company, which created the Ransome's Patent Indian Cultivator plough in India. This plough was later used in the West Indies; Jamaica in particular was cited as an example of the exchange of techniques from East to West.

Landowners in Cuba called the cultivation in rows – planting at an adequate distance that would allow the use of agricultural implements – "Louisiana-style" growing. This indicated that the landowners were looking more towards the mechanised agriculture practised in the United States, the country from

---

Leida Fernández Prieto, "Islands of Knowledge: Science and Agriculture in the History of Latin American and the Caribbean," *Isis* 104, no. 4 (December 2013): 786–97.

24   Roland T. Ely, *Cuando reinaba Su Majestad el Azúcar: Estudio histórico-sociológico de una tragedia latinoamericana; El monocultivo en Cuba, origen y evolución del proceso* (Havana: Imagen Contemporánea, 2001), 574.

which the equipment was sent, and that the wide dissemination and exchange of knowledge and practices often erased their origins. The *criollo* agronomist Álvaro Reynoso thought this method of sugar cultivation should be called "English" because it had been applied to sugar cane for the first time in English, and later French, colonies. It was introduced in Cuba by Alexandre Dumont, a French officer who emigrated after the Saint-Domingue Revolution, but who then did not become a general in the Spanish colony.

Reynoso is considered the father of Cuban scientific agriculture. He was a disciple of Justus von Liebig during his landowner-funded studies in Europe. He made a series of agricultural scientific trips in Cuba that culminated in numerous publications. Of these, the best known was the "Essay on the Cultivation of Sugar Cane" (1862), which became the leading manual for Java and Brazil but not for Cuba.[25] Reynoso's work placed agriculture as the cornerstone of the modernisation of the sugar industry despite slavery. In this text, Reynoso defined the guidelines of the integral Cultivation System that took into account various ecological, socio-economic and cultural factors, as well as the scientific procedures for producing a greater quantity of sugar. For example, he mentions drainage systems, the use of organic and chemical fertilisers, and the use of agricultural mechanics. In his essay, Reynoso used the terms "local agriculture" and "our agriculture" for the first time, as well as "backward, primitive, transhumant or emigration agriculture," because he sought virgin lands. For him, extensive cultivation was contrary to civilisation. However, Reynoso understood that the priority was to modernise the industrial factory because he had invested a lot of capital, knowledge and workers, relative to the abundance of land and the absence of the knowledge and men necessary to propagate scientific agriculture.

Reynoso participated in the "black legend" of the landowners' treatment of slaves, whom he not only identified as workers, but he also bought them and described them as "happier than European workers because they are better fed, have comfortable and healthy rooms, have infirmaries that are like the best hospitals, not due to petty calculations of interest but to a true advance in humanitarian sentiments," an opinion Cantero also held. However, Reynoso tried to dismantle Sagra's thesis on the impossibility of introducing modern agricultural equipment with slave labour because, at times, the enslaved labourers were sugar masters, carpenters, machinists and blacksmiths, much

---

25   Álvaro Reynoso, *Ensayo sobre el cultivo de la caña de azúcar* (Havana: Imprenta del Tiempo, 1862); Ulbe Bosma and Jonathan Curry-Machado, "Two Islands, One Commodity: Cuba, Java, and the Global Sugar Trade (1790–1930)," *Nieuwe West-Indische Gids* (*New West Indian Guide*) 86 (2012): 237–62.

more difficult trades. Historians do not know the level of slave agency during the introduction of agricultural technologies. Some of the manual labour on the plantations consisted of practices known to Africans, such as clearing, felling and burning, or the planting of rice and yams, because many of them came from the so-called crop belt on the west coast of Africa. Therein lies the question: Did enslaved populations reproduce or recreate African knowledge and practices on plantations in Cuba?

3   The Slave as Machine?

Traditionally, economic historiography on Cuba considers the slave as a key entity within the productive chain of sugar manufacturing, a human machine that landowners exploited and controlled in a rational way in order to obtain greater outputs and profitability.[26] From this perspective, studies deny the possibility that slaves reproduced and/or transmitted their knowledge and practices originating in Africa. Other scholars, on the other hand, demonstrate the transfer of African knowledge for the development of commercial crops such as rice and indigo in plantations in the southern United States.[27] New approaches underscore the opportunity for medical careers from the practice and study of slave diseases on Caribbean plantations.[28] According to the authors of these studies, the owners were interested in preserving the health and guaranteeing the reproduction of their primary workforce by hiring doctors and professionals who centred their studies on slaves in order to justify slavery and scientific racism. In fact, the plantations became spaces for the circulation and exchange of medical knowledge in the Atlantic, as was the case for French physician and anthropologist Henri Dumont's research on sugar plantations in Cuba.

---

26   Manuel Moreno Fraginals is still the main reference among Cuban sugar historians. See Manuel Moreno Fraginals, *El ingenio* (Barcelona: Crítica, 2002).

27   Judith A. Carney, *Black Rice: The African Origins of Rice Cultivation in the Americas* (Cambridge, MA Harvard University Press, 2001); Andrea Fesser, *Red, White, and Black Make Blue: Indigo in the Fabric of Colonial South Carolina Life* (Athens, GA: University of Georgia Press, 2013).

28   Steven Palmer; "From the Plantation to the Academy: Slavery and the Production of Cuban Medicine in the Nineteenth Century," *Health and Medicine in the Circum-Caribbean, 1800–1968*, ed. Juanita De Barros, Steven Palmer, and David Wright (New York: Routledge, 2009), 53–75; Diego Armus and Adrian López Denis, "Disease, Medicine, and Health," in *The Oxford Handbook of Latin America History*, ed. José C. Moya (New York: Oxford University Press, 2011), 424–53.

Keeping the working days for slaves very long was a tactic used by the land-owners to control and prevent possible uprisings, escapes or suicides.[29] The long duration of more than twelve hours of work, with hardly any rest and few hours for sleeping, caused multiple work accidents and cases of limb mutilation, and a higher percentage of deaths between May and June at the end of the milling. Likewise, landowners maintained a register and kept strict control over their slave workers. The *mayoral*, the person in charge of watching over them and doling out work and punishments, forced slaves to sing in order to prevent them from carrying out acts of resistance, which some authors identify as strategies for them to act as automatons in carrying out their jobs.

The degree to which slaves were objectified, the predominance of male slaves on plantations, and the young age at which enslaved people were brought onto slave ships constitute some of the historiographic theses put forward by scholars to argue the impossibility for slaves to transmit knowledge and practices originating from Africa. The analyses are based on the fact that women were the main agricultural workforce on the African continent, the low level of sexual reproduction, the overexploitation of slave labour, and possible demographic collapse, which would justify the scarce presence of mitochondrial DNA among the current Cuban population.[30] Following attestations that some African populations enjoyed forms of resistance to pathogens and certain diseases, geneticist Beatriz Marcheco analysed a significant sample of the population in Cuba. The result was that 72 per cent of the Cuban population's genes are of European origin compared to 20 per cent being of African origin, which contrasts with the high number and late introduction of enslaved Africans to the island, at least until 1867. This has led to the questioning of the myth that slavery in Cuba was relatively benign. On the contrary, Marcheco's study suggests the need to undertake a broader analysis to clarify whether there was a possible demographic collapse due to the effects of malnutrition, exploitation, suicides and infections.

The problem with these theses, especially from the perspective of economic rationality, is that they ignore the fact that slaves were people of flesh and blood; or, in other words, they perpetuate the dehumanisation and victimisation of slaves within labour relations. Moreno Fraginals pointed to a change in strategies among planters and traffickers to bring more women onto slave

---

29   For an analysis of the different strategies in the control of slaves in Cuba, see José Antonio Piqueras, ed., *Orden político y gobierno de esclavos* (Alzira, Valencia: Centro Francisco Tomás y Valiente, UNED, 2016).

30   Cesar Fortes-Lima et al., "Exploring Cuba's Population Structure and Demographic Story Using Genome-Wide Data," *Scientific Reports*, 11422 (2018).

ships, seeking a balance within the plantations around 1850, in the context of the sugar boom. Following Spivak's idea, slaves perhaps most clearly illustrate the absence of written testimonies from subordinate subjects. Even so, the records of emancipated Africans and other sources have been insufficiently explored to document the life histories of slaves and to trace the possible transmission of knowledge and practices in Cuba, beyond religious knowledge, which is much better-studied.

Daniel Rood highlights the contribution of a transnational group of "plantation experts" in adapting the technologies of the Industrial Revolution to the conditions of the tropics, as well as in forging alliances in the Upper South in the United States, Cuba, and Brazil that broke with British dominance and the circuits of the American Northeast.[31] Focusing on the manufacturing process, Rood illustrates the indispensable involvement of enslaved people in obtaining tropical expert know-how and maintaining profitability. For this, he alludes to the skills and knowledge of slaves who worked on the expansion of railways and other trades linked to their roles in the development of new technologies for the sugar mills. For example, Rood highlights the introduction and adaptation of the steam system devised by the French-American Afro-descendant Norbert Rillieux, the son of a white slave owner and a free woman of colour, whose knowledge paradoxically contributed to reinforcing racial ideologies and the dominance of slave owners.

One of the most atrocious measures implemented by landowners on Cuban plantations was linked to birth control, and was meant to guarantee the replacement of the slave labour market, given the possible end of the illicit trade and the probable labour shortage due to the low birth rates on the plantations. This measure worked against slaves' abortive practices based on their ancestral knowledge of plant properties. Fraginals stated that more than 25 per cent of slave women suffered from so-called "fallen uterus" due to the use of abortifacient plants for birth control. He pointed out that certain ethnic groups from the Congo living in Cuba used potions made with papaya fruit and leaves to induce miscarriage.

At some sugar mills, despicable *criollo* breeding spaces – a term clearly connecting the slaves with cattle – were used, dedicated to the sexual reproduction and birth control of slaves. Among his descriptions of Cuban industrial magnificence, Cantero documented this practice, for instance as it was carried

31   Daniel Rood, *The Reinvention of the Atlantic Slavery: Technology, Labor, Race, and Capitalism in the Greater Caribbean* (New York: Oxford University Press, 2017).

FIGURE 9.1   Sugar mill
SOURCE: LUIS MIGUEL GARCÍA MORA AND ANTONIO SANTAMARIA GARCÍA,
ED., *LOS INGENIOS: COLECCIÓN DE VISTAS DE LOS PRINCIPALES INGENIOS DE
AZÚCAR DE LA ISLA DE CUBA*, WRITTEN BY JUSTO G. CANTERO AND DRAWN BY
EDUARDO LAPLANTE (MADRID: CSIC-DOCE CALLES, 2005)

out at the Trinidad or Vista Hermosa sugar mill, owned by Esteban José Santa
Cruz de Oviedo y Hernández and located in a sugar region par

excellence, which had more than a thousand slaves (see figure 1): "Next to
this farm, and assisted by his group of Negroes, he has a *criollo* breeding place,
well kept by the owner, who is able to have an increase of thirty blacks year
after year .... During one half of the year the Negroes are fed viands and during
the other half they are fed corn flour, rice and beans, and often fresh beef and
pork as well, and three large meals over the course of the day. To this care is
owed the cessation on this farm of the dysentery that was previously carried
by so many individuals."[32]

The idealisation and "romantic" vision of slavery that the book transmitted
was interspersed with references to the inhuman practices of these degrading spaces, such as the rapes suffered by female slaves in sugar cultivation

32   García Mora and Santamaría, *Los ingenios*, 163. My translation.

throughout the nineteenth century. Santa Cruz de Oviedo had no legitimate children from his marriage. In 1851, twenty-six of his children from slaves were recognised. This violence contrasted with the elementary education provided: he financed some of his children to continue their instruction in New York, and six others went to study in Paris. What's more, in a case similar to Rillieux's, his eldest son inherited and perpetuated the father's sugar business, the origins of which stemmed from human trafficking.

Cantero also made detailed references to the barracks where the slaves lived, and to the *conucos*, plots of land given by the landowners to the slaves for gardening and to guarantee the mill's self-sufficiency, the surplus of which they could sell the local market and to nearby farms. This practice was carried out mainly by women, like in Africa. In the *conucos*, or "gardens" of the dispossessed, slaves grew food and raised pigs and chickens. For some authors, these spaces point to the transmission of African knowledge and practices because many of these crops were known and important in African agriculture, like the aforementioned rice and yams.[33]

Other historians suggest that the practice of the landowners of allowing the slaves the *conucos* for their self-subsistence disappeared with the generalisation of barracks in the context of industrialisation.[34] The barracks were closed buildings with separate rooms for men and women, in some cases with rooms for families, and kitchens in the centre. On the one hand, it is very likely that the two practices coexisted, especially since Cuba was not completely overrun by sugar monoculture in the nineteenth century. On the other hand, Esteban Montejo, a former maroon, affirmed in his biography the fact that even the barracks had *conucos*, located behind the buildings, to ensure the slaves' subsistence.[35]

As a control measure, landowners established racial categories through assigning tasks based on the African ethnic groups origins of the enslaved. According to Fraginals, the owners preferred the enslaved Lucumi Africans for working the mills given their supposed strength, although they were feared

33   Judith A. Carney, "African Traditional Plant Knowledge in the Circum-Caribbean Region," *Journal of Ethnobiology* 23, no. 2 (2003): 167–85; Miguel Esquivel and Karl P. Hammer, "The Cuban Homegarden 'Conuco': A Perspective Environment for Evolution and In Situ Conservation of Plant Genetic Resources," *Genetic Resources and Crop Evolution* 39, no. 1 (January 1992): 9–22.

34   Moreno Fraginals, *El ingenio*, 37; Mercedes García Rodríguez, *Entre haciendas y plantaciones: Los orígenes de la manufactura azucarera de La Habana* (Havana: Editorial de Ciencias Sociales, 2007).

35   Miguel Barnet and Esteban Montejo, *Biografía de un cimarrón* (Manchester: Manchester University Press, 2010).

for their fierceness and inclination to suicide. Similarly, he pointed out that another strategy was to separate the various ethnic groups, although Fraginals indicated that the Lucumis, Mandingas and Congos understood each other.

In 1866, a cynical book circulated in Havana comparing wage labourers in Spain and slave labourers in its colony. Europe was the clear audience for this publication. Under the initials R.J.E., Ramón J. Espinosa agreed with Reynoso that the slaves had better lives than workers, because they did not have to worry about food and medicine, which the slave owners were responsible for.[36] Espinosa included racial categories to describe the slave as being brutalised, submissive and lazy. In his opinion, blacks born in Africa who still spoke their native languages, belonged to the "true" African race, which occupied a lower rank than the Western race. Likewise, he was in favour of a racial division of labour according to ethnic groups, placing the Arará at the fore because they adapted best to European civilisation, saved up to buy their freedom, and were family-oriented and, therefore, more submissive. He defended the policy of the "good" slave owners who gave the African-born slave a pig and a plot of land because it assured their loyalty to the slave owner and a sense of belonging. According to Espinosa, the daily ration consisted of sixteen ounces of meat, sweet potatoes, bananas, yucca, taro and corn flour, almost all of which were planted by the slaves. He also recalled that two slaves were assigned to instruct the others in Christian customs from the time they were baptised, among other supposed benefits of slavery in Cuba.

For the present purposes, however, the text is particularly of interest as it allows us to follow the life stories of three enslaved Africans that confirmed the horrors of illegal human trafficking, even when this was conducted behind the veil of the supposed benignity of slavery. Nicolás, an imposed Christian name, of the Arará ethnic group, was twelve years old when he was illegally brought to Cuba on a slave ship in 1840, as part of the second slavery during the industrial sugar revolution. According to the author, Nicolás was known among other slaves for the special care and large extension of his *conuco* where he raised pigs and chickens, as well as crops that he delivered to his master and then sold, a practice that was common in the first decades of the nineteenth century. During slow times, Nicolás worked on the plantations, while in the harvest season he was a cane cutter. At the age of twenty-five, he had managed to save three thousand pesos, marrying a fifteen-year-old

---

36   Ramón J. Espinosa, *El proletario en España y el negro en Cuba* (Habana: Imprenta Militar de M. Soler, 1866).

Cuban-born *criolla*. When Espinosa published his book, Nicolás was thirty-nine years old. Between the ages of nine and fifteen, enslaved children worked in the fields with the *criollos*. At the same time, other slaves worked on his *conuco*. For the writer, Nicolás was such a successful example that he said he would not return to Africa "because he who had lived as a person could not live as a beast again," a cynical rhetoric justifying slavery in the eyes of European readers.

The second testimony was of a Carabalí ethnic couple. Filomena and Cayetano had also been forced to embark on the same illicit expedition as minors. Cayetano was a runaway slave; he was punished and he even tried to commit suicide. All this changed, according to the text, when he began working on his *conuco*. He married and became a "kind of African Rothschild," understood as such by the author because he became a moneylender – specifically, a pig broker; besides this, he had learned to read, count and write. At his death at age fifty-nine, he bequeathed his widow thirteen thousand pesos, money that the enslaved woman gave to the slave owner, who, according to the writer, returned it after putting the deceased's accounts in order. The third account is that of Antonio, a *criollo*, who was assigned to domestic service from a young age. He bought his freedom, but lost his savings after a "failed love affair," and returned to slavery.

The book was a cynical panegyric to slavery in the eyes of modern, civilised Europe. However, besides demonstrating the harshness of slavery, the three examples also show how *conucos*, trades and domestic work could offer slaves the opportunity of saving some money, with which they could buy their freedom, even though this was not the general rule. What's more, they point to the probable transmission of knowledge through agriculture practised in the *conucos*. Recent studies highlight that many of the same crops were grown in Africa and Cuba as a result of the Columbian exchange and the slave trade. Robin Law points out that the African population's diet consisted of grains such as sorghum and millet, yams, and game and fish products that were seasoned with chili pepper and ginger.[37] Many of these crops were brought to the Americas. We must remember that at some Cuban mills, food was delivered raw because the slaves preferred to season their meals. All of this warrants more detailed studies that are beyond the scope of this chapter.

---

37   Robin Law, Suzanne Schawarz, and Silke Strickrodt, *Commercial Agriculture, the Slave Trade and Slavery in Atlantic Africa* (Oxford: James Currey, 2013).

4   Labour Relations, Food, Commodities and Transatlantic Circuits

The feeding of the slaves was a central concern for landowners. The establish-ment of the *conucos* to guarantee the slaves' self-subsistence at the mills was alternated with the systematic purchase of jerky and cod on the international market. Sugar historians emphasise that the sugar mill broke with the eating habits of enslaved Africans, whose basic diet was imposed by the owners as a function of workforce maintenance and profitability.[38] Therefore, their diet was rich in carbohydrates through the intake of sugar cane itself, as well as banana, sweet potato, rice, corn, and jerky and cod as animal protein. Other studies highlight the link between medicine and food, which was common to the slave plantations of the Americas.[39] These essays relate the appearance of diseases in slaves, such as beriberi, to insufficient nutrition in their diet, although they argue that slaves' diets differed across agricultural plantations and between western and eastern Cuba.

The importation of foods that ensured animal protein in the slaves' diet illustrates the multidirectional horizontal-vertical exchanges and connections at various scales (global, regional and local) within the transatlantic slave and sugar circuits. Global food exchange also connected triangular trade, the Industrial Revolution, and the debates about nutritional science relating to the middle and working classes on both sides of the Atlantic, especially after the famine in Europe due to the potato plague in Ireland in 1845. This aspect has received little attention from scholars working in the fields of global and labour history, the history of science, commodity histories, and the history of slavery in Cuba.

Cuban landowners tended to feed their slaves with cod imports from Norway, and jerky was introduced from Tampico and the Río de la Plata region at the end of the eighteenth century. Andrew Sluyter analysed the jerky route across Brazil, Cuba and Africa.[40] In the mid-nineteenth century, the importation

---

38   Ismael Sarmiento, "Del 'funche' al 'ajíaco': La dieta que los amos imponen a los esclavos africanos en Cuba y la asimilación que éstos hacen de la cocina criolla," *Anales del Museo de América* 16 (2008): 217–36; Nitza Villapol, "Hábitos alimenticios africanos en América Latina," in *África en América Latina*, ed. Manuel Moreno Fraginals (México: Siglo XXI, 1977), 325–36.

39   Kennet F. Kiple, *Blacks in Colonial Cuba, 1774–1899* (Gainesville, Florida: University Press of Florida, 1976); Reinier Borrego Moreno, "La temible Trinidad: Esclavitud, malnutrición y beriberi en Cuba," in *Orden político y gobierno de esclavos*, ed. José Antonio Piqueras (Alzira, Valencia: Centro Francisco Tomás y Valiente, UNED, 2016), 177–204.

40   Andrew Sluyter, *Black Ranching Frontiers: African Cattle Herders of the Atlantic World, 1500–1900* (New Haven: Yale University Press, 2012).

of jerky connected Uruguay, Havana, Africa and Europe, a less studied route within historiography.

The Uruguayan cattle industry developed around the meat-curing plants (*saladeros*) where jerky was produced for the slave plantations of Brazil and Cuba. This business prospered with the illicit trade of enslaved Africans. Basque landowner Julián de Zulueta and Pedro Blanco, two notorious slave traders, resorted to the transatlantic Havana – Uruguay jerky route to supply their slave ships with jerky for the journey to West Africa.[41] For example, Zulueta commissioned Pedro Blanco to buy beef jerky at the Gallinas factory in Uruguay, where he acted as agent to Cuba's sugar producers in Africa, with the aim of feeding enslaved Africans.

In the 1840s, the German chemist Justus von Liebig argued for the possibility of industrially obtaining meat extract, a highly concentrated broth derived mainly from cattle, but he lacked the raw material supplies to launch a large-scale commercial venture. In 1859, a group of landowners of English origin had established a meat-curing plant in the town of Fray Bentos, located in western Uruguay.[42] A year later, the German engineer George Christian Giebert, who had worked on the railways and roads in Brazil, bought the land and partnered with Liebig to establish a company dedicated to industrial meat processing, following up on the chemist's proposal by introducing European machinery. Initially, the venture was registered under the name of "Societé de Fray Bentos Giebert et Companie." In 1865, it became known as Liebig's Extract of Meat Company, under Liebig's direction.

Some authors have pointed out that the venture marked the start of the Industrial Revolution in the Río de la Plata region.[43] The company took in workers from various countries. In addition, it globally connected other merchandise production chains such as salt that was imported from Cádiz. Packaged meat changed the eating habits of the working- and middle-class populations around the world. Since then, Fray Bentos has been known as the world's kitchen. In 2016, UNESCO declared the factory a World Heritage Site.

---

41   Archivo Histórico Nacional (AHN), Sección Estado, Expediente 8048. The character of Pedro Blanco inspired the novel by Lino Novás Calvo, *Pedro Blanco, el negrero* (Madrid: Espasa Calpe, 1973); María Dolores García Cantús, "Pedro Blanco, el lado oscuro de un negrero," *Hispania*, 45, no. 160(1985): 299–352; María del Carmen Barcía Zequeira, *Pedro Blanco, el negrero: Mito, realidad y espacios* (Havana: Ediciones Bolonia, 2018).

42   René Boretto Ovalle, *Historiografía de la ciudad de Fray Bentos* (Fray Bentos: Imprenta Fray Bentos, 2000).

43   Lucía Lewowicz, *LEMCO: Un coloso de la industria cárnica en Fray Bentos, Uruguay* (The Meat Industry's Colossus in Fray Bentos, Uruguay) (Montevideo: INAC, Zona Editorial, 2017).

Meat extract was successfully marketed on British and European markets just when science was gaining prominence in solving problems related to the health and nutrition of the middle and working classes, who relied on animal protein as the main nutrient in their diets. As it was easy to transport and not prone to spoilage it was used to feed sailors in the imperialist wars in Africa, and the troops during the Civil War in the United States. Jules Verne even included it as food for astronauts in one of his novels. However, its main uses were medicinal, and housewives used it to flavour food. In fact, the company edited its own cookbooks in various languages. In 1867, meat extract entered Spanish pharmacies as a fortifying digestive tonic.

Mark Finlay suggests various ways in which Liebig's persona and company may be studied in the future.[44] For example, for historians of science interested in the relationship between science and business Liebig may be of interest because he was the ideal example of a business scientist. Similarly, he may be used to more closely examine the relationship between science, medicine and nutrition, especially laboratory solutions applied to social problems. Indeed, Liebig was key in the training and formation of a group of avant-garde scientists, who introduced innovations and modernisation policies in their own countries and (former) colonies, as was the case for the aforementioned *criollo* agronomist Álvaro Reynoso in Cuba. According to Finlay, Liebig is also an interesting figure to study for those interested in observing scientists' occasionally unscrupulous behaviour. For instance, Liebig lied about some information related to his academic background and the quality of some of his products. Similarly, studying Liebig's company is worthwhile for business history, visual culture and women's history. Indeed, Liebig was one of the first to use aggressive advertising and publicity methods to advertise his products. His advertising methods connected the domestic market for women with the world of labour relations. So far, however, this relationship has been insufficiently explored.

In 1872, the Liebig Company promoted meat extract to housewives in Europe through recipes that it marketed with a series of lithographs that alluded to the places where the product was consumed. The company had commercial agents in more than fourteen countries, including Brazil and Cuba. Black servants

---

44   Mark R. Finlay, "Quackery and Cookery: Justus von Liebig's Extract of Meat and the Theory of Nutrition in the Victorian Age," *Bulletin of the History of Medicine* 66, no. 3 (1992): 404–18, and Mark R. Finlay "Early Marketing of the Theory of Nutrition: The Science and Culture of Liebig's Extract of Meat," in *The Science and Culture of Nutrition, 1840–1940*, ed. Harmke Kamminga and Andrew Cunnigham (Amsterdam: Brill, Editions Rodopi, 1995), 48–74.

were frequently represented in the advertising artwork because they were the ones who best knew the cuisine of plantation societies. As Cooper recalls, at a time when European elites thought of workers as a class, they thought of Africans as a race, which cannot be overlooked in an analysis of labour relations.[45] The company's visual representation was no exception.

The lithographs were published as collectibles in sets of six to twelve. Cuba participated with a group of six postcards titled "African Picture Cards," in which the image of slaves was associated with the consumption of the product (see figures 9.2–9.7).[46] The lithographs were published in 1899, when Cuba had ceased to be a colony of Spain and was under the occupation of the United States of America. We know that enslaved people on Cuba ate beef jerky, but was the meat extract supplied to slaves? Did it become a part of Cuban cuisine? Were recipe books published in Cuba? These questions remain unanswered. What we do know, is that the lithographs showed male and female slaves working on tobacco and sugar plantations. In other lithographs, the free coloured population was represented as, for instance, local market vendors and milk street vendors, as well as domestic servants. The women depicted in market scenes carried their baskets on their heads, like African women.

The image of enslaved Africans and *criollos* put forward on the lithographs was that of happy and smiling faces against a background of idyllic and exotic tropical landscapes, and was clearly manufactured for a European audience. For example, in the lithograph depicting the sugar plantations, the image of a slave carrying an ox-drawn cart full of sugar cane shows an idealised country landscape with traditional peasant huts. That is, the landscape does not reproduce the slave sugar plantation. Instead, it appropriates the rural landscape of Cuba with some of the typical houses of the peasants (see figures 9.2–9.7). The recipe on the back of the card was aimed at middle-class and working-class European housewives. Thus, slavery entered European cuisine, but it also associated Liebig with the Caribbean slave plantation.

The numerous lithographs featuring cooking recipes and home remedies not only linked the domestic female labour market with slave plantations in Brazil and Cuba; they also connected women around the globe, for instance connecting Andalusian women with Asian workers on pepper plantations in

---

45   Frederick Cooper, *Plantation Slavery on the East African Coast* (New Haven: Yale University Press, 1977), and *Beyond Slavery: Explorations of Race, Labor, and Citizenship in Postemancipation* Societies (Chapel Hill: University of North Carolina Press, 2014).

46   Liebig's Extract of Meat Company, *Advertising Cards* (Belgium: Antwerp, 1899–1942). See William Woys Weaver, "The Dark Side of Culinary Ephemera: The Portrayal of African Americans," *Gastronomica: The Journal of Food and Culture* 76, no. 3 (2006): 76–81.

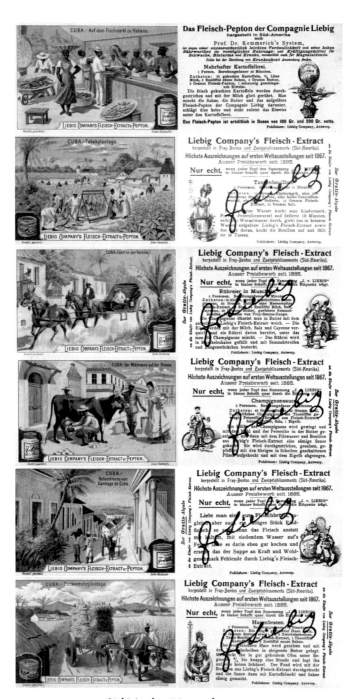

FIGURE 9.2–9.7   Liebig's advertising cards
SOURCE: LIEBIG'S EXTRACT OF MEAT COMPANY,
ADVERTISING CARDS (BELGIUM: ANTWERP, 1899)

Malaysia or housewives in the United States. Similarly, the picture cards perpetuated racial and folkloric stereotypes within the collective imagination.[47] In Spain, the cards perpetuated the image of gypsy women; in the Americas and Southeast Asia, they featured the landscape and workers of the plantations – slaves and indentured labourers, as well as male and female cooks and labourers and even the general population.

5   Conclusions

Conceptual history has highlighted the need to explore the diverse, ambiguous and contradictory meanings of the concept of "tropical agriculture." The notion was probably born with the conquest of the tropics and imperial expansion in the New World, but its greatest scope and consolidation within the language of industrial modernity occurred between the 1750s and 1870s, an era that coincided with the rise and decline of the slave plantation in Cuba. Today, many of the terms related to tropical agriculture continue to give shape to the collective imagination of the tropics and its agriculture, perpetuating notions of the dependency and underdevelopment of the so-called Global South.

In this chapter, I have outlined the main discursive elements that distinguished the creation of the concept of tropical agriculture in the period of industrial modernisation. Cuba is undoubtedly a good case study because it developed slave plantation agriculture in the middle of the golden age of the Industrial Revolution in Europe. At the same time, it had a group of erudite and active landowners who promoted and/or financed – through the private initiative of colonial institutions – the introduction of the industrial advances that were the driving force of industrial and agricultural modernity on both sides of the Atlantic. Early on, the island was connected with the transatlantic sugar and slave circuits of which the east coast of the United States and the Caribbean sugar and slave colonies (the so-called Sugar Islands) were part. Cuba also had an abundance of land and an ideal climate for cultivating sugar cane; in combination with the labour strategies used by landowners, these factors made it the "sugar queen" par excellence, according to economic historians. However, the sugar was only cultivated on certain parts of the island until the end of the nineteenth century. Therefore, the notion that Cuba's success in sugar cultivation depended on natural conditions concealed the fact that

---

47   David Ciarlo, *Advertising Empire: Empire, Race and Visual Culture in Imperial Germany* (Cambridge, MA: Harvard University Press, 2001).

colonial agriculture was an active participant in the global history of the sugar industry, because it marked the time limits of the industrial frenzy. That is, the success of the industry was affected if agricultural yields decreased due to overexploitation and collapse of ecological conditions.

My reflections, therefore, are rooted in the absence of studies on the origin and circulation of the concept of "prodigal tropical agriculture," an idea that I have been researching for several years to demonstrate that colonial agriculture was the focus of local knowledge and practices that shaped global tropical agricultural science. I argue that it was impossible to reproduce the tropics in the laboratories of the European and American industrial power centres in order to dissect, inventory and conquer them. That is, their study required what Robert Kholer has called "residential science" and the formation of what I call a tropical community of global and local agents, to collect information in situ but also to produce, correct and apply knowledge to agro-industry, which is only studied by the manufacturing sector.[48] The recruitment and hiring of transnational plantation experts in industrial centres was also key for agricultural modernity. In this process, the practices and knowledge of enslaved Africans should be considered within global history studies of agricultural labour relations. In other words, the introduction, diffusion and production of agricultural technologies in the tropics relied on and/or were negotiated between the practices and knowledge of Western science and the practices and ancestral knowledge of slave workers. The latter is of growing interest for studies on African agency within the history of slavery.

The microcosm of the slave sugar plantation illustrates the confluence of various labour Relationships, such as Asian workers, destined to produce for both global and local markets. The modernity of agriculture elucidates the connections that not only blurred borders – imperial, Atlantic/Pacific, centre/periphery – but that also made agriculture multidirectional. An analysis of these connections demonstrates that colonial agricultural modernity was jointly constructed by the same transatlantic sugar and slave agents, networks and circuits that led to the invention, circulation and adaptation of industrial capital in Europe and the United States. This chapter illuminates the central place of slaves' diet in connecting different labour relations that respond to the global taxonomy developed by Karin Hofmeester and Marcel van der Linden. At the same time, it underscores the interconnectedness between various agricultural commodity chains, the Industrial Revolution and the science of the

---

48   Robert E. Kohler, *All Creatures: Naturalists, Collectors, and Biodiversity, 1850–1950* (Princeton, New Jersey: Princeton University Press, 2013).

nutrition of workers on both sides of the Atlantic. They are all connected by the invisible thread of globalisation and the world market.

Bibliography

Alexander, Robert J. *A History of Organized Labor in Cuba*. Westport, CT: Praeger, 2002.

Armus, Diego, and Adrian López Denis. "Disease, Medicine, and Health." In *The Oxford Handbook of Latin America History*, edited by José C. Moya, 424–53. New York: Oxford University Press, 2011.

Barcía Zequeira, María del Carmen. *Pedro Blanco, el negrero: Mito, realidad y espacios*. Havana: Ediciones Bolonia, 2018.

Barcia, Manuel. *Seeds of Insurrection: Domination and Resistance on Western Cuban Plantations, 1808–1848*. Baton Rouge: Louisiana State University Press, 2009.

Barnet, Miguel, and Esteban Montejo. *Biografía de un cimarrón*. Manchester: Manchester University Press, 2010.

Barragán, Rossana, and David Mayer. "Latin America and the Caribbean." In Hofmeester and Van der Linden, *Handbook Global History of Work*, 83–110.

Bergad, Laird W., Fe Iglesias García, and María del Carmen Barcia. *The Cuban Slave Market, 1790–1880*. New York: Cambridge University Press, 1995.

Boretto Ovalle, René. *Historiografía de la ciudad de Fray Bentos*. Fray Bentos: Imprenta Fray Bentos, 2000.

Borrego Moreno, Reinier. "La temible trinidad: Esclavitud, malnutrición y beriberi en Cuba." In *Orden político y gobierno de esclavos*, edited by José Antonio Piqueras, 177–204. Alzira, Valencia: Centro Francisco Tomás y Valiente, UNED, 2016.

Bosma, Ulbe, and Jonathan Curry-Machado. "Two Islands, One Commodity: Cuba, Java, and the Global Sugar trade (1790–1930)." *Nieuwe West-Indische Gids* (New West Indian Guide) 86 (2012): 237–62.

Brennam, James P. "Latin America Labor History." In *The Oxford Handbook of Latin American History*, edited by José C. Moya, 342–63. New York: Oxford University Press, 2011.

Carney, Judith A. *Black Rice: The African Origins of Rice Cultivation in the Americas*. Cambridge, MA: Harvard University Press, 2001.

Carney, Judith A. "African Traditional Plant Knowledge in the Circum-Caribbean Region." *Journal of Ethnobiology* 23, no. 2 (2003): 167–85.

Carney, Judith A., and Richard Nicholas Rosomoff. *In the Shadow of Slavery: Africa's Botanical Legacy in the Atlantic World*. Berkeley, Los Angeles and London: University of California Press, 2009.

Casanovas Codina, Joan. *Bread, or Bullets! Urban Labor and Spanish Colonialism in Cuba, 1850–1898*. Pittsburgh, PA: University of Pittsburgh, 1998.

Ciarlo, David. *Advertising Empire: Empire, Race and Visual Culture in Imperial Germany.* Cambridge, MA: Harvard University Press, 2001.

Cooper, Frederick. *Plantation Slavery on the East African Coast.* New Haven: Yale University Press, 1977.

Cooper, Frederick. *Beyond Slavery: Explorations of Race, Labor, and Citizenship in Postemancipation Societies.* Chapel Hill: University of North Carolina Press, 2014.

Curry-Machado, Jonathan. *Cuban Sugar Industry: Transnational Networks and Engineering Migrants in Mid-Nineteenth Century Cuba.* New York: Palgrave Macmillan, 2011.

Curtin, Philip D. *The Atlantic Slave Trade: A Census.* Madison: University of Wisconsin Press, 1969.

Eltis, David, and David Richardson. *Atlas of the Transatlantic Slave Trade.* New Haven: Yale University Press, 2015.

Ely, Roland T. *Cuando reinaba Su Majestad el Azúcar: Estudio histórico-sociológico de una tragedia latinoamericana; El monocultivo en Cuba, origen y evolución del proceso.* Havana: Imagen Contemporánea, 2001.

Espinosa, Ramón J. *El proletario en España y el negro en Cuba.* Habana: Imprenta Militar de M. Soler, 1866.

Esquivel, Miguel, and Karl P. Hammer. "The Cuban Homegarden '*Conuco*': A Perspective Environment for Evolution and In Situ Conservation of Plant Genetic Resources." *Genetic Resources and Crop Evolution* 39, no. 1 (January 1992): 9–22.

Fernández Prieto, Leida. "Islands of Knowledge: Science and Agriculture in the History of Latin American and the Caribbean." *Isis* 104, no. 4 (December 2013): 786–97.

Fernández Prieto, Leida. "Crónica anunciada de una Cuba Azucarera." In *Francisco Arango y la invención de la Cuba azucarera,* edited by María Dolores González-Ripoll and Izaskun Álvarez Cuartero, 55–65. Salamanca: Universidad de Salamanca, 2009.

Fernández Prieto, Leida. "Mapping the Global and Local Scientific Archipelago: Agriculture, Knowledge and Practices, 1790–1870." In *Global Scientific Practice in an Age of Revolutions, 1750–1850,* edited by Patrick Manning and Daniel Rood, 181–98. Pittsburgh, PA: University of Pittsburgh Press, 2016.

Fernández Prieto, Leida. "Plantas, plantas y saberes en la red del tráfico negrero: Cuba-España-África." In *Cádiz y el tráfico de esclavos: De la legalidad a la clandestinidad,* edited by Martin Rodrigo y Alharilla and Maria del Carmen Cózar Navarro, 295–321. Madrid: Silex, 2018.

Fernández Sebastián, Javier, ed. *Diccionario político y social del mundo iberoamericano: Conceptos políticos fundamentales, 1770–1870.* Madrid: Centro de Estudios Políticos y Constitucionales – Universidad del País Vasco, 2014.

Ferrer, Ada. *Freedom's Mirror: Cuba and Haiti in the Age of Revolution.* New York: Cambridge University Press, 2014.

Fesser, Andrea. *Red, White, and Black Make Blue: Indigo in the Fabric of Colonial South Carolina Life*. Athens, GA: University of Georgia Press, 2013.

Finlay, Mark R. "Early Marketing of the Theory of Nutrition: The Science and Culture of Liebig's Extract of Meat" In *The Science and Culture of Nutrition, 1840–1940*, edited by Harmke Kamminga and Andrew Cunningham, 48–74. Amsterdam: Brill, Editions Rodopi, 1995.

Finlay, Mark R. "Quackery and Cookery: Justus von Liebig's Extract of Meat and the Theory of Nutrition in the Victorian Age." *Bulletin of the History of Medicine* 66, no 3 (1992): 404–18.

Fortes-Lima, Cesar, Jonas Bybjerg-Grauholm, Lilia Caridad Marin-Padrón, Enrique Javier Gomez-Cabezas, Marie Bækvad-Hansen, Christine Søholm Hansen, Phuong Le et al. "Exploring Cuba's Population Structure and Demographic Story Using Genome-Wide Data." *Scientific Reports* 11422 (2018). https://doi.org/10.1038/s41 598-018-29851-3.

Franco, José Luciano. *Comercio clandestino de esclavos*. Havana: Editorial de Ciencias Sociales, 1980.

Fuente, Alejandro de la, and Ariela J. Gross. *Becoming Free, Becoming Black: Race, Freedom, and Law in Cuba, Virginia, and Louisiana*. New York: Cambridge University Press, 2020.

García Cantús, María Dolores. "Pedro Blanco, el lado oscuro de un negrero." *Hispania* 45, no. 160 (1985): 99–352.

García Mora, Luis Miguel, and Antonio Santamaria García, eds. *Los ingenios: Colección de vistas de los principales ingenios de azúcar de la isla de Cuba,*written by Justo G. Cantero and drawn by Eduardo Laplante. Madrid: CSIC-Doce Calles, 2005.

García Rodríguez, Mercedes. *Entre haciendas y plantaciones: Los orígenes de la manufactura azucarera de La Habana*. Havana: Editorial de Ciencias Sociales, 2007.

González-Ripoll, María Dolores. "Dos viajes, una intención: Francisco Arango y Alejandro Oliván en Europa y las Antillas azucareras (1794 y 1829)." *Revista de Indias* 62, no. 224 (2002): 85–102.

González-Ripoll, María Dolores, and Izaskun Álvarez Cuartero, eds. *Francisco Arango y la invención de la Cuba azucarera*. Salamanca: Universidad de Salamanca, 2009.

Hofmeester, Karin, and Marcel van der Linden, eds. *Handbook Global History of Work*. Berlin and Boston: De Gruyter Oldenbourg, 2018.

Hofmeester, Karin, and Marcel van der Linden. "Introduction." In *Handbook Global History of Work*, edited by Karen Hofmester and Marcel van der Linden, 1–14. Berlin and Boston: De Gruyter Oldenbourg, 2018.

Kiple, Kenneth F. *Blacks in Colonial Cuba, 1774–1899*. Gainesville, Florida: University Press of Florida, 1976.

Kohler, Robert E. *All Creatures: Naturalists, Collectors, and Biodiversity, 1850–1950*. Princeton, New Jersey: Princeton University Press, 2013.

Law, Robín, Suzanne Schawarz, and Silke Strickrodt. *Commercial Agriculture, the Slave Trade and Slavery in Atlantic Africa*. Oxford: James Currey, 2013.

Leonard, Adrian, and David Pretel, eds. *The Caribbean and the Atlantic World Economy: Circuits of Trade, Money and Knowledge, 1650–1914*. Basingstoke: Palgrave Macmillan, 2015.

Lewowicz, Lucia. *LEMCO: Un coloso de la industria cárnica en Fray Bentos, Uruguay* (The Meat Industry's Colossus in Fray Bentos, Uruguay). Montevideo: INAC, Zona Editorial, 2017.

Manning, Patrick. "Slave Labour." In *Handbook Global History of Work*, edited by Karen Hofmester and Marcel van der Linden, 373 94. Berlin and Boston: De Gruyter Oldenbourg, 2018.

McCook, Stuart G. *States of Nature, Science, Agriculture and Environment in the Spanish Caribbean 1760–1940*. Austin: University of Texas Press, 2002.

Mintz, Sidney. *Sweetness and Power: The Place of Sugar in Modern History*. New York, Viking, 1985.

Moreno Fraginals, Manuel. *El ingenio*. Barcelona: Crítica, 2002.

Novás Calvo, Lino. *Pedro Blanco, el negrero*. Madrid: Espasa Calpe, 1973.

Palmer, Steven. "From the Plantation to the Academy. Slavery and the Production of Cuban Medicine in the Nineteenth Century." In *Health and Medicine in the Circum-Caribbean, 1800–1968*, edited by Juanita De Barros, Steven Palmer, and David Wright, 53–75. New York: Routledge, 2009.

Pérez de la Riva, Juan. *El monto de la inmigración forzada en el siglo XIX*. Havana: Editorial de Ciencias Sociales, 1979.

Piqueras, José Antonio, ed. *Orden político y gobierno de esclavos*. Alzira, Valencia: Centro Francisco Tomás y Valiente, UNED, 2016.

Portuondo, María M., "Plantation Factories: Science and Technology in Late-Eighteenth-Century Cuba." *Technology and Culture* 44 (April 2003): 231–57.

Puig-Samper, Miguel Ángel, Consuelo Naranjo Orovio, and Armando García González, eds. *Ensayo Político de la isla de Cuba, Alexander von Humboldt*. Aranjuez, Doce Calles: Junta de Castilla y León, 1998.

Rodrigo Alharilla, Martín, and Lizbeth Chaviano, eds. *Negreros y esclavos: Barcelona y la esclavitud atlántica, siglos XIX-XIX*. Barcelona: Icaria, 2017.

Roldán de Montaud, Inés. "The Misfortune of Liberated Africans in Colonial Cuba, 1824–76." In *Liberated Africans and the Abolition of the Slave Trade, 1807–1896*, edited by Richard Anderson and Henry B. Lovejoy, 153–73. Rochester, NY: University of Rochester Press, 2020.

Rood, Daniel. *The Reinvention of the Atlantic Slavery: Technology, Labor, Race, and Capitalism in the Greater Caribbean*. New York: Oxford University Press, 2017.

Sarmiento, Ismael. "Del 'funche' al 'ajíaco': La dieta que los amos imponen a los esclavos africanos en Cuba y la asimilación que éstos hacen de la cocina criolla." *Anales del Museo de América* 16 (2008): 217–36.

Scott, Rebecca, *Slave Emancipation: The Transition to Free Labor, 1860–1899*. Pittsburgh, PA: University of Pittsburgh Press, 2000.

Sluyter, Andrew. *Black Ranching Frontiers: African Cattle Herders of the Atlantic World, 1500–1900*. New Haven, Yale University Press, 2012.

Tomich, Dale W., ed. *New Frontiers of Slavery*. New York: SUNY Press, 2016.

Tomich, Dale W., ed. *Slavery and Historical Capitalism during the Nineteenth Century*. Lanhan, MD: Lexington Books, 2017.

Tomich, Dale W. *Through the Prism of Slavery: Labor, Capital, and World Economy*. Lanham, MD: Rowman & Littlefield, 2004.

Tomich, Dale W., Rafael de Bivar Marquese, Reinaldo Funes Monzote, and Carlos Venegas. *Reconstructing the Landscapes of Slavery: A Visual History of the Plantation in the Nineteenth-Century Atlantic World*. Chapel Hill: University of North Carolina Press, 2021.

Varela, Claudia, and Manuel Barcia. *Wage-Earning Slaves:* Coartación *in Nineteenth-Century Cuba*. Gainesville: University Press of Florida, 2020.

Villapol, Nitza. "Hábitos alimenticios africanos en América Latina." In *África en América Latina,* edited by Manuel Moreno Fraginals, 325–36. México: Siglo XXI, 1977.

Voeks, Robert, and John Rashford. *African Ethnobotany in the Americas*. New York: Springer, 2013.

Woys Weaver, William. "The Dark Side of Culinary Ephemera: The Portrayal of African Americans." *Gastronomica: The Journal of Food and Culture* 76, no. 3 (2006): 76–81.

CHAPTER 10

Dynamics of the Plantationocene

Finance Capital and the Labour Regime on British Colonial Plantations in Nineteenth-Century South Asia

Rachel Kurian

While its definition has varied over time and geography, a plantation is typically a large-scale, hierarchically-organised unit of agricultural production employing a sizable and mainly resident workforce for the cultivation of specialised crops for export, under – at least during the colonial period – foreign ownership, supervision and management.[1] It has been historically distinct from peasant production, which relied mainly on local and family labour for the production of food and associated crops.[2] By contrast, plantation production brought together and combined land, labour and capital across oceans and continents for the cultivation of commercial crops. The earliest plantations were developed by the Portuguese in the fifteenth century, who were stimulated to produce sugar on a large scale, as its price had increased in Europe with the expulsion of Muslim traders who had commanded its sale.[3] The climatic conditions for sugar were favourable in the Portuguese colonies bordering the Atlantic Ocean. An essential requisite for such production, however, was the sufficient supply of labour, which was not available in these regions. The Portuguese were familiar with the institution of slavery in the Iberian Peninsula, and, from the ninth century, the number of enslaved people in the region

---

1   B. W. Higman, "Plantations and Typological Problems in Geography: A Review Article," *Australian Geographer* 11, no. 2 (1969): 192; Colin Kirk, "People in Plantations: A Review of the Literature and Annotated Bibliography" (Research Report No. 18, Sussex, Institute of Development Studies, 1987); Frederic L. Pryor, "The Plantation Economy as an Economic System," *Journal of Comparative Economics* 6, no. 3 (1982): 288–317.
2   As noted by the labour historians Hobsbawm and Rudé in their study on the nineteenth-century English countryside, peasant production was usually located in or near villages and associated with "families owning or occupying their own small plot of land, cultivating it substantially with the labour of their members": Eric Hobsbawm and George Rudé, *Captain Swing* (London: Verso Trade, 2014), 23.
3   Sidney M. Greenfield, "Slavery and the Plantation in the New World: The Development and Diffusion of a Social Form," *Journal of Inter-American Studies* 11, no. 1 (1969): 44–57; Philip D. Curtin, *The Rise and Fall of the Plantation Complex: Essays in Atlantic History* (Cambridge: Cambridge University Press, 1998).

increased, including a rise in Moors (Muslims) through successive Christian campaigns against "infidels" and Jews.[4] The importation of black slaves from Africa began after Portuguese entrepreneurs raided Mauritania in 1444.[5] The Portuguese, who had incorporated slavery into the prevailing institution of the period – the feudal extended household – used this patriarchal, authoritarian and hierarchical structure to include more slaves in the large-scale production of sugar, laying the foundations for the "model" of plantation production.[6]

This "model" of production, which included the use of slavery, was adopted and adapted by the Spanish, Dutch and the British in their colonial plantations in the Caribbean and South America for the large-scale production of sugar as well as other tropical crops.[7] From its inception, the labour regime on plantations was permeated with class and racial hierarchies, as well as force and compulsion. The destructive and oppressive nature of the early slave plantations has been well recorded, with the planters and overseers resorting to "sadistic ferocity" and "exemplary cruelty" in their treatment of slaves, with handbooks of plantation management stressing that punishment should be meted out in a methodical and predictable way.[8] Durant has analysed the slave plantation as a social organisation in which entrenched class and race hierarchies resulted in "two distinct classes based on color and status," and in which racial prejudice and discrimination informed "distinct patterns of race relations and social inequality."[9] Similarly, Giovannetti has emphasised the significance of the slave plantation as a "race-making institution" where Africans and blacks "occupied a subordinate racial slot in the minds of European colonizers, their masters, and the general white population."[10] Within the plantations, they were placed in "a racially stratified division of labour and a racial status

4   A. J. R. Russell-Wood, "Iberian Expansion and The Issue Of Black Slavery: Changing Portuguese Attitudes, 1440–1770," *The American Historical Review* 83, no. 1 (1978): 16.

5   A. C. de C. M. Saunders, *A Social History of Black Slaves and Freedmen in Portugal, 1441–1555* (Cambridge: Cambridge University Press, 1982).

6   Greenfield, "Slavery," 45–47.

7   Curtin, *Rise and Fall*, 23–24; Greenfield, "Slavery"; George L. Beckford, *Persistent Poverty: Underdevelopment in Plantation Economies of the Third World* (London: Zed Books, 1983).

8   Robin Blackburn, *The Making of New World Slavery: From the Baroque to the Modern, 1492–1800* (London: Verso, 1998).

9   Thomas J. Durant, "The Slave Plantation Revisited: A Sociological Perspective," in *Plantation Society and Race Relations: The Origins of Inequality*, ed. Thomas J. Durant and J. David Knottnerus (Westport, CT: Greenwood Publishing Group, 1999).

10   Jorge L. Giovannetti, "Grounds of Race: Slavery, Racism and the Plantation in the Caribbean," *Latin American and Caribbean Ethnic Studies* 1, no. 1 (2006): 5–36.

hierarchy, with white owners at the top and blacks at the bottom."[11] A combination of pressures, however, such as the increasing costs of slave trade, the rise of the anti-slavery movements and the widespread protests by the slaves themselves led to slavery being abolished in the British territories in 1833, in the French territories in 1848, in the Dutch and American territories in 1863, and in the Spanish territories in 1885. But the end of slavery did not mean the end of coerced labour. After slavery was abolished in the nineteenth century, "free" migrant wage workers, recruited either through indentureship or by a contractor, were employed as plantation labourers. In analysing the system of Indian indenture, Hugh Tinker has asserted that the condition of the workers were similar, if not worse than slavery.[12] Along the same lines and stressing the continuity in the methods of labour control, Roberts has noted slavery that was a "brutal and violent institution," but that the difference between it and other forms of coerced labour, was "more a matter of degree than kind."[13] At the same time, capitalism changed with developments in industry, transport and finance in the West that, in turn, influenced plantation life and its labour regime. These changes led to increased pressure to generate profits, giving rise to a labour regime that relied on "tried means of exerting pressure in combination with resort to new forms of legal coercion."[14]

The spread of plantations gave rise to what Curtin has termed the "plantation complex," which was characterised by a set of relationships that were politically mainly controlled in Europe, made use of slave labour from Africa, and were embedded in commercial networks in Europe and North America.[15] While the specific geographical, economic, cultural and political contexts gave rise to distinct characteristics, some common features of labour control on plantations, such as the use of race, class and organisational hierarchies in production and management were retained.[16] By the seventeenth century,

---

11   Giovannetti, "Grounds of Race," 15.

12   Hugh A. Tinker, *A New System of Slavery: The Export of Indian Labour Overseas 1830–1920* (London, New York and Bombay: Oxford University Press, 1974).

13   Justin Roberts, *Slavery and the Enlightenment in the British Atlantic, 1750–1807* (Cambridge: Cambridge University Press, 2013).

14   Jan Breman, *Labour Migration and Rural Transformation in Colonial Asia.* (Amsterdam: Free University Press, 1990), 69.

15   The Dutch, British and the French adapted the Portuguese "model" to generate their own "plantation complexes" in the Caribbean: Curtin, *Rise and Fall*, 58, and Curtin, *Rise and Fall*, xi.

16   Trevor Burnard, *Planters, Merchants, and Slaves: Plantation Societies in British America, 1650–1820* (Chicago: University of Chicago Press, 2015); Orlando Patterson, "Sociology of Slavery: An Analysis of the Origins" (London: Macgibbon & Kee, 1967); Roberts, *Slavery and the Enlightenment.*

plantations which had feudal origins came to occupy a central role in promoting capitalism in the West. Several studies have shown the key role of slavery and slave plantations in supporting industrial and financial development in Britain[17] and North America.[18] Manjapra has referred to the Caribbean complex as a mixture of "ecological extraction, racism, colonialism, financial and mercantile capitalism, militarism, and agricultural science [combined] into a destructive cellular form."[19] Beckert and Rockman have argued that "slavery is necessarily imprinted on the DNA of American capitalism."[20] They emphasise the links between the labour regime on the American plantation to the country's financial and mercantile networks, arguing that it "sustained a political economy that predicated liberal capitalism's unrivalled opportunities on the unforgiving oppression of chattel slavery."[21]

More recently, in a discussion on the concept of the Anthropocene that took place in Aarhus in 2014, Donna Haraway introduced the term "plantationocene" as being more appropriate to understand the nature of plantations, through highlighting "historical relocations of the substances of living and dying around the Earth as a necessary prerequisite to their extraction."[22] According to her, it was "more efficient in the logic of the plantation system to exterminate the local labour and bring in labour from elsewhere."[23] While such a framework highlights the importance of forced labour in the spread of European power, Davis has cautioned against a "colour-blind" conception of the plantationocene, which could underestimate the significance of slave labour and "minimize the ways in which racial politics structure plantation

---

17   Eric Williams, *Capitalism and Slavery* (Chapel Hill: University of North Carolina Press, 1994); Sidney Mintz, *Sweetness and Power: The Place of Sugar in Modern History* (London: Penguin, 1986); Robin Blackburn, *Making*; Joseph E. Inikori, *Africans and the Industrial Revolution in England: A Study in International Trade and Economic Development* (Cambridge: Cambridge University Press, 2002); Catherine Hall, *Legacies of British Slave-Ownership: Colonial Slavery and the Formation of Victorian Britain* (Cambridge: Cambridge University Press, 2014); Catherine Hall and Ruth Ramsden-Karelse, "The Legacies of British Slave Ownership: Catherine Hall talks to Ruth." *Soundings* 77 (2020): 23–36.

18   Sven Beckert and Seth Rockman, eds. *Slavery's Capitalism: A New History of American Economic Development* (Philadelphia: University of Pennsylvania Press, 2016).

19   Kris Manjapra, "Plantation Dispossessions: The Global Travel of Agricultural Racial Capitalism," in *American Capitalism: New Histories*, ed. Sven Beckert and Christine Desan (New York: Columbia University Press, 2018), 361–88.

20   Beckert and Rockman, *Slavery's Capitalism*, 3.

21   Beckert and Rockman, *Slavery's Capitalism*, 5.

22   Donna Haraway et al., "Anthropologists are Talking – about the Anthropocene," *Ethnos* 81, no. 3 (2016): 535–64.

23   Haraway et al., "Anthropologists," 557.

life."[24] Extending this argument, Murphy and Schroering link plantation development to the "ever-present racial and colonial character" of world capitalism, which resulted in "differentially racialized and colonized people" from Africa, Asia and the Pacific, South and Central America being "dislocated and/or conscripted to labour with plants in Earth's topic and subtropical zones."[25] These deliberations have been significant in understanding how race and colonialism have influenced the nature of plantations and comprehending how these processes have brought about ecological and environmental destruction at the global level. As noted by Wolford in her review of the concept, the term "plantationocene" – which refers to the influence of the plantation within and beyond its boundaries – can be enriched through viewing relations within the plantation "as a set of social relations, an imperative, and an ideal that has endured around the world over the past 500 years."[26] It is important to recognise that the nature of capitalism changed over time, and that these global dynamics had consequences for the structure and labour controls of plantation life under colonialism. In addition, the labour force also underwent changes as slavery was formally abolished and replaced by migrant workers, employed on indenture or by direct recruitment. Reflecting on these different and simultaneous changes at the global and local levels will contribute to understanding the innovative nature of the plantationocene in responding to specific capitalist pressures, retaining, restructuring and renewing class, race and ethnic hierarchies and preserving force and compulsion at its core.

This chapter focuses on key features of the plantation labour regime that developed on South Asian plantations under British colonialism after the formal end of slavery in 1833. It considers the influences of the industrial and transport "revolutions" and focuses more directly on the increasing dominance of finance capital in Britain in the second half of the nineteenth century and how this influenced the ownership, management and labour relations on plantations. It pays attention to the increased demand for plantation products, the possibilities for the expansion of plantations in the peasant hinterland and

---

24   Janae Davis et al., "Anthropocene, Capitalocene, ... Plantationocene? A Manifesto for Ecological Justice in an Age of Global Crises," *Geography Compass* 13, no. 5 (2019).

25   Michael Warren Murphy and Caitlin Schroering, "Refiguring the Plantationocene," *Journal of World-Systems* 26, no. 2 (2020): 407–8.

26   Wendy Wolford, "The Plantationocene: A Lusotropical Contribution to the Theory," *Annals of the American Association of Geographers* 111, no. 6 (2021): 1622–39.

the pressure to lower labour costs to meet the demands of finance capital. The end of slavery gave rise to patterns of labour recruitment and deployment that were relatively cost-effective but that still involved the transport of migrant workers to meet the cultivation needs of commercial plantations. This chapter argues that the labour regime that emerged on the industrial plantations under British colonialism relied on historically effective methods of labour control stemming from the slave plantations, which were combined with new forms of economic, extra-economic and legal coercion to bond "free" and cheap labour in ways that favoured finance capital. In doing so, the chapter shows how the plantationocene was shaped by different actors, processes and power relations at different levels, and elaborates on the ways in which these interacted to promote the interests of British capital under colonialism while sustaining what was essentially "unfree" labour for the cultivation of commercial crops on plantations.

The argument is developed along the following lines. The key features of the slave plantation "model" are discussed, including its structure and hierarchies, and the costs of the compulsion and maintenance of the workforce. Subsequently, the role of the industrial and transport revolutions and the increasing dominance of finance capital in the nineteenth century in South Asia under British colonialism is considered, with attention being paid to the pressures placed on reducing labour costs on plantations. The chapter focuses on three characteristics of the plantation labour regime that emerged, drawing on examples from India, Ceylon and Malaya. The first is the use of migrant wage workers – either as indentured labour or contracted directly by a recruiter – which lowered the costs of maintenance and compulsion. The second is the "management style" of expatriate planters, who were mainly interested in generating short-term profits that increased their income and bonuses and had no compunction about using harsh methods of labour control to increase levels of production and productivity. The third is the increasingly interventionist role of the state in the development of the plantations through subsidies, infrastructural support and favourable laws for finance capital while not providing adequate protection for workers. In effect, the colonial state, while upholding "laissez-faire" capitalism, enabled the incorporation of bonded "unfree" labour production into plantation capitalism. In these ways, the plantationocene shows its power to sustain its dynamics in favour of capital and at the cost of labour.

1   The Labour Costs on Slave Plantations

There have been many studies that have dealt with the economics of the slave plantations.[27] Among other issues, they highlight three kinds of costs associated with the slave plantations. First, there was the cost of recruitment and transport, which included the coercion required to control the slaves on the ships, which had to be assumed by the planter.[28] These costs were also likely to have been incorporated in the profits of merchant capital from Africa, Asia and Europe, all of whom participated in slave trading in the Western Indian Ocean during the eighteenth and early nineteenth centuries – a practice that was banned by Britain in 1807, and France in 1818, which led to illegal trading.[29] Second, there was the expenditure associated with providing the slaves with food and lodging, as well as taking care of medical and insurance costs, even when they were not working on production, including when they were ill or had become old.[30] Third, there were the costs of controlling the workers: the cost of compulsion. According to the Dutch ethnologist Nieboer, plantations were "open" resource contexts, with more land available for agricultural production than the labour necessary to cultivate it, and slavery, an extreme form of compulsion, was used to meet the labour requirements of production.[31] There were costs associated with the use of violence to control and contain the workforce, including preventing slaves from running away from the plantation.

---

27   Jacob Metzer, "Rational Management, Modern Business Practices, and Economies of Scale in the Ante-Bellum Southern Plantations," *Explorations in Economic History* 12, no. 2 (1975): 123; Eugene D. Genovese, "The Political Economy of Slavery: Studies in the Economy and Society of the Slave South" (Middletown, CT: Wesleyan University Press, 2014); Williams, *Capitalism and Slavery*; Lewis C. Gray, "Economic Efficiency and Competitive Advantages of Slavery under the Plantation System," *Agricultural History* 4, no. 2 (1930): 31–47; Thomas P. Govan, "Was Plantation Slavery Profitable?" *The Journal of Southern History* 8, no. 4 (1942): 513–35.

28   Stephen D. Behrendt, David Eltis, and David Richardson, "The Costs of Coercion: African Agency in the Pre-Modern Atlantic World," *Economic History Review* (2001): 454–76.

29   Richard B. Allen, "The Atlantic and Africa: The Second Slavery and Beyond," in *Merchant Capital and Slave Trading in the Western Indian Ocean, 1770–1830*, ed. Dale Tomich and Paul E. Lovejoy (Albany, NY: SUNY Press, 2021).

30   Eugene D. Genovese, "The Medical and Insurance Costs of Slaveholding in the Cotton Belt," *The Journal of Negro History* 45, no. 3 (1960): 141–55.

31   Herman Jeremias Nieboer, "Slavery as an Industrial System: Ethnological Researches" (The Hague: M. Nijhoff, 1900). She used Nieboer's notion of closed and open resources to analyse the need for "forced labour" in post-slave situations and concluded that "compulsory" or "forced" labour existed in a situation of "open resources" even after the abolition of slavery: Willemina Kloosterboer, *Involuntary Labour since the Abolition of Slavery: A Survey of Compulsory Labour throughout the World* (Brill Archive, 1960).

Violence was essential as slaves resisted their situation, and often sabotaged equipment and committed "various other destructive acts."[32] Eric Wolf has emphasised the violence involved in the structure and nature of plantations, arguing that the plantation was, in effect, "an instrument of force, wielded to create and to maintain a class structure of workers and owners, connected hierarchically by a staff line of overseers and manager."[33] Knottnerus, Monk and Jones have used Goffman's concept of a "total institution" to characterise the slave plantations in the United States in the late eighteenth and nineteenth centuries.[34] According to them, the features that "were present to an extreme level" included "hierarchical authority structures, restricted hierarchical mobility, lack of voluntariness of membership, and mortification practices."[35] As discussed later in this chapter, many of these costs were transferred away from the plantation management with the employment of migrant workers after slavery was abolished.

2 The Industrial and Transport "Revolutions" and the Dominance of Finance Capital

From the middle of the eighteenth century, Britain experienced the First Industrial Revolution, which was most notably associated with the increased growth of large-scale manufacturing and international trade.[36] By the nineteenth century, rapid technological progress was occurring in Britain, along

---

32 John Hope Franklin and Loren Schweninger, "Runaway Slaves: Rebels on the Plantation" (Oxford: Oxford University Press, 2000). Such a viewpoint is also consistent with the notion that plantations were essentially enclave units, with the New World Group of Caribbean scholars, such as Best, Beckford, Girvan, Thomas, Brewster and Jefferson, arguing that plantations inhibited local economic development in terms of a viable domestic agriculture and also production for a regional market. In addition, the structural links between the metropole and the colonies in the eighteenth century created underdevelopment in the region. For a review of their theories, see Denis M. Benn, "The Theory of Plantation Economy and Society: A Methodological Critique," *Journal of Commonwealth & Comparative Politics* 12, no. 3 (1974): 249–60, who puts forward ideas similar to those put forward in Eric Williams' classic study of capitalism and slavery (1944).

33 Eric R. Wolf, "Specific Aspects of Plantation Systems in the New World: Community Sub-Cultures and Social Classes," *Plantation Systems of the New World* (1959).

34 Thomas Durant, "The Slave Plantation Revisited: A Sociological Perspective," in *Plantation Society and Race Relations: The Origins of Inequality*, ed. Thomas J. Durant and J. David Knottnerus (Westport, CT: Greenwood Publishing Group, 1999), 17–28.

35 Durant, "The Slave Plantation Revisited," 25.

36 Phyllis M. Deane, *The First Industrial Revolution* (Cambridge: Cambridge University Press, 1979).

with the continued expansion of manufacturing. This was accompanied by the increasing growth, wealth and political power of the British Empire.[37] Britain's share of the world's manufactured goods rose from 2 per cent in 1750 to 23 per cent in 1880.[38] These processes led to increased pressure on colonies to provide cheap wage goods and other inputs to support industrial development in Britain. Given the historical development and the nature of plantations, these were viewed as important options for the large-scale cultivation of such commodities. By 1870, Britain also experienced a "transport revolution," the clearest indicators being a "dramatic increase in travel speeds and decline in freight rates" together with significant technological advances and increased productivity in railways, canal waterways and shipping.[39] Such developments also opened up the possibilities for the expansion of commercial crops on plantations in the peasant hinterland, as food, labour, plantation products and other necessities could be transported to and from and the interior to the ports.

From the second half of the nineteenth century, there was an increased dominance of finance capital in Britain through the formation of companies that were keen to invest in the colonies if the returns were sufficiently lucrative. These developments gave rise to what Courtenay has labelled the "industrial plantation," the chief distinguishing feature of which was the high involvement of risk capital. Plantations had to compete for resources with alternative forms of investment and were successful only if investors could expect a sufficiently high return after the costs of clearing the land and buying the necessary labour and capital were taken into account.[40] There was a spread of company formation and the expansion of finance capital concerning the ownership, management, trade, production and associated services of plantation products. Under British colonialism, the industrial plantation in Asia was promoted by "sterling" companies which raised capital on the London market. As the companies developed, they often turned to agency houses to "manage" their plantations on a commission basis rather than handle their affairs from a distance.

The agency houses not only "managed" the plantations but often took care of the brokering and shipping of the commodities. These companies were also

---

37   Joel Mokyr, *The British Industrial Revolution: An Economic Perspective* (London: Routledge, 2018).

38   Robert C. Allen, *Global Economic History: A Very Short Introduction* (Oxford: Oxford University Press, 2011).

39   Dan Bogart, "The Transport Revolution in Industrialising Britain," *The Cambridge Economic History of Modern Britain* 1 (2014): 368.

40   P. P. Courtenay, *Plantation Agriculture*. 2nd ed. (London: Bell and Hyman, 1980).

often part of a business group, such as Harrisons and Crossfield, which effectively controlled branches and affiliated companies involved in trade, shipping and insurance, and even provided management services.[41] One of the earliest was the Assam Company, formed in London on 14 February 1839 – the first joint-stock industrial firm – established shortly after the annexation of Assam by the British Indian Empire in 1838, marking a shift from monopoly of trade and land revenue appropriation to exploitation of local resources to support British industry.[42] The result was a rapid amalgamation of plantations under agency houses, with agents able to assert monopolist control over how plantations were administered and supervised.[43] In Assam, just seven agency houses managed 61 per cent of all tea production, often acting as recruiters and transporters of plantation labour as well.[44] In these ways, finance capital exercised growing domination over the management of industrial plantations. The earliest spread of the new industrial plantation system outside the Americas was in the British Indian territories. They sprang up in India where tea had been grown in Assam from the 1840s. Tea and coffee plantations were important in the southern regions in the Wynaad and Nilgiris Hills from the 1850s onwards. Coffee, and subsequently tea, rubber and coconut plantations were to dominate the economic development of Sri Lanka from around this period.

The necessary investment for these companies, which operated in a competitive economic environment, was available only if plantations were sufficiently profitable on a yearly basis. This also meant that finance capital had an important influence on the organisation of production. The dominance of finance capital also meant that the owner-planter was replaced by expatriate management, the consequences of which will be discussed later. The pressure to promote profitability in the short-term mitigated against capital investment which could yield returns only in the long-term. Under these circumstances, as discussed below, the other factor of production – namely, labour – became even more significant, and the focus was increasingly on obtaining sufficient labour supply at the lowest cost possible.

---

41 Geoffrey Jones, *Merchants to Multinationals: British Trading Companies in the Nineteenth and Twentieth Centuries* (Oxford: Oxford University Press, 2002).

42 Rana Behal, *One Hundred Years of Servitude: Political Economy of Tea Plantations in Colonial Assam* (New Delhi: Tulika Books, 2014).

43 Rana Behal. "Coolies, Recruiters and Planters: Migration of Indian Labour to Southeast Asian and Assam Plantations during Colonial Rule" (Working Paper Series, Crossroads Asia, 2013), 3.

44 Behal "Coolies, Recruiters and Planters," 3.

3   Migrant Bonded Labour

The immediate shortage of labour after the abolition of slavery was met by hiring workers from China, Java and the Indian sub-continent on a system of indenture in order to meet the needs of plantation production.[45] The abuses of this system of labour recruitment have been well documented by Hugh Tinker who argued that the "world of slavery still survived; the plantation was a world apart, on its own, subject to the laws – or whims – of those in charge: the overseers and the manager or the proprietor."[46] The role of Indian indentured labour, however, needs to be embedded within the wider process of migration within and from India, to avoid what Richard Allen has termed "chronological apartheid." Instead, as Allen argues, we need to place such movements of labour within "broader historical contexts and to explore the connections between pre- and post-emancipation labour systems more fully."[47] In the nineteenth century, industrial development in British India had already given rise to a circulation of labour, and the migration of workers from rural areas for this purpose was not viewed as "a permanent exodus" but rather as "a temporary transfer" with the intention to return.[48] Similarly, indenture was largely viewed by workers as temporary migration, and their expectations did not normally extend beyond high wages and an eventual return to India.[49]

In the third quarter of the nineteenth century, indenture gave way to "free" wage labour directly recruited by an intermediary – the jobber – who dealt with the plantation manager on behalf of his "gang." From the planters, the contractor – often referred to as the *kangany* or *maistry* – received interest-free loans to advance to workers from their villages who were willing to work on the estates.[50] This system of obtaining labour for plantation work had several advantages for plantation management with regard to getting an adequate supply of labour and reducing the cost of labour. First, while in both systems the

---

45   P. C. Campbell, "Chinese Coolie Emigration to Countries within the British Empire: Studies in Economics and Political Science," *London School of Economics and Political Science*, no. 72 (London: P. S. King and Son, 1923); Douglas E. Horton, *Haciendas and Cooperatives: A Study of Estate Organization, Land Reform and New Reform Enterprises in Peru*, vol. 67 (Ithaca, NY: Cornell University, 1976); Tinker, *New System of Slavery*.

46   Tinker, *New System of Slavery*, 177.

47   Richard B. Allen "Re-Conceptualizing the 'New System of Slavery,'" *Man in India* 92, no. 2 (2012): 228.

48   J. H. Whitley, *Report of the Royal Commission on Labour* (RCL). (London, 1931).

49   K. L. Gillion, *Fiji's Indian Migrants: A History to the End of Indenture in 1920* (Melbourne: Oxford University Press, 1962).

50   Whitley, *Report*, 354.

costs of recruitment and the expenses of the journey were recovered from the worker, under indenture this meant separate transactions between the plantation manager and each worker whereas, under a "free" labour regime, the plantation only dealt with the intermediary. Second, while under indenture the labourer was bound to serve on the plantation to which he was recruited for typically a five-year period, no such restriction applied under a regime of "free" labour.

By the 1880s, while recruitment for the Assam plantations was done through the official government agents in Calcutta as well as through a labour contractor, a *sirdar*, the latter system was the preferred and cheaper option for planters.[51] Using this method, the estates were able to get labour from Bihar, Orissa, the Central Provinces and Madras[52] and even from some Telugu districts.[53] The *kangany* system was used to recruit workers to British Malaya, where there was an increased demand for labour for the sugar, coffee and rubber plantations. Labour from India was initially brought across on an indentured basis but was replaced by the *kangany* system. An employer seeking labour would send a recruiter, the *kangany*, to India advancing him the expenses for the journey. The latter would return in due course and repay the money owed to the planters, while getting a payment on the number of workers he had managed to bring across. Initial attempts were made to secure indentured labour for the coffee plantations in Ceylon, but this was soon replaced by the *kangany* system of recruitment for the tea and rubber plantations in the nineteenth and early twentieth centuries. According to Allen, around 1.5 million workers migrated to work on plantations in Ceylon and Malaya between the 1840s and the early twentieth century, usually on "short-term, often verbal, contracts," while 700,000 to 750,000 labourers migrated to work on plantations in Assam between 1870 and 1900.[54]

While the *kangany* system was important in increasing the number of workers, the planters used it also to bind the worker to the plantations through ties of indebtedness to ensure the needs of production. As advances were provided for their travel costs and these were deducted from their wages, plantation workers began their lives in debt.[55] The workers owed the passage money to

51   George M. Barker, *A Tea Planter's Life in Assam* (Calcutta: Thacker, Spink, 1884).
52   Courtenay, *Plantation Agriculture*, 65.
53   Dharma Kumar, *Land and Caste in South Asia: Agricultural Labour in the Madras Presidency during the Nineteenth Century* (Cambridge: Cambridge University Press, 1965).
54   Richard B. Allen, "Slaves, Convicts, Abolitionism and the Global Origins of the Post-Emancipation Indentured Labor System," *Slavery and Abolition* 35, no. 2 (2014): 329.
55   Whitley, *Report*, 355.

the planter via the *kangany*, allowing the latter to establish a debt-bondage among his recruits.[56] The reality, however, was that the worker was constantly in debt, and continual advances had to be paid to meet the workers day-to-day expenses. In many ways, therefore, a system of advances actually replaced the payment of wages. These advances were important in persuading workers from the Madras Presidency to migrate to work on the coffee and tea plantations in Ceylon, with families keeping the advances to pay off local debts.[57] In this manner, the system of recruitment "created an almost endemic problem of indebtedness among the workers."[58] In Ceylon, these ties of indebtedness were strengthened through the *tundu* system. The *tundu* (literally, a "note") was a piece of paper that indicated the amount of money that the worker owed the estate, who was given a legal discharge only if this payment was done.[59] However, the planters often refused to issue these discharge tickets when they wanted the workers to remain, with the *tundu* containing the "principle of indentureship," even if it was never formally given this name.[60]

These features of direct recruitment (that is, bypassing official authorities) meant that while these migrant workers were viewed as "free" labour, they were, in effect, bonded labour, tied through debts to the labour contractor, who remained the intermediary between the recruited workers and the management.[61] The *kangany* system also transferred part of the "responsibility of containing and controlling the labour force from the planter to an intermediary," with the workers effectively being "chattel labour," like under slavery.[62] Overall, it was clear that the processes involved in recruiting and controlling labour were important in securing sufficient labour when needed, as the contractor was able to recruit workers from his village, while involving the contractor in the supervision of workers meant a reduction or transference of some of the management and labour control cost.[63]

56   Ravindra K. Jain, *South Indians on the Plantation Frontier in Malaya* (New Haven: Yale University Press, 1970).

57   Roland Wenzlhuemer, *From Coffee to Tea Cultivation in Ceylon, 1880–1900: An Economic and Social History* (Leiden: Brill, 2008).

58   Kumari Jayawardena and Rachel Kurian, *Class, Patriarchy and Ethnicity on Sri Lankan Plantations: Two Centuries of Power and Protest* (Hyderabad: Orient BlackSwan, 2015).

59   Rachel Kurian, "State, Capital and Labour in the Plantation Industry in Sri Lanka 1834–1984" (PhD diss., University of Amsterdam, 1989).

60   Kurian, "State, Capital and Labour," 93.

61   Gail Omvedt, "Migration in Colonial India: The Articulation of Feudalism and Capitalism by the Colonial State," *The Journal of Peasant Studies* 7, no. 2 (1980): 185–212.

62   Jayawardena and Kurian, *Class, Patriarchy and Ethnicity*, 33.

63   Omvedt, "Migration in Colonial India," 193.

The *kangany* system also served to preserve patriarchal structures on the plantations. The expansion of tea had given rise to an increased demand for labour, and the Ceylon planters pressured the 1860 Immigrant Labour Commission to also recruit women.[64] Women in the source region, the Madras Presidency in India, were paid less than their male counterparts, and were also viewed as "steadier" and more controllable, and this proved a significant economic incentive for planters to recruit them.[65] As a result of such active recruitment and its economic advantages, women constituted the majority of the plantation workforce in colonial South Asia by the early decades of the twentieth century. Kurian and Jayawardena have used the concept of "plantation patriarchy" to analyse the gender prejudices and patriarchal norms stemming from colonialism, race, caste, ethnicity, religion and culture in the labour regime and living arrangements on the plantations in Sri Lanka that justified and normalised the subordinate status of women workers.[66] In the case of Ceylon, this was reflected in the women being placed under male authority at all levels, being paid lower wages and working longer hours than their male counterparts and also being responsible for the reproductive chores in the household, all of which helped lower the costs of production. The subordination of women was further justified with reference to Hindu religious norms.[67]

4   Expatriate Management

By the late nineteenth century, Asian plantations were mainly run by expatriate managers. According to a Royal Commission in 1931, about 90 per cent of plantations in North India and nearly all those in Madras and Burma were managed by Europeans. Plantations managed by Indians were few and generally far smaller in size.[68] Expatriate managers were, by and large, interested in making their fortunes during their stay on the plantation and returning home as wealthy as possible, and as soon as possible. The typical remuneration package combined a relatively modest basic monthly salary with a potentially

---

64   Rachel Kurian and Kumari Jayawardena, "Plantation Patriarchy and Structural Violence: Women Workers in Sri Lanka," in *Social and Cultural Dimensions of Indian Indentured Labour and its Diaspora: Past and Present*, ed. Maurits S. Hassankhan, Lomarsh Ropnarine, and Radica Mahase (Delhi: Manohar; New York: Abingdon, 2017) 25–49.
65   Kurian and Jayawardena, "Plantation Patriarchy," 32.
66   Kurian and Jayawardena, "Plantation Patriarchy."
67   Kurian and Jayawardena, "Plantation Patriarchy," 35–36.
68   Whitley, *Report*, 349.

larger supplement that was determined as a percentage of annual profits. Total remuneration was, therefore, partly a function of short-term profits.[69] For that reason, plantation managers were keen to maximise these short-term profits and were less concerned with the longer-term interests of the plantation and, in particular, of its workforce.[70] And while the modern plantation could be viewed as a "laboratory," in which methods of increasing agricultural efficiency were "developed and tested,"[71] the pressures of finance capital and plantation management prioritised increasing land productivity (through fertilisers and crop betterment) and the intensification of the labour process.

Planters often imposed slave-like forms of coercion in order to maximise their control over labour. Many planters familiar with slave labour moved from the sugar plantations they had set up in the West Indies in the 1830s and the 1840s to Asian colonies, including Ceylon, Malaya and Assam in the 1870s to 1880s.[72] Some of the cruelty employed on the Assam plantations was high-lighted in the Chief Commissioner's Annual Report on Labour Immigration into Assam in 1900. Amongst other things, this report, by Commissioner Henry Cotton, showed an increase in the mortality levels in Assam, payment of wages below the legal minimum, numerous instances of non-payment of wages, failure to provide rice at the statutory price, and failure to pay the required subsistence allowance to sick labourers. The report also mentioned instances in which rigorous punishment was meted out to labourers by magistrates, often for very minor offences. Meanwhile, European planters and managers could be acquitted even in cases that involved the murder of a plantation worker.[73] The Superintendent of Police in Kandy (Ceylon) reported that plantation workers were treated in ways that were "exceeding arbitrary and cruel," claiming conditions were even worse than "Negro slavery."[74] Thus, plantation management methods reminiscent of an earlier era had evidently survived.

---

69   Lalith Jayawardena, "The Supply of Sinhalese Labour to the Tea Industry in Ceylon" (research study, made available by the author, Cambridge University, 1960).

70   The practice of linking the manager's bonuses to the profits was also undertaken by finance capital in Southeast Asia; for instance, in the Dutch colony of Sumatra. The European staff, in particular the manager and his assistants, had "maximal interest in increasing production and lower costs": Jan Breman, *Taming the Coolie Beast* (Oxford: Oxford University Press, 1989), 79.

71   Graham Edgar and Ingrid Floering, *The Modern Plantation in the Third World* (Sydney, Australia: Croom Helm, 1984).

72   Tinker, *New System of Slavery*, 177.

73   Rana Behal, "Some Aspects of the Growth of Plantation Labour Force and Labour Movements in Assam Valley Districts, 1900–1947" (PhD diss., Centre for Historical Studies, Jawaharlal Nehru University, 1984).

74   Jayawardena and Kurian, *Class, Patriarchy and Ethnicity*, 33.

In Ceylon, the *kangany* system served to perpetuate caste-based forms of control into management. The main contractor, or the head *kangany* was usually from a "higher" caste, while the majority of workers were from a relatively "lower" caste, allowing caste divisions and controls to "pervade work arrangements."[75] Planters were also keen to transfer some of the costs of the supervision and control of the workers, a significant expense on the slave plantations, to the recruiters. Thus, the recruiter became more than the overseer on the estates; he was the intermediary between the plantation management and the workers he recruited, which gave him a powerful role in the labour management on the estates. He was also able to use his position to enforce non-economic forms of coercion to control the workers. As noted by de Silva: "His ties of caste and kinship with those whom he recruited gave a moral basis to his authority. He mediated in their family affairs and was their representative and spokesman in labour disputes. Combined with this patron-client relationship between the *kangany* and labour gang was a creditor-debtor relationship, which placed the labourers in financial bondage to him, and consolidated his leadership. As an intermediary the *kangany* was not a neutral element but a prop in the power structure of the estate community. In the eyes of the labourers he was effectively their employer."[76]

5   The Interventionist State

In spite of upholding the "laissez-faire" philosophy of capitalism, the colonial state intervened with subsidies, favourable legislation and other forms of support to promote industrial plantation capitalism, while providing poor protection and welfare for the workers. It supported the Assam plantations by providing, among other things, experimental plantations and the services of experts as well as rent-free concessions to the companies.[77] The colonial government tried to make labour available by increasing land revenue on peasant holdings so that the peasants would seek employment on the plantations. The colonial government also passed legislation supportive of plantation agriculture, such as Act VI (Bengal Council) of 1865 which granted planters the right to arrest, without warrant, workers who ran away from estates. This same Act also included measures to protect plantation workers, but these protective

---

75   Jayawardena and Kurian, *Class, Patriarchy and Ethnicity*, 41.
76   S. B. D. De Silva, *The Political Economy of Underdevelopment* (London: Routledge and Kegan Paul, 2012).
77   Behal "Some Aspects," 88–131.

measures were seldom invoked, and the colonial state took no steps to enforce them. Act I of 1882 raised the terms of contract duration from three to five years and fixed rates of pay according to work performed. This, again, enhanced the control exercised by planters over the plantation workforce, as fixing the schedule of paid tasks was left entirely to the discretion of the planters.[78]

In his 1900 Annual Report on Labour Immigration into Assam, Henry Cotton, the Chief Commissioner of Assam, reported that unfair treatment meted out to plantation workers was well known by many at the highest levels of the colonial government. The colonial state seemed to view these forms of exploitation as necessary evils that supported the profitability of European-owned and -controlled plantation enterprises. As noted in 1900 by the Chief Secretary to the Government of India, J.B. Fuller, in relation to the conditions of workers in Assam tea gardens: "The truth is of course that serious abuses must occur under a labour system which is something of the nature of slavery, for an employee who can be arrested and forcibly detained by his master is more of a slave than a servant and that these abuses are the price which has to be paid for the great advantages which has resulted from the establishment and growth of the tea industry in Assam."[79]

Even the Viceroy, Lord Curzon, accepted that labour had to suffer in order to promote plantation agriculture. According to him, "It is an arbitrary system, an abnormal system .... But it has been devised not in the main in our interests but in the interests of an enterprise with which the Government of India could but sympathise, namely, the effort to open up by capital and industry the resources of a distant and backward province."[80]

Under pressure from London to generate revenues to cover the military and other costs of ruling the colony, the local colonial government in nineteenth-century Ceylon supported plantations through the development of railways and other necessary infrastructure, as well as through subsidies, incentives, tax benefits and supplying cheap land.[81] The colonial state also intervened in Malaya through the creation of commissions that helped recruit indentured and cheap labour. As early as 1890, the European planters requested an official commission to inquire into the state of labour in Malaya and to come up with suggestions for encouraging immigration. This commission was dominated by planters whose intent was "less to improve indentured labour conditions than

---

78   Rana Behal "The Emergence of a Plantation Economy: Assam Tea Industry in the Nineteenth Century" (New Delhi: Occasional Papers on History and Society, 1985).
79   Behal "Some Aspects," 94.
80   Behal "Some Aspects," 95.
81   Jayawardena and Kurian, *Class, Patriarchy and Ethnicity*, 23–26, 35.

to obtain the government's participation in importing labour."[82] Although its recommendations were not immediately endorsed, another commission set up in 1896 reiterated them and a bill was passed in 1897 whereby these were enforced. In 1907, the Indian Immigration Committee was set up. One of its immediate tasks was to "devise a comprehensive scheme to import labour on a large-scale."[83] In reality, this meant the setting up of "quasi-official legal instruments for the centralised control of labour supply on the estates."[84] A Tamil Immigration Fund was also set up, the proceeds of which were to meet the cost of importing labour. The fund consisted of levies on employers but also contributions by the government.[85] By 1913, it was estimated that the fund had taken care of all the costs of recruitment, including the *kangany*'s recruiting allowance.[86] By 1914, the use of licences was significant in regulating the flow of workers (the *kangany* being given a licence indicating the minimum number of workers he could bring across to Malaya). The expenses of his journey as well as the allowance were given to him, the expenses for the recruits being paid out of the Fund by various officers during the course of the journey.[87] All these measures helped to ease the migration of workers from India for the growing plantation industry, and various aspects reflect the concern of the state and the management with increasing the labour supply.

Such policies and interventions indicated "that the colonial state was not a 'night watchman' laissez-faire state even though its own ideology usually stressed that it was neutral and unconcerned to interfere in such 'commercial transactions' as labour migration."[88] It was keen to maintain the supply of labour for the industrial plantations (which were, in any case, linked to the interests of the colonial powers in terms of ownership) and wished to supply cheap inputs for the Industrial Revolution in Europe with the minimum costs possible. It passed legislation that was favourable to the planting industry, set up a large number of labour inquiry commissions, and took an even more direct role in the recruitment process of labourers with the evolution of the labour-contracting system. Bureaucrats were involved in overseeing the

---

82 Norman J. Parmer, *Colonial Labour Policy and Administration: A History of Labour in the Rubber Plantation Industry in Malaya, c. 1910–1941* (New York: J. J. Augustin, 1960).

83 Parmer, *Colonial Labour Policy*, 39.

84 Jain, *South Indians*, 200.

85 Parmer, *Colonial Labour Policy*, 42.

86 Parmer, *Colonial Labour Policy*, 44.

87 K.S. Sandhu, *Indians in Malaya: Some Aspects of their Immigration and Settlement (1786–1957)* (Cambridge, Cambridge University Press, 1969); Parmer, *Colonial Labour Policy*, 51–52.

88 Omvedt, "Migration in Colonial India," 204.

process and a system of stringent control over the numbers of recruits evolved. The state also passed medical ordinances, which, by and large, reflected a concern to maintain the labour force. It was clear, however, that an important motivation was to promote plantation capitalism, and the emphasis was more on helping the planters increase the profitability of production than on protecting the workers. According to Omvedt, there was "no evidence that any such responses of the colonial state – or any legislation resulting from them – at any point contradicted the needs of plantation owners and factory owners for cheap labour."[89]

6   Unfree Labour and Colonial Capitalism: Revisiting the Plantationocene

In line with the dynamics of capitalist development in the West, and, more particularly, the increasing dominance of finance capital, the nineteenth-century British colonial plantations innovated their labour regime to include "free" waged workers after slavery had been abolished in 1833. The planter-owner was replaced by expatriate management employed by companies, and the need to generate high short-term profits to get access to investment in the global market mitigated against long-term investment and focused, rather, on trying to lower labour costs as much as possible. This was done through the employment of "free" migrant labour, initially on indenture, and subsequently recruited by contractors. Some of the costs of recruitment, labour control and supervision, which were substantial during the slave era, were transferred to the contractors and workers themselves, the latter effectively bonded through ties of indebtedness to work on the plantations. The hierarchies of the slave era, such as those based on race and class, and the use of force and compulsion, were integrated into the new order, as these had proved effective in controlling the workforce. These were supplemented by local forms of labour controls, such as those based on caste and religion. Plantation patriarchy, which had its origins in the slave era, also assumed new forms and dynamics in the industrial plantations, with women being paid less, working longer hours, doing the unpaid care work in the household and generally being placed under male supervision. Finally, in contrast to its expected role as the promoter of laissez-faire capitalism, the colonial state consciously supported the industrial

---

89   Omvedt, "Migration in Colonial India," 206.

plantation through its policies, including through subsidies and legislation supportive of plantation owners and managers rather than of workers.

While the concept of the plantationocene is linked to the dislocations and relocations of life and nature across the world for plantation production, this chapter has argued that the term can be enriched by taking into account the global and local dynamics that inform and shape its characteristics in specific contexts. It has shown that power relations and processes at different levels gave rise to specific forms of labour control in ways that benefitted finance capital under British colonialism in the nineteenth century. The labour regime that developed as a consequence reflected its historical legacy of force and compulsion which had proven effective in controlling workers in the slave era. It combined these with the prevailing hierarchies and legal coercion to serve the interests of colonial capitalism. While such changes can perhaps be viewed as part of the innovative and adaptive nature of the plantationocene to external and internal opportunities, there is little doubt these involved extreme exploitation and multiple forms of oppression of workers.

Bibliography

Allen, Richard B. "European Slave Trading, Abolitionism, and 'New Systems of Slavery' in the Indian Ocean." *PORTAL: Journal of Multidisciplinary International Studies* 9, no. 1 (2012): 1–21.

Allen, Richard B. "Re-Conceptualizing the 'New System of Slavery.'" *Man in India* 92, no. 2 (2012): 225–45.

Allen, Richard B. "Slaves, Convicts, Abolitionism and the Global Origins of the Post-Emancipation Indentured Labor System." *Slavery & Abolition* 35, no. 2 (2014): 328–48.

Allen, Richard B. "The Atlantic and Africa: The Second Slavery and Beyond." In *Merchant Capital and Slave Trading in the Western Indian Ocean, 1770–1830*, edited by Dale Tomich and Paul E. Lovejoy. Albany, NY: SUNY Press, 2021.

Allen, Robert C. *Global Economic History: A Very Short Introduction*. Vol. 282. Oxford, UK: Oxford University Press, 2011.

Allen, Robert C. *The Industrial Revolution: A Very Short Introduction*. Vol. 509. Oxford, UK: Oxford University Press, 2017.

Barker, George M. *A Tea Planter's Life in Assam*. Calcutta: Thacker, Spink, 1884.

Behrendt, Stephen D., David Eltis, and David Richardson. "The Costs of Coercion: African Agency in the Pre-Modern Atlantic World." *Economic History Review*, 54, no. 3 (2001): 454–76.

Behal, Rana. "Some Aspects of the Growth of Plantation Labour Force and Labour Movemens in Assam Valley Districts, 1900–1947." PhD diss., Centre for Historical Studies, Jawaharlal Nehru University, 1984.

Behal, Rana. "The Emergence of a Plantation Economy: Assam Tea Industry in the Nineteenth Century." New Delhi: Nehru Memorial Museum and Library (NMML) Occasional Paper, History and Society, Number XXI 1985.

Behal, R. "Coolies, Recruiters and Planters: Migration of Indian Labour to Southeast Asian and Assam Plantations during Colonial Rule." Working Paper Series No. 9, Crossroads Asia, 2013.

Behal, R. *One Hundred Years of Servitude: Political Economy of Tea Plantations in Colonial Assam*. New Delhi: Tulika Books, 2014.

Benn, Denis M. "The Theory of Plantation Economy and Society: A Methodological Critique." *Journal of Commonwealth & Comparative Politics* 12, no. 3 (1974): 249–60.

Beckert, Sven, and Seth Rockman, eds. *Slavery's Capitalism: A New History of American Economic Development*. Philadelphia: University of Pennsylvania Press, 2016.

Beckford, George L. *Persistent Poverty: Underdevelopment in Plantation Economies of the Third World*. London: Zed Books, 1983.

Bhatia, B. M. *Famines in India 1860–1945: A Study in Some Aspects of the Economic History of India.* Bombay: Asia Publishing House, 1963.

Blackburn, Robin. *The Making of New World Slavery: From the Baroque to the Modern, 1492–1800*. London: Verso, 1998.

Bogart, Dan. "The Transport Revolution in Industrialising Britain." *The Cambridge Economic History of Modern Britain* 1 (2014): 368–91.

Breman, Jan. *Taming the Coolie Beast*. Oxford: Oxford University Press, 1989.

Breman, Jan. *Labour Migration and Rural Transformation in Colonial Asia*. Amsterdam: Free University Press, 1990.

Bryce-Laporte, Roy Simon. *The Conceptualization of the American Slave Plantation as a Total Institution*. Los Angeles: University of California Press, 1968.

Burnard, Trevor. *Planters, Merchants, and Slaves: Plantation Societies in British America, 1650–1820.* Chicago: University of Chicago Press, 2015.

Campbell, P. C. "Chinese Coolie Emigration to Countries within the British Empire: Studies in Economics and Political Science." *London School of Economics and Political Science*, no. 72. London: P. S. King and Son, 1923.

Clukey, Amy, and Jeremy Wells. "Introduction: Plantation Modernity." *Global South* 10, no. 2 (2016): 1–0.

Courtenay, P. P. *Plantation Agriculture*. 2nd ed. London: Bell and Hyman. EWB/HBS/IDA: Selections, 1980.

Craton, Michael. "A Cresting Wave? Recent Trends in the Historiography of Slavery, with Special Reference to the British Caribbean." *Historical Reflections/Réflexions Historiques* (1982): 403–19.

Cumpston, Ina Mary. *Indians Overseas in British Territories: 1834–1854*. Oxford: Oxford University Press, 1953.

Curtin, Philip D., and Philip DeArmond Curtin. T*he Rise and Fall of the Plantation Complex: Essays in Atlantic History*. Cambridge: Cambridge University Press, 1998.

Davis, Janae, Alex A. Moulton, Levi Van Sant, and Brian Williams. "Anthropocene, Capitalocene, ... Plantationocene? A Manifesto for Ecological Justice in an Age of Global Crises." *Geography Compass* 13, no. 5 (2019). https://doi.org/10.1111/gec3.12438.

De Silva, S. B. D. *The Political Economy of Underdevelopment*. London: Routledge and Kegan Paul, 2012.

Deane, Phyllis M. "The First Industrial Revolution." Cambridge: Cambridge University Press, 1979.

Durant, Thomas. "The Slave Plantation Revisited: A Sociological Perspective." In *Plantation Society and Race Relations: The Origins of Inequality*, edited by Thomas J. Durant and J. David Knottnerus. Westport, CT: Greenwood Publishing Group, 1999.

Franklin, John Hope, and Loren Schweninger. *Runaway Slaves: Rebels on the Plantation*. Oxford: Oxford University Press, 2000.

Genovese, Eugene D. "The Medical and Insurance Costs of Slaveholding in the Cotton Belt." *The Journal of Negro History* 45, no. 3 (1960): 141–55.

Genovese, Eugene D. *The Political Economy of Slavery: Studies in the Economy and Society of the Slave South*. Middletown, CT: Wesleyan University Press, 2014.

Govan, Thomas P. "Was Plantation Slavery Profitable?" *The Journal of Southern History* 8, no. 4 (1942): 513–35.

Graham, Edgar, and Ingrid Floering. *The Modern Plantation in the Third World*. Sydney, Australia: Croom Helm, 1984.

Gray, Lewis C. "Economic Efficiency and Competitive Advantages of Slavery under the Plantation System." *Agricultural History* 4, no. 2 (1930): 31–47.

Greenfield, Sidney M. "Slavery and the Plantation in the New World: The Development and Diffusion of a Social Form." *Journal of Inter-American Studies* 11, no. 1 (1969): 44–57.

Hall, Catherine. *Legacies of British Slave-Ownership: Colonial Slavery and the Formation of Victorian Britain*. Cambridge: Cambridge University Press, 2014.

Hall, Catherine, and Ruth Ramsden-Karelse. "The Legacies of British Slave Ownership: Catherine Hall talks to Ruth." *Soundings* 77, no. 77 (2021): 23–36.

Haraway, Donna, Noboru Ishikawa, Scott F. Gilbert, Kenneth Olwig, Anna L. Tsing, and Nils Bubandt. "Anthropologists are Talking – about the Anthropocene." *Ethnos* 81, no. 3 (2016): 535–64.

Higman, B. W. "Plantations and Typological Problems in Geography: A Review Article." *Australian Geographer* 11, no. 2 (1969): 192–203.

Hobsbawm, Eric, and George Rudé. *Captain Swing*. London: Verso Trade, 2014.

Horton, Douglas E. *Haciendas and Cooperatives: A Study of Estate Organization, Land Reform and New Reform Enterprises in Peru*. Vol. 67. Ithaca, NY: Cornell University, 1976.

Inikori, Joseph E. *Africans and the Industrial Revolution in England: A Study in International Trade and Economic Development*. Cambridge: Cambridge University Press, 2002.

Gillion, K. L. *Fiji's Indian Migrants: A History to the End of Indenture in 1920*. Melbourne: Oxford University Press, 1962.

Giovannetti, Jorge L. "Grounds of Race: Slavery, Racism and the Plantation in the Caribbean." *Latin American and Caribbean Ethnic Studies* 1, no. 1 (2006): 5–36.

Jackson, Robert Nicholas. *Immigrant Labour and the Development of Malaya, 1786–1920: A Historical Monograph*. Kuala Lumpur: Government Press, 1961.

Jain, Ravindra K. *South Indians on the Plantation Frontier in Malaya*. New Haven: Yale University Press, 1970.

Jayawardena, Kumari, and Rachel Kurian. *Class, Patriarchy and Ethnicity on Sri Lankan Plantations: Two Centuries of Power and Protest*. Hyderabad: Orient BlackSwan, 2015.

Jayawardena, Lalith. "The Supply of Sinhalese Labour to the Tea Industry in Ceylon." Research study made available by the author, Cambridge University, 1960.

Jayawardena, Lalith. *The Supply of Sinhalese Labour to Ceylon Plantations (1830–1930): A Study of Imperial Policy in a Peasant Society*. Cambridge: University of Cambridge, 1963.

Jones, Geoffrey. *Merchants to Multinationals: British Trading Companies in the Nineteenth and Twentieth Centuries*. Oxford: Oxford University Press, 2002.

Kirk, Colin. "People in Plantations: A Review of the Literature and Annotated Bibliography." Research Report No. 18. Sussex, Institute of Development Studies, 1987.

Kloosterboer, Willemina. *Involuntary Labour since the Abolition of Slavery: A Survey of Compulsory Labour throughout the World*. Brill Archive, 1960.

Kondapi, C. *Chenchal Indians Overseas, 1838–1949*. New Delhi: Indian Council of World Affairs; Bombay: Oxford University Press, 1951.

Kumar, Dharma. *Land and Caste in South Asia: Agricultural Labour in the Madras Presidency during the Nineteenth Century*. Cambridge, Cambridge University Press, 1965.

Kurian, Rachel. *Women Workers in the Sri Lanka Plantation Sector*. Geneva: International Labour Office, 1982.

Kurian, Rachel. "State, Capital and Labour in the Plantation Industry in Sri Lanka 1834–1984." PhD diss., University of Amsterdam, 1989.

Kurian, Rachel, and Kumari Jayawardena. "Plantation Patriarchy and Structural Violence: Women Workers in Sri Lanka." In *Social and Cultural Dimensions of Indian Indentured Labour and its Diaspora: Past and Present*, edited by Maurits S.

Hassankhan, Lomarsh Ropnarine, and Radica Mahase, 25–49. Delhi: Manohar; New York: Abingdon, 2017.

Metzer, Jacob. "Rational Management, Modern Business Practices, and Economies of Scale in the Ante-Bellum Southern Plantations." *Explorations in Economic History* 12, no. 2 (1975): 123–150.

Mintz, Sidney. *Sweetness and Power: The Place of Sugar in Modern History.* London: Penguin, 1986.

Mokyr, Joel. *The British Industrial Revolution: An Economic Perspective.* London: Routledge, 2018.

Murphy, Michael Warren, and Caitlin Schroering. "Refiguring the Plantationocene." *Journal of World-Systems Research* 26, no. 2 (2020): 400–15.

Nieboer, Herman Jeremias. *Slavery as an Industrial system: Ethnological Researches.* The Hague: M. Nijhoff, 1900.

Omvedt, Gail. "Migration in Colonial India: The Articulation of Feudalism and Capitalism by the Colonial State." *The Journal of Peasant Studies* 7, no. 2 (1980): 185–212.

Parmer, J. Norman. *Colonial Labour Policy and Administration: A History of Labour in the Rubber Plantation Industry in Malaya, c. 1910–1941.* New York: J. J. Augustin, 1960.

Patterson, Orlando. *Sociology of Slavery: An Analysis of the Origins.* London: Macgibbon & Kee, 1967.

Pryor, Frederic L. "The Plantation Economy as an Economic System." *Journal of Comparative Economics* 6, no. 3 (1982): 288–317.

Reddock, Rhoda E. "Women and Slavery in the Caribbean: A Feminist Perspective." *Latin American Perspectives* 12, no. 1 (1985): 63–80.

Roberts, Justin. *Slavery and the Enlightenment in the British Atlantic, 1750–1807.* Cambridge: Cambridge University Press, 2013.

Russell-Wood, A. J. R. "Iberian Expansion and the Issue Of Black Slavery: Changing Portuguese Attitudes, 1440–1770." *The American Historical Review* 83, no. 1 (1978): 16–42. https://doi.org/10.2307/1865901.

Sandhu, Kernial Singh. S. *Indians in Malaya: Some Aspects of their Immigration and Settlement (1786–1957).* Cambridge: Cambridge University Press, 1969.

Saunders, A. C. de. C. M. *A Social History of Black Slaves and Freedmen in Portugal, 1441–1555.* Cambridge: Cambridge University Press, 1982.

Tinker, Hugh A. *A New System of Slavery: The Export of Indian Labour Overseas 1830–1920.* London, New York and Bombay: Oxford University Press, 1974.

Wallerstein, Immanuel. *The Modern World-System: Capitalist Agriculture and the Origins of the European World-Economy in the Sixteenth Century.* New York: Academic Press, 1974.

Wallerstein, Immanuel. *The Modern World-System II: Mercantilism and the Consolidation of the European World-Economy, 1600–1750.* Vol. 2. Berkeley: University of California Press, 2011.

Wenzlhuemer, Roland. *From Coffee to Tea Cultivation in Ceylon, 1880–1900: An Economic and Social History*. Leiden: Brill, 2008.

Whitley, J. H. *Report of the Royal Commission on Labour (RCL)*. London, 1931.

Williams, Eric. *Capitalism and Slavery*. Chapel Hill: University of North Carolina Press, 1994.

Wolf, Eric R. "Specific Aspects of Plantation Systems in the New World: Community Sub-Cultures and Social Classes." *Plantation Systems of the New World* (1959): 136–45.

Wolford, Wendy. "The Plantationocene: A Lusotropical Contribution to the Theory." *Annals of the American Association of Geographers* 111, no. 6 (2021): 1622–39.

CHAPTER 11

The Mistress of the Coffee Markets of the World

Slavery in Brazil and the Kangany *System in Ceylon, c. 1815–1878*

Rafael Marquese

1   Introduction

Having announced it twice one month earlier, *The Ceylon Observer* – the most important periodical in this British colony – finally published a long article by Robert Boyd Tytler on 4 October 1852.[1] Despite his young age, many considered Tytler to be one of the founding fathers of Ceylon's coffee economy. Born in Scotland, he moved to the East Indies in 1837, at the age of eighteen, after doing a three-year internship as a management assistant on coffee plantations in the Blue Mountains, Jamaica. In the following years, along with other planters and managers with previous experience in the West Indies, Tytler would help lay the groundwork for Ceylon's coffee economy by transmitting and locally adapting the agronomic knowledge that had originally been developed for Caribbean slave coffee plantations.[2]

Tytler's 1852 article, however, dealt with a different slave society. The prospects for Ceylon's coffee culture were still uncertain in the aftermath of the deep crisis of 1847–1848. Many estates founded during the investment boom between 1837 and 1845 had been abandoned, confiscated for debt or sold significantly below the original invested value. Based on a careful assessment of the fixed operating costs and average productivity of Ceylon's plantations,

---

1   I would like to thank Leonardo Marques, Alain El Youssef, Waldomiro Lourenço da Silva, Jr., Marcelo Ferraro, Rodrigo Goyena Soares, Lindener Pareto, César Bonamico, Dale Tomich and Ricardo Henrique Salles for their many suggestions and comments. This chapter is partially the result of a larger project founded by CNPq, the Brazilian research council, of which I am a fellow.
2   *The Ceylon Observer*, 6 September 1852; *The Ceylon Observer*, 30 September 1852 [United Kingdom National Archives – UNKA, CO 59/22]; I. H. van den Driesen, "Coffee Cultivation in Ceylon (1)," *The Ceylon Historical Journal* 3 (1953): 41; Tom J. Barron, "Scots and the Coffee Industry in Nineteenth Century Ceylon," in *The Scottish Experience in Asia, c. 1700 to the Present: Settlers and Soujourners*, ed. T. M. Devine and Angela McCarthy (London: Palgrave MacMillan, 2017), 163–86; "Pioneers of the Planting Enterprise in Ceylon: Robert Boyd Tytler," *The Tropical Agriculturist* 13, no. 4 (1893): 218–19.

Tytler pointed out how a fluctuation in coffee prices of ten shillings (up or down) could lead to the recovery of the industry or its definitive demise. The remarkably low prices of 1847–1848 were clearly "the natural result of production exceeding consumption." The crucial information that coffee investors in Ceylon needed, therefore, depended on the perspectives of the world coffee market, which would, in turn, be determined by the expansion or stagnation of supply in the following years. It was necessary to study rival producers, whose output was still much higher than Ceylon's at the time. According to Tytler, "with respect to Java perhaps we have little to fear or to hope for," given the inelasticity of its production under the Cultivation System. The real problem was elsewhere: "The great arbitress ... of this vital question, as she is the present overruling mistress of the Coffee Markets of the world, is Brazil with her slave labour."[3]

The main objective of Tytler's article was to start a discussion within the Ceylon commercial and planting community on creating a fund (with quotas of ten pounds each) to finance a voyage to Brazil "with the general purpose of ascertaining the actual state of affairs in that large producing country in respect of its capability of extension of cultivation and the chance it presents of holding out in the competition for supplying the market of the world with Coffee." This investigation of Brazilian coffee culture would have to concentrate on the problem of slavery. It was not clear for Tytler if "our free labour in Ceylon" would be able to compete "with that of athletic slaves who, under the lash, are made to furnish more than double the daily quota of work." The main issue was the cost of labour. Wages in Ceylon were low due to the abundant supply of seasonal workers from South India. Brazil could only maintain its position in the world coffee market if slaves remained relatively cheap in the country. News that the Empire of Brazil had ended the transatlantic slave trade two years earlier was reaching Ceylon through London. But, considering the history of the previous decades, when the transatlantic slave trade continued to be illegally carried out despite its formal prohibition, was the enforcement of the 1850 law to be trusted? Would the emperor and the Brazilian government be effectively committed to suppressing the traffic? In Cuba, a large number of slaves were relocated from coffee plantations to sugar plantations: could the same happen in Brazil after the end of the transatlantic slave trade, with an accompanying drop in coffee production?[4]

---

3 R. B. Tytler, "Coffee Production: Brazil and Ceylon," *The Ceylon Observer*, 2 October 1852 [UKNA, CO 59/22].
4 Tytler, "Coffee Production."

The seasonality of coffee production ensured that demand for labour was significantly reduced for much of the agricultural year. For this reason, unless coffee planting was combined with the production of other tropical staples, slavery was not particularly suited to coffee in Tytler's evaluation. Brazilian planters, he argued, were perhaps making the mistake of expanding their coffee plantations too much without having a proportional labour supply. That strategy was driving Brazilian planters to force their slaves to harvest indiscriminately and simultaneously "all sorts [of coffee berries], whether ripe or unripe." Hence, Brazilian coffee was priced at a much lower level on international markets. Without the transatlantic slave trade and with an estimated annual slave mortality of 10 per cent, planters "must in the end, and at no very remote date, bring themselves to a dead lock." It was this hypothesis that Tytler wanted to verify on the ground in Brazil.

Tytler's proposal lost its raison d'être almost immediately. International coffee prices had reached their lowest level in the entire nineteenth century precisely in 1847–1848. Despite some occasional fluctuations, the next thirty years would be marked by a sharp rise in prices,[5] boosting the "golden age" of Ceylon's coffee economy. But even though his plan to inspect what was happening with slavery in Brazil was not implemented, the basic premise of Tytler's article – the existence of structural relations between the coffee economy in Brazil, based on slave labour, and its Ceylon counterpart, based on a peculiar form of wage labour – was clearly correct.

These relations, however, have not been properly investigated yet. The historiography on nineteenth-century Ceylon has focused on the annual migratory flows of Tamil coolies from South India, the nature of their wage labour regime (free or coerced), their living conditions on plantations, the dual or integrated character of the plantation economy in its relations with the local peasant economy, and the ecological origins of the coffee crisis in the 1870s–1880s. Connections between the experience of slave plantations in the West Indies and post-slave plantations in the East Indies have recently attracted the attention of scholars, but research efforts in this field are still rare.[6]

5   Edmar Bacha, "Política Brasileira do café: Uma avaliação centenária," in *150 anos de café*, ed. Edmar Bacha and Robert Greenhill (Rio de Janeiro: Marcellino Martins & E. Johnston, 1992), 20; "Coffee Prices since 1845," in Alex Brown, *The Coffee Planter Manual* (Colombo: Colombo Observer Press, 1880), 165–68.

6   See, for instance, Kris Manjapra, "Plantation Dispossessions: The Global Travel of Agricultural Racial Capitalism," in *American Capitalism: New Histories*, ed. Sven Beckert and Christine Desan (New York: Columbia University Press, 2018); Kris Manjapra, *Colonialism in Global Perspective* (Cambridge: Cambridge University Press, 2020), 71–99.

The historiography on slavery in the nineteenth-century Brazilian coffee sector is massive and details its multiple economic, demographic, social and cultural dimensions. Nevertheless, the interconnections between Brazil and the other coffee zones of the world – whether slave-based or not – remain under-examined.[7]

My aim is to analyse how the different types of compulsory labour used in the nineteenth-century capitalist world economy for the production of coffee were related to and conditioned by each other. Thus, my goal is to take up the imperative articulated by Marcel van der Linden, a scholar in the field of global labour history, according to which "we should not study the different kinds of subaltern workers separately, but consider the connections between them as much as possible."[8] The present chapter, however, incorporates formal comparisons and connections into a broader integrated approach – which brings a substantive comparison and not just a typological one[9] – that shows how slavery in Brazil and the *kangany* system in Ceylon were formed by a double bundle of forces, which united and differentiated them. On the one hand, labour relations in these two spaces were deeply shaped by the global anti-slavery policies promoted by the British Empire after the end of the Napoleonic Wars. On the other hand, although coercive labour was the backbone of coffee economies in both spaces, their distinctive labour arrangements and inscription in the tropical commodity markets of the industrial capitalist world economy ultimately subordinated the fate of Ceylon to that of Brazil.

The chapter is divided into three parts. In the first part, I examine the making of the coffee economy in Brazil and in Ceylon in the first half of the nineteenth century, demonstrating how the joint forces of the industrial world economy and British anti-slavery shaped local processes and were shaped by

---

7   A good survey of the ongoing scholarship is given in Ricardo Salles and Mariana Muaze, eds., *O Vale do Paraíba e o Império do Brasil nos quadros da Segunda Escravidão* (Rio de Janeiro: 7 Letras-Faperj, 2015). I have discussed the global and comparative dimensions of the Brazilian coffee economy before, but without addressing Ceylon; see Rafael de Bivar Marquese, "Luso-Brazilian Enlightenment and the Circulation of Caribbean Slavery-Related Knowledge: The Establishment of the Brazilian Coffee Culture from a Comparative Perspective," *História, Ciências, Saúde – Manguinhos* 16, no. 4 (2009): 855–80; "Espacio y poder en la caficultura esclavista de las Américas: El Vale do Paraiba en perspectiva comparada, 1760–1860," in *Trabajo libre y coativo en sociedades de plantación,* ed. José Antonio Piqueras (Madrid: Siglo XXI, 2009), 215–52; "As origens de Brasil e Java: Trabalho compulsório e a reconfiguração da economia mundial do café na Era das Revoluções, c. 1760–1840," *História* 34 (2015): 108–27.

8   Marcel van der Linden, *Workers of the World: Essays Toward a Global Labor History* (Leiden: Brill, 2008), 36.

9   See Philip McMichael, "Incorporating Comparison within a World-Historical Perspective: An Alternative Comparative Method," *American Sociological Review* 55, no. 3 (1990): 385–97.

them. In the second part, I compare the labour arrangements adopted in coffee plantations in Brazil and Ceylon between the 1850s and 1870s, focusing on the mechanisms of landscape and labour management. Finally, in the conclusion I discuss the implementation of Tytler's plan in 1876, when the Ceylon government sent the journalist G.A. Crüwell on an inspection trip to Brazil. At the same time, they mobilised A. Scott Blacklaw, who had been working as a superintendent on a coffee plantation in Brazil since 1873, to collect additional information. In 1878, the book *Brazil as a Coffee – Growing Country* was published in Colombo, Ceylon, co-authored by Crüwell and Blacklaw. However, the contexts of Tytler's 1852 proposal and Crüwell's 1876 journey were quite different. The observations made by Crüwell and Blacklaw between 1876 and 1878 help us understand the specific nature of the simultaneous crises of slavery (but not of the coffee economy) in Brazil and the coffee economy (but not of the *kangany* system) in Ceylon.

1   The Making of the Coffee Economy in Brazil and Ceylon, 1815–1850

The first global coffee complex was part of the Ottoman economy and arose at the turn of the seventeenth century, when peasant coffee production in Yemen was connected to the large urban consuming centres of the Ottoman Empire in the eastern Mediterranean. Through a process of emulation prompted by early Orientalism, the consumption of the beverage became increasingly popular in the great urban centres of northwestern Europe at the end of the seventeenth century. The pressures of a growing Western demand on Yemen's limited supply caused coffee prices to explode in the early eighteenth century. For that reason, the colonial powers of northwestern Europe sought to appropriate the secrets of coffee production, acclimatising the tree to the conditions in their own Caribbean slave colonies. The second global coffee complex took off after the 1720s and was structured along the axis of Caribbean slave colonies/urban consumers in Northern Europe. In the second half of the eighteenth century, the volume of slave-based coffee production financed by European capital grew at an unprecedented pace, with the French colony of Saint-Domingue occupying the most prominent place. Between 1786 and 1790, its average annual coffee exports were around thirty-two thousand metric tons, which was then equivalent to around half of the world's supply.[10]

---

10   Rafael de Bivar Marquese, "A Tale of Two Coffee Colonies: Environment and Slavery in Suriname and Saint-Domingue, c. 1750–1790," *Comparative Studies in Society and History* 64, no. 3 (2022): 722–755.

The Age of Revolutions completely changed the coffee commodity chain. Despite the efforts of Touissant Louverture to recover the plantation economy after the slave revolution of 1791 and the abolition of slavery in 1794, in 1801 Saint-Domingue's coffee exports fell to about two-thirds of what they had been in 1790.[11] The Napoleonic invasion in 1802 and the Haitian War of Independence fought over the following two years created an even greater vacuum in the world coffee supply by destroying much of the coffee infrastructure and disrupting the island's connections with the North American merchants that re-exported the product to Europe. The opportunities opened by the disruption of Saint-Domingue were immediately seized upon by rival Caribbean slave colonies. Jamaica had partially occupied the space opened by the Saint-Domingue Revolution since the 1790s; after 1804, it was accompanied by Cuba, which was also dependent on slave labour.[12] In 1815, Cuba and Jamaica sent a total of around twenty thousand tons of coffee to the world market, which indicates that they had still not been able to fully fill the vacuum created by revolutionary processes in the French Caribbean.[13] The dysfunction in and transformations of the world coffee market between the 1790s and the 1800s became evident with the return to peace in 1815, when coffee prices rose to a new high.[14] In the following decades, coffee consumption in the urban centres of the North Atlantic would gain an additional and decisive impulse with the English Industrial Revolution and economic growth in the United States and Continental Europe.[15]

Britain's undisputed victory at the end of the Napoleonic Wars, with the complete dominance of the seas, placed it in a strong position to reshape the European role in overseas territories. The Dutch possessions are a case in point. In 1795, the new Batavian Republic became an ally of the Republic of France.

---

11   Robert K. Lacerte, "The Evolution of Land and Labor in the Haitian Revolution, 1791–1820," *The Americas* 34, no. 4 (1978): 453.

12   S. D. Smith, "Sugar's Poor Relation: Coffee Planting in the British West Indies, 1720–1833," *Slavery and Abolition* 19, no. 3 (1998): 68–89; Levi Marrero, *Cuba: Economia y Sociedad*, vol. 11 (Madrid: Editorial Playor, 1984), 108.

13   Mario Samper and Radin Fernando, "Historical Statistics of Coffee Production and Trade from 1700 to 1960," in *The Global Coffee Economy in Africa, Asia, and Latin América, 1500–1989*, ed. William Gervase Clarence-Smith and Steven Topik (Cambridge: Cambridge University Press, 2003). All coffee exports data cited in this chapter from now on will be taken from this source.

14   Nicolaas W. Posthumus, *Inquiry into the History of Prices in Holland* (Leiden: E. J. Brill, 1946), 75–79.

15   John M. Talbot, "The Coffee Commodity Chain in the World-Economy: Arrighi's Systemic Cycles and Braudel's Layers of Analysis," *Journal of World-System Research* 28, no. 1 (2011): 71–72.

As a consequence, the British conquered old VOC (*Vereenigde Oostindische Compagnie* – the Dutch East India Company) domains in Asia, such as the Cape Colony and Ceylon in 1796, and the island of Java in 1811. Demerara, Essequibo, Berbice and Surinam were, in turn, conquered in 1804 in the West Indies. At the Congress of Vienna, the Netherlands was seen by Britain as a key actor when it came to containing France's future revolutionary power; for this reason, the British representatives made sure to partially restore the overseas domains of the new United Kingdom of the Netherlands (Holland plus Belgium), returning Java and Surinam to it. Britain, however, retained Cape Colony and Ceylon, converting the second into a Crown Colony, and forcing the Dutch to ban the African slave trade in their colonial possessions. In Ceylon – the colonial space that interests us in this chapter – the years following the confirmation of British rule over its coast would be marked by the conquest of the Kingdom of Kandy in the interior of the island (1815–1818).[16]

Britain also played a major role in the redesign of the Portuguese Empire. In November 1807, after the Napoleonic invasion of the Iberian Peninsula, the Portuguese royal family fled to Brazil escorted by a British fleet. One of the first measures taken by the Portuguese Crown when settling in the New World was to open Brazilian ports to the so-called "Friendly Nations," which, at the time, meant Great Britain. In 1808, Brazilian slaveholders got free access to the world market, without the intermediation of Portugal's previous mercantilist policy. The 1810 Trade Treaty, which granted a series of benefits to British traders who operated in Brazilian ports, consolidated the new framework of close association between the Brazilian slave economy and the British mercantile power, crucial for its exports. On the issue of the transatlantic slave trade, however, Great Britain did not achieve the same success with the Portuguese Crown as it did with the Dutch. British manoeuvres taken at the Congress of Vienna to forbid the transatlantic slave trade to Brazil failed and, as an expression of the strength of slavery within the Portuguese Empire, Brazil was turned into a United Kingdom with Portugal and Algarve in 1816, with its headquarters located in Rio de Janeiro instead of Lisbon.[17]

---

16   John Darwin, *Unfinished Empire: The Global Expansion of Britain* (London: Penguin, 2012), 24–25, 72–73; Alicia Schrikker, *Dutch and British Colonial Intervention in Sri Lanka, 1780–1815: Expansion and Reform* (Leiden: Brill, 2007), 129–58; Patrick Peebles, *The History of Sri Lanka* (Westport, CT: Greenwood Press, 2006), 41–54; M. C. Ricklefs, *A History of Modern Indonesia since c. 1200* (London: Palgrave, 2001), 147–54; Pepjin Brandon, "'Shrewd Sirens of Humanity': The Changing Shape of Proslavery Arguments in the Netherlands (1789–1814)," *Almanack* 14 (September – December 2016), 3–26.

17   Rafael Marquese, Tâmis Parron and Márcia Berbel, *Slavery and Politics: Brazil and Cuba, 1790–1850* (Albuquerque: University of New Mexico Press, 2016), 85–93; Fernanda Bretones

Although spatially separated and very distinct from each other, these events in Ceylon and Brazil were part of a unified process of transformation of the European imperial structures during the Age of Revolutions. At the end of the Napoleonic Wars, Britain had consolidated itself as the hegemonic power of the capitalist world economy. And, for reasons that are beyond the scope of the present chapter, Britain started presenting an anti-slavery ideology – as a constitutive part of its imperial strategy – that implied an endless fight against the transatlantic slave trade at the international level and the abolition of slavery in its own West Indian possessions, followed by a looser policy of gradual abolition in its East Indian possessions.[18]

The making of the Brazilian slave-based coffee economy took advantage of the circumstances created by these revolutionary and inter-imperial conflicts at the turn of the nineteenth century. The establishment of the Portuguese royal family in the city of Rio de Janeiro played a key role in this. The Paraíba do Sul River Basin (the so-called Paraíba Valley), whose course runs from east to west paralleling to the Atlantic coast, was located in an arc within a maximum of two hundred kilometres distance from Rio de Janeiro's port. Situated between the foothills of the *Serra do Mar* and the *Serra da Mantiqueira*, the lands of Vale do Paraíba were, at the beginning of the nineteenth century, entirely covered by the tropical Atlantic Forest and with ideal altitude and climatic conditions for growing coffee.[19] At the time, Rio de Janeiro was one of the most thriving Atlantic commercial ports, with a commercial infrastructure that had been established in previous centuries for sugar and gold exports, among other products. Most importantly, with its transformation into the capital of the Portuguese Empire, Rio de Janeiro became the largest port of disembarkation for enslaved Africans in the Americas. The ample supply of local capital, merchant facilities and cheap slave labour could easily be mobilised to take advantage of the favourable post-1815 climate for coffee production, with the rapid establishment of plantations in the virgin soils of the Paraíba Valley. The growth of coffee exports from Rio de Janeiro was overwhelming. In the first half of the 1810s, the export of coffee amounted to 1,500 tons per year; in

---

Lanes, Guilherme de Paula Costa Santos, and Alain El Youssef, "The Congress of Vienna and the Making of the Second Slavery," *Journal of Global Slavery* 4, no. 2 (2019): 162–95.

18   Cf. Richard Huzzey, *Freedom Burning: Anti-Slavery and Empire in Victorian Britain* (Ithaca: Cornell University Press, 2012); Dale Tomich, "Civilizing America's Shore: British World-Economic Hegemony and the Abolition of the International Slave Trade (1814–1867)," in *The Politics of the Second Slavery*, ed. Dale Tomich (Albany: State University of New York Press, 2020), 1–24.

19   Cf. Warren Dean, *With Broadax and Firebrand: The Destruction of the Brazilian Atlantic Forest* (Berkeley: University of California Press, 1995).

1821, on the eve of Brazilian independence, these exports were already equivalent to those of Cuba: thirteen thousand tons per year.[20]

In the estimates of one economist, "between 1821 and 1850 the trend rate of growth of coffee exports was 8.47 per cent per annum."[21] In the early 1830s, the Empire of Brazil alone would reach the total volume of world coffee exports of 1790, when the Saint-Domingue Revolution started. In the last five years of the transatlantic slave trade (1845–1850), coffee exports from Brazil amounted to c. 125,000 tons per year, which made the country responsible for half of the world's supply. The Brazilian coffee economy, moreover, was now closely linked to a new consumer market, in addition to the traditional urban markets of continental Europe that continued to grow. Since the 1790s, as a neutral power in the imperial conflicts of the period, the United States had established itself as an important player in the re-exports of coffee from the Caribbean, which simultaneously allowed the creation of a solid base of coffee consumers in the country itself. However, the decisive event for the popularisation of coffee in the US was the abolition of import tariffs for the product in 1833. In the middle of the nineteenth century, driven by population growth and the so-called "Market Revolution," the US was responsible, by itself, for about a quarter of the world's coffee imports, 90 per cent of which came from a single supplier, Brazil.[22]

Perhaps the most important piece of data to understand what happened to the world coffee market in the first half of the nineteenth century is the downward trend in international prices between 1823 and 1848. This downward trend was not uniform: concerning the New York prices, for instance, there was a very strong fall between 1821 and 1830; a short recovery between 1832 and 1836; a soft fall between 1837 and 1840; and another sharp fall between 1841 and 1847.[23] These movements suggest how slave production in the Paraíba Valley was transforming the world coffee market by allowing the popularisation of

---

20 Rafael Marquese and Dale Tomich, "Slavery in the Paraíba Valley and the Formation of the World Coffee Market in the Nineteenth Century," in *Atlantic Transformations: Empire, Politics, and Slavery during the Nineteenth Century,* ed. Dale Tomich (Albany: State University of New York Press, 2020), 193–223.

21 Pedro Carvalho de Mello, "The Economics of Labor in Brazilian Coffee Plantations, 1850–1888" (PhD diss., University of Chicago, 1977), 29.

22 Tâmis Parron, "A política da escravidão na era da liberdade: Estados Unidos, Brasil e Cuba, 1787–1846" (PhD diss., Universidade de São Paulo, 2015), 244–66; Christopher David Absell, *The Bittersweet Century: Slavery, Tariffs and Brazilian Export Growth during the Nineteenth Century* (PhD diss., Universidad Carlos III de Madrid, 2019), 137–73.

23 Mauro Rodrigues da Cunha, "Apêndice estatístico," in *150 anos de café,* ed. Edmar Bacha and Robert Greenhill (Rio de Janeiro: Marcellino Martins & E. Johnston, 1992), 333.

coffee consumption through oversupply. The spread of coffee consumption among urban and rural workers in the United States and the growing urban proletariat of continental Europe reflected a broader pattern, characteristic of the third global coffee complex. The domestic consumption of coffee as part of the "invention of the breakfast," when the luxury of the eighteenth-century poor became the basic necessity of the nineteenth-century proletarian, transformed the product into a "wage-food," that is, an agricultural good, produced on industrial scale, that became part of the reproduction of the wage labour force.[24]

The growth of coffee production in Brazil between the 1820s and 1840s took place against British anti-slavery pressure. After 1822, Great Britain established two conditions for recognising the newly independent country: first, that Brazil would not incorporate the Portuguese colony of Angola as a province of its new empire; second, that it would ban the transatlantic slave trade within three years. When ratifying the anti-slave trade treaty in 1827, Emperor D. Pedro I lost political support among Brazilian slaveholders, which greatly contributed to his fall in 1831. That same year, the Brazilian Parliament passed its own national law banning the transatlantic slave trade. As a result, the number of disembarked slaves significantly decreased between 1831 and 1834. However, due to the strong demand for labour in the new coffee plantations (a direct result of the US free tax measure of 1833), from 1835 onwards the illegal transatlantic slave trade recovered with an enormous strength. Despite all British naval pressure, between 1835 and 1850 almost 550,000 enslaved Africans were disembarked at the coastal ports that served the coffee production in the Paraíba Valley. This was only possible because the Paraíba Valley coffee planters were crucial actors for the institutional construction of the Brazilian Second Empire (1841–1889), which gave them all the necessary support to confront British diplomatic and naval pressure and to keep untouched their illegal slave property.[25]

For the first time in the history of the world coffee economy, coffee producers were commanding a national state to serve all of their interests. During this period, the only coffee zone that managed to compete with slavery in Brazil was the Dutch colony of Java, whose exports were mounting to sixty thousand tons

---

24   Harriet Friedmann and Philip McMichael, "Agriculture and the State System: The Rise and Decline of National Agricultures, 1870 to the Present," *Sociologia Ruralis* 29, no. 2 (1989), 101; Dale Tomich, *Through the Prism of Slavery: Labor, Capital and the World Economy* (Boulder, CO: Rowman & Littlefield, 2004), 56–71.

25   Parron, "A política"; Rafael Marquese and Ricardo Salles, "Slavery in Nineteenth-Century Brazil: History and Historiography," in *Slavery and Historical Capitalism During the Nineteenth Century*, ed. Dale Tomich (Boulder, CO: Lexington Books, 2017), 127–69.

per year in the late 1840s. However, Dutch colonial authorities had to recreate and amplify the voc's past modalities of forced crops, the so-called Cultivation System (see Elise van Nederveen Meerkerk's chapter in this volume), in order to compete with Brazil. Cuba was well supplied by the transatlantic slave trade and had ample reserves of virgin land, but lost ground to Brazil in the global coffee markets and – as Tytler pointed out in his 1852 article – was compelled to abandon coffee production in favour of sugar. The abolition of slavery in the British Empire led to the collapse of coffee production in Jamaica. It was in this context that Ceylon started to build its coffee plantation economy at the turn of the 1840s.

Ceylon was separated from the British East India Company (EIC) posses-sions early in the nineteenth century and, therefore, lost access to its vast finan-cial resources. Established as a Crown Colony, Ceylon was of crucial strategic importance for the British Empire in Asia, but remained in deficit in its first decades. The economy of cinnamon, which had been previously explored by the Portuguese and the Dutch, was no longer profitable. In 1832–1833, as slavery was being abolished in the West Indies, London initiated a series of adminis-trative and judicial reforms to make Ceylon a self-financing colony and, if pos-sible, a lucrative one. The reformist impulse deepened in the following years, always obeying the objective of converting the island into a prosperous planta-tion colony along the lines of the West Indies and Mauritius, but without slav-ery.[26] From the beginning, coffee was conceived as a possible solution to the impasses of Ceylon's colonial economy. The native Sinhalese population had long cultivated the shrub on a small, peasant scale for commercial purposes, and the post-1815 commercial stimuli led this peasant production to quadruple in the next twenty years. However, since it was not controlled by British capital and was relatively inelastic (in 1838, its amount was still only 1,860 tons), the "peasant way" for coffee production in Ceylon was not a viable option in the eyes of the colonial power.[27]

The first issue to be tackled was the equalisation of the imperial tariffs that regulated the British market. Until 1835, coffee shipped from the East Indies paid 50 per cent more duty (9d. per pound weight[28]) than the coffee coming from the West Indies (6d.). From 1836, as part of the extensive imperial reforms introduced in the midst of the abolition of African slavery in the Caribbean,

---

26   Asoka Bandarage, *Colonialism in Sri Lanka: The Political Economy of the Kandyan Highlands, 1833–1886* (Berlin: Mouton/De Gruyter, 1983), 52–64.

27   Van den Driesen, "Coffee Cultivation," 35–41.

28   Before the decimal system, the pound sterling was divided into 20 shillings (s.), and each shilling into 12 pence (d.).

these tariffs were equalised at 6d. Foreign coffee was now to be surcharged at a rate that was two-and-a-half times higher (i.e., 1s.3d.) than the British coffee imported from the West Indies or East Indies/Ceylon.[29] The second issue to be tackled was land. The highlands of the ancient Kingdom of Kandy, which until then had been exploited secondarily by the Sri Lankan peasant communities as a complement to the rice paddy cultivation in its lower zones, saw a first wave of privatisation promoted by British colonialism. Ceylon became one of the colonial laboratories for Wakefield's thesis on the closure of the frontier – by suspending free land concessions – as a condition for the creation of commercial agriculture in open resource zones. Between 1838 and 1843, as an immediate response to the intra-imperial tariff equalisation, the abolition of slavery in the West Indies, and the rise in coffee prices within the protected metropolitan market, nearly 250,000 acres of land were sold by the British government to set up coffee plantations or for financial speculation by British investors.[30]

Most of these investments, however, were made without specific technical expertise on how to produce plantation coffee. The geo-ecological and climatic conditions of the Central Province highlands, although adequate for growing coffee, were different from those of the Caribbean, especially regarding the rainfall regime. Even experienced coffee growers, such as Tytler, were still learning how to deal with these local conditions at the turn of the 1840s, at the same time that forests were being cleared for large-scale plantations. It was also necessary to create specific labour arrangements in view of the refusal of the native Sinhalese peasantry to engage in wage labour on the new plantations.[31] The solution was finally found in the lower Tamil castes of Southern

---

29   *Report from the Select Committee on Sugar and Coffee Planting*, vol. 8 (London: Commons, 1848), xxvii – xxxi; Seymour Drescher, *The Mighty Experiment: Free Labor versus Slavery in British Emancipation* (Oxford: Oxford University Press, 2002), 145.

30   James L.A. Webb, Jr., *Tropical Pioneers: Human Agency and Ecological Change in the Highlands of Sri Lanka, 1800–1900* (Athens, OH: Ohio University Press, 2002), 76–77; Van den Driesen, "Coffee Cultivation," 43; K. M. de Silva, "The Third Earl Grey and the Maintenance of an Imperial Policy on the Sale of Crown Lands in Ceylon, c. 1832–1852: Some Influences of Edward Gibbon Wakefield's Doctrines in a Tropical Colony," *The Journal of Asian Studies* 27, no. 1 (1967): 5; *Report from the Select Committee*, vol. 6, 41–42.

31   M. W. Roberts, "Indian Estate Labor in Ceylon During the Coffee Period (1830–1880)," *Indian Economic & Social History Review* 3, no. 1 (1966): 1–52; I. H. van den Driesen, *Indian Plantation Labor in Sri Lanka: Aspects of the History of Immigration in the 19th Century* (Nedlands: University of Western Australia, 1982), 4; Rachel Kurian, "Labor, Race, and Gender on the Coffee Plantations in Ceylon (Sri Lanka), 1834–1880," in *The Global Coffee Economy in Africa, Asia, and Latin América, 1500–1989*, ed. William Gervase Clarence-Smith and Steven Topik (Cambridge: Cambridge University Press, 2003), 176–77.

India, who had long sought temporary jobs in the coastal areas of Ceylon. Attracted by the wages offered in the Central Province highlands during the first wave of coffee investments (which were comparatively low compared to other plantation zones in the British Empire, but much higher than present-day payments in India), these coolie workers, organised in gangs coming from the same villages, appointed a foreman from their own ranks – the *kangany*, a Tamil word that refers to an agricultural supervisor – to negotiate the specific labour arrangements for harvesting the coffee with the British planters or their superintendents, all of them (the coolies and their *kangany*) going back to South India at the end of the picking season.[32]

This vast mobilisation of land, labour and capital took place in less than a decade (1837–1845). It should be remembered, however, that newly planted coffee trees take from three to five years to enter full production. Precisely when the viability of these investments was to be tested, customs duties were changed in Britain. In 1842, British taxes for its colonial coffee were reduced from 6d. to 4d. per pound weight, but those of foreign coffee were reduced from 1s.3d. to 8d. – that is, practically a cut by half. The worst was yet to come: in 1844, tariffs on foreign coffee dropped to 6d., but the tariff for colonial coffee was kept at 4d.[33] This progressive tariff equalisation was a direct development of the broader free trade policy that Britain was adopting in those years. Mainly focused on the sugar and wheat markets, this policy also ended up affecting coffee, a good with a relatively small market in the metropole due to the dominance of tea. What was happening with coffee had little impact on the metropolitan economy, but its impact on Ceylon was enormous. As the British market was no longer protected, imperial and international prices tended to converge[34] right when the Brazilian oversupply was imposing a huge drop in world coffee prices (1841–1847).

Only a decade old, the coffee plantation economy in Ceylon was already at a crossroads. The problem was not only the fall in world prices, but also how to recruit labourers. In 1847 and 1848, two official inquiries – one local, the other imperial – carefully discussed the impasses of Ceylon's coffee culture.

---

32   One of the most vivid descriptions of this first labour engagement – albeit profoundly ideological – can be found in the planter's memoirs of P. D. Millie, *Thirty Years Ago, or the Reminiscences of the Early Days of Coffee Planting in Ceylon* (Colombo: A. M. & J. Ferguson, 1878), Chapter 3.

33   *Report from the Select Committee*, vol. 8, xxvii.

34   Tâmis Parron, "The British Empire and the Suppression of the Slave Trade to Brazil: A Global History Analysis," *Journal of World History* 29, no. 1 (2018): 15.

The first one looked at the conditions of the annual migration and the work performed by the Tamil coolies in the highlands of Ceylon. The vast inquiry carried out in the early months of 1847 by James Emerson Tennent, Ceylon's governor, sought to understand why the flow of coolies had suddenly and substantially decreased in 1846. Despite the almost unanimous denial of ill treatment of the coolies by planters and their superintendents, what emerged from the testimonies was an abundant documentation of practices such as whipping, arbitrary arrests within the plantations, and the suspension of payments – or even non-payment – to workers. Coolies staying in India were voting with their feet by refusing to come back to Ceylon for the next harvest. In a few testimonies, the metric for judging what was happening to the coolies in the Ceylon coffee plantations was given by the recently abolished black slavery in the West Indies.[35] The inquiry, however, remained unfinished, most likely because the coffee crisis in those years decreased the demand for labour, thus minimising the supply restriction. In the end, coffee planters (who, at one point, asked for firmer action from the colonial government to guarantee the continuous flow of coolies in the future) and authorities (who replied that Ceylon did not have a plantation slavery past like the West Indies and Mauritius did, and therefore, London owed them nothing) seemed to agree that the regulation of the annual Tamil migration as well as discipline within the plantations should be exclusively left to market forces. Nor did metropolitan abolitionists worry about what was going on in Ceylon: since it was not indentured labour, the work of coolies on the coffee plantations never came to their attention.[36]

The anti-slavery movement was, in turn, crucial for the debates surrounding the imperial inquiry. The free trade policy adopted by London in the 1840s lowered sugar and coffee prices in the British market, as it was opened to the slave product of Cuba and Brazil. Amid the so-called "Mighty Experiment" of British emancipation, the former slave colonies of the Empire were now in the midst of a deep economic crisis. In the early months of 1848, a Select Committee of the British Parliament thoroughly investigated the problem. The free trade advocates – anti-slavery or not – saw the equalisation of tariffs as the final test

---

35   Kandy's police officer, 18 January 1847: "I have no hesitation in saying and I am well convinced that this class of the population is in a much worse condition in the Central Province than the Negro Slave was described to be in the West Indies in former days as to their wants and treatment from their employers, the mode of enforcing discipline and labour and the remuneration received," UKNA, CO 54/235, fo.52. Gampola's Justice of the Peace, 8 February 1847: "their position on the Estates is nearly intolerable I may say as Egyptians Bondage or West Indian slavery," UKNA, CO 54/235, fo.102.

36   Huzzey, *Freedom Burning*, 178–79.

for the success of the abolition experiment: under the rules of free trade, would free labour be able to prove its superiority over slave labour, as the abolitionists thought it would? Or would abolition finally prove that it had been a misconceived experiment from its very beginnings? The planter and merchant interests in the former slave colonies dominated the depositions to the Committee. Throughout the survey, sugar attracted much more attention than coffee. Still, all testimonies related to coffee had agreed that Brazilian slavery was at the heart of the post-abolition coffee crisis in Jamaica and Demerara, threatening to do the same to the recently built coffee plantation economy in Ceylon.[37] The Committee's final proposal, which was in favour of returning to previous protectionist tariffs, was not taken up by the Russell Cabinet. Nonetheless, the material presented to Parliament between February and May 1848 had a direct impact on British foreign policy. The campaign against the transatlantic slave trade that the Foreign Secretary Lord Palmerston promoted in the following years was an explicit official response to the British sugar and coffee colonial lobby. In 1849–1850, the British Navy, after decades of fighting the slave trade in African waters or on the high seas, launched a frontal attack against Brazil by capturing or sinking at least ten slave ships in Brazilian territorial waters, and even threatening to directly bombard its ports. In 1850, faced with the risk of going to war with the greatest naval power in the world, the Empire of Brazil finally ended the secular – and infamous – transatlantic slave trade.[38]

The constant fall in world prices between 1823 and 1848, a direct result of brazilian supply, helped popularise coffee consumption in the North Atlantic. After 1850, however, Brazilian coffee planters no longer counted on the unlimited supply of enslaved Africans. The Brazilian Empire's commitment to ending the transatlantic slave trade, which Tytler proposed to examine in 1852, had become real and effective as early as 1851, largely because of a campaign in the British metropole that was supported by Ceylon's coffee interests. Also, in 1851, British customs tariffs for colonial and foreign coffee were finally equalised (3d. per pound weight),[39] helping to increase the consumption of the beverage in a market that had been dominated by tea since the 1730s. Between the 1850s and 1870s, as part of a cyclical upswing of the capitalist world economy, international coffee prices would rise sharply, which boosted the definitive take-off of coffee production in Ceylon. In 1850, the British colony had exported about 17,000 tons of coffee. Two decades later, that number rose to

---

37   *Report from the Select Committee*, vol. 6, 4173; vol. 7, 139–49; vol. 8, xxvii–xxxi; Drescher, *The Mighty Experiment*, 161–81.
38   Tâmis Parron, "The British Empire."
39   *The Planting Directory for India and Ceylon* (Colombo: A. M. & J. Ferguson, 1878), 46.

50,000 tons (45,000 tons of plantation coffee), closely approaching Java with its 70,000 tons per year. By then, the pace of coffee growth in Brazil had slowed significantly compared to what it had been between 1821 and 1850, but, even so, Brazil exported 208,800 tons to the world market in 1870.

2   Slavery and the *Kangany* System, 1850–1870

The patterns of labour that were created and the landscape management practices that were developed in the Paraíba Valley in the 1830s, and that quickly led Brazilian coffee to dominate the world supply, remained unchanged in the second half of the nineteenth century, despite the end of the transatlantic slave trade. In this section, I will briefly describe and contrast these patterns with the patterns of the Ceylon coffee economy.[40]

Just like in all areas of tropical agriculture, the techniques of swidden agriculture for clearing the ground for coffee planting in the Paraíba Valley and in Central Ceylon were almost the same. In the undulating hilly topography of the Paraíba Valley (*Mar de Morros de Meia-Laranja*; literally, "sea of half-orange hills"), the planting of the seedlings was done in vertically aligned, well-spaced rows, from the base to the top of the hills. The unit of area measurement used in the Paraíba Valley was the *alqueire* (11.95 acres); usually, roughly

---

40   My analysis is based on a critical reading of the agronomic literature of the period. See, for Brazil, Pe. João Joaquim Ferreira de Aguiar, *Pequena memória sobre a plantação, cultura e colheita do café* (Rio de Janeiro: Imprensa Americana de I. P. da Costa, 1836); Francisco Peixoto de Lacerda Werneck, *Memória sobre a fundação de uma fazenda na província do Rio de Janeiro*, ed. Eduardo Silva (Rio de Janeiro: Fundação Casa de Rui Barbosa/Senado Federal, [1847] 1985); "Instruções geraes para a administração das fazendas (23 de fevereiro de 1870)," in *Negro de corpo e alma: Mostra do Redescobrimento; Brasil 500 anos*, ed. Emanoel Araújo and Nelson Aguilar (São Paulo: Fundação Bienal de São Paulo, 2000); C. F. van Delden Laërne, *Brazil and Java: Report on Coffee-Culture in America, Asia, and Africa* (London and The Hague: Martinus Nijhoff, 1885). For Ceylon, see Edmund C. P. Hull, *Coffee: Its Physiology, History and Cultivation* (Madras: Gantz Brothers, 1865); William Sabonadière, *The Coffee Planter of Ceylon,* 2nd ed (London: E. & F. N. Spon, 1870); Alex Brown, *The Coffee Planter's Manual,* 2nd ed (Colombo: Ceylon Observer Press, 1880). Two memorialists also offer very valuable information: Eloy de Andrade, *O Vale do Paraíba* (Rio de Janeiro: Real Gráfica, 1989); Millie, *Thirty Years Ago*. For Paraíba Valley, I return to the analysis I have presented before: see Rafael de Bivar Marquese, *Administração & escravidão: Ideias sobre a gestão da agricultura escravista Brasileira* (São Paulo: Hucitec, 1999), 157–89, and Rafael de Bivar Marquese, "African Diaspora, Slavery, and the Paraíba Valley Plantation Landscape: Nineteenth-Century Brazil," *Review* (*Fernand Braudel Center*) 39, no. 2 (Spring 2008), 195–216. For the more specific information in this section, I will give the corresponding references.

four thousand coffee trees were planted per *alqueire*. Following the rules of the former slave coffee economy in the Caribbean, the trunks were cut to facilitate harvesting (known as "topping") by slaves, but in Brazil the side branches of the coffee trees were rarely pruned. In the first three years after the trees had been planted, maize, beans and manioc were grown between the coffee rows, both to shade them and to facilitate weeding. Manure was never used in the Paraíba Valley. The initial productivity of coffee trees planted in frontier areas was very high (from ninety to one hundred *arrobas*[41] per one thousand trees), but a few years later it was common for it to drop by one-third or even half. The productivity in the oldest coffee zones was in general around thirty *arrobas* per one thousand trees.

The size of plantations in the Paraíba Valley varied widely in terms of their spatial dimensions as well as in terms of their human scale, but available data indicates that the bulk of coffee production came from properties with over one hundred slaves and with two to three hundred *alqueires*. Comparatively, these properties were much larger than the slave-based coffee plantations in Saint-Domingue, Jamaica and Cuba. At the beginning of the exploitation of the Paraíba Valley plantations (on both small and large units), there was always much more land available for planting than was effectively used for cultivating coffee. This land structure was directly related to the landscape management strategy used there. Vertically aligned, well-spaced planting always implied rapid erosion: in about twenty years, not only would the coffee trees become unproductive, but the original soil cover would be completely lost. In response, planters periodically proceeded with new plantings on their properties; the internal landscape of the plantations thus came to resemble a patchwork quilt, with a somewhat chaotic combination of scattered coffee plantations of different ages and varying productivity, depleted land converted into pasture, and belts of diminishing forest reserves for the maintenance of the future productivity of the plantation. All of this resembled mining more than agriculture.[42]

The harvest took place in the driest and coldest months of the year, between May and October. Given the vastness of the plantations and the large number of coffee trees allocated to each worker, the planters' strategy was to extend the harvest for as long as possible, allowing the slaves to practice the so-called *derriça* – the quick harvesting of all the green, the ripe and the dry cherries at once (with leaves included), from the stem to the tip of the branch. Here, we can understand how landscape management was related to labour management

---

41   In Brazil, an *arroba* equals 14.7 kilograms.
42   Marquese, "Espacio y poder," 239–51.

through a specific spatial economy. As is always the case with slavery, the plantation labour force in the Paraíba Valley was quantitatively rigid for the whole year. Given the needs for ancillary services and the considerable number of children and elderly people on the plantations, not all slaves worked in the coffee fields. In general, field slaves comprised 50 to 60 per cent of the overall enslaved population in a given plantation. Nor did the slave owner have any means to dismiss his workers during the dead season of the agricultural cycle. The solution was to operate according to an equation which combined the production of foodstuffs during the coffee off-season (corn, beans and manioc interspersed in new coffee rows or in lower quality land, with the cultivation of rice in the lowlands in the small valleys), two to three annual weedings of the coffee fields, and overwork at the time of gathering coffee. Hence, the logic of extending the coffee harvest period with the use of the *derriça* resulted in an increasing allocation of coffee trees per slave. Compared to the Caribbean, these figures were impressive: while between one thousand to one thousand and five hundred coffee trees were usually attributed to each field slave in Saint-Domingue, Jamaica, and Cuba, this proportion more than doubled between 1830 and 1870 in the Paraíba Valley. In the second half of the century, it was not uncommon to find plantations that attributed four to five thousand coffee trees to a field slave, which also meant that these slaves would have to weed much more extensive areas, considering the large spacing between the trees.[43]

The large spacing of coffee rows, which were vertically aligned on the hills, was informed by the wish to increase the capacity to watch and control slaves. Weeding was done in gangs under the command of a foreman; the fastest slaves were placed at the last rows in order to dictate the pace of the group; if a worker was slower than the others, he or she could easily be seen by the foreman at the bottom of the hill and, consequently, punished. During the harvest, there was a minimum individual daily harvest quota for each slave based on their individual capacities and the estimated total volume of the crop. If the slave did not meet the quota, he would be whipped; if he exceeded it, he would receive small monetary incentives. As a result of these schemes, field slaves had to individually harvest from three *alqueires* of coffee (here, an *alqueire* counted as a unit of volume, equal to sixty litres) per day in bad years to up to nine *alqueires* in good years. (Coffee trees planted without shade have strong annual variations in crops). It should be stressed again that the green, the ripe and the dry cherries would all be harvested at the same time. When taken to the plantation headquarters, the cherries were placed in the vast Brazilian

---

43   Marquese, "African Diaspora."

drying platforms to dry the pulp and the parchment for up to two months, that is, until they were dry enough to be processed at the rough, but highly effective, pestle mills. The end result was low-quality, but very cheap coffee that was produced through a spatial economy focused on maximising the productivity of slave labour.

All contemporary reports – including those by A. Scott Blacklaw and G.A. Crüwell – noted the harsh daily disciplinary codes that made this brutal workload feasible. Given the absence of reliable agricultural statistics for nineteenth-century Brazil and the inner variations of the coffee agronomy, it is difficult to accurately establish the average coffee productivity per slave in the Paraíba Valley. Estimates that take the total slave population of the coffee districts – and not only the field workers – as a basis indicate an annual productivity of 1,000 to 1,200 kilograms of processed coffee per slave.[44] A detailed cliometric study focused on the specific productivity of field slaves in 1873, however, gives 2,280 kilograms of coffee per worker.[45]

Ceylon's coffee economy exhibited a clear continuity with the eighteenth-century Caribbean agronomy, but the consolidation of local agronomic techniques did not take place until the 1850s. The topography of the highlands of the ancient Kingdom of Kandy – the most suitable for coffee – was even more irregular than the Paraíba Valley and its climate was subject to the monsoon regime, which is much more humid. Here, the coffee trees were also vertically planted, but with trenches and drains in contour lines to mitigate the effects of erosion. The most common planting density used in Ceylon was c. 1,200 coffee trees per acre; in the Paraíba Valley it was c. 335. In addition to topping, the trees in Ceylon were constantly pruned because of the high planting density. In the early years of the shrubs' growth, not only was nothing planted between the rows, but weeds were also taken out by hand. Subsequently, weeding was supposed to be carried out monthly. Another major difference in relation to the Paraíba Valley was manuring, which, in Ceylon, was often practised right from the early days of a new coffee plantation. Incidentally, the topic of manure may have been the most discussed subject of the agronomic publications in the British colony; by contrast, almost nothing was written about it in Brazilian coffee manuals. In spite of all these intensive agricultural treatments, coffee

---

44 "Quadro estatístico de alguns estabelecimentos rurais da Província de São Paulo," in *Documentos com que o Ilustríssimo e Excelentíssimo Senhor Dr. José Antonio Saraiva, presidente da Província de São Paulo, instruiu o Relatório na abertura da Assembleia Legislativa Provincial no dia 15 de fevereiro de 1855* (São Paulo: Typographia Antunes, 1855); Van Delden Laërne, *Brazil and Java,* 119–24.

45 Mello, "Economics," 166.

plantations in Ceylon had a remarkably low initial productivity compared to the Paraíba Valley. In Ceylon, productivity was calculated per acre, not per coffee tree. Converting the numbers, productivity in Ceylon was always between fifteen to twenty *arrobas* per one thousand trees, regardless of whether the plantations were on virgin soil or on terrain that had already been exploited.[46]

The relatively small spatial scale of its plantations was one of the reasons that made intensive cultivation in Ceylon possible. As is almost always the case in coffee economies, there was a significant number of small coffee estates (i.e., under fifty acres) on the highlands of the Central Province, but the standard units were between one and two hundred acres (or 8.5 to 17 Brazilian *alqueires* as a unit of area). The allocation of the estate surface to coffee was overwhelming; once an estate got into full production, there were very few areas for grazing or forest reserves, and almost none for the production of foodstuffs. The basis for calculating the demand for labour was just under two coolies per acre, leaving six to eight hundred coffee trees per worker.

Intensive cultivation was also made possible by a vast supply of labour. After the 1847/1848 crisis was over, Southern Indian coolies returned to the Ceylon plantations in large numbers, this time through an arrangement directly induced by the planters or the superintendents called the "Coast Advance System," but better known as the *kangany* system (a label that appears in the British official documentation).[47] This system differed from what had been practised before (1837 to 1847). From the 1850s on, the *kangany* would receive a cash advance from the coffee entrepreneur in Ceylon, which he would use to recruit the Tamil coolies in South India. With prior knowledge of the

---

46   Ceylon's coffee economy collapsed in the 1870s, so it is not possible to estimate the long-term viability of its soils for coffee cultivation. However, these very same lands are still cultivated with tea in what is now Sri Lanka. The agricultural landscape of the Paraiba Valley was completely devastated at the turn of the twentieth century, with the massive conversion of its lands, after the coffee crisis, to extensive livestock.

47   The historiography on the *kangany* system during the apogee of coffee cultivation in Ceylon is vast. See, for instance, Bandarage, *Colonialism in Sri Lanka;* Roberts, "Indian Estate Labor"; Kurian, "Labor, Gender, and Race"; Roland Wenzlhuemer, "Indian Labour Immigration and British Labour Policy in Nineteenth-Century Ceylon," *Modern Asian Studies* 41, no. 3 (May 2007), 575–602; James S. Duncan, *In the Shadows of the Tropics: Climate, Race and Biopower in Nineteenth-Century Ceylon* (Aldershot: Ashgate, 2007), 67–99; Kumari Jayawardena and Rachel Kurian, *Class, Patriarchy and Ethnicity on Sri Lanka Plantations: Two Centuries of Power and Protest* (New Delhi: Orient BlackSwan, 2015), 165; Ritesh Kumar Jaiswal, "Mediated (Im)Mobility: Indian Labour Migration to Ceylon under the Kangany System (c. 1850–1940)," in *The Palgrave Handbook of Bondage and Human Rights in Africa and Asia,* ed. Gwyn Campbell and Alessandro Stanziani (New York: Palgrave MacMillan, 2019), 157–88.

communities and the local power hierarchies in India (being a member of those same communities or not), the *kangany* would search for lower caste coolies already enmeshed in indebtedness relations with native landlords. The higher the local demographic pressure and the more acute the periodic cycle of hunger was, the easier it would be to recruit the coolies. Attracted by money advances offered by the *kanganies*, the coolies would go to Ceylon as a gang (consisting of twenty to fifty coolies, overwhelmingly men of the same castes), temporarily leaving their families behind. The long journey from the peasant community in India to the plantation where they would work in Ceylon would take 15 to 30 days of walking (interspersed with a short boat crossing of no more than a day). Throughout the journey, the coolie would increase his debt to the *kangany* in exchange for food (exclusively rice). For every worker, the *kangany* would earn a commission upon arrival at the plantation. Recruitment in India and migration to Ceylon followed a clear seasonal pattern. The coffee harvest took place in the upper lands of the Central Province (where the bulk of Ceylon's coffee production was concentrated) from October to mid-January, and in its lower lands from August to December. The gangs arrived at the coffee plantations between June and September, returning to India between January and April. There was, therefore, a certain complementarity between the agricultural cycles of rice in India and coffee in Ceylon, which allowed the surplus of Tamil workers to move seasonally to harvest coffee without compromising the Indian economic and power structures to which they were subjected and to which most of them would return.

A plantation would mobilise different gangs, seldom from the same caste. The debt contracted by the gangs of coolies directly with their *kangany* – and not with the plantation – guaranteed immediate discipline in the labour process: the work was supervised by this *kangany*, with all the *kanganies* of the different gangs under the general supervision of a European superintendent. During the harvest, each coolie was responsible for one row of coffee plants, with a fixed task of picking three bushels of ripe fruit (= 36.36 litres, which equals c. 1.8 *alqueires* [unit of volume] of coffee in Brazil). The payment of 8d. per day only took place if the labourer picked the specified amount. If a coolie picked more, he would receive a little more money in proportion to the extra amount collected. As part of the coolies' wages, planters or superintendents provided rice rations. Wages were paid at the end of each month of work or only at the end of the harvest (the season generally lasted three months), discounting the advance given to the *kangany* for recruitment in India and transportation to Ceylon and the amount of rice rations given at the plantation. The official correspondence sent to the Colonial Office in London and the agronomic publications of the period were, in general, silent about the physical coercion of the coolies, but indirect evidence in that same documentation indicates that the whip was used with some frequency.[48] The disciplinary measure that was considered the most effective, however, was the suspension of payments, which further tied the coolie to the cycle of indebtedness that kept the entire system moving. This same logic facilitated the retention of at least one-third of the total number of annual migrants for the off-season, when they were necessary for weeding, pruning, manuring, or even for setting up new plantations. In the case of weeding, it became common to hire so-called weeding gangs, that is, coolies who would remain in Ceylon after the end of the harvests under the control of their *kanganies*, who, in turn, would be contracted by the plantations for maintenance services during the off-season. These services were paid directly to the *kangany* according to the area to be weeded.

The high humidity in the Ceylon coffee zone and the seasonal variation in the labour supply called for innovations in processing. In the Central Province plantations, the fruits were just pulped and, after only two or three days of drying, immediately sent on parchment to the port city of Colombo. In the 1830s, Ceylon's colonial administration had started to construct excellent roadways connecting the plantations to the coast. In the warehouses of Colombo's exporting houses, parchment coffee was dried in the sun and, finally, peeled in large steam-powered circular mills. This final stage was independent of the coffee crop's seasonality. In the final years of the coffee economy, about twenty thousand workers who lived on the island permanently (mostly women and children) were engaged in this job.[49]

Faced with the uncertainties inherent to the seasonal migration of coolies mobilised by the *kangany* system, Ceylon planters and superintendents always opted to recruit an oversupply of workers for the harvest. Such a strategy, in order to function, depended on the push factors of Southern India, which, in turn, resulted directly from the transformations produced by British colonialism there. The dependence of the lower castes on, and their vulnerability in relation to, the local landlords was reinforced throughout the nineteenth century, which made them particularly susceptible to being captured by the advances offered by the *kanganies*.[50] In other words, the debt nexus was the mainspring of the entire system. Indian misery allowed the coffee wages – which were very low and stable throughout this period – to be attractive enough to keep

---

48   See, for instance, the observations of Sabonadière, *The Coffee Planter of Ceylon*, 106–7.

49   *The Planting Directory*, 34.

50   Kurian, "Labor, Race, and Gender," 177–78. See also Benedicte Hjejle, "Slavery and Agricultural Bondage in South India in the Nineteenth Century," *Scandinavian Economic History Review* 15, no. 12 (1967): 71–126.

moving the sequence of *advance* (in India) – *debt* (on the way to Ceylon and during work at the coffee plantations) – *payment* (in Ceylon, so they could return to India).

What was the final result of this system in terms of labour productivity? The statistics produced by the British colonial apparatus and on the private initiative of the coffee planters themselves, which are much more reliable than those available for Brazil, suggest a slight increase in coffee production between the first and the second half of the 1860s. In this period, the annual coffee production per worker rose from 144.45 kilograms in 1861–1865 to 160.45 kilograms in 1866–1870.[51] For the sake of comparison: if we consider the total amount of slaves in the Brazilian coffee zones (and not just the actual number of field slaves in the coffee plantations), a Brazilian slave produced almost eight times more coffee than an Indian coolie. However, if this comparison takes into account only field slaves, the difference rises to almost fifteen times more.

The higher productivity of coffee trees in Brazil does not explain this sharp contrast. Its explanation lies in the distinctions between the two types of spatial economies and the fundamental differences between nineteenth-century slavery and coolie work under the *kangany* system. The logic of the spatial economy in the Paraíba Valley was based on the intensive exploitation of enslaved labourers through the extensive exploitation of natural resources; in Ceylon, the rationale was to combine intensive coffee cultivation with the extensive use of coolie labourers. This difference was not only due to the fact that their geographies and environments were distinct, but was also caused by the social relations of production that were specific to each space. Slavery was based on an interpersonal, individual relation of power between the master and the slave. The public and private determinants of this relationship, that is to say, the nature of the state and the society in question, and the nature of the social relations of force between masters and slaves established the limits for the exploitation of the slave in the labour process. at the height of the "second slavery" of the Empire of Brazil (c. 1830–1870), coffee planters in the Paraíba Valley controlled these public and private determinants with an iron fist, within a profoundly asymmetrical framework of social relations that made possible the individualisation of the slave labourer and, therefore, his greater exploitation.[52]

51   *The Planting Directory*, 22.

52   Orlando Patterson, *Slavery and Social Death: A Comparative Study* (Cambridge, MA: Harvard University Press, 1982), 172–73; Gavin Wright, *Slavery and American Economic Development* (Baton Rouge: Louisiana State University Press, 2006), 122; Rafael de Bivar Marquese, *Os tempos plurais da escravidão no Brasil: Ensaios de história e historiografia* (São Paulo: Intermeios, 2020), 207–41.

Wage labour on the Ceylon coffee plantations was undeniably coercive and, therefore, not exactly free labour, given the structuring role of indebtedness relationships for its entire system.[53] The nature of this coercion, however, was profoundly different from chattel slavery in the Americas. That is why wage labour in Ceylon could be ideologically constructed and represented as free labour by multiple actors (colonial administrators, planters, abolitionists) of the nineteenth-century British "Anti-Slavery Empire." However, for this reason, too, there were clear limits to increasing the exploitation of coolies. Each of the different gangs of coolies acted as a collectivity on the plantations, coming from the same Indian peasant communities and belonging to the same castes, and this collective character protected them to some degree. The relationships between British planters and superintendents with the gangs of coolie labourers were always established through a *kangany*, which freed the former from taking charge of the immediate control of the labour process and its corresponding supervision costs. Planters and superintendents were only interested in the quantitative and steady supply of workers, always at a low cost, and not the individual performance of each one of them. Even though the *kangany* kept each coolie in debt, he had neither the motive nor the means to individualise each labourer in the coffee labour process in order to make him or her work harder. The *kangany* received a fixed commission for each coolie that was mobilised; the coolie received a fixed daily payment for the minimum quota harvested. The monetary incentives for harvesting above the minimum quota were not so significant to stimulate coolies' overwork. After receiving their wages at the end of the coffee harvest, ending their debt relation with the *kangany*, and coming back to India with all that they could save, the coolies would return to their previous lives, moving back into all the previous ties of dependence and subordination. They would then be no longer subjected to the work of the plantation – until they were eventually forced to go back to it by the reproduction of poverty and the debt nexus within the local power hierarchies in India.

As in other times and places of the capitalist world economy, the proletarianisation of the Tamil coolie in Ceylon was thus incomplete. The slave in Brazilian coffee plantations, in turn, was indeed exploited as a proletarian

---

53   On debt and coercive labour, see Robert J. Steinfeld, *Coercion, Contract, and Free Labor in the Nineteenth Century* (Cambridge: Cambridge University Press, 2001), 20–21; Marcel Van der Linden, "Dissecting Coerced Labor," in *On Coerced Labor: Work and Compulsion after Chattel Slavery*, ed. Marcel van der Linden and Magaly Rodríguez García (Leiden: Brill, 2016), 291–322; Rolf Bauer, *The Peasant Production of Opium in Nineteenth-Century India* (Leiden: Brill, 2019), 7.

in the immediate labour process, to affirmatively answer the question posed by Sidney Mintz in a famous essay.[54] It was this apparent paradox – the slave labourer as a proletarian; the coolie wage labourer as a non-proletarian – that allowed Brazil to continue to command the world coffee market in the 1850s and 1860s, even without the previous and almost infinite supply of enslaved Africans.

3 Epilogue: The 1870s Crisis

The appearance of leaf rust disease (*Hemileia vastatrix*) in Ceylon coffee plantations in 1869 would completely change the prospects of its coffee economy in just a few years. After 1870, as the plague spread throughout the dense coffee plantations in the highlands of the Central Province, harvests began to show great oscillation, with a continuous fall in the trees' productivity (which was already low compared to Brazil). Still, in the first half of the 1870s, major investments were made with the goal of opening of new plantations. Coffee prices were high in the world market; the launching of the Colombo – Kandy railway, which had started to operate in 1867, diminished transportation costs; and, above all, everyone expected that the pest would soon pass.[55]

But it did not, and in 1875 panic set in. It was time to move with Tytler's 1852 plan. At the end of 1875, The Ceylon government sent G.A. Crüwell, an expert on agronomic and economic issues and a journalist for *The Ceylon Observer* (*co*) to Brazil. At the same time, the newspaper had already mobilised A. Scott Blacklaw as a local correspondent, an experienced Ceylon coffee superintendent who had been hired by the London and Brazilian Bank in 1873 to run a large plantation seized by debt two years earlier. The *Angélica* plantation was located in the confines of the Brazilian new coffee frontier, the so-called *Oeste Novo de São Paulo* (São Paulo's New West), whose terrain, which was less undulating than that of the Paraíba Valley, was even more fertile.[56] After visiting

---

54   Sidney Mintz, "Was the Plantation Slave a Proletarian?" *Review (Fernand Braudel Center)* 2, no. 1 (Summer 1978), 81–98. For a more forcefully theoretical argument of the slave as proletarian in the labour process, see Maria Sylvia de Carvalho Franco, "Organização social do trabalho no período colonial," *Discurso* 8 (June 1978), 145.

55   On the *Hemileia vastatrix* in Ceylon, see Webb, *Tropical Pioneers,* 108–16, and Stuart McCook, *Coffee is Not Forever: A Global History of the Coffee Leaf Rust* (Athens, OH: Ohio University Press, 2019), 36–64.

56   On the history of Angélica plantation, see the detailed and recent analysis by Joseph M. Mulhern, *After 1833: British Entanglement with Brazilian Slavery* (PhD diss., Durham University, 2018), 262–99.

plantations in the Paraíba Valley of Rio de Janeiro in January 1876, Crüwell met with Blacklaw on the *Angélica* plantation. Crüwell's stay in Brazil lasted only three months (25 December 1875 to 30 March 1876). The two would send several articles and letters to the *co* in the following years. Crüwell died in Ceylon in November 1877. Blacklaw sent his last letter to the *co* in January 1878. In that same year, the owner of the *co* gathered all this material in a single 150-page volume.[57]

This is an exceptional document on the integration of and the divergence between the coffee economies of Brazil and Ceylon, with several keen insights into what was happening with "The Mistress of the Coffee Markets of the World." First, and contrary to what Crüwell and Blacklaw themselves had initially assumed and written in their 1876 letters, by the end of 1877 it had become clear that coffee in Brazil had not been affected by leaf rust disease. Second, the internal slave trade had been operating for a quarter of a century in the opposite direction from what Tytler had predicted in 1852, by bringing slaves from economic sectors in crisis (such as sugar, cotton and cattle ranching) to the thriving coffee plantation economy in South-Central Brazil. Third, the railroads that were being built to serve São Paulo's new frontiers demonstrated that Brazil had an incalculable potential for rapidly increasing its coffee exports; its plantations were much larger and were undergoing major technical improvements when it came to the processing processes of the cherries. Fourth, observing the labour process directly, notably how many trees a coolie and a slave cultivated in Ceylon and Brazil and how much each one harvested, it was found that "the work demanded and performed by the slaves is enormous. It is beyond the utmost of what human beings are capable of performing without derangement to the physical resources of the individual."[58]

But precisely because of this last point the Brazilian coffee economy would eventually also experience a crisis. The end of the transatlantic trade in 1850 had been compensated by the internal slave trade, but after the passage of the Free Womb Law in 1871, slaves were no longer born in Brazil. With great accuracy, Blacklaw observed that, in view of the failure of the experiments with European immigrant workers on the frontier coffee plantations, "now comes the question of where to find labour to employ on the plantations of Brazil, a question which will have to be answered within the next ten years."[59] Crüwell

---

57   G. A. Crüwell and A. Scott Blacklaw, *Brazil as a Coffee-Growing Country: Its Capabilities, the Mode of Cultivation, and Prospects of Extension, Described in a Series of Letters* (Colombo: A. M. & J. Ferguson, 1878).

58   Crüwell and Blacklaw, *Brazil*, 1819.

59   Crüwell and Blacklaw, *Brazil*, 10.

reaffirmed the point, giving it a racial connotation: "The dark object in the picture is the slave question, the labour question. The colonist system, you see, is a failure. Europeans are unable to perform the work needed on coffee estates. They have tried, but they cannot do it: climatic influences prevent them."[60] In both Brazil and Ceylon, then, coffee cultivation was in crisis; however, Blacklaw and Crüwell noted that these were distinct crises: one was environmental, and the other was a crisis of the social relations of production.

In this period, there was also an ecological crisis in the Paraíba Valley due to its extensive agronomic methods. However, the prospects of Western São Paulo – still based on slavery – promised to soon surpass the old Brazilian coffee zone. Indeed, in the short run the ecological crisis of Ceylon was much more urgent. The last pages of the 1878 book explained how rising international prices during the 1870s, the recent railway expansion, and the increase in the internal slave trade had led to the establishment of new coffee plantings in the province of São Paulo. An article published in the *CO* on 28 March 1878, summarising the latest information collected by Blacklaw, predicted that if Brazil could send all the coffee it would soon be able to harvest to the world markets, "those markets would certainly be, to a large extent, 'swamped' .... All experience favours this conclusion, but Mr. Blacklaw's statements are before our readers, who can form their own judgment as to the immediate future of coffee in view of his astounding figures."[61] The prognosis proved to be right: between 1871 and 1875 and 1881 and 1885, Brazilian exports almost doubled, jumping from 174,000 to 322,000 tons per year. The consequences were immediate: international prices fell by half between 1878 and 1885 and Ceylon's coffee economy's final hour had struck.

In July 1878, Blacklaw featured as a special guest in the Agricultural Congress held in Rio de Janeiro. Called by the imperial government to identify possible solutions for the crisis of Brazilian slavery, the meeting had 456 registered planters, 279 of whom were present. At the request of the Secretary of Agriculture of the Empire, the Viscount of Sinimbu, Blacklaw presented a long and detailed lecture – in Portuguese – on the coolie work under the *kangany* system in the coffee plantations of Ceylon.[62] Interventions from Brazilian planters in the debate were recorded in the official transcript and indicate their strong

---

60   Crüwell and Blacklaw, *Brazil*, 76.
61   Crüwell and Blacklaw, *Brazil*, 144.
62   Three years before, the Brazilian government had already sponsored a Portuguese translation of the most important coffee manual written in Ceylon: Guilherme Sabonadière, *O Fazendeiro do Café em Ceylão* (Rio de Janeiro: Typographia Do Diário do Rio de Janeiro, 1875).

interest in the possible alternative that coolie labour could represent to slave labour. They were especially excited about the low wages paid to the coolies, until the decisive question came:

> A Mr Planter: – How much does each coolie produce annually? And what is the annual harvest in Ceylon?
> The Speaker replies that the coffee harvest in Ceylon is different from here. The task assigned to each coolie is two bags of 60 litres.
> A MR PLANTER: – Two *alqueires* ...[63]

Blacklaw knew the average labour productivity figures of the coolies in Ceylon and the slaves in Western São Paulo but, despite the insistence of the Brazilian planters, he chose not to present them to the Congress. A minute and a half after this dialogue (the time it takes today to read the rest of the document aloud), he ended his speech. However, information about the individual harvesting capacity of the coolies was enough. In the crisis of Brazilian slavery (1878–1888), the Indian coolie would no longer be considered an alternative. The solution would be found in an innovative state-subsidised immigration scheme, which brought in many members of the Italian peasantry, which had been devastated by the post-1870 world crisis of wheat, to work on the São Paulo coffee frontiers. A new turning point in the world coffee economy gave birth to the fourth global coffee complex, in which Latin American producers would take the place of Ceylon and Java while post-slavery, Western-oriented São Paulo would replace the Paraíba Valley, which had been ravaged by its scheme of extensive agronomy and the intensive exploitation of enslaved workers. The latter proved to be rational in the short term but profoundly irrational in the long run.

Bibliography

Absell, Christopher David. "The Bittersweet Century: Slavery, Tariffs and Brazilian Export Growth during the Nineteenth Century." PhD diss., Universidad Carlos III de Madrid, 2019.

Aguiar, João Joaquim Ferreira de. *Pequena memória sobre a plantação, cultura e colheita do café*. Rio de Janeiro: Imprensa Americana de I. P. da Costa, 1836.

---

[63]   "Conferência feita pelo Sr. Blacklaw perante o Congresso Agrícola, em 12 de julho de 1878, acerca do trabalho dos coolies," in *Congresso Agricola: Collecção de documentos* (Rio de Janeiro: Typographia Nacional, 1878), 262.

Andrade, Eloy de. *O Vale do Paraíba*. Rio de Janeiro: Real Gráfica, 1989.

Bacha, Edmar. "Política Brasileira do café: Uma avaliação centenária." In: *150 anos de café*, edited by Edmar Bacha and Robert Greenhill, 15–133 (Rio de Janeiro: Marcellino Martins & E. Johnston, 1992).

Bandarage, Asoka. *Colonialism in Sri Lanka: The Political Economy of the Kandyan Highlands, 1833–1886*. Berlin: Mouton/De Gruyter, 1983.

Barron, Tom J. "Scots and the Coffee Industry in Nineteenth Century Ceylon," in *The Scottish Experience in Asia, c. 1700 to the Present: Settlers and Sojourners*, edited by T. M. Devine and Angela McCarthy. London: Palgrave MacMillan, 2017.

Bauer, Rolf. *The Peasant Production of Opium in Nineteenth-Century India*. Leiden: Brill, 2019.

Brandon, Pepjin. "'Shrewd Sirens of Humanity': The Changing Shape of Proslavery Arguments in the Netherlands (1789–1814)." *Almanack* 14 (September – December 2016): 3–26.

Brown, Alex. *The Coffee Planter Manual*. 2nd ed. Colombo: Colombo Observer Press, 1880.

"Conferência feita pelo Sr. Blacklaw perante o Congresso Agrícola, em 12 de julho de 1878, acerca do trabalho dos coolies." In *Congresso Agricola: Collecção de documentos*. Rio de Janeiro: Typographia Nacional, 1878.

Crüwell, G. A. and A. Scott Blacklaw, *Brazil as a Coffee-Growing Country: Its Capabilities, the Mode of Cultivation, and Prospects of Extension, Described in a Series of Letters*. Colombo: A. M. & J. Ferguson, 1878.

Cunha, Mauro Rodrigues da. "Apêndice estatístico." In: *150 anos de café*, edited by Edmar Bacha and Robert Greenhill, 286–391 (Rio de Janeiro: Marcellino Martins & E. Johnston, 1992).

Darwin, John. *Unfinished Empire: The Global Expansion of Britain*. London: Penguin, 2012.

Dean, Warren. *With Broadax and Firebrand: The Destruction of the Brazilian Atlantic Forest*. Berkeley: University of California Press, 1995.

Delden Laërne, C. F. van. *Brazil and Java: Report on Coffee-Culture in America, Asia, and Africa*. London and The Hague: Martinus Nijhoff, 1885.

Drescher, Seymour. *The Mighty Experiment: Free Labor versus Slavery in British Emancipation*. Oxford: Oxford University Press, 2002.

Driesen, I. H. van den. "Coffee Cultivation in Ceylon (1)." *The Ceylon Historical Journal* 3 (1953): 31–62.

Driesen, I. H. van den. *Indian Plantation Labor in Sri Lanka: Aspects of the History of Immigration in the 19th Century*. Nedlands: University of Western Australia, 1982.

Duncan, James S. *In the Shadows of the Tropics: Climate, Race and Biopower in Nineteenth-Century Ceylon*. Aldershot: Ashgate, 2007.

Franco, Maria Sylvia de Carvalho. "Organização social do trabalho no período colonial." *Discurso* 8 (June 1978): 1–45.

Friedmann, Harriet, and Philip McMichael. "Agriculture and the State System: The Rise and Decline of National Agricultures, 1870 to the Present." *Sociologia Ruralis* 29, no. 2 (1989): 93–117.

Hjejle, Benedicte. "Slavery and Agricultural Bondage in South India in the Nineteenth Century." *Scandinavian Economic History Review* 15, no. 12 (1967): 71–126.

Hull, Edmund C.P. *Coffee: Its Physiology, History and Cultivation*. Madras: Gantz Brothers, 1865.

Huzzey, Richard. *Freedom Burning: Anti-Slavery and Empire in Victorian Britain*. Ithaca, NY: Cornell University Press, 2012.

"Instruções geraes para a administração das fazendas (23 de fevereiro de 1870)." In *Negro de corpo e alma: Mostra do Redescobrimento; Brasil 500 anos*, edited by Emanoel Araújo and Nelson Aguilar. São Paulo: Fundação Bienal de São Paulo, 2000.

Jaiswal, Ritesh Kumar. "Mediated (Im)Mobility: Indian Labour Migration to Ceylon under the Kangany System (c. 1850–1940)." In *The Palgrave Handbook of Bondage and Human Rights in Africa and Asia*, edited by Gwyn Campbell and Alessandro Stanziani, 157–88. New York: Palgrave MacMillan, 2019.

Jayawardena, Kumari, and Rachel Kurian. *Class, Patriarchy and Ethnicity on Sri Lanka Plantations: Two Centuries of Power and Protest*. New Delhi: Orient BlackSwan, 2015.

Kurian, Rachel. "Labor, Race, and Gender on the Coffee Plantations in Ceylon (Sri Lanka), 1834–1880." In *The Global Coffee Economy in Africa, Asia, and Latin América, 1500–1989*, edited by William Gervase Clarence-Smith and Steven Topik, 173–90. Cambridge: Cambridge University Press, 2003.

Lacerte, Robert K. "The Evolution of Land and Labor in the Haitian Revolution, 1791–1820." *The Americas* 34, no. 4 (1978): 449–59.

Lane, Fernanda Bretones, Guilherme de Paula Costa Santos, and Alain El Youssef. "The Congress of Vienna and the Making of the Second Slavery." *Journal of Global Slavery* 4, no. 2 (2019): 162–95.

Linden, Marcel van der. *Workers of the World: Essays Toward a Global Labor History*. Leiden: Brill, 2008.

Linden, Marcel van der. "Dissecting Coerced Labor." In *On Coerced Labor: Work and Compulsion after Chattel Slavery*, edited by Marcel van der Linden and Magaly Rodríguez García, 291–322. Leiden: Brill, 2016.

Manjapra, Kris. "Plantation Dispossessions: The Global Travel of Agricultural Racial Capitalism." In *American Capitalism: New Histories*, edited by Sven Beckert and Christine Desan, 361–387. New York: Columbia University Press, 2018.

Manjapra, Kris. *Colonialism in Global Perspective*. Cambridge: Cambridge University Press, 2020.

Marquese, Rafael de Bivar. *Administração & escravidão: Ideias sobre a gestão da agricultura escravista Brasileira*. São Paulo: Hucitec, 1999.

Marquese, Rafael de Bivar. "African Diaspora, Slavery, and the Paraíba Valley Plantation Landscape: Nineteenth-Century Brazil." *Review (Fernand Braudel Center)* 39, no. 2 (2008): 195–216.

Marquese, Rafael de Bivar. "Luso-Brazilian Enlightenment and the Circulation of Caribbean Slavery-Related Knowledge: The Establishment of the Brazilian Coffee Culture from a Comparative Perspective." *História, Ciências, Saúde – Manguinhos* 16, no. 4 (2009): 855–80.

Marquese, Rafael de Bivar. "Espacio y poder en la caficultura esclavista de las Américas: El Vale do Paraiba en perspectiva comparada, 1760–1860." In *Trabajo libre y coativo en sociedades de plantación*, edited by José Antonio Piqueras, 215–52. Madrid: Siglo XXI, 2009.

Marquese, Rafael de Bivar. "As origens de Brasil e Java: Trabalho compulsório e a reconfiguração da economia mundial do café na Era das Revoluções, c. 1760–1840." *História* 34 (2015): 108–27.

Marquese, Rafael de Bivar. "A Tale of Two Coffee Colonies: Environment and Slavery in Suriname and Saint-Domingue, c. 1750–1790." *Comparative Studies in Society and History* 64, no. 3 (2022): 722–755.

Marquese, Rafael, and Dale Tomich. "Slavery in the Paraíba Valley and the Formation of the World Coffee Market in the Nineteenth Century." In *Atlantic Transformations: Empire, Politics, and Slavery during the Nineteenth Century*, edited by Dale Tomich, 193–223. Albany: State University of New York Press, 2020.

Marquese, Rafael, and Ricardo Salles. "Slavery in Nineteenth Century Brazil: History and Historiography." In *Slavery and Historical Capitalism during the Nineteenth Century*, edited by Dale Tomich, 127–69. Boulder, CO: Lexington Books, 2017.

Marquese, Rafael, Tâmis Parron, and Márcia Berbel. *Slavery and Politics: Brazil and Cuba, 1790–1850*. Albuquerque: University of New Mexico Press, 2016.

Marquese, Rafael de Bivar. *Os tempos plurais da escravidão no Brasil: Ensaios de história e historiografia*. São Paulo: Intermeios, 2020.

Marrero, Levi. *Cuba: Economia y sociedad*. Vol. 11. Madrid: Editorial Playor, 1984.

McCook, Stuart. *Coffee is Not Forever: A Global History of the Coffee Leaf Rust*. Athens, OH: Ohio University Press, 2019.

McMichael, Philip. "Incorporating Comparison within a World-Historical Perspective: An Alternative Comparative Method." *American Sociological Review* 55, no. 3 (1990): 385–97.

Mello, Pedro Carvalho de. "The Economics of Labor in Brazilian Coffee Plantations, 1850–1888." PhD diss., University of Chicago, 1977.

Millie, P. D. *Thirty Years Ago, or the Reminiscences of the Early Days of Coffee Planting in Ceylon*. Colombo: A. M. & J. Ferguson, 1878.

Mintz, Sidney. "Was the Plantation Slave a Proletarian?" *Review (Fernand Braudel Center)* 2, no. 1 (Summer 1978): 81–98.

Muaze, Mariana, and Ricardo H. Salles, eds. *O Vale do Paraíba e o Império do Brasil nos quadros da Segunda Escravidão*. Rio de Janeiro: 7 Letras-Faperj, 2015.

Mulhern, Joseph M. "After 1833: British Entanglement with Brazilian Slavery." PhD diss., Durham University, 2018.

Parron, Tamis. *A política da escravidão no Império do Brasil, 1826–1865*. Rio de Janeiro: Civilização Brasileira, 2011.

Parron, Tâmis. "A política da escravidão na era da liberdade: Estados Unidos, Brasil e Cuba, 1787–1846." PhD diss., Universidade de São Paulo, 2015.

Parron, Tâmis. "The British Empire and the Suppression of the Slave Trade to Brazil: A Global History Analysis." *Journal of World History* 29, no. 1 (2018): 1–36.

Patterson, Orlando. *Slavery and Social Death: A Comparative Study*. Cambridge, MA: Harvard University Press, 1982.

Peebles, Patrick. *The History of Sri Lanka*. Westport, CT: Greenwood Press, 2006.

"Pioneers of the Planting Enterprise in Ceylon: Robert Boyd Tytler." *The Tropical Agriculturist* 13, no. 4 (1893): 218–19.

Posthumus, Nicolaas W. *Inquiry into the History of Prices in Holland*. Leiden: E. J. Brill, 1946.

"Quadro estatístico de alguns estabelecimentos rurais da Província de São Paulo." In *Documentos com que o Ilustríssimo e Excelentíssimo Senhor Dr. José António Saraiva, presidente da Província de São Paulo, instruiu o Relatório na abertura da Assembleia Legislativa Provincial no dia 15 de fevereiro de 1855*. São Paulo: Typographia Antunes, 1855.

Report from the Select Committee on Sugar and Coffee Planting. Vol 8. London: Commons, 1848.

Ricklefs, M. C. *A History of Modern Indonesia since c. 1200*. London: Palgrave, 2001.

Roberts, M. W. "Indian Estate Labor in Ceylon During the Coffee Period (1830–1880)." Indian *Economic & Social History Review* 3, no. 1 (1966): 1–52.

Sabonadière, William. *The Coffee Planter of Ceylon*. 2nd ed. London: E. & F. N. Spon, 1870.

Sabonadière, Guilherme. *O Fazendeiro do Café em Ceylão*. (Portuguese translation). Rio de Janeiro: Typographia Do Diário do Rio de Janeiro, 1875.

Samper, Mario, and Radin Fernando. "Historical Statistics of Coffee Production and Trade from 1700 to 1960." In *The Global Coffee Economy in Africa, Asia, and Latin América, 1500–1989*, edited by William Gervase Clarence-Smith and Steven Topik, 411–61. Cambridge: Cambridge University Press, 2003.

Schrikker, Alicia. *Dutch and British Colonial Intervention in Sri Lanka, 1780–1815: Expansion and Reform*. Leiden: Brill, 2007.

Silva, K. M. de. "The Third Earl Grey and the Maintenance of an Imperial Policy on the Sale of Crown Lands in Ceylon, c. 1832–1852: Some Influences of Edward Gibbon Wakefield's Doctrines in a Tropical Colony." *The Journal of Asian Studies* 27, no. 1 (1967): 5–20.

Smith, S. D. "Sugar's Poor Relation: Coffee Planting in the British West Indies, 1720–1833." *Slavery and Abolition* 19, no. 3 (1998): 68–89.

Steinfeld, Robert J. *Coercion, Contract, and Free Labor in the Nineteenth Century.* Cambridge: Cambridge University Press, 2001.

Talbot, John M. "The Coffee Commodity Chain in the World-Economy: Arrighi's Systemic Cycles and Braudel's Layers of Analysis." *Journal of World-System Research* 28, no. 1 (2011): 58–88.

The Planting Directory for India and Ceylon. Colombo: A. M. & J. Ferguson, 1878.

Tomich, Dale. *Through the Prism of Slavery: Labor, Capital and the World Economy.* Boulder, CO: Rowman & Littlefield, 2004.

Tomich, Dale. "Civilizing America's Shore: British World-Economic Hegemony and the Abolition of the International Slave Trade (1814–1867)." In *The Politics of the Second Slavery*, edited by Dale Tomich, 1–24. Albany: State University of New York Press, 2020.

Tytler, R. B. "Coffee Production: Brazil and Ceylon." *The Ceylon Observer*, 2 October 1852.

Webb, Jr., James L. A. *Tropical Pioneers: Human Agency and Ecological Change in the Highlands of Sri Lanka, 1800–1900.* Athens, OH: Ohio University Press, 2002.

Wenzlhuemer, Roland. "Indian Labour Immigration and British Labour Policy in Nineteenth-Century Ceylon." *Modern Asian Studies* 41, no. 3 (2007): 575–602.

Werneck, Francisco Peixoto de Lacerda. *Memória sobre a fundação de uma fazenda na província do Rio de Janeiro (1847)*, edited by Eduardo Silva. Rio de Janeiro: Fundação Casa de Rui Barbosa/Senado Federal, 1985.

Wright, Gavin. *Slavery and American Economic Development.* Baton Rouge: Louisiana State University Press, 2006.

CHAPTER 12

A Contract with Many Facets

Sharecropping and Credit Interlinkages in Southwestern Brazilian Plantations, 1840–1940

Bruno Gabriel Witzel de Souza and Rogério Naques Faleiros

1 Introduction

Terence J. Byres started his classical study on the history of sharecropping with the remarkably simple, but powerful statement that "[s]harecropping is as old as recorded history."[1][2] Extremely malleable, this labour-rental arrangement has persisted throughout human history and has been used around the globe to organise the production of the most diverse agricultural goods under radically different types of technologies and social organisations. Consequently, specific sharecropping contracts have shown extremely diverse features. Analytically, sharecropping can even be seen as a labour contract and/or a land-rental arrangement.[3] Such differentiation has important implications for the power relations established between the contracting parties, which usually

---

1 The structure of this chapter is based on the working paper "O Sistema de parceria e a formação do mercado de trabalho livre no Brasil: aspectos inerciais (1840–1930)," presented by the authors at the 40th Meeting of the Brazilian Association of Graduate Programs in Economics (ANPEC). Its conceptual framework has been updated in the current version to include theoretical discussions from the PhD thesis of Bruno Witzel de Souza.

2 Terence J. Byres, "Historical Perspectives on Sharecropping," in "Sharecropping and Sharecroppers," ed. Terence J. Byres, special issue, *The Journal of Peasant Studies* 10, nos. 2–3 (January/April 1983): 7.

3 For surveys on economic theory and history of sharecropping, see: Joseph D. Reid, "Sharecropping in History and Theory," *Agricultural History* 49, no. 2 (April 1975): 426–40; M. G. Quibria and Salim Rashid, "The Puzzle of Sharecropping: A Survey of Theories," *World Development* 12, no. 2 (February 1984): 103–14; Mukesh Eswaran and Ashok Kotwal, "A Theory of Contractual Structure in Agriculture," *The American Economic Review* 75, no. 3 (June 1985), 352–67; Keijiro Otsuka, Hiroyuki Chuma, and Yujiro Hayami, "Land and Labor Contracts in Agrarian Economies: Theories and Facts," *Journal of Economic Literature* 30, no. 4 (December 1992): 1965–2018. Byres, "Sharecropping and Sharecroppers" illustrates the use of sharecropping in various historical-geographical contexts.

include patron-client relations in the former case, or the need to set property rights over the land being cultivated in the latter.[4]

Notwithstanding such relevant particularities, the sharing of crops between one entity that holds the rights over the land and another that has the means to produce in it – and, thus, has control over (family) labour and/or agricultural implements – remains a pervasive form of organising rural relations. For instance, nowadays sharecropping tends to be used as a labour arrangement among poor families practicing agriculture in low- and medium low- income countries. Particularly in South Asia, this labour-rental arrangement is frequently interlinked with credit operations leading to modern forms of debt-peonage and to personal dependencies that not infrequently go against some of the basic principles of the Decent Work Agenda.[5]

Interlinkages with credit supply and the power relations that this implies are yet another historically ubiquitous feature of sharecropping.[6] The current chapter will look at a similar arrangement that prevailed in the southwestern Brazilian province of São Paulo from the 1840s, showing how its mechanisms of incentives and controls persisted over time and outlived the original contract to become a cornerstone of Brazilian immigration policy.

In spite of the profound socio-economic and political changes that took place in Brazil between 1840 and 1940 – including the abolition of slavery in 1888 and the substitution of a centralist empire by a federal republic in 1889 – the design and enforcement of various labour-rental contracts remained deeply influenced by the first experiments with sharecropping in the

---

4   For two illustrations in these regards, see Lee J. Alston and Joseph P. Ferrie, "Labor Costs, Paternalism, and Loyalty in Southern Agriculture: A Constraint on the Growth of the Welfare State," *The Journal of Economic History* 45, no. 1 (March 1985): 95–117; and Benedita Câmara, "The Portuguese Civil Code and the *Colonia Tenancy* Contract in Madeira (1867–1967)," *Continuity and Change* 21, no. 2 (October 2006): 213–33.

5   Smita Premchander, V. Prameela, and M. Chidambaranathan, *Prevention and Elimination of Bonded Labour: The Potential and Limits of Microfinance-Led Approaches* (Geneva: ILO Employment Sector, 2015).

6   Pranab K. Bardhan, "Interlocking Factor Markets and Agrarian Development: A Review of Issues," *Oxford Economic Papers, New Series* 32, no. 1 (March 1980): 82–98; Eswaran and Kotwal, "Theory"; Ashok Kotwal, "The Role of Consumption Credit in Agricultural Tenancy," *Journal of Development Economics* 18, nos. 2–3 (1985): 273–95; and Anindita Mukherjee and Debraj Ray, "Labor Tying," *Journal of Development Economics* 47, no. 2 (1995): 207–39. The reader interested in credit-labour-land interlinkages will find theoretical material in Avishay Braverman and T. N. Srinivasan, "Credit and Sharecropping in Agrarian Societies," *Journal of Development Economics* 9 (1981): 289–312; and Avishay Braverman and Joseph E. Stiglitz, "Sharecropping and the Interlinking of Agrarian Markets," *The American Economic Review* 72, no. 4 (September 1982): 695–715.

mid-nineteenth century. In this context, the chapter will highlight some institutional features associated with the design of the contract and its enforcement. The effective application of a labour-rental arrangement depends on the
presence of formal institutions to enforce it and on the cultural disposition to
accept the constraints it imposes on the discretionary will of the contracting
parties.[7] Both were missing for the most part in the plantations examined in
this chapter: sharecropping constituted the first form of non-captive labour
for conducting ordinary agricultural tasks during the Brazilian transition from
slavery to non-captive labour arrangements. Thus, it is not surprising that even
landowners interested in this new way of organising agricultural production
leaned towards patronage relations, reacting with scepticism – and sometimes
with rage – to the opposition of labourers, who not infrequently expressed
their dissatisfactions and burst into riots that farmers could not repress in the
same way they had been allowed to do with the slaves.

Hardly any other labour-rental arrangement has received more attention in
the historiography of Brazilian rural relations than sharecropping. As it was
the first attempt to begin the transition from slavery to free labour on economically booming plantations, there is a large body of literature – consisting of
studies that have become classics in the field – that has evaluated the evolution of sharecropping and its impacts on other types of contracts.[8] In his pref-
ace to the translation of the memoirs of the leader of a famous sharecroppers'
riot, Sérgio Buarque de Holanda inaugurated various branches of academic
research.[9] This now-classic text embedded the experiments with bonded

---

7 Bardhan, "Interlocking"; Daron Acemoglu and Alexander Wolitzky, "The Economics of
   Labor Coercion," *Econometrica* 79, no. 2 (March 2011): 555–600. An institutional approach
   embeds many of the current historical analyses of the adoption of sharecropping: Juan
   Carmona and James Simpson, "The 'Rabassa Morta' in Catalan Viticulture: The Rise and
   Decline of a Long-Term Sharecropping Contract, 1670s–1920s," *The Journal of Economic
   History* 59 (June 1999): 290–315; Juan Carmona and James Simpson, "Explaining Contract
   Choice: Vertical Coordination, Sharecropping, and Wine in Europe, 1850–1950," *The
   Economic History Review* 65, no. 3 (2012): 887–909; Samuel Garrido and Salvador Calatayud,
   "The Price of Improvements: Agrarian Contracts and Agrarian Development in Nineteenth-
   Century Eastern Spain," *The Economic History Review* 64, no. 2 (May 2011): 598–620; Samuel
   Garrido, "Sharecropping Was Sometimes Efficient: Sharecropping with Compensation
   for Improvements in European Viticulture," *The Economic History Review* 70, no. 3 (August
   2017): 977–1003.
8 This literature review is far from exhaustive; for instance, it does not consider the vast historiography on immigration that has its most common starting point in the experiments with
   sharecropping.
9 Sérgio Buarque de Holanda, "Prefácio do tradutor," in Thomas Davatz, *Memórias de um
   Colono no Brasil (1850)* (São Paulo: Martins Fontes, [1858] 1941).

labourers of the 1840s–1850s in the fields of the history of immigration and the transition from slavery to free labour in Brazil. Studies by Warren Dean, Verena Stolcke and Michael M. Hall, and Emília Viotti da Costa deepened this approach.[10] Luiz A. Corrêa do Lago extended it to show how different economic conditions led to various forms of labour arrangements across southern and central Brazil.[11] Studies of specific farms that employed sharecropping complemented these approaches, especially for those plantations that first experimented with sharecroppers.[12] Finally, Maria L. Lamounier provided the approach most closely related to this chapter, studying the institutional framework that supported non-captive labour relations in the coffee economy and how the actual enforcement of contracts led to modifications in Brazilian legislation in the nineteenth century.[13]

This chapter will revisit some of the themes of this rich literature and deepen the discussions on how the early experiments with sharecropping in São Paulo had consequences that made their effects felt at least until the beginning of the twentieth century. The goal of this chapter is to study some of the "inertial" aspects laid down by the first adoption of sharecropping. We thus advance the study of two classical hypotheses: (1) the sharecropping system proposed in the 1840s had long-standing consequences for contractual design; and (2) it influenced other labour-rental arrangements.[14] Even if completely new clauses, contracts and institutions to enforce them emerged between 1840 and 1940, various contractual mechanisms kept reappearing over time, as is demonstrated with some concrete cases. Moreover, the interlinkage of

---

10   Warren Dean, *Rio Claro: Um sistema brasileiro de grande lavoura, 1820–1920* (Rio de Janeiro: Editora Paz e Terra, 1977); Verena Stolcke and Michael M. Hall, "The Introduction of Free Labour on São Paulo Coffee Plantations," *The Journal of Peasant Studies* 10, nos. 2–3 (January/April 1983): 170–200; and Emília Viotti da Costa, *Da senzala à colônia*, 4th ed. (São Paulo: Fundação Editora UNESP, 1998).

11   Luiz A. Corrêa do Lago, *Da escravidão ao trabalho livre: Brasil, 1550–1900*, 1st ed. (São Paulo: Companhia das Letras, 2014).

12   José Sebastião Witter, *Ibicaba: Uma experiência pioneira* (São Paulo: Arquivo do Estado, 1982); José E. Heflinger, Jr., *Ibicaba: O berço da imigração européia de cunho particular* (Limeira: Unigráfica, 2007); José E. Heflinger, Jr., *A Revolta dos Parceiros na Ibicaba* (Limeira: Editora Unigráfica, 2009); and Bruno G. Witzel de Souza, "Liberdade ou grilhões? Um estudo dos contratos de parceria à luz da imigração germânica em São Paulo, 1840–1870" (Bachelor's thesis, Universidade de São Paulo, 2011).

13   Maria Lúcia Lamounier, "Formas de transição da escravidão ao trabalho livre: a Lei de Locação de Serviços de 1879" (Master's thesis, Universidade Estadual de Campinas, 1986).

14   Buarque de Holanda, "Prefácio," 34. Dean, *Rio Claro*, 164; Stolcke and Hall, "Introduction," 183.

labour-rental arrangements with credit operations remained a cornerstone of rural organisation in southwestern Brazil for this entire period.[15]

The chapter uses two sets of contracts studied by the authors in previous research. We will start with those contracts enforced in the central-western plateau of São Paulo in the 1840s–1880s.[16] In this part of the chapter, we will focus on sharecropping and its relation to contracts of fixed payments per time worked and per piece rate (*jornal* and *locação de serviços*). The second set of labour arrangements refers mainly to sharecropping and its relation to contracts for the formation of new plantations (a specific form of *empreitada*) enforced in the 1910s–1930s.[17] This set of contracts has a broader geographical coverage, including older plantations on the central-western plateau and the new agricultural frontiers in the state of São Paulo at the beginning of the twentieth century.

Before proceeding, we would like to reflect briefly on our approach. Through writing a history of *contractual changes* we adopt a formalist approach to understanding the evolution of actual *labour relations*. Non-written features that dictated the expected and actual behaviour of labourers and farmers can be retrieved partly from sources that we will use only marginally in this chapter – such as memoirs, letters and interviews, reports of governmental inspections, and the narratives of foreign travellers who visited the farms. Notwithstanding, this chapter is based on the recognition that contracts that survived in the archives framed the legally acceptable range of action of the involved parties. As such, changes in their clauses provide us with an overview – even if incomplete – of an endogenous process of learning and adaptation in daily labour relations.

The chapter is organised as follows. Section 2 provides an overview of the interconnected histories of immigration and the transition from slavery to non-captive labour arrangements in Brazil, particularly in the coffee plantations of São Paulo. Section 3 studies the structure of the sharecropping contracts proposed in the 1840s–1850s, focusing on their multidimensionality – that is, stressing that a contract that was primarily seen as a labour arrangement also

---

15   Bruno G. Witzel de Souza, "From Bonded Laborers to Educated Citizens? Immigration, Labor Markets, and Human Capital in São Paulo, Brazil (1820–2010)" (PhD diss., University of Göttingen, 2019), Chapter 2.

16   Witzel de Souza, "Liberdade ou grilhões?" Contracts researched at the *Arquivo Público do Estado de São Paulo*: Latas C07212, C07213, C07214 – Colônias, and C6045 – Contratos e Ordens de Serviço e Compras (1852–1858).

17   Rogério N. Faleiros, *Fonteiras do café: Fazendeiros e colonos no interior paulista (1917–1937)* (Bauru: Edusc/FAPESP, 2010). Contracts researched at the *Cartórios de Notas* of Araraquara, Botucatu, Campinas, Catanduva, Franca, Jaú, Lins, Novo Horizonte, Pirajuí, Ribeirão Preto, Rio Claro, São Carlos, São José do Rio Preto and São Manuel.

had a rental dimension, a mechanism of cost sharing, and an explicit interlinkage with a credit dimension. The study of the persistence and change of each contractual dimension at the beginning of the twentieth century is the object of Section 4, which complements the analysis of the contracts with information about institutional changes in Brazilian labour markets.

2   Slavery, Immigration and Non-captive Labour Arrangements in São Paulo

If the study of contracts is to serve the purpose of understanding labour relations, then it is necessary to have at least an overview of the relevant labour markets. In nineteenth-century Brazil, the history of labour was set by two intertwined processes: the sluggish abolition of slavery and the promotion of immigration – both having enormous impacts on the employment alternatives available to non-enslaved Brazilians. In 1888, slavery was abolished, unconditionally, but without any further support for the formerly enslaved population. As of 1886, mass immigration – subsidised by the provincial government of São Paulo – inserted Brazil into the global circuits of the a*ge of mass migration*. These were landmarks for a historical process that had been going on for almost a century.

A legalist approach to the history of abolition allows us to distinguish three phases that overlap with the history of immigration. The first refers to the abolition of the transatlantic slave trade and various experiments with migratory policies in the 1810s–1850s. The rise of bonded labour immigration under sharecropping contracts in the 1840s–1870s and its fade-out into new arrangements constituted an intermediary period. Finally, the abolition of slavery itself and the promotion of state-subsidised mass immigration in the 1880s–1920s crowned the process – and was also a reason for the fall of the Brazilian Crown in 1889.

The enforcement of the legislation against the transatlantic slave trade in 1850 disrupted an international circuit of labour supply that had fuelled the Brazilian plantation economy since colonial times. Since the transfer of the Portuguese Crown to Brazil in 1808 and Brazilian political independence in 1822, the Portuguese and Brazilian governments attempted to keep the slave traffic as active as possible.[18] This put Brazil at odds with the British Empire – leading to severe diplomatic tensions and maritime threats – , which opposed

---

18   Viotti da Costa, *Da senzala à colônia*, 74–86.

the traffic because its interests were now aligned with the consolidation of industrial capitalism.[19]

In this period, Brazilian immigration policy remained experimental. The prevailing practice was to recruit European households for settlement in public lands; nonetheless, experiments with other forms of immigration had already taken place, such as the recruitment of specialised labourers for public works.[20] It was only by the mid-1830s that a class of plantation owners established in the agricultural frontiers of São Paulo's central plateau started to link the category of "immigrant" to that of "agricultural labour" more directly, as an alternative to the government-led promotion of an independent class of foreign peasants in smallholdings.[21]

The responses given to the "labour question" by the coffee planters in the next period, roughly between the late 1840s and the 1870s, can, in hindsight, be seen as an expression of myopic behaviour[22] First, with the international supply of slaves cut and facing the possibility of negative natural rates of reproduction among the enslaved population, the end of slavery became a matter of time – an issue that was self-evident to the landowners. Nonetheless, the most common response of plantation owners in São Paulo was to import slaves from less economically booming provinces and regions.[23] This self-illusionary denial of an evident endpoint of slavery was, nonetheless, an individually rational response, informed by short-term concerns. After all, experimenting with non-captive labour involved many uncertainties; these landowners had made significant investments in buying slaves; and a great part of this elite's social distinction and political power came from the wealth generated by the very institution of slavery. Notwithstanding, more than a hundred landowners started experimenting with different forms of contract labour as an alternative to slavery

19   Paula Beiguelman, "A destruição do escravismo capitalista," *Revista de História* 34, no. 69 (March 1967): 149–60. Nonetheless, slavery in Brazil remained an important source of international capital – see Joseph M. Mulhern, "British Entanglement with Brazilian Slavery" (PhD diss., Durham University, 2018).

20   Sílvia C. L. Siriani, "Os descaminhos da imigração alemã para São Paulo no século XIX – aspectos políticos," *Almanack Braziliense* 2 (November 2005): 91–100.

21   See the review of the literature in Witzel de Souza, "Liberdade ou grilhões?"

22   The question about the economic rationality of plantation owners resonates in the evaluation of contractual choices: after all, did the adoption of certain arrangements result from economic calculus, institutional persistence, or simply from pure chance? For Brazilian southwestern plantations, there are two dominant views. Warren Dean conceptualises landowners as tending to favour patronage relations, while Stolcke and Hall put more emphasis on their economically rational responses to the problems at hand.

23   Dean, *Rio Claro*, 69–73; Viotti da Costa, *Da senzala à colônia*, 70.

in the 1850s–1860s.[24] These experiments were short-lived for the most part and gave way to a recrudescence of slavery in the 1870s.[25] Experimenting with contract labour in the belief that the end of slavery would come about soon was a rational response on the part of the landowners; its abandonment later on – when the scarcity of captive labour had increased even more – was, once again, individually rational in the face of the high transaction costs related to the necessary adaptations to non-captive labour.[26]

Members of the rural elite of São Paulo, whose plantations were expanding in the 1850s, made some attempts to invest in immigrant labour more systematically. However, Brazil was not a particularly attractive destination to foreign labourers, especially considering the combined prevalence of slavery, the lack of religious freedom in the officially Catholic empire, and the difficulties for the average labourer to attain landownership. Moreover, there was a general lack of experience with non-captive labour: certainly, various forms of patron-client relations with freemen executing sporadic tasks had always been present in the plantations, but not for organising ordinary agricultural labour.

A proposed solution to these problems was to interlink a labour-rental contract to a credit arrangement for poor potential immigrants, who lacked the wealth and income to cover the costs of international migration on their own. In São Paulo, the first landowner to propose this arrangement was the Portuguese-born, Brazilian senator Nicolau Pereira de Campos Vergueiro.[27] According to his contract, an immigrant household received credit from a landowner in Brazil to cover the migratory costs and subsistence expenses in the new country; the immigrant household was then obliged to repay the debt by working on the farm and sharing the annual profits of rural production under a sharecropping arrangement.[28] Known for many years as the "Vergueiro system," this contract was adapted over time and across plantations, but the

---

24 Witzel de Souza, "Liberdade ou grilhões?" 12 and Appendix I.

25 Buarque de Holanda, "Prefácio," 29–35; Viotti da Costa, *Da senzala à colônia*, Part I, Chapter 3.

26 We can trace a parallel to the West Indies here, where plantation owners preferred slaves to immigrants due to higher productivity and lower transaction costs. See Stanley L. Engerman, "Contract Labor, Sugar, and Technology in the Nineteenth Century," *The Journal of Economic History* 43, no. 3 (September 1983), 644.

27 See, in particular, Witter, *Ibicaba*; Heflinger, *Ibicaba*; and Heflinger, *A Revolta dos Parceiros*.

28 Beyond the literature reviewed in Section 1, see the contemporaneous views of: Charles Perret-Gentil, *A Colonia Senador Vergueiro* (Santos: Typographia Imparcial, 1851); Thomas Davatz, *Memórias de um colono no Brasil (1850)* (São Paulo: Martins Fontes, [1858] 1841); and Johann Jakob von Tschudi, *Viagem às províncias do Rio de Janeiro e S. Paulo* (São Paulo: Livraria Martins Editora, [1866] 1953).

aspect of credit interlinkage became a cornerstone of the Brazilian immigration policy and was crucial for the path taken in Brazil for the transition from slavery to free labour.

This specific form of peonage provided some security to landowners as a mechanism of control over labour mobility and turnover. However, such controls also caused much discontent among immigrants. Aligned with foreigners' frequently exaggerated expectations, the different readings of the sharecropping clauses by labourers and farmers led to a number of official complaints to diplomatic authorities and even to strikes. The most famous, the so-called Sharecropper's Riot, led by Swiss immigrants, took place on the very farm of Senator Vergueiro in 1856–1857 and gave rise to a series of inspections from Brazilian and international authorities. This event and other complaints by German immigrants in the province of Minas Gerais triggered the cancellation of various hiring licenses to Brazil and led to the prohibition of pro-emigration propaganda in Prussia under the Von der Heydt Rescript, which was extended to the entire German Empire later on.[29]

The riots, the alleged interference of diplomatic authorities in the labour discipline of the farms, and farmers' discontent with all these novelties were symptoms of a deeply rooted problem: the unwillingness to enforce impersonal arrangements between nominally *equal* contracting parties in a country whose economy, society and politics were primarily based on slavery.[30] Thus, in spite of many individual initiatives and various non-materialised political projects – including plans to promote the immigration of Chinese coolies – the rural economy of São Paulo in the 1870s mainly advanced through captive labour bought at high prices in other provinces and regions.

The foundation of the *Associação Auxiliadora da Colonisação* (Supportive Association for Colonisation) in the 1870s brought about some important new developments. The actual initiatives of that association had rather limited impacts, but its conceptualisation implied an important change in the migratory strategy pursued by the rural elites. The system that had been designed in the 1840s–1850s depended on a farmer who supported the hiring

---

29   Heflinger, *A Revolta dos Parceiros*, 55–63; and Witzel de Souza, "From Bonded Laborers," Appendix II.

30   A different perspective – made prominent by Viotti da Costa, in *Da senzala à colônia* – is that sharecropping had structural problems that led, on average, to a spiral of debt. Although more research is necessary in this regard, using data from Senator Vergueiro's plantation, Witzel de Souza, "Liberdade ou grilhões?" points to equilibrated contractual mechanisms, favouring the argument that the structure of contracts was not the primary problem.

of immigrants in Europe; although public funds usually backed up the credit advances made by landowners to immigrants, recruitments in Europe were decentralised. The *Associação Auxiliadora* changed that by acting on behalf of its members, increasing the potential scale and the organisational capacity of the recruitments.[31] The posterior *Sociedade Promotora da Imigração* (Society for the Promotion of Immigration) scaled up these features. Founded by leading coffee planters in 1885 and taken over by the government of São Paulo in 1892, this organisation successfully accomplished its goals of promoting pro-immigration propaganda, hiring immigrants, lodging them upon arrival and creating a centralised labour market that allowed farmers to hire labourers recently arrived in the city of São Paulo.[32]

The pressures of abolitionist activism – which included organised civil movements and mass escapes from the farms in the second half of the 1880s – and the increased demand for a secure source of cheap labour in the booming rural economy explain the foundation of these associations as the somewhat desperate answer of the planters to the final phase of abolition. Furthermore, the new elite of plantation owners was now politically better established. This led to the implementation of an official programme to subsidise immigration, which led to a massive inflow of foreigners from 1886.[33] This policy spread the costs of immigration and relieved individual planters from the insecurity of immigrants who defaulted on their obligations.

In terms of migratory inflows, the policy was a great success: between 1885 and 1919, São Paulo received a gross inflow of approximately 1.72 million foreigners, corresponding to 58.1 per cent of all entries in Brazil.[34] Nonetheless, similarly to the 1850s, planters in the 1900s kept complaining about labourers' turnover and voicing quasi-apocalyptical predictions about the consequences of the "labour crisis" (*crise de braços*) for the Brazilian economy. These complaints reflected the fact that coffee kept devouring land and labour in its march to the west: the agricultural frontiers had greatly expanded in the first decades of the twentieth century, as public policies maintained coffee prices

---

31 Viotti da Costa, *Da senzala à colônia*, 234; Witzel de Souza, "Liberdade ou grilhões?" 31–33; and Witzel de Souza, "From Bonded Laborers," 116.

32 Dean, *Rio Claro*, 152; Siriani, "Os descaminhos," 99; and Odair da Cruz Paiva and Soraya Moura, *Hospedaria dos imigrantes de São Paulo* (São Paulo: Editora Paz e Terra, Coleção São Paulo no Bolso, 2008).

33 Thomas H. Holloway, "Creating the Reserve Army? The Immigration Program of São Paulo, 1886–1930," *The International Migration Review* 12, no 2: 187–209.

34 Maria Stella F. Levy, "O papel da imigração internacional na evolução da população brasileira (1872 a 1972)," Supplement, *Revista de Saúde Pública* 8 (1974): Appendix, Table 8.

paid to producers artificially high and the western portions of the state were reached by railroad infrastructure.[35]

Contractually, an important novelty of the 1880s was the implementation of the so-called *colonato* system, which constituted the basis for rural labour relations in São Paulo well into the twentieth century. A family under *colonato* received fixed and predetermined payments for taking care of the coffee trees (or of other crops), a share of the household's annual harvest, and was permitted to practise subsistence agriculture in between the rows of new coffee trees. A study of the exact origins of each of its clauses goes beyond the scope of this chapter, but, here, one notices a substantial continuity vis-à-vis the old sharecropping arrangements, which included side payments for tasks in the lean season that became more clearly defined over time.[36]

Mass immigration also required improved institutions and organisations to regulate labour arrangements and deal with conflicts. Public responsiveness to problems on the farms was crucial for maintaining the high inflow of immigrants, as the Prinetti Decree demonstrated in 1902. This Italian decree forbade subsidised emigration from Italy after reports of abuses on the farms of São Paulo, including a riot triggered by the assassination of Diogo Salles, brother of the Brazilian president, by the Italian colonist Angelo Lungaretti, after Diogo's son attempted to "seduce" Lungaretti's sisters – which were euphemistically reported, most likely referring to verbal or physical sexual assaults.[37] Although mass immigration continued, with Portuguese and Spanish immigrants substituting the primacy of the Italians – who could still immigrate spontaneously –, the Prinetti Decree triggered debates similar to those of the Von der Heydt Rescript.

In 1906, new public initiatives included the foundation of an official agency to match labourers and farmers and to supervise the signing of contracts at the lodgings of the *Sociedade Promotora*, as well as the foundation of an

---

35   Octavio Ianni, "O progresso econômico e o trabalhador livre," in *História Geral da Civilização Brasileira*, part II, vol. 5, *O Brasil monárquico: Reações e transações*, ed. Sérgio Buarque de Holanda and Pedro Moacyr Campos (Rio de Janeiro: Bertrand Brasil, 2004), 350–74.

36   Lamounier, "Formas de transição," 31–34; and José de Souza Martins, "A imigração espanhola para o Brasil e a formação da força-de-trabalho na economia cafeeira: 1880–1930," *Revista de História* 121 (1989): 5–26. Besides classical works on the history of immigration that deal with this contract, the reader will find detailed information about *colonato* in José de Souza Martins, *O cativeiro da terra*, 9th ed. (São Paulo: Editora Contexto, 2010), Chapter 1; Maria Silvia C. B. Bassanezi, *Colonos do café*, 1st ed. (São Paulo: Editora Contexto, 2019) features an excellent case study of farm Santa Gertrudes.

37   Dean, *Rio Claro*, 173–75.

inspectorate to evaluate the travel conditions of immigrants.[38] In 1911, an umbrella organisation – the Labour Department of the State [of São Paulo] – took over these responsibilities. To carry out the task of monitoring rural labour relations, the government of São Paulo established the *Patronato Agrícola* (Agricultural Office) in 1911, whose first mandate was to "support the execution of federal and state laws concerning the defence of the rights and interests of the agricultural proletarians."[39] For this chapter, it is impotant to remark that the legislation referred to here formalised a system of "current account booklets" (*cadernetas*). According to this legislation, all accounting related to a household should be noted down not only in the farm's administrative books but also in booklets given to labourers – in which the labour contract was also written down – allowing for clearer mutual monitoring.

The timeline sketched in this section stresses the overlapping histories of immigration and the abolition of slavery in Brazil. In terms of labour arrangements, we highlighted the learning processes that took place in the half-century after the elaboration of the first sharecropping contract. While defending the thesis that sharecropping had a long-standing influence on the elaboration of other contractual arrangements, we nonetheless discussed the profound organisational changes in the recruitment, employment and monitoring of non-captive labourers in the nineteenth and early twentieth centuries. By contrasting continuities and changes in labour markets, we aimed at avoiding a schematic approach to the history of labour relations. Although specific contractual forms were more prevalent in certain periods – such as sharecropping in the 1850s, fixed payments in the 1870s, and *colonato* in the 1880s – the complex organisation of a plantation required a multitude of different actors employed under various labour regimes. Moreover, it was not uncommon to find the same actors working under different arrangements during the season, across plantations, and throughout their life cycles.[40]

---

38   Chiara Vangelista, *Os braços da lavoura: Imigrantes e caipiras na formação do mercado de trabalho paulista (1850–1930)* (São Paulo: Hucitec, 1991), 58; and Cruz Paiva and Moura, *Hospedaria*, 36–37.

39   Lei N. 1299A, 27/12/1911, Article 1 (free translation by the authors). Available at https://www.al.sp.gov.br/repositorio/legislacao/lei/1911/lei-1299A-27.12.1911.html.

40   For case studies of contractual mix and the functional division of labour in plantations, see Rosane C. M. Monteiro, "Regiões esquecidas da história: Um estudo sobre a organização da mão-de-obra em fazendas do oeste paulista no período de transição," *História Econômica & História de Empresas* 2 (August 2012): 29–52; Cláudia A. Tessari, "Sazonalidade e trabalho temporário na empresa cafeeira (oeste paulista, 1890–1915)," *História Econômica & História de Empresas* 14, no. 2 (2011): 105–43; Rogério N. Faleiros, "A fazenda Pau d'Alho de Campinas: As cadernetas como registros da contabilidade dos 'colonos' (1927–1931)," *História e Economia* 8 (January 2011): 79–94; Bruno G. Witzel de Souza and Leonardo

3   The Multidimensionality of the Vergueiro System and its Changes
      over Time (1840s–1870s)

Système du partage de récoltes (system of sharing crops); *métayer brésil-
ien* (Brazilian metayage);[41] share [of] profits and expenses of the crop;
colons partiaires (partner colonists); *systeme d'association* (system of association); Halbpacht- or *Parcerie-System* (system of share tenancy or of partnership); *Parceria-Kolonien* or *Halbpartsystem* ("Partnership" colonies or
half-part system);[42] *Parcerie-System nach dem Gesetz der Locação de serviços*
(*Vermietungsrecht*) or *Halbpachtwesen* ("Partnership" system following the
Law of *Locação de Serviços* [Rental Law] or share tenancy);[43] *Parcerie-Vertrag*
or *Teilungsvertrag* ("Partnership" contract or distribution contract)*; trabalhador parceiro na condição de um mero locador de serviços ... remunerado
pela divisão dos fructos* ("partner" worker only leasing services ... remunerated
by crop division).[44] This great variety of denominations for "sharecropping" as

          A. Santin Gardenal, "Households' Labor Income, Credit, and Expenditures in a Brazilian
          Plantation (Ibicaba, 1890–1950)" (working paper, Mimeo, 2018); and Bassanezi, *Colonos
          do café.*

41   Santos Barreto and Laveleye, *Voyages et études,* 79, attribute to Charles Reybaud the com-
          parison between the *paulista* sharecropping and the French *métayage.*

42   "Sharecropping" would be a simpler translation of the German *Halbpacht.* However, the
          radical concept of "*Pacht*" emphasises a type of rent, lease or tenancy. *Parceria* (and the
          German adaptation *Parcerie*) is the Portuguese noun for "sharecropping," which evokes
          the meaning of "partnership." Eswaran and Kotwal, "Theory," 353, stress the same mean-
          ing in the Philippines.

43   *Locação de Serviços* was the legal typification of fixed payments for hiring labourers; it pre-
          vailed as the regulatory mark for non-captive labour in Brazil until 1876. Oskar Canstatt
          incorrectly translated this as a form of rental law.

44   Nomenclatures (in order of appearance) by (1) S. Dutot, *France et Brésil* (Paris: Garnier
          Frères, Libraires-Éditeurs de Guillaumin et Cie., 1859): 122–24; (2) M. P. dos Santos-Barreto
          and Émile de Laveleye, *Voyages et études: Les Blancs au Brésil. Actualités du Brésil, sa col-
          onisation par la race blanche, les forets vierges et le far-west, religion, politique, progrès et
          avenir de ce pays* (Rio de Janeiro: Typographia da Gazeta; Paris: Gernier, frères, éditeurs;
          Louvain: D. A. Peeters-Ruelens, 1881), 79; (3) Daniel P. Kidder and James C. Fletcher, *Brazil
          and the Brazilians, Portrayed in Historical and Descriptive Sketches* (Philadelphia: Childs &
          Peterson; Boston: Phillips, Sampson, 1857), 410; (4) Charles Ribeyrolles and Victor Frond,
          Brazil Pittoresco: Historia – Descripções – Viagens – Instituições – Colonisação, vol. 3 (Rio de
          Janeiro: Typographia Nacional): 175; (5) Joaquim Manuel Macedo, *Notions de Chorographie
          du Brésil* (Leipzig: Imprimerie de F. A. Brockhaus, 1873): 372; (6) Fernando Schmid, *Über
          Handel und Wandel in Brasilien: Journalistische Skizzen; Expedition der "Allgemeinen
          Deutschen Zeitung für Brasilien"* (Rio de Janeiro: Buchdruckerei von Lorenz Winter,
          1881): 37; (7) Oskar Canstatt, *Brasilien: Land und Leute* (Berlin: Ernst Siegfried Mittler und
          Sohn, 1877): 176–77, 380–83; Oskar Canstatt, *Das republikanische Brasilien in Vergangenheit
          und Gegenwart: Nach den neuesten amtlichen Quellen und auf Grund eigener Anschauung*

first employed in the plantations of São Paulo in the 1840s–1850s indicates the novelty of the sharecropping contract and its complexity: the various names given above stress different dimensions of the contract, which were bundled together in a single arrangement.[45]

What modern scholars summarise under the term "sharecropping contracts" (*contratos de parceria*) is probably better described by the term "Vergueiro system" (*sistema Vergueiro*), which was used at the time and referred to a contract that included at least four dimensions.[46]

The contract originally proposed by Vergueiro & Co. – the firm headed by Senator Vergueiro – in 1847 included the application of crop-sharing mechanisms to three different stages of rural production. First, landowners were looking for a secure supply of labourers to take care of the coffee trees and to harvest the annual produce. Here, sharecropping acted as a labour contract that determined a fifty-fifty division of profits between the immigrant household and the farmer. Second, marketing the coffee required an initial processing of the beans on the farm, which included washing, drying, pulping, selecting and sacking them. In the 1847 contract, these tasks were divided between farmers and immigrant households via a system of crop-sharing – which implied a fifty-fifty division of the processing costs. Finally, immigrant families received plots of land to cultivate subsistence goods. The contract stipulated that the parcel of those goods sold on the market – that is, not consumed by the family itself – had to be shared with the landowner.[47] In this case, sharecropping was a form of land renting.

The term "sharecropping" in the singular thus hides the complexity of a contract according to which crop-sharing had a labour dimension, a cost-sharing dimension, and a land-rental dimension. The fourth dimension of the "Vergueiro system" was a credit interlinkage, by which the farmer covered the

---

(Leipzig: Ferdinand Hirt & Sohn, 1899), 225; (8) Moritz Lamberg, *Brasilien: Land und Leute in ethischer, politischer und volkswirtschaftlicher Beziehung und Entwicklung. Erlebnisse, Studien und Erfahrungen während eines zwanzigjährigen Aufenthaltes* (Leipzig: Verlag von Hermann Zieger, 1899), 295; and (9) João Cardoso de Menezes e Souza, *Theses sobre colonização do Brazil: Projecto de solução as questões sociaes, que se prendem a este difícil problema; Relatório apresentado ao Ministério da Agricultura, Commercio e Obras Publicas em 1873* (Rio de Janeiro: Typographia Nacional, 1875): 261–62.

45   Section based on Lamounier, *Formas de transição*, 21–49; Witzel de Souza, "Liberdade ou grilhões?"; and Witzel de Souza, "From Bonded Laborers," Chapter 2.

46   We stress "at least," because other dimensions can be identified, such as cultivation for consumption.

47   The administrations of most farms only weakly enforced this clause due to its high monitoring costs.

immigration costs of a household and bonded the labour force of all its members to the repayment of the outstanding debts.[48]

In hindsight, one notices two clear problems with this mechanism. From the labourer's point of view, the aspect of credit interlinkage implied too many uncertainties, especially for a family unaware of the working conditions on a Brazilian plantation.[49] From the farmer's point of view, the negative effect of a long-standing debt on the motivation of the workers – and their resulting productivity or willingness to default or to riot – proved to be a challenge, even if it was not a concern at first.[50]

In spite of these faults, the credit interlinkage became a cornerstone of the immigration policy in São Paulo. We consider it safe to argue that the aspect of interlinkage was the main mechanism that inserted Brazil into the *age of mass migration*, as it permitted the country to attract labourers who otherwise would not have had the economic conditions to immigrate. Brazil was thus able to attract immigrants without promoting institutional reforms, which would have been extremely costly for its ruling elites. Moreover, credit interlinkage provided landowners with a major control mechanism, securing the presence of labourers on the farm as long as there was an outstanding debt. By creating a certain degree of stability in the supply of labour, the credit dimension thus long outlived the first sharecropping contracts. The historical evidence and a theoretical illustration discussed by Bruno Witzel de Souza elsewhere point to the malleability of the credit dimension of the Vergueiro system. Under circumstances that most closely reflected the perceptions of the landowners about the contracts, it is possible to show, from a theoretical point of view, that the credit dimension could yield exactly the same benefits to the landowners, whether it was interlinked to a sharecropping contract, a fixed rent contract or a wage labour contract.[51] It is thus not surprising that this malleable dimension continued to be used to bond immigrant labour for most of the nineteenth century. Over time, various landowners substituted a fixed indenture (usually five years) for the uncertain time of the varying outstanding debts. This mechanism reduced the uncertainty involved for both landowners and labourers, but the principle of bonding labour via the coverage of immigration costs remained unaltered.

---

48   All classical authors have studied contractual changes, but a more microeconomic approach and a clearer separation of the land-rental dimension from the aspect of credit interlinkage can be found in Stolcke and Hall, "Introduction."

49   Dean, *Rio Claro*, 108–13; and Witter, *Ibicaba*, 34–35.

50   Dean, *Rio Claro*, 115.

51   Witzel de Souza, "From Bonded Laborers," 129–30, and Appendix to Chapter 2.

From 1847 to 1851, Vergueiro & Co. maintained a monopoly on recruiting bonded labourers. It is thus reasonable to assume that no great modification in the structure of sharecropping occurred. In line with the concluding remarks of section 2, however, we highlight that sharecropping was not the only non-captive labour arrangement being employed. Before the relatively successful experience of 1847, Senator Vergueiro had already hired Portuguese labourers in 1840. The current evidence – even if still inconclusive – is that these labourers had been employed under regimes of fixed payments and fixed rents; and that their tasks were organised in a gang system considered too similar to that of the slaves.[52] Moreover, it is reasonable to assume that sporadic free workers and clients had a number of verbal arrangements with the farms' administrations.[53] As such, the period of the early transition to non-captive labour arrangements was as intense in contractual experimentation as any other that we will study in this chapter.

In the early 1850s, some substantial contractual changes appeared. Vergueiro & Co. started to recruit labourers for other landowners and tightened some control mechanisms, in special those related to the bonding of immigrants. A novelty particularly opposed by international authorities was a clause that allowed the transferral of a family with its debt to another landowner, a prerogative that critics saw as a form of trading freemen. Another source of distress was the new "solidarity clause," by which each individual was responsible for the debt of his/her entire household and, hence, not allowed to stop working on the farm without consent of the farmer or until the debts had been fully repaid – a prerogative particularly harsh for young people who wanted to marry and for underage orphans. Moreover, farmers were now permitted to assign individuals to households they did not belong to by blood or kinship – and to whom the same principles of the "solidarity clause" applied.[54]

Another crucial change occurred in the division of tasks. We have seen that the 1847 contract envisaged that farmers and labourers would contribute

---

52   Tschudi, *Viagem*, 137. At this time, the Brazilian legislation explicitly regulated only one type of non-captive labour, namely "services hiring [usually per time]" (*locação de serviços*) (Lamounier, *Formas de transição*).

53   Unfortunately, we did not find labour contracts that were actually enforced before 1847; in a sense, selection bias is likely in the archiving of contracts. Relatedly, oral arrangements were probably less likely with German-speaking immigrants (as of 1847) than with Brazilians or Portuguese (as of 1840).

54   Davatz, *Memórias*, Chapter 2; Tschudi, *Viagem*, 137, 145, 191; Dean, *Rio Claro*, 99–101; and Lamounier, *Formas de transição*, 28–29. Vergueiro & Co. also started to charge 400 *réis* for each immigrant hired, a sum that was not officially stipulated in the contracts and that most farmers passed on as debt to the immigrants.

jointly to the processing of the coffee beans. In other words, the first arrangement stipulated that the fifty-fifty share was to prevail beyond the agricultural sphere and should be extended to the processing phase. It was probably daily experience on the farm that showed the unfeasibility of that earlier arrangement, with almost one hundred families simultaneously wishing to process their produce in the farm's storehouses right after the harvest. The contracts of the early 1850s now stipulated that each household would pay a fixed amount per measure of coffee beans handed in to the farm's administration – which became solely responsible for the processing operations. Beyond a formalisation of the monopsony power of landowners over the harvested produce, this clause had now established a clear functional division of labour between sharecroppers and the farm's administration: sharecroppers were agricultural labourers, while the processing became a duty of the administration alone, without the supervision or actual participation of non-captives. Moreover, this new clause implied a fixed payment within a share contract. Although all these operations most likely involved only accounting registries rather than actual monetary disbursements, the change shows the malleability of sharecropping and, in particular, its ability to accommodate side payments – a crucial feature for some of the changes we will discuss below.

A number of marginal modifications appeared as more farmers decided to experiment with the Vergueiro system. These included, for instance, variations in interest rates, in the size and obligations of side payments, in charges of extra fees, and in benefits offered to labourers – such as the duration of rent-free housing or the size of pastures for their own use. Moreover, Senator Francisco Antônio de Souza Queiroz (the son-in-law of Nicolau Vergueiro) entered the business of recruiting immigrants in Europe with a sharecropping contract marginally more advantageous to labourers than those of Vergueiro. More importantly, Senator Souza Queiroz substituted the varying nature of the contract and the undetermined period of labour-tying based on households' outstanding debts by a maximum indenture of five years. This implied that immigrant families could leave the farm upon the repayment of debts or after five years, which was certainly an asset for risk-averse labourers.[55]

In the 1860s, farmers started to remunerate non-captive labourers with simpler arrangements of fixed payments per day or per piece rate. However, in spite of the declining number of farmers employing sharecropping contracts, this form of labour arrangement remained influential. For good or ill, the Vergueiro system was the non-captive arrangement with which farmers had

---

55   Witzel de Souza, "Liberdade ou grilhões?" 114–16.

had the most experience so far. Relatedly, some influential families, such as the Souza Queiroz family, maintained classical crop-sharing clauses in their new recruitments in Europe. Finally, defending immigration to Brazil against critics – who were especially vocal in the German-speaking world – was frequently confounded with defending prevalent labour relations. On the other hand, as political debates in the 1860s made Brazil move away from the idea of recruiting Chinese coolies, the aim of bonding European labourers kept its prominence.[56] In this context, discussions in the press demonstrate that there was much lively debate going on, with ideas coming from all sides on how to solve the "labour question," that is, the reigning uncertainty on how to find new sources of cheap labour. In the 1870s, clearer propositions for crowding local markets with immigrants gained momentum, but, in practice, farmers only achieved marginally successful results based on individual initiatives to recruit labourers.[57]

Between the experiments with bonded labour (1840s–1870s) and mass immigration (1880s–1920s), the number of contracts with fixed side payments per piece rate increased, especially when it came to taking care of the coffee trees (cleaning, weeding, hoeing, pruning), including on the main farm of the deceased Senator Vergueiro.[58] These side payments diminished the uncertainties faced by immigrants, whose main source of income under sharecropping in the 1850s had been a shared yearly amount of the proceeds of the coffee harvested – a source of income subjected to many uncertainties, such as variations in coffee prices in international markets and in productivity dictated by purely exogenous agronomical and ecological conditions.[59] Many of the new contractual arrangements also attempted to diminish the possibilities for disputes and doubts, explicitly writing down the tasks and obligations of the labourers, which the original Vergueiro system did not make explicit. Together with institutional reforms – including the centralised organisations to promote immigration as well as a new regulatory mark for labour legislation enacted in 1876 – the way was paved for the appearance of the *colonato*

56   Robert Conrad, "The Planter Class and the Debate over Chinese Immigration to Brazil, 1850–1893," *International Migration Review* 9, no. 1 (Spring 1975): 41–55; Alexander C. Y. Yang, *"O comércio dos 'coolie' (1819–1920)," Revista de História* 112 (1977): 419–28; and Viotti da Costa, *Da senzala à colônia*, 184–88.

57   Witzel de Souza, "From Bonded Laborers," 111–12; and Stolcke and Hall, "Introduction," footnote 56.

58   Witter, *Ibicaba*, 43.

59   Stolcke and Hall, "Introduction," 97; and Lamounier, *Formas de transição*, 53–54.

system.[60] However, as the next section shows, the spectre of the Vergueiro system would keep haunting the plantations in many different ways.

4   Not Set in Stone, but Still Path Dependent: Influences of Crop-Sharing in the 1900s–1930s

Between 1910 and 1912, the Inspectorate of Agricultural Defence – an auxiliary body of the Brazilian Ministry for Agriculture, Industry, and Commerce – conducted a survey on the rural conditions prevailing in Brazil. Besides agro-ecological and socio-economic data, the survey also collected information on the types of labour contracts employed in each county and the average remunerations for various labour categories.[61] Unquestionably, this source has many shortcomings, particularly in its lack of clear definitions for the various labour categories. Notwithstanding, its data provide us with a unique overview of the various labour contracts that prevailed at the beginning of the twentieth century.

In table 1, we categorised the labour-rental contracts registered for the state of São Paulo. Please notice that the term "entries" in the notes accompanying the table refers to the number of times that a labour-rental arrangement was listed in the source and not to the number of counties where it prevailed, as most municipalities had more than one single arrangement listed. While they lacked a standardised methodology for listing the contracts, the *Inspectore* used an erratic combination of three categories to list the agricultural labour systems prevailing in a county. The type of labourer and the frequency of payment were registered in most cases, which allowed us to divide the table into two columns. Column A registers the categories of labourers (*camarada, colono, meeiro*, etc.), while Column B does not stipulate the type of contract, but the frequency of payment. Moreover, the *Inspectore* frequently mentioned some specific tasks or features of the contract (for instance, *colonos* who worked at a piece rate or in the cultivation of specific crops).

Even if unsurprising, a striking feature shown by Table 12.1 is the variability in labour-rental arrangements per category of worker and per frequency of payments, as well as the number of their possible combinations. As we

---

60   Stolcke and Hall, "Introduction," 179; Martins, "A imigração espanhola," 20–22; and Viotti da Costa, *Da senzala à colônia*, 240.
61   Brazil, Ministério da Agricultura, Indústria e Commércio. Serviço de Inspecção e Desfesa Agrícolas, *Questionários sobre as condições da agricultura dos 173 municípios do Estado de S. Paulo* (Rio de Janeiro: Serviço de Estatística; Inspectoria do 14º Districto, 1913), iii – vi.

TABLE 12.1   Summary of rural labour arrangements in the counties of São Paulo, 1910–1912

Column A: per category of labourer			Column B: per frequency of payment		
	Entries	%		Entries	%
Parceria	13	2.7	Contracts	62	12.68
			Yearly contracts	4	0.82
Meação	41	8.4			
Meação under contract	7	1.4	Payments by "*jornal*"	81	16.56
Meação colono	1	0.2	Daily payments (*diária*)	51	10.43
Meação empreiteiro	1	0.2	"*Jornal*" per month	5	1.02
			Monthly payments	5	1.02
Empreitada	121	27.7	"*Jornal*" per year	4	0.82
Empreitada under contract	8	1.64			
Empreitada to clear forests	1	0.20	Salaries	12	2.45
Empreitada to form plantations	1	0.20	Daily salaries	14	2.86
			Monthly salaries	4	0.82
Colono paid per year or pruning	11	2.25	Yearly salaries	2	0.41
Colono under contract	6	1.23			
Colono under contract and per year	3	0.61			
Colono under *empreitadas*	1	0.20			
Colono in coffee cultivation	1	0.20			
Colono in sugar cane cultivation	1	0.20			
Camarada per day or by "*jornal*"	17	3.5			
Camarada paid by salary	1	0.2			
Camarada per month	10	2.0			

TABLE 12.1   Summary of rural labour arrangements in the counties of São Paulo (*cont.*)

Notes: (1) 46 entries that mentioned "*etc.*" to indicate other arrangements were not included in the totals to compute the percentages of each entry; (2) Entries "*trato por ano*" and "*trato por mez*" (caring for a crop per month and per year) were included in the categories "*Jornal per month*" and "*Jornal per year*"; (3) "*Parceria*" and "*meação*" refer to sharecropping and mechanisms of crop-sharing, respectively, without stipulating if these were labour or land-rental contracts; (4) "*Contracto*" presupposes the existence of a legally binding contractual instrument; (5) "*Camaradas*" refer to service providers, usually individuals working per piece rate, but who could also be employed per time, as other rows indicate; (6) "*Empreitada*" was usually an agricultural task executed by a rural labourer (the "*empreiteiro*"); (7) "*Jornal*" is the payment for time worked (a "*jornada*"), which – as the entries indicate – could be daily (*DIÁRIA*), monthly or yearly.
SOURCE: COMPILED BY THE AUTHORS BASED ON BRAZIL (1913). PLEASE NOTICE THAT THE CATEGORISATIONS IN TABLE 1 ARE THOSE OF THE AUTHORS, NOT OF THE ORIGINAL SOURCE; ALL TABULATIONS ARE AVAILABLE UPON REQUEST

have stressed throughout, contractual mix characterised the rural economy of São Paulo since the very first introduction of sharecropping in the 1840s.[62] By the early twentieth century – with rapidly expanding agricultural frontiers – this complexity had certainly not diminished. Indeed, one sees no dominant contractual category among those listed in Table 12.1. The most frequently mentioned category was that of the *empreiteiros*, who executed tasks per piece rate (the so-called *empreitadas*), most frequently at their own risk. Nonetheless, even this category appeared only in approximately 30 per cent of the entries, with eight cases simply mentioning that their work was regulated by a "contract" and one even indicating that *colonists* executed tasks under *empreitadas.*

Somewhat more surprising is the relatively small number of *colono* arrangements listed in the survey. It is likely that many *colonos* in this survey were subsumed within the generic category of people working under "contracts" and "yearly contracts."

The *Inspectore* also listed two types of contracts that had explicit crop-sharing features. First, sharecropping (*parceria*) appeared explicitly in thirteen counties, but only made up 2.67 per cent of all arrangements listed. Second, *meeiros* and *meação* contracts were present in forty-eight counties of São Paulo and corresponded to 10.21 per cent of all arrangements listed. The term

---

62   Dean, *Rio Claro*, 96; and Lamounier, *Formas de transição*, 25.

"*meação*" refers to mechanisms of crop-sharing, but these arrangements could also refer to tenants, as was the case for the municipality of Campinas, for which the source mentions: "a few *meeiros* take care of some properties, having the rights to two-thirds of the production."

Before advancing, a word of caution is due. Even a superficial reading of the Inspectorate's survey reveals that many other labour-rental arrangements were employed on the farms but were not listed in the survey, probably because it was impossible for the *Inspectore* to cover all the farms in the regions they visited – some of which were extremely vast and difficult to reach. For forty-six out of the 173 counties of São Paulo, the published results mentioned "etc." after the last labour-rental arrangement listed, that is, the source stopped short of mentioning all "labour systems" being used in those regions (which also calls into question the completeness of the other counties). Moreover, there were internal inconsistencies in the source. For instance, under the rubric "labour systems," the *colono* contract was listed for twenty-two counties; however, this type of contract was mentioned in thirty-three counties under the heading "salaries."[63] Thus, the reader should consider the data above with caution: the survey illustrates the complex contractual mix prevailing at the beginning of the 1910s in broad strokes, but it does not provide a final picture of all labour arrangements prevailing in a particular locality, which can be gained only through the study of contracts prevailing in specific regions – the theme of the rest of this section.

Determining why crop-sharing arrangements prevailed in certain localities is a complex issue that this chapter will not deal with. Nonetheless, figure 1 shows the geographic spread of the *parceria* and *meação* contracts mentioned above across the counties of São Paulo in the early 1910s.

By discussing how contracts changed as part of a learning process that, in many cases, can be traced back to the first experiences with non-captive labour, we will see how the sample of contracts researched for the 1910s–1930s had become increasingly more detailed.[64] Notwithstanding, we warn against three misinterpretations regarding the concept of "learning" in contractual design. First, "learning" does not necessarily imply *linearity*. Indeed, many experiences in the twentieth century paralleled problems already faced in the mid-nineteenth century. Second, while the coffee economy was the motor of the Brazilian economy, the state of São Paulo had different regions in terms of

---

63   Not reported to save space. All compiled data are available upon request.
64   Faleiros, *Fonteiras do café*.

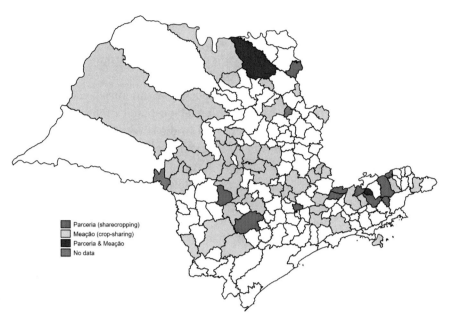

FIGURE 12.1 Sharecropping crop-sharing mechanisms across counties of São Paulo 1910–1912
Notes: (1) Municipal frontiers from 1911; (2) Missing data for Salto *Grande do Paranapanema* and *Ibiquara*
SOURCE: SAME AS IN TABLE 1, COMPILED PER COUNTY, INSTEAD OF BY NUMBER OF ENTRIES

rural specialisation.[65] Technical conditions dictated by different crops influenced contractual adoption. Finally, the contractual mix in the state implies feedback effects between different arrangements.[66] As such, sharecropping not only influenced other labour arrangements, but was also influenced by them.

With these remarks in mind, the most important feature of sharecropping and *colonato* contracts signed in the early twentieth century – in many cases under the supervision of state organisations, such as the *Patronato Agrícola* – was their level of detail when it came to settling disputes. Landowners attempted to stipulate more clearly in the contracts the behaviour they expected from labourers. For most of the nineteenth century, sharecropping contracts had determined that labourers should accept the extra-contractual bylaws of the

---

65   For a recent review of this theme, see Renato P. Colistete, "Regiões e especialização na agricultura cafeeira: São Paulo no início do século XX," *Revista Brasileira de Economia* 69, no. 3 (July – September 2015): 331–54.

66   Eswaran and Kotwal, "Theory."

farms where they lived. Although written regulations did exist on the largest and most important plantations, on the smaller and less well-organised farms written regulations were less important than the will of the landowners or patronage practices.[67] Many of the stipulations in the bylaws were incorporated into the contracts themselves at the beginning of the twentieth century. Concretely, this implied an increase in the number of punitive clauses against what farmers considered misbehaviour. For instance, a farm in the county of Pirajuí stipulated that "recidivism of abuses and insubordination against the discipline on the farm" – broadly defined – were sufficient for expelling a family without monetary compensation.[68] In the county of Novo Horizonte, a 1928 contract returned to a question that had been controversial at least since the Sharecropper's Riot, namely the discretionary power of the landowner, "during week days," to impede the entrance onto his property of anybody whom he judged improper. The same contract dealt with the recurrent problem of labour mobility and turnover: the *meeiro* was not allowed to work for anybody else if his/her tasks were not in accordance with the "good rules" of agricultural production.[69]

In a similar vein, contracts started to distinguish their various dimensions more clearly. Following a trend that had begun in the 1870s, farmers attempted to establish clearer regulations regarding the leasing of plots of land for labourers' subsistence cultivation within the farms.[70] The labour-related aspects of the contracts also started to be set out more precisely, mainly via clearer stipulations of the remunerations for each task performed by the workers, probably as a form to diminish their bargaining power between agricultural seasons.

As noted in Section 3, adding side payments to sharecropping contracts diminished the uncertainties surrounding labourers' annual remuneration. The labour dimension of sharecropping combined with peonage was risky, as the amortisation of the debt depended on the annual harvest, which was subjected to unpredictable natural conditions and economic oscillations in a number of markets. Certainly, sharecropping could generate extraordinary gains if coffee prices increased, but the reverse was also true.[71] Using data from

---

67   Lamounier, *Formas de transição*, 32–33, 40–48; Viotti da Costa, *Da senzala à colônia*, 272–74 and Witzel de Souza, "Liberdade ou grilhões?" 42, 96–97.

68   Livro de Notas n. 35, fl. 56. 2° Ofício Civil de Pirajuí, 28 November 1927.

69   Livro de Notas n. 22, fl. 156. 2° Ofício Civil de Novo Horizonte, 28 September 1928.

70   Pedro G. Tosi, Rogério Naques Faleiros, and Rodrigo da Silva Teodoro, "Crédito e pequena cafeicultura no Oeste Paulista: Franca/SP 1890–1914," *Revista Brasileira de Economia* 61, no. 3 (July – Sept. 2007): 405–26.

71   Dean, *Rio Claro*, 117.

Ribeirão Preto and Franca, Rogério Faleiros showed that sharecropping could lead to a negative variation in labour remuneration of about 35.2 per cent, while variations in *empreitadas* reached a mere 1.7 per cent.[72] As such, the mixed form of sharecropping with side payments provided a middle ground for the trade-off between expected gains and contractual risks.

A number of sharecropping contracts also started to stipulate shares that varied according to short-term junctures. In 1929, farmer João Pires Monteiro set a remuneration floor for his sharecropper: profit sharing would take place only if the price of coffee was above a certain threshold (20 *mil-réis* per *arroba*); otherwise, the labourer would pocket the yields.[73] A similar principle was applied on Figueira farm in 1919 following the 1918 frost that had severely damaged the coffee trees. The farmer set a quantity floor: a household would be entitled to one hundred per cent of the profit if the amount harvested was lower than one thousand *arrobas*; at that exact level, the family would receive two-thirds of the profit; the usual fifty-fifty share applied only if the quantity produced by the household surpassed that threshold. In 1919, farmer Vicente Ferreira applied crop-sharing for two agricultural products, setting a different floor for each. For cotton, the fifty-fifty share would be applied only if the price reached a minimum of 10 *mil-réis* per *arroba*. For coffee, the farmer stipulated a complex system of varying shares: given the expected low productivity of new coffee trees, households would earn one hundred per cent of the profit from trees younger than three years; the fifty-fifty share would apply only from the fourth year onwards – and it seems that this contract had a fixed duration.[74] Naturally, not all farmers were as responsive to labourers' demands for more security in moments of crisis, as was illustrated by a 1920 *empreitada* contract that dictated that labourers would receive no compensation for the coffee trees lost in the 1918 frost, putting the entire burden of the risk of natural disasters on the shoulders of the labourers.[75]

In a similar vein, one notices a preoccupation in defining the participation of each contracting party in the costs of processing and transporting the produce; if labourers were expected to participate in the sharing of costs, contracts now meticulously defined such operations and the size of the side payments.[76]

---

72   See in particular Faleiros, *Fonteiras do café*, 185, 240–42, 305, 396–400, 446–51.

73   Livro de Notas n. 184, fls. 24. 2° Ofício Civil de Franca, 18 September 1933.

74   Livro de Notas n. 14A, fls. 126. 2° Ofício Civil de Araraquara, 11 September 1918.

75   Livro de Notas n.107, fls. 76. 2° Ofício Civil de Jaú, 5 April 1920.

76   For clarity, we are not arguing that the first changes in the Vergueiro system in 1851 *caused* the adoption of those clauses later on. The proposition of side payments to substitute for crop-sharing as a mechanism of cost division was an answer to productive conditions. Nonetheless, that change was part of a learning process that persisted.

To illustrate, in 1918, the proprietors of Reunidas Irmãos Camargo farm, in the county of São Carlos, still charged a side payment of 400 réis per *arroba* of harvested coffee as the labourers' contribution to the processing of the beans – the fact that this amount was identical to that specified in the Vergueiro system is by chance, we assume. A 1935 contract from the county of Jaú also determined that a side payment should be made, but updated the prices and added another 1,000 réis for a general category of expenses.[77] Interestingly, another farmer in the same municipality felt the need to stipulate contractually that the processing of the beans must occur on the farm where they had been harvested, suggesting that transportation costs in the 1930s had fallen sufficiently to allow labourers to process their harvests in different farms or localities.[78]

Of course, not all forms of clearer contractual specification meant improvements in actual labour relations. Ironically, in one of the contracts found, the tendency to incorporate more detailed clauses was actually used to increase the discretionary power of the landowner. In 1925, in an *empreitada* for the planting of new coffee trees, a farmer in the municipality of Novo Horizonte determined a weekly period when labourers had to work for the maintenance and repair of his property, without remuneration.[79] This had been a thorny issue since the 1850s. In the past, due to ingrained patron-client relations, it had been unimaginable to landowners that labourers would dare to refuse to execute a task because it was not established in a contractual relation; but to the outrage of many farmers, this was precisely what happened. To circumvent this problem, the 1852 contract by Senator Souza Queiroz had outlined a list of tasks that labourers should execute – such as maintaining the water pipelines used for washing coffee beans.[80] The Central Association for Colonisation discussed this contractual response in 1854 and determined that sharecroppers should not be employed in other tasks than those they had been hired for.[81] It is remarkable that seven decades later, with slavery gone and mass immigration settled, one landowner stipulated a clause that, in practice, meant a return to his discretionary power on how to allocate labour within his farm.

---

77   Livro de Notas n. 218, fl. 11. 2° Ofício Civil de Jaú, 16 November 1935.
78   Livro de Notas n. 196, fl. 56. 2° Ofício Civil de Jaú, 28 November 1931. See also an *empreitada contract* signed in the county of São José do Rio Preto, in 1935, which stipulated higher fees charged over charts that did not belong to the farm – Livro de Notas n. 215, fl. 21. 2° Ofício Civil de Jaú, 27 July 1935.
79   Livro de Notas n.08, fl. 2556. 2° Ofício Civil de Novo Horizonte, 6 July 1925.
80   Witzel de Souza, "Liberdade ou grilhões?" 105.
81   Lamounier, *Formas de transição*, 51.

5   Concluding Remarks

The ubiquity of sharecropping as a labour-rental arrangement that for long has been considered less efficient than other available options is a theme that has fascinated generations of historians and social scientists. This chapter touched upon some of these debates by revisiting a classic historiography that deals with the adoption and evolution of sharecropping contracts in the plantations of São Paulo, Brazil, where sharecropping was the first relatively successful arrangement to make use of non-captive labour, usually foreign-born, in the early transition from slavery to free labour.

The first part of the chapter studied the multidimensionality of the original sharecropping contract in the coffee plantations of São Paulo. The Vergueiro system – as it was known by contemporaries – included a *labour dimension* that involved the sharing of profits from coffee harvesting; a *cost-sharing* mechanism for processing the coffee beans; a *land-rental* dimension for the crop-sharing of subsistence goods; and a form of *credit interlinkage* that allowed for the immigration of poor and otherwise credit-constrained Europeans. In its second part, the chapter discussed how problems with the enforcement of free labour relations led to contractual refinements at the beginning of the twentieth century – a process that was not exempt from many drawbacks. Particularly important was the incorporation of side payments into crop-sharing contracts, which lowered the uncertainties of the contracting parties.

By linking the periods of experimentation with non-captive labour (1840s–1870s) to that of consolidated mass immigration (1900s–1930s), this chapter discussed the history of contractual design within an institutionalist framework, highlighting the importance of path dependence for understanding contractual choice and enforcement. Moreover, this study aimed to show the variety of arrangements that have coexisted even in geographically narrow spaces. The evidence shows that rural labour relations are complex now and that there is no reason to hypothesise that they were simpler in the past. Adding new pieces to this already immense puzzle might blur some pictures we currently have of historical contractual design, but it will certainly contribute to a more accurate depiction of past labour-rental relations.

Bibliography

Acemoglu, Daron, and Alexander Wolitzky. "The Economics of Labor Coercion." *Econometrica* 79, no. 2 (March 2011): 555–600.

Alston, Lee J., and Joseph P. Ferrie. "Labor Costs, Paternalism, and Loyalty in Southern Agriculture: A Constraint on the Growth of the Welfare State." *The Journal of Economic History* 45, no. 1 (March 1985): 95–117.

Bardhan, Pranab K. "Interlocking Factor Markets and Agrarian Development: A Review of Issues." *Oxford Economic Papers, New Series* 32, no. 1 (March 1980): 82–98.

Bassanezi, Maria Silvia C. B. *Colonos do café.* 1st ed. São Paulo: Editora Contexto, 2019.

Beiguelman, Paula. "A destruição do escravismo capitalista." *Revista de História* 34, no. 69 (March 1967): 149–60.

Braverman, Avishay, and Thirukodikaval Nilakanta Srinivasan. "Credit and Sharecropping in Agrarian Societies." *Journal of Development Economics* 9 (1981): 289–312.

Braverman, Avishay, and Joseph E. Stiglitz. "Sharecropping and the Interlinking of Agrarian Markets." *The American Economic Review* 72, no. 4 (September 1982): 695–715.

Buarque de Holanda, Sérgio. "Prefácio do tradutor." In Thomas Davatz, *Memórias de um Colono no Brasil (1850)*. São Paulo: Martins Fontes, [1858] 1941.

Byres, Terence J. "Historical Perspectives on Sharecropping." In "Sharecropping and Sharecroppers," edited by Terence J. Byres, special issue, *The Journal of Peasant Studies* 10, nos. 2–3 (January/April 1983): 7–40.

Byres, Terence J., ed. "Sharecropping and Sharecroppers." Special issue, *The Journal of Peasant Studies* 10, nos. 2–3 (January/April 1983).

Câmara, Benedita. "The Portuguese Civil Code and the *Colonia* Tenancy Contract in Madeira (1867–1967)." *Continuity and Change* 21, no. 2 (October 2006): 213–33.

Canstatt, Oskar. *Brasilien: Land und Leute.* Berlin: Ernst Siegfried Mittler und Sohn, 1877.

Canstatt, Oskar. *Das republikanische Brasilien in Vergangenheit und Gegenwart: Nach den neuesten amtlichen Quellen und auf Grund eigener Anschauung.* Leipzig: Ferdinand Hirt & Sohn, 1899.

Carmona Juan, and James Simpson. "The 'Rabassa Morta' in Catalan Viticulture: The Rise and Decline of a Long-Term Sharecropping Contract, 1670s–1920s." *The Journal of Economic History* 59 (June 1999): 290–315.

Carmona Juan, and James Simpson. "Explaining Contract Choice: Vertical Coordination, Sharecropping, and Wine in Europe, 1850–1950." *The Economic History Review* 65, no. 3 (August 2012): 887–909.

Colistete, Renato P. "Regiões e especialização na agricultura cafeeira: São Paulo no início do século XX." *Revista Brasileira de Economia* 69, no. 3 (July – September 2015): 331–54.

Conrad, Robert. "The Planter Class and the Debate over Chinese Immigration to Brazil, 1850–1893." *International Migration Review* 9, no. 1 (Spring 1975): 41–55.

Corrêa do Lago, Luiz A. *Da escravidão ao trabalho livre: Brasil, 1550–1900.* 1st ed. São Paulo: Companhia das letras, 2014.

Cruz Paiva, Odair da, and Soraya Moura. *Hospedaria dos imigrantes de São Paulo*. São Paulo: Editora Paz e Terra, Coleção São Paulo no Bolso, 2008.

Davatz, Thomas. *Memórias de um Colono no Brasil (1850)*. São Paulo: Martins Fontes, [1858] 1941.

Dean, Warren. *Rio Claro: Um sistema Brasileiro de grande lavoura, 1820–1920*. Rio de Janeiro: Editora Paz e Terra, 1977.

Dutot, S. *France et Brésil*. Paris: Garnier Frères, Libraires-Éditeurs, 1859.

Engerman, Stanley. L. "Contract Labor, Sugar, and Technology in the Nineteenth Century." *The Journal of Economic History* 43, no. 3 (September 1983): 635–59.

Eswaran, Mukesh, and Ashok Kotwal. "A Theory of Contractual Structure in Agriculture." *The American Economic Review* 75, no. 3 (June 1985), 352–67.

Faleiros, Rogério N. *Fonteiras do café: Fazendeiros e colonos no interior paulista (1917–1937)*. Bauru: Edusc, FAPESP, 2010.

Faleiros, Rogério N. "A fazenda Pau d'Alho de Campinas: As cadernetas como registros da contabilidade dos 'colonos' (1927–1931)." *História e Economia* 8 (January 2011): 79–94.

Garrido, Samuel. "Sharecropping Was Sometimes Efficient: Sharecropping with Compensation for Improvements in European Viticulture." *The Economic History Review* 70, no. 3 (August 2017): 977–1003.

Garrido, Samuel, and Salvador Calatayud. "The Price of Improvements: Agrarian Contracts and Agrarian Development in Nineteenth-Century Eastern Spain." *The Economic History Review* 64, no. 2 (May 2011): 598–620.

Heflinger, Jr., José Eduardo. *Ibicaba: O berço da imigração Européia de cunho particular/Ibicaba: Die Wiege der privat Organisierten Europäischen Einwanderung*. Limeira: Unigráfica, 2007.

Heflinger, Jr., José Eduardo. *A Revolta dos Parceiros na Ibicaba/The Rebellion of the Sharecroppers in Ibicaba*. Limeira: Editora Unigráfica, 2009.

Holloway, Thomas H. "Creating the Reserve Army? The Immigration Program of São Paulo, 1886–1930." *The International Migration Review* 12, no 2 (1978): 187–209.

Ianni, Octavio. "O progresso econômico e o trabalhador livre." In *História geral da civilização Brasileira*. Part II, vol. 5, *O Brasil monárquico: Reações e transações*, edited by Sérgio Buarque de Holanda and Pedro Moacyr Campo, 350–74. Rio de Janeiro: Bertrand Brasil, 2004.

Kidder, Daniel, and James C. Fletcher. *Brazil and the Brazilians, Portrayed in Historical and Descriptive Sketches*. Philadelphia: Childs & Peterson, 1857.

Kotwal, Ashok. "The Role of Consumption Credit in Agricultural Tenancy." *Journal of Development Economics* 18, nos. 2–3 (1985): 273–95.

Lamberg, Moritz. *Brasilien: Land und Leute in ethischer, politischer und volkswirtschaftlicher Beziehung und Entwicklung; Erlebnisse, Studien und Erfahrungen während eines zwanzigjährigen Aufenthaltes*. Leipzig: Verlag von Hermann Zieger, 1899.

Lamounier, Maria. L. "Formas de transição da escravidão ao trabalho livre: A Lei de Locação de Serviços de 1879." Master's thesis, Universidade Estadual de Campinas, 1986.

Levy, Maria Stella F. "O papel da imigração internacional na evolução da população brasileira (1872 a 1972)." Supplement, *Revista de Saúde Pública* 8 (1974): 49–90.

Macedo, Joaquim Manuel de. *Notions de Chorographie du Brésil.* Translated by J. F. Halbout. Leipzig: Imprimerie de F. A. Brockhaus, 1873.

Martins, José de S. *O cativeiro da terra.* 9th ed. São Paulo: Editora Contexto, 2010.

Martins, José de S. "A imigração espanhola para o Brasil e a formação da força-de-trabalho na economia cafeeira: 1880–1930." *Revista de História* 121 (1989): 5–26.

Menezes e Souza, João Cardoso de. *Theses sobre colonização do Brazil: Projecto de solução as questões sociaes, que se prendem a este difícil problema; Relatório apresentado ao Ministério da Agricultura, Commercio e Obras Publicas em 1873.* Rio de Janeiro: Typographia Nacional, 1875.

Ministério da Agricultura, Indústria e Commércio. Serviço de Inspecção e Desfesa Agrícolas. *Questionários sobre as condições da agricultura dos 173 municípios do Estado de S. Paulo.* Rio de Janeiro: Serviço de Estatística; Inspectoria do 14º Districto, 1913.

Monteiro, Rosane C. M. "Regiões esquecidas da história: Um estudo sobre a organização da mão-de-obra em fazendas do oeste paulista no período de transição." *História Econômica & História de Empresas* 2 (August 2012): 29–52.

Mukherjee, Anindita, and Debraj Ray. "Labor Tying." *Journal of Development Economics* 47, no. 2 (1995): 207–39.

Mulhern, Joseph M. "British Entanglement with Brazilian Slavery." PhD diss., Durham University, 2018.

Otsuka, Keijiro, Hiroyuki Chuma, and Yujiro Hayami. "Land and Labor Contracts in Agrarian Economies: Theories and Facts." *Journal of Economic Literature* 30, no. 4 (December 1992): 1965–2018.

Perret-Gentil, Charles. *A Colônia Senador Vergueiro.* Santos: Typographia Imparcial, 1851.

Premchander, Smita, V. Prameela, and M. Chidambaranathan. *Prevention and Elimination of Bonded Labour: The Potential and Limits of Microfinance-Led Approaches.* Geneva: ILO Employment Sector, 2015.

Quibria, Muhammad Ghulam, and Salim Rashid. "The Puzzle of Sharecropping: A Survey of Theories." *World Development* 12, no. 2 (February 1984): 103–14.

Reid, Joseph D. "Sharecropping in History and Theory." *Agricultural History* 49, no. 2 (April 1975): 426–40.

Ribeyrolles, Charles, and Victor Frond. *Brazil Pittoresco: Historia – Descripções – Viagens – Instituições – Colonisação; Acompanhado de um álbum de vistas, panoramas, paisagens, costumes etc. etc.* Vol. 3. Rio de Janeiro: Typographia Nacional, 1859.

Santos-Barreto, M. P. dos, and Émile de Laveleye. *Voyages et études: Les Blancs au Brésil ; Actualités du Brésil, sa colonisation par la race blanche, les forets vierges et le far-west, religion, politique, progrès et avenir de ce pays.* Rio de Janeiro: Typographia da Gazeta; Paris: Gernier, frères, éditeurs; Louvain: D. A. Peeters-Ruelens, 1881.

Schmid, Fernando. *Über Handel und Wandel in Brasilien: Journalistische Skizzen; Expedition der "Allgemeinen Deutschen Zeitung für Brasilien".* Rio de Janeiro: Buchdruckerei von Lorenz Winter, 1881.

Siriani, Sílvia C. L. "Os descaminhos da imigração alemã para São Paulo no século XIX – aspectos políticos." *Almanack Braziliense* 2 (November 2005): 91–100.

Stolcke, Verena, and Michael M. Hall. "The Introduction of Free Labour on São Paulo Coffee Plantations." *The Journal of Peasant Studies* 10, nos. 2–3 (January/April 1983): 170–200.

Tessari, Cláudia A. "Sazonalidade e trabalho temporário na empresa cafeeira (oeste paulista, 1890–1915)." *História Econômica & História de Empresas* 14, no. 2 (2011): 105–43.

Tosi, Pedro G., Rogério N. Faleiros, and Rodrigo da Silva Teodoro. "Crédito e pequena cafeicultura no Oeste Paulista: Franca/SP 1890–1914." *Revista Brasileira de Economia* 61, no. 3 (July–Sept. 2007): 405–26.

Tschudi, Johann Jakob. *Viagem às Províncias do Rio de Janeiro e S. Paulo.* São Paulo: Livraria Martins Editora; Coleção Biblioteca Histórica Paulista, [1866] 1953.

Vangelista, Chiara. *Os braços da lavoura: Imigrantes e caipiras na formação do mercado de trabalho paulista (1850–1930).* São Paulo: Hucitec, 1991.

Viotti da Costa, Emília. *Da senzala à colônia.* 4th ed. São Paulo: Fundação Editora da UNESP, 1998.

Witter, José Sebastião. *Ibicaba: Uma experiência pioneira.* 2nd ed. São Paulo: Arquivo do Estado, 1982.

Witzel de Souza, Bruno G. "Liberdade ou grilhões? Um estudo dos contratos de parceria à luz da imigração Germânica em São Paulo, 1840–1870." Bachelor's thesis, Universidade de São Paulo, 2011.

Witzel de Souza, Bruno G. "From Bonded Laborers to Educated Citizens? Immigration, Labor Markets, and Human Capital in São Paulo, Brazil (1820–2010)." PhD diss., University of Göttingen, 2019.

Witzel de Souza, Bruno G., and Leonardo A. Santin Gardenal. "Households' Labor Income, Credit, and Expenditures in a Brazilian Plantation (Ibicaba, 1890–1950)." Working paper, Mimeo, 2018.

Yang, Alexander C. Y. "O comércio dos 'coolie' (1819–1920)." *Revista de História* 112 (1977): 419–28.

PART 3

State Intervention and Agricultural Labour Mobility

∴

CHAPTER 13

Vulnerability beyond Revolutions

Rural Workers, Former Slaves and Indentured Migrants in the French Empire

Alessandro Stanziani

In 1834, a society for the abolition of slavery, connected to the British associations, was created in Paris. Led by Duke Victor de Broglie, the French society encouraged legislative reforms, manumission and limited recognition of civil rights for *gens de couleurs*.[1] Several pamphlets and studies produced by parliamentary commissions summarised the long-standing debate over the comparative efficiency of wage labour versus slavery.[2] Contrasting estimates were produced, with some claiming the profitability of slavery and others challenging it. At the same time, new considerations arose: the profitability of slavery was said to be demonstrable only for the individual planter, but not for the "nation." Two main positions emerged; for some, slavery was an ethical and religious affair more than an economic issue. In response to this argument, anti-abolitionists replied that Africans would suffer famine if left in Africa; slavery was openly declared to be a humanitarian project.

In 1838, a new commission was set up, chaired by Alexis de Tocqueville; he produced a final report, using an enormous amount of statistical data to establish the need for immediate emancipation. Tocqueville justified this conclusion by pointing out that gradual emancipation would require special rules for a particular group of labouring people, with the attendant risk of social tensions. Instead, a general emancipation would simplify the issue. Tocqueville added some ordinary considerations about slaves' lack of motivation and low productivity. He also criticised the British solution of an apprenticeship period, which he saw as the source of undue abuses by planters and thus of social conflict.[3] In 1842, Victor Schoelcher submitted a detailed plan for abolition in which he assigned a central role to the "association principle," allowing groups of freed

---

1 "*Gens de couleurs*" was the term used for all free non-whites, that is, former slaves or non-whites born as free.

2 Adolphe Granier de Cassagnac, *De l'émancipation des esclaves: Lettre à M. de Lamartine* (Paris: Delloye, 1840).

3 Alexis de Tocqueville, *Rapport fait au nom de la commission chargée d'examiner la proposition de M. de Tracy relative aux colonies, 1839 in Œuvres completes*, vol. 3 (Paris: Gallimard, 1962).

slaves to form an association with their former masters and share the profits.[4] In 1843, the De Broglie Commission finally published three volumes of its minutes and criticised the idea of ownership of slaves as a natural right. This was acceptable for other kinds of property, but not for human beings. But it also added a new insight: the need for the strict regulation of free labour: once freed, former slaves had to be put under surveillance and strictly regulated.

In the end, the Commission opposed immediate abolition and suggested two alternative, gradual forms of emancipation, one that would take place over ten years, and another that would take place over twenty years. Opinions were also divided over the amount of compensation owed to slave owners and who should pay it.[5] In response, Schoelcher and the other abolitionist leaders intensified their action. In 1844–1845, they gained the support of workers' associations, which sent several massive petitions to the government demanding the immediate abolition of slavery. A cautious law was, therefore, adopted in 1845, encouraging manumission and the gradual purchase of freedom by slaves themselves. The slave was granted legal capacities and could, therefore, own movable and fixed property. However, this approach soon ran up against a swiftly evolving situation in the colonies as well as in France. In 1846–1847, in the West Indies, several thousands of slaves escaped from French to British islands (five thousand from Guyana to Trinidad, two thousand of whom reached their destination, and one thousand from Guadeloupe to Dominica). Planters spoke of on-going transformation through voluntary manumission under the law of 1845 and the introduction of machines and free indentured immigrants. Such an evolution would take time and legislators concluded that immediate abolition would put an end to this positive process. Nevertheless, strong state support was required to promote these dynamics.[6] Social tensions also escalated in France itself: artisans complained of increasing difficulties and urban workers protested against low wages, long working days and unstable employment. In 1847, strikes intensified in Paris and France.

We are thus confronted with a relatively well-known historical dynamic: elites were keen to support the abolition of slavery, but only on the long term and with due compensation to slave owners. Meanwhile, social unrest took the lead and pushed towards more radical politics. What was the outcome of these tensions?

---

4   Victor Schoelcher, *Des colonies françaises: Abolition immédiate de l'esclavage* (Paris: CTHS, [1842] 1998).

5   M. Jollivet, *La Commission présidée par M. le duc de Broglie et les gouverneurs de nos colonies, théorie et pratique* (Paris: Imprimerie De Boulé, 1843).

6   Général Ambert, *Abolition de l'esclavage* (Paris: Imprimerie de Guirodet et Jouaust, 1848).

Immediately after the Parisian uprising in February 1848, commissions on the abolition of slavery were formed in March and April. Led by Schoelcher, the commission advocated the immediate abolition of slavery, entitling all manumitted slaves to become French citizens. There were discussions concerning compensation for slave owners and a possible period of apprenticeship – the majority of the commission was favourable to both.[7] Meanwhile, another commission was settled to discuss the reform of labour in France. The connections between the parliamentary commissions on slavery and on labour were crucial. Several topics were common to both, including the organisation of legal courts to handle labour disputes, pensions for the infirm and the elderly, national workshops (*ateliers*), the control and punishment of vagrancy, and the length of working days. Strangely enough, at first sight, the decrees established a relation between rural workers in France, former slaves and new indentured immigrants in France's colonies. In both rural areas and the colonies, *prud'hommes* (industrial or labour tribunals) were not allowed, and justices of peace (rural low courts) were supposed to replace them.[8] Second, the worker's booklet (*livret ouvrier*), an instrument to control workers' mobility in France but which was unevenly enforced on the mainland, was introduced in the colonies in order to control "vagrancy." At the same time, a bill suggested extending the booklet to agricultural labourers; however, the measure failed to pass.

Here, a number of interesting questions arise: why did revolutionary France abolish slavery but keep former slaves and new immigrants under strong coercion and unfair rights, while criticising the British for doing so? And why were emancipated slaves and rural workers on the mainland regulated by similar rules?

These questions are tied to broader questions about the abolitionist process and revolution: countless comparisons have been made between French and British abolitionism,[9] mostly stressing the hesitant and ambiguous attitude of

---

7   ANOM (French Colonial Archives), Généralités 162 d. 1326, "Comptes rendus des séances de la Commission d'abolition de l'esclavage."

8   Jean-Claude Farcy, "Les archives méconnues de la justice civile," in *Histoire et archives: L'histoire contemporaine et les usages des archives judiciaires (1800–1939)*, ed. Frédéric Chauvaud and Jacques-Guy Petit (Paris: Champion, 1998), 397–408.

9   Robin Blackburn, *The Making of New World Slavery: From the Baroque to the Modern, 1492–1800* (London: Verso, 1998); Seymour Drescher, *Capitalism and Antislavery: British Mobilization in Comparative Perspective* (New York and Oxford: Oxford University Press, 1987); David Brion Davis, *The Problem of Slavery in the Age of Revolution, 1770–1823* (New York: Oxford University Press, 1999); Marcel Dorigny, ed, *Les abolitions de l'esclavage* (Saint-Denis: Presses Universitaires de Vincennes, 1995); Yves Benot, *La révolution française et la fin des colonies* (Paris: La Découverte, 2004); Lawrence Jennings,

the French. This chapter offers a complementary view, by arguing that the limits of the revolutionary movement as regards slavery were strongly related to the tensions on labour, and rural labour in France itself in particular. To this end, it will follow the links between indentured migrants, slaves and labourers from the late seventeenth century to the second half of the nineteenth century. This means that it will touch upon not only the revolution of 1848, but it will trace the roots of the ambiguities of this revolution back to the revolution of 1789 and its aftermath. The chapter will not discuss the entire French Empire, but will focus on Réunion Island. Even if some conclusions are common to the Antilles and the Atlantic world, we consider it worth focusing on the Indian Ocean world, where the transmutations of labour in the European colonies were confronted with the extremely blurred boundary between free and unfree labour in the whole area extending from Eastern Africa, to India and Southeast Asia.[10]

1   Beyond 1789: Institutions and Rural Labour in the Colonies, from the Seventeenth to the Mid-nineteenth Century

Like in the British Empire, in the French colonies the contract of *engagement*, or indentured service was developed in the seventeenth century. It was initially intended for white settlers whose transport expenses were advanced by employers or their middlemen in exchange for special commitment to work for several years. The *engagés* were subject to criminal penalties and could be transferred to other masters along with their contract. Owing to the close resemblance between wage earners and domestic servants and the survival of forms of domestic service into the nineteenth century, the contract of *engagement* should not be understood in opposition to these other labour relationships but, rather, as an extension and of them in the colonial situation. If we look at the contracts, then we see that, in France, the agricultural day labourer was supposed to sell exclusive ownership of his time and services to his employer; the sailor's contract extended the duration of this sale with special

---

        French Antislavery: The Movement for the Abolition of Slavery in France, 1802–1848 (Cambridge: Cambridge University Press, 2000); Nelly Schmidt, *Abolitionnistes de l'esclavage et réformateurs des colonies, 1820–1851: Analyses et documents* (Paris: Karthala, 2000).

10   Richard Allen, *European Slave Trade in the Indian Ocean* (Athens, OH: Ohio University Press, 2015); Edward Alpers, *The Indian Ocean in World History* (New York and Oxford: Oxford University Press, 2013); Abdul Sheriff, *The Indian Ocean: Oceanic Connections and the Creation of New Societies* (London: Hurst, 2014).

clauses related to voyage expenses. All these clauses were reproduced in the contract of *engagement*.[11] Moreover, the *engagé* owed his labour to his master who, in exchange, was to teach him about colonial farming.

As in nearby English colonies, during the second half of the seventeenth century an increasing number of African slaves reached the Antilles as well as Mauritius and Réunion Island.[12] In all those cases, however, indentured migrants and slaves coexisted. In the Atlantic, in 1654, two-thirds of the indentured immigrants in Guadeloupe were domestics. In 1671, one-third of the households had no slaves or servants. Half of the households had both slaves and domestic servants. It was only during the second half of the seventeenth century that the proportion of the white population sharply declined. In Guadeloupe, it fell from 80 per cent in 1654 to 50 per cent in 1664 and 39 per cent in 1684. In Martinique, the white population was 51 per cent in 1664 and dropped to 29 per cent in 1678.[13]

In Réunion and Mauritius Islands this was all the more relevant that the use of "*engagés de couleur*" (as they were designated, to stress the importance of race) developed in the eighteenth and even more in the nineteenth century. This immigration was partly linked to the need for artisans (Indian carpenters and masons) but, above all, to the demand for additional labourers at a time when, under pressure from the English, the price of slaves was constantly rising.[14] In the Indian Ocean, the French traded between 334,000 and 384,000 slaves to the Mascarene Islands between 1500 and 1850.[15] In the eighteenth and nineteenth centuries, about 200,000 slaves were imported to Réunion Island for the production of sugar, mostly from Madagascar and East Africa. Indians were also present: in 1708, the total count of adult slaves was 268–197 were men and 71 were women; 20 per cent of the men and 36 per cent of the women were Indians.[16] A century later, they comprised about 3 per cent of the total number of 54,000 slaves.

Race played an important although changing role over time; at the end of the seventeenth century, mixed marriages were extremely common: 67 per cent in 1690. The Royal Declaration of 1698 acknowledged children of mixed couples

---

11   Gabriel Debien, *Les engagés pour les Antilles 1634–1715* (Paris: Société de l'histoire des colonies françaises, 1952), 45.

12   Jean-Marie Fillot, *La traite des esclaves vers les Mascareignes au XVIIIe siècle* (Paris: Orstom, 1974); Sudel Fuma, *L'esclavagisme à la Réunion, 1794–1848* (Paris: Harmattan, 1992).

13   Frédéric Régent, *La France et ses esclaves* (Paris: Grasset 2007), 25.

14   Fillot, *La traite*.

15   Marina Carter, "Indian Slaves in Mauritius (1729–1834)," *Indian Historical Review* 15, nos. 1–2 (1988–1989), 233–47.

16   Fillot, *La traite*.

as French if they were baptised. In 1735, in Saint-Louis and Saint-Pierre, 86 per cent of estate owners were *métis*.[17] This encouraged the rate of manumission, which was relatively high on Réunion Island, in particular in the presence of kinship and family relationships between the master and the slave. As a result, unlike the American colonies, in Réunion "freed coloured people" were not counted until 1767, when most *métis* were classified as white. Here, because of the long tradition of mixed marriages, a person's social condition seemed to be more important than the colour of his or her skin.

Despite this attitude, the Revolution of 1789 and the abolition of slavery in 1794 had a limited impact on Réunion Island. Initially, the implementation of the Revolution encountered serious problems in the colonies where the "freed coloured" requested their full integration in terms of rights, while whites – not only masters and elites but also those from other countries whose rights had just been acknowledged – resisted them. The outcome differed according to place: civil rights were granted to the "freed coloured" in Mauritius, but not in Réunion Island, where they did not win their political rights until 1793.[18] At the end of the day, the abolitionist decree of 1794 was never implemented in Réunion island, where Napoleon had no difficulties in officially proclaiming the restoration of slavery.

In the 1820s as well as under the July Monarchy, two contrasting trends emerged: while in most French colonies manumission and the social conditions of freed slaves improved (in Martinique, freed slaves owned slaves and had trades[19]), there was an increase in illegal slave trafficking to the French West Indies and Réunion Island, partly in reaction to this trend and the mounting difficulties in French colonial production. An estimated forty-five thousand illicit slaves were imported to Réunion Island between 1817 and 1835.[20] A total of about three hundred thousand slaves were imported to the Mascarene archipelago between the eighteenth century and the first half of the nineteenth. Unlike the eighteenth century, East Africa and Mozambique were the main source of supply (60 per cent), with the rest coming from Madagascar (31 per

---

17 Régent, *La France*, 61.
18 Claude Wanquet, *Histoire d'une Révolution: La Réunion, 1789–1803* (Paris: Editions Laffitte, 1980–1984).
19 Fréderic Régent, *Esclavage, métissage, liberté* (Paris: Grasset, 2004).
20 Monica Schuler, "The Recruitment of African Indentured Labourers for European Colonies in the Nineteenth Century," in *Colonialism and Migration: Indentured Labour before and after Slavery,* ed. Pieter Emmer (Dordrecht, Boston and Lancaster: Martinus Nijhoff, 1986), 125–61.

cent) and the countries of southern Asia (9 per cent). These networks were to remain in place after the abolition of slavery.[21]

In Réunion Island, slaves continued to be imported until 1848, when the practice was finally abolished. However, disguised forms of slavery persisted: ships' captains transporting Indians often resorted to fraud, and contracts of *engagement* to Singapore were signed, but the *engagés* ended up being sent to Réunion Island.[22] Moreover, the French colonial administration encouraged the Indian *engagés* to migrate and tried to establish rules that were sufficiently clear to avoid trouble, but they also worried about their actual enforcement.[23] Translating those principles into action remained difficult. During the first half of the 1830s, Indian *engagés* numbered about three thousand.[24] The legal rules in force provided that the *engagés* should receive food, lodging and wages. In practice, however, the employer-landowners seldom complied with the rules. Several riots took place, against planters and, above all against their overlookers.[25]

The Indian *engagés* resisted not only by reducing the amount of work they did and by rioting, but also by taking their cases to court.[26] However, faced with the unfavourable attitude of the magistrates and the administration, Indian *engagés* formed a trade union in which the members with the best mastery of the French language played a highly active role in formulating appeals, intervening with the authorities, and so on.[27] In 1837, the trade union was prohibited.[28]

---

21 Alessandro Stanziani, *Labour in the Fringes of Empire: Voice, Exit, and the Law* (New York: Palgrave, 2018).

22 TNA (The National Archives, Kew), CO 415/9/A.221, 1827.

23 Archives départementales de la Réunion (henceforth ADR) in 57 M1, for example: "Exposé de la situation intérieure de la colonie en 1832 par le directeur de l'intérieur" and "Rapport sur les différents services de la colonie," 1828.

24 Louis Maillard, *Notes sur l'île de la Réunion* (Paris: Dentu, 1862) : 190.

25 ADR 168 M 3, Lettre du Directeur de l'intérieur concernant les Indiens mutins de l'établissement Adam, 2 August 1831; Lettre du régisseur de l'établissement de Champ-Borne, 24 July 1831.

26 Megan Vaughan, *Creating the Creole Island Slavery in Eighteenth Century Mauritius* (Durham and London: Duke University Press, 2007).

27 ANOM FM SG/Reu c 406, c 432 d 4603 à 4606 (immigration chinoise). ("FM" stands for Fonds ministériels; "SG" for Série Géographiques (geographical series), and "Reu" stands for Réunion Island; "c" is the box and "d" the file in the box).

28 Sudel Fuma, *Esclaves et citoyens, le destin de 62000 Réunionnais, histoire de l'insertion des affranchis de 1848 dans la société réunionnaise* (Saint-Denis, La Réunion: Fondation pour la Recherche et le Développement dans l'Océan Indien, 1979), 116.

At that point, the *engagés* discovered a different instrument: they became "fugitives" and "deserters."[29] Most went into town while others hid up on the hills, and still others simply moved from small to large estates, where the working and living conditions were imagined to be better. And this was partially true: large estate owners lured labouring people from neighbouring estates, particularly small ones; and then, with the help of the local police, they did not return them to their original owner.

Faced with workers' resistance and the unfair competition between planters, local authorities decided to increase the number of migrant arrivals of migrants, starting with the Chinese *engagés*. A new decree was adopted in 1843 to regulate these *engagés*: their contracts were supposed to last at least five years, and the minimum age of the *engagé* was set at sixteen; the landowners had to agree to pay wages and the return trip to China; ill treatment or a two-month delay in wage payments was sufficient grounds for the administration to nullify a contract. However, once again, estate owners seemed unwilling to comply with the rules.[30] As a result, the few dozen Chinese who arrived soon adopted the same strategy as the Indians. At first, they protested against their living conditions and overdue wages, and then they started legal proceedings or left their employers.

Again, French planters and authorities invoked rules on rural labour existing in France and which, according to them, kept labourers under the strict authority of the master. In their eyes, indentured immigrants working on plantations were a kind of rural labourers who, as already mentioned, even in France, were under a strong dependence on their master. Moreover, because of their skin colour and provenance, the subordination of migrants became even more extreme than in France. In other words, the persistent harsh living and working conditions of migrants in Réunion island had two main roots: race and the still ongoing marginality of rural workers in France itself. This is intriguing: if the French revolutions of 1789 and 1848 had an ambiguous impact on slaves, and if they provided better conditions for urban workers, why did they marginalise rural labour?

---

29   ANOM FM SG/Reu c 380 d 3288, c 370 d 3180.
30   ANOM FM SG/Reu c 406, c 432 d 4603 à 4606 (Chinese immigration).

2   Rural Labour Institutions in France across the 1789 Revolution

During the last decades, scholarship has stressed how France appears to be the first country to have abolished lifelong domestic service as well as criminal penalties in labour disputes.[31] As late as the eighteenth century, France's leading legal experts considered labour to be a service provision. Available studies show that *prud'hommes* protected the workers in the textile industry and certain urban milieus.[32] But what about the other sectors, especially agriculture?

Although the French Revolution eliminated lifelong domestic service, until 1901, rural labourers and workers could not apply to *prud'hommes*, but only to the justice of the peace. Both before and after the Revolution, legal texts classified people working in agriculture as labourers or "task workers" (*tâcherons*) or as servants in husbandry.[33] In the eighteenth century, servants in husbandry were by far the largest group of wage earners in French agriculture, just like in Great Britain. Prior to the Revolution, penalties were imposed on all labourers, pieceworkers or servants in husbandry who quit their jobs before the end of their contract or without the employer's authorisation. A variety of contractual arrangements to limit mobility existed at the time (bonuses for hardworking labourers, payment by task) along with general provisions.[34] Thus, from the sixteenth to the eighteenth century, agricultural labourers and servants were free to move about and change employers only at certain times of year – that is, according to the critical periods in the agricultural calendar.[35]

It was not the same for day labourers; the seasonal nature of agricultural labour gave rise to a significant amount of regional mobility, which was already considerable in the seventeenth century and remained high until around the end of the nineteenth century. This mobility, together with the notion of labour as service in the legal and economic culture of the time, is precisely what helps to explain the harsh penalties imposed on labourers and servants. They were not allowed to leave their masters until the end of their contract, and, if they

---

31   Alain Cottereau, "Droit et bon droit: Un droit des ouvriers instauré, puis évincé par le droit du travail, France, XIXe siècle," *Annales* 57, no. 6 (2002): 1521–57.

32   Jacques Le Goff, *Du silence à la parole: Droit du travail, société, État (1830–1985)* (Quimper: Calligrammes-La Digitale, 1985).

33   Jean-Marc Moriceau, "Les Baccanals ou grèves des moissonneurs en pays de France, seconde moitié du XVIIIe siècle," in *Mouvements populaires et conscience sociale,* ed. Jean Nicolas (Paris: Maloine 1985), 420–33.

34   Philip Hoffman, *Growth in a Traditional Society: The French Countryside, 1450–1815* (Princeton: Princeton University Press, 1996), 45–46.

35   Yvonne Crebouw, *Salaires et salariés agricoles en France, des débuts de la révolution aux approches du Xxe siècle* (Lille: ANRT, 1986).

left prematurely, they were subject to heavy penalties as well as the loss of their earnings. The master, on the other hand, could discharge them at any time.

Disputes over the wages (*gage*) of servants in husbandry and labourers was one of the areas reserved for justices of the peace,[36] especially because masters were taken at their word (until 1868), unlike their dependants, regarding any issue concerning *gages* (different from wages), wages or advances.

A labourer could leave his employer at any time or be discharged without prior notice – and without providing or claiming any compensation. In practice, however, the need to ensure workers for urgent labour had an obvious corrective effect on this rule. For example, a labourer paid by the day might be kept on for one or two weeks, or even a month or two, in summer and autumn. In some regions, incidentally, there were forms of servants' contracts for six months or a year.

Labourers remained free to offer their services to multiple farmers, if their schedules permitted. Both the wage earner and the master paid for this freedom: the day labourer's employment status was precarious and he ran the risk of seasonal unemployment, while the employer faced a possible shortage of hands during peak seasons.[37]

Lastly, domestic servants were most closely tied to their masters. What defined domestic servants and differentiated them from other agricultural wage earners was the content of the commitment, which was almost always tacit and which could not be broken "except for the most serious reasons." Domestic servants were subject to their master's will, which meant they "owed all [their] time to the master for any labour demanded." This subordination to the master's will resulted in receiving the promised *gages* in a lump sum. Without notice or compensation, the master could discharge the domestic servant for "dishonesty," "disobedience," "forgetting duties," cursing, or acts of violence. The domestic servants, for their part, complained of poor or inadequate food.[38]

Problems arose most often with regard to the *gage*. Most practices allowed the master to withhold wages equivalent to the amount of work due from the wage earner. This led to the proposal, renewed in 1848, to extend the worker's

---

36   Jean-Claude Farcy, *Guide des archives judiciaires et pénitentiaires, 1800–1958* (Paris: CNRS éditions, 1992).

37   AN (National Archvies, Paris) F 10 452 "Fixation des salaires agricoles," an II, an III; AN C 1157–61.

38   Antoine Pages, *Usages et règlements locaux, servant de complément à la loi civile et topographie légale du département de l'Isère* (Grenoble: Baratier Frères, 1855). See also the 1870 parliamentary enquiry in AN C 1157–61.

booklet (*livret ouvrier*)[39] to agricultural labourers; however, the measure failed to pass. On the other hand, if the domestic servant demanded compensation, he had no other recourse but the justice of the peace. The situation changed during the second half of the century, when the rate of disputes went up and the demand for agricultural wage earners and domestic servants increased due to emigration to the cities. Employers accused the justices of the peace of being "on the side of labourers and domestic servants"[40] – just like manufacturers during the same period accused the magistrates on industrial tribunals of being biased against them.

In short, before the Revolution, the status of French labourers and domestic servants resembled bondage; labour was assimilated to service provision. In the nineteenth century, although domestic servants and labourers were held far more accountable than their employers for breach of contract, they were no longer governed by criminal constraints, but merely by civil law. This marked a fundamental difference from the pre-revolutionary period.[41] In this context, rural labourers received far less protection than urban workers.

3 Rural Labour in France

Conventional history claims that France stagnated in growth, productivity and in regard to main economic indicators throughout the eighteenth century.[42] Over the last decades, new studies have challenged this view and have shown that there was considerable growth in eighteenth-century French agriculture.[43] We now know[44] that credit markets were fully developed in pre-revolutionary

---

39   The *livret ouvrier* was a discharge certificate; it had to certify being hired for a specific job and its completion (*quittance*) or acknowledge that the worker had not yet paid off advances received as wages and that his debt remained to be deducted from future wages by the new employer.

40   Cottereau, "Droit et bon droit."

41   Alain Dewerpe, *Le monde du travail en France, 1800–1950* (Paris: Colin, 1989); Yves Lequin and Pierre Delsalle, *La brouette et la navette: Tisserands, paysans et fabricants dans la région de Roubaix et de Tourcoing, 1800–1848* (Lille: Westhoek, 1985).

42   Patrick O'Brien and Caglar Keydar, "Les voies de passage vers la société industrielle en Grande-Bretagne et en France," *Annales ESC* 34 (1979): 1284–1303.

43   Philip Hoffman, *Growth in a Traditional Society*; George W. Grantham, "Divisions of Labour: Agricultural Productivity and Occupational Specialization in Pre-Industrial France," *The Economic History Review* 46, no. 3 (1993): 478–502.

44   Gilles Postel-Vinay, *La terre et l'argent* (Paris: Albin Michel, 1997); Philip Hoffman, Gilles Postel-Vinay, and Jean-Laurent Rosenthal, *Priceless Markets* (Chicago: University of Chicago Press, 2000).

France, and the same was true for property rights. Pluriactivity and seasonal labour markets were omnipresent.

George Grantham in particular evaluated the input of labour for the main agricultural operations in several French areas over a long period of time – roughly the eighteenth and nineteenth centuries – and concluded that labour productivity increased throughout the country during the period, particularly in intensive husbandry, and more so in tillage than in harvesting. In some areas, notably the Paris Basin, labour productivity was almost equal to the best agricultural areas in Britain at the time. The rural population decreased more slowly in France than in Britain, but more rapidly than in any other European country in the nineteenth century. This slow decrease was the result not just of the presumed protection of "peasant property" after the revolution, as conventional historiography has argued, but also of the strong coercion still exerted on rural workers. From this standpoint, the Revolution of 1789 brought much more "freedom" to urban than to rural workers.

In short, the Revolution of 1789 and the revolution in Saint-Domingue did not seem to bring much freedom to colonial workers or to rural labourers in mainland France. Both these groups were marginalised, in the colonies because from Napoleon onwards, the counter-revolutionary emancipation had been firmly established; and in France itself, because the advances of the revolution benefitted some finance, merchants and entrepreneurs, as well as limited groups of workers. Small units and rural labourers were left out. The reasons for this were both political and economic; in politics, the major divide in the world of labour was between the rural and the urban on the one hand, and between the mainland and the colonial on the other. From an economic standpoint, these attitudes were strengthened in the labour-intensive production in agriculture and in the colonies. The question is whether the revolution of 1848, the abolition of slavery and the Second Industrial Revolution changed this state of affairs.

Even as late as 1851, only 27.6 per cent of the active population was working in the industrial sector (16 per cent in 1815; 21 per cent at the end of the 1830s). In 1855–1864, production in cottage industry was still 1.6 times higher than that of industry. Market segmentation remained the rule in France until around the end of the nineteenth century and, as a result, there was no uniformity in prices, wages or skills. With a few exceptions, pluriactivity was the norm.[45]

---

45   Gérard Gayot, *De la pluralité des mondes industriels: La manufacture royale des draps de Sedan, 1646–1870* (Paris: EHESS, 1995).

Labour intensification in agriculture rose in France as well as in Britain, to such an extent that Gregory Clark came to the conclusion that, before 1850, labour intensification without any technical progress was the norm in Europe.[46] At the same time, the output and yields were far higher in Britain than in France, despite an equal increase in the number and length of working days.[47] The organisation of labour and capital explain these differences. The contribution of labour dominated French growth until at least the 1870s, if not later.

The seasonal nature of agricultural labour gave rise to a significant amount of regional mobility, which was already considerable in the seventeenth century and remained high until around the end of the nineteenth century. In 1860, about 25 per cent of the industrial labour force was still moving from one sector to another during the summer.[48] Where possible, employers could try to compensate for the loss of men by employing women, adolescents and children. Although farm wages hovered below industrial wages for most of the year, the situation was reversed during the peak season, particularly for women. Their wages were systematically inferior to those of men, but they recovered the difference during the summer in both agriculture and industry. It was as if agriculture offered a high wage for a brief period every year in order to attract workers who were usually engaged in industrial production.[49] Seasonal labour was more intensive during the periods workers spent in towns and even more for peasant-workers in cottage industry. At the same time, wages, above all real wages, stagnated.

Day labourers were commonly found in the southern Mediterranean, Alsace-Lorraine, the Île-de-France and Picardy. It is estimated that in 1862 about half of the 4 million agricultural wage earners were day labourers; thirty years later, that figure had dropped to 1.2 million. This trend was linked, in large part, to a sudden reduction in the number of small landowners between 1862

---

46   Gregory Clark, "Productivity Growth without Technical Change in European Agriculture before 1850," *The Journal of Economic History* 47, no. 2 (1987): 419–32.

47   Grantham, "Divisions of Labour," 486.

48   Thierry Magnac and Gilles Postel-Vinay, "Wage Competition between Agriculture and Industry in Mid-Nineteenth Century France," *Explorations in Economic History* 34 (1997): 1–26.

49   Jean-Pierre Bompard, Thierry Magnac, and Gilles Postel-Vinay, "Migrations saisonnières de main-d'oeuvre: Le cas de la France en 1860," *Annales d'Économie et de Statistique* 19 (1990): 97–129.

and 1892; by contrast, servants in husbandry made up an increasingly high percentage of agricultural labourers.[50]

These trends in different rural areas corresponded to those in various industrial branches; in industry, seasonal shutdowns were less frequent in capital-intensive firms. Industrial employers could either shut down production in the summer or increase wages. The decision they took depended on the branch of industry and the region. Indeed, a national market was still lacking in nineteenth-century France (at least until after the 1880s) and peasant-workers reasoned in terms of a comparison between local wages in agriculture and industry. This explains why, in departments where industrial wages were high, agricultural wages followed suit, and vice versa: workers compared and finally offset the imbalance between the two wages. For the same reason, summer shutdowns were more widespread among companies that paid their workers less than the summer wage they earned for farm labour.

This season shut-down was particularly well-suited to high labour-intensive crop areas. When labour was required at different intervals, as was the case for flax, hemp and vegetable and oil seeds, workers did not look to distant markets for compensation. In these cases, their wages would not be offset by going to distant markets.

In wine producing regions, on the other hand, workers did respond to distant higher wages, and so – to an even greater degree – did workers located in pastoral counties. In particular, those in pastoral counties – in northern France, the Vosges and parts of Normandy and Brittany – left industry in the summer to work in neighbouring grain-growing regions with excess demand – in Picardy, Champagne, Lorraine and the Paris Basin.

This situation disappeared almost entirely after 1875, when seasonal migration sharply declined. Between 1860 and 1890, the earlier practice of combining agricultural and industrial employment largely vanished. In 1860, at least five hundred thousand and probably as many as eight hundred thousand workers quit their jobs during summer. By 1890, only one hundred thousand continued to do so.

In short, after 1848, official rules on the rural labour market did not change and rural workers still were penalised compared to urban workers. However, over the years, their legal strength increased and so did urbanisation. This double movement produced slowly improving conditions for rural workers, who

---

50   Jean-Luc Mayaud, "Salariés agricoles et petite propriété dans la France du XIXe siècle," In *La moisson des autres*, ed. Jean-Claude Farcy and Ronald Hubscher (Nice: Créaphys édition, 1996): 29–56.

could now better negotiate their seasonal activities in town and in the countryside. However, during the second half of the nineteenth century, this slow progress in the condition of rural workers on the mainland seemed to be in sharp contrast with the persistent bondage of former slaves and new immigrants in the colonies.

4 Indentured Migrants after 1848

Immediately after the decrees of May 1848, the elites of Réunion Island gathered to prepare a petition and a series of documents intended to demonstrate the need to postpone abolition in order to preserve the economy and stability of the island. Otherwise, they argued, the whole population, including the slaves, would suffer from the sudden collapse of sugar production.

In 1848, the General-Commissioner of the Republic, Sarda-Garriga, was sent to the island to enforce the abolition decree. He immediately ordered the plantation owners to free their slaves and ordered the latter to respect public order and not turn into vagrants. Freedom, he declared, makes work a duty. In principle, on 20 December 1848, sixty-two thousand slaves on the island were manumitted.[51]

Indeed, when the French abolished slavery in 1848, unlike the British they did not impose an intermediate period of "apprenticeship" but, instead, practised disguised forms of enslavement. Recruitment in India, Madagascar, Mozambique and the East Coast of Africa relied on networks that had been in place since the eighteenth century. It employed the same practices as the slave trade, often involving violence, sometimes with the help of local tribal chiefs.[52]

In 1847, there were a total of 6,508 *engagés* – Indians, Chinese, Africans and Creoles. The lack of available labour encouraged several landowners to call for the importation of additional *engagés*, this time from Africa, especially since France was moving towards the abolition of slavery. Indeed, like in the British Empire in the 1830s and 1840s, the abolition of slavery in the French colonies in 1848 was followed by a revival of the *engagement* system. While only 153 African *engagés* entered into service in 1853, thereafter, on average, about 4,000 Africans arrived each year between 1851 and 1854; 10,008 were

51   ADR, 16 K 32.

52   François Renault, *Libération d'esclaves et nouvelle servitude: Les rachats de captifs africains pour le compte des colonies françaises après l'abolition de l'esclavage* (Abidjan: ARSTOM, 1976).

imported in 1858 and 5,027 the following year.[53] The routes supplying *engagés* and immigrants partly reproduced those of the slave trade and commercial networks already in place. Indian labourers were brought to the island with the help of Arab and Indian middlemen, who were often in competition with each other. Taking advantage of the British peace and their permission to sail under the British flag, Indian merchants (often from Bombay and the Malabar Coast) gained a considerable competitive advantage in transporting coolies and goods between the Indian Ocean and India.[54]

On the western route, between Réunion Island and Africa, the annexation of Mayotte opened up new supply sources in the Comoros archipelago itself, in Madagascar and on the West Coast of Africa. Between 1856 and 1866, about 8,000 *engagés,* nearly all of them from Mozambique, were transported via Mayotte to Réunion Island.[55] According to the 1866–1867 census, of the population of 11,731 inhabitants, 3,716 were Africans (31.7 per cent); the vast majority (2,245) of them were *engagés* from Mozambique.[56]

The demand for manpower was so high that Réunionese estate owners even tried to annex Madagascar; in this, they had the support of the Arab and Sakalava communities in the Mozambique Channel islands. Trading houses and transport offices in Nantes, Bordeaux and Marseille also played an active part in these operations.[57] Relying on already existing slavery and the support of the local sultans, these merchants established stable, large-scale commercial contacts in Réunion Island for *engagés* in Madagascar, Gabon, the Congo and even West Africa.[58] In 1853, France built new centres in Gabon and Senegal to expand the zone for "redeeming" *engagés*; similar operations were carried out in Zanzibar and Mozambique.[59] The "redeemed" (actually newly purchased) Madagascans and Africans finally boarded ships for Réunion Island, often

---

53   ANOM, *Réunion, tableau de l'immigration africaine à la réunion de 1848 à 1869*, C 454, d 5042 à 5074. See also Ho Hai Huang, *Histoire économique de l'île de la Réunion, 1849–1881: Engagisme, croissance et crise* (Paris: Lavoisier, 2004).

54   TNA FO 84/174.

55   ANOM, MAD C 235 D 514.

56   Edward Alpers, "A complex relationship: Mozambique and the Comoro islands in the Nineteenth and Twentieth Centuries," *Cahiers d'études africaines* 41, no. 161 (2001): 73–95.

57   Renault, *Libération d'esclaves,* 36–38, 67–70, 106–9.

58   Mohamed M'Trengoueni, "Les différentes formes de l'esclavage et leurs abolitions successives à Mayotte," in *Esclavage et abolition dans l' Océan Indien, 1723–1869,* ed. Edmund Maestri (Paris: Harmattan, 2002): 141–52. On this slave trade, notably between West Africa and Réunion Island via Mayotte, during the period from 1875 to 1890, see ANOM, C 269, D 601.

59   ANOM FM SG/Reu, C 135, several files (1035–1039 in particular); C 350, 2465–2470 (recruitments in Mozambique).

passing through the Seychelles. In all, between 1851 and 1860, 20,000 *engagés* were exported from Portuguese Africa and the same number was shipped from the Swahili coast; 10,000 landed in Réunion Island and Comoros.[60] The British ships sequestered several cargoes of *engagés* bought by the French or the Portuguese.[61] Finally, in 1861, a Franco-British agreement provided for the cessation of French prior redemption in Africa in exchange for the possibility of resorting to Indian coolies.

Initially, those put to work under contract of *engagement* were either new immigrants or local freed slaves, in almost equal numbers. Thus, in 1854, 34,650 men and 4,709 women immigrants, were added to 22,650 "local" male indentured labourers and 9,022 females. Local workers under other agreements than *engagement* were a tiny minority: 3,763 males and 3,116 females. The total number of workers came to 86,028.[62] Seasonal variations were nevertheless significant: in the first quarter of 1855, there were 61,191 workers in all, including 37,062 new male immigrants, 5,049 female immigrants, 9,545 local males and 4,785 local females. At the moment, contracts for one year (or longer) were the rule; only 1,683 workers were under shorter terms. These numbers did not reflect reality: the law required long-term contracts; the planters therefore provided this kind of contract, but they actually employed short-term workers as the seasonal variations demonstrate. In the second half of 1855, during the peak agricultural season, the number of working people jumped to 91,276, including 41,155 new immigrants, 33,228 members of the "local population" and 9,214 without a contract of *engagement*.[63]

The Second Empire imposed tighter restrictions not only on rural labourers, as we have seen, but also, and above all, on emancipated slaves and *engagés*. A contract of *engagement* was imposed on all workers in the colonies; the legal rules governing the *livret ouvrier* were widely implemented and enforced. Anyone without fixed employment (defined as a job lasting more than one year) was considered a vagrant and punished as such. The penalties were considerable, but the law was also frequently circumvented through fictitious contracts of *engagement* that some – especially women – signed with landowners who were interested in having occasional labourers.

---

60   Gwyn Campbell, ed, *The Structure of Slavery in Indian Ocean Africa and Asia* (London: Frank Cass, 2004).

61   ANOM FM SG/Reu c 382 d 3318, c. 379 d 3206; William Gervase Clarence-Smith, *The Third Portuguese Empire, 1825–1975* (Manchester: Manchester University Press, 1985).

62   ADR 10M9.

63   ADR 10M9, Statistiques du travail.

In principle, *engagés* had the right to go to court and denounce cases of mistreatment and abuse. We have seen that, under slavery, those rights had been largely ignored. Abolition did little to change those attitudes; in practice, it was still extremely difficult to make use of the rules, mainly because colonial law courts were in the hands of local elites. Thus, when immigrants went to court to denounce abuses, they were often sent back to their employer, who, at best, punished them and docked their wages for insubordination; at worst, the employer would sue them for breach of contract and slander. In the face of these difficulties, workers sometimes joined together to denounce illegal practices, but they risked being sentenced by the judge and the police to two months of forced labour in a workhouse for illicit association and breach of the peace.[64]

Following protests by Indian immigrants and the British consul, in the late 1850s, permission was given to form a union for the protection of immigrants. The union was granted the authority to inspect estates and was supposed to safeguard immigrants' legal rights. However, the union performed its mission poorly, at least until the late 1860s; inspections were seldom held, and legal assistance was offered only to those immigrants who had completed less than five years of a renewed contract. This approach provoked a counteraction on the part of immigrants and the British consul, but the initial decisions of the courts validated a conservative interpretation and rejected claims denouncing unequal treatment under the law.[65]

Contract renewals, wage payments and corporal punishment were the most common issues in the lawsuits filed by *engagés*. Unlike slaves, *engagés* had the right to return home; terms were negotiated in the contract, which was supposed to comply with the general provisions of the law. In practice, however, repatriation was difficult. During the 1850s and 1860s, a third of the indentured immigrants returned home (mostly Indians). This percentage was close to the one in Mauritius, the Caribbean, Surinam and Jamaica at the time, but it was far from the repatriation figure of 70 per cent recorded in Thailand, Malaya and Melanesia. Distance and the cost of transport were just two of the variables affecting repatriation; politics and concrete forms of integration were also important factors.[66] On Réunion Island, in particular, urban traders and certain colonial officers encouraged *engagés* to return home. The former group argued that once the immigrants had completed their commitment, they

---

64   ANOM FM SM/Reu c 379 d 3211 and c 383 d 3323.
65   ANOM FM SG/Reu c 384 d 3361.
66   David Northrup, *Indentured Labour in the Age of Imperialism, 1834–1922* (Cambridge: Cambridge University Press, 1995), 129–32.

settled in towns and engaged in illegal trade and unfair competition. Colonial administrators were inclined to support this view: the defence of public order required the repatriation of immigrants.[67]

By contrast, several employers and estate owners, especially small ones, were hostile to the resettlement of immigrants in town or their repatriation, and they pushed for the renewal of contracts. Their attitude can be explained by the fact that unlike large estate owners, they faced increasing problems in finding the financial resources, networks and diplomatic support for new recruits. For that reason, they made use of every legal and illegal means to retain workers at the end of their contracts. In particular, they seized immigrants' wages and *livrets* and added severe penalties whenever possible ("laziness" and the failure to accomplish assigned tasks in due time were the most common arguments for applying penalties). Hence, the worker's "debt" was never repaid, and the contract was protracted. Day labour standards and objectives were gradually raised so that few workers could meet them; they were thus subject to stiff penalties while working eighteen to twenty hours a day instead of the ten mentioned in contracts and official rules.[68] And as if all this were not enough, employers had no qualms about using physical force to make workers renew their commitments.

These practices had been informally denounced from the 1850s, but it was not until the 1860s that they were brought before the courts, under pressure from British diplomats and French central government authorities.[69] Even then, lawsuits often dragged on for years and involved only a very small percentage of workers. In very few cases, employers were forced to pay their workers due wages, with no damages or interest, though many immigrants were also granted permission to terminate (illegal) contracts and abuses without paying penalties.[70]

In first-level courts throughout the 1870s, no more than seven employers were sentenced each year for inflicting injuries and other violence. At the appeals court level, the figure dropped to one per year, the sole exception being four individuals convicted in 1875, but this was a single lawsuit and the three people receiving sentences were themselves immigrants working as foremen.[71]

Conversely, every year employers sued several hundred workers for breach of contract. Sentences were usually favourable to the plaintiffs, and the workers

---

67   ANOM FM SG/Reu c 382, some dozen files, and c 379.
68   ANOM FM SG/Reu c 379 d 3211.
69   ANOM FM SG/Reu c 382 d 3324, 3310, 3311, 3318.
70   ANOM FM SM SG/Reu c 379 d 3217, 3210.
71   ANOM FM SM SG/Reu c 379 d 3203.

had to face severe monetary penalties, which often translated into forced labour. Immigrants were also dragged into court for robbery, for which the sentences were very harsh – such as five years of forced labour for a stolen chicken.[72]

As time went by, the use of coercion became increasingly essential in public governmental activities such as building and repairing roads, bridges and ports. Forced labour as a disciplinary measure and workhouses were already in existence under slavery, for the punishment of slaves who were under the jurisdiction of the public authorities; accordingly, slaves were assigned to workhouses or put to work on public works projects, rather than sent to their masters to be punished. In February 1831, colonial workhouses had a total workforce of 888 (612 men, 180 women and six children) in their so-called "mobile" department, that is, forced labour performed in various parts of the island; the "sedentary" department had a total of 202 labourers (148 men, twenty-eight women and twenty-six children). The mortality rate in these activities was very high: by 1831, an estimated 303 deaths (out of 12,347 prisoners) had taken place in the workhouse since it was set up in 1826.[73] Such coercion continued after the abolition of slavery. In Saint-Leu, in 1859, there were 321 people in the public workhouses, with between seventy and eighty prison sentences per quarter. By contrast, only sixteen people were engaged in disciplinary forced labour by the end of 1858.[74]

In part, this outcome can be attributed to the violence and the poor living and working conditions of French planters, who received much less fiscal and financial support than their neighbours in Mauritius. Contingency and structural dynamics converged in a world of violence, exploitation and inequality. Violent colonialism responded not only to economic pressures and local conditions on the island, but also to the way the French managed labour and their empire.

5   Conclusion: Labour, Empire and Revolution

The French Revolution suppressed lifelong domestic bondage, whereas the nineteenth century progressively abolished slavery, first in the British colonies, and then in the French colonies. Still, this process did not accompany the rise of a free labour market between legally equal actors. In Britain, France and their colonies, workers and indentured immigrants were not disguised

---

72   ANOM FM SG/ SG Reu c 385 d 3367.
73   ADR 11 M 21, Atelier colonial.
74   ADR, 6M 1405 (ateliers disciplinaires).

slaves (as much of the literature in the nineteenth century argued),[75] but they did have an inferior legal status and far fewer rights than their masters. From this perspective, colonies were territories not only of slavery but, above all, of forms of bondage inspired by status inequalities entrenched in France itself. Status inequalities in France served as the model for those in the colonies. However, unlike Britain, where the Masters and Servants Acts opposed any kind of worker – including both domestic and rural labourers – to their masters, in France this opposition was only partially replicated before the Revolution of 1789. The difference was that, even at that time, legal differences between aristocrats, workers, peasants, merchants and the clergy overlapped with the emerging capitalist social differentiation. The Revolution consolidated this trend and provided special legal, political and social rights to estate owners, old aristocracies and new capitalists while proclaiming the equality of the whole population before the law. In practice, workers had no right to unionise or even to vote until universal suffrage in the twentieth century. Within this context, informal unions, industrial law courts and social movements were able to win some legal and social protection in some urban and industrial sectors while rural labour was marginalised. Corporatism replicated from pre-revolutionary to capitalist France. This became a source of inspiration for regulating labour in the colonies, in particular in the aftermath of the abolition of slavery. The rights of indentured immigrants and former slaves were constantly ignored in post-1848 French colonies and this was so not only under the Second Empire, that is, since 1851, but even in the aftermath of the revolution, as was shown at the very beginning of this chapter. In fact, the fragmentation of rights, interests and action of labouring people (weak solidarities between different branches of workers, deep suspicion between urban and rural workers, their joint hostility towards immigrants from the colonies) responded to the alliance between aristocrats and capitalists. The latter divided the former. As a consequence, under the Second Empire, two trends were at work: on the one hand, in commercial, trade and financial relationships, Napoleon III gradually reduced regulations and moved towards free trade and deregulated markets. On the other hand, in labour relationships, the Second Empire put severe limitations on workers' rights, sought to preserve the worker's booklet and denied the right to strike or even to unionise.

---

75   For more on this debate, see Alessandro Stanziani, "Free Labour—Forced Labour: An Uncertain Boundary? The Circulation of Economic Ideas between Russia and Europe from the Eighteenth to the Mid-Nineteenth Century," *Kritika: Explorations in Russian and Eurasian History* 9, no. 1 (2008): 1–27.

In the colonies, this attitude took a distinctly repressive turn and inequalities existed both in the law (fewer statutory rights for immigrants and non-French residents) and in the way it was implemented (legal procedures unfavourable to labouring people) as well as outside the law (unpunished abuses and violence, economic exploitation). The notion of freedom was for a world to come and it appealed to immediate exclusion as a foundation for an eventual future inclusion.

Bibliography

Archival Material

ADR (Archives départementales de la Réunion):

10M9 Statistiques du travail.

11 M 21 Atelier colonial.

168 M 3, Lettre du Directeur de l'intérieur concernant les Indies mutins de l'établissement Adam, 2 août 1831; Lettre du régisseur de l'établissement de Champ-Borne, 24 juillet 1831.

16 K 32.

6M 1405 (ateliers disciplinaires).

AN (National Archives Paris).

F 10 452 "Fixation des salaires agricoles," an II, an III; N C 1157–61.

ANOM (French Colonial Archives):

Généralités 162 d. 1326, "Comptes rendus des séances de la Commission d'abolition de l'esclavage."

FM SG/ Reu (Réunion Island Funds): c 385 d 3367; c 379 d 3211; c 380 d 3288; c 370 d 3180; c 382 d 3318; c. 379 d 3206; c 382 d 3324, 3310, 3311, 3318; c 384 d 3361; c 406; c 432 d 4603 à 4606 (Chinese immigration). c 406, c 432-d 4603 to 4606; c 135, several files (1035–1039 in particular); c 350, 2465–2470 (recruitments in Mozambique). c 379 d 3217, 3210; c 379 d 3211; c 383 d 3323.

FM SG/MAD (Madagascar Funds) c 235 d 514.

ANOM, Réunion, tableau de l'immigration africaine à la réunion de 1848 à 1869, c 454, d 5042 à 5074.

TNA (The National Archives, Kew):

CO 415/9/A.221, 1827. FO 84/174.

Printed Material

Allen, Richard. *European Slave Trade in the Indian Ocean*. Athens, OH: Ohio University Press, 2015.

Alpers, Edward. "A Complex Relationship: Mozambique and the Comoro islands in the Nineteenth and Twentieth Centuries." *Cahiers d'études africaines* 41, no. 161 (2001): 73–95.

Alpers, Edward. *The Indian Ocean in World History*. New York and Oxford: Oxford University Press, 2013.

Ambert, Général. *Abolition de l'esclavage*. Paris: Imprimerie de Guirodet et Jouaust, 1848.

Benot, Yves. *La révolution française et la fin des colonies*. Paris: La Découverte, 2004.

Blackburn, Robin. *The Making of New World Slavery: From the Baroque to the Modern, 1492–1800*. London: Verso, 1998.

Bompard, Jean-Pierre, Thierry Magnac, and Gilles Postel-Vinay. "Migrations saison-nières de main-d'oeuvre: Le cas de la France en 1860." *Annales d'Économie et de Statistique* 19 (1990): 97–129.

Campbell, Gwyn, ed. *The Structure of Slavery in Indian Ocean Africa and Asia*. London: Frank Cass, 2004.

Carter, Marina. "Indian Slaves in Mauritius (1729–1834)." *Indian Historical Review* 15, nos. 1–2 (1988–1989): 233–47.

Clark, Gregory. "Productivity Growth without Technical Change in European Agriculture before 1850." *The Journal of Economic History* 47, no. 2 (1987): 419–32.

Clarence-Smith, William Gervase. *The Third Portuguese Empire, 1825–1975*. Manchester: Manchester University Press, 1985.

Cottereau, Alain. "Droit et bon droit: Un droit des ouvriers instauré, puis évincé par le droit du travail, France, XIXe siècle." *Annales* 57, no. 6 (2002): 1521–57.

Crebouw, Yvonne. *Salaires et salariés agricoles en France, des débuts de la révolution aux approches du XXe siècle*. Lille: ANRT, 1986.

Davis, David Brion. *The Problem of Slavery in the Age of Revolution, 1770–1823*. New York: Oxford University Press, 1999.

Debien, Gabriel. *Les engagés pour les Antilles 1634–1715*. Paris: Société de l'histoire des colonies françaises, 1952.

Dewerpe, Alain. *Le monde du travail en France, 1800–1950*. Paris: Colin, 1989.

Dorigny, Marcel, ed. *Les abolitions de l'esclavage*. Saint-Denis: Presses Universitaires de Vincennes, 1995.

Drescher, Seymour. *Capitalism and Antislavery: British Mobilization in Comparative Perspective*. New York and Oxford: Oxford University Press, 1987.

Farcy, Jean-Claude. *Guide des archives judiciaires et pénitentiaires, 1800–1958*. Paris: CNRS éditions, 1992.

Farcy, Jean-Claude. "Les archives méconnues de la justice civile." In *Histoire et archives: L'histoire contemporaine et les usages des archives judiciaires (1800–1939)*, edited by Frédéric Chauvaud and Jacques-Guy Petit, 397–408. Paris: Champion, 1998.

Fillot, Jean-Marie. *La traite des esclaves vers les Mascareignes au XVIIIe siècle*. Paris: Orstom, 1974.

Fuma, Sudel. *Esclaves et citoyens, le destin de 62000 Réunionnais, histoire de l'insertion des af ranchis de 1848 dans la société réunionnaise.* Saint-Denis, La Réunion: Fondation pour la Recherche et le Développement dans l'Océan Indien, 1979.

Fuma, Sudel. *L'esclavagisme à la Réunion, 1794–1848.* Paris: Harmattan, 1992.

Gayot, Gérard. *De la pluralité des mondes industriels: La manufacture royale des draps de Sedan, 1646–1870.* Paris: EHESS, 1995.

Granier de Cassagnac, Adolphe. *De l'émancipation des esclaves: Lettre à M. de Lamartine.* Paris: Delloye, 1840.

Grantham, George W. "Divisions of Labour: Agricultural Productivity and Occupational Specialization in Pre-Industrial France." *The Economic History Review* 46, no. 3 (1993): 478–502.

Hoffman, Philip, Gilles Postel-Vinay, and Jean-Laurent Rosenthal. *Priceless Markets.* Chicago: University of Chicago Press, 2000.

Hoffman, Philip. *Growth in a Traditional Society: The French Countryside, 1450–1815.* Princeton: Princeton University Press, 1996.

Huang, Ho Hai. *Histoire économique de l'île de la Réunion, 1849–1881: Engagisme, croissance et crise.* Paris: Lavoisier, 2004.

Jennings, Lawrence. *French Antislavery: The Movement for the Abolition of Slavery in France, 1802–1848.* Cambridge: Cambridge University Press, 2000.

Jollivet, M. *La Commission présidée par M. le duc de Broglie et les gouverneurs de nos colonies, théorie et pratique.* Paris: Imprimerie De Boulé, 1843.

Le Goff, Jacques. *Du silence à la parole: Droit du travail, société, État (1830–1985).* Quimper: Calligrammes-La Digitale, 1985.

Lequin, Yves, and Pierre Delsalle. *La brouette et la navette: Tisserands, paysans et fabricants dans la région de Roubaix et de Tourcoing, 1800–1848.* Lille: Westhoek, 1985.

M'Trengoueni, Mohamed. "Les différentes formes de l'esclavage et leurs abolitions successives à Mayotte." In *Esclavage et abolition dans l' Océan Indien, 1723–1869,* edited by Edmund Maestri, 141–52. Paris: Harmattan, 2002.

Magnac, Thierry, and Gilles Postel-Vinay. "Wage Competition between Agriculture and Industry in Mid-Nineteenth Century France." *Explorations in Economic History* 34 (1997): 1–26.

Maillard, Louis. *Notes sur l'île de la Réunion.* Paris: Dentu, 1862.

Mayaud, Jean-Luc. "Salariés agricoles et petite propriété dans la France du XIXe siècle." In *La moisson des autres,* edited by Jean-Claude Farcy and Ronald Hubscher, 29–56. Nice: Créaphys édition, 1996.

Moriceau, Jean-Marc. "Les Baccanals ou grèves des moissonneurs en pays de France, seconde moitié du XVIIIe siècle." In *Mouvements populaires et conscience sociale,* edited by Jean Nicolas, 420–33. Paris: Maloine, 1985.

Northrup, David. *Indentured Labor in the Age of Imperialism, 1834–1922.* Cambridge: Cambridge University Press, 1995.

O'Brien, Patrick, and Caglar Keydar. "Les voies de passage vers la société industrielle en Grande-Bretagne et en France." *Annales ESC* 34 (1979): 1284–1303.

Pages, Antoine. *Usages et règlements locaux, servant de complément à la loi civile et topographie légale du département de l'Isère.* Grenoble: Baratier Frères, 1855.

Postel-Vinay, Gilles. *La terre et l'argent.* Paris: Albin Michel, 1997.

Régent, Fréderic. *Esclavage, métissage, liberté.* Paris: Grasset, 2004.

Régent, Frédéric. *La France et ses esclaves.* Paris: Grasset, 2007.

Renault, François. *Libération d'esclaves et nouvelle servitude: Les rachats de captifs africains pour le compte des colonies françaises après l'abolition de l'esclavage.* Abidjan: ARSTOM, 1976.

Schmidt, Nelly. *Abolitionnistes de l'esclavage et réformateurs des colonies, 1820–1851: Analyses et documents.* Paris: Karthala, 2000.

Schoelcher, Victor. *Des colonies françaises: Abolition immédiate de l'esclavage.* Paris: CTHS, [1842] 1998.

Schuler, Monica. "The Recruitment of African Indentured Laborers for European Colonies in the Nineteenth Century." In *Colonialism and Migration: Indentured Labor before and after Slavery,* edited by Pieter Emmer, 125–61. Dordrecht, Boston and Lancaster: Martinus Nijhoff, 1986.

Sheriff, Abdul. *The Indian Ocean: Oceanic Connections and the Creation of New Societies.* London: Hurst, 2014.

Stanziani, Alessandro. "Free Labor – Forced Labor: An Uncertain Boundary? The Circulation of Economic Ideas between Russia and Europe from the Eighteenth to the Mid-Nineteenth Century." *Kritika: Explorations in Russian and Eurasian History* 9, no. 1 (2008): 1–27.

Stanziani, Alessandro. *Labor on the Fringes of Empire: Voice, Exit, and the Law.* New York: Palgrave, 2018.

Tocqueville, Alexis. *Rapport fait au nom de la commission chargée d'examiner la proposition de M. de Tracy relative aux colonies, 1839.* In *Œuvres completes.* Vol. 3. Paris: Gallimard, 1962.

Vaughan, Megan. *Creating the Creole Island Slavery in Eighteenth Century Mauritius.* Durham and London: Duke University Press, 2005.

Wanquet, Claude. *Histoire d'une Révolution: La Réunion, 1789–1803.* Paris: Editions Laffitte, 1980–1984.

CHAPTER 14

Between Community Development Effort and Hidden Colonial Forced Labour

The Long History of "Communal Labour" in Gold Coast/Ghana, 1927–2010

Alexander Keese

1   Introduction

The principal idea of forced labour underlying colonial rule in sub-Saharan Africa's rural regions is well-known, but its implementation and effects remain superficially analysed for large parts of the African continent. In several studies, the view prevails that coerced labour as it was organised by the colonial authorities from the late nineteenth century onwards, somehow reproduced forms of slavery. This opinion holds partly true for concession company rule in places such as the Congo Free State, French Gabon and Middle-Congo, or the Portuguese colony of Mozambique. The connection, which existed in higher or lower degrees of intensity for those Central and South East African cases, was especially important if the agents of such concession companies channelled unfree labour into production tasks that had formerly had a connection with slave labour.[1] Then, to quote Eric Allina's ground-breaking work, it could indeed just resemble "slavery by any other name."[2] Elsewhere, however, the overlap between slavery practices, especially where they were part of local community life – and not the source of labour for European plantation complexes, which

---

[1]   Catherine Coquery-Vidrovitch, *Le Congo au temps des grandes compagnies concessionnaires 1898–1930* (Paris and The Hague: Mouton, 1972); Elioth P. Makambe, "The Exploitation and Abuse of African Labour in the Colonial Economy of Zimbabwe, 1903–1930: A Lopsided Struggle between Labour and Capital," *Transafrican Journal of History* 23 (1994): 81–104; David Northrup, "Slavery & Forced Labour in the Eastern Congo 1850–1910," in *Slavery in the Great Lakes Region of East Africa*, ed. Henri Médard and Shane Doyle (Oxford: James Currey; Kampala: Fountain Publishers; Nairobi: EAEP; Athens, OH: Ohio University Press, 2007), 111–23; Aldwin Roes, "Towards a History of Mass Violence in the Etat Indépendant du Congo, 1885–1908," *South African Historical Journal* 62, no. 4 (2010): 634–70; Malyn Newitt and Corrado Tornimbeni, "Transnational Networks and Internal Divisions in Central Mozambique," *Cahiers d'Etudes Africaines* 192 (2008): 707–40.

[2]   Eric Allina, *Slavery by Any Other Name: African Life under Company Rule in Colonial Mozambique* (Charlottesville and London: University of Virginia Press, 2012), 77–82.

were, after all, rare on the African continent – and colonial practices of forced labour was more complex. Andreas Eckert has rightly pointed out that individuals with servile status could be the first to be internally discriminated within village communities. Such discrimination could include their recruitment for forced labour tasks imposed by the colonial system, through a mechanism of picking the socially weakest individuals of the community through internal compulsory and negotiation processes.[3] However, this connection has not found much further inquiry.

Even colonial forced labour as a more general practice and experience of colonial rule has only very recently received more systematic attention. This delay in research partly has to do with research methods and the difficulty of finding sources: oral informants tended to refer to forced labour tasks in a kind of streamlined horror narrative, which frequently did not allow scholars to reconstruct the concrete experience behind it and its actual effects on local life. Conversely, detailed discussions of forced labour and the reactions to its use are often difficult to uncover from archival evidence, as the comments of colonial officials and auxiliaries, and transcribed testimony of victims, are scattered through files.[4] However, two aspects can be pointed out as essential common elements of colonial forced labour all over sub-Saharan Africa. First, a principal means of coercion were periods of mandatory service for the creation and maintenance of infrastructures – especially roads, which were often essential for the transport of agricultural products – but also sanitation in rural sectors. Forced agricultural production, mostly through cotton quotas and limited to particular regions, was also part of colonial forced labour systems, but less common.[5] Second, while colonial forced labour was abolished in the various territories in sub-Saharan Africa between 1946 and 1961, colonial administrators of different regimes remained committed to the idea of labour coercion for the greater good of both the colonies' economy and as means of teaching Africans "how to work."[6] Many of the postcolonial regimes on the

---

3   Andreas Eckert, "Slavery in Colonial Cameroon, 1880s to 1930s," *Slavery & Abolition* 19, no. 2 (1998): 140.

4   As examples of important monographs on the theme, see, for French West Africa, Babacar Fall, *Le travail forcé en Afrique-Occidentale française (1900–1946)* (Paris: Karthala, 1993), who claims to have used many oral accounts but never refers to them in the book, and, for Senegal, Romain Tiquet, *Travail force et mobilisation de la main-d'œuvre au Sénégal* (Rennes: Presses Universitaires de Rennes, 2019).

5   See Libbie J. Freed, "Conduits of Culture and Control: Roads, States, and Users in French Central Africa, 1890–1960" (PhD diss., University of Wisconsin-Madison, 2006), 100.

6   Alexander Keese, "Hunting 'Wrongdoers' and 'Vagrants': The Long-Term Perspective of Flight, Evasion, and Persecution in Colonial and Postcolonial Congo-Brazzaville, 1920–1980," *African Economic History* 44 (2016): 152–80.

African continent adopted some of the labour obligations that had been in place, framing them into new civic duties or youth services in contexts of road cleaning and maintenance.[7]

In the British colonies on the African continent, labour obligations and their coercive nature were quite differently defined. As a colonial power, the British government insisted internationally, through prompt ratification of the Forced Labour Convention C29 of the International Labour Organization in 1931, on the superior standards of British colonialism.[8] Indeed, British politicians claimed that forced labour as colonial practice had long disappeared in the African territories – or, sometimes, not so long but definitely, as in the case of the Gold Coast's Northern Province in 1927.[9] This was taken up by some older literature, while later studies showed that *corvée* labour, organised by the chiefs, was used until at least 1935, as in the case of the Ashanti Province.[10] After that, the principal and decisive claim was that rural populations in the various colonies *voluntarily* contributed to rural works, for the sake of "rural development." This colonial trope transformed, as I will discuss, into an issue of alleged community development models under Ghana's postcolonial regimes.[11] In other words, while the continuities of forced labour under later British colonialism in sub-Saharan Africa, between 1927 and the 1950s, have mostly remained unstudied, post-independence communal labour, where the term and concept continued to exist, has been framed as a benign and fully voluntary communitarian practice.

The colonial version of framing practices as benign and voluntary communitarian labour has been challenged most recently, for Kenya, by Opolot Okia, who demonstrated how the practice continued to be controlled by the colonial state after 1930, in spite of British rhetoric at the ILO level.[12] In the case of the Gold Coast, present-day Ghana, some older studies had already questioned the idea

---

7   Alexander Keese, "The Slow Abolition within the Colonial Mind: British and French Debates about 'Vagrancy,' 'African Laziness,' and Forced Labour in West Central and South Central Africa, 1945–1965," *International Review of Social History* 59, no. 3 (2014): 377–407.

8   Daniel Maul, "The International Labour Organization and the Struggle against Forced Labour from 1919 to the Present," *Labour History* 48, no. 4 (2007): 477–500.

9   Roger G. Thomas, "Forced Labour in British West Africa: The Case of the Northern Territories of the Gold Coast 1906–1927," *Journal of African History* 14, no. 1 (1973): 9–32.

10   Gareth Austin, *Labour, Land and Capital in Ghana: From Slavery to Free Labour in Asante, 1807–1956* (Rochester, NY: University of Rochester Press; Woodbridge: Boydell & Brewer, 2005), 246.

11   Sara Berry, "Questions of Ownership: Proprietorship and Control in a Changing Rural Terrain – A Case Study from Ghana," *Africa* 83, no. 1 (2013): 36–56, 44, 48.

12   Opolot Okia, *Labor in Colonial Kenya after the Forced Labor Convention, 1930–1963* (New York: Palgrave, 2019): 101–16, 127–45.

of the voluntary character of road work under British colonialism, but those studies remained isolated.[13] The critical analysis of communal labour under colonial rule has recently found even clearer expressions with a focus on the colony's Northern Province, which had been a bastion of *corvée* labour much commented on, and where the "traditional chiefs" continued to rely on imposing communal labour tasks after 1930.[14] The principal reinterpretation discussing the changes of the 1930s, and linking international pressures (through the ILO) with the goals and hesitations of colonial agents and the objectives of chiefs, focusing on the north of Ghana, but also adopting a colony-wide perspective, was recently published by Sarah Kunkel: her work offers a new standard for our understanding of these social practices and their transformations and continuities.[15]

This chapter will go into another direction. It will, first, point to evidence showing that communal labour in the British territories in Africa under colonial rule was widely (if not everywhere) a smokescreen for rural forced labour. Given that secondary roads and their maintenance were essential for the rural production sector, these experiences of compulsory work nevertheless remain an important part of the agrarian world. However, the picture is complicated by the fact that communitarian practices also existed, as mutual help during harvests, for instance. Although I will refer to some new studies on that later issue, I hold it as difficult to generalise on the absence or presence of coercion in these practices. For rural infrastructure, its creation and maintenance, the case is clear; and my results will show that, despite certain changes and modalities and massive changes in the rhetoric used, these often remained unfree practices. In other words, "communal labour" remained "forced labour" in the sector of infrastructure maintenance; moreover, while this practice, with its compulsory nature and the fact that it especially targeted the weakest elements in communities, might have reached its peak in the early 1940s, it continued to exist beyond independence in 1957 and during the subsequent independent regimes.

---

13   Kwabena O. Akurang-Parry, "Colonial Forced Labor Policies for Road-Building in Southern Ghana and International Anti-Forced Labor Pressures, 1900–1940," *African Economic History* 28 (2000): 23.

14   Alice Wiemers, "'It is all he can do to cope with the roads in his own district': Labor, Community, and Development in Northern Ghana, 1919–1936," *International Labor & Working-Class History* 92 (2017): 89–113.

15   Sarah Kunkel, "Forced Labour, Roads, and Chiefs: The Implementation of the ILO Forced Labour Convention in the Gold Coast," *International Review of Social History* 63, no. 3 (2018): 449–76.

Building on a number of interpretations for the late 1920s and the 1930s, I will then attempt to question the idea that "communal labour" was an *ongoing* forced labour practice for the Gold Coast/Ghana and see to which degree and under which forms it lived on into the various postcolonial regimes and even into the new millennium (while obviously admitting that the intensity of coercive elements is likely to have been milder from the 1940s onwards). Building mostly on archival evidence – because I hold that the same problems of interpreting labour coercion through oral interviews prevail in the Ghanaian case, and even more so for the decades after independence – I will follow the scattered indications for such labour in rural infrastructure-building and maintenance. The goal is to detect the dissonances in administrative observations, the expressions of refusal and resistance, and the voices of victims of communal labour but also of those detracting labour refusals that appear in letters and petitions. This approach is inspired by the strategies inherent in subaltern study methods.[16] My perspective will mostly rely on evidence from various southern Ghanaian regions (including the Eastern Region and the Ashanti Region) and, especially, from the Central Region for which I will interpret new, ground-breaking archival evidence. I will attempt to bring those experiences in connection with broader developments.

2   Communal Labour: From an Allegedly Accepted Development Reality in the 2000s Back to "Natural Practices" in the 1920s

In the Ghanaian media, a more recent debate on communal labour took place during the last years of the John Kufuor presidency, which, between 2000 and 2008, completed the process of removing one-party and governmental control over the news sector.[17] In 2007, the *Daily Graphic*, the principal newspaper in Ghana, published a nostalgic "call" referring to "our communal spirit." This can also be read as an appeal to return to imagined older practices of communal labour:

> It is important that we rekindle the communal spirit which drove our forebears to undertake development projects through self-help.
>   From time immemorial, that spirit moved various communities to rally around their chiefs to build roads to link them to neighbouring

---

16   Christopher J. Lee, "Subaltern Studies and African Studies," *History Compass* 3 (2005): 1–13.
17   For the situation before the change of government in 2000, see Jennifer Hasty, "Performing Power, Composing Culture: The State Press in Ghana," *Ethnography* 7, no. 1 (2006): 71.

towns and villages. Invariably, the adjoining communities also contributed towards such projects.

Self-help has been the spirit behind the construction of schools and churches which have quickened the pace of development in many communities.

Modernity and urban migration have conspired to undermine the spirit as it used to be ....

When that happens, those at home and abroad become reluctant and adopt a lukewarm attitude towards contributions towards projects which could be beneficial to the people. It is against this background that we share the call by Vice-President Alhaji Aliu Mahama that we should rekindle the communal spirit which seems to be waning.[18]

The discussion projected communal labour as a positive issue of the past, in which so-called "traditional chiefs" were sufficiently revered to enlist the constant voluntary support of their populations for communal labour projects. This vision corresponded to the ideas spread by British administrators during the colonial period, emphasising the democratic and voluntary nature of such work. The same idea was defended elsewhere in British colonial territories; it was thus by no means exclusive to the Gold Coast and to the Kenyan case interpreted by Okia. The fantasy of a communitarian development effort orchestrated by the chiefs found perhaps its clearest expression in a comment coming from the administration of the Tanganyika Mandate in 1929, a comment that already belonged to the upcoming discussion on international intervention in colonial forced labour: "The term 'forced labour' in this connection is a misnomer. There are many things which require to be done in a native village connected with its good order, sanitation, etc., where it is by far the simplest and least expensive way for the able-bodied male villagers to do them themselves."[19]

Recent work on Ghana has highlighted the initiative of locals in the colonial period, thus providing a picture that goes beyond the notion that locals were solely motivated to act for the common good of community development because of their charismatic chiefs. Using a new, exciting approach to discussing local initiative in yam producing areas, María José Pont Cháfer shows, especially through oral evidence, that successful pioneers exploring

---

18   "Our communal spirit," *Daily Graphic*, 29 May 2007, ModernGhana.com.

19   The National Archives, Public Record Office, Kew, United Kingdom (TNA, PRO), CO 822/17/7, Colonial Office, Tanganyika Department, *Memorandum on Forced Labour.* (without number), without date [received May 1929], 5.

new production opportunities for yams were quite proactive in mobilising communal labour as a communitarian exercise. Chiefs were much less important in those initiatives. Pont Cháfer's discussion rightly insists on the capacity of locals to decide to join forces in communitarian work, although in her PhD thesis the range of examples clearly focuses on harvest labour.[20] In future research, such situations would need to be clearly distinguished from situations in which local hierarchies prompted the mobilisation of communal labour.

However, during the colonial period and beyond, the role of chiefs and the issue of organising construction and maintenance processes, in which the state does not provide wages, still dominate the debate.[21] Another trope, appearing in scholarship on more recent periods, is that of the generally positive image of such obligations, even if they are initiated or imposed by a local hierarchy.[22] For a number of cases from the 1970s onwards, Sara Berry has described communal labour as an essential first element of the strategy of village notables, who used their prerogative to call for it to create a fundament for mobilising resources provided by donors.[23] Moreover, in the field of development sociology, Lauren Morris even holds that there was a major difference in attitude towards communal labour between Ghanaian public opinion of the early 2000s, where its image is allegedly positive, and that in neighbouring Côte d'Ivoire.[24] It is, therefore, crucial to take a closer look at how such practices presented themselves and were accepted by local Ghanaian populations, according to available evidence. I will examine locals' opinions and reactions through the late 1920s and 1930s, for the years during and after the Second

---

20 María José Pont Cháfer, "We, the People of the Yam: A History of Crops, Labour and Wealth from the Periphery of Ghana" (PhD diss., EHESS Paris, 2020), 222–32.

21 Kunkel, "Forced Labour," 466. In an impressive new article, María José Pont Cháfer challenges this view, holding that in the Northern Territories voluntary labour indeed took over in road maintenance. This seems to me in contradiction to the evidence discussed here (for districts in the south), but would merit a wider discussion, especially on mechanisms of obscuring coercive practices: see María José Pont Cháfer, 'From Forced to Voluntary Labour in Rural Labour in Rural Africa: The Transition to Paid Voluntary Labour on the Roads of the Northern Territories of the Gold Coast', *International Review of Social History*, first view article, 2022, doi:10.1017/S0020859022000657, esp. pp. 14–18.

22 Alice Wiemers, "'When the chief takes an interest': Development and the Reinvention of 'Communal' Labor in Northern Ghana, 1935–60," *Journal of African History* 58, no. 2 (2017): 251–53.

23 Berry, "Questions," 43–44, 49.

24 Lauren Morris, "Mediating Ethnic Conflict at the Grassroots: The Role of Local Associational Life in Shaping Political Values in Côte d'Ivoire and Ghana," *Journal of Modern African Studies* 42, no. 4 (2004): 604.

World War, and, finally, for postcolonial rural life under the Nkrumah, Busia, Acheampong and Rawlings regimes of the independent Ghanaian state.

3 The Cheap Alternative: Discussions, Experiences, and Euphemisms around Communal Labour from the 1920s to the 1950s

Colonial attitudes towards forced labour in the Gold Coast appear neatly in the service diary of the district commissioner of Bekwai, in the Ashanti Province. In early August 1927, officials Hunter and Maidment of the Agricultural Department of the colony explained to the commissioner their plans for holding an agricultural show in the district: "Force communal labour to clear a site & erect stalls. force the people to bring in exhibits & generally to do all the work." The commissioner ironically commented on their plans, but his main complaint was the organisational effort for himself, and not the negative impact of forced work on local individuals.[25] However, with the implementation of the ILO Convention C29 suddenly becoming a threat on the horizon, colonial officials in the Gold Coast started to calculate the detrimental effects of renouncing labour coercion.[26]

The Provincial Commissioner of the Central Province was plain about what he considered the dramatically negative effects of the abolition of communal labour practices. He commented on this "gloomy picture" by warning against "the effects of an enormous fall in Revenue, since communal labour could be computed in terms of cash and be considered an asset of the Colony," as only "[i]f communal road maintenance and village services are to be excluded from the Convention, there is little to worry over."[27] According to the (better-known) comment of his colleague in the Eastern Province, the whole plan was "eminently unsuitable for compulsorily abolishing a system by which the Colony obtains work for the common good of the people without undue hardship, the abolition of which the people have not asked for themselves."[28]

---

25 Public Records and Archives Administration Department, Accra, Ghana (henceforth PRAAD (Accra)), ADM 46/5/2, *Bekwai – Commissioner's Diary 1927*. (without number), without date, 72.

26 Kunkel, "Labour," 450–51.

27 Public Records and Archives Administration Department, Cape Coast Branch, Ghana (henceforth PRAAD (Cape Coast)), ADM 23/1/2437, Acting Provincial Commissioner of the Central Province to Secretary for Native Affairs of the Gold Coast, *Forced Labour*. (n° 2147/30/C.P.222/21.), 29 August 1930, 2.

28 PRAAD (Accra), CSO 14/1/34, Erskine, Provincial Commissioner of the Eastern Province, to Colonial Secretary of the Gold Coast (n° 457/C.S.), 10 November 1930, 1–2.

While hoping to see the colonial government step in to provide revenue for essential road services, the report from the Central Province nevertheless suggested to keep as many mandatory labour services as possible, including through strict sanitation rules compelling locals to guarantee village sanitation; however, the still-common recruitment of women and children for labour services was eventually to be excluded in the future.[29] To bolster the argument, the report quoted and cited extensively from the positions formulated four decades earlier by Gold Coast lawyer and Fante spokesman John Sarbah, who had insisted that "his people" would always favour labour obligations over hut taxes.[30] Here, the idea, so commonly used, that Africans in colonial contexts practically demanded labour services for themselves appears prominently for the first time.[31]

Moreover, the colonial administration was ever keener to shift the burden of internal negotiation, or compulsion, in view of local communities carrying out communal labour, to the chiefs.[32] Warning against the apparently "common misinterpretation" that labour services no longer existed, in June 1930 the District Commissioner of Dunkwa in the Central Province informed leading chiefs that they simply had to obtain local consent for the tasks which still had to be a part of daily life. How this consent was to be obtained remained open, but the message clearly pointed to the possibility of imposing the tasks on those with less protection within a village community.[33] In the Eastern Province, administrators equally accused the locals of trying to escape from village labour obligations, and they held the chiefs responsible for "convincing" the community; but, once again, this rationale left considerable room for imposing these tasks on vulnerable individuals.[34] Such tasks could eventually be avoided by the weak by moving away into cocoa zones and taking over *abusa* sharecropping labour: a system that was also characterised by certain abuses, but which established itself as a viable alternative.[35]

---

29   PRAAD (Cape Coast), ADM 23/1/2437, Acting Provincial Commissioner of the Central Province to Secretary for Native Affairs of the Gold Coast, *Forced Labour.* (n° 2147/30/ C.P.222/21.), 29 August 1930, 6.

30   PRAAD, *Forced Labour*, 29 August 1930, 3.

31   See also Wiemers, "When the Chief," 245–46.

32   Kunkel, "Forced Labour," 469–71.

33   PRAAD (Cape Coast), ADM 23/1/2438, Assistant District Commissioner of Dunkwa to Denkehene, Twifuhene, and Hemanghene (n° 1299/108/1930), 26 October 1930.

34   PRAAD (Accra), ADM 29/6/12, Acting Colonial Secretary of the Gold Coast to Commissioner of the Eastern Province in Koforidua (n° 284/36/24.), 25 September 1936, 1.

35   PRAAD (Accra), ADM 29/6/12, Walker, Acting District Commissioner of Mampong, Akwapim, to Acting Commissioner of the Eastern Province in Koforidua, *Supervision of Labour.* (n° 642/185/1930), 18 June 1936; for a more repressive variant of individuals

How powerful the coercive element within allegedly voluntary communal labour ultimately was can be demonstrated through an interpretation of the reactions that followed its disappearance in some parts of the Gold Coast in the 1940s. In Kwamang in the Ashanti Province, the "youngmen," referring to younger inhabitants of the town who had regularly been targeted for labour services, were relieved about the institution of fees and the introduction of regular paid labour for road maintenance and sanitation. This was regarded as immense progress, although it coincided with a wide array of other local conflicts, linked to the debts of stools (local chieftaincies).[36] In the Juaben Division of the Ashanti Province, the increasing anger of those being compelled to perform communal labour had strong effects, which were noted by administrators complaining that it also made the recruitment of soldiers for the Second World War much more difficult, as the chiefs, who were responsible for the recruitment, were becoming increasingly unpopular.[37] In the following years, individuals called upon for communal labour (described as "normal minor voluntary communal services" by the district commissioner of Oka-Western Akim in 1944), frequently tended to refuse to give that labour if they had already paid an annual levy.[38] At Asikuma in the Central Province, the chief recruited an alternative group of "communal labourers": he forced inmates from the Native Administration Prison to work for the Catholic mission and he (falsely) described that work as perfectly legal "maintenance of a 'juju house or place of worship.'"[39]

In the aftermath of the war, local resistance against communal labour became ever more entrenched. The region of Winneba in the Central Province offers an exemplary selection of incidents that shed light on the changing attitudes towards communal labour. In 1946, Kwesi Krampa, the Bamuhene of Agona State and three of his sub-chiefs complained that in the absence of a

---

accepting free labour, allowing them to get away from labour services, in the Portuguese colony of Mozambique, see Zachary Kagan Guthrie, *Bound for Work: Labor, Mobility, and Colonial Rule in Central Mozambique, 1940–1965* (Charlottesville: University of Virginia Press, 2018).

36   PRAAD (Accra), ADM 50/5/10, *Quarterly Report on Native Affairs – ending 31/12/40.*, 130 (without number, report bound in volume), without date.

37   PRAAD (Accra), ADM 50/5/10, *Quarterly Report on Native Affairs – ending 31/12/4*, 77 (without number, report bound in volume), without date, 1.

38   PRAAD (Cape Coast), ADM 23/1/2437, Crawford, District Commissioner of Oka-Western Akim, to Provincial Commissioner of the Central Province in Cape Coast, *Forced Labour.* (n° 565/W.A.271/35.), 15 July 1944.

39   PRAAD (Cape Coast), ADM 23/1/2437, Watson, Acting District Commissioner of Saltpond, to Provincial Commissioner of the Central Province in Cape Coast, *Forced Labour* (n° 1469/S.D. 109/1920.), 20 July 1944.

paramount chief of the state, the chieftaincy being vacant, "when such labour is called upon to be performed, the inhabitants and especially the youngsters comprising the section refused countenancing such 'CALL' on the grounds that there is no Head to impose penalty on them in their failure to attending same." They asked for a policeman to compel the locals to work in communal service.[40] The District Commissioner of Winneba had to report on the mood in the area to his superiors; he insisted that the work of clearing roads and paths "generally represents the wish of the community as a whole – and cannot strictly be called forced labour."[41] However, resistance became ever more generalised. In Krodua, J.C. Lamptey, representing the *odikro* (chief), called a number of inhabitants of the town "insurgents," as they were "refusing to obey orders given to them; this habit, discourage[s] the others to clear Roads of Krodua, and other Town improvement." In view of "making them sober and submissive," Lamptey also hoped to intimidate locals through the presence of police agents in the area.[42]

By 1951, it became clear that even the late colonial state – now with Kwame Nkrumah integrated into state activities as the leader of government affairs and the future prime minister of an increasingly autonomous territory – was not particularly concerned with replacing communal labour by remunerated, skilled road labour. In Juaben, the district commissioner remarked that nothing could be finalised in terms of road networks without the locals offering their communal labour.[43] In the case of the Ashanti Province, the pressures remaining on the shoulders of the "youngmen" were a principal issue turning the youth movement of the region away from Nkrumah's Convention People's Party and towards a regionalist opposition against Nkrumah's march to power.[44] Elsewhere, locals expected Nkrumah's government to abolish the communal labour practices when the country became independent.

---

40   PRAAD (Cape Coast), ADM 23/1/3204, Kwesi Krampa, Bamuhene of Agona State; Bamuah, Sub-Chief; Adjepong, Sub-Chief; Kwesie Nkrumah, Sub-Chief, to District Commissioner of Winneba (without number), 28 June 1946.

41   PRAAD (Cape Coast), ADM 23/1/2437, Assistant District Commissioner of Winneba to Provincial Commissioner of the Central Province, *Forced Labour* (n° 1453/260/1935.), 26 August 1947.

42   PRAAD (Cape Coast), ADM 23/1/3204, J.C. Lamptey, for the Odikro of Krodua, to District Commissioner of Winneba (without number), 1 September 1947.

43   PRAAD (Accra), ADM 50/5/10, *Quarter Ending December, 1951*, 233 (without number, report bound in volume), without date: 1.

44   Jean Allman, "The Youngmen and the Porcupine: Class, Nationalism and Asante's Struggle for Self Determination, 1954–57," *Journal of African History* 31, no. 2 (1990): 270.

4   **From Key (Voluntary) Element of the New National Community**
     Back to Pressures to Work: Communal Labour under Ghana's First
     Independent Regimes (1957–1972)

The independence of Ghana in 1957 was inscribed in a regime propaganda that called for a clear break with the hardships of life under colonial rule. In principle, this position came in combination with a clear rebuttal of the role of the "traditional chiefs" – who had, as I have shown, been essential as organisers of communal labour. However, this position was ambivalent: the Nkrumah regime had a tendency to act against chiefs that had been opponents to its road to power, but it left much room for manoeuvre for "traditional rulers" who had at an early moment joined ranks with Nkrumah's Convention People's Party.[45] Even so, "the people's" support for the nation-state project, expressed through voluntary communal labour as a development effort, was restated as an important plebiscitarian element. Labour inspectors were thus happy to confirm whenever they met such apparent enthusiasm. When E.B.K. Ampah, Jr., checked on the conditions of road labour between Tuakwa Junction and Betsingua in the Mfantsiman area of the Central Province in October 1959, he reported his very positive impressions of villagers' "willingness and readiness to provide communal labour to the maximum." The interviews with those engaging in communal labour seemed to confirm the point.[46]

It is difficult to verify up to which point the Nkrumah regime managed to maintain the relative enthusiasm of its early phase. Alice Wiemers holds that refusals against communal labour were rare in the Northern Province by 1960, as villagers sought cooperation with chiefs to create initiatives for local development.[47] However, Jeffrey Ahlman points to individual acts of resistance in the Western and Ashanti Provinces, where villagers refused to participate in communal labour, challenging the lack of the state's engagement, which contrasted unfavourably with waged labour under colonial rule.[48] The lack of thorough examination of communal labour mechanisms under Nkrumah in the historical debate corresponds to the frequently vague discussion of youth

---

45   Richard Rathbone, *Nkrumah and the Chiefs: The Politics of Chieftaincy in Ghana 1951–60* (Oxford: James Currey; Accra: F. Reimer; Athens, OH: Ohio University Press, 2000).

46   PRAAD (Cape Coast), RG 1/2/87, E.B.K. Ampah, Jr, to Regional Commissioner of the Central Region, *Tuakwa Junction – Betsingua Motor Road* (without number), 7 October 1959.

47   Wiemers, "When the Chief," 257.

48   Jeffrey Ahlman, *Living with Nkrumahism: Nation, State, and Pan-Africanism in Ghana* (Athens, OH: Ohio University Press, 2017).

services such as the Builders' Brigade, for which the coercive elements of the institution of communal labour also still need to be further studied.[49]

After the fall of the Nkrumah regime through the *coup d'état* of 24 February 1966, and the installation of a National Liberation Council, a vocal campaign took off to accuse members of the fallen regime of misdeeds, corruption and repression. It has yet to be established whether labour obligations and possible repressive mechanisms linked to those were an important part of this negative narrative.[50] The years between 1966 and 1972 are, therefore, a test case to understand how labour obligations were imagined on the level of the political elite – and what locals thought about the experience under Nkrumah and the new policies and rules that were instated. At the same time, communal labour came to be redefined as an issue of participating in the nation state, which gave local authorities a renewed claim to enforce the related practices on unwilling residents.

After the elections of 1969, which led to a new civilian government under Kofi Busia, this government pushed for the creation of a National Service Corps to include, notably, the unemployed and certain groups of school-leavers. Busia and his ministers insisted on the importance of such national service: "We haven't got the funds," he said, "to do the big things which Nkrumah did."[51]

At the same time, the architects of the National Service Corps also flirted with the idea of coercing certain groups.[52] Although the new ranks of the Busia government discussed the military-style organisation of the Nkrumahist Builders' Brigade or of the Young Pioneers as highly unpopular and held that the new institution had to be clearly distinguished from such authoritarian

---

49   Jeffrey Ahlman, "A New Type of Citizen: Youth, Gender, and Generation in the Ghanaian Builders Brigade," *Journal of Africa History* 53, no. 1 (2012): 100–2.

50   The end of the Nkrumah regime still needs much better discussion, as has been pointed out in Jean Allman, "Kwame Nkrumah, African Studies, and the Politics of Knowledge Production in the Black Star of Africa," *International Journal of African Historical Studies* 46, no. 2 (2013): 181. It is currently caught between early accounts, partly of scholars who were present during the events, like in Maxwell Owusu, *Uses and Abuses of Power* (Chicago: University of Chicago Press, 1970); Victor T. Le Vine, "Autopsy on a Regime: Ghana's Civilian Interregnum 1969–72," *Journal of Modern African Studies* 25, no. 1 (1987): 169; and later accounts, focusing on the analysis of Kwame Nkrumah's intellectual path; see: Ama Biney, "The Development of Kwame Nkrumah's Political Thought in Exile, 1966–1972," *Journal of African History* 50, no. 1 (2009): 83–84.

51   Public Records and Archives Administration Department, Ho Branch, Ghana (henceforth PRAAD (Ho)), RAO/C.1017, Ebenezer E. A. Brew, National Secretary, National Service Corps, Prime Minister's Office, The Castle, "Minutes of Meeting held at the Castle on Thursday 11th December, 1969 at 12 Noon" (without number), 6 January 1970, 2.

52   PRAAD (Ho), RAO/C.1017, "Minutes," 6 January 1970, 6.

forms of labour administration, the wider public was unconvinced. It was obvious from documents from the Volta Region, in particular, that locals feared that the Corps would be another authoritarian instrument under a different name, and that, like in Keta, volunteers were not forthcoming.[53]

In 1970, faced with a lack of enthusiasm, the administration attempted to exert pressure on locals (and local authorities) to consider their participation. The argument built heavily on the idea of communitarian obligations and their imagined precolonial past. The issue of compulsion was low key in these arguments, but it was clearly expressed that participation from village communities was expected; and it was basically left to the communities to decide how the burden was to be internally distributed:

> 2. Various reasons have made the establishment of the Service Corps necessary ....
>
> (ii) Communal labour which is the main idea behind the Corps is not new to Ghana, but you all know that in so many cases, projects have been stopped because funds or skills had been lacking, or that a particular project hastily begun, had been found to be not too relevant.
>
> (iii) It is also the Government's determination to lay the emphasis in its development programmes on the rural areas. But development, like any other good thing, cannot descend on a people like manna from heaven. The Government therefore wants every local community to take part in our efforts to build a great country.
>
> The Service Corps therefore offers a unique opportunity for this idea of participation. This also means that there is now a common yardstick by which every village and town would be judged in terms of its preparedness to help itself.[54]

Part of the argument was thus that the National Service Corps would provide a better framework for communal efforts, and help those enrolled in communal labour to eventually obtain new skills through training measures provided by the corps. However, the few sources found so far question the success of that approach. According to reports from the Central Region, villagers in several

53   PRAAD (Ho), RAO/C.1040, A.K. Otchere, Regional Administrative Officer of the Volta Region, to Secretary to the Cabinet, Office of the Prime Minister of Ghana, *Volta Region – Report for the Month ending 31st January, 1970* (n° A/ADMN/56/25), 25 March 1970.

54   PRAAD (Ho), RAO/C.1017, A.W. Parker, District Administrative Officer, to the Chiefs in Jasikan District, *Jasikan District and the National Service Corps* (n° AD.53/29.), 23 February 1970.

areas, such as Dunkwa, remained reluctant to enrol in the National Service Corps because they interpreted it as a multiplication of communal labour obligations.[55]

At the same time, through the impact of the Busia government, communal labour came to be framed differently in local power relations. The new government used a xenophobic and populist strategy in 1969/1970, leading to a general movement against immigrants and descendants of immigrants, who were redefined as "aliens" in the Ghanaian nation. Up to five hundred thousand were expelled from Ghanaian territory, although a number of these managed to clandestinely return.[56] The effects of anti-foreigner legislation and sentiments transformed communal labour into something that was locally expected and demanded from foreigners, especially in places in which they belonged to the weakest elements. An impressive number of partly anonymous, partly signed letters of denunciation illustrate this change in the appreciation of communal labour practices.

A few examples suffice to illustrate the point. In Tatali in the Northern Region, close to the Togo border, an anonymous writer targeted Nigerian resident Ali Dankali, accusing him (like others) of escaping from deportation and claiming citizenship on false grounds; in particular, the letter-writer reproached Dankali for not having encouraged the (Nigerian-descendant) youngmen to willingly accept communal labour.[57] In Ve-Agbome in the Volta Region the behaviour of Nigerian resident, Adzima Akindji, who had first evacuated his possessions from the town and left Ghana, but subsequently returned, was seen by local detractors as deplorable. In particular, his detractors, including part of the "traditional authorities," accused Akindji of having refused to provide communal labour over the years.[58]

In Asene in the Eastern Province, the Town Committee demanded the expulsion of the "aliens" and called for Northern Ghanaians living there to be

---

55   PRAAD (Cape Coast), RG 1/12/8, K. Obeng-Adofo, District Administrative Officer of Dunkwa, *Intelligence Report – Dunkwa District.* (without number), without date [February 1970]: 2.

56   Ousman Kobo, "'We are citizens too': The Politics of Citizenship in Independent Ghana," *Journal of Modern African Studies* 48, no. 1 (2010): 67–94.

57   PRAAD (Accra), RG 8/1/12, anonymous letter from Tatali via Yendi, Northern Region, to Ministerial Secretary, Ministry of the Interior (without number), 27 November 1970.

58   PRAAD (Accra), RG 8/1/17, G.S.K. Dzadu IV, Mankrado, Clemence K. Tuadi, Asafo, Koyiko, Otsyeame, to Minister of the Interior (without number), 15 January 1971.

relocated to a separate settlement, as the Committee believed that the two groups were conspiring to avoid communal labour.[59] Later enquiry by a government inspector met the vehement denials on the part of the Northern Ghanaian Dagomba population in Asene, whose spokesmen claimed that they had never tried to escape from any fair communal labour call.[60] Therefore, the argument did not always have its effects as a strategy, as many officials did not sympathise with rigid measures against non-citizens. One of the most interesting available sources, a petition by leaders of the "Muslim community" of Nsawam, in the Eastern Province, details the complaints of Northern Ghanaians and individuals who had acquired Ghanaian citizenship against a number of abuses experienced. The experience of being pressured into communal labour and threatened with repercussions in case of protest against its unfair distribution, was a key complaint: "Yet each time there was a communal labour exercise, none of them would turn up: not any one from the Akim Kotokus. Each time there was communal labour, they would be seen going round the town intimidating people with possible deportation."[61]

The impact of a new, xenophobic nationalism thus allowed local authorities to reinforce the rules of the game, which were probably not new. Communal labour had tended to hit the weakest in communities, and this situation did not change altogether after the end of colonial rule. Between 1969 and 1972, the power relations linked to the practice became dominated by xenophobia, before a new military takeover changed the direction of labour obligations, without removing them at all.

---

59   PRAAD (Accra), RG 8/1/17, Nana Kusu Bosompong, Chief of Asene; Dakurateng, District Administrator of Kwateng), Committee Chairman; Nana Boadnaah, Queenmother; for Asene Town Committee, Asene, to Minister of the Interior, *Return of Aliens to Asene* (without number), 14 February 1971, 1–2.

60   PRAAD (Accra), RG 8/1/17, C.K. Asempapa, Assistant Commissioner of the Oda Division, Ghana Police, to Inspector-General, Accra/Akim Oda, *Return of Aliens to Asene* (n° ORHQ.50/V.2/204), 4 June 1971.

61   PRAAD (Accra), RG 8/1/19, Chief Salifu Baruwa, Chief A. Mussar, Chief Hamedu Abdulai, Yakubu Banda, to E. Akuffo-Addo, President of the Republic of Ghana, *Adoagyiri/Zongo-Nsawam Muslim Community: Compliance Order Exercise and Citizens' Personal Liberties* (without number), 4 July 1971, 4.

5   **Communal Labour and Local Resistance from the Experience of the Acheampong Regime into the Rawlings Period (1972– early 1990s)**

The military regime of Ignatius Acheampong between 1972 and 1979 is diffi-cult to study, due to a relative absence of sources beyond a possible analysis of the press, which was employed as propaganda tool of the regime's strategy.[62] Choosing a path of striving for rural self-sufficiency, this regime attempted to mobilise Ghanaian citizens to take part in rural work through a year-long pro-duction exercise called "Operation Feed Yourself," in view of reaching these goals. For the first time after decolonisation, and, indeed, since the 1920s, man-datory labour tasks were employed directly in agricultural production and not only with regard to rural infrastructure. Here, rural mobilisation led to com-plaints against compulsory labour in state-driven agrarian services, although those expressions of resistance are as yet difficult to weigh.[63]

As to the wider recourse to communal labour, and local reactions, histori-ans nevertheless have access to an interesting sample of files for the Central Region, which shows the continuities and ruptures regarding such labour in the Acheampong period; observers have presented this dossier as significant at least for southern Ghana. Widespread resistance of "youngmen" appeared as frequently as a trope and as an observation, as had been the case in the 1940s. In May 1974, the Regional Commissioner received a complaint by K.K. Nyame, Lieutenant-Colonel in Tema, reporting on the behaviour of Kwame Amo, who was said to have incited locals in Gomoa Mankessim to refuse communal labour in village sanitation. The author of the letter called for severe punishment for Amo, as otherwise "the future of communal labour is doomed in my town"; he suggested sending soldiers and that Amo be "drilled openly for all to see."[64] The subject of "strangers" refusing communal labour, and their necessary pun-ishment, found its variant in 1974 through the example of "Ga man," Acquaye Dodoo, in the village of Twifu Ntaferewaso; local chiefs massively complained

---

62   Maxwell Owusu, "Economic Nationalism, Pan-Africanism and the Military: Ghana's National Redemption Council," *Africa Today*, vol. 22, no. 1 (1975): 31–50.

63   Anna Lemmenmeier, "Operation Feed Yourself: Ghana's Experiment towards Food Self-Sufficiency under Colonel Acheampong, 1972–78" (Master's thesis, University of Berne, 2012): 72–73.

64   PRAAD (Cape Coast), RG 1/11/83, K.K. Nyame, Lieutenant-Colonel, 1st Battalion of Infantry, Michel Camp, Tema, to Regional Commissioner of the Central Region (n° 1BN/332/2), 8 May 1974 [dossier page 78, vol. I].

to the authorities about "gross abuse" and the effects that his behaviour would have in the wider region.[65]

In Asebu, the chief was faced with villagers who refused to offer communal labour on the Asebu – Apewosika feeder road, causing him to call for an army unit to intimidate the wrongdoers.[66] By contrast, in the Assin District, the members of the Assin Andoe Town Development Committee challenged the policy of the chief to artificially include certain locals in communal labour obligations; this was partly a struggle of rural leaders, but also had to do with particular individuals being repeatedly targeted.[67]

Such situations found their ways into internal security reports, where district commissioners branded resistance against communal labour as typical for "subversion" and "hostility" against the authoritarian regime in Accra. For Assin, the commissioner held that "communal labour ... is the main source of providing adequate amenities under the Seven Year Development Plan." Local refusals were triggered by views of the unfair distribution of tasks, and some lawyers from Cape Coast ("human parasites," as the commissioner called them) travelled through the Central Province districts to offer legal support to villagers threatened by court measures.[68] In some cases, like in Nsaba, the pro-regime Youth Association reported the unpatriotic behaviour of the town's residents, and brought complaints about refusals to perform communal labour together with those concerning a lack of understanding of the agrarian goals of Operation Feed Yourself; in the case of Nsaba's internal conflicts, the distribution of power thus appears as different from other cases, where the "youngmen" were, rather, the target of communal labour obligations and deserted or refused to give them.[69]

---

65 PRAAD (Cape Coast), RG 1/11/83, Nana Kwame Daku II, Chairman, Ntaferewaso Village Development Committee, c/o Kojo Mensah, to District Administrative Officer of Dunkwa, *Twifu Ntaferewaso Village Affairs* (without number), 30 July 1974 [dossier page 115I, vol. II/TJ2].

66 PRAAD (Cape Coast), RG 1/11/81, Nana Amanfi V, President of Asebu Traditional Council, to Regional Commissioner of the Central Region, Cape Coast, *Application for the Assistance of Army Personnel* (n° ATC.42/PRES.1/73/1.Vol.2), 17 April 1975.

67 PRAAD (Cape Coast), RG 1/11/83, P. Sarkodie-Ebedwo, Frichi Oduroh, J.W. Asante, Kwame Nsonwaa, and Yaw Asumang of Asin Andoe and Asin Manso, to Chief Executive Officer, Asin District Council, Asin Fodo, *Assin Andoe Town Development Committee and Communal Labour* (without number), September 1975 [dossier page 177, vol. II/TJ2].

68 PRAAD (Cape Coast), RG 1/12/25, District Commissioner of Asin Atandasu, *Report on Ghana Internal Security and Civil Emergency Schemes Asin Atandasu District* (without number), without date [Dossier Pages 27–28], 1.

69 PRAAD (Cape Coast), RG 1/11/82, Office of the Secretary, Nsaba Youth Association, c/o W.O. Donkoh, Dept. of Civil Aviation, P.O. Box 87, Accra, to the Regional Commissioner, H.E. LT. Col. Baidoo, Central Regional Administration, *Nsaba Youth Association – Appeal*

Little is known about the experience under the late Acheampong regime between 1975 and 1979, and there are also no studies on the changes of communal labour practices under the Rawlings regime. Its importance appears to dwindle in some areas, perhaps partly due to massive state intervention in the economy that characterised the first ("Marxist") phase of Rawlings's government between 1981 and 1983.[70] However, structural adjustment and a pronounced lack of government funding thereafter could have reversed that trend. Evidence is scattered, but the interesting observations from a contemporary study by Joseph Ayee give some hints as to the local perception of communal labour in the late 1980s. As locals had no choice and were sanctioned in case of refusal, they tended to describe these experiences as repressive.[71]

For much of the postcolonial period, the question of compulsory labour needs additional study, beyond the simple acceptance of its allegedly benign nature. A glance at Ghana's southern provinces, and especially the Central Province, for the years 1969 to 1975 (for which a comparably good base of new sources can be mobilised), shows that the coercive elements prevailed and invited resistance. These experiences of repression were unlikely to immediately go away after 1975.

6   Conclusion: From a Colonial to a Postcolonial Institution

Labour coercion under colonial rule and labour obligations after independence were not the same thing. Frequently, the use of practices connected to colonial forced labour, ending, in most cases, in the second half of the 1940s or shortly after, involved massive abuses, leading to individuals even dying from the hardships of the work. In comparison, labour services demanded from individuals after Ghana's independence in 1957, and under subsequent regimes into the new millennium, appear relatively mild. A new national narrative wrote them into voluntary, communitarian development efforts from which the element of compulsion seemed to be lifted.

---

to *Central Regional Commissioner on Chieftaincy Affairs in Nsaba Traditional Area* (without number), 24 August 1974, 1.

70   James C.W. Ahiakpor, "Rawlings, Economic Policy Reform, and the Poor: Consistency or Betrayal?" *Journal of Modern African Studies* 29, no. 4 (1991): 594; Richard Jeffries, "Rawlings and the Political Economy of Underdevelopment in Ghana," *African Affairs* 81, no. 324 (1982): 307–17.

71   Joseph R.A. Ayee, "The Measurement of Decentralization: The Ghanaian Experience, 1988–92," *African Affairs* 95, no. 378 (1996): 37.

This vision is much too simple, as I have shown in this chapter. My analysis for the five decades between the 1920s and the 1970s, also considering some observations for the period after the re-creation of a functioning parliamentary democracy (in 2000), demonstrates the many continuities. Existing research does not make this analysis any easier: neither sociologists nor anthropologists interested in rural life in Ghana's different regions have ever managed to study the relations of power within local communities. At the start of the third decade of the twenty-first century, potential informants still buy into the narrative of a fundamental change in labour obligations from colonial rule to independent regimes. Research into the nature and the effects of communal labour in Ghana, as a coercive mechanism, therefore depends on finding local reactions to the demands from authorities that have been documented and making plausible connections between them; often, this means working within the dissonances of archival accounts. In spite of these limits, this approach helps us to gain important insights.

First, while demands for coerced labour became less widespread and less blatant in the colony of the Gold Coast during the 1930s, as a response to external pressure and to correspond to the image of a good coloniser that the British government attempted to sell in the international context, the practice did not disappear at the local level before the 1950s. British officials clearly pointed to the economic importance of the practice, and claimed it was impossible to abandon it entirely without substantial economic setbacks for the colonial (and imperial) economy. Responding to internal and external pressures, the colonial administration started to use, in the Gold Coast, what Okia has deconstructed as a smokescreen of communitarian and traditionalist arguments for Kenya. However, the arguments employed remain very close to what became the post-independence rhetoric of communal labour in Ghana, in which it was depicted as an exercise in voluntary communitarian self-help.

Second, my discussion shows (at least for the Central Province/Region and adjacent provinces in Ghana's southern half) that certain groups felt unjustly treated in the distribution of labour services, and that that was the case over the whole of the period studied here. Between 1930 and 1951, substantial groups of individuals in villages and smaller towns refused participation in communal labour, pointing to their being exploited by local hierarchies. These refusals can partly be understood as an expression of generation conflicts and as mobilisation against local chiefs who were accused to be too close to colonial rule. However, in many cases, the refusals to cooperate expressed resistance against power hierarchies that made certain groups of people the principal victims of calls for communal labour. It is possible (but this would need to be substantiated) that similar practices played a lesser role or that, if they continued to exist, they were even embraced in the enthusiasm under the early Nkrumah regime, which might have succeeded in presenting them as necessary element of nation-building. The negative vision of other labour instruments of the regime (such as the Young Pioneers or the Builders' Brigade) casts doubt on such a positive image of communal labour for the whole period between 1957 and 1966. After 1969, in a context of xenophobic nation-building, "foreigners" in all senses of the word were intimidated to bear the principal burden of communal labour. From 1972, the Acheampong regime led the practice away from xenophobic interpretation, but the compulsory elements of communal labour prevailed. They motivated locals to resist, and, in many cases, the negative view of communal labour as coercive practice appears to have maintained itself into at least the early 1990s. In general, the acts of resistance that I drew on as main source, and which have not previously been studied, clearly show that those used in communal labour rejected the compulsory nature of the practice.

Third, one might wonder if the role of communal labour changed between 1990 and 2010 – and if "all is well" now, so to speak. In the absence of studies from the field that look at power relations in rural contexts (beyond Pont Cháfer's pathbreaking study, but which, it needs to be repeated, focuses on regions that were successful in agrarian production, which eventually made communitarian efforts more logical than in many other cases), the continuity of coercive elements can only be guessed at. However, the press report on an incident from Dormaa-Ahenkro in the Brong-Ahafo Region – an incident that was not exceptional at all, apparently – where four individuals were punished with fines between GHS 96 and GHS 362 (New Ghana Cedis) and threatened with prison sentences for their refusal to take part in communal labour in 2010, shows that the logic of coercion did not totally disappear.[72] A fine between EUR 50 and EUR 194 was substantial in a rural context. This invites interdisciplinary scholars and historians alike to pay more attention to the complex and contradictory history of the exercise of communitarian labour, which was rooted in a logic of compulsion.

---

72   "Court Fines Communal Labour Evaders," *Ghana New Agency*, 1 June 2011. ModernGhana. com.

Bibliography

Ahiakpor, James C. W. "Rawlings, Economic Policy Reform, and the Poor: Consistency or Betrayal?" *Journal of Modern African Studies* 29, no. 4 (1991): 583–600. https://doi .org/10.1017/S0022278X0000567X.

Ahlman, Jeffrey. "A New Type of Citizen: Youth, Gender, and Generation in the Ghanaian Builders Brigade." *Journal of Africa History* 53, no. 1 (2012): 87–105. https:// doi.org/10.1017/S0021853712000047.

Ahlman, Jeffrey, *Living with Nkrumahism: Nation, State, and Pan-Africanism in Ghana.* Athens, OH: Ohio University Press, 2017.

Akurang-Parry, Kwabena O. "Colonial Forced Labor Policies for Road-Building in Southern Ghana and International Anti-Forced Labor Pressures, 1900–1940." *African Economic History* 28 (2000): 1–25.

Allina, Eric. *Slavery by Any Other Name: African Life under Company Rule in Colonial Mozambique.* Charlottesville and London: University of Virginia Press, 2012.

Allman, Jean. "The Youngmen and the Porcupine: Class, Nationalism and Asante's Struggle for Self Determination, 1954–57." *Journal of African History* 31, no. 2 (1990): 263–79. https://doi.org/10.1017/S0021853700025032.

Allman, Jean. "Kwame Nkrumah, African Studies, and the Politics of Knowledge Production in the Black Star of Africa." *International Journal of African Historical Studies* 46, no. 2 (2013): 181–203.

Austin, Gareth. *Labour, Land and Capital in Ghana: From Slavery to Free Labour in Asante, 1807–1956.* Rochester, NY: University of Rochester Press; Woodbridge: Boydell & Brewer, 2005.

Ayee, Joseph R. A. "The Measurement of Decentralization: The Ghanaian Experience, 1988–92." *African Affairs* 95, no. 378 (1996): 31–50. https://doi.org/10.1093/oxfordj ournals.afraf.a007712.

Berry, Sara. "Questions of Ownership: Proprietorship and Control in a Changing Rural Terrain – A Case Study from Ghana." *Africa* 83, no. 1 (2013): 36–56. https://doi.org/ 10.1017/S0001972012000708.

Biney, Ama. "The Development of Kwame Nkrumah's Political Thought in Exile, 1966–1972." *Journal of African History* 50, no. 1 (2009): 81–100. https://doi.org/10.1017/ S0021853709004216.

Coquery-Vidrovitch, Catherine. *Le Congo au temps des grandes compagnies concession-naires 1898–1930.* Paris and The Hague: Mouton, 1972.

Eckert, Andreas. "Slavery in Colonial Cameroon, 1880s to 1930s." *Slavery & Abolition* 19, no. 2 (1998): 133–48. https://doi.org/10.1080/01440399808575243.

Fall, Babacar. *Le travail forcé en Afrique-Occidentale française (1900–1946).* Paris: Karthala, 1993.

Freed, Libbie J. "Conduits of Culture and Control: Roads, States, and Users in French Central Africa, 1890–1960." PhD diss., University of Wisconsin-Madison, 2006.

Hasty, Jennifer. "Performing Power, Composing Culture: The State Press in Ghana." *Ethnography* 7, no. 1 (2006): 69–98. https://doi.org/10.1177/1466138106064591.

Guthrie, Zachary Kagan. *Bound for Work: Labor, Mobility, and Colonial Rule in Central Mozambique, 1940–1965.* Charlottesville: University of Virginia Press, 2018.

Jeffries, Richard. "Rawlings and the Political Economy of Underdevelopment in Ghana." *African Affairs* 81, no. 324 (1982): 307–17. https://doi.org/10.1093/oxfordj ournals.afraf.a097428.

Keese, Alexander. "The Slow Abolition within the Colonial Mind: British and French Debates about 'Vagrancy,' 'African Laziness,' and Forced Labour in West Central and South Central Africa, 1945–1965." *International Review of Social History* 59, no. 3 (2014): 377–407. https://doi.org/10.1017/S0020859014000431.

Keese, Alexander. "Hunting 'Wrongdoers' and 'Vagrants': The Long-Term Perspective of Flight, Evasion, and Persecution in Colonial and Postcolonial Congo-Brazzaville, 1920–1980." *African Economic History* 44 (2016): 152–80.

Kobo, Ousman. "'We are citizens too': The Politics of Citizenship in Independent Ghana." *Journal of Modern African Studies* 48, no. 1 (2010): 67–94. https://doi.org/ 10.1017/S0022278X0999022X.

Kunkel, Sarah. "Forced Labour, Roads, and Chiefs: The Implementation of the ILO Forced Labour Convention in the Gold Coast." *International Review of Social History* 63, no. 3 (2018): 449–76. https://doi.org/10.1017/S0147547917000102.

Lee, Christopher J. "Subaltern Studies and African Studies." *History Compass* 3 (2005): 1–13. https://doi.org/10.1111/j.1478-0542.2005.00162.x.

Le Vine, Victor T. "Autopsy on a Regime: Ghana's Civilian Interregnum 1969–72." *Journal of Modern African Studies* 25, no. 1 (1987): 169–78. https://doi.org/10.1017/ S0022278X00007679.

Lemmenmeier, Anna. "Operation Feed Yourself: Ghana's Experiment towards Food Self-Sufficiency under Colonel Acheampong, 1972–78." Master's thesis, University of Berne, 2012.

Makambe, Elioth P. "The Exploitation and Abuse of African Labour in the Colonial Economy of Zimbabwe, 1903–1930: A Lopsided Struggle between Labour and Capital." *Transafrican Journal of History* 23 (1994): 81–104.

Maul, Daniel. "The International Labour Organization and the Struggle against Forced Labour from 1919 to the Present." *Labour History* 48, no. 4 (2007): 477–500. https:// doi.org/10.1080/00236560701580275.

Morris, Lauren. "Mediating Ethnic Conflict at the Grassroots: The Role of Local Associational Life in Shaping Political Values in Côte d'Ivoire and Ghana." *Journal of Modern African Studies* 42, no. 4 (2004): 589–617. https://doi.org/10.1017/S00222 78X04000412.

Newitt, Malyn, and Corrado Tornimbeni. "Transnational Networks and Internal Divisions in Central Mozambique." *Cahiers d'Etudes Africaines* 192 (2008): 707–40. https://doi.org/10.4000/etudesafricaines.15471.

Northrup, David. "Slavery & Forced Labour in the Eastern Congo 1850–1910." In *Slavery in the Great Lakes Region of East Africa*, edited by Henri Médard and Shane Doyle, 111–23. Oxford: James Currey; Kampala: Fountain Publishers; Nairobi: EAEP; Athens, OH: Ohio University Press, 2007.

Okia, Opolot. *Labor in Colonial Kenya after the Forced Labor Convention, 1930–1963*. New York: Palgrave, 2019.

Owusu, Maxwell. *Uses and Abuses of Power*. Chicago: University of Chicago Press, 1970.

Owusu, Maxwell. "Economic Nationalism, Pan-Africanism and the Military: Ghana's National Redemption Council." *Africa Today* 22, no. 1 (1975): 31–50.

Pont Cháfer, María José. "We, the People of the Yam: A History of Crops, Labour and Wealth from the Periphery of Ghana." PhD diss., EHESS Paris, 2020.

Rathbone, Richard. *Nkrumah and the Chiefs: The Politics of Chieftaincy in Ghana 1951–60*. Oxford: James Currey; Accra: F. Reimer; Athens, OH: Ohio University Press, 2000.

Roes, Aldwin. "Towards a History of Mass Violence in the Etat Indépendant du Congo, 1885–1908." *South African Historical Journal* 62, no. 4 (2010): 634–70. https://doi.org/10.1080/02582473.2010.519937.

Thomas, Roger G. "Forced Labour in British West Africa: The Case of the Northern Territories of the Gold Coast 1906–1927." *Journal of African History* 14, no. 1 (1973): 9–32. https://doi.org/10.1017/S0021853700012184.

Tiquet, Romain. *Travail force et mobilisation de la main-d'œuvre au Sénégal*. Rennes: Presses Universitaires de Rennes, 2019.

Wiemers, Alice. "'It is all he can do to cope with the roads in his own district': Labor, Community, and Development in Northern Ghana, 1919–1936." *International Labor & Working-Class History* 92 (2017): 89–113. https://doi.org/10.1017/S0147547917000102.

Wiemers, Alice. "'When the Chief takes an Interest': Development and the Reinvention of 'Communal' Labor in Northern Ghana, 1935–60." *Journal of African History* 58, no. 2 (2017): 239–57. https://doi.org/10.1017/S0021853716000633.

CHAPTER 15

Agricultural Labour Regimes of Im_Mobilisation

On the Legacies of Internal and External Colonisation within Europe

Dina Bolokan

> We tend to forget that the lowest proletariat in a colonizing country always has a sub-proletariat from the colonized country, and this reality outlasts colonization.
>
> – CHRIS MARKER, *Le Joli Mai*, 1962

∴

1 Introduction

The development towards large-scale production zones in Spain and Italy has been described as the "Californization of the Mediterranean agriculture."[1] Following worker uprisings in Southern Spain and Southern Italy, surveys pointed to the prison-like working conditions in large-scale vegetable and fruit production.[2] The best known examples are the monitored reception centres, tent cities, informal "ghettos" and shanty towns in Calabria and Apulia and the "prisons of plastic" in Almería.[3] Less widely discussed are the production areas in the meat processing industry, such as the precarious working and living conditions in huge slaughterhouses in Lower Saxony in Germany. Workers have protested these conditions. Most of those who find themselves "trapped"

---

1 Anna Mary Garrapa, "Supermarket revolution y agricultura californiana: ¿un modelo en expansión?" *Interdisciplina* 6, no. 14 (2018): 155–76.

2 Among others, see NoLager Bremen and Europäisches BürgerInnenforum, eds., *Peripherie & Plastikmeer: Globale Landwirtschaft – Migration – Widerstand.* Vienna: EBF/NoLager Bremen, 2009; Irene Peano, "Ways of Making a Human Otherwise: After-Ethnography with Migrant Labourers in Italian Agro-Industrial Enclaves," in *Modos de Fazer/Ways of Making,* ed. Vítor Oliveira Jorge, 219–30. Porto: Centro de Investigação Transdisciplinar Cultura, Espaço e Memória, 2020.

3 See, for instance, Devi Sacchetto and Domenico Perrotta, "Il ghetto e lo sciopero: Braccianti stranieri nell'Italia meridionale," *Sociologia del lavoro* 128, no. 4 (2012): 153–66.

in these food production zones come from Africa, Latin America, Asia and "Eastern" Europe. Labour arrangements are based on differing legal statuses, but working and living conditions are almost always highly exploitative and subject to control.[4] While, overall, the European agricultural sector is marked by a change from small-scale farms to large-scale companies – affecting regions across Europe in very different ways – one common tendency is to increasingly employ workers from around the globe on a precarious, short-term basis.

This chapter explores a central paradox that affects the most marginalised workers and that has characterised labour and mobility regimes in the agricultural sector in Europe from the late nineteenth century onwards. On the one hand, labour regimes in agriculture and within the globalised agri-food industry carry an element of confinement, as they are marked by prison-like living and working conditions. On the other hand, these regimes are characterised by "very mobile"[5] and "flexible"[6] workers. This "hypermobility"[7] means that workers regularly change labour arrangements, often working on different farms, in different factories or even in different countries, depending on their citizenship and legal/illegalised status. I access the current labour and living conditions of the most marginalised workers through a post- and decolonial reading of what I call "differentiated regimes of im_mobilisation." These regimes of im_mobilisation[8] consist of formal organised regimes that come with quotas, bilateral agreements and further bureaucratic rules and regulations. Sandro Mezzadra and Brett Nielsons have argued that "differential inclusion" is a crucial element that must be kept in mind "to account for the actual operation

---

4   Among others, see Stefania Prandi, *Oro rosso: Fragole, pomodori, molestie e sfruttamento nel Mediterraneo* (Cagli: Settenove, 2018).

5   Monika Szulecka, "Regulating Movement of the Very Mobile: Selected Legal and Policy Aspects of Ukrainian Migration to EU Countries," in *Ukrainian Migration to the European Union: Lessons from Migration Studies*, ed. Olena Fedyuk and Marta Kindler, 51–71. Switzerland: Springer International Publishing AG, 2016.

6   Yoan Molinero-Gerbeau and Avallone Gennaro, "Producing Cheap Food and Labour: Migrations and Agriculture in the Capitalistic World-Ecology," *Social Change Review* 14, no. 2 (2016): 121–48.

7   Dina Bolokan, "On Hypermobility in the Agricultural Sector in Europe – Translocal Life Trajectories between Switzerland and Moldova," in *The Rural-Migration Nexus: Global Problems, Rural Issues*, ed. by Nathan Kerrigan and Philomena de Lima (London: Palgrave, forthcoming).

8   "Im_mobilisation" is intended to question the dichotomous separation between "being trapped" on the one hand and "being hypermobile" on the other and to show that the transitions are fluid and not contradictory. So, it is not a situation of either/or; it is both/and. Immobility is not just a counterpart to hypermobility – both are the counterpart to the free movement of people.

of the migration regime in the making in Europe." They thereby point to the effects of the illegalisation of migration and how states include people while creating "the conditions under which a racial divide is inscribed within the composition of labour and citizenship."[9] To situate this divide within global history and power relations, scholars such as Aníbal Quijano[10] and Manuela Boatcă[11] have put forward the notions of the "coloniality of power" and the "coloniality of citizenship." They refer to the establishment of an economic structure involving the abduction and transatlantic enslavement of people during European expansion and external colonisation – which was based on the radical divide of the labour force – and argue that this was the foundation of modern capitalism. Crucial to this order was the hierarchical division of people: those without any compensation whose labour was ruthlessly exploited and those whose work was waged, but who were still exploited. The creation of this global inequality was based on the newly emerged idea of "race" – a fiction that became a structuring principle in thought and affect and impacted the way societies were organised. The racist notion of biologically and culturally based differences enabled the division of people into those who were afforded rights and those who were denied rights. The concept of coloniality refers to the transmission of these racial power relations into the present times. In the same vein, Kien Nghi Ha builds a strong argument by showing that we cannot look at current labour migration in Germany without understanding the ways that labour and migration policies developed within Imperial Germany. In his analysis, he points to the need to look at the entanglements of external *and* internal colonisation within Europe.[12] Building on these implications, and thus on insights from critical border studies and post- and decolonial thought, I aim to show how today's agricultural regimes in Europe carry the inherent logic of mobilisation and immobilisation along intersectional access or lack of access to rights. Furthermore, I argue that present agricultural labour

---

9   See Sandro Mezzadra and Brett Nielson, "Borderscapes of Differential Inclusion: Subjectivity and Struggles on the Threshold of Justice's Excess," in *The Borders of Justice,* ed. by Étienne Balibar, Sandro Mezzadra, and Ranabir Samaddar (Philadelphia: Temple University Press, 2011), 191.

10   Aníbal Quijano, "Coloniality of Power, Eurocentrism, and Latin America," *Nepantla: Views from South* 1, no 3 (2000): 533–74.

11   Boatcă, Manuela, "Coloniality of Citizenship and Ocidentalist Epistemology," in "Decolonial Theory & Practice in Southeast Europe," edited by Polina Manolova, Katarina Kušić, and Philipp Lottholz, special issue, *Dversia* 19, no. 3 (2019): 55–77.

12   Kien Nghi Ha, "Spricht die Subalterne deutsch? Migration und postkoloniale Kritik," in *Die Kolonialen Muster Deutscher Arbeitsmigrationspolitik,* ed. Encarnación Gutiérrez Rodríguez and Hito Steyerl (Münster: Unrast, 2003), 56–107.

regimes and their supposedly neoliberal transformations are in fact marked by "coloniality of labor,"[13] and, thus, by power relations that date back to the mid-fifteenth century and derive from external colonisation and from semi-colonial power relations inside Europe.[14] My main argument and intervention is to prove that current differentiated regimes of im_mobilisation must be situated in the histories of imperial Europe, so as to recognise how power relations and the racialised/ethnicised international division of labour evolved within and outside of imperial Europe. I am thus interested in both continuities and changes between and within colonial and post/neocolonial agricultural labour regimes *in* Europe.

I first trace the development of worker recruitment in Europe and elaborate on how European colonisation impacted migration and labour recruitment in industrialising regions. Given my focus, a comprehensive panorama of all European countries and their specificities is not within the scope of this section. Here, I focus only on the development of state-enforced regimes of labour rotation as part of internal colonisation in Prussia, beginning in the early twentieth century. I then analyse current differentiated labour regimes of im_ mobilisation in food production in Europe. I will show how the obverse logics of confinement and hypermobility are related to the coloniality of labour and elaborate on the political economy of the (re)productive sphere and the related political infrastructure.

2   The Development of (Agricultural) Worker Recruitment Systems in Europe

In this section, I roughly map the way in which migration patterns in Europe changed as a result of colonisation and state policies on labour migration and worker recruitment. I then focus on agricultural worker rotation regimes in Prussia and look in detail at policies of internal colonisation and the racialising discourses involved.

Until the mid-twentieth century, Europe was a continent of emigration. In addition to internal European migration, from the mid-nineteenth to the early twentieth century, some fifty million people left Europe to live in settler

---

13   Manuela Boatcă, "Coloniality of Labor in the Global Periphery: Latin America and Eastern Europe in the World-System," *Review (Fernand Braudel Center)* 36, no. 3–4 (2013): 287–314.
14   Boatcă, "Coloniality of Labor."

societies, with about thirty million of these people emigrating to the United States.[15] Migration patterns in Europe changed in the 1950s during the process of decolonisation. From the 1940s, European settlers, colonial officials and soldiers returned to their colonising European home countries, followed by those that had been colonised. The largest (return) migrations took place in the 1950s and 1960s and led, for example, from India, Kenya and Malaysia to Great Britain; from North Africa to France and Italy; from Indonesia to the Netherlands; and from the Congo to Belgium. In the mid-1970s, postcolonial (return) migration also occurred in Portugal. According to estimations, between 5.5 and 8.5 million people arrived in Europe in the course of postcolonial (return) migrations.[16]

Since the First World War heralded the end of the free international labour market, state-organised, -regulated and -controlled labour migration increased within Europe, such as, for instance, from Italy to France, Luxembourg, Belgium, Germany and Austria.[17] As early as 1931, Switzerland introduced the *Saisonnierstatut* (statute for seasonal workers), which regulated short-term residence permits for workers from abroad until 2002.[18] Germany followed soon after and signed its first bilateral agreement with Italy as early as 1937, during Nazi Germany and Fascist Italy.[19] It was primarily intended to fill the need for workers in agriculture and later it became important for the sectors connected to the arms industry.[20]

---

15   Heinz Fassmann and Rainer Münz, *Migration in Europa: Historische Entwicklung, aktuelle Trends und politische Reaktionen* (Frankfurt and New York: Campus, 1996). Other sources count around fifty-five million people from "Eastern" Europe alone that moved to the US between 1846 and 1940, of which eventually 30–40 per cent returned. See Tara Zahra, *The Great Departure: Mass Migration from Eastern Europe and the Making of the Free World* (New York: W.W. Norton, 2016).

16   Klaus Jürgen Bade, *Europa in Bewegung: Migration vom späten 18. Jahrhundert bis zur Gegenwart* (Munich: Beck, 2000).

17   Sergio Bologna, "Kontinuität und Zäsur in der Geschichte der italienischen Migrationsarbeit," in *Proletarier der "Achse": Sozialgeschichte der italienischen Fremdarbeit in NS-Deutschland 1937 bis 1943,* ed. Cesare Bermani, Sergio Bologna, and Brunello Mantelli (Berlin: Akademie, 1997), 3ff.

18   See "Federal Law on the Residence and Settlement of Foreigners of March 26, 1931"; Patrick Auderset, Charles Magnin, and Rosa Brux, *Nous, saisonniers, saisonnières ... Genève 1931–2019* (Genève: Archives contestataires, 2019).

19   Bologna, "Kontinuität und Zäsur," 43ff.

20   Brunello Mantelli, "Zwischen Strukturwandel auf dem Arbeitsmarkt und Kriegswirtschaft: Die Anwerbung der italienischen Arbeiter für das 'Dritte Reich' und die Achse Berlin-Rom 1938–1943," in *Proletarier der "Achse": Sozialgeschichte der italienischen Fremdarbeit in NS-Deutschland 1937 bis 1943,* ed. Cesare Bermani, Sergio Bologna, and Brunello Mantelli (Berlin: Akademie, 1997), 259ff, 273, 386.

In the UK, a Seasonal Agricultural Workers Scheme was implemented in 1945 and was aimed at bringing in young people during the labour-intensive months. Designed to be a cultural exchange arrangement, this programme was for agricultural students from across Europe and later emerged as a way of recruiting agricultural workers to fill labour market demands.[21]

The most extensive migrations into Europe after the Second World War were into the prospering industrialised regions north of the Alps and the Pyrenees, that became immigration regions as a result of the targeted recruitment of so-called guest workers from the Southern European peripheries.[22] The rapidly growing economy and Fordist industrial production were in need of "cheap" and "low-skilled" labour. This led to the intensive recruitment of workers into "Western" and "Northern" Europe and the development of bilateral agreements based on state interests, supposedly those of the so-called receiving and sending countries.[23] The latter aimed to outsource poverty while benefitting from workers' remittances. By the early 1970s, practically all industrialising European countries had developed some sort of systematic recruitment of workers from abroad for so-called lower skilled labour.[24]

In the first phase of "guest worker" migration, Italy was an important country of origin of workers. Further recruitment agreements were subsequently set up with Spain, Greece, Portugal, the former Yugoslavia, Turkey, Morocco and Tunisia. Building on this network of bilateral recruitment agreements, a labour migration regime emerged, involving a core of up to twenty countries. The geographical expansion of this migration regime and the intensity of recruitment peaked between 1967 and 1972.[25] In France, for example, the largest groups of workers came from Portugal, Spain and Italy as well as from the North African Maghreb states. Germany initially mainly recruited workers from Italy, then

21 Erica Consterdine and Sahizer Samuk, "Closing the Seasonal Agricultural Workers' Scheme: A Triple Loss" (working paper no. 83, University of Sussex, Sussex Centre for Migration Research, 2015), 4.

22 Jochen Oltmer, "Einführung: Migrationskontinent Europa," in *Nach Übersee: Deutschsprachige Auswanderer aus dem östlichen Europa um 1900*, ed. Deutsches Kulturforum östliches Europa (Potsdam: Deutsches Kulturforum östliches Europa, 2015), 8–25.

23 Paul Gans and Andreas Pott, "Migration und Migrationspolitik in Europa," in *Handbuch Lokale Integrationspolitik,* ed. Frank Gesemann and Roland Roth (Wiesbaden: Springer, 2018), 14.

24 Stephen Castles, "Guestworker in Europe: A Resurrection?" *International Migration Review* 40, no. 1 (2006): 741–66.

25 Christoph Rass, *Institutionalisierungsprozesse auf einem internationalen Arbeitsmarkt: Bilaterale Wanderungsverträge in Europa zwischen 1919 und 1974* (Paderborn: Schöningh, 2010); Gans and Pott, "Migration und Migrationspolitik."

switched to Turkey and the former Yugoslavia from the end of the 1960s. In the Netherlands, immigration from Turkey and Morocco was most common.[26] At the beginning of the 1970s, many countries stopped recruiting workers from abroad, which put an end to the extensive institutionalisation of labour migration in Europe. Over fifteen million people had come to "Western," "Central" and "Northern" European countries by 1975.[27] In the period between 1960 and 1973, a total of about thirty million people were registered.[28] To sum up: the main migration movements in Europe in the first half of the twentieth century up until the 1970s were marked by postcolonial migration and the development of systematic labour migration policies. While the former was a mix of return migration and immigration after decolonisation with the perspective of permanent (re)settlement, the latter was intended to be short-term and dependent on labour market needs.

Kien Nghi Ha has argued that state policies of labour migration in Europe can be roughly divided into two phases. In the first phase, from the nineteenth century until the First World War, it was primarily the European semi-peripheries that served as recruitment areas. In the phase after the Second World War, recruitment areas were increasingly extended to the postcolonial world to satisfy the growing demand for workers. This tendency encompasses all colonising European countries, although the specific characteristics and implementation of labour migration differed for each country. In the 1950s, workers from England's so-called "Irish backyard" had been supplemented and, in the most marginalised labour areas, even almost completely replaced by workers from South Asia and the Caribbean. France had traditionally recruited workers from the peripheral areas of Spain and Italy and later turned to recruit workers from the formerly colonised francophone societies in Africa.[29]

In the next section, I will focus on the recruitment of agricultural workers in Prussia, as this provides important insights into internal colonisation policies in Europe. Here, it is worth mentioning that, in the period leading up to the First World War, the German Reich became the second-largest labour importing country in the world after the US. In 1910, the German Reich counted

---

26   Klaus J. Bade and Michael Bommes, "Migration und politische Kultur im 'Nicht-Einwanderungsland,'" in *Migrationsreport 2000: Fakten – Analysen – Perspektiven*, ed. Klaus J. Bade and Rainer Münz (Frankfurt am Main: Campus Verlag, 2000), 333ff.

27   Corrado Bonifazi, "Evolution of Regional Patterns of International Migration in Europe," in *International Migration in Europe: New Trends and New Methods of Analysis*, ed. Corrado Bonifazi et al. (Amsterdam: Amsterdam University Press, 2008), 107–28.

28   Rass, *Institutionalisierungsprozesse*, 9.

29   Rass, *Institutionalisierungsprozesse*, 25.

1.26 million workers from abroad, two-thirds of which came from the Polish regions of Austria-Hungary and Russia.[30]

2.1   Agricultural Workers from Abroad Before, During and After Imperial Germany

In this subsection, I trace the way labour migration policies in Germany were informed by colonial and capitalist logic. Specifically, I trace how this specific logic was kept alive by a racist and patriarchal mindset. Thus, I argue that colonial discourses that shaped imperial conquest over people and land outside of Europe shaped labour migration policies in Europe and manifested as a paradox of hyper-constrained hypermobility. Analysing different systems of coercive labour relations over the centuries in Europe (first/second slavery and first/second serfdom), Manuale Boatcă, building on Immanuel Wallerstein's world-systems theory, points to the development of "quasi-colonial relationships" between "Eastern" and "Western" Europe. Already in the mid-fifteenth century, as raw materials from "Eastern" Europe were extracted by "Western" Europe, these power relations went hand in hand with rural coercive labour in "Eastern" Europe."[31] The latter provided food and raw materials to the former, and the majority of the rural population in the exploited regions became part of the supply infrastructure for "Western" Europe.[32] Within this historical context, Manuela Boatcă expanded the understanding of the "coloniality of labor" to encompass "the complex relationships between co-existing, but not contradictory modes of labor control."[33] Adding to Aníbal Quijano's understanding of continuities between colonial and postcolonial structures of domination as "coloniality of power," Boatcă makes an important point about power relations within Europe:

> That there should be clear limits to the comparability of chattel slavery and serf labor as second slavery and second serfdom, respectively, does not mean that one should disregard obvious parallels, nor that the search for a common denominator is misguided. With respect to the social and economic consequences of the abolition of the respective labor regimes in both regions under scrutiny, it is helpful to consider them as instances

---

30   Kien Nghi Ha, "'Erdarbeiter' – 'Gastarbeiter' – 'Computer-Inder': Arbeitsmigrationspolitik und innere Kolonisierung," in *Deplatziert! Interventionen postkolonialer Kritik*, ed. Stephan Cohrs and Nadine Golly (Berlin: Wissenschaftlicher Verlag Berlin, 2008), 26.
31   Boatcă, "Coloniality of Labor," 304ff.
32   Boatcă, "Coloniality of Labor," 304ff.
33   Boatcă, "Coloniality of Labor," 312.

of the coloniality of labor of global capitalism. As a framework for studying the continuities between structures of domination, coloniality of labor could help analyze the ongoing link between labor forms and specific racial groups after the abolition of slavery in the Americas as well as the pauperization of both freed slaves and freed serfs in the Americas and Eastern Europe without tying these processes to a specific type or stage of slavery or serfdom.[34]

This quasi-colonial division of labour between "Eastern" and "Western" Europe primarily consisted of providing raw materials and foodstuffs. As society moved towards industrialisation, these power relations evolved to comprise the flow of workers. Due to their coercive characteristics and racialising qualities, these flows, I argue, were also marked by a "coloniality of labour." The case of Imperial Germany illuminates this point.

Labour recruitment to Prussia from eastern neighbouring regions, was already widespread throughout the nineteenth century, especially for agricultural work, leading historians to refer to these semi-peripheral regions as the "recruitment areas" of Prussia.[35] In the 1890s, for example, three-quarters of all labour placements in Germany were carried out by commercial agents, some of whom kept up to half of the workers' wages for their services.[36] Ruthenians and Polish workers from Galicia could be recruited officially, as no statutory ban on recruitment existed. By contrast, in Russia, commercial recruitment was banned and foreign agents were not officially allowed to recruit workers within the country. However, recruitment still took place informally and reached such an extent that the historian Klaus J. Bade has referred to these regions as the "free hunting grounds" (*freie Jagdgebiete*) of Prussia.

It is important to understand the rules and regulations that were in place and the way that labour recruitment developed along state-controlled labour rotation regimes at that time. In 1907, Imperial Germany implemented the *Karenzzeit-Regelung* (waiting period regulation), thereby introducing a rotation system that formed the basis of later "guest worker" policies.[37] Within

---

34   Boatcă, "Coloniality of Labor," 312.
35   Klaus Jürgen Bade, *Auswanderer – Wanderarbeiter – Gastarbeiter: Bevölkerung, Arbeitsmarkt und Wanderung in Deutschland seit der Mitte des 19. Jahrhunderts* (Ostfildern: Scripta Mercaturae, 1984), 444ff; Kien Nghi Ha, "Spricht die Subalterne deutsch? Migration und postkoloniale Kritik," in *Die Kolonialen Muster Deutscher Arbeitsmigrationspolitik*, ed. Encarnación Gutiérrez Rodríguez and Hito Steyerl (Münster: Unrast, 2003), 78.
36   Bade, *Auswanderer,* 460–61.
37   Klaus Jürgen Bade, "'Billig und willig' – Die ausländischen Wanderarbeiter im kaiserlichen Deutschland," in *Deutsche im Ausland – Fremde in Deutschland: Migration*

this context, a system of bureaucratic rules and regulations was developed to closely control labour mobility and recruitment. Central to this was the *Legitimationszwang* and the *Rückkehrzwang*. *Legitimationszwang* meant, above all, that immigration was strictly regulated. This means that work and residence permits were issued for a limited period of time and had to be reapplied for annually. Workers were separated into work units according to gender, and worker's children were generally forbidden to enter the country. Pregnancy was considered a breach of contract and was a reason to be expelled from Germany.[38] The *Rückkehrzwang* meant that the workers had to leave Germany at the end of the season and spend the obligatory "waiting period" (*Karenzzeit*) in winter outside the country.[39] The combination of *Legitimationszwang* and *Rückkehrzwang* meant both mobilisation and immobilisation for the workers at the same time: the *Arbeiterlegitimationskarte* (workers' identification card) had nothing in common with a visa but revealed the dual purpose of the *Legitimationszwang*: its function was to block permanent immigration while sustaining the back-and-forth transnational movement of workers. The immobilisation of workers was ensured by binding them to the workplace for the duration of the employment contract and residence permit. The reason for such a strict regulation was the fight against breach of contract by workers from abroad. Therefore, the *Arbeiterlegitimationskarte* carried two names, that of the worker and that of the employer to whom the worker remained bound for the specified period of time. In case of breach of contract, the worker was expelled from the country. The residence permit was thus tied to a specific employer, which meant that a change of employment, if a person did not agree with the working conditions or received a better offer, was forbidden, unless the previous employer gave his consent. While the worker had no right to leave, the employer could dismiss the worker at any time, for example, due to "poor work performance."[40] The "ordered rotation" applied to "unskilled" workers, such as agricultural workers from Poland (Russian Poland, Galicia), who represented the largest group of workers. The *Rückkehrzwang* did not apply

in *Geschichte und Gegenwart*, ed. Klaus Jürgen Bade (Munich: Beck, 1992), 314; Cord Pagenstecher, *Ausländerpolitik und Immigrantenidentität: Zur Geschichte der "Gastarbeit" in der Bundesrepublik* (Berlin: Dieter Bertz Verlag, 1994); Ha, "Spricht die Subalterne deutsch?" 70ff.

38   Bade, *Auswanderer*, 462.

39   See in detail: Klaus Jürgen Bade, "Land oder Arbeit? Transnationale und interne Migration im deutschen Nordosten vor dem Ersten Weltkrieg" (Habilitation treatise, Erlangen-Nürnberg, [1979] 2005), 425ff, 447ff.

40   Bade, *Auswanderer*, 462ff.

to workers from other countries, such as those from Italy who represented the second-largest group.

These differentiated policies of rotation developed as a very complex system characterised by rigid rules and regulations. They were accompanied by a flexible sub-system of "exceptions in individual cases" that varied among government districts and served the interests of employers and the national economy, but not the workers. For better control, the cards (*Arbeiterlegitimationskarten*) had different colours depending on workers' origin. Polish workers received the "red Polish card," Italian workers received a green card, those from Belgium received a blue one, and so on. The cards of the agricultural workers additionally bore a broad, coloured longitudinal line and there were special cards such as the "potato digger card." While the ever-increasing mobility of local agricultural workers and the exodus from agriculture became a mass phenomenon, workers from abroad were bound to their contracts. Thus, im_mobilisation became an institutionalised and highly controlled labour regime. So-called contract-breakers were on the police wanted list for deportation. This situation even increased the interest of agricultural employers from abroad, who were considered to be a "safe and cheap labour force" due to their precarious situation within the absence of labour laws.[41] According to Kien Nghi Ha, these working relations within the rotation system materialised through the *Legitimationskarte* (identification card) and therefore contained "elements of temporary serfdom," since neither freedom of contract nor freedom of movement existed and thus fundamental workers' rights were denied. Together with the *Rückkehrzwang*, this coercive relationship was not only an instrument of labour law but also of the police, as it provided the basis for the annual deportation of racially marked "foreigner Poles." As a consequence, labour laws of forced flexibilisation and forced rotation of employment relations were subject to strict bureaucratic surveillance and control by authorities. Above all, this shows how flexibilisation and control in labour relations developed step by step in a way that aggregated their power. These regulations built the basis for preventing workers from leaving the country or for deporting them whenever necessary. The Nazis later made intensive use of exactly these policies.[42] They could thus build their confinement practices of workers from abroad on a recruitment and migration infrastructure that had been developed, proved and tested for many decades. The "Eastern" European "hunting grounds" later changed as a result of the self-ignited world wars. Germany had to give up both

---

41   Bade, *Auswanderer*, 462ff.
42   Ha, "Spricht die Subalterne deutsch?" 75ff.

its non-European colonies and its Nazi territories, and, later, its traditional labour recruitment areas in "Eastern" Europe during the Cold War. As a result, it turned to the countries bordering the Mediterranean for worker recruitment.[43] The *Legitimationskarte* existed from 1912 onward: it was first issued by the *Deutsche Arbeiterzentrale* in the Weimar Republic, since 1927 by the *Reichsanstalt für Arbeitsvermittlung und Arbeitslosenversicherung* and, finally, by the *Bundesanstalt für Arbeit*.[44]

It is important to reflect upon how agricultural workers from "Eastern" Europe were seen within the colonial society in Prussia. Racialised as "born earth workers" (*geborene Erdarbeiter*) they were called "*Wulacker*" (from the German word *wühlen*, to grub) and even dehumanised as "low ranking Slavs."[45] While the colonial nations were establishing their rule in the colonies, Prussia employed workers from "Eastern" Europe under conditions that – following contemporary agricultural historians and recent historical work – amounted to the "existence of lawless wage slaves."[46] In addition, anti-migrant racism began to evolve during the nineteenth century, as workers from abroad were described as "floods" and "streams" flowing into Imperial Germany, thereby fuelling discourses of *Überfremdung* (racist-imbued fear of being swamped by foreigners). Scholars also contributed to these discourses in society; the sociologist Max Weber pointed to the danger of "polonisation" ("*Polonisierung*") while expressing fear of a "slavic flood" ("*slavische Überflutung*") of agricultural workers and a development that he described as a "cultural regression of several human ages."[47] Other scholars, such as Sartorius von Waltershausen, even linked the social position and the role of these workers in the German Reich to enslaved people in North America or the British West Indies and referred to workers from Italy as a "second-order working class" ("*Arbeiterschicht zweiten Grades*"). Meanwhile, other scientists, such as Max Sering – a German

43   Ha, "'Erdarbeiter,'" 25.

44   Ha, "'Erdarbeiter,'" 25.

45   Klaus Jürgen Bade, ed., *Deutsche im Ausland – Fremde in Deutschland: Migration in Geschichte und Gegenwart* (Munich: Beck, 1992); Kien Nghi Ha. "'Billig und willig': Arbeitsmigrations- und Integrationspolitik aus postkolonialer Perspektive," in *Postkoloniale Politikwissenschaft*, ed. Aram Ziai (Bielefeld: Transcript Verla, 2016), 176.

46   Ulrich Herbert and Karin Hunn, "Beschäftigung, Soziale Sicherung und soziale Integration von Ausländern," in *Bundesrepublik Deutschland 1957–1966: Sozialpolitik im Zeichen des erreichten Wohlstandes; Geschichte der Sozialpolitik in Deutschland seit 1945*, ed. Michael Ruck and Marcel Boldorf (Baden-Baden: Nomos, 2007), 685–724; Ha,"Billig und willig,'" 176.

47   Max Weber, *Die Verhältnisse der Landarbeiter im ostelbischen Deutschland* (Duncker & Humblot Reprints, 1892), 452; Max Weber, *Gesammelte Aufsätze zur Sozial- und Wirtschaftsgeschichte* (Tübingen: Mohr, 1924), 504.

agricultural economist and one of the most influential national economists of his time – argued for the necessity of "inner colonisation," thus the need to acquire colonies towards the east to be able to compete with the United States' economy.[48]

This reveals the colonial mindset of the time, which was driving the appropriation of the labour force, as with land, towards the "East." According to Kien Nghi Ha, the emergence of nation state migration policies during Imperial Germany cannot be seen as separate from the colonial policies of that time, as the ruling classes of the Wilhelminian colonial society shared nationalist, anti-Semitic, racist, social Darwinist, imperialist and militaristic ideologies.[49] Thus, it is not surprising, that dehumanising colonial ideologies impacted all spheres of society, including labour migration policies. External and internal colonisation hence developed simultaneously in Imperial Germany and are both closely linked to the racialised/ethnicised exploitation of agricultural workers and land appropriation – both in the colonies and in Europe.

State policies of labour migration and the recruitment of workers from abroad represent a way of skimming off "human capital" from the peripheries while also outsourcing the reproduction of workers to other regions. This connection is particularly evident in the national economic cost-benefit calculation in Imperial Germany. The so-called "rearing costs" were to be skimped on by these recruitment practices and appeared as "saved socialization and training costs" in the national budget during the guest worker era. It was calculated that a "guest worker" generated at least 20,000 *Deutsche Mark* (DM) per year for the national economy. In addition, billions of DM were surpluses for the German social security system, since the "guest workers" had no access to benefits.[50] At the same time, Germany argued that the implementation of the "guest worker" schemes counted as development aid for the countries of origin and was thus a contribution to their European integration.[51] In fact, the opposite took place, as the recruiting national economies received a workforce they did *not* have to (re)produce,[52] thus saving costs. Instead, the countries of origin

---

48 Max Sering was a co-founder of the Society for the Promotion of Inner Colonisation (*Gesellschaft zur Förderung der inneren Kolonisation*) in 1912 and reflected on his approach in the journal "Archive for Inner Colonisation" (*Archiv für innere Kolonisation*). See Max Sering, *Die innere Kolonisation im östlichen Deutschland* (Leipzig: Duncker & Humblot, 1893).

49 Ha, "'Erdarbeiter.'"

50 Ha, "'Erdarbeiter,'" 23ff.

51 Herbert and Hunn, "Beschäftigung."

52 (Re)productive work includes all working and caring relationships that produce current and future workers who undertake (re)productive work. It ranges from childbirth and

had to bear the losses and costs for (re)production.[53] The reduction of people to mere resources is also evident in the relationship between Nazi Germany and Fascist Italy, where Germany saw Italy as a "reservoir of manpower."[54]

According to Ha, just like discriminatory labour migration policies today, the labour migration policies that were developed in Imperial Germany can, therefore, be seen as "internal colonization," and thus as a reversal of colonial forms of expansion, which allow for the appropriation of the productive power of "Europe's internal others." This follows a logic where migrating workers are defined and treated as "freely displaceable objects of consumption."[55] Thus, while the recruitment initiatives from after the Second World War also emanated from the sending states and the German side saw their role as offering a kind of development aid, the narrative of aiming to help also has to be put into the right genealogy.[56] According to Madina Tlostanova, the "rhetoric of salvation [has continued to hide] the colonial logic of control, domination and suppression" throughout history up until today.[57] In fact, the "guest worker" regime further implemented an ethnicised/racialised division of labour, accompanied by the marginalisation of workers from abroad. The introduction of a new "layer" of migrated workers into society (Unterschichtung) – which was built on centuries of colonial experiences both outside and within Imperial Germany – actually implemented an "underclass" (Unterklasse) or "ethclass" that enabled many German citizens on the lowest rung of the social ladder to rise professionally and socially. This is the way how a neocolonial division of labour was established inside Europe. This sub-proletarianisation created an ethnicised/racialised and underprivileged class within the agricultural labour market.[58] Through various rules and regulations, the social upward mobility of migrated workers was made difficult or prevented. This logic was inscribed in

---

the upbringing of children to the care of workers after retiring from employment due to illness or old age. (Re)productive relationships include all of these, but are not limited to these tasks. They go far beyond human-to-human relations. For reflections on the political economy of (re)production, see Dina Bolokan, "Against Single Stories of 'Left Behind' and 'Triple Win': On Agricultural Care Chains and the Permanent Subsistence Crisis," *Frontiers in Sociology* 6 (2021): 1–20.

53   Ha, "Spricht die Subalterne deutsch?" 69.

54   Bologna, "Kontinuität und Zäsur," 307.

55   Ha, "'Erdarbeiter,'" 28.

56   Mathilde Jamin, "Die deutsch-türkische Anwerbevereinbarung von 1961 und 1964," in *Fremde Heimat: Eine Geschichte der Einwanderung aus der Türkei,* ed. Aytaç Eryılmaz and Mathilde Jamin (Essen: Klartext-Verlag, 1998); Herbert and Hunn, "Beschäftigung," 704ff.

57   Madina Tlostanova, "Postsocialist ≠ Postcolonial? On Post-Soviet Imaginary and Global Coloniality," *Journal of Postcolonial Writing* 48, no. 2 (2012): 130–42.

58   Ha, "Spricht die Subalterne deutsch?" 61ff., 74.

labour and migration laws with such regulations as the *Inländerprimat* (domestic primacy), that exist up until today. This legal primacy defines that workers holding German citizenship have priority over workers who do not hold German citizenship (or, EU citizens over non-EU citizens) when filling vacancies. Ha thus concludes that, although important differences existed between *Wanderarbeiter* (Weimarer Republic), *Fremdarbeiter* (Nazi Germany) and *Gastarbeiter* (post-war Germany) (itinerant/migrant worker/forced labourer, "foreign worker" and "guest worker"), which should by no means be discarded, the main elements of "guest worker" schemes stem from the labour migration legislation of colonial Germany, and their traces can still be seen today.

In other words, we can argue that these continuities, which remain analytically important, are all characterised by regimes of im_mobilisation. They adapt to different historical and political conditions and change through time and space, but carry the inherent logic of the need to maintain an ethnicised/racialised subproletariat of those who are racialised/ethnicised by internal and external colonisation.

3   Neocolonial Labour Regimes of Im_mobilisation in the Agricultural/Agri-food Sector in the European Union

This section seeks to highlight patterns and general trends in the EU that allow us to understand the colonial entanglements of current mobility regimes that accompany agricultural labour relations. These regimes manage (i.e., channel, control, restrict and repress) agricultural workers' movements, thus impacting workers' choices, overall well-being and life conditions. These new regimes of rotation and of im_mobilisation reveal how coloniality is kept alive in the way that labour is organised.

Despite huge differences in implementation, temporary worker recruitment from abroad – according to quotas on seasonal/short-term labour arrangements – have become essential parts of the agricultural and agri-food sector in many places in the European Union. The Netherlands, Norway, Ireland, Sweden, Greece, Italy, and Spain all introduced systematic recruitment of workers, including for the agricultural sector, before the beginning of the 2000s.[59] This especially applies during harvesting and planting months for vegetable and fruit production, in the agri-food industry and, for large meat

---

59   Piotr Plewa and Mark J. Miller, "Postwar and Post-Cold War Generations of European Temporary Foreign Worker Policies: Implications from Spain," *Migraciones Internacionales* 3, no. 2 (2005): 59.

and fish processing factories. Though certain recruitment programmes have persisted over the decades, such as in France (for example, "the IMOs"), many European countries restricted migration policies in the 1970s and reintroduced recruitment programmes at the beginning of the 2000s.[60] The return to temporary labour migration policies has been viewed as a partial resurrection of "guest worker" programmes.[61] It can be stated that, as an overall dynamic throughout the last decades, policies of intense labour recruitment have alternated with political measures to reduce and limit labour migration.[62] While the application of this dynamic varies among countries, the evolution of this dynamic can actually be traced back throughout the last centuries, as some insights I have given above illustrate. Nevertheless, the agricultural sector has always had a specific position within these policies: not only has this sector often been on the forefront when labour recruitment policies have been developed and implemented, but the agricultural sector has always had a special position when it came to guaranteeing the recruitment of workers from abroad in spite of overall restrictions.[63]

When most North European states extended temporary labour migration permits after the Cold War, the southern EU member states followed suit. Thus, Spain, Greece, Italy and Portugal also adopted policies to implement controlled and temporary labour migration – especially for agriculture – although the implementation varies and is very specific to each country.[64] According to Plewa and Miller, the most obvious differences relate to the historical background and prior experiences with temporary labour migration policies. While

---

60 Alain Morice and Bénédicte Michalon, "Les migrants dans l'agriculture: Vers une crise de main-d'oeuvre?" *Études rurales* 182 (2008): 9–28; Stephen Castles, "Guestworker in Europe: A Resurrection?" *International Migration Review* 40, no. 1 (2006): 741–66.

61 Plewa and Miller, *Postwar*; Castles, "Guestworker in Europe"; Sonja Nita, "Circular Migration within the EU-Moldova Mobility Partnership," in *Impact of Circular Migration on Human, Political and Civil Rights: A Global Perspective*, ed. Carlota Solé et al., United Nations University Series on Regionalism (Cham: Springer International Publishing, 2016): 23–44.

62 See The Schwarzenbach Initiative: Angelo Maiolino, *Als die Italiener noch Tschinggen waren. Der Widerstand gegen die Schwarzenbach-Initiative* (Zürich: Rotpunktverlag, 2011).

63 See Sachsengänger in Prussia: Manuela Obermaier, *Die Sachsengänger: Wanderarbeiter im Rübenanbau 1850 bis 1915* (Berlin: Dr. Albert Bartens Verlag, 1999), or for 1974 France: Plewa and Miller, *Postwar*, 64. The earliest example of this dynamic was the shutting down of the borders during Covid-19 in spring 2020 while extra regulations allowed for the recruitment of agricultural workers: Dina Bolokan, "Recruitment Infrastructure within the Agricultural and Agrifood Sector: Post-Soviet and Neocolonial Entanglements between 'Eastern' and 'Western' Europe," *Social Change Review* 18, no.1 (2020): 39–77.

64 See Plewa and Miller, *Postwar*.

the "Northern" countries were among those that recruited workers during the "guest worker" era, the southern EU countries were among those affected by large-scale emigration. The lack of experience with temporary labour immigration in the southern EU countries led them to follow the "Northern" EU countries as points of reference. Therefore, Plewa and Miller argue that labour migration policies in "unexperienced" countries did not develop from a thorough analysis; instead they imitated the post-war "Western" and "Northern" European model of temporary labour migration. Thus, Italy and Spain pursued a policy of admitting seasonal workers in the post-Cold War period that is comparable to that of former "guest worker" policies in Germany, France and Switzerland, albeit on a much smaller scale.[65]

Apart from differences in scale and types of agricultural recruitment programmes for workers from abroad, the time-limited post-Cold War labour recruitment policies remain essentially very similar, and in some cases even the same, as was the case, for instance, for the post-Second World War *Gastarbeiter* regulations. The economic objectives of both the sending and the receiving countries are the determining factors for admission, whereas the interests and needs of the migrated workers are disregarded and their rights are generally extremely limited compared to locally born workers. Depending on the country where labour is performed and on the worker's citizenship (EU/non-EU) the recruitment channel takes very different forms. In general, however, workers mostly have short-term employment contracts – if they have any at all – which are often tied to a specific geographical area, a specific occupation/sector or even to a specific employer.[66] Strong dependencies on the employer are particularly significant because it is the employer who controls events surrounding migration and legal residence in the country. The latter power relation has been referred to in migration studies as "deportability," a social and legal status that clearly reminds one of the above-mentioned serfdom-like labour and living conditions.[67] The constant threat of deportation does not only apply to illegalised workers, but also includes the precarious situation of

---

65   Plewa and Miller, *Postwar*, 65.
66   See Plewa and Miller, *Postwar*, 59ff. Also, the implementation of bilateral agreements with Moldova in the framework of circular migration policies in the EU in 2009 at first allowed people only to work in Poland and only in the agricultural/agri-food sector. Due to recruitment and labour chains (workers from Poland are largely employed in the agricultural sector in wealthier European countries), the meat and fish processing industry lacks workers and compensates with workers from other countries such as Moldova and Ukraine. See Bolokan, "Recruitment Infrastructure."
67   For deportability, see Nicholas De Genova, "Migrant 'Illegality' and Deportability in Everyday Life," *Annual Review of Anthropology* 31 (2002): 419–47.

temporary employed workers who have to leave the country if they lose their job, no matter the reason of the employment termination.

While recurring, long-term labour relations within the agricultural sector exist and, in some cases, also allow workers from abroad to settle down where they perform wage labour, most agricultural working relations are structured in a way that does not allow settling down or legalising workers' status. These agricultural labour regimes thus carry elements of hypermobility and of confinement at the same time. In what follows, I will give a few examples that show how different mobility patterns coexisted within regimes of im_mobilisation. This reveals that although the two "obverse" logics of confinement and hypermobility might appear contradictory, in fact they are inherent to these regimes and, therefore, constitute them.

3.1   Current Transnational and Transregional Rotation Regimes

Regimes of im_mobilisation can be transregional, where workers regularly change labour relations within the country, or they can be transnational, and marked by a regular crossing of national borders. In southern Italy, for example, the transregional regime can encompass picking citrus fruit in Calabria during the winter months, then working on strawberry plantations in Campania during spring, followed by harvesting tomatoes in Puglia or Basilicata in the summer.[68] This rotation regime is especially relevant to illegalised workers and even more to those seeking asylum, who live mostly in informal, so-called ghettos and shanty towns or in state/NGO-run and monitored reception centres and tent cities.[69] Many of the workers who live in these locations are of sub-Saharan African origin. While they have to be highly mobile and follow the different harvest cycles, they "found themselves 'trapped' in agriculture" – not least due to their status – and live in segregated spaces.[70] After people from

---

68   Domenico Perrotta, "Agricultural Day Laborers in Southern Italy: Forms of Mobility and Resistance," *South Atlantic Quarterly* 114, no. 1 (2015): 198.

69   The inhabitants themselves define these settlements as "ghettos." See Irene Peano, "Global Care-Commodity Chains: Labour Re/Production and Agribusiness in the District of Foggia, Southeastern Italy," *Sociologia del lavoro* 146, no. 2 (2017): 24–39s.

70   Nick Dines and Enrica Rigo, "Postcolonial Citizenships between Representation, Borders and the 'Refugeeization' of the Workforce: Critical Reflections on Migrant Agricultural Labor in the Italian Mezzogiorno," in *Postcolonial Transitions in Europe: Contexts, Practices and Politics*, ed. Sandra Ponzanesi and Gianmaria Colpani (London and New York: Rowman & Littlefield International, 2016), 151–72; Martina Lo Cascio and Domenico Perrotta, "The Intertwinement of Symbolic and Structural Violence: Migrant Agricultural Labourers in Two Regions of Southern Italy," in *Race Discrimination and Management of Ethnic Diversity and Migration at Work*, edited by Joana Vassilopoulou, Julienne Brabet, and Victoria Showunmi, vol. 6 (Bingley: Emerald Publishing, 2019), 185.

former colonised regions have crossed the Mediterranean in search of a better life, while also trying to escape persecution, economic precarity or even war, the only possibility to enter Italy is set within the legal framework of applying for refugee status, which does not allow full access to labour and civil rights or a long-term perspective. This condition has been described as the "'refugeei-zation' of the workforce" within the agricultural sector – a phenomenon that, according to Nick Dines and Enrica Rigo, and following Miguel Mellino, has to be situated within "postcolonial capitalism."[71] They thereby refer to the fact that "the hierarchization of the global workforce no longer corresponds simply to the classic international division of labour, but is also mirrored in the subal-tern inclusion of migrants within the same European space."[72]

In other cases, the rotation regimes are transnational. This especially applies to agricultural workers from "Eastern" Europe, mainly from Romania and Moldova, that represent the main workforce in Italy, as well as to workers from India, Morocco or Albania, who have officially been registered as hold-ing a regular work contract in agriculture.[73] Thus, workers from Romania are most often employed on a seasonal basis.[74] Due to the European citizenship of workers holding Romanian citizenship, labour arrangements and worker mobility are not limited to Italy, and agricultural workers regularly return to their place of origin. Although workers from "Eastern" Europe have privileged legal status, this does not necessarily lead to better labour relations or higher wages in Italy.

Analysing forms of mobility and resistance within the *caporalato* system in tomato farming in Puglia and Basilicata, Domenico Perotta observed that work-ers from Romania often work for lower wages than workers from Africa. One reason he assumes, among others, is that workers from Romania have "greater freedom" and, therefore, accept lower wages. He argues: "Their most powerful and profitable form of resistance is their mobility within Europe, their abil-ity to 'escape.'" According to Perotta, this results in the fact that workers from Romania seldom get involved in struggles around working conditions, whereas those from Africa with a precarious legal status, those that are "trapped" in this

---

71   Dines and Rigo, "Postcolonial Citizenships"; Lo Cascio and Perrotta, "Intertwinement";
      and Miguel Mellino, *Cittadinanze postcoloniali: Appartenenze, razza e razzismo in Europa
      e in Italia* (Rome: Carocci, 2013), 11.

72   Dines and Rigo, "Postcolonial Citizenships," 152.

73   Workers from India mainly work in livestock farming: see Perrotta, "Agricultural Day
      Laborers," 197; Lo Cascio and Perrotta, "Intertwinement."

74   Dines and Rigo, "Postcolonial Citizenships," 152.

area, do engage in collective protest. In some ways, their social position seems to provide a better starting point for organising.[75]

3.2   The Invisible Economy: Regimes of (Re)Production within Regimes of Im_mobilisation

This section aims to reflect on the "invisible economy." This (re)productive sphere of the differentiated regimes of im_mobilisation is where the workforce is produced and reproduced, and that is key to capitalist surplus value.[76]

Following migrant farm workers' struggles, Irene Peano investigated reproductive labour and care within large-scale agribusiness on a local basis.[77] In what she calls zones – in this case, the agro-industrial district of Foggia in south-eastern Italy – living and working conditions are segregated, racialised/ethnicised and gendered. Comparing the organisation of West-African shanty towns to "Eastern"-European settlements, Peano has shown that, while the shanty towns are mainly populated by single male farm workers, sub-Saharan African women engage in the reproduction of the labour force rather than in agricultural work. This can also include sex work, due to the lack of alternatives. Peano further concludes that "West-African women working as re/productive service providers in the zone are a few hundred with very high turnover rates just as their male counterparts."[78] When it comes to agricultural workers from "Eastern" Europe, who represent the majority, all genders are involved in agriculture. According to Peano, in Romani communities, who represent a large number of seasonal workers, women mostly travel with their next of kin. Most often, all are involved in agricultural labour, including children, and work under the same exploitative conditions as their colleagues from West-Africa. Additionally, she argues that women face a "double work regime," as they are additionally responsible for tasks such as taking care of small children, cooking and washing. Hence, Peano concludes that different degrees of dependency and thus of exploitation exist that also depend on gender and on the position within "the care-commodity chains and their re/productive labour regimes."

---

75   Perrotta, "Agricultural Day Laborers," 200.

76   For reflections on the "invisible economy," see the Iceberg Model of Capitalist Patriarchal Economics in Maria Mies and Veronica Bennhold-Thomsen, *The Subsistence Perspective: Beyond the Globalised Economy* (London, New York and Australia: ZED Books & Spinifex Press, 1999), 30–31.

77   See Peano, "Global Care-Commodity Chains"; Irene Peano. "Emergenc(i)es in the Fields: Affective Composition and Countercamps against the Exploitation of Migrant Farm Labor in Italy," in *Impulse to Act: A New Anthropology of Resistance and Social Justice*, ed. Othon Alexandrakis (Bloomington, IN: Indiana University Press, 2016), 63–88.

78   Peano, "Global Care-Commodity Chains."

However, she also emphasises that, while different workers are differently exploited in the same place and "trapped" in segregated settlements, people can find community, solidarity and a space that allows for collective organising and mutual aid.[79] So while living and working conditions within these labour regimes and "zones" are highly ethnicised/racialised *and* highly gendered, they also carry the "potential for non-commodified forms of care labour."

This "invisible economy" also carries a transregional dimension. In my own studies, I have shown how workers' families and communities that remain in their countries of origin are also part of this "invisible economy." Many people who work in the European agricultural sector operate as smallholders in their places of origin. While they harvest abroad or work in the food processing industry, other people must take care of their social responsibilities towards friends, relatives and neighbours and their agricultural subsistence, leading to agricultural care and subsistence chains. These caring communities thus subsidise food production in the countries where their friends and relatives are employed.[80]

3.3   *The Political Infrastructure of Being "Trapped" and Being Mobile*

The hierarchisation of workers has installed revolving doors in "fortress Europe," including at the "Eastern" European borders. This "just-in-time" recruitment of workers becomes possible through different bilateral agreements, such as traineeship agreements, and through co-ethnic citizenship for those who are seen as "not-quite-European" but still "culturally compatible."[81] I will now elaborate on a number of regulations that keep workers "trapped" and hypermobile, thereby reproducing the hierarchisation of workers along colonial legacies.

One such example are "circular migration" policies. They serve as one of the European Union's formal recruitment strategies for managing labour migration in low-wage sectors, such as in agriculture and agribusiness. Beginning in 2005, the EU developed Mobility Partnerships, based on which bilateral agreements between member states and non-EU-countries could be signed to

---

79   Peano, "Global Care-Commodity Chains," and see Alessandra Corrado, "Clandestini in the Orange Towns: Migrations and Racisms in Calabria's Agriculture," *Race/Ethnicity: Multidisciplinary Global Contexts* 4, no. 2, Reworking Race and Labor (2011): 191–201.

80   See Bolokan, "Against Single Stories."

81   For more on "not-quite-European" discourses and Othering processes, see Manuela Boatcă, "Thinking Europe Otherwise: Lessons from the Caribbean," *Current Sociology* 69, no. 3 (2021): 389–414; Bolokan, "Recruitment Infrastructure."

facilitate rights-based "circular migration."[82] Moldova was one of the first partnerships: a formal system of work relations between Moldova and Poland was put into place with this mobility partnership between the EU and the Republic of Moldova.[83] On this legal basis, Poland offers Moldovan (non-EU citizens) temporary work for several months per year. Due to several regulations that have been implemented since 2006, workers from other countries can be employed in Poland without the need to obtain a work permit. This so-called simplified system allowed non-EU members and workers from Russia, Ukraine and Belarus to work in Poland for three months within a six-month period. At first, this possibility was limited to the agricultural sector only – the sector most in need of a workforce – but it opened to all sectors over the following years. As Polish citizens emigrate or are regularly employed within the agricultural sector all over the European Union, this results in recruitment chains and a shortage of workers within the country. Thus, Poland currently has the highest numbers of incoming workers from abroad in the EU. Temporary workers on Polish farms and in the meat processing industry increasingly come from Ukraine, especially after the outbreak of war in 2014.[84] It can be assumed that most of the workers recruited from Moldova work in the fish and meat processing industry.[85] These workers are either employed on a temporary basis or regularly search for new labour arrangements due to very harsh labour conditions. They are thus forced to be mobile due to legal regulations or end up fleeing exploitation and refusing disastrous labour and living conditions in the hope of finding better, sustainable labour arrangements. This hypermobility – a life permanently on the move – heavily impacts workers' health while, at the same time, resulting in their exclusion from social security, permanent health insurance and the possibility of early retirement.[86] Still, such bilateral agreements based on "circular migration" policies are being promoted worldwide as a development strategy, following the colonial discourse of "aiming to help." These agreements are supported by the World Bank as well as by many sending and receiving countries. Various projects exist that have been implemented as pilot projects to test "circular migration." This, for example, allows

---

82   European Commission, *Migration and Development: Some Concrete Orientations* (2005); *On Circular Migration and Mobility Partnerships between the European Union and Third Countries* (2007).

83   Joint declaration on the mobility partnership between the European Union and the Republic of Moldova, 2005.

84   Marta Jaroszewicz, *Migration from Ukraine to Poland: The Trend Stabilises* (OSW Report, October 2018), 6.

85   Bolokan, "On Hypermobility."

86   Bolokan, "On Hypermoblity," and see Monika Szulecka, "Regulating Movement."

the recruitment of workers from Mauritius and Ghana to Italy, from Georgia to Germany, and from Morocco to Spain.[87] Most programmes are in place in low-wage sectors, such as agriculture. In some cases recruitment programmes are highly gendered, such as in the case of Morocco, where women with at least one child at home are being recruited to make sure that agricultural workers will not overstay their contracts and will, instead, go back to their children.[88]

Though the living and working relations in the agricultural sector in Southern Italy that Irene Peano refers to as "zones" are very specific, they reveal crucial patterns that are also relevant to labour conditions elsewhere in Europe.[89] The large-scale greenhouses in Almería that are known as Spain's "Seas of Plastic" and the living and working conditions in the meat processing industry, especially the large-scale slaughterhouses in Germany, are further examples of coexisting regimes of confinement and hypermobility. In these zones, workers are "trapped." They are physically "trapped," as they may lose their jobs if they leave these zones, and they are socially "trapped," because of their discrimination and segregation from society, legal status and lack of alternative employment. At the same time, agricultural workers (and those responsible for (re)production within these zones) have to be constantly on the move; this hypermobility arises when either the agricultural working relation is of limited duration or their legal status is complicated and people need to move within or outside the country or even back home. In other cases, people decide to end the working relationship because of bad health relating to the highly exploitative conditions.[90] What differs from place to place is the degree of confinement and the range of mobility. This is also applicable beyond the large-scale agribusiness "zones" and is represented within medium and small-scale agriculture, where workers from abroad are also temporarily employed. While long-term working relations do exist, a large majority of workers are only employed for several weeks or months at a time and, therefore, have to be constantly on the move. This concerns agricultural workers from abroad that

---

87   See "Circular Migration: First Batch of Mauritians to Leave for Italy," 7 May 2013, http://www.govmu.org/English/News/Pages/Circular-Migration-First-batch-of-Mauritians-to-Leave-for-Italy-in-December.aspx; IOM, "Circular Migration: Filling Temporary Labour Shortages and Promoting the Benefits of Managed Migration," YouTube video, 19:54, accessed April 2022, https://bit.ly/3PUBTRk; Anna Goos, "Manual on Circular Migration Scheme," 2016, https://bit.ly/3J7v36t.

88   Ian Barnes and Cristina Cherino, "Circular Migration and New Modes of Governance: So What Are the Consequences?" in *Państwo demokratyczne, prawne i socjalne: Studia społeczne, polityczne i ekonomiczne* (Krakow, Poland: Krakowska Akadem, 2014), 593.

89   Peano, "Global Care-Commodity Chains."

90   Bolokan, "On Hypermobility."

additionally have limited access to workers' rights – if any at all – while the local labour force can find recurrent and stable agricultural labour relations. This preference for "local" workers is inscribed into labour and migration laws with the concept of *Inländerprimat* (domestic primacy). It is, furthermore, implemented in the European Union as a dual migration system that gives priority to EU citizens.

The resulting hierarchisation of workers maintains a gendered and ethnicised/racialised division of labour according to colonial legacies. As a consequence, the most precarious workers within the agricultural sector in Europe have to work under the status of "trainee," "refugee" or "asylum seeker," or, in the worst-case scenario, have to live under illegalised living and working conditions. This, again, mostly affects workers from regions that have previously been exploited by European colonisation – in Latin America, Africa and Asia – but in some cases also encompasses people from "Eastern" European countries inside and outside the EU, such as in the former Soviet regions. Today, workers from abroad are marginalised in a similar way, as the "guest worker" regime was accompanied by the introduction of a new lower class in society (*Unterschichtung*). The existence of an underclass (*Unterklasse*)/ethclass enables citizens of a country who find themselves on the lowest rung of the social ladder to rise professionally and socially, as the stratified underprivileged class takes over the jobs the workers holding citizenship can refuse.[91]

Whether workers end up being trapped or hypermobile depends on their citizenship and legal and civil status, as well as on racialised and ethnicised forms of discrimination. How workers perceive a certain place and working relation is also bound to class, age, gender, sexuality, (dis)abilities and religion, leading to varying experiences of inclusion or exclusion. Hence, current labour and living conditions in large parts of the agricultural and agri-food sectors in Europe should be analysed as differentiated regimes of im_mobilisation that carry the inherent colonial logic of the transnational and transregional mobilisation of workers, such as their concurrent confinement/segregation.

4   Conclusion

As mentioned in the beginning, Kien Nghi Ha has argued that state policies of labour migration can be roughly divided into two phases: (1) from the nineteenth century to the First World War and (2) after the Second World War.

---

91   Ha, "Spricht die Subalterne deutsch?" 74.

While, during the first phase, the inner-European semi-peripheries served as main recruitment areas, workers increasingly came from the postcolonial world in the second phase.[92] This, of course, applies very differently to each European region depending on their role in colonisation and their later post-colonial (return) migrations. Following Kien Nghi Ha and with reference to the agricultural labour market, I argue that it is important to distinguish a third phase. This phase is characterised by the presence of workers from the postco-lonial peripheries – though not necessarily with a historical colonial link to the receiving country (which, in some cases, distinguishes it even more from the second phase) – *and* from European semi-peripheral regions, especially those that became accessible again post 1991.[93] The latter have once again become the main recruitment zone for agricultural workers, after these were lost after the Second World War and remained inaccessible during the Cold War. This is the reason that, for example, Ukraine has been referred to as "Europe's Mexico."[94] The crucial characteristic of the third phase is thus the existence of a very precarious (even illegalised) labour force, mainly consisting of workers from formerly colonised regions and "Eastern" Europe. While both are caught within differentiated regimes of im_mobilisation, and are, therefore, marked by a "coloniality of labour," it is, of course, crucial to note that these regimes cannot be equated with slavery or serfdom. I conclude, nevertheless, that these agricultural labour regimes in food production are structured by coloniality. In other words, coloniality is immanent to the differentiated and international division of (re)productive labour. This is because of the way in which this divi-sion and these regimes developed, in terms of the composition of the work-force, its racialising qualities and, above all, the position of the workers within the global economy. One of the most significant changes has been the way recruitment programmes are organised in the third phase. Instead of large-scale recruitment programmes such as in the guest worker era, multiple strate-gies and smaller recruitment programmes that target very specific local needs and interests are being applied. As I have shown, and as Plexa and Miller have also argued, macro admission programmes have been replaced by multiple microprogrammes.[95] I, therefore, agree with Hönekopps' analysis that these changes to micro-policies have allowed national economies to better manage

---

92   Ha, "Spricht die Subalterne deutsch?" 25.

93   Between 1990 and 1997, over half of all migration to the European Union states came from formerly Communist Central and Eastern Europe. See Plewa and Miller, *Postwar*, 67.

94   Franck Düvell, "Ukraine: Europe's Mexico?" *Central East European Migration Country Report 1* (Oxford: University of Oxford, Centre for Migration, Policy and Society, 2007).

95   Plewa and Miller, *Postwar,* 67.

(i.e., control) migration.[96] Still, people's movements and illegalised statuses also reveal that they cannot be fully controlled. In future studies, it would be worth focusing on how the "coloniality of labour" is challenged within these difficult conditions, to gain insight into transregional and manifold resistance practices.

Bibliography

Auderset, Patrick, Charles Magnin, and Rosa Brux. *Nous, saisonniers, saisonnières ... Genève 1931–2019*. Genève: Archives contestataires, 2019.

Bade, Klaus Jürgen. "Land oder Arbeit? Transnationale und interne Migration im deutschen Nordosten vor dem Ersten Weltkrieg." Habilitation treatise, Erlangen-Nürnberg, [1979] 2005.

Bade, Klaus Jürgen. *Auswanderer – Wanderarbeiter – Gastarbeiter: Bevölkerung, Arbeitsmarkt und Wanderung in Deutschland seit der Mitte des 19. Jahrhunderts.* Ostfildern: Scripta Mercaturae, 1984.

Bade, Klaus Jürgen, ed. *Deutsche im Ausland – Fremde in Deutschland: Migration in Geschichte und Gegenwart.* Munich: Beck, 1992.

Bade, Klaus Jürgen. "'Billig und willig' – Die ausländischen Wanderarbeiter im kaiserlichen Deutschland." In Bade, *Deutsche im Ausland*, 311–23.

Bade, Klaus Jürgen. *Europa in Bewegung: Migration vom späten 18. Jahrhundert bis zur Gegenwart.* Munich: Beck, 2000.

Barnes, Ian, and Christina Cherino. "Circular Migration and New Modes of Governance: So What Are the Consequences?" In *Państwo demokratyczne, prawne i socjalne: Studia społeczne, polityczne i ekonomiczne*, edited by Marian Grzybowski and Bogumił Naleziński, 581–600. Krakow, Poland: Krakowska Akadem, 2014.

Boatcă, Manuela. "Coloniality of Labor in the Global Periphery: Latin America and Eastern Europe in the World-System." *Review (Fernand Braudel Center)* 36, no. 3–4 (2013): 287–314.

Boatcă, Manuela. "Coloniality of Citizenship and Occidentalist Epistemology." In "Decolonial Theory & Practice in Southeast Europe," edited by Polina Manolova, Katarina Kušić, and Philipp Lottholz, special issue, *Dversia* 19, no. 3 (2019): 55–77.

Boatcă, Manuela. "Thinking Europe Otherwise: Lessons from the Caribbean." *Current Sociology* 69, no. 3 (2021): 389–414.

---

96   Plewa and Miller, *Postwar*, following Elmar Hönekopp, "The New Labor Migration as an Instrument of German Foreign Policy," in *Migrants, Refugees, and Foreign Policy: U.S. and German Policies Toward Countries of Origin*, ed. Rainer Münz and Myron Weiner (Providence, RI: Berghahn Books, 1997), 17.

Bolokan, Dina. "Recruitment Infrastructure within the Agricultural and Agrifood Sector: Post-Soviet and Neocolonial Entanglements between 'Eastern' and 'Western' Europe." *Social Change Review* 18, no. 1 (2020): 39–77.

Bolokan, Dina. "Against Single Stories of 'Left Behind' and 'Triple Win': On Agricultural Care Chains and the Permanent Subsistence Crisis." *Frontiers in Sociology* 6 (2021): 1–20.

Bolokan, Dina. "On Hypermobility in the Agricultural Sector in Europe – Translocal Life Trajectories between Switzerland and Moldova." In *The Rural-Migration Nexus: Global Problems, Rural Issues*, edited by Nathan Kerrigan and Philomena de Lima. London: Palgrave, forthcoming.

Bonifazi, Corrado. "Evolution of Regional Patterns of International Migration in Europe." In *International Migration in Europe: New Trends and New Methods of Analysis*, edited by Corrado Bonifazi, Marek Okólski, Jeannette Schoorl, and Patrick Simon, 107–28. Amsterdam: Amsterdam University Press, 2008.

Castles, Stephen. "Guestworker in Europe: A Resurrection?" *International Migration Review* 40, no. 1 (2006): 741–66.

"Circular Migration: First Batch of Mauritians to Leave for Italy." 7 May 2013. http://www.govmu.org/English/News/Pages/Circular-Migration-First-batch-of-Mauritians-to-Leave-for-Italy-in-December.aspx.

Consterdine, Erica, and Sahizer Samuk. "Closing the Seasonal Agricultural Workers' Scheme: A Triple Loss." Working paper no. 83, University of Sussex, Sussex Centre for Migration Research, 2015. https://bit.ly/2lRzgmw.

Corrado, Alessandra. "Clandestini in the Orange Towns: Migrations and Racisms in Calabria's Agriculture." *Race/Ethnicity: Multidisciplinary Global Contexts* 4, no. 2 (2011): 191–201.

Corrado, Alessandra, Carlos de Castro, and Domenico Perrotta. *Migration and Agriculture: Mobility and Change in the Mediterranean Area*. London and New York: Routledge, 2017.

De Genova, Nicholas. "Migrant 'Illegality' and Deportability in Everyday Life." *Annual Review of Anthropology* 31 (2002), 419–47.

Dines, Nick, and Enrica Rigo. "Postcolonial Citizenships between Representation, Borders and the 'Refugeeization' of the Workforce: Critical Reflections on Migrant Agricultural Labor in the Italian Mezzogiorno." In *Postcolonial Transitions in Europe: Contexts, Practices and Politics*, edited by Sandra Ponzanesi and Gianmaria Colpani, 151–72. London and New York: Rowman & Littlefield International, 2016.

Düvell, Franck. "Ukraine: Europe's Mexico?" *Central East European Migration Country Report 1*. Oxford: University of Oxford, Centre for Migration, Policy and Society, 2007.

European Commission. *Migration and Development: Some Concrete Orientations*, 2005. https://bit.ly/3x6MdPf.

European Commission. *On Circular Migration and Mobility Partnerships between the European Union and Third Countries,* 2007. https://ec.europa.eu/commission/pres scorner/detail/en/MEMO_07_197.

Fassmann, Heinz, and Rainer Münz. *Migration in Europa: Historische Entwicklung, aktuelle Trends und politische Reaktionen.* Frankfurt and New York: Campus, 1996.

Federal Law on the Residence and Settlement of Foreigners of 26 March 1931. https:// bit.ly/37jxDcC.

Gans, Paul, and Andreas Pott: "Migration und Migrationspolitik in Europa." In *Handbuch Lokale Integrationspolitik,* edited by Frank Gesemann and Roland Roth, 11–56. Wiesbaden: Springer, 2018.

Garrapa, Anna Mary. "Supermarket revolution y agricultura californiana: ¿Un modelo en expansión?" *Interdisciplina* 6, no. 14 (2018): 155–76.

Gertel, Jörg, and Sarah Ruth Sippel. *Seasonal Workers in Mediterranean Agriculture.* London: Routledge, 2014.

Goos, Anna. "Manual on Circular Migration Scheme." 2016. https://bit.ly/3J7v36t.

Ha, Kien Nghi. "Spricht die Subalterne deutsch? Migration und postkoloniale Kritik." In *Die Kolonialen Muster Deutscher Arbeitsmigrationspolitik,* edited by Encarnación Gutiérrez Rodríguez and Hito Steyerl, 56–107. Münster: Unrast, 2003.

Ha, Kien Nghi. "'Erdarbeiter'–'Gastarbeiter'–'Computer-Inder':Arbeitsmigrationspolitik und innere Kolonisierung." In *Deplatziert! Interventionen postkolonialer Kriti`k,* edited by Stephan Cohrs and Nadine Golly, 16–36. Berlin: Wissenschaftlicher Verlag Berlin, 2008.

Ha, Kien Nghi. "'Billig und willig': Arbeitsmigrations- und Integrationspolitik aus postkolonialer Perspektive." In *Postkoloniale Politikwissenschaft,* edited by Aram Ziai, 173–90. Bielefeld: Transcript Verla, 2016.

Herbert, Ulrich, and Karin Hunn. "Beschäftigung, Soziale Sicherung und soziale Integration von Ausländern." In *Bundesrepublik Deutschland 1957–1966: Sozialpolitik im Zeichen des erreichten Wohlstandes; Geschichte der Sozialpolitik in Deutschland seit 1945,* edited by Michael Ruck and Marcel Boldorf, 685–724. Baden-Baden: Nomos, 2007.

Hönekopp, Elmar. "The New Labor Migration as an Instrument of German Foreign Policy." In *Migrants, Refugees, and Foreign Policy: U.S. and German Policies Toward Countries of Origin,* edited by Rainer Münz and Myron Weiner, 165–82. Providence, RI: Berghahn Books, 1997.

IOM. "Circular Migration: Filling Temporary Labour Shortages and Promoting the Benefits of Managed Migration." YouTube video, 19:54. Accessed April 2022, https://www.youtube.com/watch?v=SRobg68z9C4.

Jamin, Mathilde. "Die deutsch-türkische Anwerbevereinbarung von 1961 und 1964." In *Fremde Heimat: Eine Geschichte der Einwanderung aus der Türkei,* edited by Aytaç Eryılmaz and Mathilde Jamin, 69–82. Essen: Klartext-Verlag. 1998.

"Joint Declaration on the Mobility Partnership between the European Union and the Republic of Moldova, 2005." https://www.eeas.europa.eu/node/5404_en.

Lo Cascio, Martina, and Domenico Perrotta. "The Intertwinement of Symbolic and Structural Violence: Migrant Agricultural Labourers in Two Regions of Southern Italy." In *Race Discrimination and Management of Ethnic Diversity and Migration at Work*, edited by Joana Vassilopoulou, Julienne Brabet, and Victoria Showunmi, 175–200. Vol. 6. Bingley: Emerald Publishing, 2019.

Lower, Wendy. *Nazi Empire-Building and the Holocaust in Ukraine*. Chapel Hill: University of North Carolina Press, 2005.

Maiolino, Angelo. *Als die Italiener noch Tschinggen waren. Der Widerstand gegen die Schwarzenbach-Initiative*. Zürich: Rotpunktverlag, 2011.

Mantelli, Brunello. "Zwischen Strukturwandel auf dem Arbeitsmarkt und Kriegswirtschaft: Die Anwerbung der italienischen Arbeiter für das 'Dritte Reich' und die 'Achse Berlin-Rom' 1938–1943." In *Proletarier der 'Achse': Sozialgeschichte der italienischen Fremdarbeit in NS-Deutschland 1937 bis 1943*, edited by Cesare Bermani, Sergio Bologna, and Brunello Mantelli, 253–392. Berlin: Akademie, 1997.

Mellino, Miguel. *Cittadinanze postcoloniali: Appartenenze, razza e razzismo in Europa e in Italia*. Rome: Carocci, 2013.

Mies, Maria, and Veronica Bennhold-Thomsen. *The Subsistence Perspective: Beyond the Globalised Economy*. London, New York and Australia: ZED Books & Spinifex Press, 1999.

Molinero-Gerbeau, Yoan, and Avallone Gennaro. "Producing Cheap Food and Labour: Migrations and Agriculture in the Capitalistic World-Ecology." *Social Change Review* 14, no. 2 (2016): 121–48.

Morice, Alain, and Bénédicte Michalon. "Les migrants dans l'agriculture: Vers une crise de main-d'oeuvre?" *Études rurales* 182 (2008): 9–28.

Nita, Sonja. "Circular Migration within the EU-Moldova Mobility Partnership." In *Impact of Circular Migration on Human, Political and Civil Rights: A Global Perspective*, edited by Carlota Solé, Sonia Parella, Teresa Sordé Martí, and Sonja Nita, 23–44. United Nations University Series on Regionalism. Cham: Springer International Publishing, 2016.

Nelson, Robert L. *Germans, Poland, and Colonial Expansion to the East: 1850 through the Present*. New York: Palgrave Macmillan, 2009.

NoLager Bremen, and Europäisches BürgerInnenforum, eds. *Peripherie & Plastikmeer. Globale Landwirtschaft – Migration – Widerstand*. Vienna: EBF/ NoLager Bremen, 2009.

Oltmer, Jochen. "Einführung: Migrationskontinent Europa." In: *Nach Übersee: Deutschsprachige Auswanderer aus dem östlichen Europa um 1900*, edited by Deutsches Kulturforum östliches Europa, 8–25. Potsdam: Deutsches Kulturforum östliches Europa, 2015.

Pagenstecher, Cord. *Ausländerpolitik und Immigrantenidentität: Zur Geschichte der "Gastarbeit" in der Bundesrepublik.* Berlin: Dieter Bertz Verlag, 1994.

Peano, Irene. "Emergenc(i)es in the Fields: Affective Composition and Countercamps against the Exploitation of Migrant Farm Labor in Italy." In *Impulse to Act: A New Anthropology of Resistance and Social Justice,* edited by Othon Alexandrakis, 63–88. Bloomington, Indianapolis: Indiana University Press, 2016.

Peano, Irene. "Global Care-Commodity Chains: Labour Re/Production and Agribusiness in the District of Foggia, Southeastern Italy." *Sociologia del lavoro* 146, no. 2 (2017): 24–39.

Peano, Irene. "Ways of Making a Human Otherwise: After-Ethnography with Migrant Labourers in Italian Agro-Industrial Enclaves." In *Modos de Fazer/Ways of Making,* edited by Vítor Oliveira Jorge, 219–30. Porto: Centro de Investigação Transdisciplinar Cultura, Espaço e Memória, 2020.

Perrotta, Domenico, "Agricultural Day Laborers in Southern Italy: Forms of Mobility and Resistance." *South Atlantic Quarterly* 114, no. 1 (2015): 195–203.

Plewa, Piotr, and Mark J. Miller. "Postwar and Post-Cold War Generations of European Temporary Foreign Worker Policies: Implications from Spain." *Migraciones Internacionales* 3, no. 2 (2005): 58–83.

Rass, Christoph. *Institutionalisierungsprozesse auf einem internationalen Arbeitsmarkt: Bilaterale Wanderungsverträge in Europa zwischen 1919 und 1974.* Paderborn: Schöningh, 2010.

Quijano, Aníbal. "Coloniality of Power, Eurocentrism, and Latin America." *Nepantla: Views from South* 1, no. 3 (2000): 533–74.

Sacchetto, Devi, and Domenico Perrotta. "Il ghetto e lo sciopero: Braccianti stranieri nell'Italia meridionale." *Sociologia del lavoro* 128, no. 4 (2012): 153–66.

Sering, Max. *Die innere Kolonisation im östlichen Deutschland.* Leipzig: Duncker & Humblot, 1893.

Szulecka, Monika. "Regulating Movement of the Very Mobile: Selected Legal and Policy Aspects of Ukrainian Migration to EU Countries." In *Ukrainian Migration to the European Union: Lessons from Migration Studies,* edited by Olena Fedyuk and Marta Kindler, 51–71. Switzerland: Springer International Publishing AG, 2016.

Tlostanova, Madina. "Postsocialist ≠ Postcolonial? On Post-Soviet Imaginary and Global Coloniality." *Journal of Postcolonial Writing* 48, no. 2 (2012): 130–42.

Weber, Max. *Die Verhältnisse der Landarbeiter im ostelbischen Deutschland.* Duncker & Humblot Reprints, 1892.

Weber, Max. *Gesammelte Aufsätze zur Sozial- und Wirtschaftsgeschichte.* Tübingen: Mohr, 1924.

Zahra, Tara. *The Great Departure: Mass Migration from Eastern Europe and the Making of the Free World.* New York: W.W. Norton, 2016.

CHAPTER 16

Cheap Labour, (Un)Organised Workers

The Oppressive Exploitation of Labour Migrants in the Malaysian Palm Oil Industry

Janina Puder

1 Introduction

Research on contemporary rural labour relations has long been neglected in Western labour sociology.[1] Current studies concerned with changing labour relations often focus on the industrial and service sectors[2] as well as on the care sector of early-industrialised Western countries.[3] Nevertheless, from a global perspective the primary sector is still an important field of employment, especially in the peripheral and semi-peripheral zones of the world.[4] With political initiatives such as the Green Economy[5] or the Bioeconomy,[6] targeted at the substitution of non-renewable, fossil resources with bio-based materials, the primary sector could gain even greater economic importance.[7] This could have an immense effect on rural labour relations in countries rich in natural

---

1 Claudia Neu, "Land- und Agrarsoziologie," in *Handbuch Spezielle Soziologien*, ed. Georg Kneer and Markus Schroer (Wiesbaden: VS-Verlag, 2010), 256–57.

2 See, for instance, John Smith, *Imperialism in the Twenty-First Century: Globalization, Super-Exploitation, and Final Crisis* (New York: Monthly Review Press, 2016).

3 See, for instance, Arlie R. Hochschild, "Global Care Chains and Emotional Surplus Value," in *On the Edge: Living with Global Capitalism*, ed. Will Hutton and Anthony Giddens (London: Vintage, 2001).

4 Henry Bernstein, *Class Dynamics of Agrarian Change*, Agrarian Change and Peasant Studies Series (Halifax: Fernwood Publishing, 2010); Saturnino M. Borras, "Agrarian Change and Peasant Studies: Changes, Continuities and Challenges – An Introduction," *The Journal of Peasant Studies* 36, no. 1 (2009): 5–31.

5 See UNEP, *Uncovering Pathways towards an Inclusive Green Economy: A Summary for Leaders* (2015).

6 See Patrick Lamers et al., eds., *Developing the Global Bioeconomy: Technical, Market, and Environmental Lessons from Bioenergy* (London: Elsevier, 2016); OECD, T*he Bioeconomy to 2030: Designing a Policy Agenda* (2019), https://www.oecd-ilibrary.org/economics/the-bio economy-to-2030_9789264056886-en.

7 Maria Backhouse et al., "Bioökonomie-Strategien im Vergleich: Gemeinsamkeiten, Widersprüche und Leerstellen" (working paper 1 Bioinequalities, Jena, 2017), https://www .bioinequalities.uni-jena.de/sozbemedia/neu/2017-09-28+workingpaper+1.pdf.

resources, as can already be witnessed in the case of Brazilian sugar cane and Southeast Asian palm oil cultivation for the production of so-called biofuels.[8]

Often, rural labour is not only characterised by the requirement of vast amounts of low-skilled labour and harsh working conditions, but also by a widespread deployment of migratory labour.[9] Whether it is seasonal labourers from Latin America employed in the United States picking lettuce, East-European workers cutting asparagus in Germany, or domestic migration of rural workers in India and Indonesia – rural labour migration can be found all around the globe. Apart from highly centralised and mechanised agricultural production,[10] labour relations in the primary sector of semi-/peripheral countries are often characterised by informality, precarity and semi-proletarianisation.[11] Thus, low-skilled rural migrant workers often constitute a particularly vulnerable segment within the working class of nation states, considering that they are usually without an advocacy group representing their interests. Typically, destination countries regulate the influx of foreign workers according to the "needs" of their national economy while sending countries encourage the out-migration of surplus labourers. By doing so, governments enable private companies to make use of a mobile labour reserve[12] as a seemingly never-ending source of cheap labour – so, too, in Malaysia.

Compared to its local manpower, Malaysia has one of the largest migrant labour forces in the world.[13] Many low-skilled migrants seeking work in

8   Kristina Lorenzen, "Sugarcane Industry Expansion and Changing Land and Labour Relations in Brazil: The Case of Mato Grosso do Sul 2000–2016" (working paper 9, Jena, 2019), https://www.bioinequalities.uni-jena.de/sozbemedia/WorkingPaper9.pdf; Janina Puder, "Excluding Migrant Labour from the Malaysian Bioeconomy: Working and Living Conditions of Migrant Workers in the Palm Oil Sector in Sabah," *Austrian Journal of South-East Asian Studies* 12, no. 1 (2019): 31–48.

9   Raúl Delgado-Wise and Henry Veltmeyer, *Agrarian Change, Migration and Development* (Warwickshire: Fernwood Publishing, 2016).

10   That is, soy production in Argentina. See Norma Giarracca and Miguel Teubal, "Las actividades extractivas en la Argentina," in *Actividades extractivas en expansión: ¿Reprimarización de la economía argentina?*, ed. Norma Giarracca and Miguel Teubal (Buenos Aires: Antropofagia, 2013).

11   Tania Li, "To Make Live or Let Die? Rural Dispossesion and the Protection of Surplus Populations," *Antipode* 41, no. 1 (2009): 66–93; Oliver Pye, "A Plantation Precariate: Fragmentation and Organizing Potential in the Palm Oil Global Production Network," *Development and Change* 48, no. 5 (2017): 942–64.

12   Florian Butollo, "Die große Mobilmachung: Die globale Landnahme von Arbeit und die Reservearmeemechanismen der Gegenwart," in *Kapitalismus und Ungleichheit: Die neuen Verwerfungen*, ed. Heinz Bude and Philipp Staab (Frankfurt am Main: Campus, 2016).

13   Archana Kotecha, *Malaysia's Palm Oil Industry* (2018), https://static1.squarespace.com/static/5592c689e4b0978d3a48f7a2/t/5b9a15db88251b25f1bc59d1/1536824861396/Malaysia_Analysis_120218_FINAL.pdf.

Malaysia stem from rural areas within the region.[14] The state actively channels these workers into jobs characterised as dirty, dangerous and degrading. This applies especially to the country's highly profitable palm oil industry. Malaysia's economy is extremely dependent on the export of palm oil – and, with that, on the constant supply of cheap labour. Over the course of centuries, Malaysia has created a segmented labour market,[15] which, in the palm oil sector, has produced (and systematically reproduced) highly mobile, but unorganised workers.[16] Legal obstacles and a perceived competition between low-skilled local and foreign rural workers have so far prevented the widespread organisation of migrant workers in the palm oil sector.

This chapter draws a connection between the working conditions of migrant palm oil workers and the problem of their union organisation within Malaysia.[17] The empirical findings included in this chapter were conducted during several field stays between 2018 and 2019 in the East-Malaysian state of Sabah as well as one online workshop with international and regional scholars and activists in June 2020. My own conclusions, drawn from participatory observations, qualitative interviews with workers, unionists and labour activists, and group discussions (see table 1), are complemented with findings from other studies concerned with labour migration in the Malaysian palm oil sector.

I will start by sketching Malaysia's labour migration regime, followed by a brief discussion of the core features and tendencies of the prevailing regime as applied in the country's palm oil industry. I argue that the state regulation of labour migration forms the precondition for an oppressive exploitation relationship between employer and migrant workers in the palm oil sector. Following Erik O. Wright, I define relationships of oppressive exploitation as relations of mutual dependence, in which one party dominates the other including, for example, measures of discrimination. Here, "the exploiter

---

14   Oliver Pye et al., "Precarious Lives: Transnational Biographies of Migrant Oil Palm Workers," *Asia Pacific Viewpoint* 53 (2012): 330–42.

15   Blanca Garcés-Mascareñas, *Labour Migration in Malaysia and Spain: Markets, Citizenship and Rights* (Amsterdam: Amsterdam University Press, 2012).

16   Janina Puder, "Entwicklung, Arbeitsmarktsegregation und Klassenstruktur in Malaysia: Eine politische Ökonomie der Arbeitsmigration," *Sozial.Geschichte Online*, no. 26 (2020), https://sozialgeschichteonline.files.wordpress.com/2020/03/04_puder_ar beitsmigration_malaysia-1.pdf.

17   Rizal Assalam, *Herausforderungen bei der Organisierung von Arbeitsmigrant*innen in den Palmölplantagen Sabahs* (2019), https://suedostasien.net/herausforderungen-bei-der -organisierung-von-arbeitsmigrantinnen-in-den-palmoelplantagen-sabahs/.

depends" directly "upon the effort of the exploited."[18] In capitalist societies exploitative oppression can be denoted by a functional devaluation of the labour power, for instance, based on citizenship to cheapen the labour power of specific workgroups. Thereby, exploitation refers to what Marx described as an antagonistic social relationship between the working class and capitalists, in which the latter appropriates the surplus labour of the former during the production process to create surplus value and accumulate capital.[19] I argue that the oppressive exploitation of migrant workers in the sector expresses itself in the difficulties of their socio-economic reproduction as well as practical and institutional hurdles to their unionisation. At the same time, however, I put forward that formal and informal strategies of collective action can advance immediate working and living conditions of migrant palm oil workers in Malaysia.

2   Mobile, Flexible, Disposable: The Malaysian Labour
     Migration Regime

Labour migration to Malaysia dates back to colonial times.[20] Encouraged by the British Crown, foreign labour became the backbone of Malaysia's early capitalist development. As local labour was either not available in sparsely populated regions or natives were unwilling to work under the harsh working conditions of colonial capitalism, the British rulers encouraged the recruitment of foreign workers from India, China and Indonesia.[21] The mobilisation of labour quickly became an essential factor for colonial Malaysia, as the country wished to develop into an important supplier of resources such as natural rubber, palm oil and cacao for the industrialising countries of the West.[22]

---

18   Erik Olin Wright, *Class Counts: Comparative Studies in Class Analysis* (Cambridge: Cambridge University Press, 2000), 11.
19   Karl Marx and Friedrich Engels, *Kritik der politischen Ökonomie*, MEW 23 (Berlin: Dietz Verlag, 1962).
20   Michele Ford, Lenore Lyons, and Willem van Schendel, eds., *Labour Migration and Human Trafficking in Southeast Asia: Critical Perspectives* (London: Routledge, 2012); Garcés-Mascareñas, *Labour Migration*; Amarjit Kaur, "Mobility, Labour Mobilisation and Border Controls: Indonesian Labour Migration to Malaysia since 1900" (paper, 15th Biennial Conference of the Asian Studies Association of Australia, Canberra, June – July, 2004).
21   Amarjit Kaur, "Labour Brokers in Migration: Understanding Historical and Contemporary Transnational Migration Regimes in Malaya/Malaysia," *International Review of Social History* 57, no. 20 (2012): 225–26.
22   Garcés-Mascareñas, *Labour Migration*, 52.

With Malaysia's independence from the British Empire in 1957 and the emergence of new state borders in the region, the young government began establishing a labour migration regime, which not only became extremely employer-friendly but also boosted economic growth significantly.[23] As the plantation sector further expanded, the cultivation of oil palms widely replaced natural rubber, and the global demand for palm oil gradually increased. In consequence, the state support of palm oil production became an important pillar of Malaysia's development strategy.[24] Today, the high versatility and energy density of palm oil makes it an attractive field of investment for the state and private actors.[25] Moreover, compared to other vegetable oils, such as rapeseed, palm oil is relatively cheap. Its low price on the global market is thus for the most part a result of the deployment of disposable cheap labour[26]provided by the state-led labour migration regime.

To understand the current working conditions of migrant workers in the Malaysian palm oil sector and the problem of their organising in the context of the prevailing labour migration regime, five core features of the regime must be determined: (1) it is characterised by the state regulation of migrant labour influx, which became increasingly flexibilised from the 1970s onwards.[27] Since then, the state has coordinated the recruitment and expulsion of migrant workers depending on the needs of capital first and foremost. In the past, during economic crises, foreign labour became constrained, oppressing workers' freedom of movement and their social rights (i.e. in the form of sudden mass deportation). In times of economic growth, however, the state lifted restrictions, in the hope of attracting higher numbers of labour migrants from within the region; (2) the regime is marked by a division of labour between low-skilled foreign workers employed in unfavourable segments of the economy and domestic workers deployed to perform better paid jobs with higher

23   Rüdiger Sielaff, "Das Mobilitätspotential der Gewerkschaften in Malaysia," *VRÜ Verfassung und Recht in Übersee* 14, no. 2 (1981): 168.

24   Puder, "Entwicklung."

25   Stéphane Bernard and Jean-François Bissonnette, "Oil Palm Plantations in Sabah: Agricultural Expansion for Whom?" in *Borneo Transformed: Agricultural Expansion on the Southeast Asian Frontier*, ed. Rodolphe D. Koninck, Stéphane Bernard, and Jean-François Bissonnette (Singapore: NUS Press, 2011), 133.

26   Ingrid Nielsen and Sen Sendjaya, "Wellbeing among Indonesian Labour Migrants to Malaysia: Implications of the 2011 Memorandum of Understanding," *Social Indicators Research* 117, no. 3 (2014): 925.

27   Kaur, "Mobility"; Johan Saravanamuttu, "The Political Economy of Migration and Flexible Labour Regimes: The Case of the Oil Palm Industry in Malaysia," in *The Palm Oil Controversy in Southeast Asia: A Transnational Perspective*, ed. Jayati Bhattacharya and Oliver Pye (Singapore: ISEAS Publishing, 2013), 120–39.

skill requirements.[28] While there are also a high number of impoverished rural households composed of natives,[29] low-skilled migrant workers in Malaysia are legally prevented from entering better paid jobs, restricting their social mobility;[30] (3) in the past, large unions required the limitation of labour migration to support skill development and career opportunities for the domestic workforce.[31] This was accompanied by the demand for higher wages in low-pay branches of the Malaysian economy.[32] By doing so, unions have in fact excluded migrant workers from the labour movement, resulting in a fragmentation of the working class; (4) unlike the advocates of the domestic workforce, companies have constantly pressured the government to let in more foreign workers to satisfy the ongoing shortage of cheap labourers, especially in the palm oil sector. From this point of view, cheap labour provides the basis for growth, development and market competition in various sectors; and (5) the state has installed high legal and political hurdles for migrant worker organisation to prevent labour unrest in low-wage segments of the economy.[33] These features do not only give evidence of the oppression and institutional discrimination of migrant workers in Malaysia, they also lay the foundation for a specific mode of exploitation as expressed in the state's palm oil sector.

In 2019, there were approximately 3.5 million documented migrants residing in Malaysia. In addition to this, between 1.46 and 4.6 million undocumented migrant workers are estimated to work illegally in the country.[34] Today, foreign workers mostly originate from Indonesia, the Philippines, Nepal, Myanmar, India and Bangladesh.[35] They primarily work in the palm oil industry, the construction sector, industrial manufacturing and the service sector (including

28   Puder, "Excluding Migrant Labour."

29   Anas Alam Faizli, *Rich Malaysia, Poor Malaysians*, 3rd ed. (Petaling Jaya: Gerakbudaya Enterprise, 2018).

30   Puder, "Excluding Migrant Labour," 43–44.

31   Michele Ford, "Contested Borders, Contested Boundaries: The Politics of Labour Migration in Southeast Asia," in *Routledge Handbook of Southeast Asian Politics*, ed. Richard Robison (New York: Routledge, 2014), 311.

32   Garcés-Mascareñas, *Labour Migration*, 196.

33   Assalam, *Herausforderungen*.

34   Joseph T. Anderson, "Managing Labour Migration in Malaysia: Foreign Workers and the Challenges of beyond Liberal Democracies," *Third World Quarterly* (2020), https://doi .org/10.1080/01436597.2020.1784003.

35   ILO, *Review of Labour Migration Policy in Malaysia: Tripartite Action to Enhance the Contribution of Labour Migration to Growth and Development in ASEAN* (Bangkok: ILO, 2016), https://www.ilo.org/wcmsp5/groups/public/---asia/---ro-bangkok/documents/ publication/wcms_447687.pdf.

home care), in jobs with low skill requirements.[36] In 2017, about 73 per cent of agricultural land was cultivated with oil palms, making Malaysia the second-largest palm oil producer in the world after Indonesia.[37] In 2012, 87 per cent of workers on oil palm plantations were non-Malaysian,[38] and mainly came from Indonesia. To escape poverty and poor working conditions in their homeland, marginalised segments of the Indonesian rural population seek employment opportunities in Malaysia. Cultural, ethnic, linguistic and religious affinities between the Indonesian and the Malaysian population, the persistent labour shortage in the Malaysian palm oil industry coupled with a surplus of low-skilled Indonesian agricultural workers, as well as wage differences between the two countries, makes Malaysia an attractive destination for Indonesian workers.[39]

The state regulation of labour migration, the accumulation model of the palm oil sector, which relies on disposable cheap labour, and the fact that sending countries encourage out-migration form the preconditions for the oppressive exploitation of highly mobile workers in the palm oil sector, as is demonstrated in the following section.

3   Oppressed and Exploited: Migrant Workers in the Malaysian Palm
       Oil Industry

In order to take up a job in Malaysia, migrants must apply for a formal work permit, which is valid for three years. The permit can be extended for up to two years. Upon the expiry of the permit, workers must return to their country of origin and reapply for a renewal if they wish to re-enter Malaysia legally.[40] As this process can be time-consuming and costly, migrant workers often over-stay their legal duration of stay or re-enter Malaysia without the proper documents, whereby they become illegalised.[41] The state grants different permits for selected branches of the economy based on the citizenship of workers,

---

36   Guntur Sugiyarto, "Internal and International Migration in Southeast Asia," in *Routledge Handbook of Southeast Asian Economics*, ed. Ian Coxhead (New York: Routledge, 2015), 281.
37   Kotecha, *Malaysia's Palm Oil Industry*, 4.
38   Pye et al., "Precarious Lives," 332.
39   Nielsen and Sendjaya, "Wellbeing, 923.
40   Pye et al., "Workers."
41   Pye et al., "Workers."

creating a government-regulated division of labour by nationality.[42] For example, Indonesian workers are mostly employed in the Malaysian agricultural and construction sector, while workers from the Philippines dominate the area of home care. Through this practice, the state segregates workers of different nationalities, preventing them from organising based on their shared interest in better working and living conditions. Migrant workers are not allowed to change jobs once they are issued a permit, which makes them highly dependent on their assigned employer.[43] If foreign workers change jobs without permission, their working permit expires. In such cases, or if their permit is withdrawn, for instance, due to an economic recession, they become illegalised. On the one hand, undocumented workers enjoy greater autonomy as they can choose jobs, pay no taxes, and it is difficult to deport them because state authorities cannot track their whereabouts.[44] On the other hand, they risk being captured by the police or paramilitary units, and being placed in detention centres, where they face being caned, fined and, eventually, deported (Expert interview 1). In addition to that, the state seeks to prevent migrants from permanently settling in Malaysia by prohibiting them from bringing their families or marrying within the country. In practice, however, these restrictions are often ignored by workers and infringements are regularly tolerated by official authorities and employers.[45] If children of migrant workers are born in Malaysia to parents who do not have the right of permanent residence, they are considered stateless, being recognised neither by Malaysian authorities nor by those of their country of origin. This leaves them extremely vulnerable to future exploitation and oppression.

The Malaysian palm oil value chain consists of roughly three different links: oil palm plantations, processing mills and refineries. Since the harvesting, rearing and care of oil palms can only be mechanised to a limited extent, a large part of the plantation work is carried out manually by migrant workers. On plantations there is typically a gendered division of labour.[46] While male workers perform physically demanding or operational tasks such as harvesting, transporting the oil palm fruit bunches, and taking care of plantation maintenance, female workers are mostly deployed to collect loose fruit, taking care

---

42   Boo T. Khoo, "The State and the Market in Malaysian Political Economy," in *The Political Economy of South-East Asia: Conflicts, Crises, and Changes*, ed. Garry Rodan, Kevin Hewison, and Richard Robison (Oxford: Oxford University Press, 2001), 181.
43   Pye et al., "Workers."
44   Garcés-Mascareñas, *Labour migration*, 84.
45   Bernard and Bissonnette, "Oil Palm Plantations," 133.
46   Oliver Pye et al., "Workers."

of the oil palm nursery, applying fertiliser and spraying pesticides.[47] Handling pesticides requires female workers to wear gear to protect their airways and skin from the toxic substances, but often companies do not provide workers with appropriate tools or protection gear (Interview 3).

In East Malaysia the minimum wage is 800 ringgits (approx. USD 195) and in Peninsular, due to the higher costs of living, 1,000 ringgits (approx. USD 244).[48] Migrant palm oil workers' wages hardly exceed this minimum wage. Migrant households can only achieve higher incomes if they pool wages earned in the palm oil sector with incomes generated through informal activities, such as selling illegally planted fruits at the weekly market (Interview 2). Empirical studies also revealed that the wages of migrant workers in the palm oil sector vary depending on whether workers are paid based on permanent contracts, whether they are day labourers or whether wages are tied to harvest quotas.[49] The income and working conditions of migrant palm oil workers thus depend on the type of employer they work for. Larger companies seek to exhaust legal provisions on minimum wages and overtime, constantly urging workers to spend more manpower than their contract provides for or by passing on taxes for working permits onto employees. Migrant workers employed by smaller companies and smallholders are routinely underpaid. In the case of small oil palm estates migrant workers are in part underemployed due to the small size of the crop area, while in harvest peak periods they are easily overworked. Male workers generally benefit from higher wages and more frequently have permanent contracts. At the same time, female workers are usually hired as day labourers, earning much less than male workers.[50] On smaller plantations, undocumented family members will often support one formally employed worker without receiving any compensation to reach otherwise unachievable harvest quotas. Irrespective of the type of employers, migrant workers periodically struggle to socio-economically reproduce their labour power and household, due to low wages and unsteady employment relationships.[51]

---

47   Vasanthi Arumugam, *Victims without Voice: A Study of Women Pesticide Workers in Malaysia* (Ulu Kelang: Tenaganita; Pesticide Action Network Asia and the Pacific, 1992).

48   In comparison, the bottom 75 per cent of Malaysian households have an average monthly income of 5,000 ringgits (approx. USD 1,230): Faizli, *Rich Malaysia, Poor Malaysians.*

49   Oliver Pye, "Deconstructing the Roundtable on Sustainable Palm Oil," in *The Oil Palm Complex: Smallholders, Agribusiness and the State in Indonesia and Malaysia*, ed. Rob Cramb and John F. McCarthy (Singapore: NUS Press, 2016).

50   Pye et al., "Workers."

51   Janina Puder, "Superexploitation in Bio-Based Industries: The Case of Oil Palm and Labour Migration in Malaysia," in *Bioeconomy and Global Inequalities: Socio-Ecological Perspectives on Biomass Sourcing and Production*, ed. Maria Backhouse et al. (London: Palgrave Macmillan, 2021).

These conditions, in which the concrete mode of exploitation of migrant palm oil workers unfolds, demonstrate the oppressive mechanisms of the Malaysian labour migration regime at work. The regulatory framework of labour migration deprives workers of the right to choose their own employer and profession. It restricts their socio-economic mobility by making them more vulnerable towards an intensive exploitation of their labour power, especially concerning female migrant workers and by tolerating undocumented family members who are available as a free labour resource. The legal status as well as the segregation of migrant workers based on citizenship create institutional and practical hurdles for union organisation. Prohibiting family reunification and denying undocumented household members access to the labour market or to education facilities leads to an externalisation of the reproductive costs and work necessary sustain the socio-economic reproduction of migrant households by the Malaysian state. To gain insights into the way in which workers are disciplined as cheap labourers in the production process by being prevented from organising as well as opportunities for resistance the following sections discuss the obstacles to and possibilities for organising migrant palm oil workers.

3.1   *Institutional and Political Barriers for Workers' Organisation*
Malaysia's constitution formally guarantees all citizens the right to join and build a trade union. However, the government restricts this right in preventing the establishment of general trade unions, blocking the emergence of a comprehensive trade union movement.[52] Since their inception, many state-approved unions have maintained a close relationship to the government. Representative positions within unions are mostly filled by high-ranking foremen and managers. The interests of less privileged workers are, therefore, systematically underrepresented. Moreover, not all workers have the same rights. Despite the fact that migrant workers with a valid working permit are formally allowed to join a union, they are prohibited from assuming representative functions; moreover, the interests of undocumented workers cannot be represented formally at all.[53] In practice, the Malaysian state has, in the past, repeatedly expelled migrant workers in response to labour unrest.[54] Politically, Malaysia's national trade union umbrella organisation, the Malaysian Trade

---

52   Stephen Castles, "Gewerkschaften und Entwicklung in Asien," *Gewerkschaftliche Monatshefte* 23, no. 7 (1972), http://library.fes.de/gmh/main/pdf-files/gmh/1972/1972-07 -a-432.pdf.
53   Assalam, *Herausforderungen*.
54   Kaur, "Mobility," 14.

Union Congress (MTUC), was outspoken in its rejection of the widespread use of migrant labour in low-wage segments of the economy until 2005.[55] Only later did it revise this position and chart a new strategic course in cooperation with various civil organisations, attempting to integrate the specific interests of migrant workers into its work.[56]

The restrictive legal framework within which unions operate in Malaysia limits the ability of migrant workers in the palm oil sector to organise. In East-Malaysia the Sabah Plantation Industry Employees Union (SPIEU) has been campaigning for the rights of migrant workers in the palm oil sector for a long time. Nevertheless, the unionisation rate of migrant workers has remained at a consistently low level since the legalisation of unions in the 1930s,[57] especially in the primary sector.[58] In principle, migrant workers employed on oil palm plantations and in mills have a certain production power.[59] If they were to stop working for only 24 hours, an entire production cycle would be disrupted, due to the need to process harvested oil palm fruits as quickly as possible, before they go bad.[60] However, even if a union manages to organise documented workers, it must ensure that a majority of 50 per cent plus at least one person (the 50+1 principle) of all workers in a company join the union in order to be recognised by the company as a negotiating partner (Expert interview 1). This refers to all production sites of the company. In concrete terms this means that if a plantation company, for instance, operates ten plantations, the 50+1 rule must be met on every single plantation. This principle proves to be an extreme organisational and logistical challenge for unions, as, besides the institutional and political hurdles of union work in the palm oil industry, there are further obstacles preventing migrant workers in the sector from organising.

3.2   Socio-spatial Isolation of Migrant Palm Oil Workers

Palm oil plantations and mills are usually located in remote areas far away from villages and urban areas. Migrant workers are compelled to reside within the plantation or close to the processing side in basic housing provided by their

---

55   Ford, "Contested Borders, Contested Boundaries," 311.
56   Ford, "Contested Borders, Contested Boundaries," 311.
57   Frederic C. Deyo, "South-East Asian Industrial Labour: Structural Demobilisation and Political Transformation," in Rodan, Hewison, and Robison, *Political Economy*.
58   Sielaff, "Das Mobilitätspotential," 160.
59   Stefan Schmalz and Klaus Dörre, "Der Machtressourcenansatz: Ein Instrument zur Analyse gewerkschaftlichen Handlungsvermögens," *Industrielle Beziehungen* 21, no. 3 (2014): 222.
60   Maria Backhouse, *Grüne Landnahme: Palmölexpansion und Landkonflikte in Amazonien* (Münster: Westfälisches Dampfboot, 2015), 72.

employers. Larger and medium-sized companies are equipped with security gates at different access points on the production site. Guards meticulously document who enters and exists the plantation at any time and will prohibit outsiders from accessing without permission. To enter the working and living spaces of migrant palm oil workers, labour activists use informal channels, pretending to visit relatives who are employed in the respective plantations or factories (Expert interview 4). One volunteer union activist reported that he tried to intercept hard-to-organise migrant workers from small and medium-sized plantations on their way to or from work to inform them about the work of the local union. In order to do so, he hides in the surrounding forests at night in fear of being attacked by thugs hired by plantation owners if he were to approach migrant workers openly during the day (Expert interview 2). This indicates that organising workers often goes along with high risks for activists themselves. Another trade union representative even reports that he has received various death threats and has been physically threatened several times because of his trade union activity (Expert interview 3).

The topographical conditions of many oil palm plantations further hinder activists trying to organise workers in far-off areas (Expert interview 3). The infrastructural accessibility of oil palm plantations varies greatly. In especially remote locations it can become challenging for workers themselves with basic means of transportation to leave and enter their workplace to meet up with other workers or even go to the weekly market. Roads are not always fully developed which makes them impassable during bad weather conditions. Public transport is rarely available and only runs irregularly. Migrant workers normally only own (if any) one or two motorcycles per household. During heavy rainfall, motorcycles are unsuitable for the plantation terrain as unpaved roads become extremely muddy. In larger companies, workers benefit from facilities such as a health clinic or small shops. As basic services and necessities are close by, many respondents mentioned that they hardly ever leave their workplace. One female worker even revealed that she never left the estate she works on since she was born there (Interview 1). These circumstances bind migrant workers to their immediate surroundings most of the time.

It is common practice among employers to seize the passports of their migrant workforce for alleged "security" or "bureaucratic" reasons. In reality, companies will hold the passports of migrant workers to prevent them from running away because of low wages and bad working conditions. Out of fear of getting arrested when leaving the plantation or mill site without carrying their passport when caught by the police or paramilitary units, migrant workers will mostly stay at their workplace and residence. Therefore, holding the passport of migrant workers gives companies the power to exercise control over the movement of their workers, isolating them from the "outside world," as this statement of a male worker exemplifies: "Without [my passport] I cannot go anywhere .... [Taking my passport is] the same as chaining my arms and legs, I become paralysed." (Interview 2)

The socio-spatial features of plantations and mill sites function as tools for plantation and mill owners to control migrant workers, binding them to their workplace and eliminating workers' capacity for organisation. In practice, it enables employers to discipline workers to keep their labour power disposable and prevents migrant workers from getting in touch with other migrant workers possibly employed on better terms. Thus, sharing information and experiences, both regarding different income and working conditions as well as concerning the enforcement of workers' rights and unionisation, is of central importance in this respect.

3.3   The Power of Information: Workers' Rights in the Workplace

The lack of access to information about labour rights and residence regulations expose workers to intensive exploitation and the disregard of rights by employers. When migrant workers were asked whether they had received a formal employment contract at the beginning of their current employment relationship, many workers reacted with uncertainty. Often there was confusion about the exact content of the documents they signed, as exemplified by this statement from a mill worker: "We just have to sign [what the company presents to us, J. P.] .... We don't read it all because the documents are very thick." (Interview 5) Trade union representatives described in various formal and informal conversations that the lack of access to information about workers' rights and their own legal status, illiteracy among workers, as well as the employers' refusal to cooperate with union representatives and labour activists, represent particular challenges for organising migrant plantation and mill workers (Group discussion 1). As a consequence, the majority of workers are not aware of basic rights, such as the minimum wage, protective clothing or safety training, but also the right to hold their own passport.

There is a lack of official complaint possibilities for migrant workers in case of labour rights abuse. Official bodies such as embassies or the Malaysian ministry of Human Resources usually take no initiative when it comes to supporting migrant workers in enforcing their rights. A representative of an Indonesian Workers' Union, who supports Indonesian plantation workers in Malaysia, described the following case, which exemplifies the inactivity of state authorities in Malaysia: in the East Malaysian state of Sabah a group of Indonesian migrant workers employed at a larger oil palm plantation company, demanded the payment of outstanding wages. Since their employer had not met wage demands for several months, the workers threatened to go on strike. As a result, they were immediately dismissed and replaced by new migrant workers. With their termination, the migrant worker group did not only lose their jobs but also their homes and residence permits. In desperate need of help, they turned to the Indonesian embassy to avoid deportation custody and to sort out the options for receiving their withheld wages. Despite several requests, they did not receive any response from the Indonesian authorities. Only by putting public pressure on the embassy by involving the trade union, a regulated return of the workers to Indonesia could be organised. While the workers were not forcibly deported, they still had to leave Malaysia without receiving the wages they were legally entitled to (Expert interview 3). While this case demonstrates the seeming unwillingness or inability of state authorities to provide migrant workers with information and support them in enforcing their rights, it also proves the importance of trade union involvement.

Nevertheless, most of the time, unorganised workers – who make up the majority of migrant plantation and mill workers – bridge information deficits and uncertainties about their options for action through their social networks.

3.4   Individual Coping Mechanisms in Dealing with Socio-Economic Precarity

Because of fear of repression by employers or the state as well as a lack of knowledge and experience in dealing with trade unions, migrant workers tend to deal with legal conflicts and work-related problems through social networks.[61] These networks have a specific material dimension: not only do they mediate employment relationships and serve as a resource for exchanging information about working conditions under different employers and labour rights, they also undermine the prevailing labour migration regime in the Malaysian palm oil sector to some extent. Accordingly, undocumented migrant workers in particular, whose specific concerns can only be represented by official interest representatives with great difficulty, resort to informal social structures to sort out adequate employment opportunities, which helps them remain undiscovered (Interview 4). Drawing on the work of James C. Scott,[62] Oliver Pye describes such practices as a form of "everyday resistance" of migrant workers against exploitative labour conditions and precarious living conditions.[63] The term refers to a variety of practices employed by

---

61   Puder, "Excluding Migrant Labour," 42–43.
62   James C. Scott, "Everyday Forms of Resistance," *The Copenhagen Journal of Asian Studies* 89, no. 4 (1989): 33–62.
63   Pye, "Plantation Precariate."

subaltern classes, who, in a political environment of intensive state oppression, are not supposed to attract attention and whose actions, therefore, do not openly appear as class struggles.[64] In contrast to class struggles organised from below, which attack the ruling classes and their institutions in a targeted, open manner, the term "everyday resistance" aims to capture the spontaneous struggles of precarious agricultural workers. However, everyday resistance is not necessarily detached from organised forms of class struggle but, rather, builds an analytical bridge between open class confrontation and the hidden, subversive acts of oppressed classes.[65] It is an expression of workers' struggle at the micro level, which, although not (yet) collectively coordinated, may create the cultural preconditions and necessary experiences for future class struggle at the macro level.[66]

Trade unions are gradually learning to make use of the existing informal social networks. Activists report that they are beginning to establish contact with previously hard-to-organise migrant palm oil workers through Community Learning Centers (CLC), a type of educational facility funded by non-governmental organisations or public institutions for the undocumented children of migrant palm oil workers:

> Most CLCs are founded on the initiative of migrant women. Interestingly, some of the founders and teachers are themselves palm oil workers .... [L]ocal teachers have a strong interest in workers' rights because they themselves have had experiences as plantation workers .... [T]hey have experience in advocating for migrants with the civil authorities. They also have the ability to bond with workers because they have that experience themselves and because they discuss with them to get them to let their children go to school .... These CLC teachers can play a crucial role in giving workers a basic education in workers' rights. To do this, they themselves must first be well trained. Since the CLCs are located in the middle of the plantations, teachers have a much better chance of introducing the idea of a common struggle and a union to the workers in the daily confrontations with them.[67]

---

64   Scott, "Everyday Forms of Resistance," 33–34.
65   Stellan Vinthagen and Anna Johansson, "Exploration of a Concept and Its Theories," *Resistance Studies Magazine*, no. 1 (2013): 1–46.
66   Scott, "Everyday Forms of Resistance."
67   Assalam, *Herausforderungen*.

The particular importance of unionisation in the palm oil sector is evident when comparing the basic labour rights of migrant workers in a large company with those in the rest of the companies of the case study. In contrast to medium-sized companies and oil palm smallholders, the workers of the large palm oil company studied during the fieldwork have been represented by a trade union for several decades. The incomes of all workers employed by the company are formally regulated by collective agreements, which the union regularly renegotiates with the company. Workers also benefit from basic occupational health and safety measures, paid vacation days and sick leave. This was explicitly not the case in other types of companies. Here, working conditions and income depend directly on the bargaining position of migrant workers vis-à-vis their employers. If, for example, migrant workers fall ill and they do not get paid as a consequence, the socio-economic reproduction of their labour power and their household is immediately threatened. While individual coping mechanisms and personal networks can help unorganised workers to gain access to better employment opportunities or financial support in particular situations, the unionisation of migrant palm oil workers opens up possibilities for a widespread and profound advancement of working and living conditions. Nevertheless, the current influence and success of trade unions with regard to the enforcement of labour rights and the improvement of the working and living standards of migrant palm oil workers in Malaysia is still limited by the state.

Against the backdrop of the outbreak of the Covid-19 pandemic in 2020, informal networks and cooperation between Indonesian and Malaysian union representatives have gained even greater importance in dealing with vulnerable migrant workers in situations of severe crisis. Due to the topicality of the crisis at the time of the completion of this chapter, the following excursus can only depict this in a fragmentary way. Nevertheless, it is intended to provide some insight into the changing working and living conditions of migrant workers under the impact of the current global crisis and the crucial role of trade unions in ensuring the survival of migrant workers and their families during this time. The account is based on media reports as well as reports of workers and trade union representatives in the context of an online discussion with various labour and environmental organisations active in Southeast Asia and Germany in which I participated at the end of July 2020.

4   Excursus: Workers' Organisation during the Global Pandemic

With the outbreak of the pandemic, large parts of the Malaysian economy came to a halt. This resulted in a shutdown of palm oil production and thus a sudden mass release of migrant workers. Over the course of the crisis, many documented workers lost their working permits and, with that, their shelter, leading to their immediate expulsion.[68] Undocumented migrants were put into deportation camps to be sent back to their country of origin, without a chance to comply with the necessary hygiene rules to reduce the risk of infection and without medical care.[69] Migrant workers were publicly stigmatised both in Malaysia and in their countries of origin, as they were seen as a group with a high risk of infection, due to their anticipated mobility, their lack of access to medical care and their general living conditions on the plantations and mill sites. Many documented migrants who lost their jobs due to the pandemic either refused to return to their country of origin, as they feared not being able to return, or simply could not afford the travel expenses.

Labour and humanitarian activists have reported that many companies stopped paying wages when production was halted. Consequently, affected migrant workers, especially those lacking access to transportation, could no longer adequately supply themselves with food or other essential goods.[70] They were completely left to their own devices by both their employers and the Malaysian state. Vulnerable migrant groups such as day labourers, outsourced and undocumented workers, were particularly affected by this. In addition, many workers were cut off from medical care, which was previously provided on the plantation sites. Other reports from workers and trade union activists revealed that some plantation companies only rudimentarily implemented the general rules of hygiene and continued to do "business as usual" during the pandemic. In unionised plantations, however, it was possible to obtain continued payment of wages, ensuring that workers were housed and basic health care could be maintained.

---

68   Adam Minter, "Corona Virus Is Bringing out the Worst in Malaysians," *Bloomberg*, accessed 5 December 2020, https://www.bloomberg.com/opinion/articles/2020-05-15/coronavirus-is-bringing-out-the-worst-in-malaysians.

69   Jason Santos, "Trapped and Abandoned: The Fate of Sabah's Illegal Migrant Workers," *Free Malaysia Today*, accessed 5 December 2020, https://www.freemalaysiatoday.com/category/nation/2020/04/09/trapped-and-abandoned-the-fate-of-sabahs-illegal-migrant-workers/.

70   TPOLS, "The Condition of Palm Oil Workers amidst Covid-19 Pandemic," *Palm Oil Labour Network*, accessed 5 December 2020, https://palmoillabour.network/the-condition-of-palm-oil-workers-amidst-covid-19-pandemic/.

The oppressive exploitation of (unorganized) migrant workers becomes especially visible during crisis. The drastic expulsion of many migrant workers, their stigmatisation, leaving them without sources of income and shelter, their obstructed access to medical care in case of illness and the fact that they were left to figure out strategies to survive without any direct help from the Malaysian state nor their country of origin, demonstrates the discriminatory handling of migrant labour power.

5   Conclusion

The connection between difficulties in reproducing migrant palm oil workers labour power and households and the high proportion of unorganised migrant workers is conditioned by oppressive social, institutional and political mechanisms disciplining Malaysia's migratory labour reserve. In this chapter it was argued that, through the prevailing labour migration regime, the Malaysian state creates the precondition for oppressive exploitation relationships in the palm oil sector. The segmentation of the labour market, the segregation of migrant workers by citizenship, the discrimination of migrants in terms of union organisation and the flexibilisation of labour migration constantly disciplines and devaluates the labour power of migrant workers, keeping their labour power cheap and disposable.

The working and living conditions of low-skilled migrant workers in the palm oil sector outlined in the context of the labour migration regime indicate that migrant workers in Malaysia not only occupy a deprivileged position on the labour market, which channels them into unfavourable, underpaid segments of the economy; it also demonstrates a certain form of oppression of migrant workers in terms of legal status and the enforcement of basic rights. This raises the question of what possibilities migrant workers have to resist their oppressive exploitation.

In many cases, the organisation of migrant workers in the palm oil sector is hampered by workers' fear of being deported if they join a union as well as by a lack of experience in dealing with trade unions. Companies are able to make use of production localities to seize control over migrant workers. Whether it is documenting workers' movements through a guarded gate while, at the same time, preventing labour activists from getting in touch with them, more indirect measures such as installing basic facilities on the production site or seizing worker's passports, allegedly for their own safety: these practices effectively shield workers from the outside world, making them immobile and hindering their organisation. Furthermore, it was argued that isolated workers

have limited access to crucial information about legal rights, residency requirements and contractual conditions, making it hard to share experiences among
migrant workers without a third party such as a trade union initiating such
a process. This makes migrant workers particularly vulnerable to oppressive
exploitation and labour rights abuse by their employers.

Even though possible entry points for the mobilisation of migrant workers in Malaysia are blocked by companies and the state working in tandem to
suppress labour unrest in the palm oil sector, workers are able to organise by
establishing informal social networks for coping with immediate difficulties or
sharing information. Thus, informal networks may create the preconditions for
union work, particularly concerning hard-to-organise migrant workers without previous knowledge or experience working with unions. At the same time,
trade unions can learn from informal support networks and thus improve the
success of organising. The importance of organising migrant palm oil workers did not only become obvious in the differences in working conditions of
unionised versus non-unionised palm oil producers but, especially, during crisis. While the disposability, discrimination and devaluation of migrant workers
by the Malaysian state and employers became apparent during the unfolding
of the crisis dynamics of the global pandemic, it also revealed the importance
of trade union support in ensuring the survival of migrant palm oil workers
and their dependants.

TABLE 16.1   Interviewees' occupation and data and location of interviews

Interview no.	Occupation/function	Date and location
Interview 1	Plantation workers (female, loose fruit picker)	8 March 2018
Interview 2	Plantation worker (male, various tasks)	9 March 2018, Sandakan
Interview 3	Plantation worker (female, various tasks)	9 March 2018, Sandakan
Interview 4	Plantation worker (female, maintenance)	14 March 2018, Tawau
Interview 5	Mill worker (male, press station), mill worker (male, oil station), mill worker (female, clerk)	15 March 2018, Kunak

TABLE 16.1 Interviewees' occupation and data and location of interviews (*cont.*)

Interview no.	Occupation/function	Date and location
Group discussion	Participants: Workers, scholars, trade union representatives, a labour activist and environmental activists	5–7 April 2019, Tawau
Expert interview 1	Trade union representative	14 March 2018, Tawau
Expert interview 2	Trade union representative	5 April 2019, Tawau
Expert interview 3	Trade union representative	10 May 2019, telephone interview
Expert interview 4	Non-governmental organisation representative	6 May 2017, Kuala Lumpur

Bibliography

Anderson, Joseph Trawicki. "Managing Labour Migration in Malaysia: Foreign Workers and the Challenges of beyond Liberal Democracies." *Third World Quarterly* (2020): 1–19. https://doi.org/10.1080/01436597.2020.1784003.

Arumugam, Vasanthi. *Victims without Voice: A Study of Women Pesticide Workers in Malaysia*. Ulu Kelang: Tenaganita; Pesticide Action Network Asia and the Pacific, 1992.

Assalam, Rizal. *Herausforderungen bei der Organisierung von Arbeitsmigrant*innen in den Palmölplantagen Sabahs*. Accessed 13 April 2019. https://suedostasien.net/her ausforderungen-bei-der-organisierung-von-arbeitsmigrantinnen-in-den-palmoelpl antagen-sabahs/.

Backhouse, Maria. *Grüne Landnahme: Palmölexpansion und Landkonflikte in Amazonien*. Münster: Westfälisches Dampfboot, 2015.

Backhouse, Maria, Kristina Lorenzen, Malte Lühmann, Janina Puder, Fabricio Rodríguez, and Anne Tittor. "Bioökonomie-Strategien im Vergleich: Gemeinsamkeiten, Widersprüche und Leerstellen." Working paper 1, Bioinequalities, 2017. https://www.bioinequalities.uni-jena.de/sozbemedia/neu/2017-09-28+workingpa per+1.pdf. Accessd 16th of September 2022.

Bernard, Stéphane, and Jean-François Bissonnette. "Oil Palm Plantations in Sabah: Agricultural Expansion for Whom?" In *Borneo Transformed: Agricultural Expansion on the Southeast Asian Frontier*, edited by Rodolphe D. Koninck, Stéphane Bernard, and Jean-François Bissonnette, 120–51. Singapore: NUS Press, 2011.

Bernstein, Henry. *Class Dynamics of Agrarian Change*. Agrarian change and peasant studies series. Halifax: Fernwood Publishing, 2010.

Borras, Saturnino M. "Agrarian Change and Peasant Studies: Changes, Continuities and Challenges – An Introduction." *The Journal of Peasant Studies* 36, no. 1 (2009): 5–31.

Butollo, Florian. "Die große Mobilmachung: Die globale Landnahme von Arbeit und die Reservearmeemechanismen der Gegenwart." In *Kapitalismus und Ungleichheit: Die neuen Verwerfungen*, edited by Heinz Bude and Philipp Staab, 215–36. Frankfurt am Main: Campus, 2016.

Castles, Stephen. "Gewerkschaften und Entwicklung in Asien." *Gewerkschaftliche Monatshefte* 23, no. 7 (1972): 432–39.

Delgado-Wise, Raúl, and Henry Veltmeyer. *Agrarian Change, Migration and Development*. Warwickshire: Fernwood Publishing, 2016.

Deyo, Frederic C. "South-East Asian Industrial Labour: Structural Demobilisation and Political Transformation." In *The Political Economy of South-East Asia: Markets, Power and Contestation*, edited by Garry Rodan, Kevin Hewison, and Richard Robison, 283–304. Oxford: Oxford University Press, 2006.

Faizli, Anas Alam. *Rich Malaysia, Poor Malaysians*. Petaling Jaya: Gerakbudaya Enterprise, 2018.

Ford, Michele. "Contested Borders, Contested Boundaries: The Politics of Labour Migration in Southeast Asia." In *Routledge Handbook of Southeast Asian Politics*, edited by Richard Robison, 305–14. New York: Routledge, 2014.

Ford, Michele, Lenore Lyons, and Willem van Schendel, eds. *Labour Migration and Human Trafficking in Southeast Asia: Critical Perspectives*. London: Routledge, 2012.

Garcés-Mascareñas, Blanca. *Labour Migration in Malaysia and Spain: Markets, Citizenship and Rights*. Amsterdam: Amsterdam University Press, 2012.

Giarracca, Norma, and Miguel Teubal. "Las actividades extractivas en la Argentina." In *Actividades extractivas en expansión: ¿Reprimarización de la economía argentina?*, edited by Norma Giarracca and Miguel Teubal, 19–44. Buenos Aires: Antropofagia, 2013.

Hochschild, Arlie R. "Global Care Chains and Emotional Surplus Value." In *On the Edge: Living with Global Capitalism*, edited by Will Hutton and Anthony Giddens, 130–46. London: Vintage, 2001.

ILO. *Review of Labour Migration Policy in Malaysia: Tripartite Action to Enhance the Contribution of Labour Migration to Growth and Development in ASEAN*. Bangkok: ILO, 2016. https://www.ilo.org/wcmsp5/groups/public/---asia/---ro-bang kok/documents/publication/wcms_447687.pdf. Accessed 16 September 2022.

Kaur, Amarjit. "Mobility, Labour Mobilisation and Border Controls: Indonesian Labour Migration to Malaysia since 1900." Paper presented at the 15th Biennial Conference of the Asian Studies Association of Australia, Canberra, June – July, 2004.

Kaur, Amarjit. "Labour Brokers in Migration: Understanding Historical and Contemporary Transnational Migration Regimes in Malaya/Malaysia." *International Review of Social History* 57, no. 20 (2012): 225–52.

Khoo, Boo Teik. "The State and the Market in Malaysian Political Economy." In *The Political Economy of South-East Asia: Conflicts, Crises, and Changes*, edited by Garry Rodan, Kevin Hewison, and Richard Robision, 178–205. Oxford: Oxford University Press, 2001.

Kotecha, Archana. *Malaysia's Palm Oil Industry*. 2018. https://static1.squarespace.com/static/5592c689e4b0978d3a48f7a2/t/5b9a15db88251b25f1bc59d1/1536824861396/Malaysia_Analysis_120218_FINAL.pdf. Accessed 16 September 2022.

Lamers, Patrick, Erin Searcy, J. Richard Hess, and Heinz Stichnothe, eds. *Developing the Global Bioeconomy: Technical, Market, and Environmental Lessons from Bioenergy*. London: Elsevier, 2016.

Li, Tania. "To Make Live or Let Die? Rural Dispossession and the Protection of Surplus Populations." *Antipode* 41, no. 1 (2009): 66–93.

Lorenzen, Kristina. "Sugarcane Industry Expansion and Changing Land and Labour Relations in Brazil: The Case of Mato Grosso do Sul 2000–2016." Working paper 9, Jena, 2019. Accessed 5 December 2020. https://www.bioinequalities.uni-jena.de/sozbemedia/WorkingPaper9.pdf.

Marx, Karl, and Friedrich Engels. *Kritik der politischen Ökonomie*. MEW 23. Berlin: Dietz Verlag, 1962.

Neu, Claudia. "Land- und Agrarsoziologie." In *Handbuch Spezielle Soziologien*, edited by Georg Kneer and Markus Schroer, 243–61. Wiesbaden: vs-Verlag, 2010.

Nielsen, Ingrid, and Sen Sendjaya. "Wellbeing Among Indonesian Labour Migrants to Malaysia: Implications of the 2011 Memorandum of Understanding." *Social Indicators Research* 117, no. 3 (2014): 919–38.

OECD. *The Bioeconomy to 2030: Designing a Policy Agenda*. 2019. Accessed 5 December 2020. https://www.oecd-ilibrary.org/economics/the-bioeconomy-to-2030_9789264056886-en.

Puder, Janina. "Excluding Migrant Labour from the Malaysian Bioeconomy: Working and Living Conditions of Migrant Workers in the Palm Oil Sector in Sabah." *Austrian Journal of South-East Asian Studies* 12, no. 1 (2019): 31–48.

Puder, Janina. "Entwicklung, Arbeitsmarktsegregation und Klassenstruktur in Malaysia: Eine politische Ökonomie der Arbeitsmigration." *Sozial.Geschichte Online* 26 (2020): 45–70. https://sozialgeschichteonline.files.wordpress.com/2020/03/04_puder_arbeitsmigration_malaysia-1.pdf. Accessed 16 September 2022.

Puder, Janina. "Superexploitation in Bio-Based Industries: The Case of Oil Palm and Labour Migration in Malaysia." In *Bioeconomy and Global Inequalities: Socio-Ecological Perspectives on Biomass Sourcing and Production*, edited by Maria Backhouse, Rosa Lehmann, Kristina Lorenzen, Malte Lühmann, Janina Puder, Fabricio Rodríguez, and Anne Tittor, 195–215. London: Palgrave Macmillan, 2021.

Pye, Oliver. "Deconstructing the Roundtable on Sustainable Palm Oil." In *The Oil Palm Complex: Smallholders, Agribusiness and the State in Indonesia and Malaysia*, edited by Rob Cramb and John F. McCarthy, 409–41. Singapore: NUS Press, 2016.

Pye, Oliver. "A Plantation Precariate: Fragmentation and Organizing Potential in the Palm Oil Global Production Network." *Development and Change* 48, no. 5 (2017): 942–64.

Pye, Oliver, Ramlah Daud, Yuyun Harmono, and Tatat. "Precarious Lives: Transnational Biographies of Migrant Oil Palm Workers." *Asia Pacific Viewpoint* 53 (2012): 330–42.

Pye, Oliver, Ramlah Daud, Kartika Manurung, and Saurlin Siagan. "Workers in the Palm Oil Industry: Exploitation, Resistance and Transnational Solidarity." Köln, 2016. https://www.asienhaus.de/archiv/user_upload/Palm_Oil_Workers_-_Exploitation_Resistance_and_Transnational_Solidarity.pdf. Accessed 16 September 2022.

Rodan, Garry, Kevin Hewison, and Richard Robison, eds. *The Political Economy of South-East Asia: Conflicts, Crises, and Changes*. Oxford: Oxford University Press, 2001.

Saravanamuttu, Johan. "The Political Economy of Migration and Flexible Labour Regimes: The Case of the Oil Palm Industry in Malaysia." In *The Palm Oil Controversy in Southeast Asia: A Transnational Perspective*, edited by Jayati Bhattacharya and Oliver Pye, 120–39. Singapore: ISEAS Publishing, 2013.

Schmalz, Stefan, and Klaus Dörre. "Der Machtressourcenansatz: Ein Instrument zur Analyse gewerkschaftlichen Handlungsvermögens." *Industrielle Beziehungen* 21, no. 3 (2014): 217–37.

Scott, James C. "Everyday Forms of Resistance." *The Copenhagen Journal of Asian Studies* 89, no. 4 (1989): 33–62.

Sielaff, Rüdiger. "Das Mobilitätspotential der Gewerkschaften in Malaysia." *VRÜ Verfassung und Recht in Übersee* 14, no. 2 (1981): 157–70.

Smith, John. *Imperialism in the Twenty-First Century: Globalization, Super-Exploitation, and Final Crisis*. New York: Monthly Review Press, 2016.

Sugiyarto, Guntur. "Internal and International Migration in Southeast Asia." In *Routledge Handbook of Southeast Asian Economics*, edited by Ian Coxhead, 270–99. New York: Routledge, 2015.

TPOLS, "The Condition of Palm Oil Workers amidst Covid-19 Pandemic," *Palm Oil Labour Network*, accessed 5 December 2020, https://palmoillabour.network/the-condition-of-palm-oil-workers-amidst-covid-19-pandemic/.

UBA. *Arbeit und Qualifikation in der Green Economy.* 2014. https://www.umweltbundes amt.de/publikationen/arbeit-qualifikation-in-der-green-economy. Accessed 16th of September 2022.

UNEP. *Uncovering Pathways towards an Inclusive Green Economy: A Summary for Leaders.* 2015.

Vinthagen, Stellan, and Anna Johansson. "Everyday Resistance: Exploration of a Concept and Its Theories." *Resistance Studies Magazine,* no. 1 (2013): 1–46.

Wright, Erik Olin. *Class Counts: Comparative Studies in Class Analysis.* Cambridge: Cambridge University Press, 2000.

Index

Printed in the United States
by Baker & Taylor Publisher Services